An Introduction to Syntactic Analysis and Theory

An Introduction to Syntactic Analysis and Theory

DOMINIQUE SPORTICHE
HILDA KOOPMAN
EDWARD STABLER

WILEY Blackwell

This edition first published 2014

Registered Office
John Wiley & Sons, Ltd, The Atrium, Southern Gate, Chichester, West Sussex, PO19 8SQ, UK

Editorial Offices
350 Main Street, Malden, MA 02148-5020, USA
9600 Garsington Road, Oxford, OX4 2DQ, UK
The Atrium, Southern Gate, Chichester, West Sussex, PO19 8SQ, UK

For details of our global editorial offices, for customer services, and for information about how to apply for permission to reuse the copyright material in this book please see our website at www.wiley.com/wiley-blackwell.

Library of Congress Cataloging-in-Publication Data

Sportiche, Dominique.
An introduction to syntactic analysis and theory / Dominique Sportiche, Hilda Koopman, Edward Stabler.
pages cm
Includes index.
ISBN 978-1-4051-0016-8 (cloth) – ISBN 978-1-4051-0017-5 (pbk.)
1. Grammar, Comparative and general–Syntax. 2. Generative grammar. I. Sportiche, Dominique, author. II. Koopman, Hilda Judith, author. III. Stabler, Edward P., author.
P291.S57 2013
415–dc23

2013015034

A catalogue record for this book is available from the British Library.

Cover image: © Fotosearch
Cover design by E&P Design

Set in 9.5/11.5pt Galliard by SPi Publisher Services, Pondicherry, India
Printed in Singapore by C.O.S. Printers Pte Ltd

3 2015

To Noam with gratitude beyond words, whose influence is found on every page, and whose charismatic ideas have made intellectual life exciting, Chomsky-style.

Contents

Additional and updated materials are available at www.wiley.com/go/syntacticanalysis

Acknowledgments

This book was written more slowly than we anticipated, over years of teaching syntax to advanced undergraduate students and graduate students at UCLA. This means many people have contributed to it in many different ways. We would like to thank:

- Robin Clark who inspired a very first attempt to write an uncompromising introduction to contemporary syntactic theory. We hope you will like the result.
- The generations of students at UCLA and elsewhere, whose reactions, positive and negative, have forced us to work harder.
- The colleagues who have used earlier versions of this book and gave us very valuable feedback: Ora Matushansky, Léa Nash, and Elena Soare at Université Paris 8, Vincent Homer at École normale supérieure in Paris, Maire Noonan at McGill University, Chris Collins at NYU, Greg Kobele at the University of Chicago, and Benjamin George, Peter Hallman, Anoop Mahajan, Keir Moulton, Robyn Orfitelli, and Martin Prinzhorn at UCLA.
- Three colleagues who gave us extremely extensive comments: Joseph Emonds, Chris Collins, and Leston Buell. We tried our best to incorporate your many suggestions.
- The anonymous reviewers who provided encouragement, and criticisms that we tried to address.
- Our teaching assistants who have experienced the effects of earlier versions from the trenches and our graduate students, whose comments made this book much better than it could ever have been without them: Natasha Abner, Byron Ahn, Melanie Bervoets, Ivano Caponigro, Isabelle Charnavel, Vincent Homer, Tomoko Ishizuka, Ananda Lima, Robyn Orfitelli, Dave Schueller, Sarah van Wagenen, Jun Yashima.
- The many colleagues whose work and taste have influenced us in too many ways to list and who are also part of this book: Alec Marantz, Anna Szabolcsi, Barry Schein, Benjamin Spector, Danny Fox, Gennaro Chierchia, Guglielmo Cinque, Hagit Borer, Henk van Riemsdijk, Isabelle Charnavel, Jean Roger Vergnaud, Jim Huang, Joseph Aoun, Luigi Rizzi, Maria Luisa Zubizaretta, Maria Polinsky, Martin Prinzhorn, Michal Starke, Misi Brody, Morris Halle, Norbert Hornstein, Philippe Schlenker, Richard Carter, Richard Kayne, Tim Stowell, Vincent Homer, Viola Schmitt.
- Last but not least, Noémie and Sophie who, as often the sole native speakers of English close by, have suffered endless torment over acceptability judgments. If you read this book, you will perhaps feel that the end justified the means.

1
Introduction

Linguistics is a domain in which language is studied. The notion of language is a common sense notion. In general, a common sense name is not sufficient to characterize a field of research, as there may be many different fields studying more or less the object referred to by the same common-sense name. For example, one can study the oceans from the point of view of a marine biologist, a climate oceanographer, a plate tectonics physicist, a zoologist, a botanist, or a chemist. To get a more precise idea of the field of linguistics, it is necessary to define the type of questions that one is asking about the object of study. Most of what modern linguistics studies falls under the heading of the study of the "language faculty" that human beings possess as part of their human biology. The capacity for language shared by all normal members of our species includes, among other things, the ability to physically manifest thoughts, to linguistically express diverse and original ideas, in diverse and original ways. This faculty also underlies the ability to understand others, to have coherent conversations, and to deduce other people's intentions from their utterances. These properties of language point to a field where the object of study is some mental property of individuals. So linguistics is a part of individual psychology, viewed in contemporary research as part of the study of the human brain.

Investigating this complex and often mysterious faculty appears a daunting task. One way to start is to try to formulate sensible questions about the output of our linguistic capacity – the sounds, the words, the sentences – so as to provide a framework within which incremental knowledge about this faculty can be gained.

1.1 Where to Start

We can start by looking at a simple case of basic linguistic behavior in an individual. When I hear language, my ears are sensing small, rapid variations in air pressure. This vibration, sound, is transformed into nerve impulses that travel to my brain, where the signal is somehow decoded and transformed into an idea, a thought. This is speech perception, or recognition. A similar process occurs in users of sign language: a visual signal is somehow decomposed and converted into an idea. Inversely, when I speak, an idea in my mind is physically manifested through speech or visual signs: this is speech production. These simple observations raise many questions. What exactly goes on when we produce or recognize speech? How does perception or production unfold in real time and how is this coded in brain tissue?

An Introduction to Syntactic Analysis and Theory, First Edition.
Dominique Sportiche, Hilda Koopman, and Edward Stabler.

To understand language processing in the brain, we aim to understand how it rapidly changes state in ways that we can interpret as analytical steps in decoding the linguistic signal. How does the brain do this, exactly? In engineering jargon, we are faced with a problem of "reverse engineering," a common problem for industrial spies. We have a machine – a body, particularly a brain – capable of accomplishing a certain task and we try to understand how it works and how it could be built. We have similar questions in vision, acoustic processing, and other domains of cognitive science. Note that our question is not simply how a particular ability could be produced or imitated in principle. Rather, we aim to identify how it is really produced in the human language user.

This "reverse engineering" problem is very difficult to approach directly. First, to find the physical mechanisms responsible for some ability, we need to have a good understanding of the basic properties of that ability. For example, studies show that certain areas of the brain (Broca's and Wernicke's areas, etc.) are active when we perform certain kinds of linguistic tasks, but to decipher what exactly they are doing, what computations are being performed, we need to know a lot about what these tasks involve. To obtain this kind of understanding, we must initially approach the problems of production and perception abstractly.

We start with the hypothesis that, stored in our mind somehow, we possess some information about certain basic things, some atoms of information that we can deploy in given contexts. As a starting point, we could assume that these atoms are "words" or something similar, such as *table* and *book*, and *eat* and *curious*, and *the* and *before*, and further that these elements have phonetic properties, or instructions on how to physically realize the atoms through speech, as well as meanings, a pairing of the elements to bits of thoughts.

So when it comes to expressing a thought to someone else, a simple story is that I search in my mind for the words corresponding to what I want to talk about and string them together in a particular way to express the thought. Of course, this string of words has to be physically manifested, as in speech or signing, which means that a signal has to be sent to the motor centers that coordinate physical gestures of the mouth or the hand, as the case may be.

Similarly, successful perception of a sentence might be achieved by an electrical signal sent to my brain by the hearing system, which is then segmented by my brain into words, each corresponding to a bit of thought. As my brain receives the particular sequential arrangement of these words, it can also calculate what the combination of the words in the sentence means as a whole.

We can schematize these processes with the following flow chart:

sounds ↔ ordered sets of words ↔ meanings

If we go from left to right, we have a crude model of spoken language perception, from right to left a crude model of spoken language production. If we replaced "sounds" with "signs," we would have crude models of sign language perception and production.

Understanding how this could work, even at an abstract level, is not easy. For example, it is imaginable that the rules governing how sounds are composed into ordered sets of words in a particular situation depend on what the hearer is looking at when perceiving the sounds. This would mean that we have to worry the visual system and how it relates to the linguistic system. This is why we decide to concern ourselves with an even more abstract problem, and will not investigate how the flow chart above really works, how it unfolds in real time. Instead, we will ask: What **necessary linguistic** properties does the language processing task have? By **linguistic**, we mean that we are going to abstract away from the influence of visual clues or background knowledge about the world, and (initially at least) focus on grammatical properties (akin to those found in traditional grammar books). By **necessary**, we mean that we will concentrate on properties that hold across all normal uses of the language, properties that linguistic computations must respect in order to yield the linguistic phenomena we observe.

Here is a sample of more precise questions about necessary linguistic properties:

- Do all orders of words yield meaningful expressions (in the way that all orders of decimal digits represent numbers)? If not, why not?
- Do meaningful word sequences have any structure beyond their linear, temporal ordering? If so, what kind of structure, and why would this structure exist?
- How are the meanings of a sentence determined by (or restricted by) the meanings of its component parts?

The discovery that speech can be symbolically transcribed, can be written down, is certainly among the most momentous human discoveries ever. It allowed the transmission of information across distances and across generations in ways that were never before possible.

> In the famous 1632 *Dialogue Concerning the Two Chief World Systems* written by Galileo Galilei one of the characters, Sir Giovanni Francesco Sagredo, "a man of noble extraction and trenchant wit," so marvels about this invention: "But surpassing all stupendous inventions, what sublimity of mind was his who dreamed of finding means to communicate his deepest thoughts to any other person, though distant by mighty intervals of place and time! Of talking with those who are in India; of speaking to those who are not yet born and will not he born for a thousand or ten thousand years; and with what facility, by the different arrangements of twenty characters upon a page!"

What is less obvious is that this invention is also a theoretical discovery about human psychology: the structure of language, the nature of this system, allows thoughts to be transmitted in this way. One fundamental aspect of this discovery can be stated as follows: the speech signal – even though it is a continuous physical phenomenon – namely a continuous variation of air pressure for normal speech, or continuous motion for sign language – can be represented with a finite (sometimes small) number of discrete units. A particularly striking example of this property is illustrated by alphabetic writing systems, as the quote in the box opposite emphasizes: with a small number of symbols – letters – they can very effectively (partially) code speech. Informally speaking, it is clear that this segmentation of the speech signal occurs at various levels of "graininess." Alphabetic writing systems segment the speech signal in very small units of writing, while Chinese characters or Egyptian hieroglyphic writing systems segment it in somewhat larger units. That this segmentation can occur at various degrees of "magnification" can be illustrated with the following string:

these books burned

Evidence confirms that English speakers segment and analyze this expression at some levels roughly like these, where the number in the leftmost column indicates the number of units in its line (and the first line is written in phonetic alphabet and is meant to represent the sequence of sounds found in this string):

12	ð	iː	z	b	ʊ	k	s	b	ə	r	n	d
6	Demonstrative		Plural	Noun			Plural	Verb				Past
3	Demonstrative+Plural			Noun+Plural				Verb+Past				
2	Subject							Predicate				
1	Sentence											

Linguists have extensively documented the relevance of such segmentations for our understanding of language structure. Hypothesizing that these modes of segmentation, these different "levels of magnification," correspond to real psychological properties of the speech signal, we will need to at least answer the following questions about each level as part of understanding how our flow chart above really works:

- What is the inventory of the smallest pieces, the atomic elements, that are assembled at each level?
- What are the rules or principles that govern how these units can be assembled?

Traditionally, linguists have postulated the following divisions: Phonology studies the atoms and combinations of sounds; Morphology considers the atoms and how words are built; and Syntax considers how words are put together to form phrases. Of course, this preliminary division into such subdomains may not be correct. It could be that the atoms of syntax are not words but morphemes, and that the rules of combination for morphemes are the same as the rules of combination for words. If this were the case, there would really be no distinction between morphology and syntax. Or morphology might be part of phonology. (These kinds of proposals have been seriously explored.) But we will start with this traditional picture of the components, modifying it as necessary. In fact, where syntax books start with words, this book will start with morphology, i.e. the structure of words.

These two questions – what are the atoms of language, and how are they combined – characterize very well what this book is about. We view language as a system of symbols (e.g. sounds, which are paired up with meanings), and a combinatory system, where symbols combine to yield more complex objects, themselves associated with meanings. Here we concentrate on how aspects of this particular symbolic combinatory system are put together: this is a technical manual that almost exclusively worries about how to investigate and characterize the combinatory structure of morphological and syntactic units.

Even though the scope of this book is relatively narrow, the research perspective on language it embodies is part of a much broader research program that tries to characterize cognitive functions. The questions we address here are limited to the structure of the syntactic and morphological combinatory systems but, as will become clear, a substantial amount is known about these systems that suggests that non-trivial principles regulate how it works. This in turn raises all sorts of questions which we will not address but that are central research questions: how is this system put to use when we speak or understand? How much computational power is needed to master such a system? Is language fundamentally shaped by our communicative intentions? Where do the fundamential principles of language structure come from? Are they innate? Are they learned? Are they completely specific to language, or only partially so, or not at all? Are they specific to humans? Or only partially so? How did they appear in our species? Suddenly? Progressively? By themselves?

The approach to the study of language described above took off in the mid 20th century and is now a dynamic field incorporating an increasing panoply of methods or tools, from the methods used by traditional grammarians and language fieldworkers, to laboratory methods originating in experimental psychology, to neuro-imagery, to mathematical methods imported from pure and applied mathematics, to statistical tools and the tools of modern genetics. Noam Chomsky, pictured here on the left, presently (2013) Institute Professor at the Massachusetts Institute of Technology is the most influential pioneer of this research perspective and agenda and the research methods that carry it out.

In conjunction with other mental or physical properties? All these questions are (on their way to) being investigated in the rapidly developing field of cognitive science.

It is important to emphasize that apart from framing questions about language in a useful way, the new, systematic methods of investigation have met with great success. It is fair to say that in the past 50 years, our knowledge of linguistic structures has increased at a pace unparalleled in the history of linguistics. Because this approach to language is relatively young, progress is rapid and our progressively increasing understanding means that new, better hypotheses emerge all the time, sometimes revealing inadequacies of previous assumptions.

1.2 What this Book is and is Not, and How to Use It

First, a book like this one, which tries to provide a snapshot of our current state of understanding, is to a certain extent bound to be or to become incorrect as research progresses. It is thus important to remember that although the results described herein are sound and reasonable, most important are the methods used to reach them.

As was stated, this book is a technical manual focusing on syntactic and morphological structures. It is not meant to be exhaustive. Nor is it meant to be a systematic introduction to the relevant literature. Because the field progresses rapidly, notions once thought to be useful or important no longer play a prominent role. In general we do not discuss them. Other notions are not included because they are too advanced for such an introductory book. Rather we aim to provide a reasoned introduction to the central tools and concepts that seem necessary and well justified by the research of the past 50 years.

Although this book uses quite a bit of formal notation, it does not, by design, present a formalized theory of syntax, except in the last chapter. In that chapter, a complete formalization is introduced. This formalization of a part of our linguistic system has allowed researchers to precisely investigate important issues, like the expressive power of our model of the combinatory system. It has also allowed us to prove results showing that this model is in principle well behaved with respect to a number of important measures, like parsability and learnability.

The main text of this book is definitely anglocentric, focusing on English. This is in part due to the fact this book grew out of class notes written for English-speaking students in syntax classes at the University of California at Los Angeles. But the focus on English is motivated by the field: supporting the conclusions reached requires sophisticated argumentation and thus requires looking in depth at an individual language. English is the best and most deeply studied language by a wide margin, so it is not unreasonable to think that there is a greater chance that deep, perhaps universal, properties of language have been discovered, and that some of the results have wide, perhaps universal, validity. This anglocentricity is also somewhat illusory, as a very substantial amount of how English is analyzed today is, and will continue to be, informed by in-depth work done on other languages, most notably by work in the 1960's on the Romance languages, the other Germanic languages, and Japanese, and by more recent work on an ever expanding variety of languages spanning all language families and broad regions of the planet. Theoretical research is crucially informed by cross-linguistic research, and it is our firm belief – buttressed by the life-long personal experience of working on a wide variety of human languages – as well as the very large number of studies that bear on a wide variety of languages, that the methods and tools introduced here are reliable, productive, and necessary for the study of any natural human language.

From a practical standpoint, we intend this book to be readable on its own, by anyone, even those without any prior knowledge of linguistics. Since this is a technical manual, it should be read slowly, making sure to the greatest extent possible that nothing is left unclear. To this end, it is essential to do exercises. This cannot be overemphasized. The exercises are meant to let the reader check that the content relevant for them has been mastered. Additionally, the exercises may sometimes introduce results not discussed in the body of the chapters, or discuss alternatives to hypotheses previously adopted.

Wherever possible and accessible, we try to show how the conclusions reached connect with other modes of investigation of cognitive capacities, such as the (neuro-)psychology of learning and processing and computational approaches.

Scattered in the chapters are three types of box. They have different functions, indicated by their titles. Boxes marked "Practice" indicate points at which particular practice should be done. Shaded boxes should be read and paid particular attention to: they highlight important information. Material in double-ruled boxes is not critical to the reading of the chapter. These boxes introduce, discuss, or anticipate more advanced material. Read with this material, the book is a pretty advanced introduction to current theorizing and results.

While the emphasis in this book is on methods of investigation, the current results are important too. In general we summarize both at the end of each chapter in a section entitled "What to remember."

1.3 Further Reading

Reading original literature in syntactic theory can be difficult. The original literature by now spans more than 60 years. As mentioned in the Introduction, this field is very young, progress has been and continues to be rapid. In this time span, many discoveries have been made, sometimes making earlier work obsolete, new notations are constantly introduced to encode new understanding, making earlier notations opaque. At the moving frontiers of knowledge, several hypotheses, incompatible with each other, were and are simultaneously entertained. All this contributes to making reading the original literature difficult. It is important to replace the literature in its time: what exactly was the particular theoretical understanding then? What was known and what was not? What did the overall model look like? What were the particular questions linguists were worrying about, and what technical vocabulary or notation was used to talk about the phenomena discussed? As part of language, the meaning of words sometimes shifts, and technical vocabulary or notation evolves.

We recommend to the reader to first carefully work through the (relevant parts of this) textbook, and read only general background or foundational literature. Only once a good understanding has been gained of the properties that any linguistic theory will have to account for, should a start be made with the original literature.

General resources There are many textbooks and handbooks that can be used to complement the current textbook. We list a selection of general syntax textbooks, some of which are helpful to prepare reading the literature of what was broadly understood at the time they were published: Van Riemsdijk and Williams (1986), McCawley (1998), Haegeman (1994), Ouhalla (1994), Culicover (1997), Roberts (1997), Carnie (2002), Adger (2003), Radford (2004), Hornstein, Nunes, and Grohmann (2005).

In this general context, the site http://tgraf.bol.ucla.edu/timeline.html is a useful resource: Thomas Graf attempts to provide an annotated timeline of how new anlytical or theoretical ideas were introduced in generative linguistics. In addition, the reader may also want to check out the Blackwell Series "Classic Readings in Syntax," currently in development, as well as the very useful Blackwell Companion to Syntax: (Everaert and Riemsdijk, 2006).

For a current assessment of the general results of the generative enterprise, written for a broad general public, the collection of articles about core ideas and results in syntax in the *Lingua* volume edited by Luigi Rizzi (2013) is particularly noteworthy.

For descriptive grammars, or grammars informed by work in the type of syntactic framework broadly construed we have described, we mention the following selection of works, often the result of collaborations of many linguists, comprising multiple volumes or thousands of pages, and by no means exhaustive: (Hualde and De Urbina, 2003) for Basque, (Haeseryn and Haeseryn, 1997) for Dutch. (Huddleston and Pullum, 2002) on English, (Renzi, 1988–1995) for Italian, and (Demonte Barreto and Bosque, 1999) for Spanish.

There are other, valuable introductory books at various levels and with different objectives. The following are general, fairly systematic introductions to the research program we pursue: Anderson and Lightfoot (2002), Baker (2001), Chomsky (1975), Jackendoff (1995), Lightfoot (1982), Pinker (1994). It is also a good idea to look around the Internet, in particular for Noam Chomsky's writings.

Finally, we highly recommend the site http://ling.auf.net/lingbuzz maintained by Michal Starke. It is a searchable, openly accessible repository of scholarly papers, discussions, and other documents for linguistics. Current research in its various subfields – most relevantly syntax and semantics – is continually being uploaded by researchers.

2

Morphology: Starting with Words

Our informal characterization defined syntax as the study of rules or principles that govern how words are put together to form phrases, well-formed sequences of words. The crucial elements in this informal characterization – "words," and "rules or principles" – have common-sense meanings independent of the study of language. We more or less understand what a rule or principle is. A rule or principle describes a regularity in what happens. For example, "If the temperature drops suddenly, water vapor will condense," is a rule of natural science. This is the notion of rule that we will be interested in. It should be distinguished from the notion of a rule that is an instruction or a statement about what should happen, such as "If the light is green, do not cross the street." As linguists, our primary interest is not in how anyone says you should talk. Rather, we are interested in how people really talk. Before considering rules for building phrases and sentences, we will consider the structure of words.

In common usage, "word" refers to some kind of linguistic unit. We have a rough, common-sense idea of what a word is, but it is surprisingly difficult to characterize this precisely. It is not even clear that this notion allows a precise definition. It could be like the notion of a "French language." There is a central idea to this notion but, as we try to define it, we are led to making arbitrary decisions as to whether something is part of French or not. Fortunately, as we will see later, we may not need a precise version of the notion "word" at all. Nevertheless, these common-sense notions provide a reasonable starting point for our subject. So we will begin with some of the usual ideas about words: objects of the kind that can be more or less isolated in pronunciation, that can be represented by strings of letters separated by blank spaces, and that have meanings.

As we will see, some evidence has been put forth to the effect that words are *not* the basic units of phrases, not the atomic units of syntax. Instead, the atoms, or "building blocks" that syntax manipulates would be smaller units, units that we will see later in this chapter. We will also see that that there are reasons to think that the way these units are combined is very regular, obeying laws very similar to those that combine larger units of linguistic structure. But we begin by looking at properties of words as we have informally characterized them, and see where this leads. As mentioned above, the subdomain of linguistics dealing with word properties, particularly word structure, is called *morphology*. Here we will concentrate on just a few kinds of morphological properties that will turn out to be relevant for syntax. We will briefly introduce the following basic ideas:

- Words come in categories.
- Words can be made of smaller units (morphemes).

An Introduction to Syntactic Analysis and Theory, First Edition.
Dominique Sportiche, Hilda Koopman, and Edward Stabler.

- Morphemes combine in a regular, rule-governed fashion:
  a. To define the regularities we need the notions of head and selection.
  b. The regularities exhibit a certain kind of locality.
- Morphemes can be silent.

2.1 Words Come in Categories

The first important observation is that there are different types of words. This is usually stated as the fact that words belong to different categories, where categories are nouns, verbs, adjectives, prepositions, adverbs, determiners, complementizers, and other things. Some of these are familiar from traditional grammar (like nouns and verbs), others probably less so (like complementizers, or determiners).

Open class categories: have a large number of members and new words can be (more or less freely) created in these categories.

Noun (N)	table, computer, event, joy, action
Verb (V)	run, arrive, laugh, know, love, think, say, spray
Adjective (A)	big, yellow, stable, intelligent, legal, fake
Adverb (Adv)	badly, curiously, possibly, often

Closed class categories: have a limited number of members, which can be enumerated. Speakers cannot really create new members in these categories.

Preposition (P)	on, of, by, through, into, from, for, to, with
Determiner (D)	the, a, this, some, every
Numerals (Num)	one, two, three, ten, thirteen
Complementizers (C)	that, if, whether[1] for
Auxiliaries (V)	have, be, (some instances of) do
Modals (v or M)	will, would, can, could, may, might, shall, should
Coordinators (Coord)	and, or, but
Negation/Affirmation (Neg/Aff)	no, not, too, so

The way these categories are given above is rather coarse grained, but will be good enough for our purposes. They will eventually need to be refined. For example, there are many different "subcategories" of verbs, some of which are distinguished in dictionaries: transitive, intransitive, and so on. Most dictionaries do not specify refinements of categories other than verbs, but these are needed too. For example, there are many different kinds of adverbs:

Manner Adverbs	slowly, carefully, quickly
Degree Adverbs	too, enough
Frequency Adverbs	often, rarely, always
Modal Adverbs	possibly, probably

Notice also that the degree adverb *too* in *This is too spicy* is not the same word as the affirmative *too*, mentioned above, in *That too is a word!*. Similarly, the complementizer *for* in *For you to eat it would be a mistake* can be distinguished from the preposition *for* in *He cooked it for me*.

There are also important distinctions among the determiners:

Articles	a, the
Demonstratives	that, this, these, those
Quantifiers	some, every, each, no

In fact, all of the categories mentioned above have significant subcategories.

[1]This is what we will assume for now. We will modify this on p. 291 in a way that does not affect any conclusion based on the categorial status of *whether* as C.

Open and closed class categories: In closed class categories, there is no option of freely adding new members. In open class categories there is, but the mechanism by which new items are introduced may not the same for all categories. While new nouns come into the language all the time – e.g. *television, quark, google, carmageddon* – it is less clear how creation takes place within other open class categories. It may be that new verbs, adjectives, or adverbs come into the language only derivatively. Thus it may be that verbs or adjectives or adverbs are never created out of nothing. For example, perhaps the verb *google* can only appear because there is a noun *google*, a new adjective must always be of a form such as noun-y, and an adverb derived from an adjective, e.g. "adjective"-ly. For an example of recent research on this, see chapter 9 of Kayne (2010).

This classification of words into categories raises fundamental questions:

- What are these categories, that is, what is fundamental basis for distinctions between categories?
- How do we know that a particular word belongs to a particular category?

Traditionally, the categories mentioned above are identified by semantic criteria, that is, by criteria having to do with what the words mean. A noun is sometimes said to be the name of a person, a thing, or a place; a verb is said to be the name of an action; an adjective the name of a quality; etc. There is some (probably very complicated) truth underlying these criteria, and they can be useful. However, a simple minded application of these criteria is not always reliable or possible. Sometimes words have no discernible meaning (the complementizer *that*), nouns can name actions (e.g. Bill's repeated *betrayal* of his friends), and verbs and adjectives can denote states (John *fears* storms = John is *fearful* of storms).

It is important to keep meaning in mind as a guide, but in many cases we will need more reliable criteria. The most fundamental idea we will use is the following: **a category is a set of expressions that all "behave the same way" in the language**. And the fundamental evidence for claims about how a word behaves in a particular language is its distribution: where it can appear, and where it leads to nonsense or some other kind of deviance.

2.1.1 Affixes are often category and subcategory specific

In morphology, the simplest meaningful units are often called *morphemes*. By "meaningful" here, we mean either "semantically meaningful" in the sense of being paraphrasable by an idea, or else "indicating a grammatical property." For example, the plural morpheme *-s* in English is semantically meaningful, standing for the idea of plurality. But morphemes are sometimes mere indications of grammatical properties, as in the accusative case ending *-m* in Latin (*rosa-m*), or the case marker *o* in Japanese. These elements typically mark a direct object, but do not otherwise contribute anything to the meaning. (In English, the case marking of pronouns – as in *she/he* vs. *her/him* – is not recognizable as a separate affix.) We will mostly concentrate on semantically meaningful morphemes in this section.

A distinction is often drawn between morphemes that can occur independently, *free morphemes*, and *affixes* or *bound morphemes* that can only appear attached to or inside another element, its host.

An affix that is attached at the end of its host is called a *suffix*; at the beginning of its host, a *prefix*; inside its host an *infix*; and at the beginning and end a *circumfix*. The distinction between free and bound is a property having to do with pronunciation autonomy: it is a phonological property.

Words can have more than one morpheme in them. We see this for example in English plurals that are indicated by the affix pronounced [s] or [z] or [ɨz]:

book	book-s	...s
table	table-s	...z
friend	friend-s	...z
rose	rose-s	...iz

It is mostly just nouns that can be pluralized, though a small number of other items have plural forms as well, like demonstratives (*this, these*) and some pronouns like *one* (*this one, these ones*). However, in English, the ability to be pluralized comes very close to being a distinctive property of nouns. Thus, if a word can be pluralized (and is not a demonstrative or a pronoun), it is a noun.

Notice that the characterization of this suffix is partly semantic. So for example, we know that the *-s* at the end of *reads* in the following sentence is not the plural affix, but some kind of 3rd person singular agreement marker, since it appears only with 3rd person singular subjects. In the following example, we mark the unacceptable form with an asterisk in the following:

She read-s the newspaper. They/I/you read/*read-s the newspaper.

This verb form does not refer to a plurality of readings. If it did, it would do so regardless of whether the reader is singular or plural. In English, there is no plural version of any verb, or of any preposition (e.g. **for-s*), or of any adjective *big-*s*. If a word can be pluralized (and is not a demonstrative or a pronoun), then it is a noun.

Remark on linguistic terminology: Just as we are using the notion "word" in an informal way, we are using terms like "sentence", "subject", "object", "pronoun", and "agreement" in informal ways. For the moment, this is sufficient to allow us to know what we are talking about, but we will progressively define all these terms systematically. Here is some help with recognizing the subject of a sentence:

- The subject of the sentence precedes the auxiliary or the finite verb in simple declarative sentences like, *The girls are busy playing tennis. The girls will be invited. Such books are easy to sell. Playing tennis is fun.*
- The subject determines agreement on the verb in the present tense. *They like* vs. *she like-s*. Agreement is particularly visible with the irregular verb *be*: *I am/she is* vs. *you are/they are*.
- Subjects have a special case form (nominative), visible in English pronouns. So we can say *They swim* with the nominative pronoun *they*, but not, as a full sentence, **Them swim* (accusative) or **Their swim* (genitive).
- The subject follows the complementizer *that, if, whether*, but precedes the auxiliary or the verb in sentences like *They thought that Bill's mother's friends were waiting.*
- A subject immediately follows the auxiliary in yes/no questions: *Are Bill's mother's friends waiting?*.

Note again that the asterisk is used to indicate that a sentence or other expression is unacceptable. We will have much more to say about all these things later.

While, in English, a word that can be pluralized is a noun (unless it is a demonstrative or pronoun), the reverse does not always hold. If some word cannot be pluralized, it does not follow that it is not a noun. Some nouns, so-called mass nouns (like *furniture*, *milk*, or *rice*), can only be pluralized with great difficulty. And when they are pluralized, their meaning shifts in a subtle way. While *the books* refers to a group of books, *the rices* would usually refer to a set of **types** of rice. There is clearly a lot more to say about the difference between mass nouns and count nouns. (See Chierchia, 1998) for a good overview.) Yet, mass nouns are still nouns, as they otherwise have the distributional properties of nouns. Thus the ability to accept the plural suffix seems to generally be a reliable diagnostic of "nounhood," but failure to pluralize does not imply that a word is not a noun.

While pluralization picks out nouns, other affixes pick out different categories. English can modify the way in which a verb describes the timing of an action by adding affixes:

I dance	present tense (meaning habitually, or at least sometimes)
I danc-ed	past tense
I am danc-ing	present *am* progressive *-ing* (meaning I'm dancing now)

In English, only verbs can combine with the past tense or progressive affixes. This then can be used as a diagnostic test: if a word can combine with a past or progressive affix, it is a verb. The progressive affix is pronounced as *-ing*. There are other *-ing* affixes that we will not be concerned with, such as the one that enables a verb phrase to act as a subject or object of a sentence:

His reaching the top surprised me a lot

Clearly, in this last example, the *-ing* does not express the idea that the *reaching the top* is going on now, as we speak. It expresses some sense that can be roughly paraphrased as *the fact that he reached the top surprised me*. Note that although even the most irregular verbs of English have *-ing* forms (*being, having, going*), some verbs sound very odd in progressive constructions:

?He is liking you a lot *She is knowing the answer

Could we conclude from this oddness that *like* or *know* are not verbs? No. We can see that *know* and *like* are verbs by using the past tense test. The situation with *like/know* in the progressive is similar to the one we encountered above, when we saw that some nouns did not seem to allow pluralization. This kind of situation holds quite frequently, and that is why we use the following slogan:

An isolated negative result is usually **uninformative** by itself

This is a slogan (and only a slogan) to help you remember that it is difficult to interpret the isolated failure of a particular test (we refer to this as *experimental failure*). The reason is that we do not know where the failure comes from. It could be due to factors that have nothing to do with the property we are investigating; in the example above, whether *like* and *know* are members of the category V. (For example, Newton's gravitation law would not be disconfirmed by a dropped object not falling vertically: it could be affected by wind, or by a magnet, etc.). For the same reason, it is difficult for experimental methodology to simply predict absence of change. If one found no change, this could be because nothing changed, or it could be because the experimental methods did not suffice to detect the change. Now, this does not mean that a negative result is never informative. We will see many cases where it is, such as when there is a systematic pattern of failures. But keep in mind that caution is in order.

Linguistics as cognitive science: In making our judgments about phrases, labeling them "ok" or "*" as we have done above, we are conducting quick, informal psychological experiments on ourselves. To decide what to conclude (e.g. whether an affix can go on a word), we are constantly asking ourselves whether this string or that string is acceptable. These are simple psychological experiments. We are relying on the fact that people are pretty good at judging which sequences of words make sense to them and to other people with a similar linguistic background, and we rely on this ability in our initial development of the subject.

Obviously, a science like physics is not like this. Useful experiments about electromagnetic radiation or gravitational forces typically require careful measurements and statistical analysis. Many linguistic questions are like physics in this respect too. For example, questions about how quickly words can be recognized, questions about word frequencies, questions about our ability to understand language in the presence of noise – these are things that typical speakers of a language will not have interesting and accurate judgments about, and so require more involved experimental methods. But questions about the acceptability of a phrase are different: we can make good, reliable judgments about this. There is a recent study by Sprouse and Almeida (2011), whose title says it all: *The 469 data points that form the empirical foundation of generative syntactic theory are at least 98% replicable using formal experiments.*

Of course, we require our linguistic theory to make sense of our linguistic judgments *and* ordinary fluent speech in "natural" settings *and* the results of careful quantitative study. In this text, we will occasionally make note of ways in which our account of syntax has been related to aspects of human abilities that have been studied through other means.

In this sense, linguistics is an experimental science trying to uncover something about the knowledge of language somehow stored in our mind. When we start with our judgments about language, though, there are at least three respects in which we must be especially careful. First, we want a theory of our judgments about the language, and every speaker of the language has access to an enormous range of data. It is unreasonable to expect linguistic theory to explain all this data at the outset. As in other sciences, we must start with a theory that gets some of the facts right, and then proceed to refine the theory. This is particularly important in introductory classes: there will be counterexamples to many of our first proposals! Some of these will turn out to be merely apparent, but others are serious. We will carefully set aside some of these, to come back to them later. A second issue that requires some care is that sometimes our judgments about the acceptability of particular examples are not clear. When this happens, we should look for clearer examples to support our proposals. Sometimes we cannot find such examples, which simply means that we have reached one of the limitations of this method of investigation, and we can try other methods. A third problem facing our development of the theory is that there are at least slight differences in the linguistic knowledge of any two speakers of the same language, no matter how closely these speakers are related. Ultimately, our linguistic theory should account for the variation that is found, but initially, we will focus on central properties of widely spoken languages. For this reason, we will often speak as if there is one language called "English," one language called "French," and so on, even though we recognize that each individual's language is different.

2.1.2 Syntactic contexts sensitive to the same categories

Surprisingly, the categorization of words that is relevant for affixation is also relevant for simply determining where a word can appear, even without affixes. The distribution of a word is an indication about its "syntactic" properties, properties determining the role the expression plays in the formation of phrases. Our categories provide a first classification of these roles. Words of the same category play similar roles and so will typically have similar distributions. Distributional evidence is very useful but is not always easy to manipulate. For example, consider the context or "frame" indicated here:

This is my most ______ book

Suppose we try to plug single words in the blank space. Certain choices of words will yield well-formed English phrases, others will not.

ok: interesting, valuable, recent
* John, slept, carefully, for

This frame only allows adjectives (A) in the space, but not all adjectives can appear there. For example, we cannot put *alleged* or *fake* there. (Remember: a negative result is uninformative by itself.)

One property that some nouns have is that they can appear in a single word slot following a determiner like *the*:

the ______ is here
ok: book, milk, furniture
* big, grow, very

As another example, the following context seems to allow single words only if they are verbs:

When will John ______ ?

Here is an example of a context in which we could be misled:

John is ______
nice *nices
president *presidents

Both elements of the first column, *nice* and *president*, can occur in this context, but they do not belong to the same category. As indicated in the second column, *president* unlike *nice* can be pluralized. Therefore *nice* is an A, while *president* is an N. We must be careful: this context allows both adjectives and nouns (and other things too)! Some frames are thus good test frames for specific categories, others are not.

The possibility of occurring in frames like the ones listed here provides a first way to classify words into categories that will be relevant to syntax and morphology. In morphology, we will see that affixes are sensitive to category, and compounding is sensitive to category as well. Why should the possibility of having a certain affix correlate with the possibility of occurring in a certain frame? We will get some insight into fundamental questions like this in the next chapters.

2.1.3 Modifiers

The options for modification provide another way to identify the categories that are relevant for both word formation (morphology) and phrase formation (syntax). Here we use a mix of semantic and syntactic factors to figure out what modifies what, in a familiar way. For example, a word that modifies a verb is probably an adverb of some kind, a word that modifies a noun is probably some kind of an adjective, and so forth for other categories (square brackets with a subscript indicate the category of a word):

category	modifier		example
V	Adv	[$_V$ stop]	stop *suddenly* (a way of stopping)
N	A(djective)	[$_N$ stop]	*sudden* stop (a type of stop)
P	Intensifier	[$_P$ in] the middle	*right* in the middle, *smack* in the middle
A	Degree	[$_A$ sad]	*very* sad, *too* sad, *more* sad
Adv	Degree	[$_{Adv}$ sadly]	*very* sadly, *too* sadly, *more* sadly

For example, we can observe that the following sentence allows a modifier to be introduced:

John was shooting → John was shooting accurately

Assuming we have independently established that *accurately* is an adverb, and since shooting accurately is a way of shooting, we can conclude that in this sentence, shooting is a verb (V). On the other hand, in

I resent any unnecessary shooting of lions

we conclude from the fact that *unnecessary* is an adjective, and from the fact that an unnecessary shooting is a type of shooting, that in this sentence, shooting is a noun (N). The reverse process works as well:

John shot → John shot sloppily

Since *shot* is the past tense of *shoot*, we know that *shot* is a verb in this sentence. Since *sloppily* modifies it, we may conclude that *sloppily* is an adverb.

2.1.4 Complementary distribution

Another, perhaps more surprising, kind of evidence for two words having the same category is available when the two words are in **complementary distribution**, by which we mean that in a given context, either one of the two words may occur but not both simultaneously. This is a good indication (though certainly not foolproof) that these two items belong to the same category.

For example, only certain words can occur in the frame below:

	____	books
ok	the	
ok	these	
*	the these	
*	these the	

We see that *the* and *these* are in complementary distribution: both appear in the same context and, if one appears, the other cannot. This suggests that there is just one structural position there, a position that can be filled by one or the other. Consequently, this is evidence that these elements have the same category, in this case the category we call determiners (D). On the other hand, we have

ok: the book
ok: blue books
ok: the blue books

So we see that *the* and *blue* are not in complementary distribution, and nothing much follows from this.

Like our other tests for category, this one is not foolproof. Consider these examples:

ok: the book
ok: John's book
* the John's book
* John's the book

> **Do categories really exist and if so what are they?** In what follows, we continue to use category labels, both traditional ones such as N, V, etc., and less traditional ones such as C, D, etc. We should be aware, however, that this may just be a convenient approximation.
>
> What kind of issues could arise for this idea? First, there is the question of whether categories are primitives of linguistic analysis or derived concepts. If the latter, if they can be entirely defined on the basis of other properties, then in a sense they have no real theoretical status: they are just convenient shorthand. If the former – the traditional, but by no means the obviously correct, view – they cannot be defined from anything more basic.
>
> A second question is whether or not the labels that we are using are really accurate. That is, similar distributions could sometimes result from distinct properties. It is quite possible (in fact likely) that the inventory of categories we have is far too crude. Thus, it may be that categories are like chemical compounds: they are made up of smaller pieces (like molecules or atoms in chemistry), which combine to form more complex structures. Under such a view Ns could be like a class of chemicals (say metals), with many subclasses (e.g. ferromagnetic metals), and the system of classes could admit of cases where an item has properties of multiple classes, so belonging to an "intermediate" category (e.g. conductive plastic polymers, which have both metal and non-metal properties).

We see that *the* and *John's* are in complementary distribution, but later we will provide reasons to reject the view that they are the same category – something slightly more complicated explains the complementary distribution in this case. Note, however, that meaning can be a guide here: *John's* expresses a kind of meaning (e.g. possession by John) that seems quite unlike the meaning expressed by *the* or *these*.

2.2 Words are Made of Smaller Units: Morphemes

We defined a *morpheme* as a meaningful atom (as having semantics or representing a grammatical property) that is maximally simple, that is, with no meaningful subparts. For our purposes here, this will be a good enough approximation. A word will be called *complex* if it contains more than one of these atoms. The part of a word that an affix attaches to is called a *stem*, and the *root* of the word is what you start with, before any affixes have been added.

English morphology is not very rich compared to most of the world's languages. It has some prefixes:

pre-test, ex-husband, dis-appear,
un-qualified, re-think, in-accurate

It has suffixes:

test-s, test-ed, test-able, nation-al-iz-ation

It seems to have a few, more peripheral, infixes:

fan-fucking-tastic	can mean roughly "really fantastic"
edu-ma-cation	can mean roughly "a less worthy education"

Many other languages (apparently) have infixes that play more central roles in the grammar. For example, in Tagalog, a language spoken in the Philippines by some 10 million speakers, one use of *-um-* is illustrated by forms like these (Schachter and Otanes (1972), 310):

ma-buti	b-um-uti	ma-laki	l-um-aki	ma-tanda	t-um-anda
"good"	"become good"	"big"	"get big, grow"	"old"	"get old, age"

English does not seem to have circumfixes (though possibly *em-bold-en*, or *em-bigg-en* from the Simpsons, might qualify), but Dutch has. Dutch past participles have two parts flanking the verbal root, *ge- -d*:

ge-genereer-d	ge-werk-t	ge-hoor-d
"generated"	"worked"	"heard"

English does have a form of affixation that involves certain verb forms exhibiting sound changes in the base in past tense (*run/ran, swim/swam, come/came, meet/met, speak/spoke, choose/chose, write/wrote*), but other languages like the Semitic languages (Arabic, Hebrew), make much heavier and more regular use of this kind of change. For example, in Standard Arabic, the language of some 250 million speakers (Ratcliffe (1998), 77),

qalbun	quluubun	najmun	nujuumun	kalbun	kilaabun
"heart"	"hearts"	"star"	"stars"	"dog"	"dogs"

English also has some affixes that are "supra-segmental," applying prosodic changes like stress shift above the level of the linguistic segments, (the phonemes): (pérmit/permít, récord/recórd).

Reduplication, repetition of all or part of a word, is another form of affixation. English does not regularly have this in its morphology, but many of the world's languages do. For example, take Agta, another Philippine language spoken by several hundred people (Healey, 1960: 7):

takki	taktakki	ulu	ululuda	mag-saddu	mag-sadsaddu
"leg"	"legs"	"head"	"heads"	"leak"	"leak in many places"

Although there are many kinds of affixes, we find that they have some properties in common across languages.

Note on orthography: We will almost always use the standard Roman alphabet and conventional spelling (when there are any such conventions), sometimes augmented with diacritics and phonetic characters to denote the expressions of various languages, even when those languages are conventionally written with non-Roman alphabets. For example, we will usually write *Cleopatra* because that is the conventional spelling of the word in English, rather than the phonetic [kliopætrə] or the Egyptian hieroglyphic . Throughout, it is important to remember that our primary focus is each individual's knowledge of his or her own *spoken* language. We use our own conventional English orthography to denote the words of each individual's language.

2.3 Morphemes Combine in Regular Ways

Morphology addresses the many questions that arise from these linguistic units. What kinds of affixes are there? What kinds occur in English? What are their combinatory properties? Do complex words have any form of internal organization?

2.3.1 Compositionality

The *Oxford English Dictionary* has an entry for the following word:

> **denationalization**: 1. The action of denationalizing, or the condition of being denationalized. 2. The action of removing (an industry, etc.) from national control and returning it to private ownership.

This word is not very common, but it is not extremely rare either. People with a college education, or regular readers of the newspapers, are likely to be familiar with it. But even a speaker who is not familiar with the word is likely to recognize that it is a possible word, and can even make a good guess about what it means. How is this possible? We can identify five basic and familiar building blocks, the morphemes making up this word:

de-nation-al-ize-ation

The word *nation* is a free morpheme, and we can see that it is an N, since it can be modified by adjectives, and it can bear plural morphology. Taking this as the root, the meaning of *denationalization* is then built progressively from the meaning of its morphological parts:

Nation-al characterizes a property that a **nation** can have, as in ***a national anthem***. **Nationalize** means "make **national**." **De-nationalize** means "undo the **nationalizing**." So **denationaliz-ation** is the process or the result of **denationalizing**, that is of removing the national character of something.

The property of words that allows them to be broken down in this way is called compositionality. Roughly, it means that meaning is progressively computed by general rules, so that once that we have computed the meaning of say *nationalize*, *nationaliz-ation* is just going to add the meaning of *-ation* (whatever that is) to the already computed meaning of *nationalize* by a general rule of meaning combination. It would, for example, be a surprise if *de-nationalize* meant to undo a personalization. No, that's what *depersonalize* means.

Sometimes however, compositionality fails. We call words and phrases that are not derived compositionally **idioms**. Imagine, for example, a species of blueberries which produces white berries. These can be marketed as white blueberries: thus a *blueberry* is not necessarily a berry that is blue. In such a case, it seems that we still have two morphemes, *blue* and *berry*, but their combined meaning is idiomatic, that is, it does not result from the general rules of meaning combination. Other times, it is less clear how to decide how many morphemes are in a word, as in examples like *speedometer*, or *cranberry*, where *cran* for many speakers only occurs in combination with *berry*. Investigating this problem in depth is beyond the scope of this chapter.

2.3.2 Affixation

When we look closely, the situation seems even more remarkable. There are 5!=120 different orderings of the five morphemes in *de-nation-al-ize-ation*, but only one order forms a word. That's a lot of possible orders, all given in Figure 2.1, but somehow, speakers of English are able to recognize the only ordering that the language allows. That is, we claim:

(1) A speaker of English, even one who is unfamiliar with this word, will only accept one of these sequences as a possible English word.

This is an empirical claim that we can verify by checking over all the orderings in Figure 2.1. (In making this check, we use our "intuition," but we expect that the claim would also be confirmed by studies of spontaneous speech and texts, and by psychological studies looking for "startle" reactions when impossible morpheme sequences occur, etc.)

What explains the fact that English speakers only accept one of these possible orderings? First, it cannot simply be memorization (like having encountered "denationalization" but none of the others) since some speakers are unfamiliar with this word. If they are familiar with it, we could try another one, even a non-existing word (e.g. denodalization from node – nodal – nodalize, etc.). Our theory is that English speakers, and speakers of other human languages, (implicitly) know some regularities about word formation. What are the regularities that a speaker needs to know in order to accept *denationalization* and reject the other 119 forms?

de- nation -al -ize -ation
* nation -al -ize de- -ation
* -al de- nation -ize -ation
* -al nation -ize -ation de-
* -al -ize de- nation -ation
* de- -al -ize -ation nation
* -al -ize -ation de- nation
* nation de- -ize -al -ation
* nation -ize -al -ation de-
* -ize nation de- -al -ation
* de- -ize -al nation -ation
* -ize -al nation de- -ation
* -ize de- -al -ation nation
* -ize -al -ation nation de-
* nation -ize de- -ation -al
* de- -ize nation -ation -al
* -ize nation -ation de- -al
* -ize de- -ation nation -al
* -ize -ation nation -al de-
* -ize -ation de- -al nation
* de- nation -al -ation -ize
* nation -al -ation de- -ize
* -al de- nation -ation -ize
* -al nation -ation -ize de-
* -al -ation de- nation -ize
* de- -al -ation -ize nation
* -al -ation -ize de- nation
* nation de- -ation -al -ize
* nation -ation -al -ize de-
* -ation nation de- -al -ize
* de- -ation -al nation -ize
* -ation -al nation de- -ize
* -ation de- -al -ize nation
* -ation -al -ize nation de-
* nation -ation de- -ize -al
* de- -ation nation -ize -al
* -ation nation -ize de- -al
* -ation de- -ize nation -al
* -ation -ize nation -al de-
* -ation -ize de- -al nation
* nation de- -al -ize -ation
* nation -al -ize -ation de-
* -al nation de- -ize -ation
* de- -al -ize nation -ation
* -al -ize nation de- -ation
* -al de- -ize -ation nation
* -al -ize -ation nation de-
* nation -ize de- -al -ation
* de- -ize nation -al -ation
* -ize nation -al de- -ation
* -ize de- -al nation -ation
* -ize -al nation -ation de-
* -ize -al de- -ation nation
* de- nation -ize -ation -al
* nation -ize -ation de- -al
* -ize de- nation -ation -al
* -ize nation -ation -al de-
* -ize -ation de- nation -al
* de- -ize -ation -al nation
* -ize -ation -al de- nation
* nation de- -al -ation -ize
* nation -al -ation -ize de-
* -al nation de- -ation -ize
* de- -al -ation nation -ize
* -al -ation nation de- -ize
* -al de- -ation -ize nation
* -al -ation -ize nation de-
* nation -ation de- -al -ize
* de- -ation nation -al -ize
* -ation nation -al de- -ize
* -ation de- -al nation -ize
* -ation -al nation -ize de-
* -ation -al de- -ize nation
* de- nation -ation -ize -al
* nation -ation -ize de- -al
* -ation de- nation -ize -al
* -ation nation -ize -al de-
* -ation -ize de- nation -al
* de- -ation -ize -al nation
* -ation -ize -al de- nation
* nation -al de- -ize -ation
* de- -al nation -ize -ation
* -al nation -ize de- -ation
* -al de- -ize nation -ation
* -al -ize nation -ation de-
* -al -ize de- -ation nation
* de- nation -ize -al -ation
* nation -ize -al de- -ation
* -ize de- nation -al -ation
* -ize nation -al -ation de-
* -ize -al de- nation -ation
* de- -ize -al -ation nation
* -ize -al -ation de- nation
* nation de- -ize -ation -al
* nation -ize -ation -al de-
* -ize nation de- -ation -al
* de- -ize -ation nation -al
* -ize -ation nation de- -al
* -ize de- -ation -al nation
* -ize -ation -al nation de-
* nation -al de- -ation -ize
* de- -al nation -ation -ize
* -al nation -ation de- -ize
* -al de- -ation nation -ize
* -al -ation nation -ize de-
* -al -ation de- -ize nation
* de- nation -ation -al -ize
* nation -ation -al de- -ize
* -ation de- nation -al -ize
* -ation nation -al -ize de-
* -ation -al de- nation -ize
* de- -ation -al -ize nation
* -ation -al -ize de- nation
* nation de- -ation -ize -al
* nation -ation -ize -al de-
* -ation nation de- -ize -al
* de- -ation -ize nation -al
* -ation -ize nation de- -al
* -ation de- -ize -al nation
* -ation -ize -al nation de-

Figure 2.1 120 orderings, only 1 is intelligible

1. The speaker needs to know each of the five morphemes, *de-*, *nation*, *-al*, *-ize*, *-ation*.
2. The speaker needs to know what kind of morpheme each one is. Is it free? If not, then is it a prefix, suffix, etc.?

ok: nation-al	*-alnation	-al is a suffix
ok: pre-test	*test-pre	pre- is a prefix

This is something that, by convention, we often indicate with preceding or following hyphens, as we have done here.

3. Since an affix is a morpheme that is not "complete," it must attach to something (which is traditionally called a stem). Let's call the thing it needs a *complement*. So the speaker needs to know what kind of thing the affix can attach to, what kind of "complement" it requires. For example:

   ok: national-ize symbol-ize *speak-ize *in-ize

   The *-ize* suffix combines with adjectives or nouns of a certain kind, but not with verbs or prepositions. This property is called *c-selection*, for "category selection." The affix *-ize* needs to combine with stems of certain categories, namely A or N. This is actually the property that we used earlier with the past tense and progressive suffixes to determine membership in the category V: these affixes c-select V. There may be other kinds of selection too, as we will see later.
4. The speaker knows that an affix must combine with something "next to it," something adjacent. For example, we can form *nation-al-ize*, but we cannot realize this as *nation-ize-al* as follows:

   ok: nation nation-al nation-al-ize *: nation nation -al *nation-iz-al

   When suffixing *-ize*, we cannot suffix it to *nation* after *-al* has attached in this way. Affixation is not allowed to "see" inside *national*, so it cannot suffix *-ize* to *nation*.
5. The speaker needs to know what kind of thing results from combining an affix with a complement, in order to be able to decide what the result is allowed to combine with:

nation-al is an adjective	*-al* turns a N into an A (N-al meaning roughly, of or having to do with N)
nation-al-ize is a verb	*-ize* turns an A into a V (meaning "make V" – a causative reading)

   How do we know *nation-al* is an A? If we have established that *-ize* generally suffixes to adjectives, one reason is that *-ize* can suffix to it. But there are of course other reasons: the other tests mentioned above converge on this conclusion.

In sum, a speaker who knows the following things will only find one analysis of *nation-al-iz-ation*:

nation:	free, N		
-al:	suffix,	c-selects N,	to form an A (X-al means pertaining to X)
-ize:	suffix,	c-selects A,	to form a V (A-ize means cause to be A)
de-:	prefix,	c-selects V,	to form a V (de-V means the reverse of V)
-ation:	suffix,	c-selects V,	to form a N (V-ation refers to an event of V-ing)

We will call this kind of specification of these basic properties of morphemes *lexical entries*.

We will elaborate our lexical entries in various ways as we proceed. Notice that the third column of the entries above, the specification of what the affixes select, is only approximate. It is true that *-al* can combine with the noun *nation* to form that adjective *national*, but this affix cannot select just any noun:

$[_N$neighborhood$]$ *neighborhoodal | $[_N$honesty$]$ *honestial

It appears that this suffix will only attach to nouns that are either simple roots – that is, atomic nouns, those that have no morphological parts, or else nouns that end in *-ion*, *-ment*, or *-or* (but not necessarily to all such nouns viz. **city-al*, **suitor-al*):

natur-al	relation-al	environment-al	mayor-al
season-al	exception-al	fundament-al	behavior-al

We see that *-al* is very particular about which nouns it can select. It selects roots and non-roots, but only certain ones. So our lexical entry for this suffix needs to be augmented, and it is not clear how to specify its requirements exactly. One proposal is that nouns ending in *-ion, -or, -ment* are in a special family of "latinate" nouns, (nouns that have been borrowed from French which ultimately goes back to Latin) and these are what are selected. Adopting this view, we could say:

-al: suffix, c-selects $N_{latinate}$ to form an A (X-al means pertaining to X)

Rather than name the families of nouns in this way, we will simply annotate our entries with the range of accepted kinds of nouns:

-al: suffix, c-selects N (-ion, -or, -ment) to form an A (X-al means pertaining to X)

Surveying the suffixes in English, Fabb (1988) finds that a number of them have special "latinate" requirements:

-al:	c-selects N to form A (-ion, -or, -ment)	natur-al
-ion	c-selects V to form N (-ize, -ify, -ate)	realizat-ion, relat-ion
-ity	c-selects A to form N (-ive, -ic, -al, -an, -ous, -able)	profan-ity
-ism	c-selects A to form N (-ive, -ic, -al, -an)	modern-ism
-ist	c-selects A to form N (-ive, -ic, -al, -an)	formal-ist
-ize	c-selects A to form V (-ive, -ic, -al, -an)	special-ize

Other suffixes select roots only in certain categories:

-an,-ian	c-selects root N to form N	librari-an, Darwin-ian
	c-selects root N to form A	reptil-ian
-age	c-selects root V to form N	steer-age
	c-selects root N to form N	orphan-age
-al	c-selects root V to form N	betray-al
-ant	c-selects root V to form N	defend-ant
	c-selects root V to form A	defi-ant
-ance	c-selects root V to form N	annoy-ance
-ate	c-selects root N to form V	origin-ate
-ful	c-selects root N to form A	peace-ful
	c-selects root V to form A	forget-ful
-hood	c-selects root N to form N	neighbor-hood
-ify	c-selects root N to form V	class-ify
	c-selects root A to form V	instens-ify
-ish	c-selects root N to form A	boy-ish
-ism	c-selects root N to form N	Reagan-ism
-ive	c-selects root V to form A	restrict-ive
-ize	c-selects root N to form V	symbol-ize
-ly	c-selects root A to form A	dead-ly
	c-selects root N to form A	ghost-ly

-ment	c-selects root V to form N	establish-ment
-ory	c-selects root V to form A	advis-ory
-ous	c-selects root N to form A	humor-ous
-y	c-selects root A to form N	honest-y
	c-selects root V to form N	assembl-y
	c-selects root N to form N	robber-y

And some English suffixes select a range of root and non-root forms:

-er	c-selects V to form N	kill-er, dry-er, class-ifi-er
-able	c-selects V to form A	manage-able, re-do-able, class-ifi-able
-ist	c-selects N to form N	art-ist, unifi-cation-ist
-ary	c-selects N to form A (-ion)	revolut-ion-ary, legend-ary
-er	c-selects N to form N (-ion)	vacat-ion-er, prison-er
-ic	c-selects N to form A (-ist)	modern-ist-ic, metall-ic
-(at)ory	c-selects V to form A (-ify)	class-ifi-catory, advis-ory
-y	c-selects N to form A (-ence)	resid-ence-y (usually a noun), heart-y

The whole collection of knowledge that a speaker has about morphemes, the collection of lexical entries, is called a lexicon. It will contain information about morphemes of the sort shown here and more. We can think of the lexicon as the place in memory where all this information is stored.

The mental representation of the lexicon: Note that if lexical information is placed in memory as we describe it, other evidence should confirm that it is really stored there, in the form we propose.

In fact, this question is getting a lot of attention from quite a variety of perspectives. There is some evidence that frequently used words, even if they can be decomposed into a sequence of two or more morphemes, are represented in their complete forms (Baayen, Dijkstra, and Schreuder (1979); Bertram, Baayen, and Schreuder (2000)), and so there is increasing interest in how people figure out the meanings of rare and novel complex words. Novel forms are often studied with various kinds of "wug" tests (Berko, 1958), which are tasks designed to indicate how subjects interpret word forms that they have never seen or heard before. A good review of current thinking and some recent proposals can be found in Trueswell et al. (2013) and Medina et al. (2011).

2.3.3 Word structure

The last section made the following claim:

(1) Only one ordering of the five morphemes in *de-nation-al-iz-ation* produces a possible English word.

The proposal was that (1) is explained by the assumption that English speakers know some basic facts about the five morphemes, facts that are represented in lexical entries like this:

nation:	free		
-al:	suffix,	c-selects N,	to form an A (X-al means pertaining to X)
-ize:	suffix,	c-selects A,	to form a V (A-ize means cause to be A)
de-:	prefix,	c-selects V,	to form a V (de-V means the reverse of V)
-ation:	suffix,	c-selects V,	to form a N (V-ation refers to an event of V-ing)

With these lexical entries, we get the following derivation, and no other:

nation → national → nationalize → denationalize → denationalization.

Derivations like this are standardly represented by a *tree*.

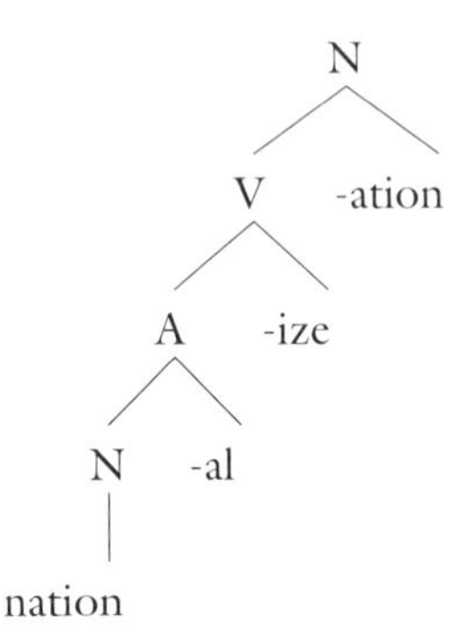

Linguists traditionally draw "trees" like this, upside-down, with the root on top and all branches going out in the downward direction. Each point that is labeled with a word or a category is called a *node*, and the node at the top of the tree is called the *root of the tree* (not to be confused with the root of a word). So the tree shown above has eight nodes, and the one at the top is the root. The four *nodes* along the bottom of the tree are called *leaves*. The four nodes that are not leaves are *internal nodes*. When a node has a branch downward to another node, it is called a *parent* or *mother* node, and the node at the end of this branch is called its *child* or *daughter*. A node is said to *dominate* another node if the second one is a descendant of the first one in the obvious sense (i.e., daughter of, or daughter of daughter of . . .). Two nodes with the same parent are called *siblings* or *sisters*.

We can read a lot of information off the tree, repeated here:

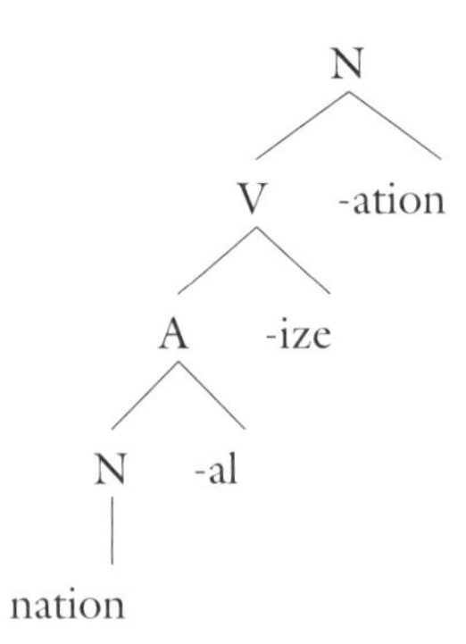

- We can see that anything dominated by a single node is a unit of some kind.
- We can see that *-al* takes N as a complement (that is, as something that "completes" it) on its left to form an A.
- We can see that *-ize* takes a (non-root) A on its left to form a V.

- Ve can see that *-ation* takes a (non-root) V on its left to form a N.
- We can see that the node V dominates all the nodes A, -ize, N, -al, nation.

It is important to realize that the information in this tree is just a compact way to include all of the information given by the following set of trees:

N	A	V	N
|	|	|	|
nation	national	nationalize	nationalization

An equivalent way of representing the information given in this tree is by means of the more compact labeled bracket notation:

$$[_N[_V[_A[_N \text{ nation}] \text{ -al}] \text{ -ize}] \text{ -ation}]$$

These structural representations are useful in that they represent many claims at once in a compact way.

2.3.4 Selection and locality

Section 2.3.2 proposes that a speaker who can make sense of the word *denationalization*, especially a speaker who is seeing it for the first time, must know five things, briefly repeated here:

1. how each morpheme is pronounced;
2. what kind of morpheme it is (free, or else prefix, suffix . . .);
3. if an affix, what it c-selects;
4. if an affix, that the c-selected element must be adjacent to the affix;
5. if an affix, what kind of thing results after c-selection.

And we can see these things in the proposed lexical entries:

1	2	3	5
nation:	free		
-al:	suffix,	c-selects N,	to form an A (X-al means pertaining to X)
-ize:	suffix,	c-selects A,	to form a V (A-ize means cause to be A)
de-:	prefix,	c-selects V,	to form a V (de-V means the reverse of V)
-ation:	suffix,	c-selects V,	to form an N (V-ation refers to an event of V-ing)

But notice that the lexical entries leave something out. The lexical entries leave out the piece of knowledge (4), that the selected element must be next to the selecting affix! Why is this left out?

Notice that, from the perspective of our trees, (4) amounts to the requirement that the branches of a tree do not cross. That is, we do not allow trees like this:

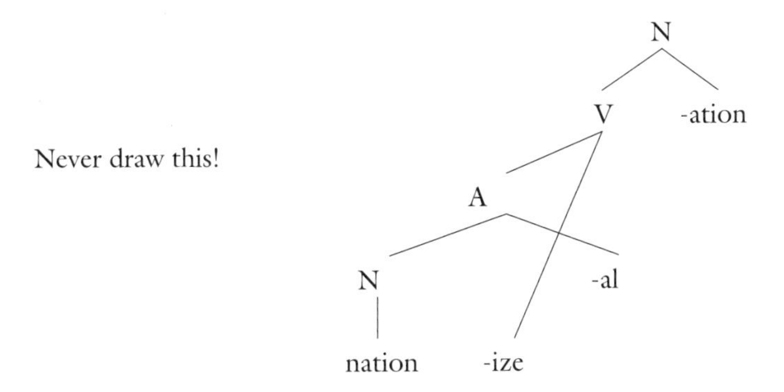

Branches cannot cross. These structures are not like mobiles, which can be flattened out on a page.

What is this property? Our trees implicitly encode two distinct type of information. First they tell us what morphological subunits there may be in a given word. Anything dominated by a single node is a unit of some kind. But they also implicitly tell us that the leaves of the tree are sequentially ordered. (Sequential order is also called temporal order.) The prohibition against branches crossing is a principle about how complex units, i.e. elements made up of parts, can have their parts temporally realized. The requirement that branches do not cross is tantamount to the requirement that morphological structure be respected by the sequential ordering.

Infixes, supra-segmental morphemes, and circumfixes look like they might be counterexamples to this idea that branches cannot cross, that is, the idea that morphological structure must be respected by temporal ordering; but really they are not, since infixes go inside the element they select, not on one side or the other. That is, they are never ordered between already combined morphemes. Moreover, infixes usually seem to want to be close to one edge or the other, and their temporal position seems conditioned **not by morphological properties or boundaries but by phonological ones**. Some recent theories claim that these elements are actually suffixes or prefixes which get pronounced "inside" their complements for phonological reasons (Prince and Smolensky, 1993). Supra-segmental morphemes also appear to hover at the right or left edge of their hosts, i.e. where prefixes or suffixes occur. Here it is just an issue of the expression of the morpheme (tones must dock on vowels). Finally, circumfixes often consist of a string of morphemes, all in a sisterhood relation. We refer to this sisterhood relation as a local relation.

What is not found: There is another property that seems to be related to the relationship between morphological structure and temporal order. We never find morphological trees in which:

i. a given node has more than one mother;
ii. a mother has more than two daughters;
iii. any node lacks a mother.

These situations would be exemplified by the following trees, respectively:

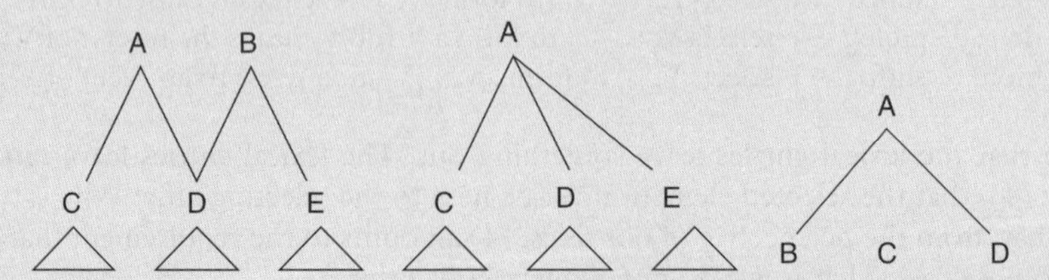

Non-existence of these trees could be derived if temporal ordering "mirrors" morphological structure. Just as a word c-selects one affix, perhaps a node with two mothers cannot be linearly ordered with respect to the rest of the structure, for example. Trees in general then obey the following conditions:

i. every node but one (the "topmost") has a mother; and
ii. no node has more than one mother.

The idea that c-selection branches cannot cross in morphology appears to be correct. We began with the observation that this property was not included in the lexicon, and now it is easy to see why. This property is not specific to any lexical item. Rather, it is a general property of how these linguistic structures are assembled.

There is another, related, fact that is very important:

Affixes cannot c-select for an element which is not a sister.

This is an empirical claim, but one that is slightly more abstract than the claim made in (1) in Section 2.3.3. We can see that this one is true by the kind of information we needed to provide in all the lexical entries listed above. No lexical entry ever imposes a requirement on a part of the word structure it is not a sister to. Because this claim is more abstract, depending on the correctness of our claims about lexical information, it is a little more difficult to defend, especially since, as we observed earlier, our proposed lexical entries are only approximate.

It may help to consider an affix that would clearly violate this locality claim. Let's construct a hypothetical case. It would be a suffix, say *-astial* (very much like *-ation*), that could combine with a verb to yield a noun, but only if this verb was itself derived from an adjective.

-astial: suffix, c-selects V derived from A to form an N

Here is a diagram illustrating what such a suffix would do:

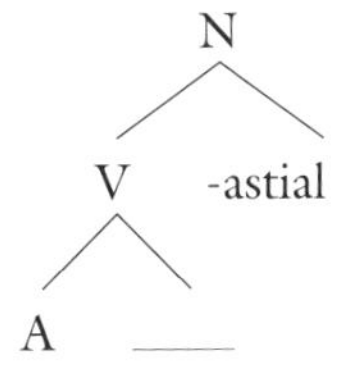

Such affixes do not seem to exist: to check whether c-selection is satisfied, we never need to look very far in the tree. Selection is checked in a **local environment**. Affixes never need to look down into the structure of the selected category. (We will get further confirmation for this idea below, in Section 2.3.6.) As we will see in the following chapters, this simple hypothesis can be maintained through a surprising range of data, and has far-reaching consequences for our theory. We give it a name:

Locality of Selection Hypothesis (to be revised): Selection is *local* in the sense that an item can only select properties of its sister(s).

If this is true, as it seems to be, then we would like to know why this very general property holds. Informally speaking, it suggests that the information inside a unit (that is, a constituent of a tree) is invisible or opaque from the outside, as if it had been compiled. We will return to such questions much later (see the discussion of cyclicity in Chapter 10).

Probing why locality of selection holds illustrates an important point. We are not content to just have correct descriptions of the phenomena we look at. We also want to try to understand why they turn out the way they do, rather than in some other conceivable way. Thus, we always start by asking such questions as: how are things organized? Is it true that they are organized this way, or that way? Can we confirm this by types of experiments other than speakers' judgments? These are basic descriptive questions. But then we turn to questions of explanation: why are these true things true? How should language be structured so that these things follow from its basic design?

Practice

Consider these words:

(i) undeniability (ii) remagnetize
(iii) post-modernism (iv) disassembled

For each of these words:

1. list all the morphemes in the word;
2. give lexical entries for each morpheme in the simple style shown in Section 2.3.2;
3. draw the tree representation of the word structure;
4. say how many nodes are in the tree;
5. say how many leaves are in the tree.

2.3.5 Compounds

We have switched from talking about words to talking about morphemes. Now we can see that many of the things that we pre-theoretically call words are actually complex. We do not call affixes "words," because they are bound morphemes, and words are "free." That is, words are relatively independent of the morphemes that occur on either side of them. Some words are simple, that is, free morphemes, but many other words are complexes of roots and affixes.

It is also possible to obtain words by combining words. These are called *compounds*. In English, compounds are sometimes written with spaces or hyphens between the elements, and sometimes there are no spaces or hyphens. Sometimes the meaning of a compound is *idiomatic* (not predicted in regular ways by the meanings of its parts), and sometimes it is compositional (the meaning is determined in the usual way by its parts).

compound	category	idiomatic?
babysit	V	yes
bartend	V	no
part supplier	N	no
anti-missile missile	N	no
kitchen towel rack	N	no
writer club address list	N	no
boron epoxy rocket motor chamber instruction manual	N	no

When we look at English compounds, we notice a striking pattern:

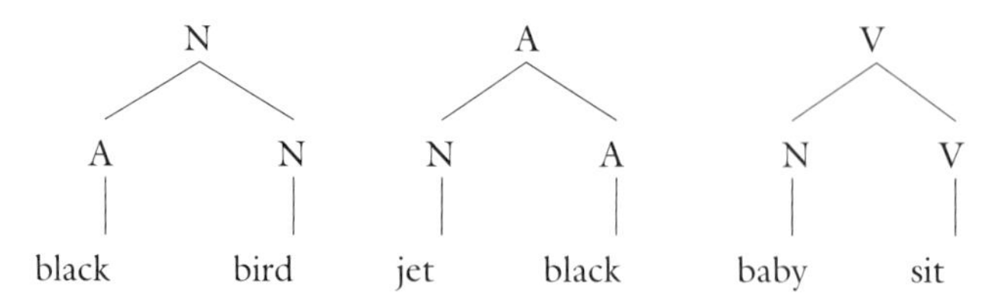

The category of the compound word is determined by the category of the right-hand member: thus *blackbird* is an N, not an A, by virtue of the fact that the right-hand member of the compound is N. This property is referred to as the Right-Hand Head Rule (Williams, 1981). We call the element that determines the category of the compound the head:

Head: The head of a constituent is the element that determines the properties of the constituent.

Informally speaking, we can say that the properties of the head are the properties of the whole. This notion of head plays a central role in morphology and in syntax.

The English Right-Hand Head Rule (RHHR): The rightmost element of a compound is the head of the compound.

More abstractly, then, in a compound word, the properties of the compound are predictable from the right-hand head rule, as illustrated below:

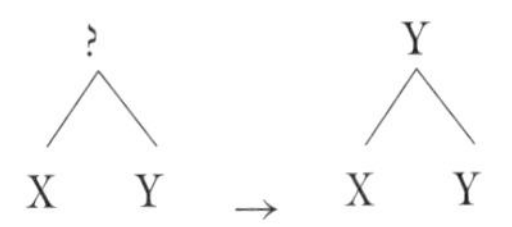

Thus, the language learner does not have to learn what category each new compound has: this is determined by the basic property of morphology expressed by the RHHR. The right-hand head rule was discussed in a famous 1981 article by Edwin Williams, who as of 2013, was a Professor of Linguistics at Princeton University.

The rightmost element determines not only the category of the compound, but other properties of the compound as well. Notice that the right-hand element determines whether the compound is singular or plural in English:

towel racks, sail boats	(plural)
parts supplier, salesman	(singular)

In languages in which nouns are marked for gender, like German, it is the right-hand member of a compound that determines the gender.

der Tisch	"the table, the desk"	(masc)
die Lampe	"the lamp"	(fem)
die Tisch Lampe	"the desk lamp"	(fem)

The right-hand element also determines the basic semantic properties of the compound. For example, an apple pie is a type of pie, jet-black is a type of black, and a blackbird is a type of bird. This takes us again to the distinction between modifiers and modifiees. In all these cases, the rightmost element is the head, which is being modified, while the leftmost element modifies it and acts as a satellite of this head.

2.3.6 The categorial status of affixes

We might ask if the right-hand head rule is specific to compounds, or if it applies more generally, to all complex words. Suppose we have a complex (=non-root) word whose rightmost morpheme is a suffix. If the RHHR applied, this suffix should determine the properties of the derived word and in particular its category. If it is a prefix, it should never determine the properties of the complex word. Reviewing all the English examples discussed above, this does seem to be the case. Consider the lists of English suffixes at the end of Section 2.3.2. We see that many suffixes change category, and those that do not change category often change meaning significantly. For example, *-er* changes V to N in *killer*, and while *-hood* does not change category in *neighborhood*, the meaning is changed significantly. A neighbor is a person, but a neighborhood is not.

With prefixes, on the other hand, the situation is quite different. Prefixes do not seem to change the category of the stem that they attach to, and it is for this reason that it is difficult to determine their category. Perhaps *re-* is an adverb; its meaning is similar to *again*. And *pre-* which may be a P, similar to *before*.

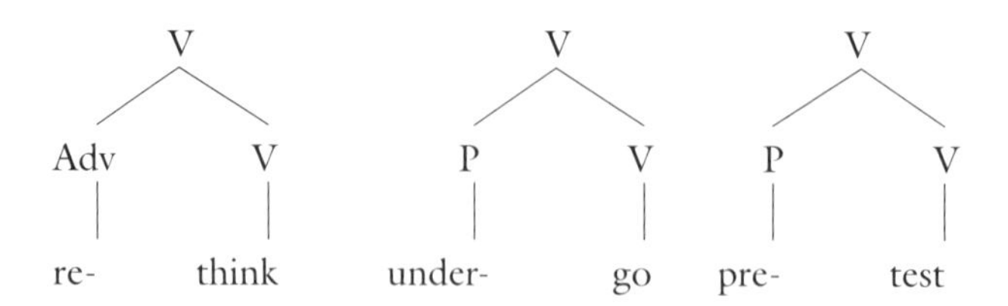

Another example is the following:

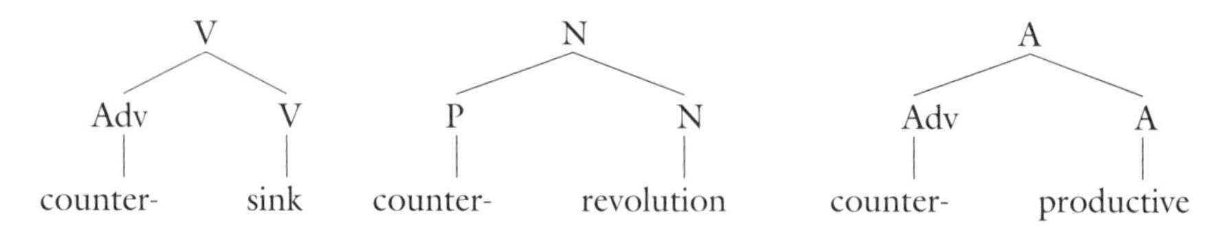

In each case the category of the result is entirely determined by the rightmost element, not by the prefix.

de-	combines with V, stays V	de-activate, de-generate, de-foliate
re-	combines with V, stays V	re-do, re-elect, re-subscribe, re-invent
anti-	combines with N, stays N	anti-Democrat, anti-climax, anti-matter
un-	combines with V, stays V	un-do, un-wrap, un-tie, un-
post-	combines with A, stays A	post-modern, post-graduate
dis-	combines with V, stays V	dis-entangle, dis-bar, dis-believe
under-	combines with V, stays V	under-go, under-coat, under-expose
ex-	combines with N, stays N	ex-marine, ex-husband
pre-	combines with A, stays A	pre-mature, pre-natal

It is reasonable to conclude that prefixes stand in a different relation to the stems they attach to than suffixes do. So let's say that prefixes are "modifiers" of those stems, in a sense that we will return to.

Suffixes, on the other hand, are able to change the category, and they occur on the right side. So they seem to obey the right-hand head rule. This strongly suggests that each suffix is of a particular category and transmits its category to the whole word, exactly as in compounds.

Let us thus assume that both free and bound morphemes belong to categories, so *-er* is an N, *-able* an A, and *-ness* an N. According to the right-hand head rule, the resulting word will have the same category as the affix, since it occurs in the head position of the derived word:

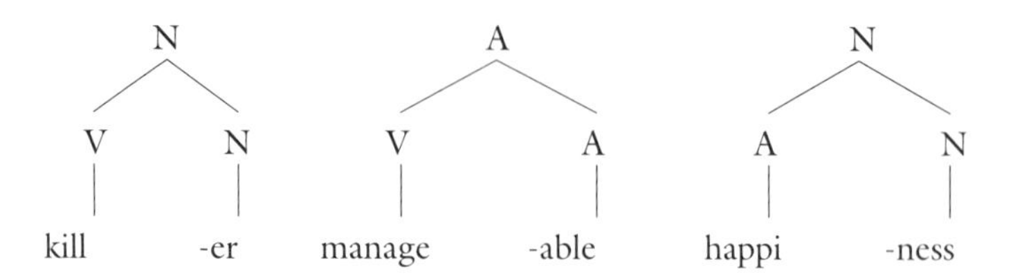

We conclude that suffixes are like words: they belong to particular categories. Thus *-er* is a noun, which happens to be a bound morpheme, meaning something like "who Xes," or "what Xs," not a free morpheme like [$_N$book]. And *-able* is a bound A (meaning something like "which can be V-ed"), and *-ness* is a bound N (meaning something like "the fact of being A"). We accordingly extend the RHHR from compounds to all words:

The English Right-Hand Head Rule (RHHR): the rightmost element of a word is the head of the word.

This perspective on affixes extends even to the so-called *inflectional affixes*, those that mark singular/plural and tense and in other languages, case (nominative/accusative/genitive/etc.), agreement, noun class, etc. These affixes tend to appear outside of the other affixes (often descriptively called "derivational" affixes) which were the focus of attention in the previous sections. But it appears that our account of derivational affixes extends straightforwardly to inflectional affixes. For English, the right-hand head rule, if fully general, predicts:

- past tense *-ed* is of a certain category (say, the category T for tense);
- a past tense verb is also of the category (T).

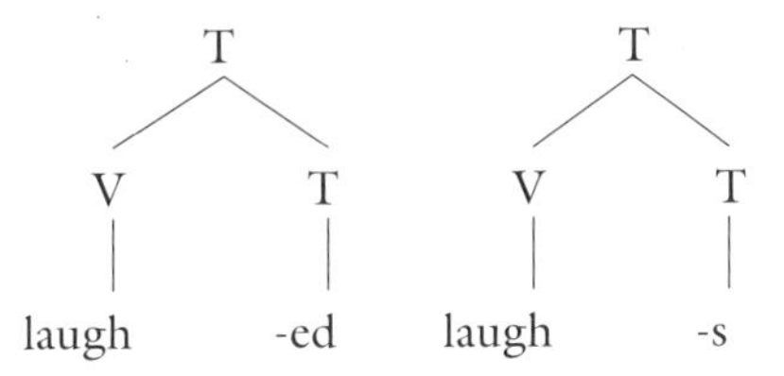

Similarly, we are led to postulate that plural *-s* is of the category number, as is the plural noun it forms:

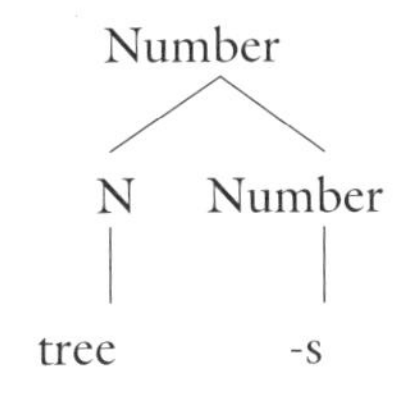

We can now put the account of affixes together. Suffixes like *-er* can be given the following simplified lexical entries (leaving the meaning specification aside):

er,	bound,	N,	c-selects for V,	(meaning)
able,	bound,	A,	c-selects for V,	(meaning)
s,	bound,	Number,	c-selects for N,	(meaning)

It is a property of heads that they determine the environment in which they occur: heads c-select for their sisters. In words and compounds, heads occur in the rightmost position, it follows that complex words with *-er* will surface as V-er (*manag-er*, and not like **er-manage*, *manage-able*, not **able-manage*).

The lexicon no longer needs to say what category is formed by the suffixes, since it is always just the category of the suffix itself. Note that there is an asymmetry between prefix and suffix c-selectors. A suffix S c-selects its complement C, and S is the head of the resulting C+S combination. A prefix P may c-select its complement C, but it is the complement that is the head of the result of P+C.

On p. 31, we promised some additional support for the locality of selection hypothesis in this section. Consider again the properties that English suffixes select for. These include not only the category of the sister, but also whether the sister is a root, or whether it is the member of a particular subcategory. For example, *-al* selects an N that is a root or a latinate noun ending in *-ion*, *-or*, *-ment*. Notice that these are properties determined by the head of the N, when it is complex, and never properties of the non-head constituents of the N. Consequently, it is plausible that these are properties of the N, as expected by the locality of selection, and in fact required by locality of selection.

2.4 Apparent Exceptions to the RHHR

There are some apparent exceptions to the RHHR that deserve attention. Some may turn out to be real once we understand how they work, but others are only apparent. We discuss a few cases here.

2.4.1 Conversion

One highly productive method of forming words in English is by conversion or zero derivation. Conversion creates new words without the use of a "visible" or "pronounced" affix.

noun	derived verb
father	father
butter	butter
ship	ship
nail	nail

What is the relation between the noun *father* and the verb *to father*? Following our conventions, we can write:

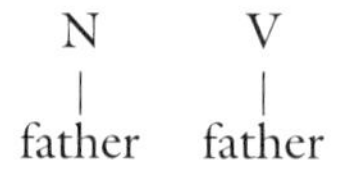

As we have done before, we can combine these two representations into one, giving an equivalent representation of these two trees, which would also express directly the relation between them:

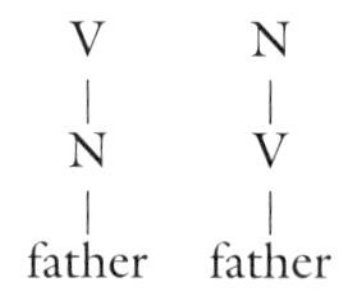

These say that the word *father* is either a verb derived from a noun or a noun derived from a verb. Note that there clearly has to be a derivation of some sort since, apart from the category change, the noun and the verb differ in other ways, like meaning and syntactic requirements (for example, the verb requires an overt complement). An alternative is to suppose that the verb is derived from the noun (or vice versa – this needs to be argued for) by postulating a silent affix: we can suppose that the verb *father* has a verbal head, but one that is silent. By the right-hand head rule, this head must be a suffix; it must be in the right-hand position. We will represent this silent verb head by *e*, where by convention, *e* denotes something that is phonetically *empty*, not pronounced.

Silent elements? Postulating silent elements is sometimes seen as controversial, so it is important to reflect a little bit about what this involves. There is no *a priori* reason why morphemes should be pronounced, just as there is no *a priori* reason why natural objects that science postulates should be visible or audible or directly perceptible in any way. Postulating a silent morpheme is no different from postulating that some stem has the silent property N (it is a noun) that can be seen by an affix. What matters are the reasons we have for postulating such objects, e.g. the effect that their presence would have on observable phenomena and how explanatory all this is. That said, if speakers postulate the existence of silent morphemes, some scenario must ultimately be provided as to how they (unconsciously) reach such a conclusion: how the presence of such silent morphemes is inferred by the language learning algorithms.

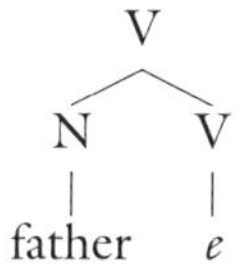

The alternative is to say that the derivation from one to the other takes place without any affixation. Why say that there is a silent V in these cases, rather than this alternative? First, it seems eminently reasonable to think there are silent morphemes in other cases, as this allows us to simplify our picture of word structure in a number of respects. One such case is the present tense morpheme. Postulating a silent present tense morpheme allows us to say that just as *laugh-ed* and *laugh-s* have the category tense (T), the present tense form *laugh* has the same category:

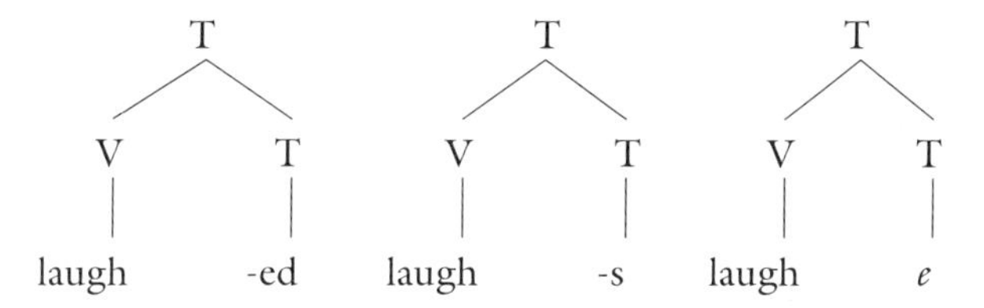

The same would go for the past or present tense form of the verb *father*: the empty V c-selects for N as its sister, and then T c-selects the V as its sister, as we see in the tree representation below:

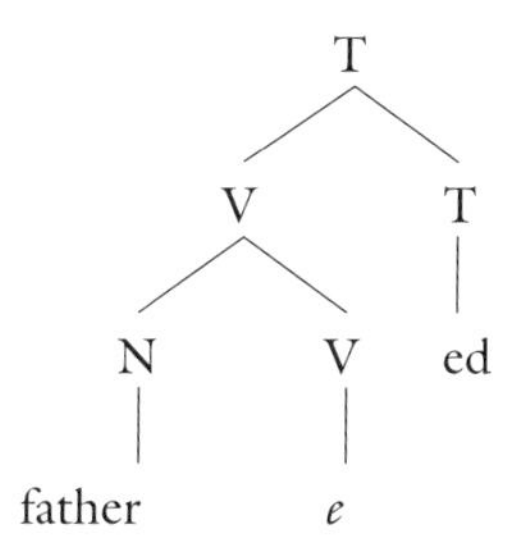

Note that *-ed*, as a bound morpheme, needs to be affixed to something. As long as the V sister of *-ed* above has some phonetic material in it somewhere, the *-ed* suffix counts as bound.

But an even stronger reason is the following: if verbs such as *father*, *wet*, *dry*, . . . , which are respectively related to the noun *father*, the adjective *wet*, and the adjective *dry*, are derived by affixation of a silent morpheme, it means that they are not roots; they are complex. This makes a prediction: no affixes that attach only to verb roots should be able to attach to these elements. This seems to be true:

steer-age	*wet-age	*dry-age	*father-age
betray-al	*wet-al	*dry-al	*father-al
defi-ant	*wet-ant	*dry-ant	*father-ant
annoy-ance	*wet-ance	*dry-ance	*father-ance
forget-ful	*wet-ful	*dry-ful	*father-ful
restrict-ive	*wet-ive	*dry-ive	*father-ive
establish-ment	*wet-ment	*dry-ment	*father-ment
advis-ory	*wet-ory	*dry-ory	*father-ory
assembl-y	*wett-y	*dry-y	*father-y

These results are all "negative" in the sense discussed earlier. That is, they are cases where a certain kind of combination turns out not to be possible. What is important here is that this failure is not an isolated instance. It is systematic and it is **predicted** by the silent affix proposal. Failure by itself is uninformative, but failure that a theory predicts is informative (although it is of course not demonstrative, or a proof in a mathematical sense, but rather a strong presumption).

We can give two further reasons in favor of the silent morpheme theory of conversion. First, unlike the verbs like *father*, nouns such as *father* should be roots. And indeed, some can be host to a root-selecting affix such as *-hood*: *father-hood*. Second, if homophonous nouns and verbs were simply both at the same time, we might expect to find affixes picky enough to select them and nothing else. This is never found. If, on the other hand, the verbs are derived from the nouns by the affixation of a silent morpheme, locality of selection would make the N property invisible to the outside: we predict that such verbs should not behave differently from non-converted verbs. And, indeed, they never do.

If we adopt the silent affix approach, many facts make sense. For example, silent affixes often contribute to the meaning of a word in exactly the same way as pronounced affixes. We find, for example, both silent and pronounced causative affixes:

wet	"to make wet"
dry	"to make dry"
empty	"to make empty"
short-en	"to make short"
normal-ize	"to make normal"
domestic-ate	"to make domestic"

What makes this comparison even more interesting is that adjectives like *wet*, *dry*, and *empty*, which combine with the empty causative, never combine with pronounced causatives (Beard, 1998):

* wett-en	* wet-ize	* wet-ate
* dry-en	* dry-ize	* dry-ate
* empty-en	* empty-ize	* empty-ate

And furthermore, the words that take pronounced, "overt" causative affixes typically do not also allow the empty causative affix (though *short* occurs as a V with another meaning):

* She shorts the dress
* She normals the distribution
* She domestics the animals

These latter facts can be explained by the assumption that words rarely allow two different causative affixes, just as they rarely allow two different plurals, or two different past tense forms.

When we started looking at conversion, it was not clear why we did not start with the verb *father* and derive the noun *father* by adding a silent head noun as affix. *A priori*, this is an equally viable option and one that is also consistent with the RHHR. Other reasons need to be brought to bear on this choice. For example, perhaps the meaning of the verb is more complex; it seems to include that of the noun but not vice versa. Thus, the noun concept may be more primitive than the verb concept (for example, *buttering* literally means "spreading butter;" while *butter* need not be defined in terms of buttering: the object butter can exist without there being any buttering but the converse is not possible). Another consideration is this: often going from the noun to the verb adds properties: for example the verbs *hammer* or *saddle* both allow and require complements (hammer something, saddle something). The reverse operation would remove properties. We may *a priori* prefer on general grounds a system that is "purely additive" because it is simpler: there is no option of ever changing anything. But we have seen clear empirical reasons for this choice: if nouns were derived from verbs, the verbs would be roots and some of them should sometimes allow the affixation of root-taking affixes, contrary to what we just saw. Similarly, the nouns should not be roots and should not allow root-selecting affixes, again contrary to what we just saw.

2.4.2 Further problems

For some compounds in English, none of the audible morphemes appear to determine the properties of the compounds as a whole. These are referred to as "bahuvrihi" compounds, or as "exocentric" compounding:

cutthroat daredevil redhead

The word *cutthroat* is an either an N (meaning a killer), or an A (meaning aggressive, murderous), but it is not a kind of throat. And the word *redhead* does not mean a type of red, nor a type of head, but rather a person with red hair. The question is how these compounds should be represented. We could assume that they have the following representations:

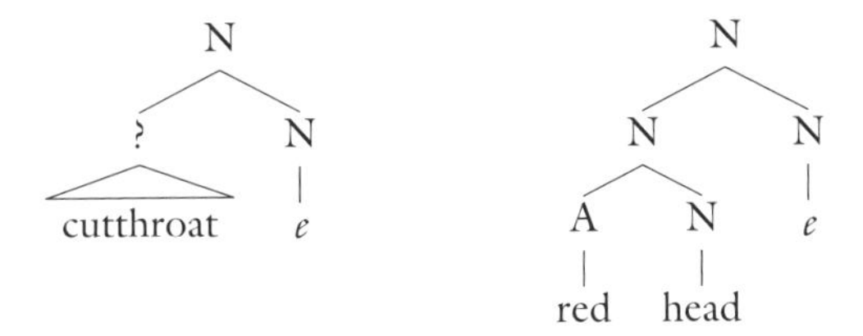

The idea that some parts of language structure may be unpronounced is a theoretically important one, and we will use it in the syntactic theory of the following chapters as well, so it is worth reflecting on the role this hypothesis plays.

2.5 Morphological Atoms

We have reached rather abstract conclusions about the nature of morphological atoms. We have defined morphemes, that is the atoms of word formation, as maximally small meaningful units. We have focused on morphemes that are "meaningful" in the sense of having a "relatively readily identifiable" meaning or function. (But note that case endings such as nominative or accusative in languages like Latin or German, or case particles such as Japanese *-ga* or *-no*, do not obviously have meanings attached to them.)

It should be kept in mind that the atoms of morphology can sometimes be quite opaque (but this is not a problem as long as there is a reasonable procedure to discover them). For example, the past of the verb *go*, which is *went*, is plausibly composed of a verbal root V with the meaning of go, and a past tense suffix: **went = Vroot + Past**. This combination just happens to be irregular in its pronunciation. Such a case is the phonological counterpart of what happens when compositionality of meaning does not hold: it is a **phonological idiom**, pronounced without audible subparts. The existence of such idioms makes the task of discovering the ultimate atoms of morphology much harder, as it is in principle possible for any word that does not look or sound like it is compositionally complex, to nevertheless be composed of more than one unit (just like *went*, or the verb *dry* with a silent causative morpheme). This shows that there is no one-to-one correspondence between groups of sound units and morphological units. All this raises non-trivial issues regarding how language learners can discover the atoms and complexes of a language. Since we are building a psychological theory, ultimately some reasonable procedure must be provided to explain how this happens.

2.6 Compositionality and Recursion

We have proposed that speakers can understand complex words like *re-write*, *un-natur-al*, and *de-nation-al-iz-ation*, even if they have never heard them before, so long as they know the meanings of the morphemes and how morphemes can be assembled in English. This is a kind of "compositionality," an idea about the importance of considering how the properties of words are composed from their parts. We can express the hypothesis this way:

Compositionality in Morphology: The morphological, syntactic, and semantic properties of (at least some) complex words are determined by their parts and how those parts are assembled.

When we put morphemes together, we have seen that some morphemes, like *-al*, are very precise about what they will combine with, while others, such as *-er* and *re-*, are not very demanding at all. A morpheme that can combine with a wide range of things is said to be *productive*. The English affix *-al* is not very productive, while English noun compounding is very productive: almost any sequence of nouns can be a compound.

The existence of productive affixes in a language opens the possibility for *recursion* in the morphology of the language. That is, there can be words of a given category that have other words of exactly the same category as a proper part; the category can *recur* more than once in a single word. This happens in English noun compounds, obviously, but it also happens to a slightly more limited extent in affixation. For example, you can *re-do* something, and sometimes you have to *re-re-do* it. After that, it begins to sound silly, but one might even say that you have to *re-re-re-do* it. Similarly, from *denationalization*, we could form *denationalizational* (pertaining to a denationalization), and *denationalizationalize* (making it so), and *denationalizationalization* (the process or result of making it so), and so on. It seems that the language does not have any kind of rule that draws a sharp line that determines how many affixes are allowed. Rather, the language seems to allow any number of affixes, or any number of words in a compound, and the reason that we do not find words with a billion prefixes or a billion nouns in them is explained not by rules of grammar but rather by non-linguistic factors like the limitation of human memory, human attention span, limitations in human life, or just limitations in human sense of humor. In any case, we find this very powerful kind of structure in words:

Recursion in Morphology: Morphology can have recursive affixation and recursive compounding. When this happens, the language has infinitely many words.

How can this be? If humans are finite, how can they know languages with infinitely many words? This is possible because complex words can be understood compositionally, on the basis of lexical entries for finitely many morphemes. This very important idea even applies in the theory of word structure.

2.7 Conclusion

2.7.1 Summary

Here are some important conclusions of this chapter:

1. The linguistic signal is discrete at various levels of analysis, such as phonology, morphology, and syntax. At each level, we have (perhaps different) atoms and rules combining these atoms.
2. The rules of morphological combination, the morphological combinatorics, have the following properties:
   a. they are recursive: they can produce infinitely long strings;
   b. they are compositional;
   c. they produce tree-like structures;
   d. they use notions such as head and selection;
   e. the notion of selection used is local: it is sisterhood in a tree.

To arrive at these conclusions, we started by looking at "words," but this notion did not play much of a role in the end. This is fortunate, since we do not know exactly what words are. What matters more, it seems, are morphemes. Morphemes are semantic and grammatical atoms that belong to specific categories. Morphemes can c-select and modify other elements. In a string formed from more than one morpheme, the morpheme that is the head of this string plays a determining role.

2.7.2 What to remember

You should know what we mean by *morpheme*, and what we mean by *bound* and *free* morphemes. You do not need to memorize the suffixes of English, but given examples of words containing (derivational or inflectional) suffixes or prefixes, you should be able to provide the *lexical entries* for their morphemes, and explain why certain morphological forms turn out the way they do. You should be able to draw the hierarchical, compositional structures of words with *tree diagrams*. You should understand the notion of *head*, and the properties of heads. Heads determine the properties of the constituents they form. Know the *right-hand head rule* (RHHR) for English. Heads c-select for their dependents (i.e. heads select for the category of the element they combine with). You should know what *selection* and *c-selection* mean, how to determine the *(c-)selection* property of a particular morpheme, and how *(c-)selection* translates into a local tree configuration. You should understand the reasons for concluding that some morphemes are silent.

2.7.3 Puzzles and preview

We have introduced some basic ideas that a theory of morphology must include, but we are far from having addressed, let alone solved, many of the complex analytical problems arising in morphology. In some examples, such as *cutthroat* in Section 2.4.2, we left a question mark on the triangle above it: it seems that the head of this compound could be *cut* (which combines with *throat*, or at the least, it seems this compound contains a substructure with *cut* c-selecting for *throat*). A similar conclusion seems reasonable for words such as *enslave, enlarge* where the *-en* part seems to play the role of head. Understanding exactly what happens here and what it means for the generality of the RHHR would require more discussion than we can afford here (but see Chapter 12 for further discussion).

As we will see, syntax builds units in much the same way as morphology (selection is local, heads determine the category and properties of the constituents/phrases they are part of), but the processes superficially differ in the following ways:

- syntax builds and manipulates phrases;
- morphology uses stems and roots, not phrases: *[[the bar] tend];
- the c-selected element in morphology precedes the head (*baby sit*), while in the syntax, it follows. (*I saw my little sister*, and not **I my little sister saw*);
- finally, syntax is slightly more opaque than morphology because various kinds of "distortions" can make it appear that selection is not local (see Section 3.7).

There is much more to say about morphology, and we will return to some of the issues in later chapters, particularly in Chapter 12. For now though, we turn our attention to syntactic objects: phrases.

2.7.4 Further exercises

(1) Plurals, affix order, and locality

(i) We might call someone who thought that the most important thing in linguistics was classification, a "classificationist." There are three Ns in the structure of *class-ifi-cation-ist,* the noun *class,* the noun *classification* and the noun *classificationist.* Draw a tree structure for this word that has three nodes labeled N.

(ii) The plural morpheme *-s* c-selects for N, as we see for example in:

So we might expect that in *class-ifi-cation-ist,* any of the three Ns could either be plural or not. That is, we would expect all of the following eight forms to be good, but in fact, only two of them are possible:

ok: class -ifi -cation -ist (singular, singular, singular)
ok: class -ifi -cation -ist -s (singular, singular, plural)
*: class -ifi -cation -s -ist (singular, plural, singular)
*: class -ifi -cation -s -ist -s (singular, plural, plural)
*: class -es -ifi -cation -ist (plural, singular, singular)
*: class -es -ifi -cation -ist -s (plural, singular, plural)
*: class -es -ifi -cation -s -ist (plural, plural, singular)
*: class -es -ifi -cation -s -ist -s (plural, plural, plural)

That is, we can only pluralize the whole word, and when we do that, the plural morphology must of course attach to the whole word and appear at the right edge, since branches cannot cross. We should be able to explain why can't we pluralize the nouns *class* or *classification* in this word.

One possible explanation could be this: the impossible forms would be excluded if *class-es* and *classification-s* were not nouns, but some other category, say Pl (for Plural). So then *-s* would be a suffix taking an N as sister and turning it into a category called Pl. Since *-al* takes an N as sister, it could not affix to *nation-s.*

Draw the tree for *class-ifi-cation-ist-s* using the category Pl, and write the lexical entries for all the morphemes in this word structure.

(iii) List at least four other possible English words (words formed from a root and affixes) that have more than one noun in them and, for each, say which nouns can be pluralized.

(If you are not an English speaker, check with an English speaker to make sure your claims about the possibilities for plurals are right.)

(iv) Is it plausible that plural nouns and singular nouns are really different categories? To answer this.

a. List at least two different frames where plural nouns but not singular nouns can occur.

b. Are there any suffixes that select Pl?

(2) Compound

Consider the following words:

a. noun compound formation rules
b. heavy metal superstar
c. web browser software monopoly
d. fish-food-like

For each of these words

(i) What is the category of the whole word?
(ii) Give one distributional justification supporting your answer to the previous question.
(iii) Draw the tree representation of the word structure in the style shown in Sections 2.3.5–2.3.6, showing the categories for suffixes.

A General Note on "Benglish" problems.

Benglish problems are based on hypothetical languages/science fiction-like scenarios. These exercises allow testing of whether basic concepts are understood, and what type of cross-linguistic variability one may expect to find. Each time, they may give rise to further questions: are languages with expected properties attested or not (and if not, could this be accidental, or not)? Students could follow up with term papers and check out the predictions for a particular language, a group of languages, or explore if the predictions can be tested against available data in online websites like WALS Atlas of Language Structures (WALS http://wals.info/), or The Syntax of the World's Languages, SSWL http://sswl.railsplayground.net/, http://www. terraling. com/.

(3) Benglish 1: Yenglish

Yenglish is a hypothetical language which is *exactly* like English *except* for the following two properties:

a. Nouns in Yenglish come in two classes (genders): masculine (ms) and feminine (fem).
b. Yenglish compounds differ systematically from English compounds: Yenglish has (many many) compounds of the following type with indicated meanings:
   (1) a. house book (Meaning: "library" *not* "book for/in the house")
       b. house prayer (Meaning: "church" *not* "prayer performed at home/for the home")

(i) What (if any) would the head of the compounds in (1a) and (1b) be? Why?
(ii) If *house* is a feminine noun and *book* and *prayer* a masculine noun, what do you expect the gender of the compound to be? Masculine, feminine, both, neither? Why?

(4) Benglish 2: Lenglish

Lenglish is a hypothetical language that is exactly like English (same affixes, same selection requirements, same pronunciations) except for the following: where English has the RHHR, Lenglish has a left-hand head rule:

Left-hand head rule (LHHR):
In any complex word, where X is the head, X is to the *left* of Y.

Translate the following English forms into Lenglish:
For all Benglish problems here and below: always start with the English trees, then apply the LHHR consistently. The leaves will lead you to a Lenglish translation.

a. globalizations
b. tablecloths
c. reundergo
d. twenty-fifth

(5) **Benglish 3: Frenglish**
Frenglish is a hypothetical language that is exactly like English (same affixes, same selection requirements, same pronunciation, same local selection) except for the following: where English has the RHHR, Frenglish has the following two rules:

(Right/left)-hand head rule ((R/L)HR):
i. In any complex word, where X c-selects Y, X is to the *right* of Y.
ii. In all other complex words, if X is the head, X is to the *left* of Y.

Translate the following English words into Frenglish:
a. globalizations
b. tablecloths
c. restaurant ticket
d. reundergo

(Note: If you know or speak any language that has patterns that resemble Frenglish, you may want to further investigate if this rule makes the right empirical predictions or not.
Advanced: if such languages are not found, what can you conclude? Why would this be the case?)

(6) **Benglish 4: Ahenglish**
Consider a hypothetical language called Ahenglish, which maximally resembles English (the same affixes, same pronunciations, same selection requirements, which must be satisfied in every complex word) but instead of the usual locality and the RHHR it has the following principle:

Alternate-head hand rule (AHHR):
In any complex where head X c-selects Y, X and Y are not adjacent unless there is no other option.

So in this language, any complex containing an affix combining with some category W to form Z must contain a W, but requires that W not to be non-adjacent if possible. With this idea, how would you translate the following four words into Ahenglish? Proceed by first constructing the English structures, then apply the rule systematically.

a. undeniability
b. remagnetize
c. fish-food-like
d. web browser software monopoly

(Note: You may want to investigate or speculate whether this rule makes the right predictions for the space of language variation or not.)

(7) **Structural ambiguity**
The word *unlockable* as used in the sentences below is ambiguous.

a. (I would like to lock this door), but it is unlockable.
b. (I would really like to unlock this door/game); fortunately it is unlockable.

(i) What is the category label of *unlockable*?
(ii) Paraphrase the meanings in (a) and (b).
(iii) Construct two (licit) word structures for *unlockable* and pair them up with their paraphrases. Write the paraphrases under them. Label each node.
(iv) Give the lexical entries for (a) and (b). (Make sure to include pronunciation, bound vs. free, category, and c-selection, as done in the main text.)
(v) Discuss whether and how each tree structure(s) respect the RHHR and the principle of locality of selection.
(vi) We can, in principle, entertain more than one way to treat such ambiguities. Of the two hypotheses below, which one is most consistent with what you found in (i–v)? Why?
  (A) This word has two different constituent structures: each structure has a unique (i.e. unambiguous) interpretation.
  (B) This word always has an invariant structure; its ambiguity is unrelated to the constituent structure, but arises from other factors. (For example: it could be learned in school, it could be due to another type of rule. ...)

(8) Compound

(i) How many meanings do we *expect* the following expression to have? (You do not need to give the meanings, just the number of meanings expected and explain why we expect this number.)

kitchen lamp shade protector

(ii) Explain why we do NOT expect this expression to designate a kind of lamp or a kind of shade.

2.7.5 Further reading

A good starting point for an exploration of word structure and morphology are the textbooks of Spencer (1991), Booij (2005), and Baker (2001). The more advanced student may want to explore: Anderson (1992), Baker (1988), chapter 2 of Di Sciullo and Williams (1987), Emonds (2000), Selkirk (1983), Spencer and Zwicky (1998), and Halle and Marantz (1994). For further references see also the references cited under Chapter 12.

3
Syntactic Analysis Introduced

Typical human language users have a remarkable ability to analyze sounds and other gestures in a certain very sophisticated way. One of our main goals in studying language is to understand how this is done, and how this ability arises in the human mind. This objective defines our field of linguistics as a branch of cognitive psychology. Of course, cognition depends on neurophysiology, and neurophysiology depends on the physics of organic matter, and so linguistics is ultimately part of the scientific study of the natural world. Like these other sciences, it is experimental.

One of the ways to study language is to look first at an organism's (i.e. a person's) linguistic "input" and "output." Examining the linguistic input we can explore, in the first place, the physical properties of linguistic signals. The relevant output includes our linguistic behavior, but also all the other changes and behavior that are caused by language: what we say, how we say it, how we react to what we hear, etc. From these, we can infer something about the distinctive contribution made by the organism, and ultimately something about how the distinctive biological and cognitive properties of the organism make the acquisition and use of language possible.

From this perspective, our first assumptions about morphological structure are already surprising. For example, suffixes are not readily distinguishable in the input, when they are there at all. When suffixes are pronounced, they are always pronounced with other things, and in fluent speech there is generally no clear acoustic boundary between stems and affixes. To make matters worse, we've seen reason to say that some suffixes are not pronounced at all. So any properties of affixes must be inferred by some kind of analysis of the linguistic input that we can perform. Recall that auditory input is just a slight variation in air pressure that can be detected by the eardrum, and visual input is a pattern of light hitting the retina. Neither air pressure variations nor arrays of light intensities and colors explicitly represent nouns or adjectives, or tense or plural affixes. The step from the perceived signal to the linguistic description is a very substantial one. The same is true in vision generally: the step from an array of light colors and intensities to the recognition of object edges and shapes and movements is a very substantial one, though it is something we can do effortlessly even when parts of the objects are not visible.

The basic strategy for studying language and other cognitively mediated behavior is roughly as follows. Suppose that we think that the cognitive agent has some internal representation or state R, which is causally involved in the production of certain behaviors. Because we don't have direct access to such an internal representation, we can only study it by looking at how it influences or is influenced by other things; so we look for or set up some situation in which we think R will interact with other systems or processes S, the choice of which is only limited by our ingenuity in designing

An Introduction to Syntactic Analysis and Theory, First Edition.
Dominique Sportiche, Hilda Koopman, and Edward Stabler.

informative experiments. In that setting, we observe what happens, call it O. Our conclusions about R come from reasoning about what it must be in order to explain the fact S+R⇒O. Clearly, this reasoning is indirect, and so it is very important to look for converging evidence on the nature of R, evidence coming from a wide range of interactions S and results O. Little by little, we get an idea of the nature of R, and we can then consider why R would be this way.

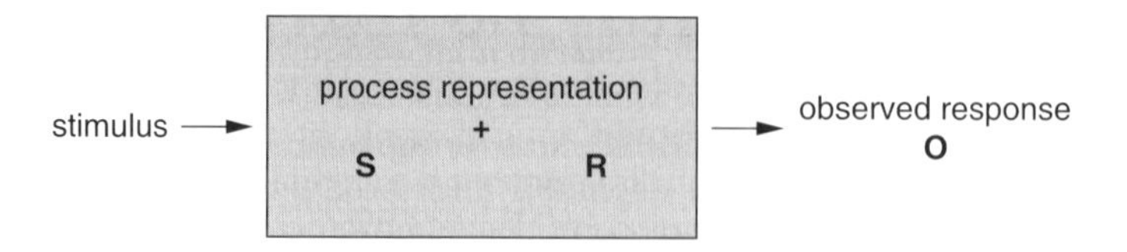

3.1 Word Order

The experiments we conduct here are perhaps surprising at first. We will take a linguistic string, say a word, or a phrase of several words, and we ask speakers certain questions about it. Then we continue by distorting it in some way and we ask speakers what they think of the result; what they think of the distorted string. We then try to attribute structure to this string in order to have an explanation of why speakers have the judgments that they have, and we consider as wide a range of strings and distortions as possible.

We have already seen this in the judgments about morpheme sequences used in the last section. When speaking English, a native speaker of English produces words and morphemes in a particular order. The affix *-al*, of category A, must follow the N, say *nation*, to which it affixes. Distorting the structure by reversing the stem and affix results in something unacceptable, something that would not occur in a typical conversation, something that would produce a "startle" reaction in a typical English-speaking listener if it were placed in an otherwise ordinary context:

ok: national * alnation

Even though speakers recognize words and sentences without really thinking about them, it is easy to make them aware of the fact that they know that words must occur in a certain order. To take another example, consider a typical English speaker confronted with the following strings:

(1) a. The clever snake disappeared into a hole in the ground
b. Hole into disappeared ground the the in clever a snake
c. The snake clever disappeared into a hole in the ground
d. Le serpent malin disparut dans un trou dans le sol

An English speaker will judge (a) as fine i.e. fully acceptable, (b) as incomprehensible, (c) as possibly comprehensible but not quite well-formed, and (d) as human speech but not much else (for speakers who do not know French: (d) is a translation of (a) into French). The differences between (a), (b), and (c) are (possibly among other things) judgments about word order, and they are the kind of thing that our theory of syntax should explain. How do we account for the fact that only certain temporal orders of words are acceptable? What is it that speakers know, perhaps tacitly, unconsciously, that explains this?

There is a familiar line of reasoning about this, which can be expressed in the following point–counterpoint fashion:

First idea: People remember things, and so there is no particular mystery about their language abilities. They have heard many words, and many word sequences, and they can remember them, or at least a very large number of them. Whenever they speak, they pick one of them that corresponds to what they want to say. They will judge a sentence as unacceptable if they think it is not something they have heard (or at least not very similar to something they have heard). An extreme form of this reasoning would postulate that speakers have somewhere in mental storage all of the sentences of their language (and perhaps even of all languages ever spoken).

Rebuttal: There are infinitely many well-formed phrases in the language. We can see this by the fact that, given any acceptable phrase, we can make a longer one that still conforms to the grammar:

the book
the book on the chair
the book on the chair in the library
the book on the chair in the library on the hill
the book on the chair in the library on the hill by the quad
...
I am happy
I think I am happy
you say I think I am happy
Bill knows you say I think I am happy
I heard Bill knows you say I think I am happy
...
John left
John and Bill left
John, Harry and Bill left
John, Bill, Harry and the Frenchman who painted the living room left
...

Not all strings can be stored in memory because we would need infinite storage capacity, and we usually assume that humans are finite discrete (that is not infinitely fine-grained) creatures, with finite memories.

Unconvinced: We can agree that speaking or understanding is not just a matter of selecting the right strings in a mental storage containing all possible strings of a given language (or of all possible languages). This would indeed seem to require infinite storage capacity. But the phrases that any human could actually speak or understand are bounded in length. No human will ever be capable of even listening to a sentence that is a billion words long, let alone making any meaningful judgment about whether it is acceptable or not; so can we really draw an important conclusion about human language abilities based on the idea that language is infinite? No human ever manipulates more than a finite number of strings in a lifetime; it is in principle imaginable that speakers have in mental storage at least all the strings used in their lifetime perhaps because they have heard them before (otherwise, this state of affairs looks suspiciously like a colossal coincidence).

Better rebuttal: When you look at human language use, it is true that some utterances are repeated frequently (like *How are you?* and *I'm fine thank you*). But when we study the matter more carefully, we find that the range of sentences that people actually produce is very large and very varied, so much so that of all the sentences people say, well over half of them are sentences that are likely to be spoken or written only once.

One way to see this is in studies of the large bodies of texts that are electronically accessible. These texts are not literal transcriptions of what people say, of course, but they provide a reasonable representation of the kinds of things people might say or read and judge to be acceptable. For example, one collection of texts that linguists have studied is called the "Penn Treebank 2" (Marcus, Santorini, and Marcinkiewicz, 1993), a collection of more than one million words of text, mainly from the *Wall Street Journal*. It turns out that in this large collection of articles and other texts, more than 99% of the sentences occur only once. In spite of that, in spite of the fact that most sentences you read in the newspaper are ones that you have never seen before (and ones that you will never see again), they are acceptable, and indeed intelligible.

So the idea that the acceptable sentences are the ones you remember hearing before is not even close to being right.

Convinced, but with another proposal: OK, so let's agree that speakers do not judge acceptability or understand sentences just by remembering them. But we have already seen that words fall into categories, so maybe, instead of remembering the sequences of words that they have heard, they remember frames, that is, they remember the sequences of categories that they have heard before. For example, hearing

The dog chased the cat

the speaker remembers that a sentence can be formed from the sequence D N V D N, and from

The cat scratched the dog on the nose

the speaker remembers that a sentence can be formed from the sequence D N V D N P D N, and so on. A sentence is judged acceptable only if it has a sequence of categories that has been heard before. Note first that this does not reduce the number of strings to remember (this can be proved), so it would not help for the know-all-strings-of-all-languages hypothesis.

Not good enough: This idea cannot be right either. First of all, it is just not true that any sequence D N V D N is an acceptable sentence:

*Those air put a compliments.

And in the second place, there are many sequences of categories that are so rare that you will hear them only once if at all, yet nevertheless they can be acceptable and meaningful.

Furthermore, we want to explain not only the difference between "acceptable" and "unacceptable" structures, and our ability to interpret these and recognize relations between them, but we also want to explain the gradient between "perfectly acceptable" and "totally unacceptable." (A "semi-acceptable" example might help justify this.) No theory with any hope of explaining these things starts with the assumption that judgments are based on remembered category sequences.

What seems to be minimally required is the hypothesis that linguistic knowledge involves recursive rules that are not sensitive to properties like length: among the properties of the linguistic engine, there exist finite devices that allow strings of morphemes to be infinitely long **in principle**, even though there are finitely many morphemes in a language and even though strings of infinite length are not produced in reality.

From the simple ideas of this argument, we will now try to work our way towards a more adequate account of what each speaker knows about his or her language. We proceed incrementally, beginning with relatively simple ideas and then developing them as necessary. Our focus will be on syntax, which concerns, roughly, matters having to do with the order of words and morphemes in phrases.

3.2 Constituency

One idea that comes up in the little argument above is that in acceptable English sentences, certain types of strings can be iterated any number of times. For example, watch the sequence of categories in these sentences:

I saw the book	pronoun V D N
I saw the book on the chair	pronoun V D N P D N
I saw the book on the chair in the library	pronoun V D N P D N P D N
I saw the book on the chair in the library on the hill	pronoun V D N P D N P D N P D N

It seems the sequence [P D N] can be repeated, iterated, any number of times. As far as the structure of the language is concerned, we can always add one more sequence. (Of course, we will always stop before a billion words, but this is for reasons that are not linguistic.) Note that we cannot iterate just P D or D N.

I saw the book	pronoun V D N
* I saw the book the chair	pronoun V D N D N
* I saw the book on the chair in the	pronoun V D N P D N P D
* I saw the book on the in the chair	pronoun V D N P D P D N

What explains this? It seems that P D N forms a kind of unit that has special properties, such as the possibility of being repeated in certain contexts.

One of the fundamental discoveries about the syntax of natural languages is that languages are *chunky*: words are organized into chunks or blocks or units that "rules" (such as the iteration rule we just mentioned) can manipulate as blocks. We have already encountered chunkiness: the spoken linguistic signal – a complex, slight fluctuation in air pressure – is segmented into sound chunks by our nervous system.

The *phonemes* are relatively small chunks; *morphemes* tend to be bigger (but they are sometimes pronounced with zero or just one phoneme); a *word* can be a complex of many morphemes; and a *phrase* like *P D N* is bigger still. In the previous chapter (Chapter 2), we depicted the morphological structure of complex words by putting the morphemes that form a unit under a single node in a tree representation. We called such units constituents. We can depict the composition of syntactic elements into larger ones in the same way, as we will see.

This will be our initial focus: constituent structure, what ingredients go into building constituents, how to test for constituency, and how to interpret problems with the constituency tests. Here, our first step will be an attempt to find out the way things are, i.e. how sequences of morphemes get organized into constituents, or "chunks." In subsequent chapters we will try to understand why the complexes are organized in these ways.

We begin with a simple, preliminary definition:

Constituent: A *constituent* is a string that speakers can manipulate as a single chunk.

Notation: If a string of words or morphemes is a constituent, we will represent this constituency by grouping all the words or morphemes as daughters of a single mother node in a tree representation:

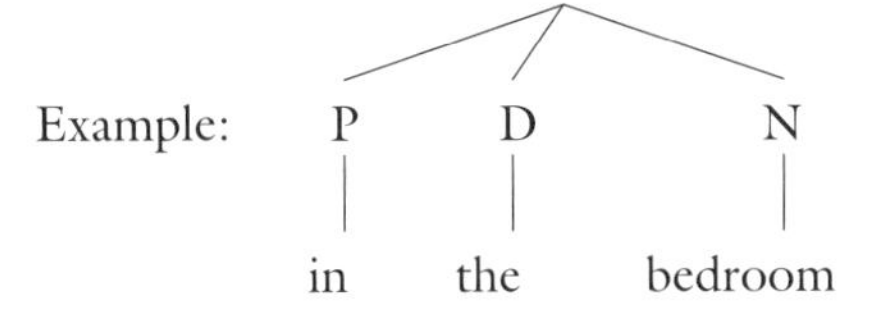

equivalently: $[[_P\text{in}][_D\text{the}][_N\text{bedroom}]]$

There is structure here that we are not representing. One thing we have seen is that *bedroom* is morphologically complex:

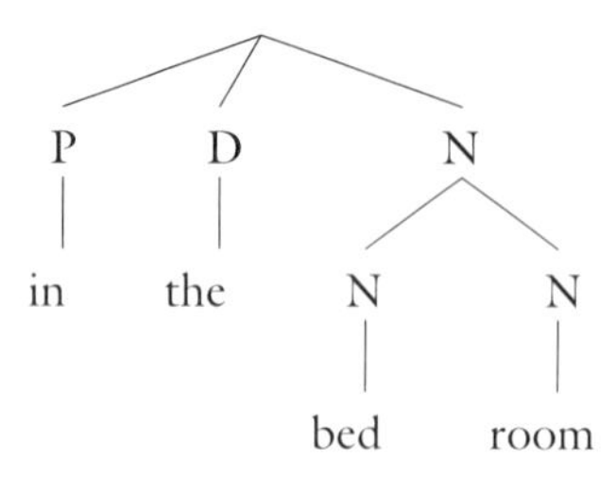

equivalently: $[[_P\text{in}][_D\text{the}][_N[_N\text{bed}][_N\text{room}]]]$

This is not an innocent difference. One question that will become relevant later is this: which of these two trees is relevant for syntactic analysis? If the first, then it would mean that syntax does not care that *bed room* is composed of two nouns, and it never needs to look inside this kind of word, or inside words in general. If the second, then syntax does care. We will see that, at least in some cases, syntax does care about the morphemes inside of what we usually regard as single words.

To begin the search to discover how things are, we will try partially answer some of the following questions:

- What are constituents and how do we determine what they are? What are the basic elements of syntax, the "syntactic atoms"? How do we go about deciding? In the case of morphemes and words, we had access to fairly reliable judgments about where the boundaries between constituents were. These judgments were supported by distributional properties of words and morphemes. Judgments are less secure when it comes to larger syntactic constituents (although with practice, things improve). We will use all sorts of tools to discover constituency.
- Do constituents cluster into subgroups, and how do we determine subgroup membership? In the case of morphology, we saw that both morphemes and words cluster in subgroups according to the category they belong to. In the present case, we have the same question. Do syntactic constituents fall into nameable subgroups with significant common properties? A further question is whether these categories are new, or if they are the same categories already seen in morphology. Anticipating our conclusion, we will discover that there is a small set of syntactic constituent types, and that new labels are needed, as syntactic constituents do not behave like word or morpheme level categories. We will see that corresponding to the word level categories A, N, V, P, D, C, T, Num (=(plural, and singular) Number), etc., there are syntactic constituents of type AP, NP, VP, PP, DP, CP, TP, NumP . . . (where the P is read *phrase*, so a DP is a determiner phrase). We will need to explain why we have such a correspondence, and we will also discover that there may be still other constituent types.

3.3 Syntactic Productivity

In the previous chapter (Chapter 2), to get a sense of how limiting the rules of morphology are, we observed that there is only one ordering of the morphemes in *denationalization* that yields a possible word in English. To get an analogous perspective on the syntactic restrictions on phrases, consider the following sentence:

This girl in the red coat will put a picture of Bill on your desk before tomorrow

This sentence has 17 words.

There are 17!=355,687,428,096,000 possible reorderings of these words. How many reorderings of these words are also good sentences? It might seem at first that there are only a handful.

For each length n, the number of well-formed expressions with n morphemes is called the *density* of a language, and the study of this mathematical notion has a long history (Salomaa and Soittola, 1978). A language is sometimes said to be *slender* if there is some fixed number k such that for every number n, the number of well-formed expressions of length n is no more than k. With a moment's reflection, it is easy to see that English and other human languages are not at all slender. In human languages, the number of sentences increases exponentially with the length of the strings.

It is easy to show that English has exponential density. We already have an easy way to show this, because we observed in Chapter 2 that English noun compounding is very productive. For example, the nouns *bulletin* and *board* combine to form *bulletin board* = "a board for posting bulletins," but they can also combine to form the less usual *board bulletin* = "a bulletin about the board." There can also be a *bulletin bulletin* = "a bulletin about bulletins," and even a *board board* = "a board having to do with other boards in some way, for example, a board that has lists of other boards on it." And so on. In general, English allows free noun compounding. Suppose there were just 2 nouns. Then we could make 4 noun compounds of length 2, 8 compounds of length 3, and so on. With 2 nouns, there are 2^n compounds of length n. Human vocabulary sizes are difficult to estimate, but certainly every reader of this text knows many thousands of different nouns. Suppose you know $10,000$ nouns. Then your language would let you consider $10,000^n$ compounds of length n. And so now if we consider just singular noun compounds, and put them into just the following frame, all the results will be syntactically acceptable (though they will often be semantically and pragmatically very odd):

the ______ appeared

If you know at least $10,000$ nouns, then each one can go into this frame, so there are at least $10,000$ sentences that are 3 words long. Using all the 2-word noun compounds, there are at least $10,000^2$ sentences that are 4 words long. And in general, for any $n > 1$ there are actually many more than $10,000^n$ different sentences of length $n + 2$, since the ones formed by this frame are a tiny fraction of the whole English language. This is an exponential number of sentences.

Noun compounding is usually regarded as a morphological process, forming compounds whose internal structure is not relevant to phrase structure, but syntax is much more like English noun compounding than it is like English affix-stem morphology: it is very productive.

Estimating the number of reorderings of a particular sentence like

This girl in the red coat will put a picture of Bill on your desk before tomorrow

is a little more complicated than estimating the number of noun compounds, because the principles restricting the combinations are much more complex, as we will see. However, making rather conservative assumptions about the possible combinations allowed, we can use a "parsing algorithm," a program that finds the syntactic structures of a sequence of morphemes, to calculate that more than 29,859,840 reorderings of this sentence are syntactically acceptable (though they might be pragmatically and semantically odd). We will consider several of these reorderings in the next few pages. This number of acceptable orderings represents about one 8.4 millionth of a percent of the possible 17! orderings (the corresponding ratio for the word *denationalization* from the Chapter 2 is 1 out of 5!, about 0.83 percent, but with only 5 morphemes). This is indeed a very small proportion, which indicates that syntax imposes very significant restrictions on how the words in sentences can be ordered. Still, it is quite a remarkable property that such a large number of possible orderings exist with only 17 words. This shows that syntax is very constraining but also shows amazing productivity. This productivity allows language to be a very flexible and expressive tool, as we will see.

3.4 Substitution

We now start to address the issue of determining constituency: what strings behave as chunks? We need to set up experiments that will help us answer this question. One possible way to determine whether a string of words forms a unit is to show that it behaves like something that we have good reason to believe is a unit. A reasonable candidate is a word. Perhaps we can show that certain strings behave like a single word. If such a string does, then it is reasonable to conclude that it is a constituent, because it behaves like a single word and it is plausible to assume that a single word is a constituent.

To be as safe as possible (we cannot be totally safe), we want the substituting words to have no internal structure. That is, ideally it is preferable to use single words that are roots (otherwise we would not be as sure that we are not substituting our string for something made of more than one unit), though this is not always possible.

- Given a well-formed string S that we are trying to analyze.
- Select a substring SUB.
- Replace SUB in "kind" by (what looks like) a monomorphemic word (a word with no internal structure).
- If the result R is well-formed, we conclude that SUB is a constituent.
- As usual, if the result is ill-formed, we conclude nothing at all, although we may want to understand why the substitution failed.

First, note that we say *replace SUB* ***in kind***. Like in any other experiment, there is a danger that the experimental result is sensitive to several different variables. In general we want to minimize as much as possible interference by factors that are not relevant for establishing constituency. One way to try to minimize noise is to select our substitution so that it introduces as little perturbation as possible. In particular, we will want to make sure that S and R are as similar in meaning as possible. We will try to make this a little bit more precise below.

Minimal pairs: when we make a substitution in a sentence for the purpose of testing constituency, we want to keep the same meaning. As mentioned, this is an attempt to come as close as possible to making **a single change** in order to be able to interpret the result of the substitution more easily. This is a very general strategy. To demonstrate that a particular factor plays a role in linguistic (or other) analysis, we want to construct a **minimal pair** illustrating this effect. Here is an example drawn from phonology. We mentioned earlier that the plural suffix -s is pronounced differently depending on what noun it is suffixed to, viz. *rug/rugs* vs. *pit/pits*. In the former, the suffix is pronounced *z*, in the second it is pronounced *s*. But the difference between *rugs* and *pits* is not so clear: it could have to do with the fact that the initial consonant sound is *r* rather than *p*. The following minimal pairs shows what the real regularity is:

> *pit/pits* vs. *bit/bits*: In both the suffix is pronounced *s*. The only difference between *bit* and *pit* is the initial consonant. This is a minimal pair and it shows that the initial consonant quality plays no role.
> *cap/caps* vs. *cab/cabs*: This is another minimal pair. The only dissimilarity is the final consonant of the noun, and it does make a difference: the suffix is pronounced *s* with cap and *z* with cab.

Now let's look at an example drawn from syntax. Traditional grammars report that, in English, regular verbs show agreement in number with a 3rd person singular subject in the present tense: an *-s* suffix must appear on the verb:

These movies frighten me
John frightens me

Both of the following sentences are well-formed:

Flying planes frighten me
Flying planes frightens me

They seem to form a minimal pair only differing in the presence of the agreement suffix (*-s*). Is the traditional grammar rule wrong?

No, because this is not a minimal pair: the form of the subject in the two sentences is the same, but their meaning is quite different. The former means "planes that are flying frighten me" and the second means "the action of flying planes *frightens* me." And not vice versa. The rule is safe (and notice that our paraphrase of the meanings reveals what is going on: in the first, the subject is "planes" which is plural, while in the second, it is something like "the action," which is 3rd person singular).

It is not always possible to construct minimal pairs. Nevertheless, we should always try.

It is important to remember that the way we interpret the results of such psychological experiments is itself part of the theory, a hypothesis to be verified or corroborated. As a result, we may wonder whether we have some *a priori* grounds to believe that such a hypothesis is warranted. Here is a consideration that seems to lend support to this interpretation: recall the type of morphological trees we came across:

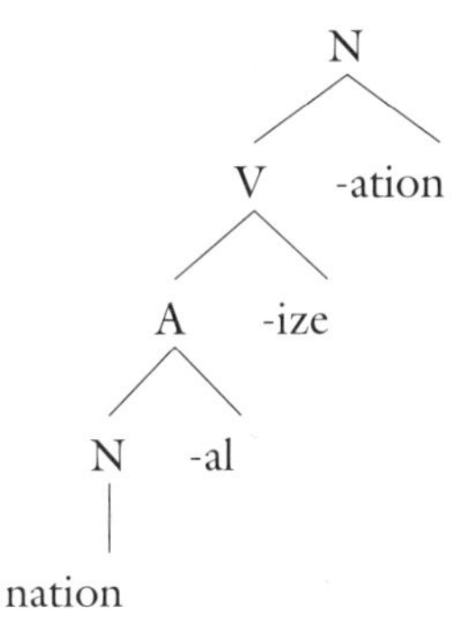

In such a tree, there are several constituents, namely *nation*, *national*, *nationalize*, and *nationalization*. We also saw that some trees are disallowed:

Never draw this!

N
V -ation
A
N -al
nation -ize

This illustrates a correlation between "being a constituent" and "forming a temporally continuous string." For example, in the first tree, *national* is both a constituent and a continuous string, while in the second (ill-formed) tree, the non-constituent *nation* + *ize* cannot be realized as a continuous string. The suggests the following conclusion: constituents **normally** form continuous strings (though we should be careful because of the existence of circumfixes and infixes).

Now if a test seems to apply equally well to continuous strings as to non-continuous strings, it would not seem like a very promising test for constituency. If, on the other hand, such a test only applies to continuous strings, it would look like a good candidate for picking out those strings that form constituents. Substitution with a single (monomorphemic) word does seem to have this property: it always applies to continuous strings. Thus our interpretation of the substitution experiment seems *a priori* reasonable.

We are now ready to experiment on one of our sentences above. We will try to see whether we can replace any string of words by a single word and still get a sentence that is both acceptable and a close synonym. We will call this *substitution with a single word*. Here are some acceptable substitutions:

(2) a. { ~~This girl in the red coat~~ / she / Mary } will put a picture of Bill on your desk before tomorrow
b. This girl in the red coat will put { ~~a picture of Bill~~ / it } on your desk before tomorrow
c. This girl in the red coat will put a picture of Bill { ~~on your desk~~ / there } before tomorrow
d. This { ~~girl in the red coat~~ / one } will put a picture of Bill on your desk before tomorrow
e. This girl in the red coat will put a picture of Bill on { ~~your desk~~ / it } before tomorrow
f. This girl in the red { ~~coat~~ / one } will put a picture of Bill on your desk before tomorrow

Consider the first substitution of *the girl in the red coat* with *she*. Recall that we want to introduce as little perturbation as possible. One requirement that we would like to impose is the following: substitution should preserve truth values (across contexts of evaluation, that is, non-accidentally).

We can explain this as follows. Suppose that the first sentence is true, that is, suppose it is an accurate description of a particular state of affairs. We will want substitution to preserve this character of truth, this truth value. To this effect, the pronoun *she* should be understood to mean the same as *the girl in the red coat*, that is, to refer to the same person. Conversely, if the sentence was false to start with, it should remain false after substitution.

This requirement provides some support for the idea that the sequences that were replaced are units, constituents. That is,

(3) a. *This girl in the red coat* is a constituent
b. *a picture of Bill* is a constituent
c. *on your desk* is a constituent
d. *girl in the red coat* is a constituent
e. *your desk* is a constituent
f. *coat* is a constituent (we knew this already).

Given these hypotheses, we can draw a tree with some structure above the words:

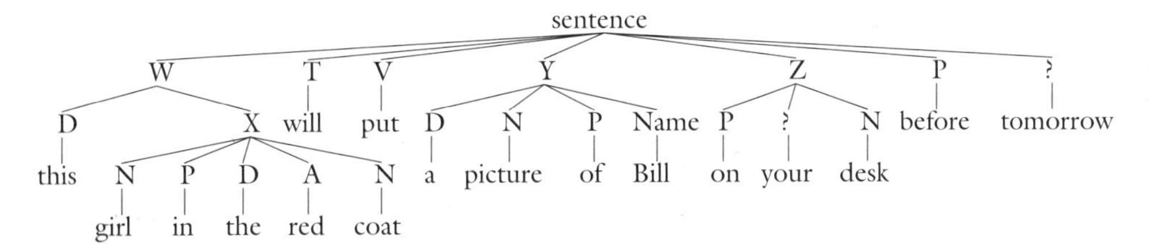

(Notice that we have labeled the new constituents W, X, Y, Z. We will introduce conventional names for these units later.)

The structure in this tree can also be represented by bracketing:

[$_W$D [$_X$N P D A N]] T V [$_Y$D N P Name] [$_Z$P ? N]] P ?
this girl in the red coat will put a picture of Bill on your desk before tomorrow

This is a first idea about the structure of the sentence, an idea that we can attempt to confirm with converging evidence from other types of experiments.

> **Test interpretation**: It is important to realize that such substitutions do not unambiguously tell us that anything that can be replaced by a single word will necessarily be a constituent. Whether this is the correct interpretation can only be determined *a posteriori*. When evidence from many such experiments is interpreted, and we have succeeded in constructing an overall coherent picture, we will be more certain that this interpretation of the experiment is the right one. As we will see, the interpretation we give to substitution above does seem to be correct in most cases.

Notice that successful substitutions indicate that the initial phrase and its substitution share a distributional property, and so we have some evidence for expanding our previous hypotheses as follows:

(4) a. *This girl in the red coat, she, Bill, Mary,* have the same category
b. *a picture of Bill, it,* have the same category
c. *on your desk, there,* have the same category
d. *your desk, it,* have the same category
e. *girl in the red coat, one,* have the same category
f. *coat, one,* have the same category.

By the transitivity of identity, we can conclude from (b) and (d) that *a picture of Bill, your desk,* and *it,* all constituents, belong to the same category. We could indicate this in the tree by labeling the three relevant nodes with the same label. For reasons that will become clear later, we choose this label to be DP, for "determiner phrase." We can replace the Y in our tree above by DP.

The last two types of constituent, (e) and (f), are interesting because, by transitivity, *coat* and *girl in the red coat* belong to the same category as well. This category cannot be N, since we can show that the latter string does not behave like an N. For example: we cannot pluralize the whole expression, **[girl in the red coat]-s* even though this expression would be like a count noun. We can put the plural affix *-s* after *coat*, but that pluralizes just the noun *coat*. We can indicate this in the tree by labeling the three relevant nodes with the same label. For reasons that will become clear later, we choose this label to be NP, for "noun phrase."

Note also that since *Bill* and *this girl in the red coat* belong to the same category, they have to share some property, for example some distributional property. Substitute one for the other and get an acceptable string:

(5) a. This girl in the red coat will put a picture of Bill on your desk before tomorrow
b. Bill will put a picture of this girl in the red coat on your desk before tomorrow

Note that this swapping is possible because we have independently established that these two strings are constituents of the same category, where in this particular case the meaning of *this girl in the red coat* is held constant. It is **not** true that swappability by itself entails that the swapped strings are constituents, and constituents of the same kind. By (4a), we might expect to be able to do the same with *she*, but something makes this impossible:

(6) a. She will put a picture of Bill on your desk before tomorrow
b. *Bill will put a picture of she on your desk before tomorrow

We could conclude from this that our hypothesis (4a) is false, but this is not necessary without further analysis. This observation does show that *Bill* and *she* do not have exactly the same distribution, but they may still have enough in common to be in the same category. As we observed in the Chapter 2: we typically cannot draw strong conclusions from isolated negative results. "Isolated negative results are uninformative." This is because there are many possible explanations for why they arise.

Notice that the acceptable pronoun in the place of *Bill* is *her*:

(7) a. She will put a picture of Bill on your desk before tomorrow
b. Bill will put a picture of her on your desk before tomorrow

In fact, in these contexts, *she* and *her* are in complementary distribution: where one occurs, the other cannot (and of course we cannot have both at once, as in (f) below):

(8) a. She will put a picture of Bill on your desk before tomorrow
b. *Her will put a picture of Bill on your desk before tomorrow
c. *She her will put a picture of Bill on your desk before tomorrow
d. Bill will put a picture of her on your desk before tomorrow
e. *Bill will put a picture of she on your desk before tomorrow
f. *Bill will put a picture of she her on your desk before tomorrow

Since they also make the same contribution, picking out a salient female referent, this suggests the conclusion:

(9) *she* and *her* are not only the same category, but are tokens of the same morpheme. Which one can occur depends on syntactic context.

We should make this more precise, defining when one form or the other is required, and explaining why we find this alternation. This turns out to be enormously important, but we postpone further discussion of it until we have understood more about constituency.

Substitution with a word can take us quite far regarding the structure of our example sentence. We saw that the string *your desk* can be replaced by the pronoun *it*, preserving well-formedness and truth value. The same thing can be done with the string *the red coat*, suggesting that this string is a constituent. The meaning of the pronoun is not the same in the two cases, but it seems reasonable to assume by transitivity that these two constituents are of the same kind, since they can be replaced by the same element. Being of the same category is consistent with the fact that they are swappable. For example,

(10) a. This girl in the red coat will put a picture of Bill on your desk before tomorrow
b. This girl in your desk will put a picture of Bill on the red coat before tomorrow
c. This girl in the red coat will put a picture of Bill on your desk before tomorrow
d. This girl on your desk will put a picture of Bill in the red coat before tomorrow

By the same reasoning, we could conclude (by transitivity in the case of *there*):

on your desk, there, in the red coat belong to the same category (called PP).

We can accordingly replace the label Z in our tree on p. 53 with PP.

Similarly, we have substitutions and swapping to indicate that *Bill* and *your desk* are of the same category, which we have called DP:

(11) a. This girl in the red coat will put a picture of Bill on {~~your desk~~ / Bill} before tomorrow
b. This girl in the red coat will put a picture of Bill on your desk before tomorrow
c. This girl in the red coat will put a picture of your desk on Bill before tomorrow

We can conclude by transitivity that all of the following have the category we are calling DP:

your desk, it, Bill, this girl in the red coat, a picture of Bill, the red coat, she, her

It would be very easy to show by exactly the same reasoning that the category DP includes pronouns such as *I, me, you, she, her, he, him, it, they, them, we, us*. Substitution with a pronoun is, as you would expect, often called *pronominalization*.

We can now redraw our tree with more labels and more structure:

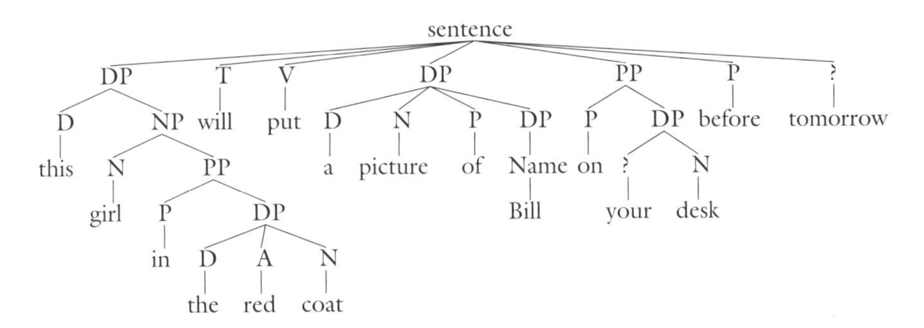

Recursion: Notice that we now see recursion in the syntax: here the subject DP properly contains another DP. We will see much more recursion in the syntax as we examine more constructions. This important property is at the root of the fact that the set of well-formed sentences in human languages is infinite. It has also been argued to play a fundamental role in human cognition; see Hauser, Chomsky, and Fitch (2002).

It is important to note that there are many substitutions that we are not interested in, because they fail in one way or another. For example, they may change the meaning of the constituent (and thus the truth value of the sentence under consideration) in some subtle or fundamental way. Consider for example the following substitution:

(12) a. This girl in the red coat will put a picture of Bill on your desk before tomorrow
b. This girl there will put a picture of Bill on your desk before tomorrow

The resulting sentence is fine but the meaning has changed. *There* does not really replace *in the red coat*. *There* suggests that we are talking about a girl in a certain location, while *in the red coat* does not. Because of this, we cannot be sure that the swapping works for principled reasons rather than accidentally. The conclusion that *in the red coat* is a constituent may be correct (and in fact it is), but the reasoning leading to it is not sound.

As another example, we can replace the whole string *girl put a picture of Bill on your desk before tomorrow* by *did*:

(13) a. This girl will put a picture of Bill on your desk before tomorrow
b. This did

The sentence that results is acceptable, but it is unlike the original in a fundamental way: the word *did* does not play the same role in the sentence as the string it replaces. Similarly for the replacement

(14) a. This girl will put a picture of Bill on your desk before tomorrow
b. Clean your desk before tomorrow

These substitutions of substrings with a word are not ones we are interested in.

Note finally that we can try the reverse operation (that is, replace a single word by a longer string).

(15) a. This girl will put a picture of Bill on your desk before tomorrow
b. This girl will put a picture of Bill on your desk before the day after tomorrow

This may be taken to suggest the strings *tomorrow* and *the day after tomorrow* belong to the same category, and actually they do: they both are DPs. However, this kind of substitution is not so easy to interpret. For example, although the substitution below yields a perfectly good sentence, the two indicated substrings do *not* belong to the same category:

(16) a. This girl will put a picture of Bill on your desk before tomorrow
b. This girl will put a picture of Bill on your desk before Monday because it is important

What goes wrong here is that we have not replaced *tomorrow* with a word that plays the same kind of role in the sentence that *tomorrow* does. *Tomorrow* and *the day after tomorrow* both designate a particular day. But the string *Monday because it is important* does not designate a particular day. The meaning of the sentence has been much more radically altered and it now means:

This girl will put a picture of Bill on your desk before tomorrow, and she will do so because it is important that she does so

There are other, more subtle, ways in which substitution may fail as a constituency test. Consider the following examples:

(17) a. John wanted to say that he had not done it
b. John wanted to deny that he had done it

These two sentences seem synonymous and one can go from the first to the second by substituting *say ... not* with *deny*, which looks like it has no internal structure. Does this mean that the string *say not* forms a constituent? This is not a continuous string, so *a priori* we would like to say no (and, this looks correct: it is not a constituent). But then why does the substitution test fail to diagnose constituency? This a difficult question and we can only give a partial answer at this point.

Informative substitutions should have a kind of general validity. The substitution under discussion is limited to exactly these two strings: it must be the verb *say* and *deny*. If we substituted *write* for *say*, for example, the substitution would not work as the sentences are not synonymous:

(18) a. John wanted to write/shout that he had not done it
b. John wanted to deny that he had done it

Substitution of *deny* with *say ... not* is thus not good enough. Quite generally then, if substitutibility depends on a particular lexical item, we should be very cautious.

Similarly, consider the following examples:

(19) a. John bought a couple of books
b. John bought two books

For many speakers, these two sentences seem synonymous and one can go from the first to the second by substituting *a couple of* with *two*, which looks like it has no internal structure. Does this mean that the string *a couple of* forms a constituent? This is a continuous string so it is *a priori* unclear whether this is the right conclusion (it is not in so far we currently know). Why then does the substitution test fail again as a diagnostic of constituency? Again, this substitution does not have general validity. It only applies to this specific pair.

What this illustrates is that informative substitutions are substitutions that work in sets of sentences in which we can substitute a variety of strings by the same word, each time preserving truth values. You can check this for yourself for the substitution tests below.

In sum, we have drawn these conclusions about substitution and related matters:

- The substitutions we are interested in replace a substring by a word, where that word plays the same kind of role in the sentence as the original string did, as we saw when we considered example (16). To try to guarantee this sameness of role, we require that the substitution be structured so as to preserve both the well-formedness and truth value of the original sentence. In addition, we require that the substitution be general enough.
- Strings that can be manipulated as chunks under such substitution are constituents.
- The kind of word that can be substituted for a string indicates its category:
  - substitution with a pronoun indicates that the constituent is a DP;
  - substitution with *one* or *ones* indicates that the constituent is a NP;
  - substitution by *there* in its locative sense can indicate that the constituent is a PP.
- String substitution failure is not a test for non-constituency.
- Substitution with a string longer than one word is not necessarily one that preserves constituency.
- The pronunciation of certain elements depends on their surroundings (for example, the 3rd person plural pronoun can be pronounced either *they* or *them* or – as we will see – even *their*).

3.5 Ellipsis

Now we look at a different kind of substitution that seems to treat strings of words as chunks, namely substitution with the null string, also known as *ellipsis*. An illustration of this is given in the following exchanges between A and B:

A says: That girl in the red coat will not put a picture of Bill on your desk before tomorrow
B replies: Yes, but this girl in the red coat will put a picture of Bill on your desk before tomorrow

Alternatively, B could have replied with either of the following:

(20) a. Yes, but this girl in the red coat will.
b. Yes, but this girl in the red coat will before tomorrow

What is interesting in these answers is the nature of what is understood, even if it is left unsaid. We can indicate it as follows:

(21) a. Yes, but this girl in the red coat will ~~put a picture of Bill on your desk before tomorrow~~
b. Yes, but this girl in the red coat will ~~put a picture of Bill on your desk~~ before tomorrow

One way of interpreting what has happened here is to say that, under certain discourse conditions, substitution of some string with a null string or silent string is felicitous. Such a substitution is called deletion or ellipsis (ellipsis just means omission of understood material). As usual, since we want to control what we are doing as much as possible, we also want to restrict the experimental variables as much as possible. One condition that we impose is that ellipsis be done in those discourse contexts in which an antecedent sentence is present. Then we want to keep the same intended meaning, that is, with the crossed out parts **necessarily understood**, and **understood in the same way** as in the antecedent sentence. In other words, we again require that the pair of sentences with or without ellipsis be true or false in the same situations, that is, have the same truth value.

When is ellipsis possible? Note that none of the following replies by B would be acceptable (there are many more that would not be acceptable) with the intended meaning, that is with the crossed out parts understood:

(22) a. * this girl ~~in the red~~ coat will put a picture of Bill on your desk before ~~tomorrow~~
b. * ~~this~~ girl in the red coat will ~~put a~~ picture of Bill on your desk before tomorrow
c. * this girl in the red coat will put ~~a picture~~ of Bill on your ~~desk before~~ tomorrow
d. * this girl in the red coat ~~will put a picture of Bill~~ on your desk before ~~tomorrow~~

A simple generalization we can make over these impossible cases of ellipsis is that ellipsis only seems to be able to affect a continuous string, that is, a string of words or morphemes that is not interrupted (linearly, or more precisely, temporally) by another string.

Why should this be true? We can reason as we have before. We have seen when we looked at our morphological trees that branches are not allowed to cross. This has the effect that elements that are part of a constituent cannot be separated by elements that are not part of this constituent. In other words, elements in a constituent must form a continuous string. Whenever we see that some process can only affect a continuous string, it is natural to think that it is *because* it can only affect constituents.

There are of course other restrictions too, if we want to keep the intended meaning, that is, with the crossed out parts understood:

(23) a. * this girl in the red coat will ~~put a picture of Bill~~ on your desk before tomorrow
b. *this girl in the red ~~coat will put a picture~~ of Bill on your desk before tomorrow
c. * this girl in ~~the red coat will~~ put a picture of Bill on your desk before tomorrow
d. *this girl in the red coat will put ~~a picture of Bill on your desk~~ before tomorrow
e. *this girl in the red coat will put a picture ~~of Bill on your desk before tomorrow~~

In these cases, the crossed out elements form continuous strings, but still do not form constituents. Substitution with a null string seems to be possible only when it replaces continuous substrings that are constituents. Again, this is a reasonable interpretation, but we will only know that it is the right interpretation when we have constructed a coherent picture taking into account lots of such experiments. As we will see, this interpretation is actually well supported, even in some cases where the results of certain ellipsis experiments would seem to indicate otherwise (e.g., gapping, to which we will return).

For the moment, however, let us proceed under the assumption that this interpretation is correct. Then, from the previous examples of successful ellipsis in (20), we conclude:

a. *put a picture of Bill on your desk before tomorrow* is a constituent.
b. *put a picture of Bill on your desk* is a constituent.

The possibilities for ellipsis are actually more restricted than we have seen. It appears that this ellipsis process is restricted to applying to particular types of constituents. For reasons that are not immediately apparent, we will suppose that the ellipsis process at work here only applies to one type of constituent, which we call a VP, for "verb phrase."

Putting all these observations together, we get the following additional constituent structure for our example:

this girl in the red coat will [$_{VP}$[$_{VP}$put a picture of Bill on your desk] before tomorrow]

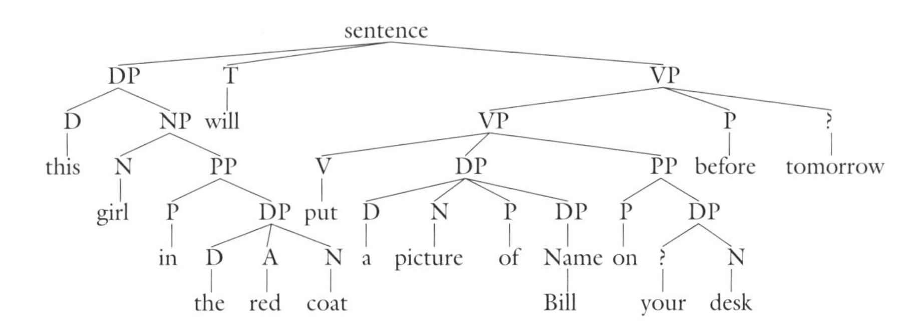

VP ellipsis (or VP deletion) is typically found in discourse contexts such as those below. In each case, the string following the coordination (*and* or *but*) contains some element that is contrasted with another element in the string preceding the coordination. We note them both in bold.

a. **This girl** will buy bread and **that one** will ~~buy bread~~ too
b. **This girl** will not buy bread and neither will **that one** ~~buy bread~~
c. **This boy** must not go to school, and **his father** must not ~~go to school~~ either
d. **This boy** must not go to France, but **his father** must ~~go to France~~
e. This actress **must** play in this movie and she **will** ~~play in this movie~~
f. Can **Mary** win the race and will **she** ~~win the race~~?
g. **This girl** will buy bread and so will **that one** ~~buy bread~~

Example (f) is called a yes/no question because it is a question that can be answered by yes or no. This is an interesting and important construction to which we will return in Chapter 6. Following that point, you should also be able to make sense of the fact that the string following the coordination in (b) and (g) looks like a yes/no question preceded by *neither* or *so*.

Note also that ellipsis is not necessary: the elided material can sometimes be pronounced. When it is, it must be pronounced with a very flat and low toned intonation (indicated with light gray font and underlining below):

(24) **This girl** will buy bread and **that one** will [buy bread] too

Another example of VP ellipsis is found in **Tag Questions**. Here are some illustrations:

(25) a. This girl will not buy bread, will she ~~buy bread~~?
b. Sean Penn can act well in many kinds of movies, can't he ~~act well in many kinds of movies~~?

The tag part is what comes after the comma. Informally, the way it is formed is as follows:

i. Take the yes/no question equivalent of the statement preceding the comma.
ii. Change the polarity of the statement (make it negative if it was positive, positive if it was negative).
iii. Pronominalize its "subject."
iv. Apply VP-ellipsis to the VP after the comma.

There are other types of ellipsis too. One kind of ellipsis applies to what we have called NPs:

John liked the wide red carpets he saw yesterday, but I preferred these { wide red carpets / red carpets / carpets / ones }

John liked the wide red carpets he saw yesterday, but I preferred these { ~~wide red carpets~~ / ~~red carpets~~ / ~~carpets~~ / ~~ones~~ }

Because ellipsis here applies to something we know independently to be a constituent (since it can be replaced by the single word *ones*), this kind of ellipsis suggests the following:

- The strings *ones, carpets, red carpets, wide red carpets* all belong to the same category (which we may assume for the moment to be NP).

As a consequence we are led to postulate the following structures for the following strings:

these $[_{NP}$carpets]
these $[_{NP}$red $[_{NP}$carpets]]
these $[_{NP}$wide $[_{NP}$red $[_{NP}$carpets]]]

Note that it is not true that this kind of ellipsis can apply every time a constituent is an NP, as we have discussed earlier. (The cases in which this kind of NP-ellipsis can or cannot apply are not yet fully elucidated.)

Another example of ellipsis occurring inside DPs or NPs is illustrated below:

John liked Mary's { wide red carpets / red carpets / carpets } but I preferred Bill's { ~~wide red carpets~~ / ~~red carpets~~ / ~~carpets~~ }

Strings like *Mary's wide red carpets* or *Mary's carpets* behave like DPs (they can be replaced by the pronoun *them* for example). Within *these, those* strings that could be replaced by *one* earlier, can be elided if they follow a string like *Bill's* within a DP. We conclude that this kind of deletion can target the strings we have called NPs.

One last type of ellipsis (which not all speakers accept) is illustrated below:

(26) a. That boy will buy a picture of Bill before tomorrow and *this girl in the red car will buy a picture of Bill before tomorrow* too
b. That boy will buy a picture of Bill before tomorrow and this girl in the red car ~~will buy a picture of Bill before tomorrow~~ too

This suggests that the string *will buy a picture of Bill before tomorrow* is a constituent in the italicized sentence for *those speakers who accept it*. As a result, we have to modify our tree to include this new constituent, (for which we will later see other evidence), which we will call T′. We will see later that the label has something to do with T (tense):

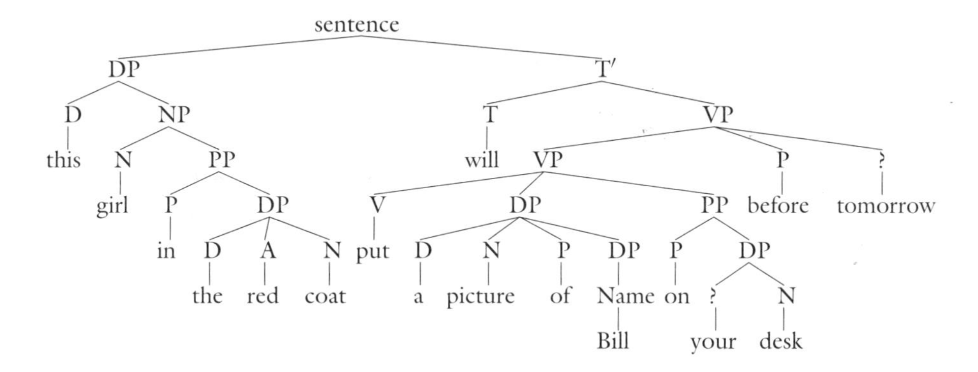

Replacement by *do so*: There is also another good constituency test called *do so* replacement. It is a kind of substitution, but with two words. Normally, this is not at all reliable, but in this particular case it is. (Advanced students should revisit this point after Chapter 12.) Here is an example:

A says: That girl in the red coat will not *put a picture of Bill on your desk*
B replies: Yes, but this girl in the red coat will (do so)

Here the string *do so* is interpreted as standing for the italicized string in the previous sentence. Notice that we put parentheses around *do so* to indicate that the reply is fine without it. If we leave it out, it is a case of VP ellipsis. This shows that *do so* replacement is also a test that singles out VP constituents.

3.6 Coordination

We now turn to a different kind of way to determine constituent structure. Again, we distort sentences in particular ways, trying to locate those substrings that seem to behave as chunks, and interpret the effects of the distortion as indicating whether or not these chunks are units.

We have looked at various distortions of this sentence:

This girl in the red coat will put a picture of Bill on your desk before tomorrow

Among the conclusions we have reached about this sentence (and variants thereof) are these:

- *put a picture of Bill on your desk before tomorrow* and *put a picture of Bill on your desk* are both VPs;
- *your desk, it, Bill, this girl in the red coat, a picture of Bill, the red coat, she, her, I, us, me, you, him, he* are all DPs;
- *on your desk, there, in the red coat,* are all PPs.

The fact that both *this girl in the red coat* and *you* belong to the same category allows us to perform the following substitution successfully:

$$\left\{\begin{array}{c}\text{This girl in the red coat}\\ \text{you}\end{array}\right\} \text{ will put a picture of Bill on your desk before tomorrow}$$

Now if we wanted to say these two sentences, there would be more economical ways to convey the content without having to repeat most of it twice. One way could be to use VP ellipsis, but this is appropriate only under certain conditions where we want to contrast certain types of information. What if there were no contrast? A very simple strategy, used to an enormous extent, is coordination. We could say:

You and this girl in the red coat will put a picture of Bill on your desk before tomorrow

This immediately raises the question: when are we allowed to use coordination? A natural answer immediately suggests itself: in the case above we see that we have coordinated two constituents of the same kind (we know this because *she* can be substituted for *This girl in the red coat* preserving well-formedness and truth value, and *she* and *you* both are DPs). We can make the following hypothesis:

We can coordinate two elements if:

i. we can say each of the two sentences independently;
ii. these two sentences have identical parts and dissimilar parts;
iii. we can substitute one dissimilar part for the other, preserving acceptability.

Point (iii) indicates that if one of the two dissimilar parts is a constituent, both are constituents of the same kind (the substitution test). This suggests the following interpretation of the possibility of doing string coordination, which generalizes this reasoning:

Coordination Test: If we have two acceptable sentences of the form *A B D* and *A C D* – where A, B, C, and D represent (possible null) substrings – and the string *A B and C D* is acceptable with the same meaning as *A B D and A C D*, this is evidence that *B* and *C* are both constituents, and constituents of the same kind.

To see how this works, let us perform this test on our example. Let

A= Ø (that is the null string, also noted *e*)
B= you
C= this girl in the red coat
D= will put a picture of Bill on your desk before tomorrow

Note that the test is stated for the coordinator *and*, but it is also true for the coordinator *or*, as we see in the following sentence, for example:

(27) a. You will put a picture of Bill on your desk before tomorrow
b. This girl in the red coat will put a picture of Bill on your desk before tomorrow
c. This girl in the red coat or you will put a picture of Bill on your desk before tomorrow

In fact, *but* is also a coordinator, one that indicates some contrast:

(28) a. This girl in the red coat will put a picture of Bill on your desk before tomorrow
b. No boys will put a picture of Bill on your desk before tomorrow
c. This girl in the red coat but no boys will put a picture of Bill on your desk before tomorrow

Here are a few more examples of how we can reason:

(29) a. This girl in the red coat will put a picture of Bill on your desk before tomorrow
b. This girl in the red coat will put it on your desk before tomorrow
c. This girl in the red coat will put it and a picture of Bill on your desk before tomorrow
d. This girl in the red coat will put a picture of Bill on your desk before tomorrow and this girl in the red coat will put it on your desk before tomorrow

The last two examples have the same meaning: we conclude that *a picture of Bill* and *it* are constituents of the same kind. (We had previously concluded that they were both DPs, so we are glad to see it confirmed.)

(30) a. This girl in the red coat will put a picture of Bill on your desk before tomorrow
b. This girl in the red coat will put a picture of Bill in the mailbox before tomorrow
c. This girl in the red coat will put a picture of Bill in the mailbox and on your desk before tomorrow

We conclude that *on your desk* and *in the mailbox* are constituents of the same kind. (We had previously concluded that one of them was a PP, so again we have confirmation.)

(31) a. This girl in the red coat will put a picture of Bill on your desk before tomorrow
b. This girl in the red coat will put a picture of Bill on your desk after the dinner
c. This girl in the red coat will put a picture of Bill on your desk before tomorrow and after the dinner
d. This girl in the red coat will put a picture of Bill on your desk before tomorrow and this girl in the red coat will put a picture of Bill on your desk after the dinner

The last two examples have the same meaning: we conclude that *before tomorrow* and *after the dinner* are constituents of the same kind. They also are PPs of a certain kind termed temporal PPs, because they say something about when the "putting" takes place.

Coordination confirms another conclusion we had already reached:

(32) a. This girl in the red coat will put a picture of Bill on your desk before tomorrow
b. This girl in the red coat will eat her breakfast before tomorrow
c. This girl in the red coat will eat her breakfast before tomorrow and put a picture of Bill on your desk before tomorrow

The last example means the same as the conjunction of the first two: we conclude that the strings *eat her breakfast before tomorrow* and *put a picture of Bill on your desk before tomorrow* are constituents, and of the same kind. This helps us gain confidence both about the viability of using VP-ellipsis, and about the viability of using coordination as a test for constituency. This is the constituent we called VP.

Coordination confirms one more conclusion we had already reached:

(33) a. This girl in the red coat will put a picture of Bill on your desk before tomorrow
b. This girl in the red coat will eat her breakfast before tomorrow
c. This girl in the red coat will eat her breakfast and will put a picture of Bill on your desk before tomorrow

The last example means the same as the conjunction of the first two: we conclude that the strings *will eat her breakfast* and *will put a picture of Bill on your desk* also are constituents of the same kind. This corroborates the conclusion we had earlier reached using ellipsis (for some speakers). This is the constituent we called T′ (pronounced "tee-bar" or "tee-prime").

It would seem *a priori* that the coordination experiment is a variation of the substitution experiment, but it is in fact more general. The reason is that we may be able to coordinate two strings, neither of which is replaceable by a single word. One such example is the coordination of T-bars (T′) or VPs seen above. The fact that coordination gives corroborated results even when substitution is not (indirectly) involved can be taken to mean that coordination is a good constituency test quite generally.

Furthermore, coordination gives us information about the nature of the coordinated constituents: recall that this came from the fact that we started with cases of coordinated strings in which the strings could each be replaced by single words of the same category (e.g. pronouns). So the strings were concluded to be of the same category as well. But now we see that even when the constituents cannot be replaced by single words (VP′ and T′) we have independent evidence that they are of the same category too. So it is reasonable to take the phrase "of the same kind" to mean "of the same category." This is what we will do from now on, pointing out problems that may arise.

The coordination experiment, and its interpretation described above, is an extremely powerful investigative tool because it seems to rarely fail. (It is actually conceivable, given what we know, that it never really fails.) It is also perhaps the only experiment in which failure seems to be straightforwardly meaningful. We will tentatively assume this last point, but will discuss it below in more detail (and it is probable that for everything we will see here, this will work).

But before we formulate how to interpret coordination failure, we need to take care of two problems. First, in many cases, coordination will fail because of an interference with agreement: coordination of two singular DPs yields a plural DP. When we coordinate DPs, we must make sure that we "fix" agreement. This is usually very easy to do (but in some cases it is not entirely obvious). Here is an illustration:

(34) a. John is sick
b. Bill is sick
c. * John and Bill is sick
d. fixed agreement: John and Bill are sick

Second, coordination of parts of words often fails (but not always):

(35) a. pre-test, anti-nuclear, en-large, nation-al, redd-en, electron-ic, inventive-ness
b. post-test, pro-nuclear, en-able, government-al, black-en, magnet-ic, clever-ness
c. [pre or post]-test, [anti or pro]-nuclear, *en-[large and able], *[nation and government]-al, *[red and black]-en, *[electron and magnet]-ic, *[inventive and clever]-ness

It would be interesting to investigate what causes these failures. Here, we will simply exclude from consideration cases involving bound morphemes.

(36) **Interpreting Coordination Test Failure**: If we have two acceptable sentences of the form *A B D* and *A C D* where none of A, B, C, and D are bound morphemes, and the string *A B and C D* is not acceptable (even after we have fixed agreement), then it is not true that: *B* and *C* are both constituents and constituents of the same kind. That is, coordination failure means that one or more of the following is true:
i. B is not a constituent, or
ii. C is not a constituent, or
iii. B and C are not of the same kind.

Here are some examples:

(37) a. This girl in the red *coat will* put a picture of Bill on your desk
b. This girl in the red *dress must* put a picture of Bill on your desk
c. *This girl in the red *coat will* and *dress must* put a picture of Bill on your desk

From the failure we can conclude at least one of the interpretations in (i–iii) in (36) must be true, for at least one of the strings *coat will* or *dress*. Actually, neither *coat will* nor *dress must* is a constituent.

(38) a. This girl in the red coat will put a picture of Bill on your desk
b. This boy on the blue coat will put a picture of Bill on your desk
c. *This girl in the red or boy on the blue coat will put a picture of Bill on your desk

From the failure we can conclude at least one of the interpretations in (i–iii) in (36) must be true, for at least one of the strings *girl in the red* or *boy on the blue*. Actually, neither of these are constituents.

3.6.1 Structure of coordinated constituents

How would we draw the tree structure of a sentence like:

(39) a. John and Mary will play with Henry and with Sue

We know that *John* is a DP, and so is *Mary*. *John and Mary* is also a constituent of course of the same kind as *John* or *Mary*. This means that the string *John and Mary* in this sentence would have the following structure (where Conj is an abbreviation for the category Conjunction):

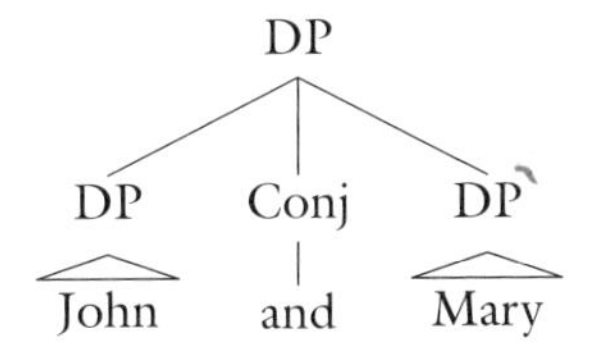

More generally the coordination of two constituents of some arbitrary type X will yield a larger constituent of type X:

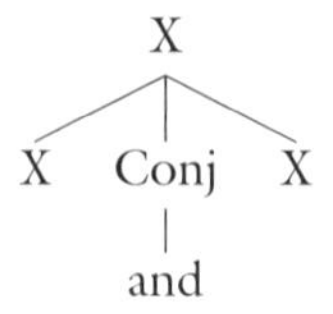

In the case of the sentence above, we would get (where the label TP "Tense Phrase" stands for sentence):

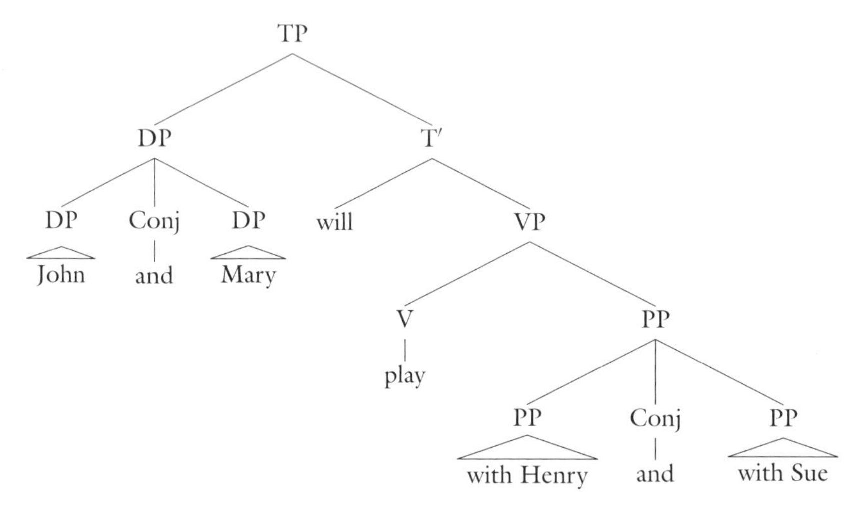

This leads to a question: how many ways are there to draw the tree for the string *John and Mary and Sue*? There are three ways: try to draw them all.

3.6.2 Right node raising and gapping

Anyone using coordination and ellipsis as constituency tests is likely to run into such puzzling constructions as right node raising and gapping. Since these constructions pose particular problems for the claims we have made so far, it is useful to be familiar with them. The analysis of these constructions is an advanced topic, but the basic problem they raise for the interpretation of the constituent tests so far is easy to describe.

Right node raising
Sometimes it appears that a portion of the string can be shared by two coordinated constituents to its left:

(40) a. They play unusual music, and I listen to unusual music
b. They play and I listen to unusual music

(41) a. I love boba ice milk tea but you hate boba ice milk tea
b. I love but you hate boba ice milk tea

(42) a. She may have defrosted the roast and should have defrosted the roast
b. She may have and should have defrosted the roast

The underlined element is said to be "right node raised." A relevant question here is whether the coordinated portions are each constituents of the same kind. Given what we have said so far about coordination, we have no choice but to accept this conclusion, even though for (40b), it leads to the first constituency instead of the bracketing we can get from VP-pronominalization (*do so*), VP-ellipsis or VP-coordination.

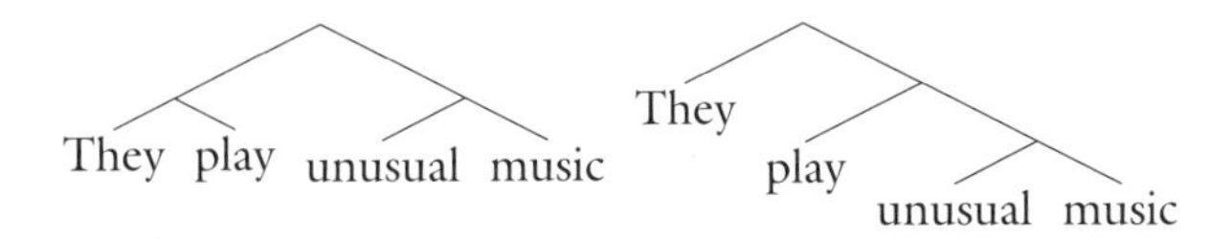

What sense can we make of this? If coordination is indeed always a reliable test for constituency, it means that this sentence and other sentences can have **more than one possible structural analysis**. We can reveal one analysis by using VP coordination or VP ellipsis, and another one by using right node raising. This conclusion is largely correct, though we are not yet equipped to understand its impact.

To avoid confusion with "standard" coordination, and to be led to apparently conflicting results regarding constituency, it is useful to know how to recognize right node raising so as **not** to use it at this stage. A good diagnostic distinguishing standard coordination from right node raising is intonation. Contrast the following examples:

(43) a. They play and I listen to unusual music
(44) a. I love the frappucinos from North Campus and your boba ice milk tea

The second example can be read with a "flowing" continuous intonation. The first, however, seems to require some kind of a pause after each conjunct, as if we were anticipating that something that normally immediately follows will not.

Gapping
In coordinated structures, we find a kind of ellipsis called **gapping**, which also seems to lead to the conclusion that strings can have two different constituent structures.

John will go to the movies and **Sue** ~~will go~~ to the theater

In this case, there are two pairs of elements that contrast with each other – the emboldened words and the underlined pair.

Applying the tests we have discovered so far, we find the following structure for the first conjunct (you should be able to support this structure by using VP ellipsis or coordination, or *do so* replacement).

John [will [go [to [the theater]]]]

Suppose we interpreted gapping as straightforwardly revealing constituency, in the sense that what appears to be elided is a constituent, as we have done so far.

Constituency of the right node raised string?
Another question concerns the shared portion, the right node raised string. After we have looked at movement later in this chapter, it will appear rather natural to suggest that:

(45) Right node raised elements are constituents.

The analysis of right node raising constructions is debated, and the particular claim in (45) is controversial (Abbott, 1976; McCawley, 1982; Postal, 1998; Runner, 1998). Assuming it to be correct would lead us to the unsurprising conclusions that *unusual music* and *boba ice milk tea* and *defrosted the roast* are constituents, but the test is controversial because of examples like the following (in which the constituency of each underlined string is debated):

(46) a. Smith loaned a valuable collection of manuscripts to the library, and his widow later donated a valuable collection of manuscripts to the library

(*Continued*)

b. Smith loaned and his widow later donated a valuable collection of manuscripts to the library

(47) a. I borrowed big sums of money from the bank, and my sister stole big sums of money from the bank

b. I borrowed and my sister stole big sums of money from the bank.

We will not discuss this question here. However it is worth knowing that consistent analyses can be constructed of such facts once a better, more advanced understanding of the principles of syntactic constituency is developed.

We should then also conclude that the first occurrence of the string *will go* is a constituent. The tree representation we would obtain would include:

John [will go] [to the theater]

This would seem to indicate that such a sentence can have two different syntactic constituent analyses. This kind of constituency cannot be represented in a single tree of the type we have used for morphology. But it is easy enough to represent what is going on by saying that this sentence is associated with **two** trees, in which case the sentence would be structurally ambiguous as follows:

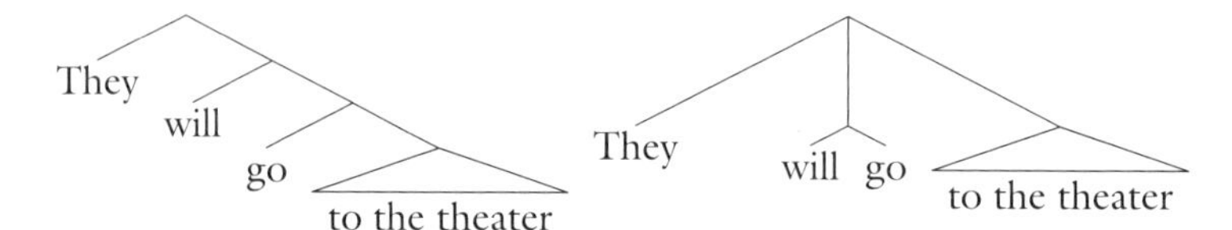

All sorts of new questions now arise. For example, this may mean that this sentence has these two structures simultaneously. Or else it may mean that sometimes the sentence has the structure indicated by the curly brackets below, and other times it has the structure indicated by the straight brackets below, but not both at the same time:

Sue [will [go [to [the theater]]]]
Sue {will go} [to [the theater]]

Are there systematic relations between these tree structures or not? Can sentences have more than two tree structures? How common is it for sentences to have two (or more) tree structures?

We will leave these questions aside for the moment and systematically ignore the curly bracket structures. To understand what happens in the case of gapping, we need to understand a lot more about syntactic organization. We briefly return to these issues in Chapter 8 where we show how to understand these constructions, and in some detail in Chapter 11, where the differences between VP ellipsis and gapping are discussed.

3.7 Movement and Other Distortions

We now turn to other classes of experiments to determine constituent structure. They involve various kinds of distortions that we impose on strings.

3.7.1 Topicalization

Consider the following pair of sentences:

(48) a. This girl in the red coat will put a picture of Bill on your desk before tomorrow

b. Before tomorrow, this girl in the red coat will put a picture of Bill on your desk ~~before tomorrow~~

Both sentences are acceptable. Their conditions of use are different of course. The first one could be a natural, neutral answer to the question: what do you think will happen? The second would be a less neutral answer to this question. However the second could be a natural answer to the question: what do you think will happen before tomorrow? Saying this sentence assumes that the topic of the exchange is about *before tomorrow*, and provides a comment about it. This is why this construction is called topicalization. It is said with a special prosody and a pause, encoded here by the comma between *tomorrow* and *this girl*. We informally refer to the string *before tomorrow* as having been topicalized. The two sentences in a pair like (a) and (b) are systematically related: we can construct the second one by taking a piece of the first and putting it at the front of the sentence. We will not explore this construction as thoroughly as we did ellipsis, but the same conclusion applies: topicalization only can affect continuous strings, and so it is reasonable to conclude:

Topicalization can only affect constituents.

As usual, we have no guarantee *a priori* that what counts as a constituent for topicalization is what counts as a constituent for ellipsis, coordination, pronominalization, etc. Constituency here just means "behave as a unit with respect to the experimental conditions we are presently observing." We return to this point at the end of this chapter.

Here is a sample of cases in which we have successfully topicalized various constituents (respectively DP, PP, VP, NP).

(49) a. This girl in the red coat will put the picture of Bill on your desk before tomorrow
b. The picture of Bill, this girl in the red coat will put ~~the picture of Bill~~ on your desk before tomorrow
c. On your desk, this girl in the red coat will put a picture of Bill ~~on your desk~~ before tomorrow
d. Put a picture of Bill on your desk, this girl in the red coat will ~~put a picture of Bill on your desk~~ before tomorrow
e. Put a picture of Bill on your desk before tomorrow, this girl in the red coat will ~~put a picture of Bill on your desk before tomorrow~~

The topicalization found in the last two case is sometimes called **VP-preposing**, for obvious reasons.

The following example is a case of topicalization of a constituent type we have not yet seen, which we will call CP, for "complementizer phrase":

(50) a. Mary should know that you must go to the station
b. That you must go to the station, Mary should know ~~that you must go to the station~~

And here is a sample of cases in which topicalization fails: all the following examples are deviant because we tried to topicalize discontinuous strings:

(51) a. * This your, ~~this~~ girl in the red coat will put a picture of Bill on ~~your~~ desk before tomorrow
b. * Will Bill, this girl in the red coat ~~will~~ put a picture of ~~Bill~~ on your desk before tomorrow
c. * Red picture desk, this girl in the ~~red~~ coat will put a ~~picture~~ of Bill on your ~~desk~~ before tomorrow
d. * your tomorrow, this girl in the red coat will put a picture of Bill on ~~your~~ desk before ~~tomorrow~~

Here are some cases in which topicalization fails even though we have concluded that the topicalized strings are constituents:

(52) * Girl in the red coat, this ~~girl in the red coat~~ will put a picture of Bill on your desk before tomorrow
(53) * Will put a picture of Bill on your desk before tomorrow, this girl in the red coat ~~will put a picture of Bill on your desk before tomorrow~~
(54) * Picture of Bill, this girl in the red coat will put a ~~picture of Bill~~ on your desk before tomorrow

What can we conclude from this regarding constituency? No significant conclusions follow from what we know so far. Trying to understand the causes for this set of failures under topicalization is an advanced and fascinating topic. We return to this question in Chapter 10.

Finally, here are some cases in which topicalization fails because we tried to topicalize non-constituents (remember, however, that these sentences do not allow us to conclude that these strings are not constituents; this conclusion will be reached by other means):

(55) * The red, this girl in ~~the red~~ coat will put a picture of Bill on your desk before tomorrow
(56) * Of Bill on, this girl in the red coat will put a picture ~~of Bill on~~ your desk before tomorrow
(57) * Will put, this girl in the red coat ~~will put~~ a picture of Bill on your desk before tomorrow
(58) * Your desk before, this girl in the red coat will put a picture of Bill on ~~your desk before~~ tomorrow

Not all constituents can be topicalized: topicalization is picky. English topicalization is useful for determining constituency of DPs, VPs, CPs, and PPs.

3.7.2 Cleft constructions

Here are some examples of the cleft construction:

(59) a. John wants to look at your notes after class
b. It is your notes that/which John wants to look at after class
c. It is after class that John wants to look at your notes
d. It is John who wants to look at your notes after class
(60) a. Ann bought a first edition of Richard III for $1000
b. It was Ann who bought a first edition of Richard III for $1000
c. It was a first edition of Richard III that Ann bought for $1000
d. It was for $1000 that Ann bought a first edition of Richard III

In this construction, the word *it* appears as subject, *be* as the verb, and more material follows. Consider the following pair:

(61) a. This girl in the red coat will put a picture of Bill on your desk <u>before tomorrow</u>
b. It is <u>before tomorrow</u> that *this girl in the red coat will put a picture of Bill on your desk* ~~before tomorrow~~

Both sentences are acceptable. Their conditions of use are different of course. The first one could be an answer to the question: *what do you think will happen?* The second could not be. However, the second could be a reaction to the statement *This girl in the red coat will put a picture of Bill on your desk before Tuesday*. Saying this sentence roughly assumes agreement between the discourse participants that the girl in the red coat will put a picture of Bill on your desk. What the speaker of this sentence contributes is the information that this will take place before tomorrow. The underlined constituent is called a *focus*, and the italicized portion the *presupposition* (because the speaker of this sentence presupposes that the discourse participants know about it). There are many constructions involving a notion of focus. This is just one of them. (We will see another one shortly: so-called "pseudocleft" constructions.) It is called a *cleft construction* and the *focus* is also called the *clefted string*. As is now familiar, we will interpret the fact that clefting can only affect continuous strings as an indication that the focus must be a constituent:

(62) The focus of a cleft construction is a constituent.

The clefting experiment takes the following form:

- Starting from some acceptable string of the form *ABC* (with A or C possibly null strings) we form the new string:

  it BE B that AC

  Where BE stands for any form of the verb *be* such as *is* or *was*.
- If the result is acceptable, this is evidence that B is a constituent of ABC; if the result is unacceptable, we conclude nothing (but we might want to investigate further to find out what went wrong).

Here are some more examples in which we perform the test above, letting the underlined string be the focus B:

(63) a. Mary saw the tall man coming from England
b. it is the tall man coming from England that Mary saw ~~the tall man coming from England~~

This result is fine, so we conclude that *the tall man coming from England* is a constituent. (You should be able to verify this conclusion in other ways: substitution, coordination, etc.)

(64) a. Mary saw the tall man come from the back
b. * it is the tall man come from the back that Mary saw ~~the tall man come from the back~~

This result is not acceptable. We cannot conclude anything.

The cleft construction will help identify DPs and PPs, but it is not so good for the other kinds of constituents. Consider this application of our test, for example, where we use — instead of striking out the clefted constituent:

(65) a. This girl in the red coat will put a picture of Bill on your desk before tomorrow
b. It is a picture of Bill that this girl in the red coat will put — on your desk before tomorrow
c. *It is put a picture of Bill on your desk before tomorrow that this girl in the red coat will —

3.7.3 Pseudoclefts

In the pseudocleft construction, what looks like an interrogative clause appears in subject position, and a focused element appears at the end of the sentence, following a form of the verb *be*.

(66) a. What John wants to look at — now is your notes
b. What Mary bought — was a first edition
c. *What Mary gave — was a book to John
d. *What Mary donated — was a lot of money to Amnesty

The underlined elements are said to be focused and pseudoclefted (moved to the end) here. Cleft and pseudocleft constructions fulfill similar functions of "focusing" a constituent of the correspondingly simpler sentence, though the two constructions differ considerably with regard to the class of cases in which they can be employed. For many speakers the pseudocleft construction is only possible with *what* (as opposed to *who*, *where*, etc.), and correspondingly the focused element is restricted to constituents of types that can serve as answers to a question with *what* (the symbol % is used to indicate that there is some variation in judgment across speakers):

(67) a. It was Alice that John was talking to
b. % Who John was talking to was Alice
(68) a. It is to Cleveland that John drove the truck
b. % where John drove the truck is to Cleveland
(69) a. It's because he was tired that Mary yelled at you
b. % Why John yelled at you is because he was tired

In this respect the cleft construction is less restricted than the pseudocleft construction: all types of DPs and PPs cleft freely. However, the cleft construction and the pseudocleft construction do not test for the same types of constituents. The cleft construction only works well for DPs and PPs, but the pseudocleft construction works well for a variety of other constituents: A(djectivals), P (APs), VPs, and CPs (*to*-infinitivals or tensed CPs – i.e. CPs with tensed verbs or modals):

(70) a. John became deathly afraid of flying
b. ?* It is deathly afraid of flying that John became
c. What John became was deathly afraid of flying (AP)
(71) a. John told us that he wants to quit school
b. ??It is that he wants to quit school that John told us
c. What John told us is that he wants to quit school. (CP)
(72) a. John promised to be gentle
b. ?* It is to be gentle that John promised
c. What John promised is to be gentle (CP)
(73) a. Mary will arrive tomorrow
b. *It is arrive tomorrow that Mary will
c. What Mary will do is arrive tomorrow (VP)

Like cleft constructions, pseudoclefts can be used to determine constituent structure, since, as is now familiar, we will interpret the fact that pseudoclefting can only affect continuous strings as an indication that the focus must be a constituent:

The focus of a pseudocleft construction is a constituent.

The pseudocleft experiment takes the following form:

- Starting from some acceptable string ABC (with A and C possibly null strings) we form the new string:

  what AC BE B

  Where BE stands for any form of the verb *be* such as *is* or *was*.

- If the result is acceptable, this is evidence that B is a constituent of ABC.
- If the result is unacceptable, we conclude nothing (but we might want to investigate further to find out what went wrong).

Here is an example where we perform the test above, letting the underlined string be the focus B:

(74) a. Henry wants the book which is on the top shelf
b. What Henry wants is the book which is on the top shelf

This result is acceptable, so we conclude that *the book which is on the top shelf* is a constituent (here a DP). (You should be able to verify this conclusion in other ways: substitution, coordination, etc.)

A variant of the pseudocleft experiment can be used to isolate VPs. It goes (approximately) as follows:

i. Starting from some acceptable string ABC (with A and C possibly null strings) we form the new string:

What A DO C BE B

(The notation DO and BE means that the verbs *do* and *be* can also be in the past or the future.)

ii. If the result is acceptable, this is evidence that B is a VP constituent of ABC; if the result is unacceptable, we conclude nothing (but we might want to investigate further to find out what went wrong).

For example:

(75) a. This girl in the red coat will put a picture of Bill on your desk before tomorrow
b. What this girl in the red coat will do is put a picture of Bill on your desk before tomorrow

This result is fine, so we conclude that *put a picture of Bill on your desk before tomorrow* is a constituent, a VP. (You should be able to verify this conclusion in other ways: substitution, coordination, etc.)

Note finally that there is a construction closely related to the pseudocleft, which we may call the **inverted** pseudocleft. It is identical to pseudoclefting except that the two strings around the verb BE are inverted. It could be stated as follows:

i. Starting from some acceptable string ABC (with A and C possibly null strings) we form the new string:

B BE what AC

(The verb *be* can also be in the past or the future.)

ii. If the result is acceptable, this is evidence that B is a constituent of ABC; if the result is unacceptable, we conclude nothing (but, as always, we might want to investigate further to find out what went wrong).

The following sentences are the inverted pseudoclefted counterparts of the examples in (67a) and (68a) above. Often, the judgments on the % marked pseudoclefts sentences we encountered earlier improve when we invert the pseudocleft:

(76) a. %Who John was talking to was Alice
b. Alice was who John was talking to

(77) a. %Where John drove the truck to is Cleveland
b. Cleveland is where John drove the truck to

(78) a. %Why John yelled at you is because he was tired
b. %Because he was tired is why John yelled at you

3.8 Some More Complex Distortion Experiments, Briefly

There are many other distortion experiments, some of which will be used and investigated in the following chapters. Here we briefly mention a few of them.

3.8.1 Wh-movement

Wh-questioned strings are constituents. Consider, for example, the sentence:

(79) Henry wants to buy these books about cooking

Is the string *these books about cooking* a constituent? Notice that a determiner like *these* can often be replaced by a wh-determiner like *which* (with appropriate, "echo question" stress, as in the following example):

(80) Henry wants to buy *which* books about cooking?

Without echo question stress on *which* however, the questioned element must be moved to the front of the expression, with further adjustments (the appearance of tensed *do* before the subject, and removing tense marking from *buy*):

(81) Which books about cooking does Henry want to buy?

From the point of view of meaning, it is clear that we have questioned what Henry wants to buy here, and so it is plausible that *which books about cooking* has the same category as *these books about cooking*. We conclude that both are constituents, supposing, as usual, that the affected subsequence of words must form a constituent in order to be moved as a unit like this.

3.8.2 Heavy constituent shift

One more distortion that can be useful for identifying constituents, but which has some surprising properties, is heavy constituent shift, often referred to as Heavy NP Shift (even though it may not move NPs!). This construction has the surprising property that it seems to be sensitive to the "size" or "weight" of the constituent involved, moving only "heavy" enough ones to the right. Consider the following sentences, in which we try to move the phrase that refers to what is sent all the way to the right edge of the sentence:

(82) a. I sent it to you
b. * I sent to you it
c. * I sent to you recipes
d. ? I sent to you the recipes from the paper
e. I sent to you <u>the recipes from the paper that I told you about yesterday</u>

The underlined element is said to be "heavy NP shifted." What we would like to propose is the following, which should seem totally unsurprising given the previous proposals:

(83) Heavy shifted elements are constituents.

Again, this idea is slightly controversial, with some linguists reasonably arguing that because of its weight sensitivity, heavy shift must have some special status. Perhaps it is not part of the syntax of human languages at all, but maybe something to do with phonology (or perhaps some theory of "rules of pronunciation" that goes beyond what phonology traditionally encompasses, but then the fact that it does seem to affect only what other constituency tests identify as syntactic constituents would call for some special explanation).

3.9 Some More Practice

The general mode of investigation we follow is this: we select a string of words (say a sentence, but it does not have to be). We manipulate the string with various processes (such as substitution, movement, coordination, ellipsis), and we find that some results are well formed (and some even mean the same thing as the original) while others are not well formed (or they have meanings unlike the original sentence). To explain this, we postulate that the manipulated subsequences form constituents, pieces of the structure. Once we are practiced with the constituency tests, we can quite quickly get to some hypotheses about the structure of a sentence.

Example: Take a sentence like the following:

(84) Bill's mother's friends are waiting at the restaurant

Just to take some first steps. Is this sentence a constituent? It must be a constituent because it can be coordinated with a constituent (of the same type).

(85) Bill's mother's friends are waiting at the restaurant and Mary is on her way to the movies

The string *Bill's mother's friends* must be a constituent as well: what is called the subject of the sentence. We can substitute the pronoun *they*, which is a single word, and preserve meaning (when we take *they* to refer to Bill's mother's friends). It is thus plausibly a DP, since pronouns diagnose DPs.

(86) They are waiting at the restaurant

It can be coordinated with single items:

(87) [Bill's mother's friends] and [John] are waiting at the restaurant

It can be clefted:

Cleft: It was [Bill's mother's friends] [that/who were waiting at the restaurant]

Notice that the focus position in a cleft can only hold a single constituent, though the single constituent can be complex, like a coordinate structure:

(88) a. It was John [that was waiting at the restaurant]
b. *It was John Bill [that were waiting at the restaurant]
c. It was John and Bill [that were waiting at the restaurant]

Proceeding in this way, we can and will further dissect the structures of sentences like this in the next chapters.

Practice

Draw the tree structure for the following sentence:

1. The boy will bring my mother Bill's most recent book about global warming when he can.

a. For each constituent you draw, provide one experiment justifying your conclusion.
b. Don't draw any constituents you cannot justify.

3.10 Some Other Evidence of Constituency

We have seen how various kinds of substitution, deletion, and distortion manipulations suggest that language has a chunky structure. These tests can be applied by any speaker in just the moment or two it takes to reflect on the input and output strings. Since it is quite challenging to make sense of the results of these tests, as we will see in the next chapters, tests like these have been a source of controversy for linguists. When these tests became well recognized in the 1960s, it was important to explore whether the tests actually provided indications of the structural properties evidenced by other sorts of linguistic tasks. These early explorations were by and large successful, and are worth remembering here. They can be found in Fodor, Bever, and Garrett (1976).

In the first place, one constituent that has been taken for granted in the way we have approached language is the *sentence* itself. (Go ahead and demonstrate that the sentence is a constituent with the diagnostic tests presented in this chapter.) Almost all of our examples have been these things we call "sentences," but is there really evidence that this unit is a valid one for theories of how we acquire and use our language? It is conceivable that this notion is just taught to us in school, and although we learn how to use the notion there, maybe it does not really play any significant role in models of human language acquisition, perception, or production.

In fact, there is abundant evidence that a structural unit very close to the one we call a "sentence" is important in a wide variety of linguistic tasks. For example, even the simple task of remembering a sequence of words is significantly easier if the sequence forms a sentence, even if the sentence is semantically and pragmatically nonsensical (Marks and Miller, 1964). For much more evidence, see the studies reviewed, for example, in Fodor, Bever, and Garrett (1976) or Townsend and Bever (2001).

What about the constituent structures we seem to find inside the boundaries of sentences? At least for the main outlines of our proposals, the evidence again is abundant that these structures play an important role in memory, perception, production, and acquisition of language. We will briefly mention just a few kinds of studies.

3.10.1 Perception of click position

One important kind of study was developed by Ladefoged and Broadbent (1960) and Fodor and Bever (1965). They found that if short bursts of noise, clicks, are played in the background while a sentence is being perceived, the click will often sound like it is in a position different from its actual, acoustic position. In particular, the click will sound like it is closer to a major constituent boundary than it really is.

sentence:	that he was happy was evident from the way he smiled
structure, by our tests:	[that he was happy] [was evident from the way he smiled]

(This is just a broad constituent structure, our tests tell us more about structure than this.)

spoken sentence:	that	he	was	happy	was	evident	from	the	way	he	smiled
click position:				*							
perceived position:					*						

In fact, the researchers discovered that this illusion persists even if you know exactly where the click is, having put it there yourself.

3.10.2 Memorization errors

After having subjects memorize lists of sentences, Johnson (1965) measured the probability that a particular word was incorrectly recalled, and showed that the probability of error increased substantially at the beginning of each phrase in the sentence:

sentence:	the	tall	boy	saved	the	dying	woman
structure, by our tests:	[the	tall	boy]	[saved	[the	dying	woman]]
probability of error:							

sentence:	the	house	across	the	street	is	burning
structure, by our tests:	[the	house]	[across	the	street]	[is	burning]
probability of error:							

The vertical bars indicate the probability of error at the place in the string right above it.[1] The higher the bar is, the higher the probability of error. The correlation between probability of error and phrase boundaries is clear. Many other studies of sentence recall show similar effects.

3.10.3 Neurophysiological correlates of syntactic analysis

It is not surprising that certain distinctive kinds of events occur in the brain during language processing tasks of various kinds. What is more surprising is that some of these brain events produce distinctive electrical potentials detectable by sensors placed on the scalp (ERP), or by differential neural activity detectable by functional magnetic resonance imaging (fMRI) or positron emission tomography (PET). These studies evidence localization of neural activity associated with syntactic analysis. The image on the left below shows PET activation of a prefrontal area of the brain in language production and when syntactic errors are noticed (Indefrey et al., 2001). On the right, a figure shows a region of fMRI activation implicated in syntactic analysis (Christensen and Wallentin, 2011).

[1] The heights of the bars in these tables were set using the results reported in table 2 of Johnson (1965, p. 472).

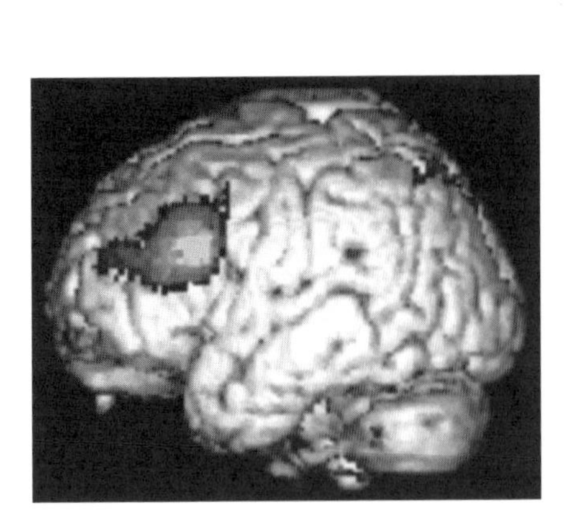

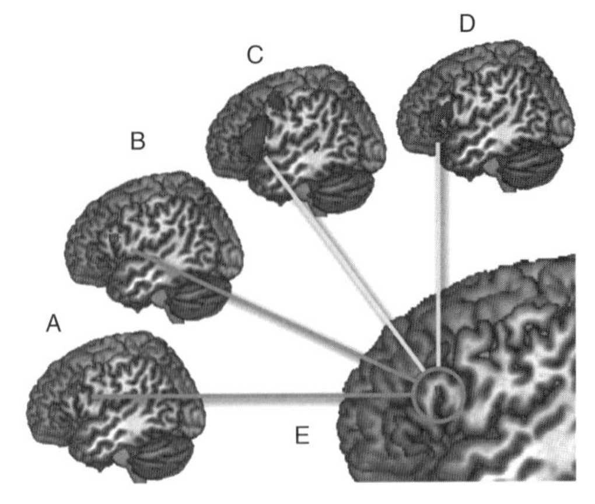

Other studies show that distinctive neural activity occurs when syntactic anomalies are detected and when syntactic complexity increases (Kang et al., 1999; Featherston et al., 2000; Embick et al., 2001; among others) where these notions of anomaly and complexity are defined in structural terms like those developed in this and the following chapters. Pallier, Devauchelle, and Dehaene (2011) find exceptionally direct fMRI evidence in support of hierarchical structures of the kind developed here, by discovering regions where activation increases with the size of the constituents.

3.11 Conclusion

In this chapter we have demonstrated that linguistic strings are segmented into syntactic constituents. We have illustrated the constituency tests, how to use them, how to apply them, what can be concluded from negative results, and how to proceed with seemingly conflicting results. The tests listed below probe the syntactic structures of strings in English.

3.11.1 Summary

Substitution: if a string S can be replaced by a single word, this is evidence that S is a constituent. In particular:
- **Pronominalization**: if a string S can be replaced by a pronoun, this is evidence that S is a DP
- *One* **substitution**: if a string S can be replaced by *one*, this is evidence that S is an NP
- *Do so* **substitution**: if a string S can be replaced by *do so*, this is evidence that S is a VP.

Ellipsis: if a string S can be deleted, this is evidence that S is a constituent.

Coordination: if a string S can be coordinated with a word (or phrase), this is evidence that S is a constituent, a constituent of the same category as the word (or phrase) it is coordinated with.

Movement: if a string S can be moved to another position (typically, all the way to the right or to the left), this is evidence that S is a constituent. In particular:
- **Topicalization**: DPs, PPs, VPs (VP preposing)
- **Clefting**: DPs, PPs
- **Pseudoclefting**: VPs, APs, DPs, ...
- **Wh-movement**: DPs, PPs
- **Right node raising**: ...
- **Heavy shift**: DP.

Important caveat: when an experiment does not successfully apply to S, the reasons for failure could be extremely varied. As a result, it does not show that S is not a constituent.

Can these very same tests be applied to probe the syntactic structures of other languages, or even to all human languages? The answer here is yes, in principle: these tests are part of the basic toolkit of any linguist. However, for each language, it must be determined what tests yield information. Imagine, for example, that a language lacks a pseudocleft construction, or allows only full clauses to be coordinated. This would restrict the use of that test for the language in question. Linguists working on some specific language might develop new tests that were informative for the language under study, but possibly these tests may not reveal much about the structure of English or, more often, yield interesting puzzles of comparative syntax. New tests are constantly being developed as the formal understanding of the properties of language become more and more precise. By the end of this book, we will have introduced and motivated a much broader inventory of tests, a quite sophisticated toolbox for the description and formal analysis of the syntax of any language.

3.11.2 What to remember

First, it is important to remember that linguistic strings are segmented into syntactic constituents. Second, it is important to understand what constituency tests are, what constituency tests there are, to know how to apply them properly, and to understand their limits (e.g. that failure is hard to interpret). Finally, it is very important to understand the concept of minimal pair: this is crucial for how reasoning can lead to sound conclusions.

3.11.3 Puzzles and preview

When we consider the results of all the constituency tests we have introduced, a remarkable conclusion emerges: in general, we do not find contradictions. The tree structure that we are led to postulate **for a given string** by one of these tests is consistent with the tree structures identified by the other experimental conditions. Informally, consistency among a set of tree structures means that for all the trees, a given node has the same mother node. This convergence is a strong indication that the interpretation we give to each experiment is on the right track.

There are however two cases which do not seem to fit with these conclusions: gapping and right node raising. Let us exemplify the problem with the sentence:

Mary will buy these books

Every test except gapping or right node raising will suggest the following constituent structure:

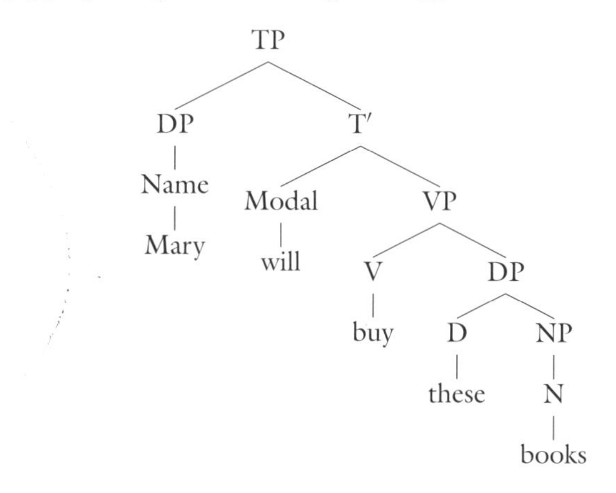

But gapping, as in:

Mary will buy these books and Sue these magazines

would suggest the following constituency:

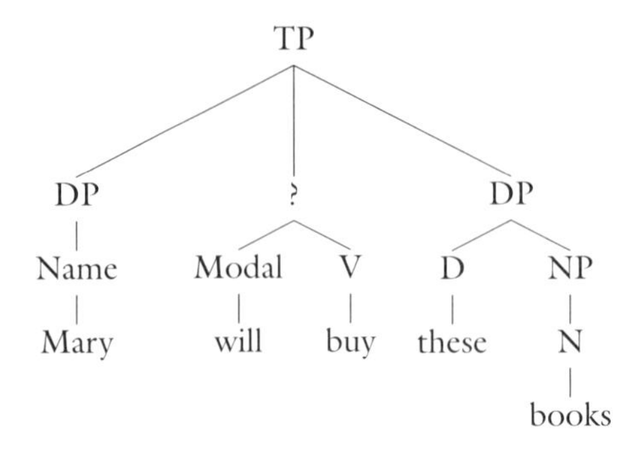

And right node raising, as in:

Mary will buy and Sue will sell, these books

would suggest the following constituency:

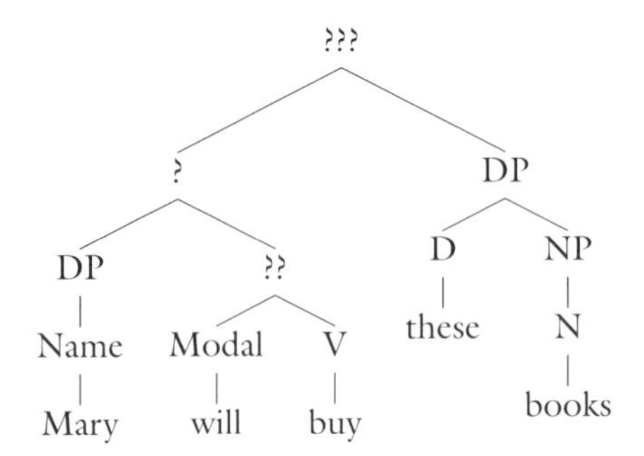

We see that the DP node, which dominates the string *these books*, has several different mother nodes among the trees: in the first tree, this node is VP, in the second it is TP, and in the third, it is ???. This is why we put gapping and right node raising aside for the moment until we have developed analytical tools to gain some understanding about what is happening here.

In the coming chapters, we will first refine our knowledge about what kind of constituents exist, and next explore why we find these, rather than other, possible groupings.

3.11.4 Further exercises

Testing skills: constituent analysis (with or without labels), tree drawing (only what can be motivated), applying tests, interpretation of tests.

(1) Early constituent structure
Draw as much of the tree structure as you can for the following sentence under the following guidelines.

(1) The men will bring me Bill's newest book about the universe when they have received it in the mail.

(i) For each constituent you draw, provide one experiment justifying your conclusion.
(ii) Don't draw any constituents you cannot justify. This may mean that your structures will (temporarily) look less developed than the ones you may have been taught in other linguistics classes!
(iii) The only experiments you can use are: substitution with a pronoun, substitution with *one/ones, do so, there, then* (assume *then* substitutes for a PP), and coordination. (Be sure to use them exactly as they are stated in the chapter.)
(iv) You should only label the nodes that you know how to label because of your experiments.

(2) Constituency tests
Using VP ellipsis and "do so" substitution in as many ways as you can, indicate what conclusions can be drawn about the following examples.

(1) a. I will fix the computer for Karim
b. I will eat spaghetti on Sunday with Marco
c. I will speak to Hector about this
d. Jessica loaned a valuable collection of manuscripts to the library

(If you are not a native English speaker, you should check your judgments with one. Mention anything that seems especially tricky or difficult.)

(3) Tree drawing
Draw trees for the sentence below.

(1) She gave him the key to Bill's bicycle

Your trees should reflect the facts listed below:

(i) She gave him the one to Bill's bicycle
(ii) *She gave him it to Harriet's motorcycle
(iii) *She did so the key to Harriet's motorcycle

(4) Structural ambiguity
The sentence below is ambiguous; it has two different structures.

(1) I will watch the girl with binoculars
(i) Paraphrase the two meanings of this sentence.
(ii) Draw two different trees for this sentence, and pair each tree up with the meaning of each sentence. Assuming that *will* has category T – don't worry if you are not sure about how to label all the nodes.
(You should be able to defend your trees using constituency tests, but you only need to explain the tests requested in (iii).)
(iii) Explain how at least one of the tests supports the structure in the first tree but not the second, and how at least one test supports the structure in the second tree but not the first.
(iv) When we replace the string *the girl* with *her*, we find the following:

(2) I will watch her with binoculars
(v) This sentence is well-formed, but no longer ambiguous! Explain why.
(Hint: start with the meaning this sentence has, and pair up the meaning with the corresponding tree.)

(5) **Right node raising**
Examples (46) and (47) (from the box in Section 3.6.2) are repeated below, with the underlined string in (b) right node raised. This is puzzling if right node raising applies to constituents.

(1) a. Smith loaned a valuable collection of manuscripts to the library, and his widow later donated a valuable collection of manuscripts to the library
b. Smith loaned and his widow later donated a valuable collection of manuscripts to the library

(2) a. I borrowed big sums of money from the bank, and my sister stole big sums of money from the bank
b. I borrowed and my sister stole big sums of money from the bank.

(i) Why are these examples puzzling? (Hint: compare what the coordination test suggests about this structure with what other tests tell us.)
(ii) Why exactly do (1b) and (2b) make RNR controversial as a constituency test?

(6) **On categories and silent heads**
Here is a quote from p. 12:

Thus, if a word can be pluralized (and is not a demonstrative or a pronoun), it is a noun.

We are interested in the category of the word *poor* as used in the examples below:

(1) a. The poor(*s) are only getting poorer
b. The rich(*es) are just getting richer
(i) Since *poor* cannot be pluralized, can you conclude it is not a noun? Discuss (1 to 2 lines), and make sure to consider the following plurals:

(2)

singular	*plural*
child	children
mouse	mice
man	men
moose	moose

(ii) The word *poor* can combine with the determiner *the*, as shown in (1). Is this sufficient evidence to conclude that *poor* is a noun?
In the answer to this question, you must take the examples in (3) into account: each holds ingredients for the answer. The answer itself can be short.
(iia) What do the examples in (3) show about the category label of *poor*?

(3) a. The extremely poor (citizens)
b. The poorest (citizens) are living in the city

(iib) What do the examples in (iv) tell you about adjectives in English?

(4) a. Big(*s) balloons
b. The poor(*s) people are just getting poorer
c. The rich(*es) kids are just getting more spoiled
d. The poor(*s) are only getting poorer
e. The rich (*es) are just getting richer

(7) **English *-s* and '*s***
English has two morphemes that sound the same *-s* and '*s*, but that interact differently with their local environments and have different (non-overlapping) meanings and distributional

properties. How should these be modeled exactly? This exercise walks you through the differences.

Consider the *-s* in :

(1) a. shark-s
b. Some big shark-s
c. Scary shark-s with sharp teeth
d. Queens of England.
e. *[Queen of England]-s

and the *'s* in (2):

(2) a. The shark's teeth
b. The children's teacher
c. The queen of England's gown
d. The girl that I met's father

(i) Does *-s* in (1) attach to an N or to some bigger phrase that contains the N? (We will call this phrasal unit a DP.) Justify your answer, using the examples in (1). (One to two sentences should suffice.)
(Be careful, if a DP ends in the head N and the *'s* appears at the end, we cannot determine whether *'s* is attaching to the end of the head N or to the end of the entire DP.)

(ii) What does *-s* in (1) add to the semantics of the element it attaches to? (One sentence.)

(iii) Can -s attach to any other element/phrase to mean the same thing? If so, which categories or phrases? (Consider (1) and (2), but also the categories of verb (V) (such as *destroy),* adjective (A) (such as *beautiful),* adverb (Adv) (such as *probably),* and preposition (P) (such as *under).* Don't just say yes or no. You have to show why, using ungrammatical examples for A, Adv, and P.)

(iv) Look up the lexical entry for *-s* in Section 2.3.6, p. 31, and write it down.
What, if anything, do we need to say to exclude the ungrammatical examples in (iii)?
Next consider *'s* in (2):

(v) Does *'s* attach to an N or to an NP/DP. Justify your answer, using the examples in (2).

(vi) What is the meaning of the forms that have *'s*? Consider strings like:

(3) a. Mary's leg
b. Sally's sister
c. My friend's keys
d. Last night's storm
e. The city's destruction
f. Bill's sudden departure
g. Mary's picture of Susan that Jim owns
h. Mary's picture that Jim took

(Be careful! The answer to this question is quite a bit longer. Proceed by paraphrasing and organizing the meanings of these DPs. Do not simply say that this morpheme always indicates possession! There is much more to it than that.)

(vii) Why is it difficult to determine the syntactic label for *'s*?
(viii) Examine the examples below:

(4) a. *The Mary's key
  b. *Mary's the key
  c. Mary's key
  d. The key
  a. List which elements are in *complementary* distribution.
  b. Why is it reasonable evidence for the fact that *'s* is a special kind of D (i.e. has the label D)?

(viii) Give its category, and list its local syntactic environment (left and right daughter of 's). Do we need to say anything special about why (2d) is allowed in some varieties of English, but (5) is excluded (in all English dialects)?

(5) a. * [To John]'s car
  b. * [Nice]'s car

(8) **VP preposing (hierarchical order of locative and temporal phrases in Dutch)**
Dutch, contrary to English, does not have VP ellipsis. But Dutch does allow fronting of a verbal constituent, a process called VP fronting. Assuming VP fronting, what can you learn about the structure of the underlined string in (1a) below? (You only need to worry about the syntactic structure of the underlined constituent for the purposes of this exercise.)

Note: For further information, Dutch is a "verb-second " language, which means that the finite verb is in second position in root clauses (after chapter 6, you will see why this is analyzed as a case of V-to-T-to-C-movement).

(1) a. de kinderen zullen zeker volgende week op de markt bloemen kopen
  the children will.PRES.PL certainly next week at the market flowers buy
  b. *kopen zullen ze volgende week op de markt bloemen
  buy will.PRES.PL they next week at the market flowers
  c. bloemen kopen zullen ze zeker volgende week op de markt
  flowers buy will.PRES.PL they certainly next week at the market
  d. op de markt bloemen kopen zullen ze zeker volgende week
  at the market flowers buy will.PRES.PL they certainly next week
  e. volgende week op de markt bloemen kopen zullen ze zeker
  next week at the market flowers buy will.PRES.PL they certainly
  f. ?*volgende week bloemen kopen zullen ze zeker op de markt
  next week flowers buy will.PRES.PL they certainly at the market
  g. *zeker volgende week op de markt bloemen kopen zullen ze
  certainly next week at the market flowers buy will.PRES.PL they

On the basis of these examples:

(i) what do each of (1b), (1c), (1d), (1e), and (1f) show about the constituent structure in (1a)?
(ii) Give a tree structure just for the underlined part in (1a) that allows you to account for all the examples in (1b)–(1f). If it does not, say where it fails, and how you could fix it.
(iii) What can you conclude about the constituency of sentences that contain locative and temporal phrases?

3.11.5 Further reading

Any syntax textbook will at least have a list and (some) discussion of constituency tests, as these are part of the standard toolkit of syntacticians. To learn more about the properties of the particular constructions underlying the constituency tests, a good place to start is the Blackwell Companion to Syntax (Everaert and Riemsdijk, 2006), an important reference resource organized by case studies (70 in all), that offer an overview of the empirical facts and theoretical insights.

4
Clauses

We now examine the structure of various types of constituents in more detail, beginning with "clauses": sentence-like structures that are commonly described as having a "subject" and a "predicate."

Through the tests that we used to detect constituency, we have established the existence of all sorts of higher order units in sentences, units larger than single words. We have labeled some of these DPs, PPs, or VPs, etc. To a certain extent this is justified. Just as we called all the words or morphemes sharing some properties (e.g. the ability to be put in the plural) nouns (N), it seems legitimate to have a label for those things that can be replaced by a pronoun such as *she*, *he*, or *it*: DP. Yet, we have not offered any justification for the choice of particular names. Would it have made sense to use VP for the elements we label DP? In particular, is there a relationship between these phrasal labels and the corresponding word level categories – DP to D, VP to V, PP to P, etc.? As we will see, the answer is positive. In this chapter we will discuss this question by examining various types of clauses and clausal complements. The notions of **head**, **sister**, and **selection** introduced in Chapter 2 will play an important role, so this may be a good time to review these notions.

4.1 Full Clauses: CPs

We have an informal understanding of what a sentence is. Here are some examples:

(1) You will see this
(2) The girl will put a picture on your desk
(3) Mary reads mysteries
(4) The visitors will leave
(5) John is snoring
(6) The visiting team won the race

These sentences are all more or less constructed like the first one or the second one. As we saw in the previous chapter, they have the following (approximate) structure, and we have given them labels in anticipation of the discussion in this chapter. Here we turn to the reasons these nodes are labeled the way they are:

An Introduction to Syntactic Analysis and Theory, First Edition.
Dominique Sportiche, Hilda Koopman, and Edward Stabler.

(7)

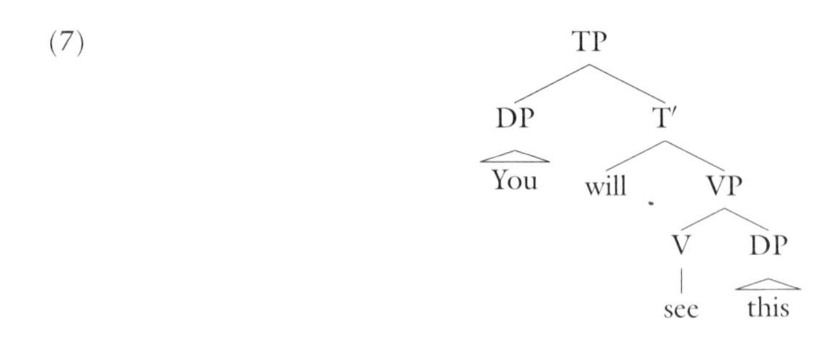

(8)

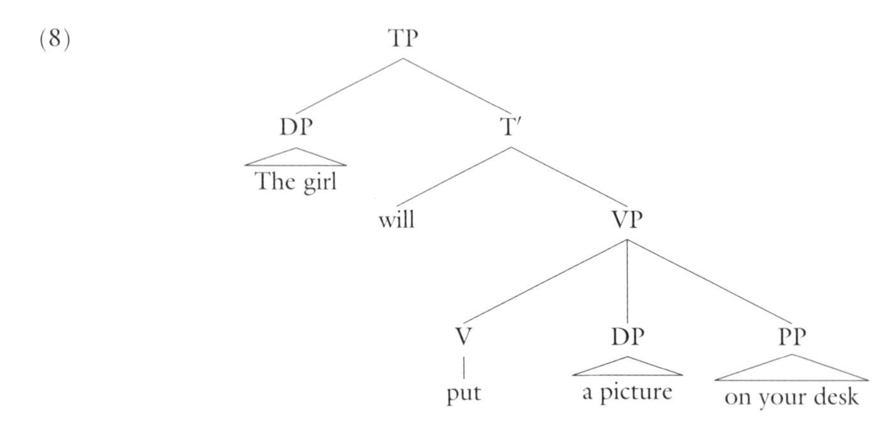

Interestingly, these sentences can occur as subordinate clauses, that is, as parts of a larger sentence (see examples below). This is another important case of syntactic recursion: the recurrence of a category X inside another X.

(9) You will see [that the girl will put a picture on your desk]
(10) I doubt [that Mary reads mysteries]
(11) He said [that the visitors will leave]
(12) The fact [that John is snoring] is informative
(13) [That the visiting team won the race] could surprise them

Practice

It is a good idea to practice constituency tests whenever there is a claim that something is a constituent. In the present case, there is a new test we can use: *so* or *this* or *that* replacement. Thus we have the pairs (i) and (ii), as well as (iii) and (iv), preserving both well-formedness and truth values:

i. You will see [that the girl will put a picture on your desk]
ii. You will see this (*namely that the girl will put a picture on your desk*)
iii. He said [that the visitors will leave]
iv. He said so (*namely that the visitors will leave*)

Now you should practice. Try to corroborate the constituency of CP using pronominalization with (*it*), coordination, or one of the clefting constructions.

As we will see shortly, it is easy enough to identify these bracketed strings as constituents with the help of the tests introduced in the previous chapter. We will begin by investigating the kind of constituent we call "*that* CPs," where CP is short for C(omplementizer) P(hrase). These phrases contain a C, like the *that* in (9), which is followed by a constituent that we called TP, a T(ense) P(hrase). The name CP evokes some connection with C, and the name TP a connection with T, but we have not yet seen why these are good names for these constituents.

The first thing to do is to run constituency tests.

If we apply our constituency tests to various parts of sentence (9), and apply the labeling conventions given so far to the various nodes, we end up with the tree below. This should not be surprising because this sentence is composed of the sentences in trees (7) and (8). What we have done is to take the first sentence, a TP, add *that* in front of it, and put the result inside the second tree in place of *this*. Why should we label the third "?" as CP, *that* as C, and the whole sentence as TP? And why use T′? Is there a connection with T, and if so what is the connection?

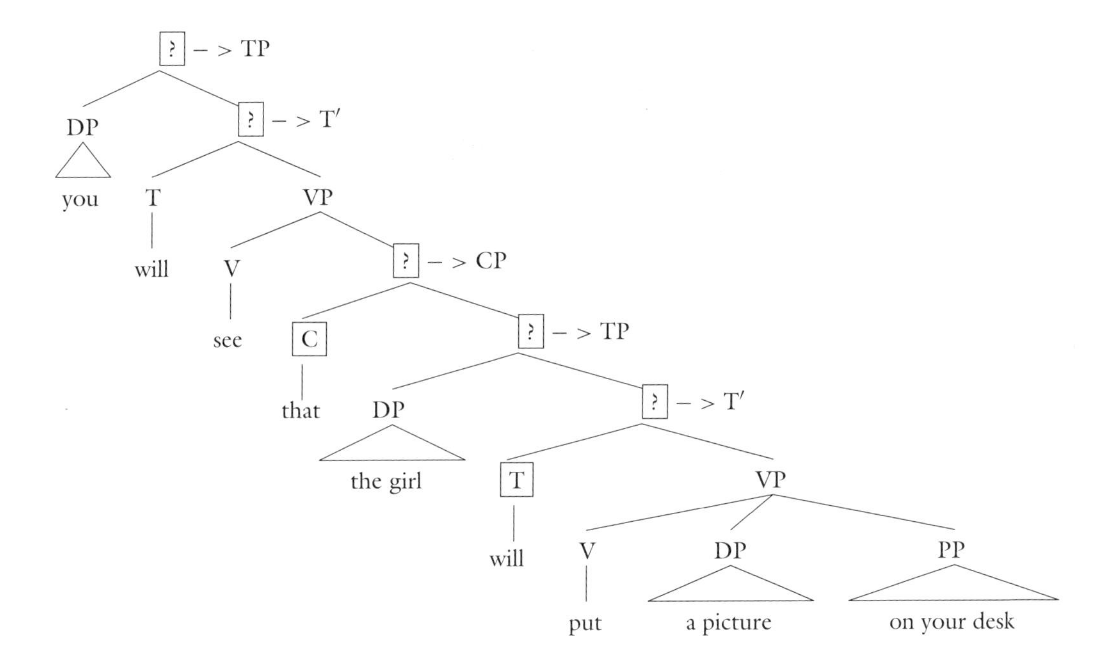

We now turn to justifying why each of the boxed ? should be labeled as indicated in the tree. This in turn will tell us why the very top node of the whole tree should be labeled as indicated here as well.

Notice that the C *that* has a different distribution from what is usually called a "demonstrative" *that*, two examples of which are given below:

(14) I like that student
(15) That is what you should see

The demonstrative occurs in a position where other determiners can occur (*the*, *a*, *this* . . .), but no determiners or other demonstratives can go in the position of *that* in the tree drawn above. This difference in distribution is why we will distinguish demonstrative *that* from C *that*.

The C *that* has a special role which we will understand better once we compare it with the distribution and function of some other complementizers.

It should be easy to verify that the bracketed CP constituent above forms a constituent with the verb *see*, as our tree structure expresses.

> **Practice**
>
> Try VP topicalization, *do so* replacement, VP ellipsis, or coordination with another VP to corroborate this last assertion.

This makes it reasonable to assume, as we have done, that this constituent is a sister of the verb *see* in (9). Various other verbs can occur here too, but the range is restricted. It depends on the type of verb.

(16) You will { see / believe / hope / say / claim / whisper / *kick / *sleep / *run } that the girl will put a picture there

Verbs that occur most naturally in this context are "verbs of saying and believing," which describe a relation between a subject and a proposition of some kind. Informally speaking, a proposition describes a state of affairs that can be true or false. For example, the sentence *John is here* describes a state of affairs that can be true or false. One can say or have an attitude toward these propositions (such as believing it or doubting it). These "attitude" verbs are different from verbs that denote physical actions or states.

We see above that some verbs can combine with *that*-CPs and others cannot. This is a typical property of heads and their sisters, as we have seen in Chapter 2: heads (in this case Vs) can select for their sisters (in this case *that*-CPs). This property is sometimes called subcategorization.

Some verbs allow different elements to occur in the position where *that* is found.

(17) John must know { that / if / whether } she will leave

(18) John may think { that / *if / *whether } she left

(19) John will wonder { *that / if / whether } she left

It is easy to show that the strings following the verbs *know*, *wonder*, and *think* are constituents, which are sisters of V, and form a VP constituent with these verbs. Since this variation in allowable complement is determined by the verb, it reflects a property between the verb head and its sister.

How should these constituents be labeled? How do we determine the identity of a constituent? One way is to use an experiment that unambiguously applies to a known constituent type. We have assumed that VP preposing or VP ellipsis is like this. Substitutability with a personal pronoun is characteristic of DPs (and now with the personal pronoun *it*, of CPs too) while *one*-replacement identifies NPs. Another powerful option is coordination, since successful coordination seems to require categorial identity of the conjuncts.

This last approach immediately allows us to draw the conclusion that the strings *that she left* and *whether she will come back* are of the same category, so both are CPs if the first one is.

(20) John knows that she left
(21) John knows whether she will come back
(22) John knows that she left and whether she will come back
(23) John knows that she left and John knows whether she will come back

So, we are dealing with two phrases of the same type, but we have not yet seen why we call them CPs, and not VPs or TPs, or why we should label *that/if/whether* as C.

There are other important ways of trying to establish the identity of a category or a constituent that can answer this last question. First, note that very roughly, (17) shows that you can know the content of a proposition (*that she left*) or the answer to some kind of question (*whether she left*); (19) shows that while you can wonder about a question, you cannot wonder a proposition; and (18) shows that you can think a proposition, but not a question. That is, it seems that Cs play an important role in specifying whether the constituent is a question (an "indirect question") or an assertion of some kind.

They seem to play the same role, namely typing the entire constituent. This suggests that they are instantiations of the same category, and we call this category C: it always combines with what we have called a sentence, a TP.

The idea that these are the same category also receives some support from the fact that (in English) only one of these elements can occur at a time, even with verbs like *know* or *say* that allow any one of the three to occur:

(24) You should say { that / if / whether / * if whether / * that if / * whether that } she left

This is what we called complementary distribution in Chapter 2. This fits with the idea that there is a single structural position that can be filled with any one of these elements, but not more than once.

In these examples, we begin to see the justification for calling expressions like *that she left* constituents, whose properties are determined by the little words we are calling Cs, which quite surprisingly play a critical role in determining the type and distribution of CPs. In this sense Cs are heads, which determine the category of the phrase in which they occur. We can now also understand why verbs combine with different types of CPs as a selectional property. Verbs are heads that can select for properties of their sisters. Since the type of CP is determined by the type of C, verbs can select for different types of clausal complements.

This will now also tell us why we don't call a CP a DP, or a VP, or some other category. The CP has a pronoun and a verb in it too – so why not? This is because the constructions above are not sensitive to changes in their subjects, that is, changes from the pronoun DP to something else:

(25) a. John knows {that / if / whether} {she / the student / all ten of the people I know} left

b. John wonders {*that / if / whether} {she / the student / all ten of the people I know} left

c. John thinks {that / *if / *whether} {she / the student / all ten of the people I know} left

The distribution of the CPs is not sensitive to changes in the VP either:

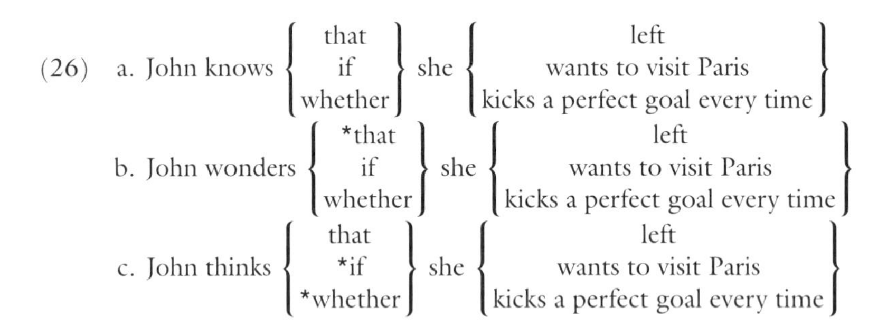

If a CP is a well-formed string, changing something in its VP to yield another well-formed string is (in general) not going to change where this CP is going to occur. The element that determines where the CP can occur in all of these constructions is the C. This is a property that we have already encountered in the chapter on morphology, with the notion **head**. Recall that the head of a constituent had the following properties:

(27) a. The **head** of a constituent tells us the category of the constituent.
b. The **head** of a constituent tells us the distribution of the constituent (the grammatical context in which it can appear).
c. The **head** of a constituent also selects certain constituents to combine with.

The relation that we have identified between C and CP corresponds to this second property.

Naming categories: The C is the **head** of the CP because it determines the internal structure of the CP, and it determines the distribution of the CP. This is similar to the heads of words we saw in morphology. This is why we call the phrase a CP.

In all the examples above, the complementizers combine with what we informally called a "sentence" in the previous chapters, but if we extend our survey of clauses a little further we find that there may be some variation here too. This will lead us to why we should call that constituent a TP, where different types of T determine different types of TPs.

So far we have seen that CPs can occur as the right-hand sister of V:

(28) a. John asked [whether she left]
 b. I doubt [if she kicks perfect goals every time]
 c. They think [that she can do it]

The same CPs can also occur as subjects of sentences, as we see in examples like these:

(29) a. [whether she left] is most unclear
 b. [That the girl put a picture there] proves her guilt

So it looks like both CPs and DPs can be subjects of sentences. (Recall that both the notion of sentence and the notion of subject are used informally until we define them later.)

Now compare the following examples to the structures above:

(30) I prefer <u>for the girl to put a picture there</u>
(31) What I prefer is <u>for the girl to put a picture there</u>
(32) <u>For the girl to put a picture there</u> would surprise you

In (30), it seems that a certain kind of attitude or "preference" is being described as holding between the subject and the proposition, or state of affairs, of the girl putting a picture there. In (31), we see that the string following the verb can be pseudoclefted, and in (32) that it can can occur as the subject of other sentences too, sentences similar to those in (29). What is the internal structure of this string? The coordination test yields the following results:

(33) [For [[the girl to put a picture there] and [Bill to remove it]]] would be surprising

This shows that *for* takes *the girl to put a picture there* as its sister, and forms a constituent that has the distribution of other CPs. This means (30) is very similar to the structure of (9), with *for* a C, as in the following tree for (30), similar to the tree for (9) that is displayed here:

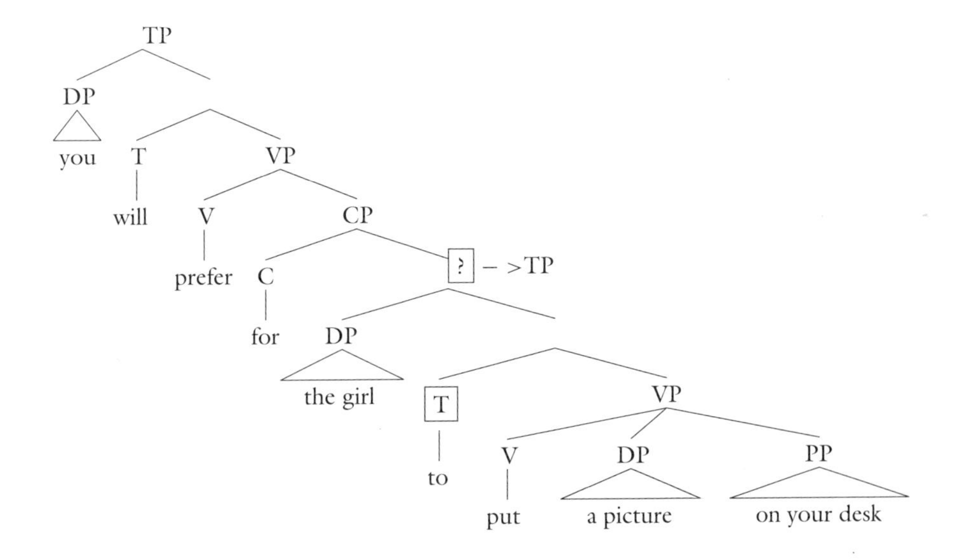

Here the verb *prefer* has a CP with the complementizer *for* as its sister, while in this tree we had the verb *see* with the complementizer *that*. The only surprising idea here is that *to* should be labeled *T*, the way *will* is in the earlier tree.

If we take *for* to be a complementizer, it should be in complementary distribution with other complementizers. It is not so easy to see right away (because the other complementizers seem to occur with a different sentence type – tensed instead of infinitive) but we will see later that this is correct. Furthermore, we would expect that such CPs that have *for* as complementizer should occur in environments in which other CPs do not. We will see this later as well.

We took for granted from the start the existence of a category C, but it should be noted that this is not a category found in traditional grammar. This is, in part, because recognizing the underlying unity of a subset of "subordinating conjunctions" is not all that easy without the kind of formal tools we are using. Our conclusion owes much to Bresnan (1979).

4.2 Tense Phrase

Let us now turn to the fact that we labeled *to* as *T*. We can support this idea, by noticing that when this *to* occurs, neither *will* nor any other tense (future, present, past) can occur. *To* and other tenses are in complementary distribution.

(34) a. I prefer [for [the girl to win]]
 b. * I prefer [for [the girl to will win]]
 c. * I prefer [for [the girl to wins]]
 d. * I prefer [for [the girl to won]]

Furthermore, the verb *to win* is the infinitive, tenseless form of the verb, and so from this perspective, it is not unnatural to think that *to* fills the tense position as a kind of "zero" value. If T is filled with *to*, the clause is *infinitival.*

We can also see that when the C *for* is present, *to* is required as well. Similarly, when *that* is present a finite T is obligatory as well:

(35) a. For the girl *will/to win tomorrow is important
 b. That the girl will*to win tomorrow is important

VP ellipsis provides further support for the view that the position of *to* is outside of the VP, exactly the way *will* is. Like the *will* in *that*-clauses, the *to* cannot be elided:

(36) a. that Ann will go out every night is expected, but I cannot believe that Sophie will ~~go out every night~~
 b. * that Ann will go out every night is expected, but I cannot believe that Sophie ~~will go out every night~~

(37) a. For Ann to go out every night is expected, but I wouldn't like for Sophie to ~~go out every night~~
 b. * For Ann to go out every night is expected, but I wouldn't like for Sophie ~~to go out every night~~

We are led to distinguish two types of clauses: tensed (or finite) clauses, in which there is an indication of the relative time at which what the clause talks about takes place (for example, *John will leave* means John's leaving will take place in the future); and tenseless or infinitival clauses in which there is no overt indication. In a simple clause, the content of the T node indicates how the event we are talking about is placed in time. In infinitival clauses, there is no indication of how to place the event in time. This is why infinitivals are called "tenseless," even though they have a constituent of category T.

Just like there are different kinds of nouns (say mass and count), there are different kinds of Ts. To distinguish the T found in tensed clauses and the T found in tenseless or infinitival clauses, we will tag the first with the feature +tense and the second with the feature −tense.

Homophony: Like the complementizer *that*, the infinitival *to* could be confused with other words that sound the same, i.e. words that are "homophonous," so we need to be cautious. For example, in (38), we see that *to* can occur as a preposition, in a position where other prepositions could occur:

(38) Let's walk {to / on / near} the beach

Notice that none of these other prepositions could replace the T *to* in (30). There are also other words that sound the same but are spelled differently, words that clearly cannot appear in the structural position T:

(39) I run on the beach {too / also}

(40) He works {too / extremely} hard

(41) The {two / three} sunbathers went swimming

The infinitival *to* has a special role in the grammar, a role that it plays in the T position, which is related to the tense of the clause.

Summarizing, we see now that there is a range of complementizers (*that, if, whether, for*), which combine with certain clausal constituents:

(42) a. I hope [that [Mary wins]]
b. They know [if [Mary won]]
c. I wonder [whether [Mary will win]]
d. They prefer [for [Mary to leave]]

We notice that the subject *Mary* can be replaced by other subjects like:

(43) I hope that {the student / some exciting person / no one from Antarctica} wins

And the verb phrase *wins* can be replaced by other verb phrases with finite verbs:

(44) I hope that Mary {wins / kicked a perfect goal / gets a chance to have a vacation in Antarctica}

What the complementizers care about is not what the subject is nor what the VP is, but what the tense is:

(45) They hope
[that [Mary { will win / won / wins / *to win }]]

(46) They prefer
[for [Mary { *will win / *won / *wins / to win }]]

So what should we call the constituents like *Mary will win* or *Mary to win*? We call them TPs, because their distribution is primarily governed by their tense. They can occur as a main sentence or with *that* if and only if they have a non-zero "finite" tense, which we write as +tense (future, present, past), and they can occur with *for* only if they are infinitival, written as −tense.

While *that* and *if* require finite +tense TP, and *for* requires a −tense TP, we can see that *whether* allows either:

(47) a. John wonders whether Mary will win
b. John wonders whether to win

(48) a. Whether she will win is a question Mary never considered
b. Whether to win is a question Mary never considered

We will return to explore more of the properties of these different structures later, but for now, hopefully some of the basic outlines of clause structure are becoming clearer and simpler than they may have seemed at first.

Our constituency tests showed that the TPs within CPs have a structure as in the following:

What selects what? Given that the complementizer *that* only co-occurs with tensed clauses and the complementizer *for* only co-occurs with tenseless clauses, we could have entertained another hypothesis, namely that a verb like *think* selects a +tense T, which in turn selects a complementizer like *that*, while a verb like *hope* selects a −tense T which in turn would select a complementizer like *for*. This would mean the complement of V is a TP not a CP, and that this TP would contain a C as initial element. In other words, there are two hypotheses (where the arrows indicate selection):

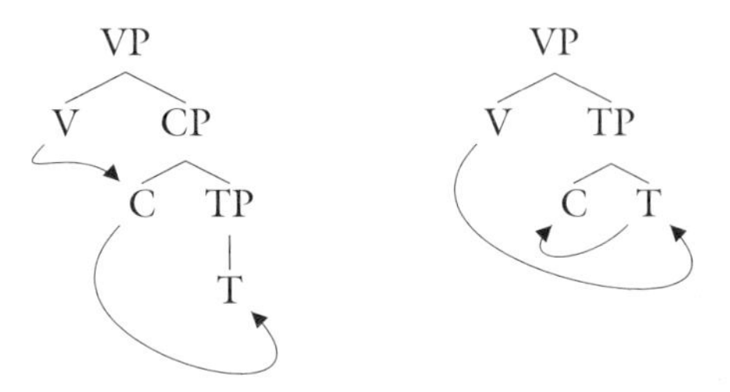

Why did we adopt the leftmost analysis? The rightmost alternative hypothesis would run into problems. First, note that certain verbs do not care about the tense of their complement clause, e.g. *wonder*.

(49) I wonder whether you left early
I wonder whether to leave early

They do, however, very much care about the complementizer they occur with. Here *whether* is allowed, but not *that*. Second, the rightmost alternative would make an incorrect prediction with the verb *think* or similar verbs: they allow tensed clauses as complements but disallow certain complementizers (e.g. *if*) that are allowed to occur with tensed clauses. Again, it seems that the verb does care about the complementizer itself. The hypothesis that the complement of a verb is a CP headed by C seems more justified.

(50) DP T V [$_{CP}$ C [$_{TP}$ DP [T VP]]]

We now have the label TP, because the T determines the distribution of the phrase, but what should we call the constituent [T VP]? This element contains the T that we would like to regard as the head of the TP, and a sister VP, so we call this constituent a T′ (tee-bar) to distinguish it from TP, which is larger, and from T, which is just the head. So we have justified the labels for many of the constituents in the trees shown earlier in this chapter:

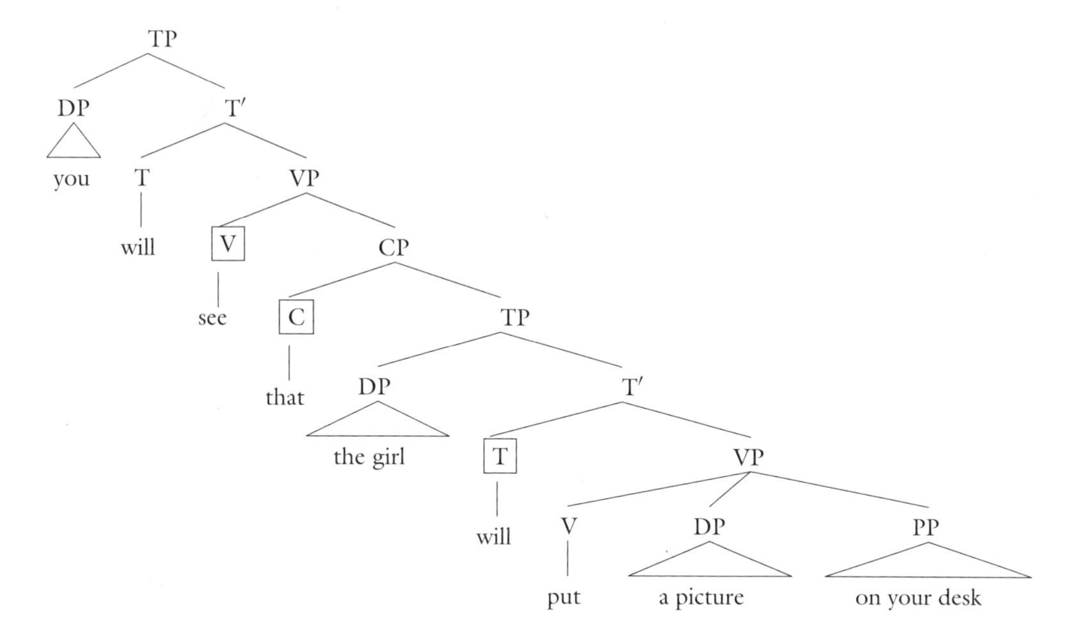

We find the observed variability between clause types is due to the boxed categories (the heads) and their relations to their sisters (their complements). Also as in morphology, heads select for their sisters. Also as in morphology, this selectional property will be coded in the lexical entry of these heads.

V	C	T
see	that	+tense (will, etc)
prefer	for	−tense (to)
ask	if	+tense
ask	whether	T
	that	will +T
etc.		

We have now seen that English has various **complementizers**: *that, if, whether, for*. The complementizers *that* and *if* differ from *for* in that the former can only occur with +tense TPs, and the latter can only occur with −tense TPs. To code this fact, let us mark *that* and *if* as +tense and *for* as −tense. As for *whether*, it is compatible with either +tense or −tense TPs, so we leave it unmarked for the feature tense. The complementizers *if, whether* form CPs that express "indirect questions." To distinguish them from the others, we can mark *if* with the feature +q (for question) and *whether* with +wh, +q (because *whether*, like many English question words such as *who, what, where, when* begins with "wh"). The complementizers *that, for* introduce declarative or non-interrogative CPs, which we mark with the feature -q.

This gives us the following approximate lexical entries for these complementizers:[1]

[1] We will modify the entry for *whether* at the end of Section 10.2 in a way that does not affect any conclusion based on the categorial status of *whether* as C.

that:	C	free	[+tense]	[−q]	selects finite +tense TP complement
if:	C	free	[+tense]	[+q]	selects finite +tense TP complement
for:	C	free	[+tense]	[−q]	selects non-finite −tense TP complement
whether:	C	free		[+q]	selects TP complement

Notice that we have labeled the roots of the trees above as TP. We could have labeled them as CP with a silent C (responsible for the clause type) as well. While the latter may well be correct – the list above is in no way an exhaustive list of English Cs – this is of little consequence for our introduction, and we will continue to label these as TPs.

TPs and CPs are both called *clauses*, and we have seen that the term "sentence" usually refers to a tensed TP. A clause that is not contained in any other, so the topmost one in our trees, is called the *main clause* (or *root* clause, *matrix* clause, or *independent clause*). A verb with present or past inflection is often called a finite verb, and the smallest clause containing such a verb, or a modal like *will, would* ... a finite clause. A clause that is contained in another is said to be an *embedded* or *subordinate* clause.

4.3 Conclusion

4.3.1 Summary

Based on what we have discovered so far, we have some general results about heads and constituents and their internal structure.

Let us first return to consider the role of heads of phrases. Repeating (27) from Section 4.1:

(51) The **head** of a constituent:
a. determines the category of the constituent;
b. determines the distribution of the constituent (where it can occur); and
c. selects certain constituents to combine with.

In CPs, we see now that the head C does not simply combine with sentences, but cares about the tense of the constituent it combines with, and so we call these constituents TPs.

Syntactic heads and labeling:
In sum, both CPs and TPs are constituents with syntactic heads. Syntactic heads have these properties:

i. Heads are word level categories (remember the word level categories are: C, T, N, V, P, D, ...).
ii. If an element is the head of a string, the maximal string whose distribution is "controlled" by this element is a constituent.
iii. There is only one head per constituent.
iv. Every constituent has a unique head.
v. Since constituents are continuous strings, the maximal string under the distributional control of a head must be a continuous string.

None of these properties are necessary. These are empirical claims about how human languages work.

In general, our convention for labeling constituents will be this:

- A head of category X sometimes combines with certain other constituents and controls the distribution of the whole complex.
- The maximal extension of the string that is controlled by the head in this way is called the *maximal projection* or *phrasal projection* of this head, and is labeled XP.

(Sometimes the head X of a phrase is labeled X^0 (read "X-zero"), and sometimes the maximal projection XP is called X^{max} or X^2 or $\overline{\overline{X}}$.)

In examples (9), (29), and the others considered above, we have seen TPs with the following internal structures:

$[_{TP}$ DP $[_{T'}$ T VP$]]$ $\qquad$ $[_{TP}$ CP $[_{T'}$ T VP$]]$

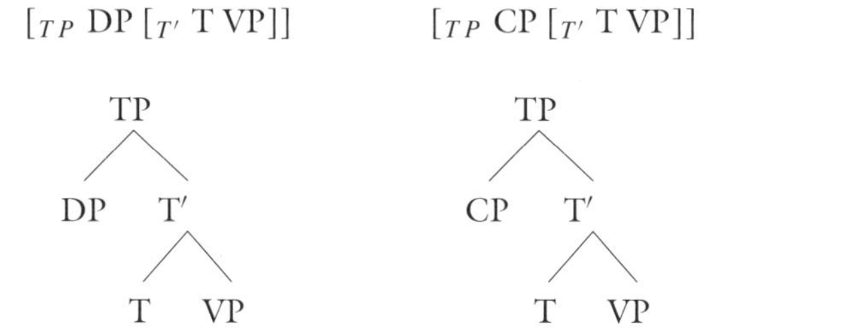

The DP or CP sister of T′ is called the *subject* or *specifier* of T or TP. We use these notions in the structural sense: the subject of the TP is the constituent which is a sister of T′ and a daughter of TP. The VP sister of T is called the *complement* of T.

Generalizing, we will use these structural, configurational terms to refer to constituents like this for all categories X:

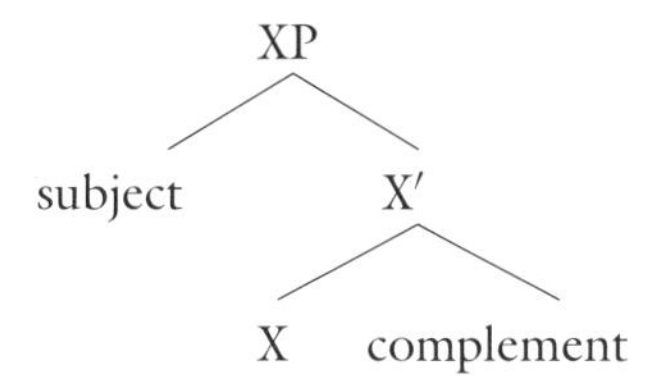

A constituent that is a sister of X is called a "complement" of X or XP. A constituent that is a daughter of XP and sister of X' is called a "specifier" or "subject" of X or XP.

On the notion "subject": In this discussion, the subject of a clause was a DP or CP that occurs in a particular configuration, as left sister to T′. One property that subjects have in English is agreement with the finite verb (with regular verbs of English, this is visible only in the 3rd person singular present tense). We will see a number of other properties of the structural subject position later.

In the linguistic literature, the term *subject* is used in many different ways, and so it is important to pay attention to what is meant here. The notion just defined is a purely structural one, and one that is much less common than the notion of "logical subject" or "agent" of a sentence, roughly, the person or thing that does or causes the action described by the verb.

For example, in our sense of "subject," *Mary* is the subject of (52), but *the paper* is the subject of (53), even though the agent of the action is the same:

(52) Mary cuts the paper easily
(53) The paper was cut by Mary
(54) The paper cuts easily

In (54), *the paper* is again the subject, even though the agent of the action is not mentioned at all. Constructions like (52) are called "active" constructions. Constructions like (53) are called "passive" constructions, and constructions like (54) are called "middle" constructions.

In the clauses we have considered so far, T almost always has an (audible) subject (the single exception we have seen was in CPs such as *whether to win*, to which we will return later). T always has a complement VP (though we have already seen that this VP can be "elided" in VP ellipsis constructions). A +tense T requires a nominative subject, while a −tense T requires an accusative subject when it has one.

(55) a. [That he won the race] could surprise them
b. * [That him won the race] could surprise them
c. [For him to win the race] would surprise them
d. * [For he to win the race] would surprise them

This is the *case* property we mentioned earlier, which is visible on pronouns in English: *he* is in the nominative case (glossed as NOM, *him* is in the accusative case (glossed as ACC).

Just as we did for Cs, we code these properties in the lexical entry for the different Ts we have seen so far, with () indicating optionality of the material in parentheses:

will:	T	free	[+tense (future)]	selects NOM subject	selects VP complement
to:	T	free	[-tense]	(selects ACC subject)	selects VP complement

4.3.2 What to remember

The most important thing to remember is how we reasoned. We established constituency with tests. We discovered that, in CPs and TPs, there is particular element – the head – that plays a distinguished role and after which these constituents are named. Although we have established this on the basis of English, similar relations hold in a great number of languages from different linguistic families, and suggest our conclusions have fairly general validity (e.g. Arabic, Basque, Dutch, French, Japanese, Malagasy, Navaho, and Swahili).

It is important to remember:

- how to recognize heads and their properties;
- how TPs and CPs are put together;
- the general format that is suggested for phrases, as well as the definitions of subject and complement.

4.3.3 Puzzles and preview

We have carefully avoided some questions that we will return to later. For example, what is in the position of the tense (T) in sentences like (a) and (b), below?

(56) a. John saw Mary
b. Harry likes movies

In sentences like these, it looks like tense and the verb are not separated the way they are in the future,

c. John will leave

or in infinitive clauses:

d. [For Mary to leave on time] is important

To understand this, we will first have to take a closer look at VP structure. Other puzzles that naturally come up but have not yet been discussed are:

- Do CPs have subjects?
- Why do some tenseless TPs lack a subject?
- Are there other kinds of CPs or TPs beyond those we have seen?
- Is this notion of head valid for other syntactic phrases?

We will return to these important puzzles, beginning with the last. Remember that languages are immensely complex and exhaustivity is not our objective. What is most important is developing skills for reasoning about linguistic structures.

4.3.4 Further exercises

(1) Tree drawing
Consider the following sentence:

(1) No student should forget that some phrases will be complicated

(i) Draw a complete tree for this sentence, using the labels introduced in this chapter.
(ii) For each T in this sentence, provide at least one example showing that it can be coordinated.
(iii) For each VP in this sentence, provide at least one example showing that it can be coordinated.
(iv) For each VP in this sentence, provide at least one example showing that it can be elided.
(v) Confirm the constituency of the embedded CP using each of the following tests:

(2) a. topicalization
b. a cleft construction
c. a pseudocleft construction

(vi) For each element of category T, show whether this element can be coordinated with *to*, and explain what the results mean. (Remember that coordination is one of the tests for which both success and failure are meaningful.)

(2) Tree drawing
Consider the following sentence:

(1) For you to succeed will be no surprise

(i) Draw a complete tree for this sentence, using the labels introduced in this chapter.
(ii) For each TP in this sentence, provide at least one example to show that it can be coordinated.
(iii) For each T in this sentence, provide at least one example to show that it can be coordinated.
(iv) For each VP in this sentence, provide at least one example to show that it can be coordinated.

(3) Tree drawing
Draw a complete tree for the following sentences: *(would, may,* and *could* are in complementary distribution with *will)*:

(1) a. I would hate for the movie to be boring
b. Bill may ask you if you could put this book on the shelf
c. Anne wondered whether Bill would read the book

(4) Head and selection
Explain, by appealing to the notion *head* and *selection,* by what principle(s) the following examples are excluded. (Do not answer how these sentences should be fixed.)

(1) a. *For he/him would go to the movies could be possible
(cf. For him to go to the movies could be possible)
b. *They said that Bill to talk a lot
(cf. They said that Bill would talk a lot)

(5) Benglish problem
Ienglish (hypothetical language) is exactly like English, except for the lexical entry of *if:*

(1) a. English *if:* C, free [+tense], [+q], select finite +tense TP complement
b. Ienglish *if:* C, [+q], free, selects TP complement

Which of the following examples do you predict to be possible or excluded in English and in Ienglish? (And why?)

(2) a. Bill wants very much for Sue to drink a martini
b. Bill wondered if he should drink a martini
c. Bill wondered if to drink a martini

(6) *If* clauses
Consider the following example:

(1) If you would give him some money, he would go to the store.

Use constituency tests and propose a reasonable structure for this example. Make sure you consider the following examples:

(2) a. He would go to the store if you would give him some money.
b. Bill told Mary that if you would give him some money, he would go to the store
c. If you would give him some money he could go Europe, and she could go to Mexico

(There is a follow up in Chapter 8.)

4.3.5 Further reading

The presentation in this chapter departs from the historical development, and does not mention *Phrase Structure Grammars*. Discussion of these can be found in any introductory textbook.

A note on T and C as heads: it took time to appreciate the general significance of the notion of head, as applying to T and C and to bound morphemes; It came around 1981 for bound affixes (Williams, 1981), 1981 for T (Stowell, 1981), and 1986 for C (Chomsky, 1986). Important work on the structure of the clause leading up to this work, include Bresnan (1979), and Emonds (1976). For introduction of D as the head of DP see Abney (1987), and Postal (1969) for an early proposal.

5
Other Phrases: A First Glance

5.1 Verb Phrases

In the previous chapters, we arbitrarily used the label VP for the constituent that T selects. Given the structural hypotheses and labeling conventions described in the previous chapter, we now know something about why the label VP is chosen: we therefore expect that the fundamental properties of this constituent are determined by a V, which is its head. In particular:

- The distribution of the constituent we call VP is determined by its V.
- The formation of the VP is determined by what the V selects.

In other words, the verb plays the primary role in determining where this VP can occur in a string and what is required internal to the VP.

We have already seen evidence that the V is the crucial element in determining the distribution of the constituent selected by T. For example, in the following sentences, we see many different kinds of constituents in the constituent following T, but the element they all have in common is a V:

(1) a. The girl [[$_T$will] [sleep]]
 b. The girl [[$_T$will] [put a picture on your desk]]

Two notions of VP: Note that we have two notions of VPs. One is well defined and properly named: a constituent whose head is a V. The other is an informal usage: the constituent subject to what we called VP preposing or VP ellipsis. We should make sure that these two notions coincide, or continue to coincide once we gain a finer understanding of the structure of VP (see Chapter 12). As a first approximation, it looks like they do: VP properly named – that is VP the constituent with V as head – is the complement of T. It is also the complement of T that is targeted by VP ellipsis or VP topicalization. We see some initial justification for this by noting that whenever there is a preposed VP, there is always another sentence in which this preposed VP is a complement of T, as the following pairs illustrate.

(2) a. [Sleep], the girl will
 b. The girl [[$_T$will] [sleep]]
 c. [put a picture on your desk] the girl [$_T$will]
 d. The girl [[$_T$will] [put a picture on your desk]]

The systematic relation found between the members of such pairs is a very important one, called Movement. This will be discussed in Chapter 8.

An Introduction to Syntactic Analysis and Theory, First Edition.
Dominique Sportiche, Hilda Koopman, and Edward Stabler.

c. I [[$_T$should] [know whether they [[$_T$will] [put a picture on your desk]]]]
d. I prefer for them [[$_T$to] [put a picture on your desk]]
e. I wonder whether [[$_T$to] [put a picture on your desk]]

Although a verb may sometimes come alone as in (1a), often it does not.

Practice

You should be able to show that this V is also a VP.

The other material in the VP is also determined primarily by the verb: the verb is the head of the VP and determines its internal structure.

A quick survey of various verbs immediately reveals that verbs vary quite a lot. There are many different types of verbs, and verbs differ from each other in many different ways.

(3) elapse, *elapse a book, *elapse to Bill, *elapse that Mary slept
*examine, examine a book, *examine a book to Bill
*send, send a book (to Bill), send Bill a book, *send that Mary slept
*put, *put a book, *put on the table, put a book on the table

We will analyze some of this variety over the course of this book, always with an eye to discovering the underlying organization.

Here we start exploring the internal structure of some of these VPs more carefully. We start with the surprising conclusion that we reached earlier (see Section 3.5, p. 59), that the sentence

(4) this girl will put a picture on your desk before tomorrow

has two VPs in it. Let's review the arguments for this.

The evidence that (4) has two VPs comes from constituency tests:

Two ways of doing VP ellipsis:

a. that girl will put a picture on your desk before tomorrow, but this girl will ~~put a picture on your desk before tomorrow~~ too
b. that girl will put a picture on your desk before tomorrow, but this girl will ~~put a picture on your desk~~ before tomorrow too
c. * that girl will put a picture on your desk before tomorrow, but this girl will ~~put a picture~~ on your desk before tomorrow too
d. * that girl will put a picture on your desk before tomorrow, but this girl will ~~put~~ a picture on your desk before tomorrow too

Two corresponding *do so* substitutions:

a. that girl will put a picture on your desk before tomorrow, but this girl will do so too
b. that girl will put a picture on your desk before tomorrow, but this girl will do so before tomorrow too

Coordination of these two constituents:

a. this girl will put a picture on your desk and leave before tomorrow
b. this girl will put a picture on your desk before tomorrow and leave

There are some other constituency tests that can apply too. Topicalization of a VP, which we've also called *VP preposing*, gives similar results:

(5) a. Think about linguistics all night, she does ~~think about linguistics all night~~
b. Climb to the top, they do ~~climb to the top~~

This construction sounds rather stilted to some speakers, but for others it is fairly natural. (Yoda, of *Star Wars* fame, uses this construction a lot, saying things like: "Mind what you have learned. Save you, it can.") With this test, we get further confirmation for our two VP hypothesis, since we can prepose in two ways:

Two ways to apply VP preposing:

a. Put a picture on your desk before tomorrow, she will ~~put a picture on your desk before tomorrow~~
b. Put a picture on your desk, she will, ~~put a picture on your desk~~ before tomorrow
c. * Put a picture, she will, ~~put a picture~~ on your desk before tomorrow
d. * Put, she will, ~~put~~ a picture on your desk before tomorrow

These tests provide converging evidence for a structure like this:

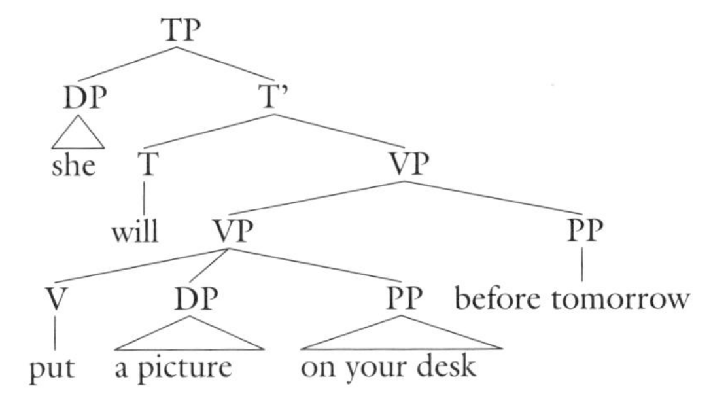

In this tree, the DP [a picture] and the PP [on your desk] are complements of V in the sense defined in Chapter 4: both are required by the verb *put* as complements, hence they are sisters of V. When a V has a single DP complement, it is called a "direct object" because the relation between this DP and the V is not mediated by any grammatical particle or head.

The status of the PP [before tomorrow] in the tree above is more surprising; it is not an immediate sister of V because it is in a different VP: it is a sister of the VP headed by V. This kind of element is called an *adjunct* or *modifier* of the V (or VP), whether it is on the right or the left, and it forms structures of the following kind (with X=V).

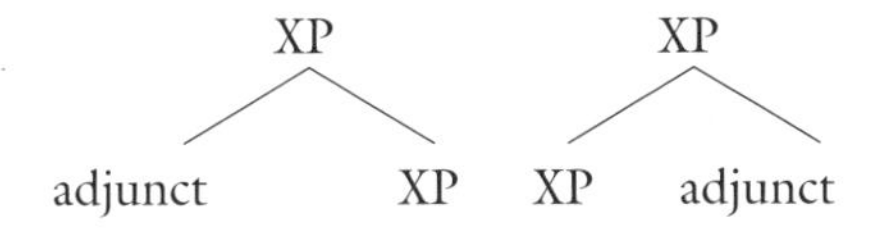

Terminology: We can now clarify some terminological usages. We now have a difference between **complements** and **adjuncts**. These are syntactic differences that are structurally coded. A complement is a sister to the head that selects it. An adjunct is a sister to a phrase. These syntactic differences correspond to different meaning relations. As we will see below, a complement is specifically selected by a particular head while an adjunct entertains a looser relation with its phrase. To emphasize the meaning difference – the semantic difference – we distinguish arguments and modifiers. An adjunct is a **modifier**: it semantically modifies its phrase. A complement is an **argument** of the head that selects it. It fills a required slot in the lexical entry of the head. This is why, in Chapter 2, we called (some) prefixes modifiers.

Constituency arguments like the ones used on the previous example show that the bracketed phrases below are adjuncts too (we add their traditional names which refer to the meanings):

(6) a. John can go to the market [on his bike] (manner adjunct)
b. My niece could write me letters [before her third birthday] (temporal adjunct)
c. My nephew could write letters to his parents [with a fountain pen] (instrumental)

For all these sentences, the VP has the following structure:

$$[_{VP} [_{VP} \text{V} \ldots] \text{PP}]$$

where the indicated PP is both inside a VP and outside a VP. And the same constituency arguments show that various kinds of constituents can be VP adjuncts, not just PPs:

(7) a. John can go to the market [quickly] (manner)
b. Mary should buy some flowers [for her mother to arrange] (purposive)
c. My niece could write me letters [more faithfully] (manner)
d. My nephew could write letters to his parents [every week] (temporal)

In English, complements always follow their heads, but adjuncts may precede or follow their host (subject to some restrictions that we will not explore):

(8) a. John can [quickly [go to the market]]
b. My niece could [more faithfully [write me letters]]
c. ?My nephew should [every week [write letters to his parents]]

In (8a), for example, the AdvP [quickly] is a VP adjunct that precedes the VP.

General differences between complements and adjuncts

There are some general differences between complements and adjuncts that can help determine whether a constituent is one or the other. In the end though, the only thing that matters is how the different constituents behave with respect to the tests.

We will further discuss the three bullet points below.

- Complements are selected in a way that adjuncts are not: the existence of entities that are referred to by complements is implicit in the specific meaning of the verb. This is not the case for adjuncts. This does not mean that there are no selectional relations between the head of a VP and an adjunct adjoined to VP. We will discuss some examples later in this chapter.
- Adjuncts are (almost) always only optionally present, while complements are most of the time (but not always) obligatorily present (we discuss complement omission in a framed box in Section 5.1.1).
- Complements cannot be iterated, while some adjuncts can be (with various results).

V complement adjunct order:
Since complements are required by V, and adjuncts combine with the VP, complements should be closer to the head, adjuncts further out. We expect to find only the order [[V Compl] Adjunct] when both occur on the same side of the V. (Try to see if this holds for the other categories we will discuss in this chapter.)

(9) My aunt will put the flowers there quickly/?* My uncle will put the flowers quickly there
(10) My aunt will criticize the country harshly/* My aunt will criticize harshly the country/My aunt will criticize harshly any country that spies on its citizens

Often the direct interpretation of this test poses problems because of various reordering processes which need to be taken into account.

(11) a. * John can go [to the market] [to India]
b. * Mary should buy [some flowers] [some bread]
c. * My niece could write me you letters
d. * My nephew could write [letters] [the postcards] [to his parents] [to his brother]
(12) a. Mary should buy some flowers [at 5 o'clock] [on Sunday]
b. My niece could write me letters [next year] [before Thanksgiving]
c. John can go to the market [on his bike] [on a truck]
d. My brother slept [next to the car] [on the floor]

Meaning differences between complements and adjuncts
We have seen how constituency tests allow us to identify adjuncts, but, at least in most cases, the constituents picked out by these tests have a distinctive property, which is expressed in the following hypothesis:

(H) Complements denote entities that are required and **specific** to the state or the action or the event that the verb refers to, while adjuncts are not **specifically** required in this way.

Ambiguity and compositionality:
Note that the last example is ambiguous. Under one interpretation, *the car is on the floor*, there is no iteration: the second adjunct is inside the first one. But there is another meaning (*the car is not on the floor (it is on a car lift)*): for these there is iteration. The relation between structure and meaning is systematic: this is an example of the important principle of **compositionality** that we mentioned in Chapter 2.

The notion of being "specific to" the meaning of the verb is sometimes quite clear.

Take the verb *visit* for example. For a visit to take place, there must be a visitor and someone or someplace visited: two entities are required. One of these is the subject, and the other is the complement:

(13) Pelé visited his uncle

A visit may also occur at some particular time and place. But every event (including visits) takes place at some time or in some place, so if you mention the time or place at which an event takes place, it is with an adjunct: *in Brazil* (a locative adjunct), or *every morning* (a temporal adjunct).

Consider the verb *put*: for putting to take place, there must be someone who does the putting, some object that is moved, and a location that the object is moved to. Note that the location in this case is specifically required by the meaning of the verb *put*. So in

(14) Mary put the ice cream in the fridge

the phrases *the ice cream* and *in the fridge* are both complements of *put*.

The reader is invited to check intuitions about the verbs in the following sentences, for example, against the results of constituency tests:

(15) She sold the car to Sam for five dollars
(16) She ran the car on propane from Reno to Vegas
(17) She built the house with her own hands from bricks and mortar
(18) The process changed the substance from solid to liquid to gas to energy
(19) We associated their subsidiaries with our corporate office
(20) I bicycled around France

There is another way in which adjuncts can often reliably be identified. Consider again an example like:

(21) Mary drank [some beer] [in the barn] [from six to nine]

Are the three bracketed constituents arguments or adjuncts? The previous tests would show that the first one is a complement of the verb (it is part of the smallest VP containing the verb) but the other two are adjuncts. If someone drank, we can say that a drinking event took place. Now notice what we can and cannot say about this event using the pronoun *it* to refer to the event itself:

(22) It was in the barn *or* it took place in the barn
(23) It was from six to nine *or* it took place from six to nine
(24) *It was some beer *or* it took place some beer

It is possible to say of this event that **it was X** or **it took place X** if X in an adjunct but not otherwise. This provides a different way to help decide whether a constituent is a complement or an adjunct. Note that we cannot say for (21) either:

(25) *It was Mary

So [Mary] is not an adjunct (in fact it is not a complement either, but rather a subject, of TP).

Of course, eventually, we would like to know why this "event" test works. One observation we can make here is that this test does not work well with stative verbs, like *fear* or *love*, which denote ongoing psychological states. (This could be related to the fact that states do not happen or take place.)

5.1.1 V complements

This understanding of the distinction between complements and adjuncts does not change the fact that different kinds of verbs select different complements. We have already seen, for example:

Some verbs select wh-CP, among other things

(26) a. They wonder [whether Mary will run]
b. They wonder about this
c. They wonder

Some verbs select *that*-CP, among other things

(27) a. I know [that she runs]
b. I know this
c. I know
d. I said [that she runs]
e. I said that
f. *? I said

Some verbs select *for*-CP, or DP

(28) a. I prefer [for Mary to run]
b. I prefer [this]
c. * I prefer
d. I said [for Mary to run]
e. I said [this]

> **Practice**
>
> Show that the embedded CPs in these examples are complements, not adjuncts.

In the first chapters, we gave a lot of attention to sentences with the verb *put*, which exemplifies the following class of verbs:

A few verbs select a DP and a locative-PP, and require them

(29) a. I put the book on the shelf
b. * I put the book
c. * I put

There are other verbs that allow the same two complements, DP and locative-PP, but none of these others require them: *arrange, immerse, install, lodge, mount, place, position, situate, stash, stow*.

Quite a few verbs do not need to have any DP complement at all; these are traditionally called "intransitive" verbs. Here are some examples: *arrive, appear, go, matter, sleep, sneeze....* Some intransitive verbs cannot have any complement at all, for example the verb *elapse*..

Why are some selected arguments optional? Why do some verbs, like *surround*, select and require a complement? One possibility is that this is simply listed in the lexicon, a totally arbitrary, accidental convention that varies from one language to another. It turns out that there is some variation across languages, but that the variation even in a given language is not what one would expect if the choice were totally arbitrary. One instance of this kind of phenomenon is sometimes called the "implicit object alternation." It seems that sometimes when a verb appears without a complement, we already know a lot about what kind of thing the complement would have to be:

(30) John ate (food or something similar) – would be weird in a context where "John ate his shoes")
(31) John knows (a proposition)
(32) John asked (a question)

These seem to contrast with verbs where the object cannot be dropped:

(33) * John needed
(34) * John criticized

And there seem to be intermediate cases that are okay if the discourse context provides some indication of what the object is:

(35) John saw (complement implicit in context)
(36) John told (complement implicit in context)

For cases like (30–32), some linguists have proposed a process in the lexicon that allows for complement-less occurrences of verbs when their complements are predictable, a lexical "saturation of an argument position" (Jackendoff, 1990; Rizzi, 1986). It is rather hard to pin this kind of proposal down enough to make it empirically testable, but there have been attempts using statistical studies of large collections of different kinds of texts (Resnik, 1993).

There are also transitive verbs: verbs that take a direct object (a DP complement), possibly together with other elements. These select DP (and some require it), for example *see, like, surround, give*.

There are many other patterns of behavior in the verbal system of English. Exploring and understanding them goes way beyond what we can do here – see for example, Levin (1993) which characterizes hundreds of different classes.

5.1.2 V–adjunct compatibility

We have seen that verbs are sensitive about their complements. For example, some verbs take direct objects while others cannot. We have already encountered this property, which we call selection. We will return to a systematic exploration of the properties of selection in syntax in Chapter 8.

It might seem at first that a similar sensitivity is not found between adjuncts and the content of the VP they adjoin to. In the example below, we see that the adjunct phrase *on Sunday*, which seems to say something about the time of an event, is acceptable with a wide variety of verb types:

(37) It mattered on Sunday
(38) I saw John on Sunday
(39) I put the book on the desk on Sunday

But these are a bit misleading. It is easy to find cases where only certain verbs or verb phrases allow certain kinds of adjuncts, i.e. where the possible occurrence of an adjunct is sensitive to the verb that heads the VP to which it adjoins.

(40) a. I saw John with a telescope
b. ?* It mattered with a telescope
(41) a. John hits nails with a hammer
b. ?*John fears storms with a hammer

This illustrates the fact that the presence of a PP interpreted as an instrument (here *with a telescope*, or *with a hammer*) requires that the verb denote an action with an agent.

Here is another illustration, this time with temporal modifiers like *for an hour*, and *within an hour*, which provide important insights into what is sometimes called the "aspectual structure" of verbs or verb phrases. The following examples provide a first indication of some basic distinctions:

Telic verbs or verb phrases refer to events that have a culmination point, or an end point:

(42) a. Mary will complete her exam within an hour
b. *Mary will complete her exam for an hour

(43) a. The alpinist will reach the top of the mountain within an hour
b. *The alpinist will reach the top of the mountain for an hour

The event of completing the exam has a natural end point: when the exam is done; that of reaching the top too: exactly at the instant that the top is reached.

Atelic verbs or verb phrases refer to events without a natural end point:

(44) Henri will paint the floor for an hour

(45) I will read linguistics for an hour

We see that some kind of selection is at play here too.

One conclusion to remember, and to which we will return, is that a head selects its complements and its subject. In addition there are selectional relations involving adjuncts too.

5.2 Determiner Phrases

We will not discuss other categories in as much detail, but the basic reasoning is essentially the same as in the previous cases. Consider these examples:

(46) The book

(47) Bill's book

(48) The description of Bill

(49) Mary's description of Bill

(50) The destruction of the city by the barbarians

(51) The barbarian's destruction of the city

(52) Mary's knowledge that the barbarians will destroy the city

Notice that all of these can appear as the subject of a sentence, where they can be replaced by pronouns, coordinated with known DPs, and so on. We have already classified *the* as a determiner (D) and *book* as a noun (N). But notice that in the position of *book* in (46), we can have phrases like:

(53) a. Beautiful book
b. Book about dragons
c. Book that I told you about yesterday

We will accordingly assume (and it should be easy to corroborate this conclusion by using constituency tests) that these are all phrases, noun phrases (NP), and so we conclude that the determiner *the* selects noun phrase complements. The structure of (46) is therefore something like this:

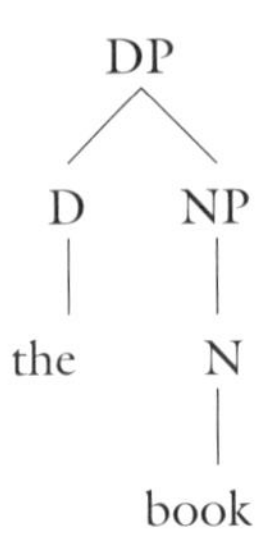

(Actually, this is a simplification that we will modify later, but it is good enough for the moment. As before, this structure is not wrong, it is simply underspecified.)

Examples (47–52) require more careful consideration. A phrase like *Bill's* in (47) is often called a genitive (the so-called Saxon genitive), or a DP with genitive case. English DPs that contain genitives, like (47–52), have some interesting properties. First note that the genitives are in complementary distribution with determiners (as we saw in Chapter 2):

(54) a. The book
b. Bill's book
c. * Bill's the book
d. * The Bill's book

The same would be observed with other determiners such as *this, that, each,* etc. This would initially suggest that *Bill's* is also a D, but the examples above already show that the genitives can be complex phrases, full DPs.

So how can it be that genitive phrases like *Bill's* are in complementary distribution with simple determiners? An easy idea is to conclude that *Bill's* contains a determiner that is in complementary distribution with other determiners. The obvious candidate is *'s*. If it is a D, we must add that it requires a DP on its left. Again, a natural assumption (which can be justified) is that it takes a subject, a DP specifier:

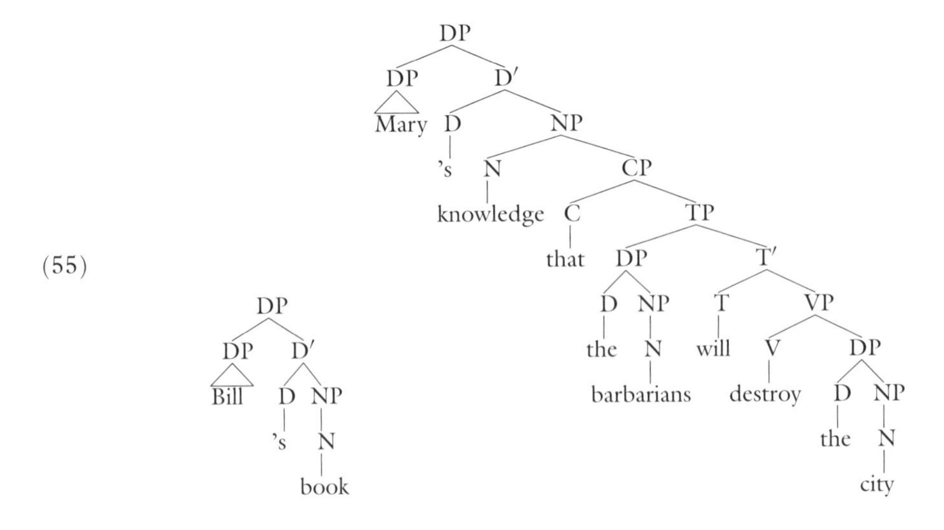

This accounts for the complementary distribution with determiners like *the, a, this, that, these*, because the genitive marker *'s* is a determiner by itself. There is only one D slot per DP (at least in English), and so if it is filled by *'s*, it cannot also be filled with *the*.

Note that this structure expresses the fact that *'s* is pronounced after a DP. This DP should behave as a constituent. And, indeed, it does. It can be coordinated – *[[Bill] and [Mary]] 's father*, and it can be a complex DP – *[the king of England]* 's hat. However, it cannot occur in a cleft construction.

(56) a. *It is Bill's that I know father.
b. *It is Bill that I know 's father

What can we conclude from this failure? (56a) is expected to fail, given the structure. *Bill's* is *not* a syntactic constituent, and only constituents can occur in the cleft position. Though drawing any conclusions from the failure of (56b) is difficult, it cannot be because *Bill* is not a constituent under the proposed structure, as we know it is from other tests. It might be because *'s* needs support within the DP (it is not a free morpheme, but a bound one of a different nature than past tense *-ed*, often called a phrasal affix), or it might be due to some entirely different reason(s) (see Chapter 10). Whatever the explanation for (56b), the structure in (55) leads to the expectation that no English speakers should accept (56a). It is mute on the issue whether some speakers might accept (56b) or not (some speakers reportedly do).

The situation is further complicated in English by the existence of genitive pronouns: *my, your, his, her, its*, etc. Recall that we have already seen nominative and accusative pronouns: they distribute like DPs, but are pronounced one way or another depending on where they occur. This variable pronunciation is a contextual property called Case (with a capital letter), so named because many languages express it by case markers. Our proposal for genitive pronouns will be similar: the particular shape of these elements is dependent on context.

[Bill] + 's	→	Bill's
[the girl] + 's	→	the girl's
[who] + 's	→	whose
[him] + 's	→	his
[her] + 's	→	her
[it] + 's	→	its
[we] + 's	→	our
[they] + 's	→	their
[my] + 's	→	my

The way to understand what happens here is roughly as follows: the D *'s* selects a subject DP which must be in the genitive case. In general, when this subject is a pronoun, this D remains silent (and the pronoun is genitive, like *my*). But under certain circumstances (when the NP complement of D is absent or elided), this D appears. Notice that the standard spelling convention does not write the apostrophe in some of these cases. For this reason we box the 's in the examples below:

(57) a. I like this book of Bill's, of your[s], of her[s], of his, of our[s], of their[s].

Note also that the first person genitive pronoun is irregular (i.e. here *my* combines with */-n/*, an ending found in genitive forms in other Germanic languages, cf. Dutch *mijn* "my") instead of *'s*:

[my] + 's → mine (not *my's)

This elaborates the pronominal paradigm of English as follows:[1]

	1s	2	3s masc	3s fem	3s neut	2p	3p
nominative (subject of T)	I	you	he	she	it	we	they
genitive (subject of D)	my	your	his	her	it	our	their
accusative everything else (in English)	me	you	him	her	it	us	them

We thus see that Ds can have complements (NPs) and they can have subjects too (genitives). We also see that they select their complement (it must be an NP) and select their subject if they have one (e.g. the *'s* D selects a (genitive) subject).

Are there adjuncts to DP? Yes. It is natural to treat elements like *only* or *even* or *all* as DP adjuncts:[2]

(58) a. [The student] left
b. [Only the student] left
c. [Even the student] left
d. [All the students] left

(59) a. I saw [the student]
b. I saw [only the student]
c. I saw [even the student]
d. I saw [all the students]

Another kind of DP adjunct is the "appositive relative clause" – a type of CP – as in:

(60) a. [John, who I saw yesterday,] will visit us
b. I wrote to [John, who I saw yesterday]

5.3 Noun Phrases

Here are some examples of NPs:

(61) a. Student
b. Brilliant student
c. Student with long hair
d. Student of physics
e. Student of physics with long hair
f. Description
g. Description of Bill
h. Gift of candy to the children
i. Claim that John stole her purse

[1] A further relevant distinction between strong and weak pronouns (*him: [hIm]*, vs *[əm]*) is not included.
[2] In the case of "even" and "only," many intricate questions arise that we cannot address here. See e.g. Kayne (2000).

The "replacement by *one*" constituency test demonstrates that (61b) and (61c) contain two NPs, as the reader can conclude from the results of the test below:

(62) a. I saw the brilliant [student]
b. I saw the brilliant one

(63) a. I saw the brilliant student with long hair
b. I saw the brilliant [one] with long hair
c. I saw the one with long hair (one=[brilliant [student]])

In the example below, *physics* is not an NP; it is an N part of a compound.

(64) a. I saw the physics student
b. * I saw the physics one

Notice what we get if we try to apply *one* replacement to a proper part of (61d):

(65) a. I saw the student of physics
b. ?* I saw the one of physics

(66) a. I saw the student of physics with long hair
b. I saw the one with long hair
c. ?* I saw the one of physics

Failure by itself is uninformative, but here we can explain it if we have an adjunct–complement distinction in NPs: [of physics] is a complement, while [with long hair] is an adjunct. This can be corroborated by the semantic relation between *student* and *physics*, which is absent between student and an adjunct (such as *with long hair*, *from Mexico*): it is part of the meaning of *student* that he/she studies something. No such specific relation holds with the adjuncts. There are only two NPs in [student of [physics]], but there are four NPs in [[student] with [long [hair]]]. This is reflected in the number of NP nodes in the trees below:

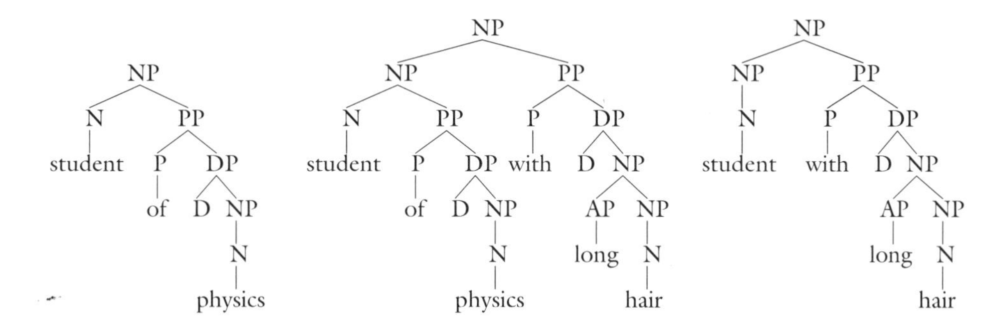

Apart from the number of NPs here, these trees have some other features that we have not yet justified. First, we have indicated that the complements of the prepositions in these structures are DPs: it is easy to see that they satisfy our constituency tests for DPs (replacement by pronouns, etc.). And since there is no overt D in these DPs, **we have taken the step of putting in an silent D** – a step analogous to assuming silent affixes, and again something we should justify.

These issues will be discussed again later, but for the moment, the main point is that there are N complements and NP adjuncts, just as there are V complements and VP adjuncts. Since complements combine with the N, and adjuncts combine with the NP, complements should be closer to the head, and adjuncts should follow them. We expect to find only the order [[N Compl] Adjunct] when both occur on the same side of the N. This expectation is borne out in English:

(67) A student of physics with long hair
(68) *A student with long hair of physics

In fact, the analogy between phrases formed by the noun *student* and the verb *to study* is quite striking. Notice also the analogy between the complements of *gift* in (61h) and the complements of the verb *give*. And the similar analogy between the complements of the noun *claim* in (61i) and the complements of the verb *claim*. When there are verb/noun pairs like these, the verb and the noun have very similar complements (but not identical: nouns do not take bare DPs as complements). Clearly, these are not arbitrary coincidences; there is something regular happening here.[3]

The way we determine what is a complement and what is an adjunct in NPs is very much like the way we do this for VPs. Complements to N correspond to entities specifically required by the meaning of the noun. If the noun is transparently related to a verb, start by checking what the complements of the verb are. If the verb takes a complement, it is a good indication for our purposes here that the related noun does so too.

In sum, D always requires a complement with an N, so we say N is the head of NP. As for internal structure, we notice that *of physics* is a natural complement for *student*, but not natural for the noun *solid* or *table*, and that adjuncts like *with long hair* are possible with *student* but awkward with the noun *description*. So the adjuncts and complements depend on the choice of N; again we conclude that N is the head of NP.

ok: Gift of candy to children
* Student of candy to children

Complements of N can be PPs or CPs. Adjuncts in NP can be found to the left (e.g. adjectives) or the right (e.g. PPs). Other adjuncts include complex APs like [$_{NP}$[$_{NP}$man] [$_{AP}$ fond of cookies]], and restrictive relative clauses which are CPs, as in [$_{NP}$[$_{NP}$man] [$_{CP}$ who is fond of cookies]].

A further way to identify some adjuncts: There is another way in which adjuncts can often be reliably identified, similar to what we saw in the case of verbs. Consider an example like:

(69) The [big] student [of physics] [with long hair] [in the library]

Are these four bracketed constituents arguments or adjuncts? Overall, this DP is designating a student, a particular kind of entity. Now notice what we can and cannot say about this entity:

(70) He is big
(71) * He is with long hair
(72) *He is of physics
(73) He is in the library

It is possible to say of this entity that *it/he is X* if X is an adjunct and not otherwise. This provides a different way to help decide whether a constituent is a complement or an adjunct. It is worth nothing that *with long hair* is an adjunct, though (71) is bad: this means that the test picks out a sufficient but not a necessary property of adjuncts. As usual, isolated negative results are hard to interpret.

[3]How to understand the appearance of *of* was an important area of research topic in the late 1970s and early 1980s. See Jackendoff (1977), Chomsky (1981), and Chomsky (1986). Kayne (1994) opened up a completely new line of research on this topic. We will not directly address this important work here, but see Section 6.8.3, p.145 for some relevant remarks.

5.4 Adjective Phrases

Here are some examples of APs:

(74) a. Sad
b. Very sad
c. Proud of Bill
d. Extremely fond of cookies
e. Interesting to whales
f. Proud that Mary succeeded

All of these can occur, for example, in the frame

He is/remains ______ .

We will assume that the PPs in (74c–74e) and the CP in (74f) are complements. This is reasonable given the selection effects we observe: *sad* disallows *of*-PPs; *proud* and *fond* take PPs with *of* but not with *to*, while *interesting* does the reverse; *proud* allows a CP while *fond* does not. Similarly, we will take expressions of degree like *very*, *extremely* to be adjuncts (on the left in English).

5.5 Prepositional Phrases

We will not discuss PPs in any detail. What we say below will suffice for our purposes. This should not be taken to mean that PPs are simple. As with everything in language, they are incredibly intricate (for a glimpse of this complexity, see the (advanced) Koopman (2000), pp. 204–60).

Examples of PPs:

(75) a. Up
b. Up [the rope]
c. In [the south]
d. From [the country]
e. From [under the rug]
f. Right [against the grain]
g. Exactly [under the tree]
h. Before [John came]
i. With [John sick]

Some elements of this category take no complement at all, as the *up* of *look up*. Others may take as complements DPs, PPs, or perhaps even TPs, as in the last example. (This is probably actually a CP with a silent *that*, but this is harder to show; we will return to this question later.)

We will take adverbs like *right, exactly* to be (left) adjuncts.

5.6 Ways to Talk About Tree Geometry

Now that we have concluded that strings are structured in constituents in all sorts of ways, it is useful to talk about the geometrical relations between elements in our trees, for example, what contains what. To this end, it is important to understand these basic terms:

Nodes: The points (e.g., TP, VP, D′, N, etc., and the points labeled with words) are called nodes.

Branches: The lines connecting points in a tree are called branches (or less frequently arcs).

Dominate: A node A dominates another node B, if A is connected to B by a downward path along the branches. If you can trace from A to B by following branches and never going up the tree, then A dominates B. Dominate is synonymous with contain.

Immediately Dominates: A immediately dominates B if and only if A dominates B and there is no other node that dominates B and does not dominate A.

Mother: A node A is the mother of a node B if and only if A immediately dominates B.

Sister: Nodes are sisters just in case they have the same mother.

Root: The topmost node in a tree is the root. More formally, the root is the one node in a tree that is not dominated by any other node.

Precede: A node A precedes another node B if and only if A does not dominate B and A occurs to the left of B in the tree structure.

5.7 Conclusion

5.7.1 Summary: heads and lexical entries

We saw in Chapter 2 that language users must represent some basic facts about the morphemes of their languages, the "atoms" of morphology. For example,

read	free	V	
prefer	free	V	
-able	bound	A	c-selects V
-er	bound	N	c-selects V
-s	bound	Number	c-selects N
re-	bound	Adv?	modifies V

Then we saw that the result of affixation does not, in general, need to be listed in the lexicon, because it is determined by the right-hand head rule (RHHR) which predicts the category of the result. We also noticed that the relation between stems and suffixes is different from the relation between stems and prefixes: in this table we have called the latter "c-selects" and the former "modifies" to code the fact that they correspond to what we call adjuncts in syntax.

In the last couple of chapters, we saw that these lexical entries for morphemes become elaborated with their syntactic properties. This comes in part from the observations made first in Chapter 3, that phrases contain heads too. In Chapter 4 we saw that particular syntactic constituents, clauses, can be regarded as phrases with heads. For example, the CP *that Mary will read* has the head *that*, and the TP *Mary will read* has the head *will*. These constituents are asymmetric: for example T takes a VP complement and forms a T′ with it. This T′ then combines with a DP subject. And this is the only way this happens (e.g. T doesn't combine with DP to form a T′). This must be coded somewhere, and we code this in the lexical entry of elements of the T category.

In this chapter, we have extended this perspective through a range of categories: VP, DP, NP, AP, PP. We saw, for example, that there are different kinds of verbs. To describe what was concluded, we will have to elaborate the lexical entries of these verbs (like the other categories) with specifications of syntactic properties, as we did for C and T in Chapter 4. For Cs and Ts, we get lexical entries like these:

that	free	C	c-selects TP[+tense]
if	free	C+q	c-selects TP[+tense]

for	free	C	c-selects TP[-tense]
whether	free	C+q[4]	c-selects TP[±tense]

For determiners, we were led to postulate the following lexical entries. These will be gradually expanded in the course of the next couple of chapters.

the	free	D	c-selects NP	example: "the book"
this	free	D	c-selects NP	example: "this book"
that	free	D	c-selects NP	example: "that book"

We also saw that the genitive *'s* needs a DP subject, a specifier, and we have not yet considered how to represent this requirement.

Selection:
To distinguish this kind of selection from c-selection, which we reserve for complements, let us call this simply *selection* or *selection for subject*. For now, this is just terminology, though there are good reasons for distinguishing this, and these will become apparent later. C-selection corresponds to what is sometimes called subcategorization.

's	bound	D	selects subject DP	c-selects NP	example: "Bill's book"

Also we saw that D can have adjuncts: e.g. elements such as *all*, *only*.

Less easy was the case of verbs, as they come in many varieties, and distinguishing complements – which are c-selected – from adjuncts – which are not – can be tricky. Here are some lexical entries. The c-selection properties (with "c" standing for *category* or *complement*) are elaborated below

elapse	free	V		example: "time elapses"
read	free	V	(c-selects DP)	examples: "I read," "I read the book"
put	free	V	c-selects DP, PP	example: "We put it over there"

Verb phrases can also combine with adjuncts. The relation between verbs or verb phrases and their adjuncts is different from the relation between verbs and their complements. Selection is involved, but we will not elaborate the lexical entries here. No V selects more than two or three complements, but it is less clear if there is a limit on the number of adjunct modifiers a verb can have.

Selection of subjects:
We have seen +tense and some Ds (like *'s*) select for subjects. Do verbs (and nouns, etc.) select subjects? In one sense, yes, and in another, no. No, because there does not seem to be a subject that a verb V requires **within its VP**. But yes in another sense:

a. The boy will read
b. *The boy will rain

These two sentences constitute a minimal pair: one is fine and the other is not, and the only difference is the choice of the verb. So the verb has something to say about the subject of T. For now, we will not code this in our lexical entries, but we will return to this important question in the next chapter, and also in Chapter 9.

[4]This is what we will assume for now. We will modify this on at the end of Section 10.2 in a way that does not affect any conclusion based on the categorial status of *whether* as C.

Turning to nouns, here is a small sample:

student	free	N	(c-selects (*of*)-PP)
claim	free	N	(c-selects *that*-CP)
question	free	N	(c-selects CP[+q])

Adjective phrases appear to be adjuncts for Ns. Adjectives themselves vary in the requirements on what can appear internal to their APs:

solid	free	A	
proud	free	A	(c-selects [*of*-PP] or CP)

Adjectives also allow adjuncts: *very, extremely*. Prepositions vary too:

up	free	P	(c-selects DP)
of	free	P	c-selects DP

Prepositions also allow adjuncts: *right, just*.

5.7.2 What to remember

Most important is the conclusion that syntactic constituents are headed, just like morphological units, and that the notion of head that we need is the same.

We have introduced some important distinctions. Heads relate to other constituents in different ways. They can take arguments (realized as complements), and some so far can select subjects. They can be modified by adjuncts. As in morphology, the properties of heads are coded in their lexical entries.

Knowing how to distinguish complements from adjuncts is important. To do this, thinking about their respective meaning contribution is important, but most important of all is understanding how to use constituency tests that ultimately reveal how exactly arguments or adjuncts fit into the structure. Arguments that are complements are systematically closer to the head than adjuncts, which combine with bigger units: phrases.

We also got a somewhat more systematic view of the role played by case morphology. The choice of a particular pronominal form depends on its syntactic position and the type of head. This is very general across languages and can be quite informative.

5.7.3 Puzzles and previews

One puzzle we mentioned is the question of whether verbs select subjects. We partially return to this question in the next chapter, but its full impact will take us some time to appreciate.

In addition, the quick survey we have taken of various phrases reveals a number of general properties of constituents that will be important later:

1. In every one of the categories we have looked at, the complements (if any) follow the head, and the subject (if any) precedes the head.
2. For all categories X of heads, there is a regularity about what kind of phrase is formed: a head X always forms an X′ or XP after combining with its complements. Clearly this should not need to be included in every lexical entry, but should be stated as some kind of general rule analogous to (but not the same as) the RHHR of morphology.

We explore this in the next chapter.

5.7.4 Further exercises

(1) NP/DP constituency
General instructions:

(i) Try to label all the nodes, but do not worry if you do not know how to label some of them.
(ii) Recall that constituent structure is such that lines do not cross and every node but the topmost has one and only one mother.
(iii) You may ignore word-internal structure.
1. Draw the trees of each of the following underlined strings (you can assume they are constituents).
   a. The old men
   b. The women and men
   c. The women and old men
2. The following underlined string is ambiguous:
   d. He is looking for very old or new editions.

(iv) Paraphrase each of the two meanings.
(v) Give two tree structures and clearly indicate which meaning corresponds to which structure. (hint: look at your trees for (1)).

(2) Apostrophe '*s*, prenominal genitives
Draw the trees for the following DPs. You may use triangles for proper names. Make sure your trees encode the basic constituency! Start by paraphrasing the meaning of each example, and apply your constituency test. (Don't go too quickly: (c) and (d) are tricky.)

(1) a. Bill's house
b. Bill and Susan's house
c. Sue's brother's house
d. Her father's brother's house

(3) Ambiguity
The following example is ambiguous.

(1) A cousin of Bill's brother
(i) Paraphrase the meanings.
(ii) For each meaning, give a corresponding tree structure.
(iii) We replace *Bill* with *who*, and form the following *wh*-question.
(2) Whose brother did you meet a cousin of?
This question is unambiguous: one of the meanings in (1) is no longer available.
(iv) Provide an account of why you think this would be the case. (Hint: this requires thinking which of the two structures can survive under wh-question formation). Make your reasoning explicit.

(4) Ambiguity and disappearing readings
The following sentence is structurally ambiguous; it has two different structures.

(1) They will slap the portly cook with the hat
(i) Paraphrase the two meanings of this sentence.
(ii) Draw two different trees for this sentence, and pair each tree up with the meaning of each sentence. (You should be able to defend your trees using constituency tests,

so check you know how to motivate each constituent you draw, but you only need to explain the tests requested below.)

(iii) Explain how at least one of our tests supports the structure in the first tree but not the second, and how at least one test supports the structure in the second tree but not the first.

(iv) If we replace *the* string *the portly cook* with *him*, the ambiguity disappears. Explain why.

(2) They will slap him with the hat

Suppose that in a Prenglish (a hypothetical language), pronouns can be NPs. This is different from English, where pronouns are DPs.

(v) Give two structures that you expect to be acceptable in Prenglish, but not in English. (Hint: consider the internal structure of NPs, and draw your trees.)

(vi) What would be the prediction about ambiguity for (2) in Prenglish? Do you think it will be ambiguous or not? Why?

(vii) If we replace *hat* with *which hat*, we get the following English unambiguous sentence:

(3) Which hat did they slap the portly cook with?

What reading disappears? Why? Is this expected or not? Why or why not? (You will revisit this puzzle in exercise 5 in Chapter 10.)

(viii) Do you expect English and Prenglish to behave differently in this respect, all other things being equal?

(5) VP constituency

Consider the following three sentences.

(1) a. The girl will [sleep] (cf. example (1a) of this chapter)
b. The girl will sleep on the couch
c. The girl will sleep on the couch tomorrow

(i) The verb is the only element following T in (1a). Use at least two different tests to show that the bracketed constituent also behaves as a VP. Draw the tree to the best of your abilities.

(ii) Apply constituency tests to the string *sleep on the couch* in (1b), draw its tree, and discuss on the basis of your results, if *on the couch* is a constituent, and if it is an adjunct or a complement (or neither).

(iii) Use at least two constituency tests to determine the structure of (1c), and draw its tree.

(iv) A fellow student proposes the following substructure for *sleep on the couch tomorrow*. There are some serious problems with this tree! It is your task to figure out what they are. What is wrong with the following structure? (This question is not about labels).

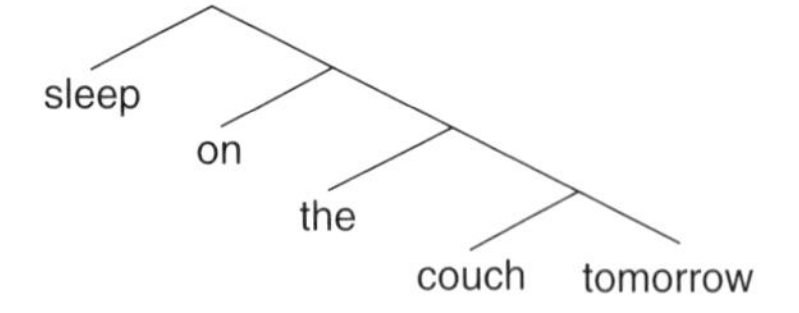

(v) What properties does this structure fail to express? (Consider your answers above. How is *on the couch* treated in this particular tree? What is its sister? What is the sister of *tomorrow*?) Compare this proposal with your own. Does it fare better?

(vi) If we replace *the* with *which* in the structure above, could this result in the question "Which couch will you sleep on tomorrow?" Explain your answer.

(6) VP/DP Constituency

Draw the tree for (1) below. Make sure your tree reflects the facts in the examples below each numbered example. The facts given there do not necessarily represent all the information you need to know to draw the tree; rather, they are guidelines for the potentially tricky parts.

(1) Doris might include the announcement about the reception in the revised invitation.
  a. Doris might include it in the revised invitation
  b. *Doris might include it about the reception in the revised invitation
  c. Doris might do so in the revised invitation
  d. Doris might do so
  e. Doris might include the one about the reception in the revised invitation
  f. Doris might include the announcement about the reception in the revised one
  g. Doris might include the announcement about the reception in it

(7) Complements and adjuncts (in DPs)

We have seen that complements form a constituent with a head, and adjuncts form a constituent with a phrase (which can be a phrase that contains a complement and the head).

Complements (like direct objects) are required because of inherent properties of the head; adjuncts in general are not required in this way. Because of this, complements combine with the head before adjuncts do.

Sometimes it is difficult to decide if some constituent is a complement or an adjunct. This is true for complements of noun phrases/DPs for example.

Look at the examples below and, for each, state which constituent combines with the head first (irrespective of right–left order) and explain any ungrammatical sentences.

List which PP you would call a complement and explain why.

(1) a. Student of linguistics from Russia
  b. A professor of linguistics from Russia
  c. A textbook of linguistics from Russia
  d. *A knife of linguistics from Russia
  e. *A thief of linguistics from Russia
  f. A student/professor/textbook/knife/thief/table from Russia
  g. *A student from Russia of linguistics
  h. * Professor from Russia of linguistics
  i. A linguistics student from Russia
  j. A Russian linguistics student (with the meaning in (1g))
  k. *A linguistics Russian student

(2) a. The Russian one
  b. *The linguistics one
  c. ?? One of linguistics from Russia
  d. One from Russia.

Based on your findings, what structures would you give to (3a), (3b) and (3c)? Why? Why do you think (3d) is excluded?

(3) a. An Italian student of math
  b. A math student from Italy
  c. An Italian math student
  d. *An math Italian student

5.7.5 Further reading

The presentation in this chapter departs from the historical development, and does not mention *Phrase Structure Grammars*. Discussion of these can be found in any introductory textbook.

A note on T and C as heads: it took time to appreciate the general significance of the notion of head, as applying to T and C and to bound morphemes. It came around 1981 for bound affixes (Williams, 1981), 1981 for T (Stowell, 1981), and 1986 for C (Chomsky, 1986). Important work on the structure of the clause leading up to this work, include Bresnan (1979) and Emonds (1976). For introduction of D as the head of DP see Abney (1987) and Postal (1969) for an early proposal.

6
X-bar Theory and the Format of Lexical Entries

6.1 Review: The Model of Morphology

We start out with a review and update of the model of morphology discussed in Chapter 2, and use it to raise specific and general questions about the model of syntactic organization. Fundamentally, morphological entities arise as the output of a combinatory system comprised of atoms and rules of combination.

1. The **atoms** of morphology are morphemes. Morphemes were defined as the simplest meaningful units (where meaningful is defined as having a semantic or a phonological interpretation). They are classified in categories. Morphemes have intrinsic properties, specified in their lexical entries, the collection of which is the **lexicon**. For a given morpheme, these properties include:
   a. its category;
   b. the kind of elements it selects;
   c. its contribution to meaning;
   d. its phonological shape (i.e. whether and how it is pronounced);
   e. whether it is bound or free (also a phonological property).
2. These atoms (the morphemes) can be assembled into complexes (which we can think of as molecules). These molecules have an internal structure that can be represented by labeled trees (with lines that do not cross).
3. Molecules and atoms can be further compounded to form still larger entities, again representable by labeled trees.
4. We will call the operation of combination **Merge** (Chomsky, 1995a). Merge can be seen as a function mapping n-tuples of trees (a set of trees) into a new or **derived** tree (what is meant here will be become clear over the course of the book).
5. Well-formed trees – the output of the Merge operation, arise as a result of the interaction between the following properties:
   a. **Lexical** properties of individual atoms determine the environments in which they can occur.
   b. **Locality**: If an atom selects an element, it acts as a head. This head must have the selected element or a molecule headed by the element as a sister. Selection is local in the sense that it is restricted to operating under sisterhood.

An Introduction to Syntactic Analysis and Theory, First Edition.
Dominique Sportiche, Hilda Koopman, and Edward Stabler.

c. **Binary branching**: In morphological trees, a mother node has at most two daughters. In other words Merge is a binary function: it is restricted to merging two trees into a new one.
d. **Right-hand head rule (RHHR)**: The head of a morphological constituent is (normally) the right daughter of this constituent.[1]

Note that the commonsense notion of "word" does not include compounds and certain other sorts of complexes, which linguistic investigation reveals to be of the same sort as their simpler variants. For example, the complex noun compound *bull dog park* has essentially the same morphological and syntactic properties as the morpheme *park* does – it is a noun. We call these categories N, V, A, P, D, C, Adv, and T, "word level" categories.

All these components interact to determine morphological structures, as indicated by this diagram:

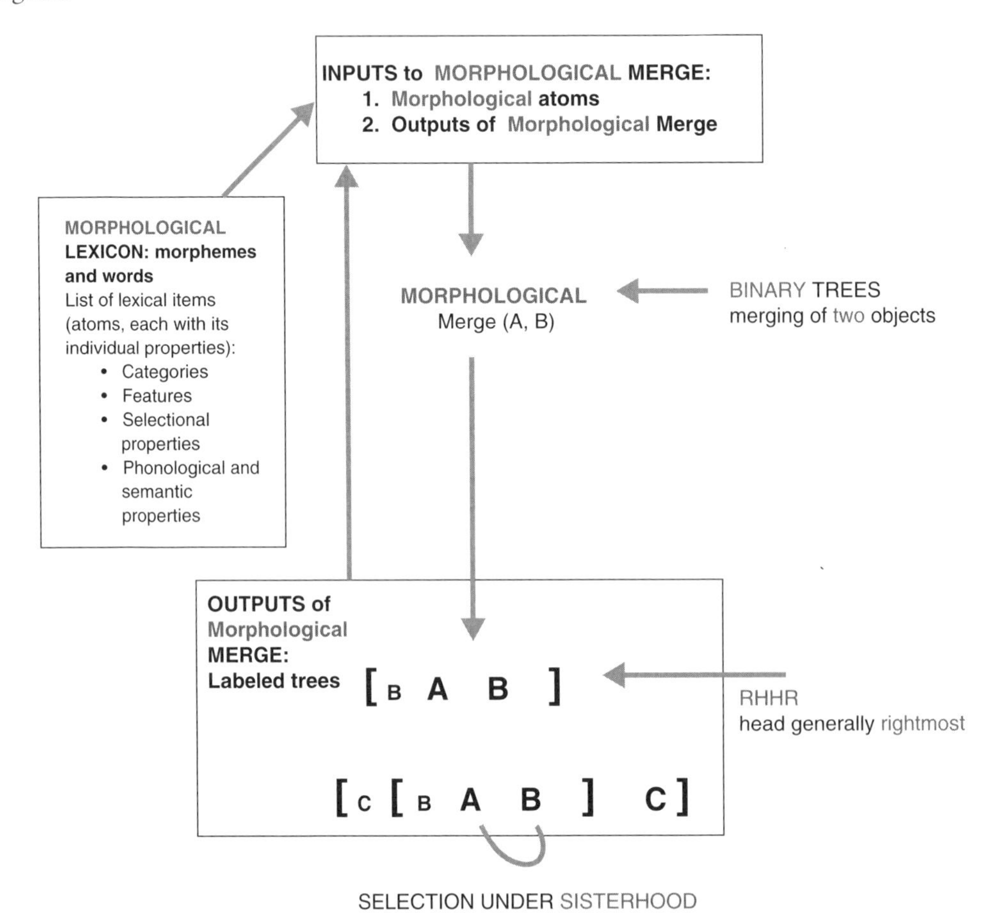

Figure 6.1 Model of the morphological component

The sizes of the components of this figure are not "to scale": the lexicon is vast, with all the morphemes that the speaker is acquainted with – many thousands for a normal adult

[1] The relation between hierarchical structure and head positioning is an open question. Here we take it that the RHHR is a property of English morphology, though some other languages appear to use a left-hand head rule for the positioning of the heads.

speaker – while the combinatory rules are extremely simple and few in number. Yet the generative power of the system, its capacity to produce infinitely many objects, lies with the rules, and so the output box should be infinitely large as should the input box, which contains both the lexicon and the outputs of the Merge operation.

The division of labor between the lexicon and Merge:
Since the set of morphological objects comprises the lexicon and the output of Merge, an important task is to determine what is responsible for what: if we observe a particular grammatical property, is this a property of some lexical entry, or is it a property of the merging algorithm and the general properties that constrain it? Of course, we cannot answer this question *a priori*, but here we give some guidelines. Something that appears in the lexical entry of some atom is an idiosyncratic property of this atom. Something that emerges because of Merge is a general property of a derived object, which arises in a systematic fashion from the component parts of the object. In effect, this is a consequence of the compositionality property that we have discussed, which addresses how the meaning of non-atoms is calculated, but which is actually much more general: all properties of the whole are computed by general rules from the properties of its parts.

This gives us boundary conditions on what property comes from where, hence on what property should be listed in the lexicon. By definition, properties listed in the lexicon are idiosyncratic, unpredictable, and specific to particular items.

Lexicon: Lexical entries only contain unpredictable information about atoms.

What is predictable and what is not is not known *a priori*. Naturally, there are idioms (both in phonological combinations and in semantic combinations) – perhaps very numerous – and these idiomatic properties will be listed in the lexicon in some way (exactly how to do this is an important, actively investigated, theoretical question which we cannot discuss here but we will address in Chapter 12). But in many instances, we do not know what is regular and what is not.

As a starting strategy, we will list in lexical entries whatever is necessary to make the system work, that is, to produce only well-formed outputs with Merge, given what we know at this stage about how Merge functions. This will tend to produce "rich" lexical entries. We will revise these as our understanding develops, because some apparently atomic elements may turn out not to be atomic after all, and some properties will migrate away from the lexicon. We will make regular remarks about this in the coming chapters.

CONVENTION: To make lexical entries more readable, we will sometimes include information that is not unpredictable. We will be explicit about this.

6.2 Building a Model of Syntax

Let us now consider how to build a model of syntax, given what we have discovered so far. Much is unclear at this point in our investigation, but by comparing the model of morphology and syntax, we can raise questions that lead to new investigations.

Before we begin, let's survey where we stand and point to where we're headed. We've introduced constituency tests and used them on many different strings. As a result, we've found many many types of phrases in English (and clearly, this kind of complexity is not peculiar to English). In fact, the situation looks rather frightening, because there seem to be many different kinds of structures already. However, beginning with this chapter, some theory will be introduced that reveals a surprising simplicity and uniformity behind the range of diverse constructions that English and other languages allow.

This chapter will concentrate on trying to understand the logic behind some of the basic regularities that we discuss. It will focus on the following issues: what is the rule system that underlies our phrases? What are the atoms of syntax? What are the properties of atoms and how should these be represented? Is there a notion of Merge? Does selection play a role? Is there a principle of locality of selection in syntax? If yes, what is its form? Are trees binary branching? Is there an equivalent to the RHHR in syntax? As we will see, this will lead us to one major concept introduced and explored in this chapter: X-bar theory, which is the syntax analogue of the RHHR.

To start with, given the conclusions of the two previous chapters, it should be immediately clear that syntax looks very much like morphology in many respects. Syntax is also a combinatory system with atoms and combinatory rules. It is a generative system building phrases by combining syntactic trees with each other. This means that there is a Merge operation. The notion of head plays a crucial role, which means that selection is important. In the following section, we will discuss the notion of head in syntax, then the analogue to the RHHR, and finally the question of how selection works in syntax.

6.3 Headedness

By experimentally probing the structure of various strings (e.g. by means of constituency tests), we have reached a number of conclusions about syntactic constituent structures. Some of them are fairly obvious, others less so. The basic idea is that phrases, like words, include a distinguished element, a head, that determines the fundamental properties of the phrases. Spelling some of the components of this proposal out more systematically, we get:

(1) a. Each phrasal constituent has a head.
b. This head is always a morpheme or a word (a D, an N, etc.).
c. There is never more than one head per constituent.
d. Every morpheme or word is the head of some constituent.
e. In general, no non-constituent has a unique head.

We will discuss (a) below in Section 6.5 and (b) in Section 8.3.1. We have not seen any reason to doubt (c) as there are no convincing cases in which a constituent has two heads jointly determining its fundamental properties. Property (d) is obviously true, since at the very least, each morpheme is the head of itself. As for (e), it has not been explicitly discussed before, but consider the properties of a string that does not form a constituent, such as the underlined parts of the string here:

(2) The driver of the car thinks that Mary should leave Dallas for Boise tomorrow

Here the whole discontinuous string is not a constituent, but it can be split into two unconnected continuous parts, each of which is a constituent with its own head (you should be able to name them by now). Or take the following example:

(3) Her **little sister** *will* disagree with her

We are dealing with a continuous string that does not form a constituent but which again can be split into two constituents, one in bold and one in italics, each of which has its own head. Finally in the following case:

(4) The girl he met at the **fundraising party** *will* **very surely** call him

We are dealing with a continuous string that does not form a constituent but that can be split into three independent constituents, two in bold and one in italics, each of which has its own head.

6.4 Internal Organization of Constituents

If we look at the internal organization of the constituents we have found so far, we see a lot of similarity. For example, looking at the TP and DP below:

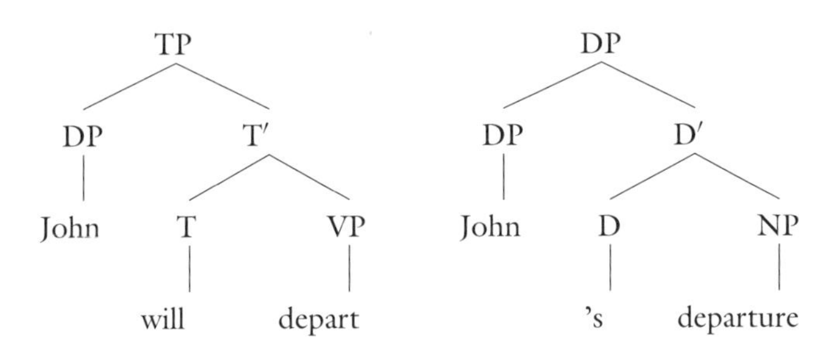

Both phrasal categories TP and DP can be composed of a DP subject or specifier and a constituent T′ or D′. T′ and D′ themselves are each made of the head, T or D, followed (in English) by the complements of T (namely VP) or D (namely NP). This similarity in structure also holds for adjuncts. For example, a PP adjunct to a VP together with a VP forms a new VP (as in [[leave the city] early]) while an adjunct AP to an NP joins with that NP to form a larger NP (as in [big [picture of Bill]]).

This suggests a certain cross-categorial uniformity: the internal organization of phrases is always the same, regardless of the choice of head.

This conjecture rests on generalizations over a great number of different chunks of constituent structures in English and other languages, and is described as X-bar theory, building on proposals of Chomsky (1970). X-bar theory is the set of principles that tells us how any particular phrase HP is allowed to be internally structured, a sort of general blueprint to which phrases must conform (the way it is actually constructed will depend on the choice of the head, H, because it also depends on the selectional properties of H). Research of the past forty years suggests that this conjecture is true. So current linguistic theory conjectures that these regularities are true of every bit of English (and of other human languages in general).

In full generality, the principles of X-bar theory elaborate on the basic ideas in (1) as follows:

(5) a. Each phrasal constituent has a head.
  b. This head is always a morpheme or a word (a D, an N, etc.).
  c. A constituent has a unique head.
  d. Every morpheme is the head of some constituent.
  e. In general, no non-constituent has a unique head.
  f. Labeling conventions:
    a. A constituent whose head is labeled H (e.g. a category symbol) has a label containing the symbol H.
    b. Such constituents are labeled H, H′, and HP[2] in order of increasing size (HP includes H′, which includes H etc.). They are called **projections** of H.
  g. Definition: The largest constituent with head H is, for **ease of reference only**, notated HP (other times H^{max}), and is called **the maximal or phrasal projection of H**.

[2] In the literature, they are also sometimes notated as H, H′, H″, H‴ (read H, H-prime, H double prime, etc. or H, H-bar, H double bar), etc., that is an H with one or more bars above it.

h. HP (or H^{max}) can have at most two daughters: one is a projection of H, the other is called the **specifier or subject** of H.
i. H′, or H-bar, consists of the head H and some sisters. These sisters (if any) are called the **complements** of H.
j. HP can also consist of an HP and a sister constituent called an **adjunct** to H (or to HP).
k. Adjuncts, complements, and specifiers/subjects are themselves phrasal constituents.

While the basic principles (a)–(e) have close analogues in morphology, (f)–(k) seem to only apply to syntax. Note the following hypothesis is implicit in the notation described in what precedes.

> The Two Level Hypothesis: In everything that follows, we will suppose, as we have seen for TP and DP above, that a head has at most two projections: heads merge with complements first, the result merges with subjects/specifiers.

As a result, the structures allowed by the theory can be depicted with tree fragments as follows. In general, the left-to-right order of the branches is **not** specified by X-bar theory, only the hierarchical structure is. In effect, the structure can be regarded as a mobile: adjuncts can appear on the left or right of the XP they modify; subjects can be the left or right sisters of X′, and complements can be left or right sisters of X.

Here are the prototypical phrase types allowed by X-bar theory.

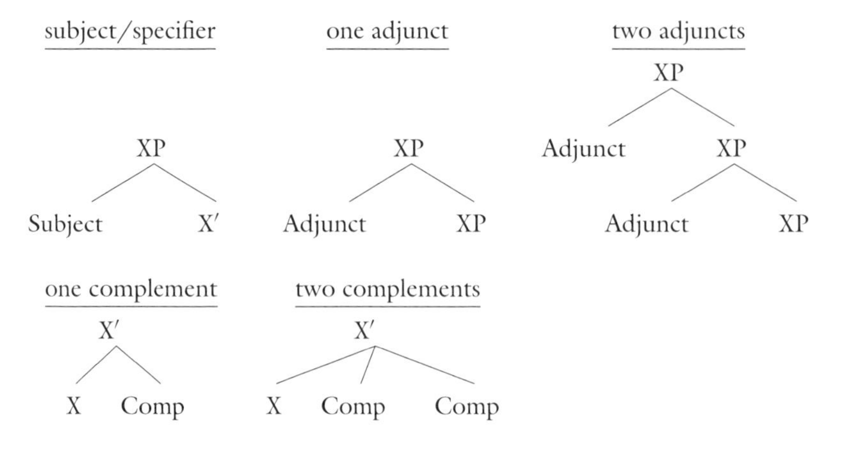

So the overall look of a phrase is this:

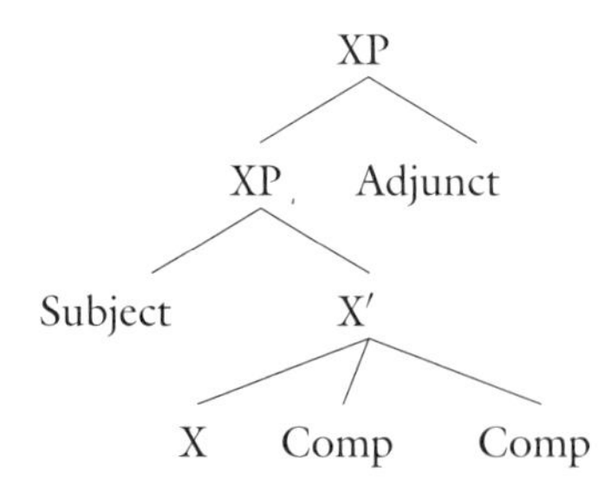

An XP can have zero or more adjuncts, zero or one subject, and zero or more complements, but it always has a head X.

The X-bar conjecture holds for hierarchical organization within phrases. But clearly, languages differ in word order. This variation is often handled by postulating that individual languages have specific settings, called **parameters**, which are responsible for the observed variability between languages with respect to the relative orders of constituents. We return to this in Section 6.10.

The version of X-bar theory we have given above is very close to the final version we will adopt, but is not quite the last word. Some revisions – which will make X-bar theory even simpler – will be introduced in Chapter 12 once we understand syntactic structures better. But we can already point to one aspect that will need attention: we define HP as the largest projection of H, but sometimes we have two HPs simultaneously, like when HP has an adjunct. How is this possible? We will see ways to make sense of this in Chapter 12.

> **Adjuncts**: We treat adjuncts as attached to HP. This assumption comes from the results of VP ellipsis or VP preposing. This structure will be good enough for everything we do in this book and we will represent adjuncts consistently in this way, and so should you. You should be aware, however, that sometimes the literature treats adjuncts as attached to H′ instead. There are substantive underlying issues here, which we cannot really discuss (but see the framed box below for some further discussion). You might want to revisit this issue after Chapter 12.

Let us end this section with some remarks about notation and conventions. It is important to realize that the following trees all convey exactly the same information, and so can be used interchangeably:

(a) NP
book

(b) NP
N
book

(c) N
book

(d) NP
N′
N
book

In such cases, if the N does not have a subject or a complement, the largest constituent with N as head is the N itself. Still, to make trees more legible, we adopt the notation in (a) or (b). This can sometimes be useful. In the following trees, (a) and (b) are equivalent but (b) does not clearly show what the head of the whole DP is (it is *'s* and not *John*), while (a) does.

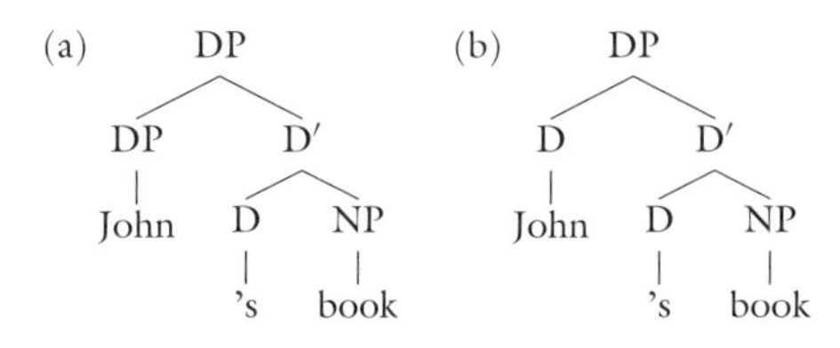

> **Advanced remarks**: First, deciding between whether adjuncts merge with an HP to form an HP, rather than to an H′ forming H′ is complicated. It is a question of which of an adjunct or subject is "higher" in the tree in a given phrase, i.e. whether a subject combines with the head complement constituent first, and the adjunct second, or the other way around. Settling this is particularly difficult. In addition, it may well be that both are correct, and that adjuncts can occur in either position, and even as adjuncts to a head. If such is the case, we need to develop accounts of where adjuncts can occur in particular cases.
>
> Second, suppose we have some lexical item **LI** of category H within some HP. When we write $[_H \text{ LI}]$, we are saying that LI is of category H (another term for the category H is the **label** of H, i.e. H is called the **label** of LI). Here HP is defined as the largest projection of LI, that is, the largest constituent within the structure with H as the head. But how is H′ (or H-bar) defined? H′ is the constituent containing the head and the complement(s), if any. If a head H has both a subject and a complement, H, H′, and HP are all distinct. In English, this results

in an HP with subjects and complements being on opposite sites of the head.

Let's take an example where this HP is itself a complement of a V, as in (a):

(a) [V [HP XP [H′ H YP]]]   (b) [V [HP XP H]]   (c) [V [HP H YP]]

If H has no complement, the tree is (b), and if the head has no subject, the tree is (c). We have defined a complement as a sister to the head H, and a subject as a non-adjunct phrasal daughter to the projection HP. Applied blindly, these definitions will treat XP in (b) or YP in (c) as both a complement and subject. Is this a problem? One thing at stake is the relative ordering of XP, YP, and H in such cases in a language like English, since subjects precede the head, while complements follow it. Another question is whether we can distinguish two kinds of predicates taking a single argument (the answer here will be yes). These are advanced questions that we will ignore here, but can be addressed when we have a better idea of verbal structure after Chapter 12.

In English, complements follow the head and subjects precede the head, as shown here, but this may vary across languages, and is not part of X-bar theory. This property of English allows us to sometimes use the following **abbreviated notation** for our tree representations of **English**: when an XP has either no subject or no complements and only in these cases, we can leave the X′ out of the tree diagram, since no ambiguity can result in this case. **We will understand that right sisters of a head are complements, and that the left sister of a head is a subject.**

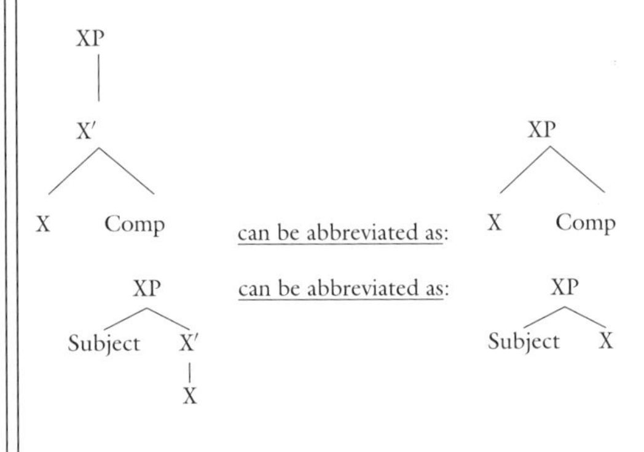

6.5 Some Consequences

X-bar theory should be true of every single phrase, and these principles are so basic we expect them to hold in other languages too. If we find an apparently headless syntactic (or morphological) constituent, we should find evidence that there is a silent head. And it is natural to expect subjects, complements, and adjuncts for every category type. If some categories do not have all these components, we would like to understand why.

6.5.1 Silent heads: D

According to this, some of the structures we have already seen must contain silent heads. For example, English common count nouns cannot be used without a determiner, unless they are plural. (These D-less plurals are called "bare" plurals.)

	definite	indefinite
sg	the bear	a bear
pl	the bears	bears

There are definite and indefinite determiners, and singular and plural NPs. But there is a gap in this system: there is no plural indefinite D with plural NPs. These bare plurals occur in DP positions, where they can give rise to indefinite readings, as in (6), where we make a claim about some books in general, or generic readings, as in (7), where we make a claim about typical or "generic" beavers:

(6) Mary bought books
(7) Beavers build dams

In such sentences all the underlined plurals must be DPs, as the coordination and substitution-with-a-pronoun tests show:

(8) Mary bought [[books] and [the trade magazines]]
(9) Can beavers build dams? Yes, they build them all the time.

But there is no visible D. This is exactly where a silent D would fit well. An indefinite silent D (a covert counterpart to *some*) would regularize the determiner system in English. In addition, these silent Ds actually have meanings, and are heads in this way: they determine the kind of DP we are dealing with (indefinite, or generic), and thus determine the distribution of the DP. For example, note that *dams* in direct object position does not have a generic meaning in the sentence above, while *beavers* in subject position does not have an indefinite reading. The sentence cannot mean that some beavers build typical dams; rather it must mean that typical beavers build some dams.

Pronouns and proper names do not co-occur with Ds, but distribute as (definite) DPs.

(10) John will see you * John will see the you

Since proper names and pronouns behave like definite DPs, by X-bar theory, they must contain at the very least a D and they must contain at least a (silent) NP, since Ds always select NPs. How this should be done is an interesting but advanced topic (discussed in work by Giuseppe Longobardi, a professor in Trieste, Italy, and by Ora Matushansky, a researcher in Utrecht, the Netherlands). Here, we will not elaborate further. We will generally represent proper names and pronouns as DPs, e.g. with a triangle or not:

6.5.2 Silent heads: T

Clauses (TPs) are constituents, and what is selected from the outside is T. Furthermore, this T also determines the kind of subject the TP has (nominative) and the presence of a VP within TP. As we saw in Chapter 2, T can also be a silent head, as with the English present tense. While past tense is systematically manifested as the suffix *-ed*, future T as *will*, and infinitive [-T] as *to*, we see below that the present tense T is usually a silent head (except in the 3rd person singular when it is manifested as the suffix *-s*).

Present	Past	Future
I wash myself	I wash**ed** myself	I **will** wash myself
you wash yourself	you wash**ed** yourself	you **will** wash yourself
she wash**es** herself	she wash**ed** herself	she **will** wash herself
he wash**es** himself	he wash**ed** himself	he **will** wash himself

we wash ourselves	we wash**ed** ourselves	we **will** wash ourselves
you wash yourselves	you wash**ed** yourselves	you **will** wash yourselves
they wash themselves	they wash**ed** themselves	they **will** wash themselves

6.5.3 Silent heads: C

Consider the following examples:

(11) John thinks that I left
(12) John thinks I left
(13) John whispered that I left
(14) * John whispered I left

Some speakers of English allow this last form, while others do not. Note that we don't mean this to be the same as: *John whispered: "I left."* In the intended form, leaving is about me, the speaker, but in this other case, leaving is about John.

How do we analyze the apparent optionality of *that*? There are two options we could consider:

(15) a. some Vs (like *think*) select either a CP or a TP;
b. these Vs select CPs but sometimes allow the C to be silent (i.e. there is a silent C – call it silent *that*, and write it ~~that~~).

There are many reasons, some of them complex, to choose the second option.

One suggestive line of reasoning is this. On either hypothesis, we would like to explain why certain verbs allow both a silent ~~that~~ and an overt *that*, while other verbs require a non-silent *that*. But notice that under (15b), the data above support the idea that a verb with a tensed TP complement *always* also allows a CP complement. Why should this be the case? There is nothing in (15a) to lead us to expect this. But under (15b), this is expected, since the proposal is that the tensed CP without an overt complementizer actually has a silent *that*. Hence the second option is preferred.

Furthermore, if we look at languages other than English, (15a) leads to the expectation that other languages should also have verbs selecting TPs.

The second idea (15b) predicts that languages that lack an equivalent of silent *that* will not allow TP complements. The latter prediction seems correct. For example, in languages like Dutch and French the complementizer is obligatory.

> **What drives selection?** Why should there be this expectation? There is quite a bit of correspondence between the selectional properties of similar items in different languages. What is behind this is the idea that category membership of a constituent is related to the meaning of this constituent, and selection for a complement, for example, is rooted in the meaning of the selector. Thus, if English *after* and French *après* mean more or less the same thing, we should expect that they would select the same kind of XP. Jane Grimshaw, professor at Rutgers, and David Pesetsky, professor at MIT, have shown that it is difficult to reduce selection to meaning (otherwise, our lexical entries could be considerably simplified) so perhaps this expectation is unwarranted, and should be qualified, all other things being equal.

Dutch: Ik denk dat Jan vertrokken is, *Ik denk Jan vertrokken is
I think that John left is, I think that John left is
"I think John left, I think that John left"

French: Je ne crois pas que Jean est parti *Je ne crois pas Jean est parti
I NEG believe not NEG John is left I NEG believe NEG John is left
"I don't believe that John left, I don't believe John left"

We see another consequence in cases like the following, where it might seem that Ps can take TP complements:

(16) a. Before [$_{TP}$ John left]
b. After [$_{TP}$ John left]

However, the previous discussion suggests that the correct structure may instead be:

(17) a. Before [$_{CP}$ ~~that~~ [$_{TP}$ John left]]
b. After [$_{CP}$ ~~that~~ [$_{TP}$ John left]]

Again, a look at other languages, as well as some evidence internal to English, suggests the second option is correct: Ps take CP complements, not TP complements.

Dutch: a. voor[dat Jan vetrokken is]
before.that John left is
b. na[dat Jan vertrokken is]
after.that John left is
French: a. après [que Jean soit parti]
after that John is left
b. avant [que Jean soit parti]
before that John is left

As we see, Dutch spells "after" and C as one word, *nadat*, and French as two, *après que*. Orthographic conventions can be arbitrary: someone had to decide where to put spaces on paper. Our intuitions as readers and writers may tell us that these are one word in Dutch but two words in French, and such intuitions sometimes trick the linguist. In this case it seems clear that the intuitions come from the writing system. However, from a formal standpoint, the analysis of such strings is the same: in neither language do the P and C form a single constituent, as the bracketing above indicates.

6.6 Cross-categorial Symmetries

X-bar theory claims that all phrases are organized in the same uniform way. If we interpret this as radically as possible, we should expect total parallelism between phrasal types.

Table 6.1 summarizes our findings so far.

We see many differences between categories: for example, Cs seem to take no subject, no adjuncts, and only one kind of complement (TP). If the radical interpretation of X-bar theory is right, either we should find reasons for these differences, or we should find that there are really no differences at all. Here is a list of some of the differences. We will investigate some of these differences in subsequent chapters, and update the table above periodically. The reader may want to complete the table every time we find a new category.

(18) a. Missing subjects in C, P, A, V, N.
b. Different subject options for DP and TP.

Table 6.1 Syntactic elements: Heads, Subjects and Complements

	C	T	D	P	A	V	N
subjects	?	DP CP	DP	?	?	?	?
complements	TP	VP	NP	DP PP CP	PP CP	DP PP CP AP mult	PP CP
adjuncts	?	AdvP?	CP	AdvP	DegP	PP AdvP	PP AP CP

c. Different categories take different numbers of complements, different kinds of complements, and different adjuncts:
- C, T, D, P, and A take only one complement at a time, V and N can take several complements (not represented in chart above).
- C, T, and D take only one type of complement each, which no other category takes as a complement.
- P, V, N, and A take several kinds of complements.
- A and N allow PP and CP as a complement, but V and P allow DP, PP, and CP as a complement.

In a sense, C, T, and D pattern alike with respect to complementation, but not with respect to subjects. They also pattern alike in being "closed categories." No new determiner, tense, or complementizer can be freely created the way new nouns, adjectives, or verbs can. Ps, Vs, Ns, and As pattern very much alike in not allowing subjects and allowing several kinds of complements. In this latter respect, Vs and Ps pattern like each other (PPs, DPs, and CPs as complements) and Ns and As also do (PPs and CPs but no DPs as complements). But Vs and Ns pattern alike in allowing more than one complement at a time. Vs also seem to be unique in that no other category so far seems to take an AP as complement. As for Cs, it could be that they allow no adjunct because C lacks the kind of meaning that could be modified by an adjunct.

6.7 Subjects Across Categories: Small Clauses

Table 6.1 reveals that there are some cross-categorial similarities but also lots of categorial dissimilarity. The most striking dissimilarity is that lots of categories seem to lack subjects, or specifiers.

We will look into this matter more carefully and discover that there are more kinds of subjects than this table suggests.

Consider sentences such as the following:

(19) a. Mary prefers her ice cream in a cone
b. She considers John proud of his work
c. Henry found Bill sad
d. They saw Bill leave

What kind of constituent structure should we give them? The following examples are close paraphrases:

(20) a. Mary prefers that her ice cream is in a cone
b. ? She considers that John is proud of his work
c. Henry found that Bill is sad
d. Henry saw that Bill left

In both the former and the latter sets of examples, the main verb (*prefer, consider, find, see*) is naturally regarded as naming an event that involves two essential things, the subject (an "experiencer"), and the state of affairs toward which the experiencer has some kind of mental attitude (the "theme"): preference, consideration, discovery, sight. Given that the presence of these two entities (the experiencer and the state of affairs) seems required by the meaning of these verbs, and that the state of affairs is named by the CP in (20), what is the structure of the sentences in (19)?

We can probe the question with constituency tests. These indicate that the material following a verb in (19) forms a constituent, as shown by the positive results below. (There are also negative results, but remember that while the negative results raise puzzles, by themselves they do not generally allow us to draw any definite conclusions. We will get a full picture of these negative cases in Chapter 12.)

Coordination:
a. Mary prefers her ice cream in a cone
Mary prefers her pancakes cooked
Mary prefers her ice cream in a cone and her pancakes cooked
b. She considers John proud of his work
She considers Sam expendable
She considers John proud of his work and Sam expendable
c. Henry found Bill sad
Henry found Sue happy
Henry found Bill sad and Sue happy
d. They saw Bill laugh
They saw Sue leave
They saw Bill laugh and Sue leave.

Pseudoclefts:
a. What Mary prefers is her ice cream in a cone
b. * What she considers is John proud of his work
c. * What Henry found is Bill sad
d. * What they saw is Bill laugh

Wh-movement:
a. What does Mary prefer? (Answer: her ice cream in a cone)
b. What does she consider? (*Answer: John proud of his work)
c. What did Henry find? (?Answer: Bill sad)
d. What did they see? (?Answer: Bill laugh)

As always, we should eventually probe why some tests fail but, for now, the coordination test provides evidence that the following parts of the sentences in (19) are constituents:

(21) her ice cream in a cone
John proud of his work
Bill sad
Bill leave

We will see additional evidence for this analysis in Chapter 7. Our next question is this: what is the category of these constituents? In each case, it looks like we have a DP, which looks like a "subject" of some kind, followed by a "predicate" of some kind: a PP in (a), APs in (b) and (c), and a VP in (d). But there is no evidence of any tense on these elements, nor is there even any verb for a tense element to attach to in (a)–(c). However, the DP in each case is understood as having the property described by the predicate, very much like in simple clauses. It thus seems natural to suppose that we have PPs, APs, and VPs with subjects. That is, the structures of (19) could be something like the following. (We show only the relevant portions of the trees.) These structures will be revisited in Chapters 10 and 12.

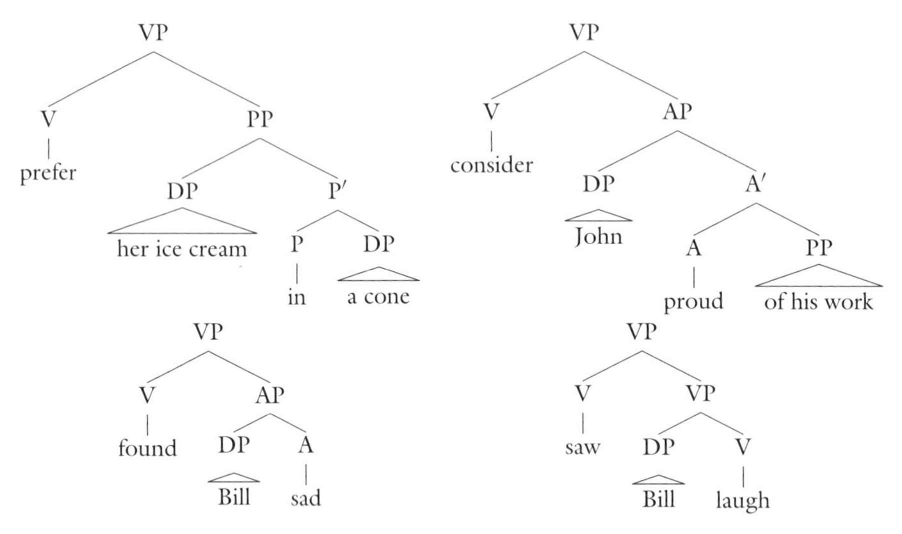

We have now found that more categories take subjects than we had seen before. The first row of the table can now be updated below.

	C	T	D	P	A	V	N
subjects	?	DP CP	DP	DP	DP	DP	?

There still remains some asymmetry – for example, we have not (yet) found cases where Cs have subjects – but we will see later in Chapter 8 that this asymmetry disappears as well, thus boosting our confidence that X-bar theory is on the right track. (There is evidence for N subjects too, but they raise some tricky issues, so we leave them aside.)

Although the term *small clause* was initially coined by Edwin Williams, the structural analysis we have presented draws on works by Timothy Stowell (pictured), currently (2013) professor at UCLA, whose pioneering work on phrase structure has been very influential (see Stowell, 1978, 1981).

6.8 Lexical Entries

Syntactic structures like the trees above are determined in part by the properties of syntactic atoms. Our starting assumption is that the syntactic lexicon, the collection of syntactic atoms, is different from the morphological lexicon since we take it to contain only the words. Indeed, some words are morphemes, and thus morphological atoms, but others are produced by the morphological component.

Just like in morphology, we need to represent the relevant properties of the syntactic atoms, in particular, selectional properties.

Recall that we strive to include only unpredictable properties in lexical entries, although we may also include information that is predictable but makes lexical entries easier to read. One such type of unpredictable information concerns thematic relations and theta roles, which the following section introduces.

6.8.1 A short primer on thematic relations

Notice that the semantic relation between the subject and the verb, or the verb and its first complement, is different in these two pairs of sentences:

(22) a. John kicked Bill
b. John fears Bill
(23) a. Mary sent Bill to Laredo
b. Mary gave Bill a book

In the first sentence, John "does" something, performs an action, but not in the second, which describes John's state of mind. There is a difference even though both are subjects. In the second pair, Bill has changed location as a result of the sending, but not as a result of the giving. There is a difference even though both are direct objects. Selection is sensitive to these differences. For example, the choice of subject (as we saw in Chapter 5) or object depends on the verb:

(24) The boy will read/*The boy will rain
(25) Mary thought *the house/that it was raining

This type of selection is sometimes called **s-selection** for "semantic selection," and can be coded by indexing a selected constituent with what is called a **theta role**, a term that identifies the meaning relation between the constituent and the predicate that selects it. To this end, we will informally use terms like **Agent**, **Theme**, **Cause**, **Possessor**, **Location**, **Goal**, **Experiencer**, and **Beneficiary**. Each term names a meaning relation that holds between a verb or a predicate and one of its arguments, thus coding s-selection. These theta roles are also called thematic roles. These terms do not really have a theoretical status, but are convenient shorthand. We will regularly add these to our lexical representations in subsequent chapters, in order to make lexical entries easier to read or interpret.

Cause: a cause (*The rock broke the window, This made him cry*).

Agent: a person or entity (intentionally) causing or doing something (*John (intentionally) broke the window*).

Experiencer: a sentient being in or acquiring a psychological state (*John fears storms, Storms frightened John, Mary saw Bill*).

Location: is a location (*John sleeps in his bed, Mary danced on the beach*).

Goal: is a location that is an endpoint (*John sent Bill books*).

Beneficiary: a beneficiary (*John baked a cake for Mary, John baked Mary a cake*).

Possessor: is a possessor (*Susan has a book, Susan owns books, These books belong to Susan*).

Possessee or possessed: what is possessed (*John owns books, John's books*).

Theme: something that undergoes a change (e.g. of location) (*John sent Bill books*) or that is progressively affected as the event denoted by the verb progresses (*John read a book*), (*Three minutes elapsed*), etc. Often more broadly used as a wastebasket for things that do not fit anywhere else e.g. *John is tall*, *Mary thinks that it is raining*.

As we mentioned, such labels play no analytical role in anything we will discuss. It is worth mentioning, however, that the following principle known as the **Theta Criterion** (Chomsky, 1981) is sometimes referred to in the literature.

Theta Criterion: Every argument bears one and only one theta role.

Whether it is true (particularly the "only one" part) or useful is a controversial matter. In Chapter 9, we will see one instance in which the validity of the theta criterion is questioned.

6.8.2 The general format of lexical entries

Here we describe the kind of information we will include in the lexical entries of syntactic atoms, the notational conventions we will use, and some examples. We (try to) list only properties that are not predictable by general rules or principles. These entries will be revised any time we gain further understanding of these questions of predictability (see e.g. Section 12.2).

If we take the structures discovered so far as representative, the lexical entry for an item, say W, contains at least the following kinds of information:

1. The form of W (this is a phonological property, whether or not it is pronounced (non-pronunciation will be indicated by /e/).
2. The category (e.g. T, D) and subcategories (e.g. +tense, +definite) of W (subcategories are also called features).
3. The number of arguments W takes (if any: if it is zero, we do not indicate anything).
4. The semantic relationship, if any, between W and each of these arguments. We code these as theta roles (e.g. goal, possessor), and occasionally refer to these as s-selection (selection for a semantic property like "animate"). These may be predictable on the basis of the meaning of W, but we will not worry about this question.
5. The phrasal category (e.g. TP or AP) that syntactically realizes each of these arguments (that is, the c-selectional properties of W).

   This kind of information appears not to be generally predictable, given minimal pairs such as *wait* and *await*. These appear to be synonyms, but *wait* takes a PP complement as Theme (*wait for Bill*), while *await* takes a DP complement (*await Bill*) (see also the framed box in Section 6.5.2).
6. The syntactic configuration in which these arguments are syntactically realized (i.e. as subject complement). We will say that the argument realized as subject, if there is one, is *selected as a subject* (or sometimes we will just say *is selected*). We adopt the following convention: the DP or CP selected as the subject will be underlined. For complements, we will use c-selection, also known as subcategorization.

   The reason this information needs to be specified is that it does not appear to be generally predictable, given pairs such as *own* and *belong*. These seem to express the same relation, but the possessee is a subject in one (*This book belongs to John*) and a complement in the other (*John owns this book*). (This does not mean that it is unpredictable in all cases, a point we will return to in Chapter 12.)
7. Additional morphological properties, e.g. if the item is a free or bound element. From here on, we will only indicate when an item is bound. An absence of specification indicates that it is free.

8. Additional semantic information about the item. This is of course an important but complex set of properties, but we will not worry very much about it. We implicitly rely on the reader's knowledge of English. For example, this information is what would distinguish a verb like *reach* (which only allows an adjunct like *in an hour* but not one like *for an hour*), from a verb like *paint* (which may allow either e.g *paint the door in/for an hour*).

As an illustration, let us start with a partial lexical entry for the verb *prefer*. The entry could look like the following without abbreviation (note that we do not indicate what is not selected):

prefer V selects a DP experiencer as subject c-selects a PP theme as complement free [meaning]

With our notational conventions, it will look like this:

prefer V $\underline{DP}_{exp}$ PP_{theme}

Of course, this verb can appear in different contexts. Taking this into account, there would be several lines in the lexical entries, as below (or in a more compact form, with slashes (/) separating options):

prefer V $\underline{DP}_{exp}$ PP_{theme}
$CP[for]_{theme}$
$CP[that]_{theme}$
prefer V $\underline{DP}_{exp}$ $PP_{theme}/CP[for]_{theme}/CP[that]_{theme}$

Here are examples of (partial lexical entries) for some other verbs:

consider	V	$\underline{DP}_{exp}$	AP_{theme}
find	V	$\underline{DP}_{exp}$	AP_{theme}
see	V	$\underline{DP}_{exp}$	VP_{theme}/DP_{theme}
laugh	V	$\underline{DP}_{agent}$	
eat	V	$\underline{DP}_{agent}$	(DP_{theme})

The lexical entry for *prefer* reads as follows. The phonological string */prefer/* is a V, it is free (since it is not marked as bound), it selects for a DP experiencer subject, (this is indicated by the underlining convention), and it selects for either a PP small clause complement (which is interpreted as the thing preferred – *a theme*), or a CP headed by *for*, or a CP headed by *that*. (Note how we specify the particular subtype of XP that is selected, e.g. a CP headed by *for* for *prefer*.) We do not always indicate the thematic role and omit it when things are clear. Note finally the parentheses around the complement of *eat*. This verb does select a complement, but its presence is not obligatory (the sentence *Natasha is eating* is well formed). The parentheses code this optionality.

This points to an obvious and very general requirement. Unless we put parentheses around an item selected by a head, this

Subcategorizing subjects?
We code in our lexical entry the category of the subject selected by *prefer*. In other words, we implicitly assume that subjects are c-selected (or to use an equivalent terminology, subcategorized). We will continue doing so for ease of readability, but it should be noted that this information is in fact redundant: knowing what the verb is, is sufficient to predict the category of its subject.

Terminology: What we notate, for example, as "a V c-selecting a PP as a complement" was historically notated as a feature of the form [___+ PP]. This coded a context in which the V could fit, and was called a *subcategorization feature*, meaning that such a V belongs to the subcategory of V fitting in the blank in this subcategorization frame. This usage created the verb *subcategorize (for)*, which is used like *c-select*.

selected item must appear in any well-formed structure containing that head. This requirement is called the **Projection Principle**.

Projection Principle: Properties of lexical items must be satisfied (in syntactic structures).

We will return to the question of how the projection principle is implemented when we discuss locality of selection. It should be clear that this principle is very general. While we concentrate here on its effects on how syntactic trees are built, it should be clear that it applies equally in morphological tree building.

6.8.3 More lexical entries

A lexical entry is in part a snapshot of its distribution: constructing a lexical entry always starts with an investigation of the local environments in which the item can occur. We now provide illustrations of both lexical entries and the kind of reasoning we apply to decide what goes in them, along with some examples that we have already encountered.

More verbs
We have considered paradigms like this:

(26) a. *Mary sends, Mary sends a book (to Bill), Mary sends Bill a book . . .
b. Time elapses, *Bill elapses, *Time elapse a book, *Time elapses to Bill
c. *Bill examines, Bill examine a book, *Bill examine a book to Mary, *Sincerity examines a book
d. *We put, *We put a book, We put a book on the table
e. We think that it is raining, *We think for it is raining, *we think if it is raining
f. We wonder whether it is raining, We wonder if it is raining, We wonder that it is raining

The verb **send** is a predicate that takes three arguments (a three place predicate). It relates an agent (the sender, realized as a subject), a theme (what gets sent, realized as a DP complement), and a goal (the recipient, realized either as a PP headed by *to* or as a DP).

send V $\underline{\mathrm{DP}_{agent}}$ DP_{theme}, $(\mathrm{P(to)\ DP})_{goal}$

Note how we put parentheses around the preposition to indicate that it is optionally present and how we put parentheses around (to DP) to indicate that this argument is optionally present.

The verb *elapse* takes one argument as subject (it is a one place predicate). It selects a theme subject, specifically, one that refers to durations.

elapse V $\underline{\mathrm{DP}_{theme}}$

The verb *examine* is a two place predicate. Its two arguments are interpreted respectively as Agent (who does the examining) and Theme (what is examined). The agent argument must be a DP subject (and because it is an agent it must be animate), and the theme must be a DP.

examine V $\underline{\mathrm{DP}_{agent}}$ DP_{theme}

Here are lexical entries for the verbs *think* and *wonder*:

think V $\underline{\mathrm{DP}_{agent}}$ $\mathrm{CP[that]}_{theme}$
wonder V $\underline{\mathrm{DP}_{agent}}$ $\mathrm{CP[+q]}_{theme}$

Adjectives
Let us consider adjectives appearing in small clause structures, as in (19). The adjective *proud* can optionally take a complement headed by the P *of*, (*proud* (*of/*about his painting*)), but the adjective *sad* does not, though it allows an optional *about* PP complement (*sad* (*of/about the results*)). Both allow a DP subject, as shown in adjectival small clauses, but do not require it (as in *I saw a proud/sad man*):

proud	A	(DP_{exp})	(PP_{of})
sad	V	(DP_{exp})	(PP_{about})

Can these entries be simplified? It turns out that the first one can. Note that unlike Vs or Ps, As and Ns never take a DP complement. How come there is such a gap? Note also that when we have pairs of related verbs and nouns as in destroy/destruction, finalize/finalization, the verb takes a DP complement and the noun always takes an *of* PP complement. We can make sense of the gap: Ns take DP complements – like related verbs – but there is a general rule that such a DP must be preceded by *of*. More generally, Ns and As do take DP complements, but this general rule of *of* insertion applies. This means that the presence of *of* is predictable so that the lexical entry for *proud* (and for relevant nouns and adjectives) could really be adjusted to the following:

proud A DP_{exp} DP

However, since we will not really discuss how this follows, we will code *proud* as selecting for *of*.

Complementizers
Here are the lexical entries of some complementizers we have already seen:

that	C	+tense	TP[+tense]
if	C	+tense, +q	TP[+tense]
for	C	–tense	TP[–tense]
whether	C	+q	TP

These entries contain unnecessary information. First note that if C is +tense, it selects a +tense TP, if it is -tense, it selects a -tense TP, and if it is unspecified for +/–tense, it does not impose a requirement on TP. It is in fact generally true that the nature of TP is thus entirely predictable on the basis of the tense specification of C. We could remove the tense specification on TPs throughout. But we can go even further, as Cs always take a TP complement: this is an intrinsic part of being a C. We can therefore simplify these entries as follows:

that	C	+tense
if	C	+tense, +q
for	C	–tense
whether	C	+q

Clearly, the +/–tense specifications are needed since, in effect, this is what drives the choice of the right TP. How about the feature +/–q? The following **minimal pair** shows it is needed to distinguish a verb like *think* from a verb like *know*.

(27) a. John thinks that/*whether Bill left
b. John knows that/whether Bill left

Tense: infinitive to, *present, past, future*

Let us now turn to the category tense. Here is what we could initially state for the Ts we have seen (as usual, we notate the present T as *e* and the past T as *ed* to suggest how they are pronounced; we could also notate them as "pres" and "past"):

will	T [+tense]		$\underline{DP_{nom}/CP}$	VP	meaning: future
e	T [+tense]	bound V	$\underline{DP_{nom}/CP}$	VP	meaning: present
ed	T [+tense]	bound V	$\underline{DP_{nom}/CP}$	VP	meaning: past
to	T [−tense]			VP	

Clearly, the tense specifications are needed. But we can omit VP since all Ts select a VP. So we simplify these entries as follows:

will	T [+tense]		$\underline{DP_{nom}/CP}$	meaning: future
e	T [+tense]	bound V	$\underline{DP_{nom}/CP}$	meaning: present
ed	T [+tense]	bound V	$\underline{DP_{nom}/CP}$	meaning: past
to	T [−tense]			

Now not all Ts select a subject, but note that all tensed Ts select a subject, and the options are the same for all: a nominative DP, or a CP. In principle we should able to simplify these entries. How to do so turns to be a tricky question though and will only become clear in Chapter 12. We leave the entries as they are for now.

Part of the problem here comes from the fact that verbs also select the subject of TP. Another side of it is this: a TP with *to* can also have a DP subject, e.g. *for him/*he to be unhappy is unusual*, where the form of the DP is not nominative, but accusative. Should we add to the lexical entry of *to* that it allows a subject DP or not? This question can only be answered by further investigation. We find infinitives with and without subjects in our inventory of structures, e.g. *for Mary to be happy, to be happy*. This could be coded as a lexical property of *to*, i.e. it could optionally select for an accusative DP subject, but this optionality is conditioned by other factors, as seen in the following: (*for *(Mary) to be happy, I consider [*(Mary) to be a happy person], *John to be on time is surprising*). Since we see either the C *for* or V play a significant role in the possible presence of *Mary*, this is not a property that is controlled by the lexical item *to*, hence it will not be coded as a lexical property of *to*.[3]

Notation: In **(Mary)* the star is on the parentheses. This means that the parentheses are disallowed: *Mary* must be present. In *(*Mary)* the star is on *Mary*. This means that *Mary* disallowed: *Mary* must be absent.

6.9 The Projection Principle and Locality

As we saw, the lexical requirements of the elements appearing in a syntactic tree must be satisfied. Following Chomsky (1981), we called this relatively obvious but fundamental requirement the Projection Principle:

[3]This raises the question where this property should be coded: in general it is a property that is assumed to be coded as a property of Ps and certain Cs, called Case (Chomsky, 1981).

Projection Principle: Properties of lexical items must be satisfied.

We now ask: how must such properties be satisfied? Among the properties are syntactic selectional properties. By examining the phrases we have found, and by looking at what is impossible, we can find out what contexts lead to satisfaction. As in morphology, we see these properties must be satisfied "locally" in a tree.

We have already observed numerous cases where a syntactic head imposes selection requirements on other constituents of phrases: each item selects a distinctive kind of complement, subject, and adjunct. Consider the following examples:

(28) a. *[that Bill came] elapsed
b. *Henri wonders the bathtub
c. *Sue put
d. *Sophie will theater

Each example is deviant because some lexical requirement of some item is not satisfied:

(a) *elapse* requires a DP subject
wonder does not tolerate a direct object DP, it requires a +q CP complement
put requires two (pronounced) complements: a DP (theme) and a PP (normally denoting a location)
will takes a VP complement, not an NP

But now consider the following examples:

(29) a. *Time is sure that Bill elapsed
b. *Mary wonders that John said if Bill left
c. *Henri told Sue in the drawer that Bill put socks

They are all seriously deviant. Let us examine them in turn:

(30) a. The adjective *sure* requires an animate subject, and there is such a subject in the structure, namely *Bill*. And the verb *elapse* requires a subject that talks about time, and there is such a subject in this sentence namely, *time*. What goes wrong here is that the subject that *sure* requires must be the subject of its clause in the structure. Similarly, the subject that *elapse* requires must be its own subject, not the subject of some other verb.
b. *Wonder* requires an *if*-clause as a complement, and there is one, namely *if Bill left*. And *say* requires a *that*-clause as a complement, and there is one, namely *that John said if Bill left*. Again we have the same problem: if a verb requires something as a complement, this complement must be realized in the structure as the verb's own complement, as its sister.
c. *Tell* wants a DP complement and a CP complement, while *put* wants a DP and a PP. This PP cannot occur as a complement of *tell* instead.

The general idea then is this: if a head requires a complement, this complement must be realized as the head's own complement, i.e. as its sister. We have illustrated this with verbs, but this is a very general property.

Local satisfaction of lexical requirements can also be illustrated with a C like *that*, which requires its own complement to be a tensed TP.

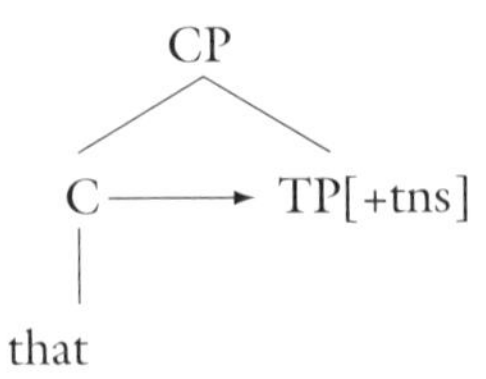

Another illustration can be given for T. We have seen that a [+tense] T requires a nominative subject. This is what differentiates the following two sentences:

(31) a. She will win the race
b. *Her will the race

The subject of a tensed clause in English must be in the nominative case. The nominative form of the 3rd person singular feminine pronoun in English is *she*, not *her*. We can state this requirement by saying that a [+tense] T requires a nominative subject as *its* subject.

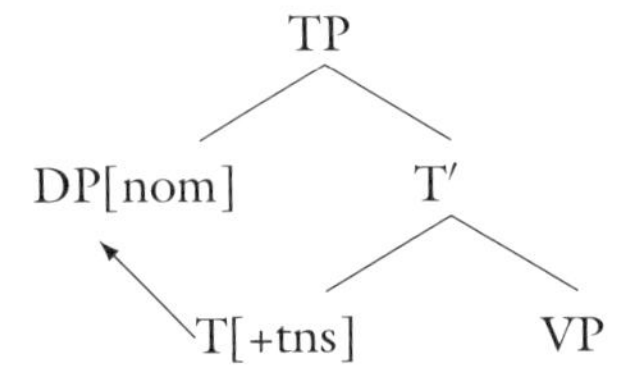

And another example involving D:

(32) a. John's book
b. * John the book, *John $D_{ind,pl}$ books
c. * 's book

A *-'s* D head of a DP (call it DP-'s) requires a DP subject (32a), but neither *the* nor the silent indefinite plural D does (32b). (32c) is ill-formed because this subject *must* appear as the daughter of DP-'s.

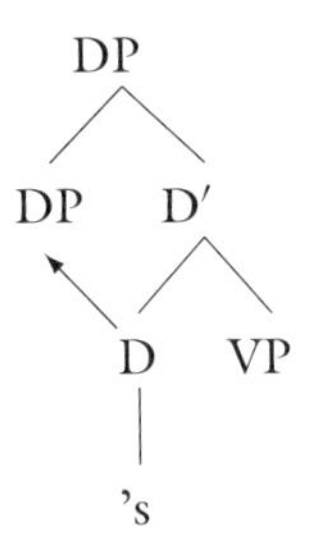

The same is true of adjuncts. An adjunct like *for an hour*, which can modify a VP like *paint the house* but not a VP like *reach the top*, can occur as an adjunct to the VP it modifies, and not to some other VP occurring in the same sentence. This gives us a simple picture of the Locality Requirement on Selection:

(33) **Locality of Selection for Syntax (preliminary)**:
a. If α selects β as complement, β is a complement of α.
b. If α selects β as subject, β is the subject of α.
c. If α selects β as an adjunct, β is the adjunct to α.

In our discussion of small clauses in Section 6.7, we have seen that the subject of verbs, adjectives, and prepositions satisfy this locality requirement, which suggests a very simple statement of locality of selection: selected elements must appear within a projection of the selector.

However, there is a major complication. We have also seen that if a verb in a (non-small) clause requires a subject, this subject must be the subject of the very clause whose VP is headed by this verb. For example, in the case of the verb *elapse* above, its subject appears as the subject of the TP containing the VP.

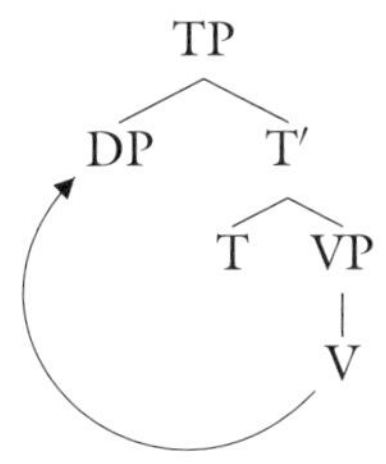

So there is a locality condition, a restriction on where c-selection requirements can be satisfied, but it is not a simple one.

> Technically, the modification we introduced above to deal with subjects does not work. Let us accept it as is for now. We return to this in Chapter 9, when we will have all the necessary ingredients to understand what is happening. There we will see that, superficially, the picture is obscured by structural distortions (which we will call movement or Move). Once we factor these out, simplicity will be restored.

(34) **Locality of Selection for Syntax (preliminary):**
   a. If a α selects β as complement, β is a complement of α.
   b. If a α selects β as subject, β is the subject of α or the subject of the clause containing α.
   c. If α selects β as an adjunct, β is the adjunct of α.

6.10 Cross-linguistic Variation

X-bar theory says something about how subjects and complements, and heads and adjuncts, are hierarchically organized in a given category, but does not entirely predict linear order. For example, there is no reason why a complement could not precede its head.

If we let subjects, heads, and complements order freely in a given category, there are six possible orders:

SHC HCS HSC SCH CHS CSH

But if X-bar theory is correct, some of these orders should be excluded, even though X-bar theory says nothing about the order of sisters. Because X-bar theory says that a head combines with its complement first, we predict that the subject cannot intervene between them. This excludes the two orders:

HSC CSH

However, when the head is the V in a simple clause, and we consider the order of V, subject, and object, we see that the first of the excluded orders corresponds to the common language type VSO, which describes languages in which typical neutral clauses have the verb first, then the subject, then the object. Mechanisms other than simple X-bar structure will be needed to explain this, and, as we are already seeing, mechanisms that distort simple X-bar orderings are independently motivated (and ubiquitous). We return to this question in the next chapter.

In English, all categories seem to follow the same order: SHC. This may suggest that the order is fixed once and for all in a given language and all categories in this language conform to it. If true, we would expect that when we turn to another language, all categories in it should conform to a unique order.

The linguist Joseph Greenberg compiled word order information about normal or basic word ordering in about 30 languages. He stated many findings as being universal among languages[4] (Greenberg, 1978). Some of these putative universals remained true after his study was extended by others to a much larger set of languages. See, for example, Dryer (1992). Among these are the following two observations:

Universal 2: In languages with prepositions, the genitive almost always follows the governing noun; in languages with postpositions, it almost always precedes.

Universal 4: With overwhelmingly greater than chance odds, languages with normal SOV order are postpositional.

One way to interpret Universal 4 is that there is a correlation between the order of the verb with respect to its complement and the order of the preposition with respect to its complement. This is what is expected if X-bar theory is correct and ordering is fixed once and for all for each language.

It is easy to verify Universal 2 for English, if we count under "genitive" *of*-complements to nouns, as in *student of chemistry*.

A language that standardly places a head before its complements is called Head-Initial. Head-initial languages include English, Zulu, Arabic, and many others. A language with the complement before the head is called Head Final, and languages of this type include Japanese, Turkish, Korean, and Quechua.

That there is cross-categorial uniformity is not predicted by X-bar theory itself, since X-bar theory does not, for example, constrain whether a complement should precede or follow its head. Greenberg's universals do not say "always," they say "almost always" or "with overwhelmingly greater than chance odds." This means that there appear to be mixed languages, for example, those with a certain order in one category but a different order in another (German is verb-final but complementizer-initial, has prepositions, not postpositions). There are even languages that allow both orders for the same category, like Dutch, whose PPs can be prepositional or postpositional. That there should be any serious tendency or correlation is surprising. It may suggest that further analysis is required. One possibility is that the system is regular, but the regularities are obscured by distortions, the very distortions responsible for obscuring the simplicity of Selection Locality.

The geographical distribution of basic constituent orders appears to be non-random too, which is to be expected since people that live near each other will tend to be linguistically (and genetically) closely related. The SOV languages cover most of Asia except the southeast, most of New Guinea, and most of North America (excluding American English, of course), except for parts of the northwest and Central America. SVO is found across central Africa, Europe, and parts of Asia. For maps of SVO and other related language features see, for example, Haspelmath et al. (2005).

[4]This notion of universal should not be confused with another usage, which is universal grammar or UG, the set of universal principles that characterizes the human language faculty.

6.11 Conclusion

6.11.1 Summary: the model of syntax

We are now in a position to provide an overall picture of our syntactic model. This is not the final version (one major ingredient is missing, which we will introduce in Chapter 8, and some further modifications will be entertained in Chapter 12) but its basic architecture is not going to change. This is what we have so far:

- We take the **atoms** of syntax to be words, that is the well-formed outputs of the morphological component. As a result, the categories of syntactic atoms are the same as the morphological categories. The *syntactic* lexicon includes all these atoms with their individual properties.
- These atoms (the words) can be assembled into complexes (syntactic molecules). These syntactic molecules have an internal structure that can be represented by labeled trees (with lines that do not cross).
- We call the operation of combination **Merge**. Merge can be seen as a function mapping n-tuples of trees (a set of trees) into a new or **derived** tree.
- Syntactic molecules and atoms can be further compounded to form still larger entities representable by labeled trees. This means that syntactic Merge is **recursive**.
- Well-formed trees – the output of (repeated) Merge operations, arise as a result of the interaction between the following properties:
  i. Lexical properties of individual atoms determine the environments in which they can occur, in accordance with the **Projection Principle**.
  Projection Principle: Properties of lexical items must be satisfied.
  ii. **Locality of selection**: If an atom selects an element, it acts as a head. This head must have the selected element or a molecule headed by the element as its complement or its subject, or as the subject of its TP. Selection is local in the sense that there is a maximal distance between a selector and what it selects.
  iii. **n-ary branching**: In syntactic trees, a mother node can have many daughters because Merge is an n-ary function: it can merge several trees into a single new one. In practice, there are no more than three or four daughters to a single mother.
  iv. **X-bar theory**: The hierarchical organization of syntactic trees is conjectured to be constrained by X-bar theory: across categories, a head X takes zero or more complements, zero or one subjects, and zero or more adjuncts. The head X forms a constituent with its complements: X′. X′ in turn forms a constituent with its subject: XP. XP can form XP constituents with its adjuncts.

> **Practice**
>
> Compare the picture of the model of syntax with the picture of the model of morphology: note all similarities and differences.

Note that we have not included **ellipsis** in our syntactic model. Ultimately, it should be included. One concrete way (by no means the only one – there are alternatives) of thinking about the ellipsis operation is as follows: the output of syntactic Merge is a labelled tree. Ultimately, it must be converted into a phonological representation. Ellipsis can be thought of as allowing (certain) constituents to remain silent, to have no phonological output.

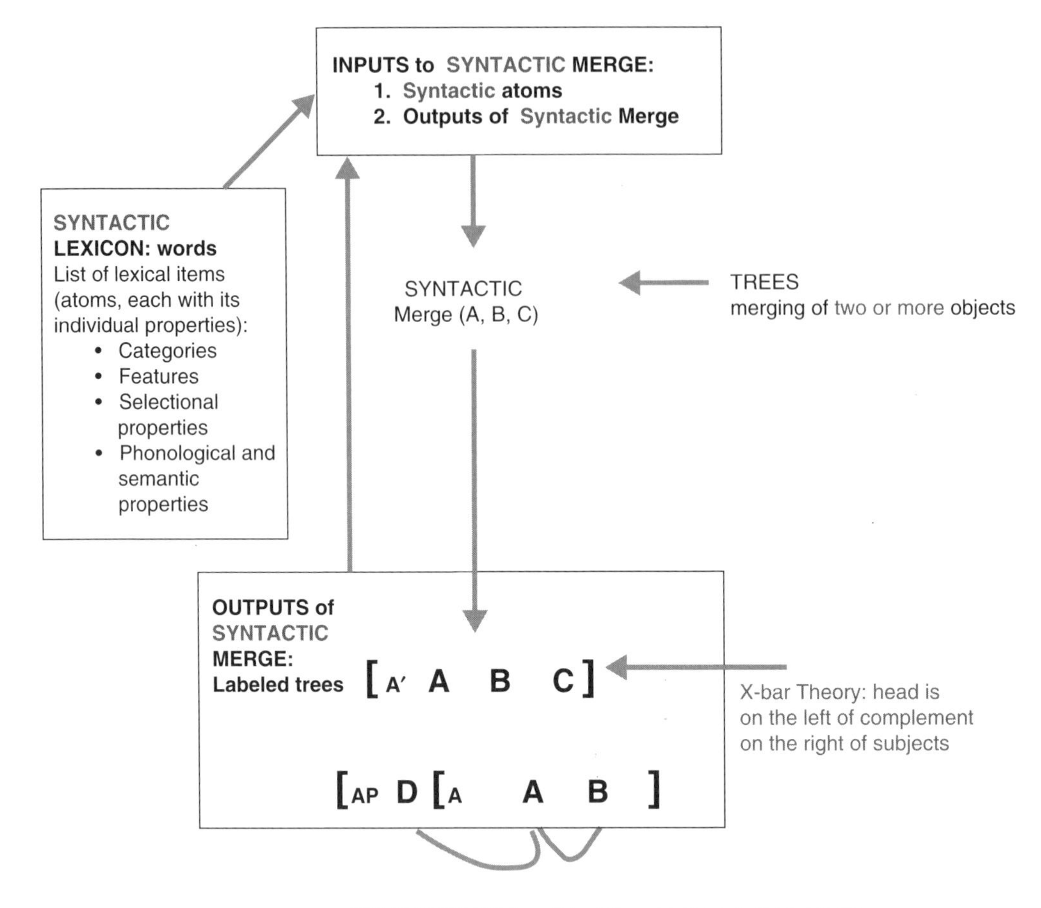

Figure 6.2 Model of the syntactic component

6.11.2 What to remember

We are starting to accumulate quite a few results. It is important to keep in mind how we got here and what the major results are. We have made extensive use of the constituency tests introduced earlier. It is essential to be familiar with them in order to understand what is at stake in X-bar theory. In turn, it is important to know and to be clear about the explicit claims of X-bar theory. To do this, one must be able to fluently use the basic terms used to talk about tree geometry.

You should know the basic architecture of the models of syntax and of morphology: what pieces there are, what their function is, and how they interact with each other. You should also know how and why we decide to code particular observations as we do. In particular, it is essential to remember that what goes into the lexicon is unpredictable information.

6.11.3 Puzzles and preview

It is puzzling how similar the models of syntax and morphology are: same basic organization, same kind of operation of Merge, which can be recursively applied. Still, they are substantial differences: binary vs. n-ary Merge, RHHR vs. X-bar theory, different kinds of atoms. Another difference has to do with how local selection is. We come back to the kind of questions this raises in Chapter 12.

The comparative lack of simplicity and elegance in our syntactic version of locality of selection is addressed in Chapter 8. As we will see, locality of selection appears to be massively violated, but only in very specific ways. We will require an understanding of these violations to simplify how locality should be characterized.

6.11.4 Further exercises

(1) NP or DP?

Consider the following coordinated sentence:

(1) Mary puts apples in the fridge in Los Angeles, but she puts them on the table in New York

(i) What is the label of the constituent that is coordinated? Why?

(ii) The first sentence contains two locative PPs. Apply constituency tests and draw the first conjunct in the tree. Discuss if:
  a. *in the fridge,* as used in this sentence, behaves as a complement or an adjunct;
  b. *in New York,* as used in this sentence, behaves as a complement or an adjunct.

(iii) Should the maximal projection of tomatoes in the above sentence be labeled NP or should it be an NP contained in a DP? (Hint: use the clue in the sentence!).

(iv) Draw a hypothetical structure consistent with your findings.

(v) If there is a DP, what would the head of the DP be? Discuss how this relates to the discussion surrounding silent Ds in the main text.

You may also want to bring in the following examples in your discussion:

(2) a. Does Mary like brownies? Yes, she likes them.
  b. Mary likes brownies and the other things you prepared for her.
  c. Monkeys are mammals. They live in the forest.
  d. Did your niece put the ballot in the box?
  e. Oh sure! Yes, she went over there and put the ballot in the box she did!
  f. *Oh sure! Yes, she went over there and put the ballot she did in the box.

(2) Samoan determiners

Samoan, a Polynesian language spoken in Samoa and Western Samoa, and in immigrant communities elsewhere, has singular and plural "indefinite" (similar to *a* or *some* in English) and "definite" determiners (like *the* in English). (The distribution of these determiners is slightly different from English, with the definite determiner occurring in some contexts where English uses an indefinite, but this is not important for this particular exercise.)

The distribution of these determiners is shown below. The determiners are glossed by their Samoan form in small caps. The third line is a free translation. Note that only the pronounced parts of Samoan are glossed in the second line, which is the important line for the analysis. It is important to keep in mind that sometimes heads can be silent: this information cannot be reliably found in glosses, since linguists will have to do linguistic detective work to deduce their presence.

(1) a. ʔaumai se maile
  get SE dog
  "Get (me) a/some dog"

  b. ʔaumai ni maile
  get NI dog
  "Get (me) (some) dogs"

c. ?aumai le maile
get LE dog
"Get(me) the dog"

d. ?aumai maile
get dog
"Get (me) the dogs"

Examine these examples very carefully and then answer the following questions, referring back to the examples.

(i) Does Samoan make a distinction between singular and plural nouns?
(ii) Compare (a), (b), (c), and (d), and describe how singular and plural are indicated.
(iii) Given its meaning, what would you label this category?
(iv) Give the lexical entries for *se, ni,* and *le,* assuming that they combine with an NP sister, using the format presented in Section 5.7.1. (You can use +def to refer to definite and –def to refer to indefinite.)
(v) What to make of (1d)? Would it be insightful to conclude there is a silent head in (1d)? What would the category and lexical entry for this head be? (Cf. Section 6.5).
(vi) Briefly compare the Samoan D system with the English D system for the four sentences above. What does your comparison suggest about the distribution of silent categories cross-linguistically?

Does it look predictable? Arbitrary? If particular instances of Ds can be silent, how many other different types of (audible) determiner systems could we in principle expect to find in the world's languages? (Answer this question under the (almost certainly too simple) assumption that Ds can be +def or –def, singular or plural.)

(3) Optionality and adjuncthood

Since the prepositional phrase *to me* can be omitted in the following example:

(1) John seems (to me) to be smart

a student concludes this shows that *to me* in the above sentence is an adjunct. Is this a correct conclusion? Explain your answer (one or two sentences).

(4) Obligatoriness and complementhood?

The English verb "to word" requires the presence of the following constituents:

(1) a. Bill worded the letter carefully
b. * Bill worded carefully
c. * Bill worded the letter

From this, a linguist concludes that "carefully" is a complement of the verb "to word."

Is this conclusion justified? If it does, "carefully" should behave as a complement and combine with *word* as a sister. Apply constituency tests and show whether this conclusion finds independent support or not. Then draw your conclusion.

(5) Theta roles

For each of the underlined verbs or adjectives below, list the elements it c-selects and the role of these elements.

(1) The short-circuit <u>caused</u> the fire
(2) Mary is <u>looking</u> for Mr. Right
(3) Moritz <u>is accustomed</u> to <u>finding</u> strange people hiding in his closets

(4) Denis prefers for the understudy to bring him his socks
(5) The landlord took the candy from the baby
(6) The office informed Mary that her visa had expired
(7) Doris was pleased with the results of her sinister plan
(8) Max returned every bicycle to its rightful owner
(9) It turned out that Regis preferred the Merlot
(10) The officer gave Mary directions to the opera

6.11.5 Further reading

The development of X-bar theory sketched in this chapter is approximately the understanding that was reached in the early to late 1980s. For further readings see Chomsky (1970) where the fundamentals of X-bar theory are first outlined, as well as Emonds (1976), Jackendoff (1977), Stowell (1981), Stowell (1983), and Baker (2003).

The Projection Principle is introduced in the very important Chomsky (1981), which laid the foundation for the development of the Principle and Parameters theory of syntax of the 1980s.

There is a very large literature dealing with thematic relations. For an excellent overview and discussion of some central issues, see Baker (1997). See also Pesetsky (1995) for an illustration of the kind of analytical problems one faces in theta theory (in this case concerning *psychological* or *psych predicates*).

The principles of X-bar theory, together with word order parameters, yield different surface word order typologies. X-bar theory leads to the expectation that OV languages and VO languages are symmetric images of each other. The advanced and very important Kayne (1994) challenges this view. Kayne shows (among many other things) that the theoretical expectations of such a theory are not borne out. The general points in this book can be appreciated with a basic understanding of X-bar principles, but many chapters in the book require a deeper understanding of how surface structures are put together, and an appreciation for the complex interactions that characterize the syntax of human languages. This book is also notable for setting out to derive the principles of X-bar theory, and putting the derivation of X-bar theory squarely on the general research agenda. This is further taken up in Chomsky (1995a), where a theory of *Bare Phrase Structure* is introduced. Bare Phrase Structure is in essence adopted throughout the remainder of the present book.

7
Binding and the Hierarchical Nature of Phrase Structure

We have described a model of syntax in which structures are "projected" to locally satisfy lexical requirements in a way that conforms to the requirements of X-bar theory. According to this model, the constituents of a sentence stand in hierarchical relationships of containment, which can be represented with a tree.[1]

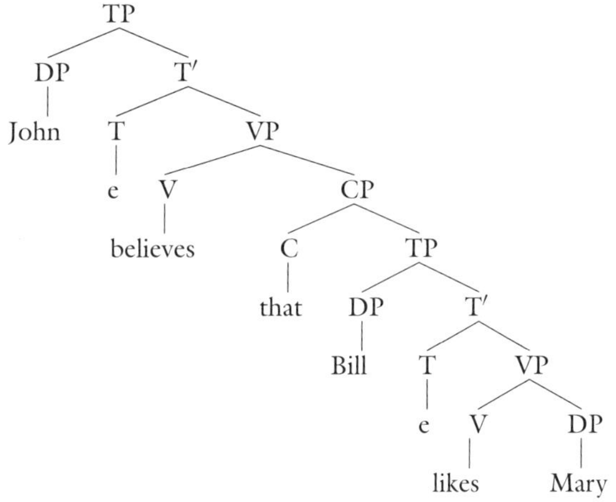

TP
DP T′
John T VP
e V CP
believes C TP
that DP T′
Bill T VP
e V DP
likes Mary

These hierarchical structures are constructed by satisfying the lexical properties of items entering into the structures, in accordance with the principle of locality of selection. These structures are independently justified by constituency tests.

[1] A careful look at the tree above shows that the present tense verb *believes* is placed under V. This should be surprising, since we have argued in Chapter 2 that *believes* should have the structure *[T [V believe] pres]* and that T should be under T in the tree and select VP etc. **In this chapter only**, we will ignore this issue, as it has no bearing on anything we discuss here, and we will draw trees as above. We will deal with verb placement properly in the following chapter. Recall also that as discussed on p. 133 in Section 6.4, we often omit the X' level when it makes no difference to what we are discussing, to keep the trees simpler. No ambiguity is created in these examples in English, since complements always follow the head while subjects precede it.

An Introduction to Syntactic Analysis and Theory, First Edition.
Dominique Sportiche, Hilda Koopman, and Edward Stabler.

One of the major results in this chapter will be some surprising confirmation for these structures, as well as new tools to investigate constituent structures, which come from some observations about how sentences are interpreted.

When we want to refer to a particular person, the person named "John," we sometimes use the DP *John*, but not always. We may also use a description that uniquely identifies him to our "audience," by using, for example, a DP like *the young boy who lives next door*. We could refer to someone named John by using any of the underlined expressions below:

(1) a. John came in.
b. Then, John left
c. He took his umbrella
d. He hurt himself with it when he tried to open it
e. The idiot can't even open an umbrella!

We can refer to John by using the name *John*, a pronoun *he*, a reflexive *himself*, or even an epithet like *the idiot*. We can also use the pronoun *it* to refer to John's umbrella. Thus we can paraphrase the last three sentences in the following very awkward way (although in the last one, we lose some information – namely that the speaker thinks John is an idiot):

(2) a. ?* John took John's umbrella
b. ?* John hurt John with John's umbrella when John tried to open John's umbrella
c. John can't even open an umbrella!

Because they stand for nominal expressions, reflexives (and reciprocals) and pronouns are called the class of pronominal expressions. Since a name or a description could be used to refer to a particular individual or an object, we may wonder why a language like English (or any other human language) bothers to have pronouns or reflexives at all. One motive is probably the conversational principle that you should be no more specific about things than necessary (especially with regard to matters that are already obvious!), but we will also see later that certain ideas cannot be expressed just with names or descriptions. Pronominal expressions play a fundamental role in human languages. In general, a pronoun or an epithet can be used to refer to some person if there is some reasonable way to find out who the pronoun is referring to. For example, we have already seen that we can use the pronoun *he* in a sentence to refer to John, if John was previously mentioned. We can also use a pronoun in a sentence to refer to John if the DP *John* is used elsewhere in the same sentence, or even if John has never been mentioned before, as in:

(3) a. John said he was sick
b. The TA who graded him says that John did really well

We can indicate that *John* and *he* or *him* refer to the same person by putting a "subscript" or "index" i on each of the phrases, which is interpreted as saying that each of these refers to an individual i. This is just a convenient notation: if two phrases have the same index, they are meant to be **coreferential**, to refer to the same entity (real or fictional, in some sense that we will not try to be too specific about). If they have different indices, they are meant to refer to different objects, to be **non-coreferential**.

We will assume for the moment that reference is exclusively a property of DPs (not of nouns, adjectives, NPs, or CPs). In this text, an index is thus always going to be an index on a DP.

Accordingly, the two sentences above can be rewritten as:

(4) a. John$_j$ said he$_j$ was sick
b. [The TA who graded [him]$_j$]$_k$ says that John$_j$ did really well

If the pronoun in the first sentence does not refer to John, we would write:

(5) John$_j$ said he$_k$ was sick

Certain combinations, however, seem impossible. For example, even if John has been mentioned previously in the discourse, or made prominent in some other way, the following sentences (a) and (b) are impossible, even though (c) and (d) are fine:

(6) a. * Himself should decide soon
b. * Mary wrote a letter to himself last year
c. He should decide soon
d. Mary wrote a letter to him last year

Similarly, in the case in which John has not been mentioned in previous discourse but is mentioned in the sentence, the following sentences are impossible:

(7) a. *John$_j$ hurt him$_j$
b. *John$_j$ says Mary$_k$ likes himself$_j$
c. *Herself$_j$ likes Mary$_j$'s mother$_k$
d. *He$_j$ heard that [the idiot]$_j$ should win.
e. *He$_j$ saw John$_j$

In this chapter, we will investigate a small number of the problems raised by such sentences. A second chapter (Chapter 13) will go into these matters more deeply.

It turns out that the description of these patterns depends on the structures of the sentences. This is a nice surprise, since we did not consider these patterns at all in our earlier development of syntactic theory. The fact that the theory nevertheless provides the structures we need to describe these new patterns constitutes strong independent evidence that we are on the right track.

7.1 Anaphors

Languages contain a class of **anaphoric** items. The reference of these elements cannot be determined by examining them the way we do with *Mary* (which refers to the salient person called Mary) or *the boy next door* (which refers to the salient boy next door). Pronouns are anaphoric: they depend on something else for their interpretation, e.g. a pointing act or an antecedent in the discourse. A core class of anaphoric elements in English are reflexives pronouns, (*myself, yourself, herself, himself, itself, ourselves, yourselves, themselves*) and reciprocals like *each other*. We use the term **anaphors** to refer to reflexive pronouns and reciprocals, and the term **pronoun** to refer to personal pronouns *he, him, it, I, me*, etc.

7.1.1 Reflexive pronouns

Reflexives and reciprocals seem to differ minimally from pronouns: they cannot be used unless there is a coreferential DP in the same sentence:

(8) a. [Mary]$_i$ likes [herself]$_i$, *[Herself]$_i$ likes [the movie]$_i$
b. [Our rabbit and the neighbor's cat]$_i$ like [each other]$_i$
c. [The boys]$_i$ fought with [each other]$_i$, * [Each other]$_i$ went to the store$_i$

The reflexive in the first sentence refers to the same entity as the subject *Mary*, and the reciprocal indicates mutual reference in a group of some kind. That is, the sentences roughly mean:

(9) a. ?* Mary likes Mary
b. Each of our rabbit and the neighbor's cat likes the other
c. Each of the boys fought with (some of) the other boys

Let's begin exploring the distribution of reflexives, i.e. where they can occur and where they produce nonsense, with some simple sentences. A first point is illustrated by these examples:

(10) a. I saw $John_j$. * Sue_i likes $himself_j$.
b. I saw $John_j$. * $Himself_j$ was laughing.

The point is the following:

(11) A reflexive must be coreferential with another DP, its antecedent, *in the same sentence*.

Another basic point is illustrated by these examples:

(12) a. The boy_i likes $himself_i$
b. * The boy_i likes $herself_i$
c. * The boy_i likes $themselves_i$
(13) a. The $girls_i$ like $themselves_i$
b. *The $girls_i$ like $themself_i$
c. * The $girls_i$ like $herself_i$
d. * The $girls_i$ like $yourselves_i$

The point here is:

(14) A reflexive must *agree* with its antecedent in person, number, and gender.

English reflexive anaphors are (at least) bimorphemic: they apparently consist of a pronoun + *self*. Ignoring complex cases, the pronominal part of the reflexive anaphor must agree in person, number, and gender with its antecedent, the *self* part only agrees in number. (Note that the pronoun does not agree in case with the antecedent (*he likes heself.) We will not explore the internal structure of reflexives here, but we will see later (e.g. in Chinese, Chapter 13) that it may play an important role in understanding the distribution. From such a study, we may hope to understand why reflexives behave the way they do. For now, we will simply leave this question aside and treat reflexives like pronouns and names – that is, as DPs without internal structure.

Now we get to the tougher issues. Why are the following simple examples no good? They satisfy our requirements (11) and (14):

(15) * $Himself_i$ likes $John_i$
(16) * $John_i$'s mother likes $himself_i$

We might try explaining (15) by hypothesizing that the reflexive is in the wrong case (it should perhaps be in the nominative case – we could expect *heself*, *Iself*, which, interestingly, do not exist), or that the antecedent must precede the reflexive, but neither of these ideas would account for (16). It turns out that a different, unified account for these two cases is possible, one that we can find by comparing the structures in which the reflexive cannot find an antecedent, like (16), with structures like (17) below, which is fine. A box around the DP identifies the DPs we are concerned with.

(17)

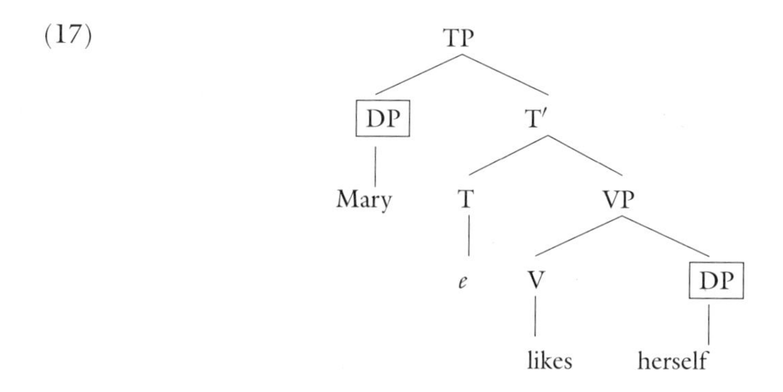

Now compare the tree (18) for sentence (16):

(18)

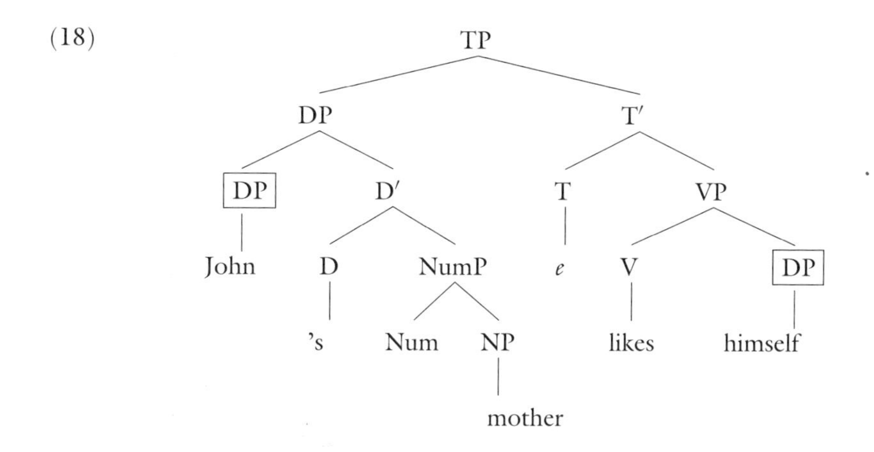

There is a simple proposal about the relevant difference between these structures: roughly, the reflexive must be included in the constituent that is a sister of the antecedent. Or from the point of view of the anaphor, when searching for its antecedent, a reflexive can only choose an immediate child of one of its ancestor nodes. It cannot search inside the children of its ancestors. This idea is usually expressed using a basic structural relation called **c-command** (where the "c" is meant to evoke "constituent"), an important notion which we will see over and over again later:

C-command: Node X **c-commands** node Y if a sister of X dominates Y.

This relation can be illustrated graphically with a simple tree. It is the relation between X and anything under a sister of X, here Z, which dominates everything under the triangle below, e.g. Y:

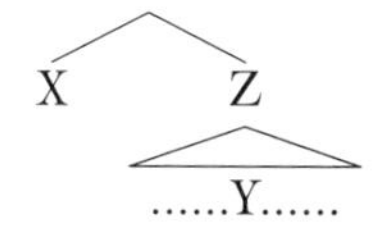

Figure 7.1 Configuration where X c-commands Y

The importance of c-command: The notion of c-command is extremely important. It pays attention to the geometry of the tree, and thus can corroborate or help discover constituency. It plays a role in a great variety of phenomena, syntactic and semantic. We will make extensive use of this notion in Chapter 11. Although geometric dependencies were appealed to before, the importance of this particular notion was discovered by Tanya Reinhart in her 1976 Ph.D. dissertation, a version of which was published as Reinhart (1983). Note that this relation does not care about node labels. To check c-command, it is sufficient to draw a constituent tree without any labels. We will do this occasionally.

We can now state the following principle:

(19) The DP antecedent of a reflexive must c-command the reflexive.

So the DP *John* in (16) with tree (18), is not a possible antecedent because it does not c-command the reflexive: indeed, the constituent sister to the DP is D′, and this D′ does not contain the reflexive DP. Notice that the requirement (19) also explains why (15) is deviant: in (15), there is no DP at all that c-commands the reflexive. (The reader might want to check that this is true.)

So now we have three special requirements associated with reflexives: (11), (14), and (19). These explain the following data:

(20) John_i believes that Bill_j saw himself_j
(21) * John_i believes that Bill_j saw himself_k

(20) is okay because the reflexive has the c-commanding antecedent DP *Bill*, with which it agrees in person, number, and gender.

Practice

Draw the tree structure of (20) to verify this. The relevant part will be the embedded clause. Its tree structure looks very much like (17).

(21) is deviant because the indices indicate that we are trying to interpret the reflexive as having no antecedent in the sentence at all – and that is ruled out by (14). There is, however, a third possible way of interpreting this sentence, which we can make more transparent by including indices:

(22) * John_i believes that Bill_j saw himself_i

This sentence is deviant. If we replace the reflexive by a name (*?John$_i$ believes that Bill$_j$ saw John$_i$*), the result is very awkward, but one can make sense of the result.

None of our three conditions are violated in this last sentence. What then explains the deviance of this example? Looking at the structure for (22), we can see that the DP *John* is a possible antecedent in the same clause; it c-commands the reflexive, and the antecedent and the reflexive agree in person, number, and gender.

A natural idea about (22) is that the antecedent *John* is "too far away" from the reflexive – there is a closer one available, namely the DP *Bill*. Even if there is no closer alternative, the sentence remains deviant, as in the following sentence, in which *Mary* is of the wrong gender to function as an antecedent for *himself*:

(23) * John_i believes that Mary_j saw himself_i

One natural hypothesis would require that the antecedent and the reflexive be "clausemates" in the following sense:

(24) The reflexive and its antecedent must be in all of the same TPs.

In (22), we see that there are two TPs. One of them is the whole sentence, while the other is just *Bill saw himself.* Since *John* is not in the smaller TP but the reflexive is, they are not close enough together. (24) properly rules this example out. (Check: is this compatible with our earlier examples too?)

The antecedents we have considered so far have all been DP subjects of TP. Since DPs can occur in other positions too, it is important to consider whether our requirements properly handle everything. A DP can be the complement of a verb, the complement of a preposition, or the subject of a DP. Can any of these positions c-command reflexives? The object of a verb does not c-command the subject of the verb, but it can c-command DPs in other complements. One construction that is like this is when an object DP is the antecedent of a prepositional object. It looks like we make the right prediction about these cases:

(25) Mary revealed John$_i$ to himself$_i$
(26) * Mary revealed himself$_i$ to John$_i$

We can check this on the following constituent tree (which shows just enough tree geometry) where the arrow indicates c-command:

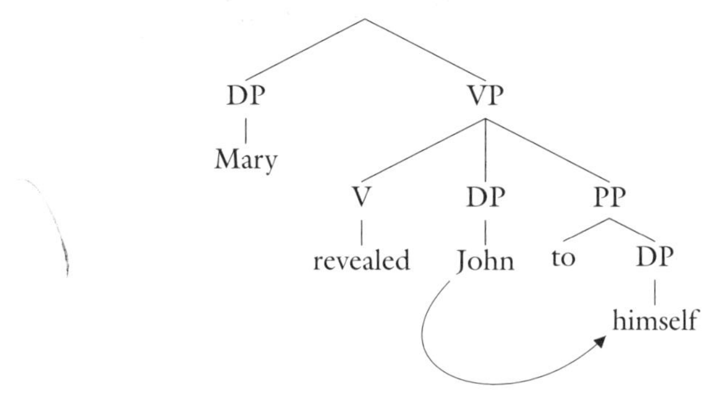

The DP has as sister the PP that includes the reflexive: the DP c-commands the reflexive, but not vice versa.

DPs can have subjects, just as TPs. When we consider the subject of a DP in subject position, we get the following cases right:

(27) Mary$_i$'s pictures of herself$_i$ surprised Bill
(28) I noticed John$_i$'s excessive appreciation of himself$_i$

In (27), the DP *Mary* does not c-command *Bill*, but it does c-command *herself.*

Practice

To follow the arguments and convince yourself, it is important to try and draw the structure of (27) and the examples below.

The first step is always to figure out the structure. For complex strings, determine what the main V is. How many arguments does it require? Which one is the subject? Which one is the object? In (27), is *Mary's picture of herself* a constituent? (Use a constituent test.) What is the internal structure of this string?

The special requirements on reflexives listed so far capture a wide range of their distributional facts. But there is another a context that we do not yet make the right predictions about. Compare (27) with this example:

(29) a. Mary$_i$ noticed John$_j$'s excessive appreciation of himself$_j$
b. * Mary$_j$ noticed John$_j$'s excessive appreciation of herself$_i$

Why is (29b) so much worse than (27)? When we hit a surprise like this, the first step to figuring out what may be going on is to consider the structure carefully:

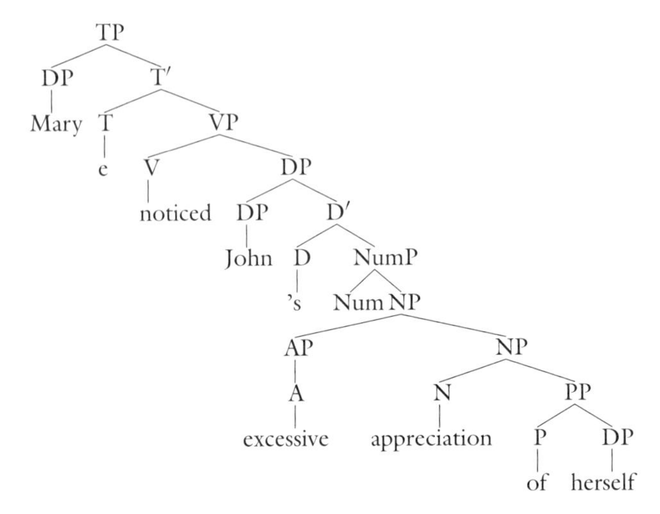

Notice that in this tree, both DPs *Mary* and *John* c-command the reflexive, and they are in all the same TPs (since there is only one TP, namely, the whole sentence). But now it is tempting to treat this case in exactly the way we handle the following:

(30) *[$_{TP}$ Mary$_i$ noticed that [$_{TP}$John excessively appreciates herself$_i$]]

This sentence is itself ruled out because the reflexive and the subject are not in all the same TPs. But we can see that the TP here [*John excessively appreciates herself*] is similar to the DP [*John's excessive appreciation of herself*], and so the DP, like the TP, seems to be able to prevent the reflexive from seeking an antecedent outside of it. We can capture this similarity with the following modification:

(31) The reflexive and its antecedent must be in all the same TPs and in all the same DPs.

The idea here is that a DP defines the same kind of local domain as a TP does: reflexives must find their antecedents in these local domains. We may wonder why TPs and DPs are singled out in this fashion. One answer immediately suggests itself: those are the two types of constituents that we have seen that have subjects. It is thus plausible that it is the very fact they have a subject that makes them local domains. We could modify (31) to:

(32) The reflexive and its antecedent must be in all the same XPs that have subjects.

Statements (31) and (32) make different predictions. Suppose we have a DP without a subject that contains a reflexive. According to the first statement, the antecedent of this reflexive should nevertheless be found within this DP. Not so according to the second. The following sentences show that the second statement is better:

(33) a. John$_k$ loved [the new pictures of himself$_k$]
b. I showed Mary$_k$ [several portraits of herself$_k$]

Both of these sentences are fine under the indicated coindexing even though the reflexive is inside a bracketed DP without a subject. This shows that the presence of a DP-internal subject is crucial, not the DP boundary itself.

To review, we have suggested that reflexives have the following four special requirements.

(34) a. A reflexive must be coreferential with another DP in the same sentence, its antecedent.
b. A reflexive must agree with its antecedent in person, number, and gender.
c. The DP antecedent of a reflexive must c-command the reflexive.
d. The reflexive and its antecedent must be in all the same XPs that have a subject.

The first of these requirements is semantic: it refers to how the reflexive is interpreted. The second is a general requirement imposed on coreferential DPs. It also applies to the relationship between a name or a description and a pronoun when they corefer. The reason for it is clear: person, number, and gender specifications restrict the referential options of DPs. Agreement means that the reflexive or the pronoun and its antecedent must be restricted in the same way to be able to corefer. The third and fourth requirements clearly involve the syntactic configurations in which the reflexives appear: these configurations restrict where reflexives can occur, and provide independent confirmation of our syntactic analyses.

A fundamental result: This is a fundamental result of contemporary syntactic theory. We see systematic correlations between our conclusions regarding constituency based on the tests discussed in Chapter 3 and the geometrical predictions made by c-command.

The first, third, and fourth requirements are usually grouped together and given the name of **Principle A** (or sometimes **Condition A**) of the Binding Principles, also referred to as the **Binding Theory**.

Principle A: An anaphor needs a c-commanding antecedent which is in all the same XPs with a subject.

(This formulation of Principle A is a bit "wordy." Further introduction and clarification of terminology in Section 7.1.3 will lead to the following final statement "an anaphor must be bound in its domain.") These four restrictions on reflexives provide an account of our first examples of reflexives, and it will turn out that we have set the stage for explaining similar examples with pronouns (see Section 7.2). We have also set the stage for explaining the much more complex examples that we will see in subsequent chapters.

Why not . . . ? Why this proposal rather than some possible alternatives?

Alternative 1: Part of the rationale behind Principle A was that the reflexive seemed "too far away" in examples like (22) and (30). So why not formulate Principle A as Principle A′ below?

Principle A′: The antecedent of an anaphor must be the closest c-commanding DP in the sentence.

Alternative 2: In fact, why can't we replace both (34c) and Principle A with this even simpler idea:

> Principle A″: The antecedent of an anaphor must be the DP that is closest to it in terms of the number of words. (This would mean only the linear string would be relevant.)

Let's explore how these alternatives fare. Both account for the data in our examples (22) and (30), as the antecedent of the reflexive is the closest DP both in terms of the structure (it is the first DP that c-commands anaphor) and in terms of words.

(35) a. (=22) * John$_i$ believes that Bill$_j$ saw himself$_i$
b. John$_i$ believes that Bill$_j$ saw himself$_j$

(36) a. (=30) * Mary$_i$ noticed that John excessively appreciates herself$_i$
b. Mary$_i$ noticed that John$_j$ excessively appreciates himself$_j$

However, these two contexts do not discriminate between the different hypotheses. We need to look at contexts where they all make different predictions. Here are some examples in which Principles A′ and A″ make the wrong predictions. Consider this one:

(37) a. Mary$_i$ appreciates only [[John] and herself$_i$]
b. ?? Mary$_i$ appreciates [John$_j$ and himself$_j$]

Here, A′ and A″ both incorrectly predict that (37a) should be bad. Since (37b) is also bad (perhaps because it is just a weird thing to say, not because it is ill-formed), one may think that the closer DP *John* does not count. It is easy to see, however, that this cannot be the case.

(38) a. Mary$_i$ described Bill to herself$_i$
b. Mary described Bill$_i$ to himself$_i$

And consider these cases:

(39) a. * The man who interviewed [Nelson Mandela]$_i$ appreciates himself$_i$
b. [The man who interviewed Nelson Mandela]$_i$ appreciates himself$_i$

(40) a. * The biographer of [Elizabeth Bishop]$_i$ appreciated herself$_i$
b. [The biographer of [Elizabeth Bishop]$_i$]$_j$ appreciated himself$_j$

Here A′ and A″ have a different problem: the DP *the biographer of Elizabeth Bishop* and the DP *Elizabeth Bishop* both end at the same position and have the same structure. This means they are the same distance from the reflexive (in terms of number of words), showing the number of words for is irrelevant. Hence A″ does not work. Instead, in these cases, only one of the DPs is a possible antecedent – namely, the c-commanding one, as our Principle A requires.

7.1.2 Reciprocals

The proposals about reflexives also extend to reciprocals – there are some well-known differences but we mostly set them aside here. The general point is that reciprocals are also anaphors in English, and thus subject to Principle A above. The earlier example of a reciprocal is repeated below, with its intended meaning spelled out underneath:

(41) a. [Our rabbit and the neighbor's cat]$_i$ like [each other]$_i$
b. [Our rabbit *x* and the neighbor's cat *y*] are such that [*x* likes *y* and *y* likes *x*]

A reciprocal requires an antecedent that is plural.[2] This antecedent must c-command the reciprocal, and it must be close enough: within all the same XPs that have a subject, exactly like reflexives:

(42) a. John$_i$ heard their$_j$ criticism of each other$_j$
b. John$_i$ heard their$_j$ criticism of themselves$_j$

(43) a. * They$_i$ heard John$_j$'s criticism of each other$_i$
b. * They$_i$ heard John$_j$'s criticism of themselves$_i$

(44) a. John heard that they$_i$ criticized each other$_i$
b. John heard that they$_i$ criticized themselves$_i$
c. *They$_i$ heard that John$_j$ criticized each other$_i$
d. *They$_i$ heard that John$_j$ criticized themselves$_i$

We will not explore the internal structure of reciprocals and, like reflexives, treat them as pronouns and names – that is, as DPs without internal structure.

Practice

Go through all the examples of this chapter and replace each instance of a reflexive by a reciprocal and each instance of an antecedent by a plural DP. The status of each resulting sentence should be the same as before the change.

7.1.3 Summary and reformulation

The previous section considers how anaphors, i.e. reciprocals and reflexives, relate to their antecedents in English sentences, as in the following simple examples:

(45) a. John$_i$ likes himself$_i$
b. The students$_k$ boys are proud of themselves$_k$

Antecedents of reflexives can be names (*John, Mary, etc.*) or descriptions (*the student, a book, etc.*). They can also be quantified DPs, like the following, which allows us to express things that really cannot be expressed in any other way.

(46) a. Everyone here$_i$ likes himself$_i$
b. No Italian spy$_k$ betrayed himself$_k$

These sentences cannot be paraphrased the way we did for names or descriptions, as (a) and (b) show below. This would give a completely different meaning.

(47) a. Everyone here likes everyone here # wrong meaning!!
b. No Italian spy betrayed no Italian spy # wrong meaning!!

Rather they seem to stand for a list of statements. Thus, if the people in the room are Albert and Lucille, the first sentence expresses the conjunction of the following sentences:

(48) a. Albert likes himself
b. Lucille likes herself

[2] Unlike reflexives, reciprocals do not wear their number marking on their sleeves. Even if they are not marked plural, they require a plural antecedent, probably because of the meaning of "other" they contain.

Similarly, if there are two Italian spies, say Marco and Leonardo, the second sentence expresses the conjunction of the following sentences:

(49) a. Marco did not betray himself
b. Leonardo did not betray himself

To convey the meanings of such sentences, we use a more complex type of paraphrase (using what is called a variable, noted as x here):

(50) a. If x is a person here, x likes x — or alternatively:
b. For every person x, x likes x
c. If x is an Italian spy, x did not betray x — or alternatively:
d. For no Italian spy x, x betrayed x

The powerful expressive capability which we see here in reflexives (which we will also find with pronouns) is very important and is found in some form in all human languages. (See Section 7.7 for discussion of a number of these languages.) This may well be one reason why languages have reflexives and pronouns.

For such cases like (47), it is a bit strange to talk about "coreference", i.e. of "referring-to-the-same-objects-as" between the reflexive and its antecedent. This is particularly clear in the case of the sentence *no Italian spy betrayed himself*. What does the DP *no Italian spy* refer to?

How to compute the meaning of such expressions is a very interesting question. We need to be precise about this if we want to understand how exactly such DPs function as antecedents for reflexives and reciprocals (or even pronouns). But this is not a question we will address here. We will simply assume that the antecedent does its job of determining how the reflexive is interpreted without spelling it out in detail.

Because coreference is not quite the right notion, we modify our terminology. We will say that an anaphor needs to be **bound**, by which we mean that the anaphor has to be c-commanded by and coindexed with its antecedent DP. (The term **bound** as defined here should not be confused with the meaning of *bound* as in bound morpheme.)

(51) A DP is **bound** (by its antecedent) just in case there is a c-commanding DP which has the same index.
(52) The **domain** of a DP anaphor is the smallest XP with a subject that contains the DP.

These notions encode the most important conclusion to remember, namely that the way anaphors are associated with their antecedents depends on the syntax. We can now reformulate our findings using these notions:

Agreement: An anaphor must agree with its antecedent in person, number, and gender (not case).

Principle A: An anaphor must be bound in its domain.

Principle A combines three requirements that were stated separately in the previous sections:

a. an anaphor must have an antecedent; and
b. the antecedent must c-command the anaphor; and
c. the antecedent must be in the domain of the anaphor, i.e. it must be in all the same XPs with a subject as the anaphor.

The "domain" in which an anaphor must find its antecedent can be indicated in a tree. Consider again a few examples like the following:

(53) a. I_i heard $John_j$'s criticism of $himself_j$
b. * I_i heard $John_j$'s criticism of $myself_i$
c. $John_j$ heard that I_i criticized $myself_i$
d. * I_i heard that $John_j$ criticized $myself_i$

We can indicate the domain of a reflexive by putting a box around the nodes that are in the same XPs with a subject as the reflexive. This is called the **domain of the reflexive**. It will always be the smallest XP with a subject that contains the reflexive.

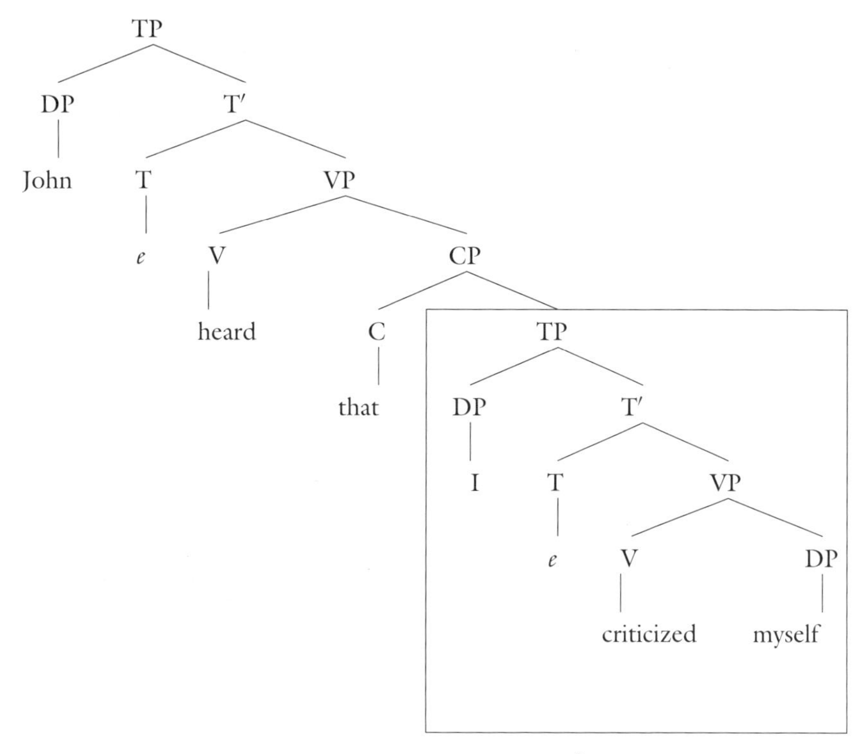

This perspective on binding and domains is still simplified,[3] but it will suffice for the moment.

7.2 Pronouns

7.2.1 Basic Principle B

If we collect a sample of the examples considered in the previous section and change the anaphors to simple accusative pronouns, in most cases the good sentences become bad and the bad ones become good:

(54) a. $Mary_i$ likes $herself_i$
b. *$Mary_i$ likes her_i

[3]We remind the advanced reader that at this point VP-internal subjects have not yet been introduced and motivated.

(55) a. [Our rabbit and the neighbor's cat]$_i$ like [each other]$_i$
b. * [Our rabbit and the neighbor's cat]$_i$ like them$_i$

(56) a. [The boys]$_i$ fought with [each other]$_i$
b. * [The boys]$_i$ fought with them$_i$

(57) a. I saw John$_j$. * Bill$_i$ likes himself$_j$.
b. I saw John$_j$. Bill$_i$ likes him$_j$.

(58) a. I saw John$_j$. * Himself$_j$ laughs.
b. I saw John$_j$. He$_j$ is laughing.

(59) a. The boy$_i$ likes himself$_i$
b. * The boy$_i$ likes him$_i$

(60) a. The girls$_i$ like themselves$_i$
b. * The girls$_i$ like them$_i$

(61) a. * John$_i$'s mother likes himself$_i$
b. John$_i$'s mother likes him$_i$

(62) a. * John$_i$ believes that Bill$_j$ saw him$_j$
b. John$_i$ believes that Bill$_j$ saw himself$_j$

(63) a. John$_i$ believes that Bill$_j$ saw him$_i$
b. * John$_i$ believes that Bill$_j$ saw himself$_i$

There is clearly a regularity here. Pronouns seem to be in complementary distribution with anaphors. (We will see that this is not quite true below, but it covers all the cases we have seen so far.) We can summarize this symmetric behavior by stating that:

> If a relation between an anaphor and an antecedent is fine, replacing the anaphor by a pronoun with the same antecedent yields a deviant result. And vice versa, if a relation between an anaphor and an antecedent is deviant, replacing the anaphor by a pronoun with the same antecedent yields a fine result.

Adopting this tentative approximation, we can account for the distribution of pronouns by requiring them to satisfy a condition called **Principle B** or **Condition B**, which is the opposite of that which anaphors need to satisfy.

Principle B: A pronoun cannot be bound in its domain (i.e. it cannot have a c-commanding antecedent in its domain).

Note that Principle B says nothing about whether a pronoun needs an antecedent or not. In fact, it is fine for a pronoun to lack an antecedent altogether in a given sentence. The principle only states that if a pronoun has a c-commanding antecedent, this antecedent must be outside the domain of the pronoun, i.e. outside of the smallest XP with a subject that contains the pronoun.

Practice

Go through all the examples in this section, draw their tree, and make sure that Principle B applies as it should.

7.2.2 A complication: lack of complementary distribution

Principle A and Principle B taken together predict that pronouns and anaphors should be in complementary distribution. In truth, complementarity between pronouns and anaphors fails in some contexts:

(64) a. They$_j$ like [[**their**$_j$] **books**]
b. They$_j$ like [[**each other**$_j$]'s books]

The domain of the DP pronoun *their* or the DP reciprocal *each other* is the same: it is the first XP with a subject containing them, i.e. the direct object DP (in bold), yet both examples are fine. Principle B correctly fails to rule out the first sentence. But Principle A predicts that the second sentence is ill-formed (since the antecedent of the reciprocal is the subject of the sentence and thus not in the domain of the anaphor). One standard approach to this problem allows the domain for anaphors to be slightly larger than what we have assumed: anaphors can keep looking a bit further in search of a c-commanding antecedent, so as to satisfy Principle A of the binding theory. The idea then is to make sure that in the anaphor's domain, there is at least one c-commanding antecedent DP. Principle A and B and the notion of domain for a pronoun are left unchanged. We just modify just the notion of *domain* for an anaphor:[4,5]

(65) The **domain** of a DP **pronoun** is the smallest XP with a subject that contains the DP.
(66) The **domain** of a DP **anaphor** is the smallest XP that has a subject *and that has a DP c-commanding the anaphor.*

It should be clear how this modification allows the anaphor in (64b) to seek as antecedent the subject of the clause.

> **Practice**
>
> Draw the tree for (64b). Treat *each other* as a DP with a triangle.

7.3 Non-pronominal Expressions

This chapter started out with a list of ill-formed sentences:

(67) a. *John$_j$ hurt him$_j$
b. *John$_j$ says Mary$_k$ likes himself$_j$
c. *Herself$_j$ likes Mary$_j$'s mother$_k$
d. *He$_j$ heard that [the idiot]$_j$ should win
e. *He$_j$ saw John$_j$

The deviance for the first three now follows from Principle A and Principle B, but not for the last two: in both cases, *he* obeys Principle B, as there is no c-commanding DP antecedent in the TP.

[4]As things stands, this predicts the following should be well-formed: *They$_j$ like [[**theirselves**$_j$]'s books]. Why this form is impossible is currently still not well understood. We will not discuss this problem further here.
[5]A technical note: in (64b), we would not want the anaphor *each other* to count as c-commanding itself. If it did, the modification we just introduced would have no effect. In order to avoid this, we should define the relation of c-command as being non-reflexive, prohibiting any node from c-commanding itself.

Note that the deviance of these sentences remains, even if we separate the pronoun and the name further. This suggests that there is no notion of "domain" involved:

(68) a. * He_i saw John_i/* He_i knows that Mary_j likes John_i/*He_i said [I know [that Mary_j likes John_i]]
b. * She_i likes [the student]$_i$/* She_i knows that Mary likes [the student]$_i$/*She said that they know that Mary likes [the student]$_i$

Proper names (like *Mary*), descriptions (like *the man on the corner, my brother*) or epithets (like *the idiot*) are not pronominals. They are sometimes called **R-expressions**, where the "R" suggests "(independently) referential." Non-pronominal expressions cannot be bound in the way anaphors and pronouns can. However, they may be coindexed with preceding pronouns:

(69) a. * He_i said that Peter_i took the car
b. After you spoke to him_i, Peter_i took the car
c. The builder of his_i house visited Peter_i

What distinguishes (69a) from (69b) and (69c)? In both environments the pronoun precedes the name *Peter*, so that cannot be the reason. The structural relations between the pronoun and the name are different though. *He* c-commands *Peter* in (69a), but does not in (69b) and (69c). We can describe these observations in a preliminary fashion, by stating that non-pronominals cannot be c-commanded by a coindexed pronoun, that is, non-pronominals cannot be bound.

Unlike what happens with Principle A and B, this requirement is not limited to any domain, but goes all the way up to the root node:

(70) a. * He_i said that John_i would leave
b. * He_i said that Mary thought that you talked to the person who saw Peter_i

And when the antecedent is a c-commanding name or description, the sentences are deviant too:

(71) a. *? John_i said that John_i would leave
b. * The student_i said that Mary thought that you talked to the person who saw Peter_i

So we have the following requirement on R-expressions, which we call Principle C, or sometimes Condition C:

Principle C: An R-expression cannot be bound.

7.4 Binding Theory Summarized

We have considered the constructions in which reflexives and pronouns are bound, where "bound" means that their reference is determined by a c-commanding antecedent. The basic facts we have discovered can be summarized in the following simple binding theory, which was proposed in this form by Chomsky (1981).

Principle A: An anaphor must be bound in its domain.
Principle B: A pronoun must be free (= not bound) in its domain.
Principle C: An R-expression cannot be bound.

The domain of an anaphor is the smallest XP-containing a DP c-commanding the anaphor which has a subject. The domain of a pronoun is the smallest XP containing a pronoun that has a subject. (Characterizing the domain precisely proves to be difficult, but this simple characterization works for many cases.) We also noticed the agreement requirements:

Agreement: Pronouns and reflexives agree with their antecedent in person, number, and gender.

A number of tricky issues have been set aside but, as a first approximation, this formulation of the binding theory provides a powerful analytical tool to probe syntactic structure.

7.5 Small Clauses and Binding Theory

Recall that we found subjects across categories when we postulated small clause constituents in Section 6.7. This conclusion can be further confirmed by the Binding Theory. Remember that the domain of a DP is the set of nodes included in the smallest XP with a subject that contains the DP. Now that we have more subjects than we thought, we should be able to check these new kinds of constructions. We find exactly the behavior that the binding theory predicts:

(72) a. * John_j heard [Mary describe himself_j]
b. John_j heard [Mary describe him_j]
(73) a. John heard [Mary_j describe herself_j]
b. * John heard [Mary_j describe her_j]
(74) a. * Mary_j considers [John proud of herself_j]
b. Mary_j considers [John proud of her_j]
(75) a. Mary considers [John_j proud of himself_j]
b. * Mary considers [John_j proud of him_j]

Intuitively, to find the domain of an anaphor or a pronoun, we locate the DP in the tree and move up the structure until we find an XP with a subject. This is the domain. A pronoun cannot have a c-commanding antecedent in this domain. For an anaphor, the domain must also contain a DP that c-commands it, and the anaphor will have to be bound in that domain.

> **Practice**
>
> Go through each of the examples above and verify how the binding theory correctly predicts the pattern of data.

The following example is consistent with the notion of binding domain we have introduced for anaphors:

(76) John_i considers himself_i proud of Mary

The analysis above suggests that [*himself*$_i$ *proud of Mary*] is an AP with a subject. The domain of the anaphor, however, extends to the main TP since this AP does not contain a c-commander of the anaphor. When we examine complements of the verb *believe*, we will see that the same reasoning leads to the same conclusion for sentences like the following:

(77) John_i believes himself_i to be proud of Mary

Small clauses and binding puzzles:
The following example seems to pose a problem for the notion of binding domain we introduced for pronouns:

(79) * John$_i$ considers him$_i$ proud of Mary

The domain of the pronoun should be limited to the AP. Within this AP, it is free. The sentence should be fine, contrary to what we observe. Extending the domain would get us into trouble in other places, like (80) below, in which coreference between the pronoun and the subject of TP is fine:

(80) They$_i$ like their$_i$ books

Providing a fully fledged account of this problem is beyond what we can do here. Let us note simply that in order to distinguish the two examples, it is useful to note that in the latter example, the case (genitive) of the pronoun is determined internally to the domain of the pronoun, but in the former example, the case is determined by the verb, which is external to the domain of the pronoun. We will leave this a puzzle for now, but will return to these questions in Chapters 10 and 13.

For exactly the same reason, the following example is wrongly predicted to be well-formed:

(78) * John$_i$ believes (that) himself$_i$ is proud of Mary

We leave this as a puzzle for now, but return to it in Chapter 13.

7.6 Some Issues

We have only begun to develop our syntactic model, but even just considering the kinds of constructions we have talked about so far, we can spot some tricky issues for our Binding Theory. We will briefly mention some of them, but leave a more careful development of the theory for later.

7.6.1 Coreference without binding

We proposed that R-expressions cannot be bound. What then of the following sentences:

(81) a. That$_i$ is [a bird]$_i$
b. That$_i$'s [the truth]$_i$
c. He$_j$ is John$_j$

There are many such cases.

(82) [Bob Dylan]$_i$ is [Robert Zimmerman]$_i$
(83) [Ice-T]$_i$ and [Tracy Marrow]$_i$ are [the same person]$_i$

What should we say about these? They look like Principle C violations. There are a number of complex issues here, but one main idea is that coreference between these DPs is the very point of the meaning of these sentences: coreference is asserted. So in a way, there is coreference not because of binding, but because of the meaning of the verb. That is, two expressions can be coreferential when they are related to a verb (e.g. *be*) that requires it, even if there is no binding. This implies that these strings are good if there is no coindexing.

Here is a similar case. Imagine a party in which most people come in casual clothes but one guy comes in a white tuxedo, and everyone notices the guy in the white tuxedo. Now suppose we know that John was at the party. Then we can say

(84) John saw him. John saw the guy in the white tuxedo, since everyone did!

But what if John was the guy in the white tuxedo (and maybe we didn't know it)? Then what we said really has forbidden coreference relations:

(85) $John_i$ saw him_i. $John_i$ saw [the guy in the white $tuxedo]_i$.

These look like Principle B and C violations. Again, what we want to say here is that there is no binding, but just a kind of "accidental" coreference: two expressions end up being coreferential just because of the circumstances, even when it is not intended or assumed by the speaker. In this case, clearly, it is not a result of binding theory that the expressions are coreferential. Note that, in a way, this case is the opposite of the previous case. In the previous case, coreference was asserted by the speaker and that was fine. Here it is not asserted nor assumed, and it is fine too.

7.6.2 Quantified antecedents

Like anaphors, pronouns can relate to an antecedent in a way that cannot be characterized as involving coreference: they can take their referential value from some other DP even if this DP does not have a reference. As we have seen with reflexives, coreference will give the wrong result. Let us illustrate this again. Unlike anaphors, pronouns can have antecedents in the previous discourse, or, like anaphors, somewhere in the same sentence, so long as the DP is not c-commanding the pronoun or inside the domain in which the pronoun cannot be bound (i.e. so long as there is no violation of Principle B):

(86) $John_i$ was lying on his_i bed. He_i was dreaming.
(87) $John_i$ believed he_i could get elected

In such cases, their semantic value is that of the antecedent. The sentences above have the following paraphrases:

(88) John was lying on his bed. John was dreaming.
(89) ? John believed John could get elected

But is this always possible? The answer is negative on two counts.

First the semantic value of the pronoun is not always that of the antecedent. Instead, we have to use a different way to represent the meaning of the sentence (intended to capture the idea that these sentences really stand for a list of statements). Using # to indicate a meaning that a sentence does not have, we can illustrate this with the following examples, in which the coindexing is intended to indicate what the interpretation of the pronoun depends upon:

(90) $Everyone_i$ thinks he_i is smart
 a. # Everyone thinks everyone is smart
 b. For every person x, x thinks x is smart
(91) Who_i in this class thinks he_i is smart
 a. # Who in this class thinks who in this class is smart
 b. For which person x in this class is it the case that x thinks that x is smart

These special translations, these formulas, are needed when the antecedent of the pronoun is a non-referential expression. Unlike proper names such as *John* or *Anna*; or definite descriptions (so called because they describe an object and are [+definite]) such as *the president of the committee*, or *this girl*, or *my Armenian neighbor*; or indefinite descriptions like *a man I met yesterday*, which, in context, pick out real or imaginary objects in the world; non-referential expressions, such *nobody* or *many people*, do not. Among non-referential expressions, we find quantified expressions (typically DPs with a D such as *no*, or *every*, or *each*), such as *several people, few books, no boy, any house, each day, everyone from Singapore, who, which book about ants*, and *how many sandwiches.*

As we saw earlier, these formulas can code the fact that these sentences, in a way, stand for lists of sentences. Suppose that in the sentence below, we understand the pronoun *they* to include Heather, Isabelle, and Marie.

(92) They did not believe they would get elected

If we replace the subject with the quantificational expression *none of the women* "for no x, x is a woman" (Heather, Isabelle, Marie), as the variable x cycles through the various values it can take, the pronoun each time takes the same value as this variable. Thus, in this context, the following three sentences are equivalent:

(93) They did not believe they would get elected
(94) (None of the women)$_i$ believed she$_i$ would get elected
(95) Heather$_i$ did not believe she$_i$ would get elected and Isabelle$_k$ did not believe she$_k$ would get elected and Marie $_k$ did not believe she$_k$ would get elected.

Not having to use an explicit list is particularly useful because such lists could in principle be infinite (even uncountably so) as in:

Every real number can be squared

This is an important property that natural languages have since it allows us to talk about infinitely many things.

Second, these cases have something else that is special. Compare the following pairs:

(96) a. Descriptions of Bill$_j$ usually please him$_j$
b. *Descriptions of [every girl]$_j$ usually please her$_j$
(97) a. The mayor of John$_j$'s hometown wrote to him$_j$
b. * The mayor of everyone$_j$'s hometown wrote to him$_j$

(98) a. I showed your description of John$_j$ to him$_j$
b. * I showed your description of [every boy]$_j$ to him$_j$

These facts suggests that the binding relation between a pronoun and its (non-referential) antecedent is sensitive to structure. Pronominal binding seems to work when the non-referential antecedent c-commands the pronoun, it fails when there is no c-command.

(99) **Condition on Pronominal Binding**: If a pronoun has a quantified expression as antecedent, the pronoun must be c-commanded by this antecedent.

One particularly striking case of this requirement is given in the coordinated structures below, or the two discourse fragments that follow:

(100) [[John$_j$ came in] and [he$_j$ was wearing a hat]]
(101) [[Nobody$_j$ came in] and [*he$_j$ was wearing a hat]]
(102) John$_j$ came in. He$_j$ was wearing a hat.
(103) Nobody$_j$ came in. *He$_j$ was wearing a hat.

The second sentence of the second fragment has the quantified antecedent *nobody*, but there is no c-command, so binding is prohibited.

Note finally that in a sentence in which the antecedent of the pronoun is not a quantified expression, there should now be two ways to think about its meaning:

(104) Mary$_i$ thinks that she$_i$ is smart
(105) ?Mary thinks that Mary is smart
(106) For *x* Mary, *x* thinks *x* is smart

It turns out that this is correct and we can illustrate the difference very simply: the missing VP in the following VP ellipsis case can be interpreted in the two different ways indicated (we will not discuss this in any detail):

(107) Mary$_i$ thinks that she$_i$ is smart and Bill does too
(108) = Bill thinks Mary is smart
(109) = Bill thinks he (Bill) is smart

Putting in the two versions of the meaning of (104) explains why:

(110) ?Mary thinks that Mary is smart, and Bill does think that Mary is smart too
(111) If *x* is Mary, *x* thinks *x* is smart, and if *x* is Bill, this is true too (Bill thinks that Bill is smart)

VP ellipsis can thus give rise to ambiguity. The first meaning is called the **strict identity** reading because the pronoun in the missing VP is interpreted exactly like its counterpart in the antecedent VP. In the second meaning, the pronoun is interpreted differently than its counterpart. This meaning is called the **sloppy identity** reading.

7.6.3 VP ellipsis

On the topic of VP ellipsis, interesting complications arise in constructions where both ellipsis and binding relations are involved. Consider these facts, for example:

(112) I$_i$ like Mary$_j$ and she$_j$ likes me$_i$
(113) * I$_i$ like Mary$_j$ and she$_j$ does too

Why is (113) bad? A natural idea is that it violates Principle C. Our treatment of VP ellipsis works fine here, in that it makes the right predictions:

(114) * I$_i$ like Mary$_j$ and she$_j$ does [like Mary$_j$] too (intended: she likes herself too)

Even though the VP is elided, i.e. is just marked as unpronounced, *Mary* is present in the structure and the meaning. It is also present in the structure that Principle C can see and is thus subject to Principle C!

This does not extend to more complex cases, raising interesting questions (which we will not further discuss here, but the problem can be appreciated):

(115) I$_i$ think John likes Mary$_j$ and she$_j$ does too
(116) I$_i$ think John likes Mary$_j$ and she$_j$ does [think that John likes Mary$_j$] too
(117) I$_i$ think John likes Mary$_j$ and she$_j$ does [think that John likes her$_j$] too

Vehicle change:
This phenomenon whereby an unpronounced element can behave not exactly like its antecedent but instead, for example, like a pronominal equivalent of this antecedent, is called **Vehicle Change**. It is discussed in a variety of contexts, pertaining to the interaction of binding theory and ellipsis (as in e.g. Fiengo and May, 1995), but also in the contexts of movement dependencies that we discuss in Chapter 8. In this last context, it raises questions about how to understand exactly what the trace of movement is, and in particular the so-called **Copy Theory of Traces**. See for example Safir (1996) or Fox (2002).

We would expect example (116) to be ill-formed, because, at some level, it has the structure of the second sentence. Instead, (116) is good, and it seems as if the elided name is allowed to be treated like a pronoun in this case (so like example (117)).

7.7 Cross-linguistic Variation

The binding relations described here are based on modern English. How generally valid are they? This is a difficult question. Superficially, other languages have different properties. It would be nice to have a binding theory that specified exactly the range of variation that could be expected in any language, the range of variation that is really due to the facts about how people determine binding relations. Unfortunately, linguistic theory has not yet reached this stage. To provide an initial impression of the kind of significant extensions and revisions needed for binding in other languages, we provide a quick sample of some of the variation found.

7.7.1 Reflexives

There is a lot of variation in the form of reflexive, and many languages have more than one way to express the reflexive. Often, reflexivity is expressed by a bound morpheme: Russian *-sja*, Swedish *-s*, Icelandic *-sk*, Fulani "middle voice morphemes," Maasai *-a*, Quechua *-ku*.

Quechua:

(118) Riku-chi-ku-ni
see-cause-self-1s
"I caused myself to be seen," or "I gave myself away"

In other languages, there are special unstressed pronouns, called "clitics," that express reflexivity. Take French:

Jean lave l'enfant	Jean se lave	Jean s' est lavé
John washes the-child	John self washes	John self is washed
"John washes the child"	"John washes himself"	"John has washed himself"

Many languages have "simple" reflexives: French *se, soi*, Dutch *zich*, Icelandic *seg*, Japanese *zibun*, Mandarin Chinese *ziji*:

French	Dutch	Chinese
Quand on parle de soi	Jan waste zich	Lisi hai-le ziji
When one speaks of (one)self	John washed self	Lisi hurt-ASP self

Some of these same languages have complex reflexives that consist of more than one morpheme as well:

Dutch	Chinese
Jan zag zichzelf	Lisi hai-le taziji
John saw himself	Lisi hurt-ASP himself

The distribution of the anaphor seems to depend, at least in part, on its morphological complexity. For example, the simple anaphors like *ziji* in Chinese or *zibun* in Japanese differ from the English *himself* in that they can take an antecedent outside the TP that contains it ("long-distance anaphors"). Complex anaphors do not allow this, even in the same languages:

Chinese:

(119) Zhangsan$_i$ renwei [Lisi$_j$ hai-le ziji$_{i,j}$]
Zhangsan think Lisi hurt-ASP self
"Zhangsan thought that Lisi hurt himself/him"

(120) Zhangsan$_i$ renwei [Lisi$_j$ hai-le taziji$_{*i,j}$]
Zhangsan think Lisi hurt-ASP self
"Zhangsan thought that Lisi hurt himself"

Japanese:

(121) Tarooi$_i$ga Hanako ni [[zibun$_i$ Amerika e itta] koto o]
Taroo NOM Hanako DAT self America to go. PAST that
hanasanakatta
tell.NEG.PAST
"Taro did not tell Hanako that he had been to the States"

Many questions arise concerning the distribution of anaphors. How exactly should long-distance anaphora be treated? Why does the form of the anaphor matter for the distribution? What precisely is the local relation to antecedent, and what semantic role can the antecedent have? What syntactic function must it have? We answer some of these advanced questions in Chapter 13.

7.7.2 Pronouns

Just as the behavior of anaphora is complex cross-linguistically and certainly not as straightforward as our binding theory leads us to expect; the distribution of pronouns is complex too. Again, some very brief remarks.

Pronouns can be like DPs in their distribution, roughly occupying the same positions as lexical DPs (as is the case in English), or they can be bound morphemes (subject or object "agreement" morphemes). Sometimes, we find "portmanteau" morphemes that express subject and object agreement at the same time, where no individual parts can be distinguished:

Inuktitut, West Greenlandic:

(122) taki-va-ssinga
see-IND-you(PL)me
"I saw/see you(pl)"

Maasai, Eastern Nilotic:

(123) ´ɛ-dɔ̀l-ɨ́tà toret
3S-see-PROGR Toret
"he is looking at Toret"

(124) kɨ́- dɔ̀l-ɨ́tà (kɨ́- = he-you or you-me)
he.you- see- PROGR,
or you.me-see-PROGR
"he is looking at you", or "you are watching me"

(125) ɨ́-dɔ̀l-ɨ́tà toret
you-see-PROGR Toret
"you are watching Toret"

In many other languages, pronouns are expressed as clitics:

French: Je te l' ai donné
I you it have given

Czech: Karel mi je dal
Karl to.me them gave

Some languages allow a pronominal subject to be absent (these languages are called Null Subject or "pro-drop" languages):

Spanish: Lo hemos cantado
it have.1.PL.PRES sung
"We have sung it"

Some languages allow sentences without any overt agreement or pronoun present:

Japanese: yonda
read-PAST
"He/she/I/you/they read"

Some languages have interesting pronominal systems that show distinctions that do not exist overtly in English. Dogrib, an Athapaskan language of Northern Canada, has a pronominal form that is referred to as the 4th person. This pronoun needs a c-commanding antecedent, and thus may not occur in the environment below (this is what it has in common with an anaphor):

Dogrib: * ye-zha shïː£¡eti
ye-son 3.ate
"Her son ate"

But when it has an antecedent, it must be disjoint from it (this is what it has in common with a pronoun):

John$_i$ ye$_{*i,j}$-mo e?i
John *ye*-mother 3.saw
"John$_i$ saw his$_j$ mother"

Many native American languages have 4th person pronouns or agreement markers; in general, their distribution has not been studied very extensively.

Some languages have two series of 3rd person pronouns. This is the case of Abe, a Kwa language spoken in the Ivory Coast (Niger-Congo). One series basically behaves as English pronouns, but the other series does not at all. For example:

Abe "o-series" behaves like English pronouns:

(126) yapi$_i$ wu o$_{i,j}$ wo n
Yapi saw his dog D

Abe "n-series" behaves differently:

(127) n_i wu n_i wo n
he saw he dog D
"He saw his dog"

(128) Yapi$_i$ wu n$_j$ wo n
Yapi saw n dog D
"Yapi$_i$ saw his$_j$ dog"

Nothing in our binding theory leads us to expect this. Clearly, if we want to explore the kinds of binding relations that the human mind can create and recognize, figuring out binding systems in diverse languages will be very important.

7.7.3 R-expressions

You might think that while pronouns and anaphors might vary from one language to another, names and descriptions and other R-expressions are probably basically the same in all languages, at least with respect to their binding properties. That is, you might think: as in English, R-expressions in language generally cannot be bound. But even this does not seem to be true. Lasnik and Uriagereka (1988) report that in Thai, sentences like this are perfectly fine:

(129) cɔɔn$_i$ chɔ̂ɔp cɔɔn$_i$
John likes John
"John likes himself"

(130) cɔɔn$_i$ khít wâa cɔɔn$_i$ chàlàat
John thinks that John is smart
"John thinks that he is smart"

Looking further into this, it turns out that the restrictions on binding R-expressions are not simply missing. Rather, they appear to be different. That is, there are cases of R-expression binding that are bad:

(131) * khǎw$_i$ chɔ̂ɔp cɔɔn$_i$
he likes John

(132) * khǎw$_i$ khít wâa cɔɔn$_i$ chàlàat
he thinks that John is smart

It appears that, in Thai, an R-expression can be bound, but not by a pronoun. Looking back at English, it seems that maybe we have the same contrast, but it is partly hidden by the availability of reflexives:

(133) John$_i$ likes himself$_i$
(134) * John$_i$ likes John$_i$
(135) ** He$_i$ likes John$_i$

7.8 Learning About Binding Relations

The binding conditions outlined above are rather abstract, and obviously most children do not get any explicit instruction about them, so how are they acquired? That is, how do children come to use the pronouns and anaphors in their language correctly? This question has been extensively investigated, with a number of surprising results. One surprise is that children belonging to various linguistic groups interpret reflexive pronouns in accordance with Principle A by the time they are about 3–4 years old, regardless of whether the expression of the reflexive is a clitic, as in Spanish, or a full word, as in English (Padilla, 1990; McKee, 1992). What is more surprising is that other binding principles seem to arise very differently. McKee (1992) tested and compared the ability of Italian and English children to understand sentences like these:

1. Lo gnomo lo lava
   the gnome him washes
   "The gnome washes him"
2. Mentre la gnoma era sdraiata, la puffetta la copriva
   while the gnome was lying-down, the smurf her covered
   "While the gnome was lying down, the smurf covered her"

For adults, in sentence (1), the antecedent of the pronoun cannot be local (or intraclausal, labeled IC), the antecedent must be non-local (or extraclausal, XC). Testing sentences like (1) and (2) to see what antecedents the children allowed, the Italian children aged 3–4 performed almost like adults on a simple task, but the English children of the same age had considerably more trouble: the *yes*'s and *no*'s in the table represent the adult grammars.

	1IC (no)	1XC (yes)	2IC (no)	2XC (yes)
Italian children, %correct	85	97	90	97
English children, %correct	18	93	38	93

What this indicates is that English children often incorrectly assume that a pronoun can be locally bound, both in a single clause sentence (1IC) and in a two clause sentence (2IC). It appears that the difference is due, at least in large part, to the fact that in languages like English (and Russian and Icelandic), the pronouns are full words, while in languages like Italian and Spanish, the pronouns are clitics. Why would this matter for pronouns but not for reflexive pronouns? It appears that the answer is rather complex, and these questions are still under study.

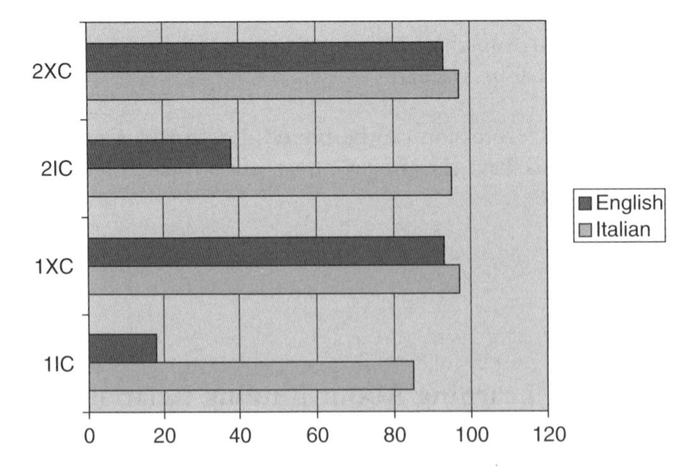

Figure 7.2 Percentage of correct identification of binding possibilities for Italian clitics and English pronouns for 30 Italian and 60 American children aged 2.6 to 5.5, in 1 or 2 clause stimuli when antecedent is local (IC) or non-local (XC), from McKee (1992)

There are also experimental studies that try to establish what children know about Principle C and how early they know it. A good example of this is the psycholinguistic work conducted by Steve Crain and his collaborators, and reported in Crain and Thornton (1998) . By constructing appropriate experimental situations, they manage to put children in a situation of deciding whether they accept or reject violations of Principle C. Amazingly, it seems that children are able to detect and reject violations of Principle C as early as 2 or 3 years old. (A lot depends here on the experimental materials and study: it is always a good idea to go back to the original studies and form your own opinion.)

The search for universals and for their origins: One question that linguists are very interested in, is whether there are non-obvious properties that are true of all languages. Of particular interest are properties that do not seem to stem from general cognitive traits, or from other non-linguistic considerations. For example, every (known) human language is a combinatory system in which there are units of combination at various levels of magnitude (phonemes, morphemes, phrases, etc.). That humans possess such systems is of course extremely important and interesting, but perhaps they are not specific to language, nor even to cognition. The same could be said for Greenberg's universal tendencies that we discussed in Chapter 6: they could arise because regularity or predictability makes understanding easier.

A good candidate for a non-trivial linguistic universal is the following subcase of Principle C:

(136) An R-expression cannot be bound **by a pronoun**.

As far as we know, it holds in every human language (in which c-command has been properly verified). Here are some examples:

*English: *He thinks that John will win*
*Italian: *pensa che Gianni vincerà*
*Modern Hebrew: *hu ma'amin she John yenaceax/he thinks that John will-win*
*Thai: *khaw khit waa coon chálàát/he thinks that John is smart*
*Gungbe: *e vedo do Kofi na wa/he believes that Kofi will come*
*Mohawk: *wa-hi-hrori-'tsi Sak ruwa-nuhwe'-s/I told him that she likes Sak*

7.9 Conclusion

7.9.1 Summary

Most important in this chapter is the relation between constituency and referential possibilities. We are starting to see some serious analytical results, suggesting that we are building a correct, coherent picture of the structure of English (and other languages). To account for possible and impossible referential dependencies, we have introduced the very important notion of c-command. And we have formulated a number of principles (Principles A, B, C and the condition on pronominal binding) that regulate such dependencies.

Binding theory adds a new type of experiment to the analytical toolkit. In binding theory experiments, we keep the syntactic structures constant, then for each DP position (and there are many), we try different types of DP (anaphor, pronoun, name, non-pronominal expression). Then we examine the referential dependencies: where binding is possible, and where is it not.

7.9.2 What to remember

You should of course know what English pronouns and reflexives are. Most importantly, you should know:

1. what the anaphors are and what an R-expression is;
2. how c-command is defined and how to apply it;

3. the technical meaning of **binding** and being bound;
4. the formulation of the binding conditions;
5. how to compute the binding domain of an anaphor and of a pronoun.

7.9.3 Puzzles and preview

We have explicitly left some questions unresolved. These will take some time to address properly. A lot remains to be done, not only to accommodate the full complexity of the English system, but also to extend our findings to other languages. We will address some of these questions in Chapter 13 on Advanced Binding, where we go into these issues in much more depth.

7.9.4 Further exercises

(1) Binding

In each of the sentences below, state the binding domain of the anaphor and indicate whether the sentence is expected to be grammatical or ungrammatical with the co-indexed antecedent.

(1) a. The manager gave Mary$_i$ a raise because he appreciates herself$_i$
b. The museum bought Doris$_i$'s portrait of herself$_i$ from the collector
c. Alice guessed that Max$_i$ found himself$_i$ a new apartment
d. That Max found his sister$_i$ a new apartment pleased herself$_i$
e. The diplomats$_i$ discussed the plan while [each other]$_i$'s spies slipped out the door

(2) Binding

Consider the following sentence:

(1) *He$_i$ asked Sue if you thought John$_i$ would get the job

State in precise terms why the indicated co-indexation fails. (Your answer must make use of/refer to the two binding theory principles that come into play here.)

(3) Binding

Consider the following sentences.

(1) John$_k$'s younger brother thinks he$_k$ should leave
(2) *Mary$_k$ declared that herself$_k$ would go to the castle on Sunday
(3) *They$_k$ saw Mary look at each other$_k$
(4) *He$_k$ does not accept the fact that Susan admires the teacher$_k$

(i) Draw the surface tree for each sentence.
(ii) Show for each of the ungrammatical sentences if it should be excluded by the binding theory (and not for some other reason).
(iii) Then explain why they are well-formed or ill-formed. (Be precise. Say exactly which principle is violated (or satisfied) and exactly how it is violated. Be sure to consider both of the indexed DPs. For example, your answer should say something about *John$_k$* and about *he$_k$* in (1).)

(4) Binding and c-command

Explain why one of the two sentences below is **predicted** to be ill-formed and the other is not. (Pay attention to the indices. You will need to provide rough trees to answer this question.)

(1) a. They showed [each participant]$_j$ an evaluation of his$_j$ performance
b. They showed the participants from [each state]$_j$ an evaluation of its$_j$ economy

(5) Binding and c-command

What is the **predicted** status of the following sentences? Explain your answers. (Pay attention to the indices. You will need to provide rough trees to answer this question.)

(1) a. They showed John$_j$ to his$_k$ friend
b. They showed his$_k$ friend John$_j$
c. They$_k$ wondered which pictures of [each other]$_j$ they$_m$ had showed to them$_n$
(i) if $j = k$
(ii) if $j = m$
(iii) if $j = n$

Note: Take the domains for Principles A and B as defined below:

Principle A: smallest XP with a subject, where this subject is not the anaphor or does not contain the anaphor.
Principle B: smallest XP with a subject.

(6) *His own*

The facts below show that the expression *his own* (and *her own, their own,* etc.) has one property in common with anaphors but not another. What is anaphor-like about *his own* and what is not anaphor-like?

(1) a. *Mary found his own keys
b. John found his own keys
c. John thought that Mary had found his own keys

(7) Binding (Yodish)

(i) Discuss what problem(s) the following examples pose for the binding theory. (Assume that the sentences in (1) are examples of 'Yodish," the (invented) language spoken by the Jedi master Yoda in Star Wars) while (2) is a plain English example.)
(ii) Discuss a way in which binding theory could be satisfied in the following.
(1) Yodish: a. Talk to each other they should
b. Talk to each other who should
(2) English: Which book about himself should he read?

(8) Benglish problem: binding theory

Senglish (a hypothetical language) is in all relevant aspects identical to English, except for the way Principle A of the binding theory works. In Senglish, Principle A is formulated as follows:

Principle A (Senglish version):
An anaphor must have a c-commanding subject antecedent within domain D (where domain D is defined as the smallest TP that contains the anaphor and a subject in [Spec, TP]).

(i) Given Principle A for Senglish, predict the patterns of grammaticality for each of the examples in (1a)–(1g) below. This means you need to state for each example if it is expected to be grammatical or ungrammatical in Senglish, and for each example explain why.

(1) a. They write stories about themselves
b. I told them stories about themselves
c. They told me stories about themselves
d. I listened to their stories about themselves
e. They liked my stories about themselves
f. They said that I liked themselves
g. After they left I saw themselves

7.9.5 Further readings

Binding theory as developed in this chapter is based on Chomsky (1981). For earlier work on pronouns and anaphors, see Postal (1971), Jackendoff (1972), Chomsky (1973), and Lasnik (1976).

A number of important references are also found in the body of the chapter, and we repeat them here: Reinhart (1983), Safir (1996), Fox (2002), Lasnik and Uriagereka (1988), and McKee (1992).

To pursue the topic of binding theory further, there is a more advanced, specialized textbook Büring (2005), which you should be able to read once you have covered Chapters 8, 11, and 13. It provides a thorough and comprehensive introduction to modern binding theory but includes semantics in some chapters, so it is perhaps best to have some training in that domain.

8
Apparent Violations of Locality of Selection

8.1 Setting the Stage

Human linguistic abilities resemble visual abilities in certain respects. For one thing, we cannot help using them. If I pronounce this sentence clearly and audibly and you hear it, you cannot help recognizing it as an English structure. In the same way, if you look at an image like the one in Figure 8.1, even though it is a two-dimensional spatial array of thousands of more or less gray points, you cannot help seeing it as a very simple three-dimensional scene with a small number of objects: one sphere and four cylinders.

Notice that the objects in the foreground present themselves as spatially continuous parts of the image. We could replace these objects with others and still have an intelligible scene. But notice the cylinder that is "farthest away" presents itself in two discontinuous pieces, since another larger cylinder is standing on end in front of it. If we wanted to replace that cylinder, we had better remove both parts of the image at once. And the base of the larger cylinder standing on end is obscured too, but we naturally assume that it's there.

In the preceding chapters, we have been considering linguistic structures, which, in their spoken form, also present themselves in two dimensions: acoustically, one dimension is time and the other is air pressure. Like the structure of visual images, there is nothing about the structure of sentences that imposes any strict bound on how large they can be (language is recursive, as we've seen), but crucially, as in the image, the constituents of sentences stand in significant relationships to one other. We have been trying to identify linguistic constituent structure by seeing which pieces we can switch, move around, or remove, without changing the structure significantly, or rendering it unintelligible.

These constituency tests yielded many kinds of phrases. An examination of these phrases revealed that they are structured in a very simple fashion, with their internal properties determined by the head. Heads combine first with complements, and then with subjects. Adjuncts merge with the projection that is formed. X-bar theory encodes the idea that all syntactic categories are hierarchically organized in a similar fashion. Consequently the overall look of every phrase is as below (though how the relations are linearized is determined by parameters in each individual language).

An Introduction to Syntactic Analysis and Theory, First Edition.
Dominique Sportiche, Hilda Koopman, and Edward Stabler.

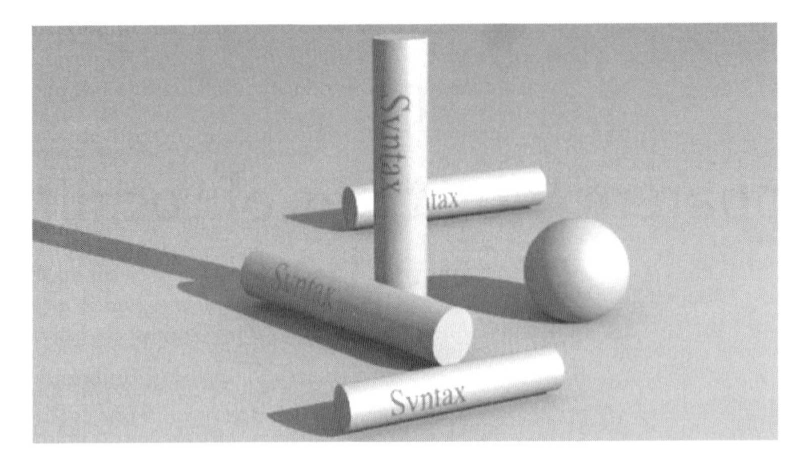

Figure 8.1 Inferred shape of non-visible parts

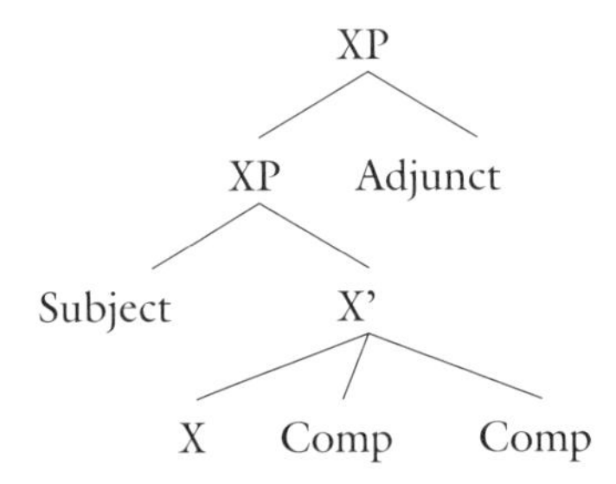

In Chapter 7, the workings of the binding theory confirmed the plausibility of these hierarchical structures. Up to now, in these first experiments, the assumption of continuity has been a valuable first approximation but, as with images, we ultimately need to allow for constituents that are **discontinuous** and relationships that are only partly revealed by the pronounced words. Language and vision are alike in these respects. The most important part of the analogy is this: certain sequences of word or morphemes, like the array of light intensities in the image, allow a surprisingly simple description, but sometimes this simplicity is obscured.

Once we discovered that there were constituents, and that different constituent types were internally similar (X-bar theory), we asked where constituents came from and built a simple theory: constituency arises from the combination of the Merge operation and the requirement that lexical properties of atoms be locally satisfied. That is, we get constituents from the combination of Merge, the projection principle, and locality of selection (LoS). Specifically, the idea that constituents form continuous substrings is a direct reflection of the local character of selection. In a nutshell, the logic of this is as follows: if **a** selects **b** as its complement, **a** must be merged with **b**, so **a** and **b** form a constituent and are adjacent. Contiguity, constituency, and locality of selection go hand in hand.

It turns out this correlation does not always hold. In fact, discontinuities abound: violations of locality of selection can be observed in almost any sentence or string. We study these violations in this chapter and show that surface strings have more than one tree associated with them, and these are related by the **Move** or **movement** operation.

Here are some of the discontinuities we discuss in this chapter, with the parts that belong together in boxes. They are listed in the order they will be discussed.

(1) Violations of Locality:

[The pictures of Bill], she [put] on your desk	Topicalization
Mary [studie] -s [Swahili]	Tensed verbs
[Mary] studi [[$_T$ -ed]] Swahili	
[Will] Mary [study Swahili]?	Questions
[Which pictures of Bill] did she [put] on your desk	Wh-questions
[Time] seems to [elapse] slowly in the tropics	Raising to subject
[Susan] wanted to [sleep]	Control
[Time] will [elapse] more slowly in the tropics	Simple clauses

In each case, a selectional relation holds between the two parts in the boxes.

Establishing selectional relations:
To show that there is a selection relation between two items, we show that they must co-vary, that is, changing only one of them can make the sentence deviant unless we change the other one as well, leaving everything else unchanged. The pairs of strings so constructed constitute minimal pairs. In this chapter, we will practice many ways of doing this.

Even if we don't yet know how to draw the trees for all these sentences, we do know enough to show that in each case (except the last one), locality appears violated.

Below, we indicate the minimum amount of structure that we have established must be there, and this is enough to show the existence of these violations.

(2) a. The pictures of Bill [$_{TP}$ she [$_{VP}$ put on your desk]]
b. [$_{TP}$ Mary [$_T$ will [$_{VP}$ study Swahili]
c. Which pictures of Bill did [$_{TP}$ she [$_{VP}$ put on your desk]]
d. [$_{TP}$ Time [$_{VP}$ seems [$_{TP}$ to [$_{VP}$ elapse slowly in the tropics]]]]
e. [$_{TP}$ Susan [$_{VP}$ wanted [$_{TP}$ to [$_{VP}$ sleep]]]]

Practice

Make sure you understand why the principle of LoS appears to be violated. For each of these sentences, draw its tree as well as you can, leaving unattached what you do not know how to attach. Then verify that in each of the trees, the LoS condition is indeed not satisfied.

8.2 Topicalization: A First Case of Movement

To give a flavor of how Movement works, let us look at topicalization. It looks like the structures of the acceptable sentences (2a) and (2c) violate LoS: we expect the direct object of the verb to immediately follow the verb. How can we account for this observation? Giving up LoS is not an option. We would lose an explanation for all the facts that led to it. The only reasonable option is to loosen it up: we need to allow some violations of locality of selection, but in a restricted fashion. But how, exactly, do we reformulate the principle? To guide us to the right answer, consider the following fundamental observation:

> Whenever we observe a violation of LoS between two items in a structure, there (almost always) exists another structure in which LoS between these very same elements is not violated. The converse is not true.
>
> In other words, the set of linguistic structures is not homogeneous from the point of view of selection. There is a **fundamental asymmetry** between the set of structures in which LoS is satisfied and the set of structures in which it is not.

In the case of topicalization, the following pair is representative of this very general observation:

(3) a. She put the pictures of Bill on your desk
b. The pictures of Bill, she put on your desk

The second sentence is possible only if the first is. How do we express the systematic relation between such pairs of sentences? How do we explain this asymmetry? The simple idea we will pursue is this: to express the idea that the second sentence is only possible because the first is, we postulate that **the second sentence is built on the first one**. More precisely, we postulate that the second sentence is the same as the first except that the object has been "moved" to the front of the clause, and we impose LoS only on the first sentence, before the object has been moved.

So technically, we associate two structures with sentences (2a): a structure S1, which we will call the **underlying structure** or **underlying tree**, and a **derived** or **surface structure** S2, which is the **derived** or **surface tree** yielded after movement.

We impose LoS only on S1:

S1:		she put	[the picture of Bill] on your desk
			⇓
S2:	[The picture of Bill]	she put	[~~the picture of Bill~~] on your desk

To derive S2 from S1, we apply the operation **Move**, which maps structure S1 onto structure S2 by displacing the phrase, *the picture of Bill*, to the front. More generally, Move is an operation that takes a tree as input, and produces another tree, in which some piece of structure has been displaced.

Topicalization (which is both the name of the construction, as well as the name of the particular instance of the Move operation) is our first example of movement. It is a type of XP movement (i.e. it moves DPs, PPs, VPs, etc.) that was informally introduced in Section 3.7.1.

Suddenly, many new questions arise. One immediate question that arises is the following: what surface structure do we get when we apply topicalization? We will not investigate this question in detail. It suffices to assume that the topicalized phrase is an adjunct to TP. This is at least consistent with the position of topicalized constituents in embedded clauses:

(4) Mary thinks $[_{CP}$ that [the picture of Bill] $[_{TP}$ she put on your desk]]

Here, the topicalized phrase (underlined) is sandwiched between the C *that* and the TP boundary. But more general questions arise as well. First, are there other kinds of movement? If so, what kinds of movement are there? In this chapter, we will add other types of movements to our inventory of processes, namely other examples of XP movement, as well as affix hopping or 'T-to-V', V-to-T, and T-to-C (called head movement). All these movements relate underlying trees to surface structures.

Second, can anything move anywhere? If yes, would this void the idea that there is LoS? It turns out that, in fact, movement is tightly constrained. For example – and this is one of the tests we used in Chapter 3 – movement only moves constituents, or strings that can independently be shown to be units. **Understanding when and how movement is allowed is exactly understanding when and how locality of selection can be violated.** In later chapters, we will, to a certain extent, investigate movement theory, the questions of when movement is allowed or required, and how it takes place. These questions are very actively investigated in current research, and we will progressively gain understanding of them (particularly in Chapter 10). For now, we start by investigating the different violations of locality, guided by our principles.

8.3 Head Movement

8.3.1 The distribution of English verbal forms

Our first serious investigation of Movement deals with the syntactic relationship between T and V in English. This is a topic that has been intensely studied since Chomsky's seminal work (1957). In what follows, we present and justify a particular analysis of this relationship. There exist alternative theories in the research literature, but they all must have the basic ingredients we will postulate, in some form or another.

Tensed verbs

One problematic case for X-bar theory that we have been systematically avoiding is the distribution of English simple present and past tense forms. Rather than two independent words, present and past tense verbs bundle together the T head and a V sister to its left. They are morphologically complex. In Chapter 2, we concluded that they had the following structure (where *past* and *pres* stand for past and present tense morphemes):

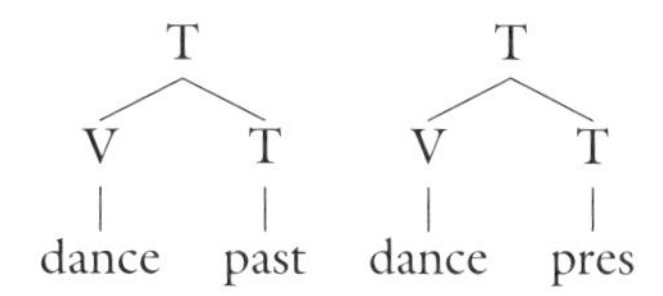

Very good, but compare the following two structures:

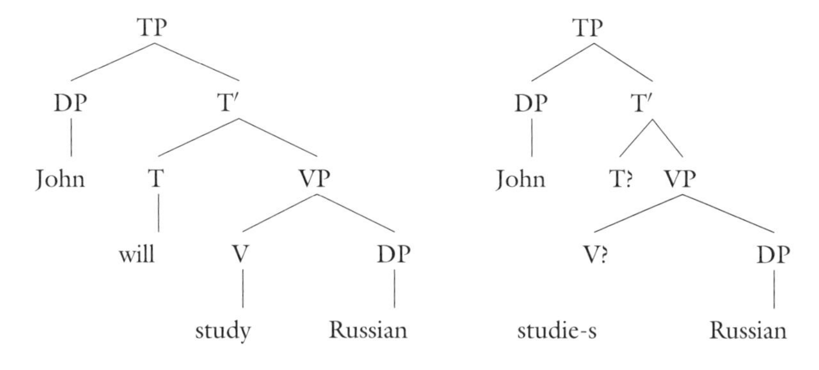

There is no problem in the left tree, but how do we build the right tree? Where should *studies* go? X-bar theory and locality of selection lead us to expect structures like the following:

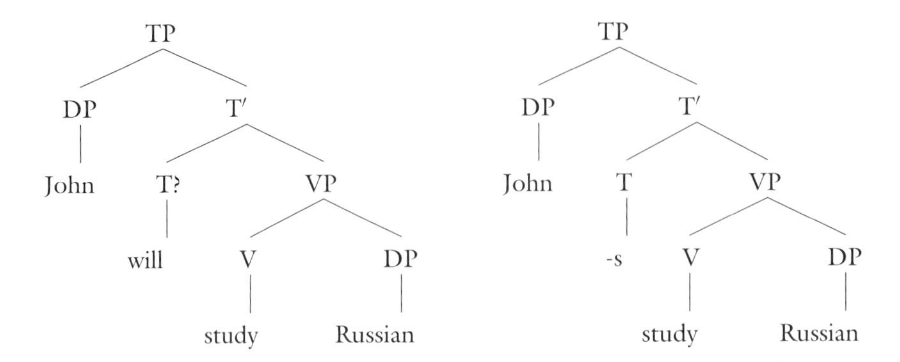

These trees correctly represent the relations between heads and phrases, each properly identifying its phrasal projection and determining its properties. In particular the presence of T and hence TP follows from the presence of the lexical properties of T (which selects a nominative subject, and a VP complement). But the trees do not capture the way in which the heads are actually pronounced: the leaves of the rightmost tree cannot be pronounced as **John s study Russian*. We can already identify a reason why: the lexical properties of the bound T head are not satisfied. T requires a V sister on its left. There has to be another tree in which V and T have been put together. This means that the pronounced string should be associated with (at least) two trees, an underlying tree like the one above, and a derived tree that leads to the correct pronunciation. In other words, we expect that a movement process is involved, which puts V and T together.

Let us see if we can justify this idea.

What Move operation could transform the first tree into the second? There are two natural ideas:

(5) a. the V *study* moves up to T;
b. the T affix *-s* moves down to V.

Both operations will turn out to exist, but for different subclasses of verbs, the former for auxiliary verbs (like *be* and perfect *have*), the latter for all other English verbs.

Notice that we can distinguish between these proposals by putting something between T and V, like an adverb, as in these structures:

(6) a. T Adv VP
b. John will carefully study the report
c. ?*John carefully will study the report

This shows that the adverb appears most naturally between T and V. It is a left VP adjunct. If the verb were moving out of the VP and up to T, we would expect the inflected verb to show up on the left of the adverb. If T moves to V, we would expect the inflected verb to show up on the right of the adverb. This second prediction is correct:

(7) a. John carefully studies the report
b. * John studies carefully the report

So we get the following trees, the one without movement on the left and the one with movement on the right:

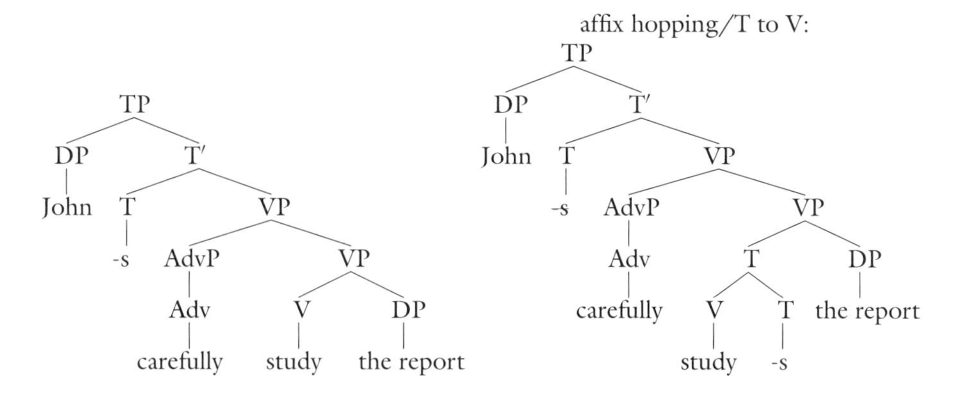

The movement of T onto the verb is called **affix hopping**, following Chomsky (1957), or **T-to-V**. These rules are specific instances of a general movement type known as **head movement** (movement of small, roughly word-size pieces of structure). Note how we represent the vacated head of T by the crossed out *-s* morpheme that has hopped.

> **Crossing lines**: Note that, in effect, the tree that results from this movement is a tree in which lines cross, since the T node is attached to the right of the verb form and the V node is attached to the left of the tense suffix. So syntactic trees do show some kind of crossing lines after all.
>
> Movement is a way to describe when and how this kind of crossing takes place. A sentence can be associated with two distinct trees, neither of which has crossing lines. The crossing is done by the Move operation transforming the first tree (in which locality of selection is satisfied), into the second, in which the selectional property of the T morpheme is locally satisfied.

Interaction of T-to-V and VP ellipsis

The proposal that such sentences are associated with two trees is confirmed by VP ellipsis tests. The tricky part is the existence of the first, underlying, tree, without T-to-V, which is more abstract:

Consider the following examples:

(8) a. She [$_T$will] [use paints]
b. I wonder if she will [use paints].
c. Yes, she will/* yes, she/*yes, she will use
d. Yes, she will, *use paints*

(9) a. She [[$_V$use] -ed $_T$] paints
b. I wonder if she used paints
c. Yes, she did/* yes, she/*yes, she used/*yes, she paints
d. Yes, she did, *use paints*

The very first question here is how (8c) and (8d) are related to (8a) and (8b). In the first set this is clear: VP ellipsis is involved. In the second set, the part missing in (9c) looks exactly like the elided VP in the first set, not bigger, nor smaller. It includes the verb without tense and the direct object. This leads to the natural assumption that VP ellipsis has applied in both (9c) examples. The missing part can even be present, as long as it is read with a flat intonation and preceded by a pause, as in the (d) examples.

We can confirm this with right node raising:

(10) a. I understand she used, and will use, special kinds of paint
b. Indeed, she did, and she will, *use paints*

Here the elided VP is shared.

The odd and fundamental fact of this paradigm is that, superficially, VP ellipsis has applied to what looks like a non-constituent in (9a): it has removed the verb, but not the tense affix on the verb, which appears on the dummy verb *do*. *Do* is called a dummy or grammatical verb because it does not have the meaning or the distribution of the main verb *to do*, which appears in a sentence like *she did her homework*. It only occurs in specific syntactic environments, and can co-occur with any main verb, including main verb *do*, as in *she didn't do her homework*. The process responsible for the appearance of *do* is generally called "*do*-support", with "*do*" supporting T, following Chomsky (1957).

We can make sense of this if we assume that VP ellipsis has applied to the underlying tree: in it the verb and the object form a constituent. This predicts that the constituents making up the verb phrase and determining the properties of the VP (*use* + *paints*) are not pronounced, **but the T should be**. And it is. So VP ellipsis applies to a structure where the T is not included in the VP: the underlying tree.

The affix hopping hypothesis allows the following understanding: VP ellipsis only elides VP material. It cannot apply once T has hopped onto V. But it can apply to an underlying tree (produced by the normal merging operations, but without movement). This leaves the T affix stranded, but the affix requires a V sister. English allows the insertion of dummy verb *do* to serve as support for this stranded affix (with a rule called ***do*-support**), or ***do*-insertion**. As we will see shortly, the rule of *do*-support applies in other environments where the affix is stranded for reasons other than VP ellipsis.

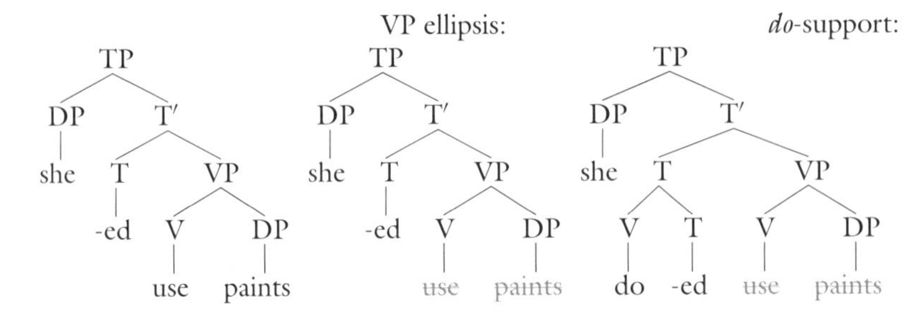

> **Morphology and syntax**: VP ellipsis, a phenomenon sensitive to syntactic structure, can slice a tensed verb and delete the verbal part but not the tense part. Or, equivalently, a bound T morpheme appears by itself as head of a syntactic phrase prior to affix hopping, as in the second tree above. This undermines the picture we have given of the model of syntax, as it shows that a bound T morpheme can correspond to a **syntactic** atom, with word formation *following* syntactic structure building, not *preceding*. We return to this issue in Chapter 12.

Negation

Some convergent evidence that leads to the conclusion that finite main verbs like *study* are not in T, comes from tensed verbs in negative sentences. First, we note that negation *not* occurs between T and its VP complement.

(11) a. They will not know it
b. They will not have gone to the store

But finite main verbs cannot follow or precede negation by themselves. Instead the dummy verb *do* must appear preceding *not*, and the verb is not tensed at all. (The dummy verb *do* should not be confused with the verb that means *to do (to act)*; dummy verb *do* has a purely grammatical function without thematic structure, while main verb *do* requires an agent as a subject and a theme. Consider: *John didn't do so.*)

(12) a. They did not know it
b. *They did not knew it/ *They do not knew it
c. *They not knew it
d. *They knew not it

How do we describe this? Given what we previously concluded, it suffices to assume that T-to-V does not and cannot apply in such sentences. This assumption explains why the main verb fails to carry any tense marking. Furthermore, the present and past T affixes are now stranded, but they need V sisters to bind to. Just as in the case of VP ellipsis, *do*-support kicks in.

Of course, we would like to know why the presence of negation blocks T-to-V. This complex question is still being actively debated and we will not discuss it here; it has to to do with the general issue of when Move is allowed to apply.

> **Negation** in natural languages is an incredibly complex phenomenon. Here we limit ourselves to the distribution of the morpheme *not*. But even for this narrow topic, there are difficult problems. One is the distinction between what is sometimes called *constituent* vs. *sentential* negation, illustrated by the following pair:
>
> a. Peter will not be anxious
> b. Peter will be not anxious
>
> Here we are only concerned with sentential negation, which we can recognize in several ways. Here are two of them:
>
> First, sentential negation can contract as *n't*, but constituent negation cannot:
>
> a. Peter won't be anxious
> b. *Peter will be n't anxious
>
> Second constituent negation allows a negative tag question, while sentential negation does not.
>
> a. Peter will be not anxious, won't he?
> b. *Peter will not be anxious, won't he?

How does negation fit into the structure of the sentence? This question raises extremely complex issues, some of which are briefly addressed in Section 8.3.4. Negation distributes like a preverbal adverb on the VP complement of T: we will treat it as an adjunct to the VP complement of T.

As a convention, we will just notate *not* as Neg (rather than NegP) and treat it as an adjunct to VP here (see p. 133 in Section 6.4). You can still see it is an adjunct because of the labeling below. This is a simplification, but sufficient for our purposes.

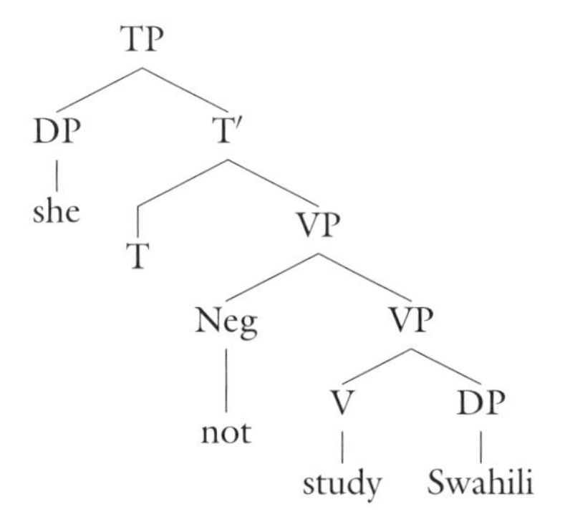

Auxiliaries

Are all tensed verbs in English put together by a rule of T-to-V? The answer is negative. The pattern we saw with the verb *study+-s* in (7) holds for all verbs with the exception of a number of auxiliary and modal verbs that can be enumerated. English allows multiple auxiliary verbs to appear in the same clause – a modal, a form of the perfect auxiliary *have*, and a form of *be* can all occur in the same sentence:

(13) John will have been eating cake

VP ellipsis tests confirm that when we have multiple verbs like this, we seem to have multiple VPs:

(14) * Mary won't have been eating cake, but John
(15) Mary won't have been eating cake, but John will
(16) Mary won't have been eating cake, but John will have
(17) Mary won't have been eating cake, but John will have been

Furthermore, we notice that the verb after auxiliary *have* must be in **past participle** form, which in English often ends with *-en* or *-ed*:

(18) John has (eaten/taken/hidden/stolen/shown/baked/left/advertised) the cake

In contrast, the verb after auxiliary *be* must be in **present participle** form, ending with *-ing*:

(19) John is (eating/taking/hiding/stealing/showing/baking/leaving/advertising) the cake

These dependencies between the particular auxiliary and the form of the following verb can be coded by taking their lexical entries to be like this:

will: T, +tense, DP_{nom}
have: V, VP[past participle], perfect
be: V, VP[present participle], progressive

The entry for *have* reads as follows: *have* is a V which c-selects a VP complement headed by the past participle form of the verb. It signals "perfect." These lexical requirements are met in the structure below (for sentence (13) above):

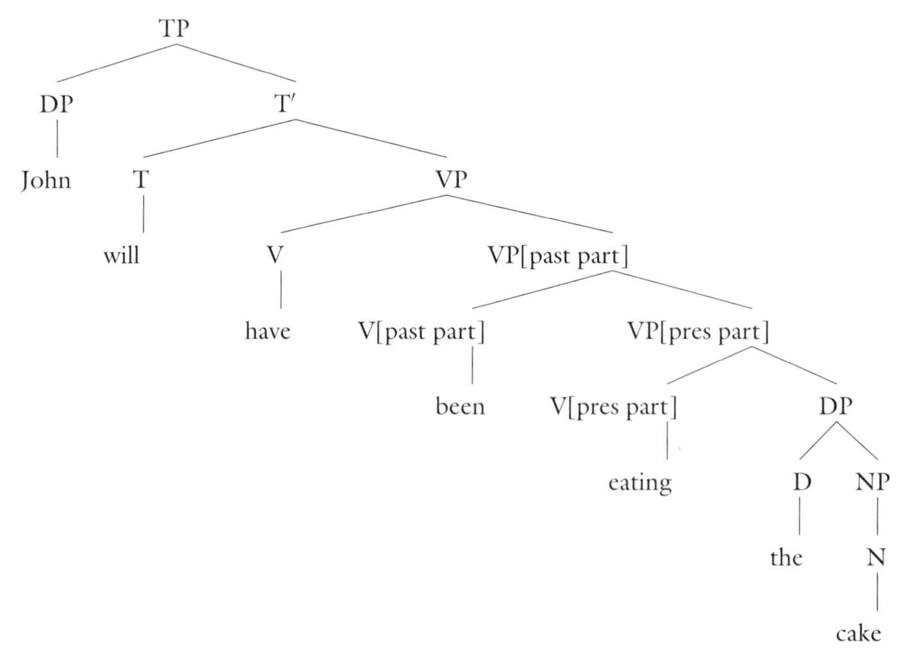

Notice that there are several different VPs in this structure, and that they are marked differently (as a bare VP, a past participle, a present participle). Each VP conforms to X-bar theory, and each could be modified by an adjunct like *enthusiastically*, so we can account for many of the positions in which the adverb could naturally occur.

(20) a. John will enthusiastically [$_{VP}$have been eating cake]
b. John will have enthusiastically [$_{VP}$been eating cake]
c. John will have been enthusiastically [$_{VP}$eating cake]
d. * John will have been eating enthusiastically cake

The following examples show that auxiliary verbs *have* and *be* can, like all English verbs, be inflected for tense and, when they are, they must appear to the left of the negation (which we could contract in each case to make sure that we are dealing with sentential negation). In particular, *do*-support is excluded:

(21) a. * John studies not Russian
b. John does not study Russian
c. John had not studied Russian
d. * John did not have studied Russian
e. John is not studying Russian
f. *John does not be studying Russian

These verbs do not behave like main verbs. A simple way of explaining what happens is to postulate that, unlike main verbs, these verbs are allowed to move to T by a rule **V-to-T** (short for **V-to-T movement**):

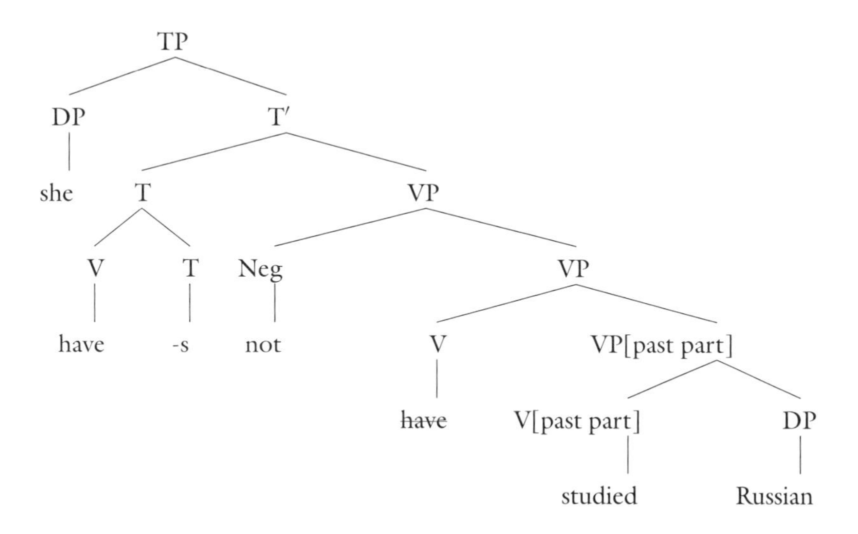

This simple idea derives the paradigm: since auxiliary verbs can move to T, T is not longer stranded and *do*-support is not needed.

The behavior of modal verbs like *would, can, could, may, might, shall, should* (as well as dummy *do* of *do*-support) mirrors that of auxiliary verbs *have* and *be* with a twist: they are **defective** verbs, i.e. they do not allow the full paradigm that regular verbs do. They have only +tensed forms, and no other verbal forms (*to can swim/*canning swim ...). We can code this in their lexical entries by marking them as requiring a +tense T sister. As a result, they must always undergo V-to-T.

Last resort: Now we just saw that *do*-support is not needed. But why can't it apply anyway, yielding the ill-formed examples (21d) and (21f)? Equivalently, why must V-to-T apply if it can? These questions are ones about when Move can or must apply, and they are somewhat beyond the scope of this chapter. One way to think about the mechanism involved is in terms of last resort: insertion of dummy material is not allowed unless there is no alternative.

Since a sentence contains only one T, these modals are in complementary distribution: only one can occur per T.

In languages closely related to English, modal verbs are regular and can carry non-finite verbal morphology. The excluded English example below is fine in other Germanic languages, like Dutch. (If you are familiar with any other language, you may want to check how it behaves in this respect.)

(22) * Viola must can swim/ *Viola will can swim
OK(Dutch) Viola moet kunnen zwemmen/ Viola zal kunnen zwemmen
OK(Dutch) Viola must can.INF swim.INF/ Viola will can.INF swim.INF
"Viola must be able to swim"/"Viola will be able to swim"

8.3.2 Subject–aux inversion: T-to-C movement

The regular modal–*have–be* pattern of auxiliaries, where each auxiliary verb selects a VP and determines the form of its sister, is apparently disrupted in yes/no questions:

(23) a. John will/should/must/can [$_{VP}$ go to school]
b. Will/Should/Must/Can John [$_{VP}$ go to school]?
(24) a. John has [$_{V[past\ part]}$ gone] to school
b. Has John [$_{V[past\ part]}$ gone] to school?
(25) a. John is [$_{V[pres\ part]}$ going] to school
b. Is John [$_{V[pres\ part]}$ going] to school?

This question-forming process is often called **subject–auxiliary inversion**. When there is a finite main verb, the yes/no question requires *do*, suggesting that ***do*-support** has applied:

(26) a. John goes to school
b. *Goes John to school?
c. Does John go to school?

An argument from complementary distribution
How should such strings be analyzed? A cue to the correct analysis is given by the contrasts found between Standard American English and Belfast English, as analyzed in Henry (1995). These two varieties of English form embedded yes/no questions differently. The first sentence is the standard one, and it is available in both types of English; the second is only available in Belfast English.

(27) a. I wonder whether Mary will work for Microsoft
b. I wonder will Mary work for Microsoft

Whereas the standard way is to introduce the embedded clause with a +q C (selected by *wonder*), Belfast English can form embedded yes/no questions the same way that they are standardly formed in main clauses, that is, by subject–aux inversion. There is a restriction however: when there is an overt lexical complementizer, embedded subject–auxiliary inversion is disallowed:

(28) a. I wonder whether/if Mary has worked for Google
b. *I wonder whether/if has Mary worked for Google
c. *I wonder has whether/if Mary worked for Google

How can we make sense of this? Why should there be **complementary distribution** between an inverted auxiliary or modal verb and a complementizer? The natural idea is that they compete for the same position. In this case, subject–aux inversion involves movement of the auxiliary verb to the C position: if the C position is filled by an overt +q C, as required by the embedding verb (see Chapter 4), the movement cannot happen. If C is not filled by an overt +q C, the auxiliary verb can move to C.

Let us make this more precise. First, even if there is no audible C, there must be a silent C to satisfy the selectional properties of the embedding verb. Second, this silent C must be +q for the same reasons. Third, the auxiliary moves to this +q C: this means that unlike overt +q Cs such as *whether* and *if*, this silent +q C is an affix that requires a sister. In other words, we have the following derivation involving T-to-C:

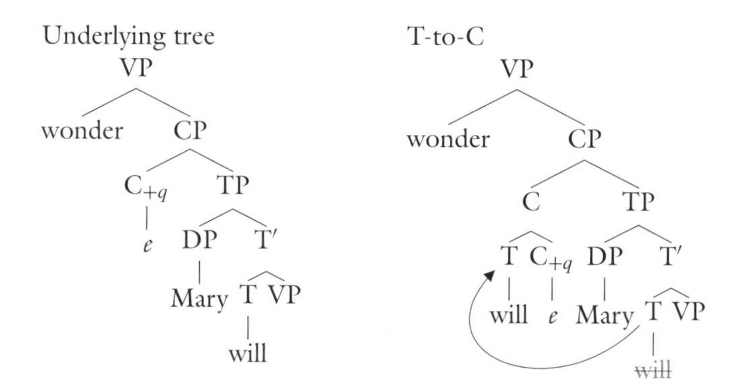

But now, notice that the CP we get in the rightmost tree is exactly what we need for main clause yes/no questions in both varieties of English. So we assume that the silent +q C that occurs in embedded clauses in Belfast English also occurs in main clause yes/no questions.

To summarize, English has a silent +q C (which we can refer to as Cq) that can occur in main clauses and is an affix, whose lexical entry can be given as follows:

e: C, +q, bound, +tense

Note that this C must be marked +tense, as matrix yes/no questions are limited to finite clauses.

> Note that movement allows a single constituent to enter into local processes at various different points in the structure: a constituent can satisfy some requirements before movement, e.g. selection, and some other properties after movement. We will systematize this conclusion later, once we know a little bit more about movement.

Questions with finite have *and* be

Here we sketch the derivation for the following question: "*Has Mary studied Swahili?*" First, we build a regular TP, in which *have* undergoes V-to-T. This TP in turn is merged with the +q silent C, which triggers T-to-C. Rather than using three trees to depict the three individual steps, we depict them all in the single tree below:

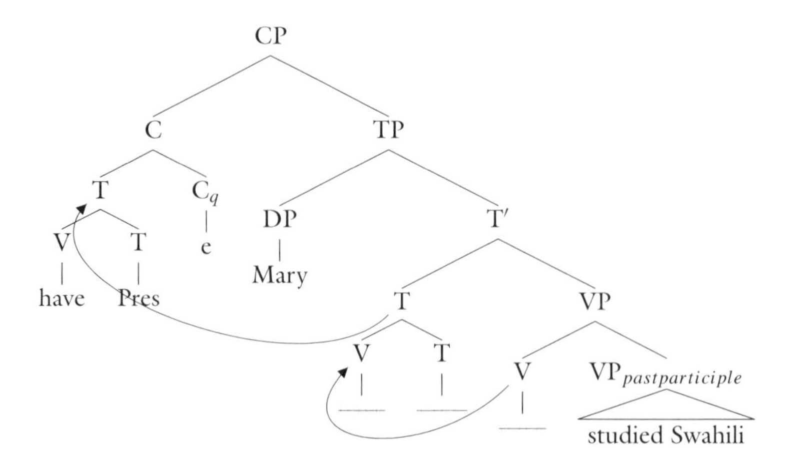

Questions with do*-support*
Let us now turn to the last case, namely the pair:

(29) a. She went there
b. Did she go there?

How is the question formed? We already have all the ingredients necessary to do this, so we can give a step-by-step description of how Merging and Moving gets us the right output. We first build a TP, then Merge a +q C. T then moves to C, and since T is a bound affix, *do*-support must apply. This is illustrated in the following table. We discuss questions that this raises immediately below it:

1		[she	[-ed	[go to the store]]]
2		⇓ Merge Cq		
3	[Cq	[she	[-ed	[go to the store]]]]
4		⇓ T-to-C		
5	[-ed Cq	[she	[	[go to the store]]]]
6		⇓ *Do*-support		
7	[do -ed Cq]	[she	[	[go to the store]]]]
8		⇓ Idiomatic pronunciation rule: do+ed= did		
9	Did	she		go to the store?

These derivational steps are straightforward. Note the last step, which gets us from (8) to (9): the past tense form of *do* is idiomatically "pronounced" *did*. Here is a tree illustrating the result:

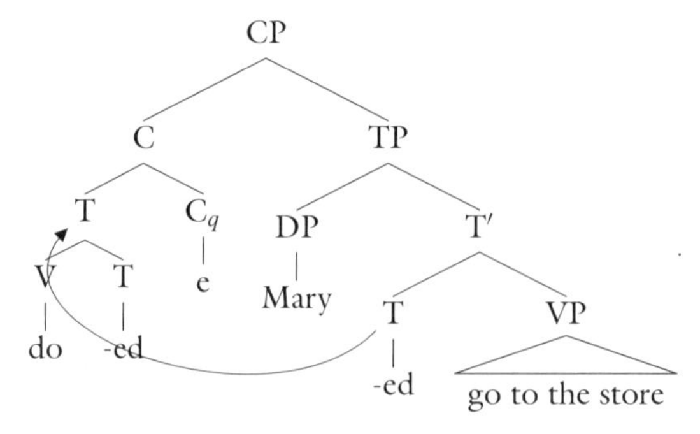

This works, but still, we would like to know why it works in this way, rather than in some other conceivable way. Here are some questions worth pursuing.

Why didn't affix hopping (= T-to-V) apply at step 1? Answer: if it had applied, T would have moved to V, and then when Cq was merged as in step 2, T would not have been available to move to C. Why not? If T had moved to V, forming the T *go+ed= went*, this new T could move to C to provide a host for the affixal +q C. But note that, in this case, moving the T in VP to C has it skipping over the head T of TP. This type of head movement is prohibited quite generally. We will return to this general prohibition, known as the **Head Movement Constraint**, in Chapter 12.

Wait, why can't the movement go through that intermediate T position? Answer: we do not know yet when movement is possible or permitted. We will see that there are several conditions on movement. One of them, which we will discuss later in Section 8.6, is that movement is triggered only as a means to satisfy some selectional property. Moving the T (+ the verb) back through the place where it came from would be disallowed, because that step would not meet this requirement.

8.3.3 Head movement in DPs

The preceding section discussed the distribution of finite verb forms, Ts, and Cs in some detail. We now turn to plural nouns, more specifically the question of how plural nouns are formed, and how they fit in the structure of DPs. Recall that we concluded in Chapter 2 that, just like tensed verbs, plural nouns have an internal structure:

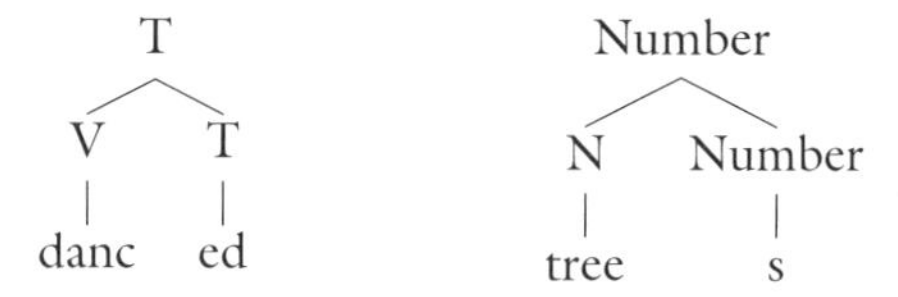

We just saw that the formation of the tensed verb is actually due to the syntactic operation of T-to-V. How about the formation of the plural noun? We will conclude that it is also formed by a syntactic operation.

The first step is to ask ourselves how this could be. If a syntactic operation is involved, there must be a category Number in our tree, and a NumberP, and so on. Can this be justified? The answer is positive. To see this we need to examine the selectional properties of determiners.

We have seen various determiners: *the, this, every, each, these, some, a*, among others, and two silent Ds (a plural indefinite and a plural generic D, which were introduced in Chapter 6, Section 6.5.1), and we probed the constituent structure of DPs in Chapter 5. So far, we have assumed that Ds select for NP sisters, an assumption that a more careful examination shows to be incorrect.

First, note that the choice of a D does not really seem to specifically influence the kind of N it takes. But different Ds often require that the N has a certain number (singular or plural), or no number at all (i.e. mass nouns). Take *each*, which requires a singular noun (cf. **each books, OK each book*), or take the indefinite or the generic silent Ds we saw, which are only compatible with plural count nouns (compare *beavers usually build dams/* beaver usually build dam*). This suggests that Ds quite generally select a category "Number," and since the number follows the D, NumberP should be selected as a complement to D. Now the number information appears on N (in English) so Number in turn should take a NP as its complement.

We find further support for the location of NumberP as the right sister of D by looking at the location of number sensitive expressions, such as numerals – *two, three*, etc. These are found between the D and NP adjuncts. Numerals presumably enter into selectional relations with the Number head: they precede prenominal adjectives, and in turn combine with plural nouns.

the [NUMBER [interesting book-s]
these three NUMBER interesting book-s
the many NUMBER interesting book-s
these two NUMBER red balloons
*these red two NUMBER balloons (with neutral intonation)

Thus, the D selects NumberP as its sister, and Number takes NP as its sister. Adjectives are adjoined to NP, and the plural Number head *-s* ends up as a suffix on N.

From now on, we abbreviate the head **Number** as **Num**, and its projections Number′ and NumberP as **Num′** and **NumP**.

The resulting structure [D Num A N] is very similar to what we found in clauses, with [C T Adv V]. This parallel raises the question of how Num and N get together. Since the plural noun *follows* adjectives, it seems the suffix lowers to N (Num-to-N), just the way we had T-to-V. Indeed, N to Num movement (parallel to V-to-T movement) would have produced the linear string D (two) Num N-PL A, *the two balloons red* and this is clearly not a correct description for English.

Properties of Number: Number, or Num, can be [± count]. If it is [−count], it selects mass nouns (like water, sand, etc.), which cannot be pluralized, it is [−plural] (see (14)). If it is [+count], it can be [+plural] or [−plural] (or "singular"). If it is [+plural], this Num is pronounced as the bound morpheme *-s* on the N in English. If it is singular, we will assume here that it is silent.

Lexical entries for Ds will then look like the following (using the function of the D to indicate a silent head):

the	D	+def,	Num +count
GEN	D	Num +plural, or −count[1]	
INDEF	D	−def,	Num plural
each:	D,	Num singular	

Naturally, the various Number heads will also have lexical entries, here using the symbol e to indicate a silent head. One possible idea is that Number affixes in the DP are like the tense affixes in TP. They are members of the category Num, and undergo Num-to-N movement, just like T affixes undergo T-to-V.

e	Num [sg], N,
/-z/:	Num [pl], N, bound

Taking all this into account, a phrase such as *these three red balloons* will have something like the following structure:

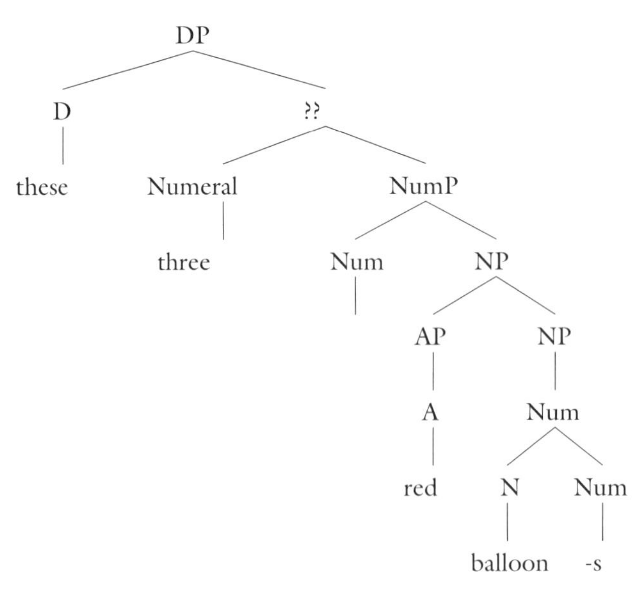

[1]The silent generic D combines not only with plural count nouns but also with singular mass nouns as in *vodka is distilled*.

First, note that we have indeed elected to move Num to N by head movement. The reason is that the number affix and the noun occur to the right of the adjective, which, as an NP adjunct, marks the left boundary of the NP. This reasoning is identical to what led us to T-to-V (taking into account VP adjunct placement).

Second, note the question marks on the node dominating numeral and NumP. Clearly, there are selectional relations between numeral and Num but this could be realized in a variety of ways: numerals could be subjects of Num, or left adjuncts to NumP (or even – which we will not do here – take NumP as complements to a numeral head, though this would require modifying the lexical entries for Ds).

Finally, this structure allows a natural treatment of *one* replacement. As we saw, the minimal constituent that *one* replaces is an NP (it is a good idea to review the DP section in Chapter 5), but it can apply to any NP. *One* can also host the plural morpheme, so it is natural to assume that *one* is an N that takes no complements or subject, so it is both an N and an NP. These facts together yield the following paradigm, as can be easily verified:

(30) these three big red balloons
(31) these three big red ones (*replacement of the NP [balloon]*)
(32) these big ones (*replacement of the NP [red [balloon]]*)

8.3.4 Head movement: summary

We have now seen four instances of the Move operation applying to a head: V-to-T, T-to-V, T-to-C, and Num-to-N. We will encounter more instances in Chapter 12.

What to remember for verbal forms
Fundamentally, postulating movement is meant to handle superficial violations of locality of selection: we see, for example, a T morpheme inside VP, outside of the selection reach of C, even though it is selected by C; we conclude that T has moved from the position where it is selected to the position where it appears. The English C/tense/auxiliary/verb system is a quite complicated. You should understand and know how to analyze the different verbal forms in English, and how to find out if T-to-V or V-to-T has applied. This is what we discovered in the preceding sections:

Distribution of tensed verb forms in English:

in T: the tensed forms of : perfect auxiliary V (perfect *have*, the auxiliary *be*), and the modals *will, would, can, could, may, might, shall, should*, as well as dummy *do.*
in VP: all other tensed forms
in C + q: only elements that can occur in T can occur in the C region in questions
***do*-support in T**: rescues stranded affixes that cannot combine with V, satisfies bound nature of T or + q C.

You should also understand why DPs contain NumPs, what the relation of Num to numerals and to plural morphology is, and why this can be analyzed as Num-to-N movement.

Head movement puzzles and preview
The analysis of English verb forms and the existence of movement raise new questions and puzzles, some of which we will progressively address. It is important to remember that understanding the logic behind a superficially strange system like the English verbal system is only a first step. We also want to understand why the system works the way it does. Is it accidental, or is it in fact regular? Does it reflect general rules of how human language functions? For example, since we need movement, we can ask ourselves: what is allowed to move? To where? Under what conditions?

We will return to these questions. Below are a couple of examples of puzzles we would like to understand.

A brief note on rule interactions: Recall that VP ellipsis can apply to various VPs in a sentence. We also saw that *do*-support can serve to "rescue" a stranded affix, as in

Mary didn't finish the cake, but Joe finished the cake
but Joe did ~~finish the cake~~
* but Joe

When VP ellipsis does not apply, the proposal was:

Joe -ed finish the cake
↓affix hopping
Joe finish-ed the cake

When it does, we postulated:

Joe -ed finish the cake
↓VP ellipsis
Joe -ed ~~finish the cake~~
↓do support
Joe do-ed ~~finish the cake~~

Notice what must be disallowed though:

Joe -ed finish the cake
↓affix hopping
Joe finish-ed the cake
↓VP ellipsis
Joe ~~finish-ed the cake~~

VP ellipsis must apply before T-to-V. Why? How can we obtain these results without just describing or stipulating them? We know that in general, it is not true that ellipsis applies before Head Movement. In some languages, like Irish (a VSO language) (McCloskey, 1991), Swahili (Ngonyani, 1996), Brazilian Portuguese, and possibly Japanese, Head movement can apply before VP ellipsis, although here, Head Movement is V to T. This is an outstanding puzzle.

The following puzzling case may suggest that it is. Consider these examples:

Othello wasn't listening to Iago but she was listening to Iago
but she was ~~be listening to Iago~~
* but she did ~~be listening to Iago~~

We cannot delete the verb *be* and repair with the structure *do*-support. Let us examine a prohibited sequence:

* she -ed be listening to Iago
↓VP ellipsis
she -ed ~~be listening to Iago~~
↓do support
she do-ed ~~be listening to Iago~~

Thus, here we obtain the result that V-to-T movement of *be* must precede *do*-support, just like in Irish or Brazilian Portuguese.

There are other outstanding puzzles too. One well-known one relates to a difference between auxiliary VPs and main VPs with respect to the possibility of deletion:

John was here, and	Mary will be here too
	*Mary will ~~be here~~ too
John has left	but Mary shouldn't ~~leave~~
	*but Mary shouldn't ~~have left~~

Affix hopping: Affix hopping (i.e. T-to-V movement) is puzzling, because it looks like it constructs structure inside an already constructed structure, or lowers one part of the structure onto another. There are some reasons to believe that this should not be allowed, which then raises the question as to how the effects of affix hopping are possible. Two solutions are often adopted: one is that the content of T can be realized on its sister by a non-syntactic rule (see Emonds, 1987; Marantz, 1988). This moves the problem from the syntax to the postsyntactic "spell-out" component (sometimes called phonology). Another solution is one in which all morphology is presyntactic, i.e. the verbs start out with all their morphology (see Chomsky, 1993). This removes the problem of word formation from the syntax and shifts it to the lexicon and the morphology. It is fair to say that problems of affix hopping have not yet found a satisfactory theoretical answer.

More about the representation of sentential negation: At this point, there are two available options for the treatment of negation (Neg). Either Neg is a head combining with an XP complement, (roughly Alternative A), (in which case it could in principle have a subject), or Neg is an adjunct to VP, as we have adopted in Section 8.3.1 for our purposes (Alternative B).

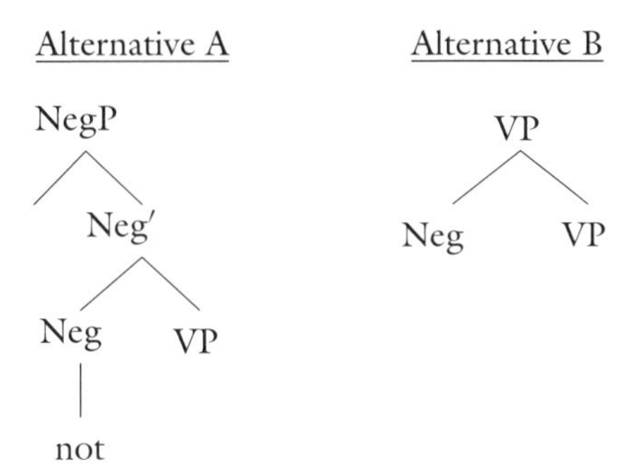

It turns out that this is a very difficult question to settle. Both proposals have been pursued, as well as mixed proposals (where some negative items enter into the configuration into A, others into B). All proposals have both merits and problems, and we briefly point these out.

Here are some reasons in favor of Alternative A, using the tools that we have developed so far. Consider VP ellipsis first:

(33) a. John will endorse the treaty,
but George will not ~~endorse the treaty~~
b. Will George indeed not endorse the treaty?
He will indeed not ~~endorse the treaty~~
c. *He will indeed ~~not endorse the treaty~~
d. He will indeed ~~endorse the treaty~~

Thus, by looking at VP ellipsis, we see that the polarity of the clause (whether it is negative or not) must always be overtly expressed in the remnant and can never be recovered in the way VP adjuncts can be recovered under VP ellipsis.

VP preposing shows the same:

(34) He says he will not endorse the treaty; and indeed
[endorse the treaty] he won't
*not endorse the treaty he will

But this also holds for VPs that host auxiliaries *have* and *be*. Again, we see that the constituent we have identified as VP fails to show some distributional properties of VP. As before, failure of constituent tests does not show conclusively that the constituent is not a VP.

There are also some arguments in favor of B. In morphology we were led to assume that Neg was a modifier/adjunct: since Neg (*un-/in-*) did not change the category of the word. This suggests that we should treat *not* in the same way, as a modifier of VP: negation turns the VP into a negative VP. There is also an argument from locality of selection: we have treated T as c-selecting VP, and this should translate into sisterhood. Under Alternative A, negation seems to intervene between T and VP, and sisterhood would need to be loosened. Under Alternative B, no problem arises. However, this alternative does not lend itself to a natural account for why affix hopping cannot apply over *not*.

8.4 Detecting Selection

Clearly, selection plays a very important role in driving the shape of syntactic structures and diagnosing the presence of movement. How exactly do we determine that there is a selection relation between different items? This is not always easy. For example, when we discussed the internal structure of DPs, we modified our earlier assumptions (which seemed natural since the Ds we knew were always accompanied by NPs) about what Ds select. We have already made some remarks about this in Section 5.7.1. This is what we turn to in this section.

8.4.1 Covariation

One of the main ways way of determining what selectional relations hold in a tree is to systematically investigate what covaries with what. For example, one typical way we have done this is by:

i. selecting a verb;
ii. asking what entities the verb relates;
iii. finding what strings of morphemes correspond to these entities.

Typically the verb requires that these strings have certain properties: that they refer to animate objects, or are concrete, etc. (selection) or that they be DPs or PPs or CPs etc. (c-selection). We conclude that we have a selectional relation when the content or the category of the string is dependent on which verb we picked. An example that will be useful later is:

(35) Time seems to elapse slowly in the tropics

We select the verb *elapse*. It is a one-place predicate. It attributes a property (that of elapsing) to an entity denoting a duration. It is the DP *time* that refers to this duration. We have a selectional relation between the V *elapse* and the DP *time*, as we can see by trying to vary just the subject:

(36) * Mary seems to elapse slowly in the tropics

But note that that an appropriate replacement of the verb *elapse*, e.g. *speak*, re-establishes well-formedness:

(37) Mary seems to speak slowly in the tropics

While useful, the above method is not entirely foolproof, as we will see in the next chapter. The problem can be illustrated with the following sentence: *Time makes itself elapse/*Gold makes itself elapse /OK Gold makes itself shine*. By parity of reasoning we could conclude, wrongly, that *elapse* selects *time* in this sentence too. What is happening is that the embedded verb selects its subject (*itself*) which must be bound by the subject of the clause, giving the effect of covariation without there being selection **imposed by lexical properties**.

It is thus prudent to use other ways to establish the existence of selectional relations **imposed by lexical properties**. Sometimes, there are more specific ways to determine that we have such a selectional relation between two positions in a tree. Here we review a few that will be handy later.

8.4.2 Very tight selection: idiom chunks and weather *it*

These are cases in which, typically, a verb selects its object so tightly that this object needs to be a specific word, rather than a range of possible words, and the meaning of the whole unit is special, e.g. not compositional at all, or perhaps just metaphorical.

pull strings = use one's connections (metaphorical)
take care of = care for (non-compositional: there is no taking going on)
lend assistance = help (non-compositional: there is no lending going on)

In the following sentences, we see a portion of an idiomatic expression, an **idiom chunk**, separated from other parts of the idiomatic expression:

(38) a. How many strings did you say she had to pull in order to do that?
b. How much care do you think he would be taking of his patients under those circumstances?

These stranded idiom chunks clearly illustrate that we are dealing with a case of non-local selection in these sentences: we conclude they must involve movement (here: wh-movement, to which we return in the next section).

Certain idiom chunks do not even occur at all outside of the idiomatic expressions. One example is the word *headway*, which only occurs as part of the idiom:

make headway = progress

This idiom can occur in sentences like this:

(39) How much headway is he likely to make

The fact that in all these cases, the tightly selected N does not appear in its "selected position" immediately implies that movement has taken place.

Another case of very tight selection is illustrated by atmospheric verbs such as *rain, snow*, etc. These verbs have the peculiarity that they allow as subject so-called weather *it*, which resembles (but actually behaves slightly differently from) pleonastic *it* (as in *it seems that* ... to which we will return), in that both seem to lack meaningful content. The distribution of weather *it* in conjunction with atmospheric verbs can be used to detect selectional relations. For example, consider the following two sentences:

(40) * Mary persuaded it to rain
(41) Mary expected it to be raining

This illustrates selectional differences: if *it* was solely selected by *rain* in both cases, we would not expect this difference. We return to such cases in Chapter 9.

8.4.3 Case

As we saw earlier, case is a property that DPs have, which depends on the syntactic position in which they occur. In English, it is only visible on certain pronouns, but many other languages show case on almost all DPs: German, Latin, Japanese, and Finnish, among others.

Nominative:	* they saw Bill	*them saw Bill	*their saw Bill
Accusative:	* Bill saw they	Bill saw them	* Bill saw their
Genitive:	* they cat saw Bill	* them cat saw Bill	their cat saw Bill

The particular case a DP gets is tied to the position it occurs in:

Nominative: subject of tensed T, so it is property selected by tensed Ts
Accusative: complement of V, so it is a property selected by (certain) Vs
Genitive: subject of DP, so it is a property selected by the "possessive" D

Again, the following examples lead to the postulation of movement, since we observe non-local selection:

(42) a. Who left Bill
b. * Whom left Bill
(43) a. Who did Bill leave
b. Whom did Bill leave

In English, the form *whom* is accusative, not nominative, while the form *who* can be anything. The contrast between the (b) forms receives an explanation under movement analysis, where *whom* moves from its selected position as object of *leave*. Again, this is an instance of **wh-movement**.

8.4.4 Existential constructions

Certain other words are restricted to occur in very specific environments too. The word *there* has a use in which it does not designate a location:

(44) a. There were three firemen available
b. There is no largest prime number
c. Is there anything to do today?
d. There are two main characters in the novel

This non-locative *there* is called *existential*, because it attributes or (with negation) denies existence (whether real or fictional) of some entity or situation. Existential *there* is very restricted in its distribution. It does not get stressed (no pitch accent), and it can occur as the subject of a clause with certain main verbs but not all:

(45) a. There are three firemen available
b. ? Suddenly, there arrived two strange men
c. * There stabbed an animal
d. * There ran many people

It does not seem to occur as complement:

(46) a. * Mary judged there (object of V)
b. * You should sit before there (object of P)
c. * I had a realization of there (object of N)
d. # I ate there (object of V, OK only with locative *there*)

An exact description of this phenomenon would require somewhat more background than we have at the moment. However, a simple approximate description of the restriction on existential *there* can be given as follows:

(47) Existential *there* can only occur as subject of a clause with certain main verbs.

Here are some reasons why we are justified in calling *there* a DP and the subject of the clause. First, it is involved in subject–auxiliary inversion (i.e. T-to-C):

(48) a. There were seven people in the room
Were there seven people in the room?
b. There were several doctors available
Were there several doctors available?

The second is that it behaves like a subject in the "tag-question" construction (see p. 60) that we see here:

(49) a. Rodney was eating some squid, wasn't he?
b. There is a man ready to jump from the roof, isn't there?

It may be that the structure of an existential *there* sentence such as (44a) involves a small clause complement of the verb *be*, with *there* as subject:

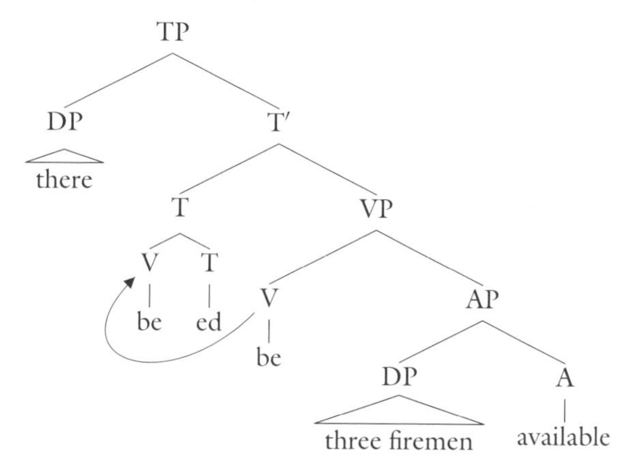

8.5 Phrasal Movements

We started this chapter with a list of constructions in which locality of selection is violated, beginning with an investigation of topicalization, and showed that the rules of movement allow violations of locality of selection to be "merely apparent," since movement can change an underlying tree into a surface tree. We stress again that understanding when and how movement is allowed is exactly understanding when and how locality of selection can be violated. In the previous sections, we discovered quite an inventory of instances of movement. Thus far, these include movement of XPs (so far, topicalization) and particular instances of *head movement* – V-to-T, T-to-V, T-to-C, and Num-to-N. We now turn to the remaining cases, repeated below. This will allow a reformulation and simplification of the principle of locality of selection, and provide further insight into how structures are built.

(50) Violations of Locality:

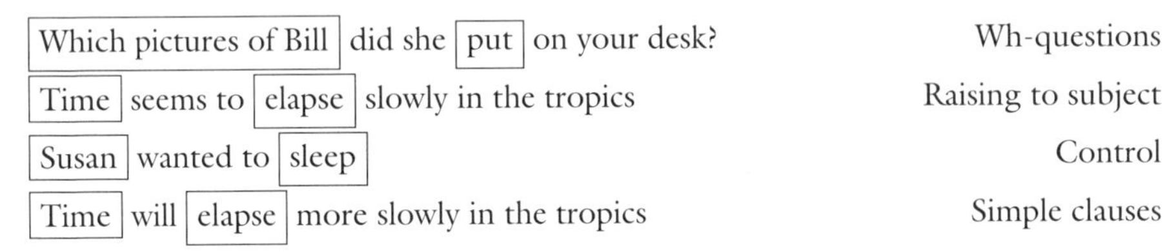

8.5.1 Wh-questions

We have already seen in Section 8.4 two reasons to postulate wh-movement in wh-questions (based on idiom chunk distribution and case distribution). For example, the two sentences we relate now are wh-questions:

(51) a. You put [which picture of Bill] on his desk?
b. [Which picture of Bill] did you put on his desk?

(The first of these examples is pronounced with a special "echo-question" intonation, with emphasis on *which*, and it is only appropriate in certain contexts.) The verb *put* selects a complement DP, a theme, and also a locative PP. In the latter case, Move has applied after selection to separate the DP complement from the verb:

S1: You put [which picture of Bill] on his desk?
⇓
S3: [Which picture of Bill] did you put on his desk?

Wh-movement moves wh-phrases, that is, phrases containing a wh-word like *which, what, who, how, why*. The result is interpreted as a request for information, not as a statement. To the right of the preposed object, we find a string that (apart from the preposed object) looks exactly like a yes/no question. We therefore analyze that string in the same way as a yes/no question: an auxiliary or modal verb, or some form of *do*, which is placed into the position C by T-to-C movement, as we discussed in Section 8.3.2. Note that this silent C is marked +q, making the structure into a question, as desired.

Where do wh-phrases move to in wh-questions? We now know they raise past C since they are found to the left of a T that has raised to C: the natural conclusion is that they raise to the **subject** (or specifier) position of CP. One reason is that there can be only one preposed wh-phrase to the left of C (it * where which picture of Bill did you put): if it were an adjunct to CP, why not have two? The other reason is related to the requirement that the preposed phrase contain a wh-question word. On analogy with the agreement between the subject of a clause and T in person and number, we can hypothesize that this requirement reflects an agreement relation between the +q C and its subject: the preposed wh-phrase must contain a question word because it needs to count as +q too.

Here then is the wh-movement Move step. First, the structure is built up in a regular way, so that the properties of TPs, DPs, and all phrases are satisfied. When we merge the +q C, its bound property is satisfied by T-to-C, and we get to the following stage:

Did you put which pictures of Bill on his desk?

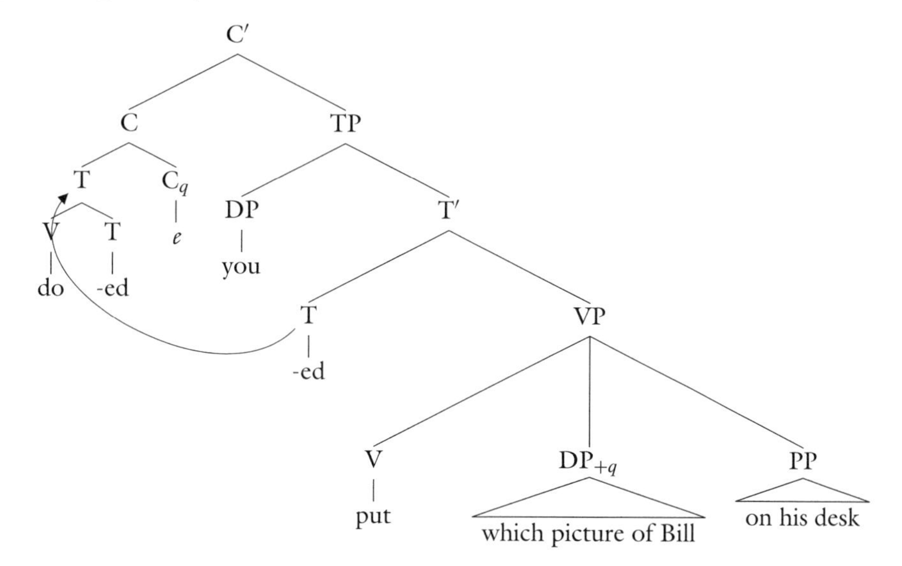

Next, wh-movement can apply to yield the surface tree for the sentence (51b):

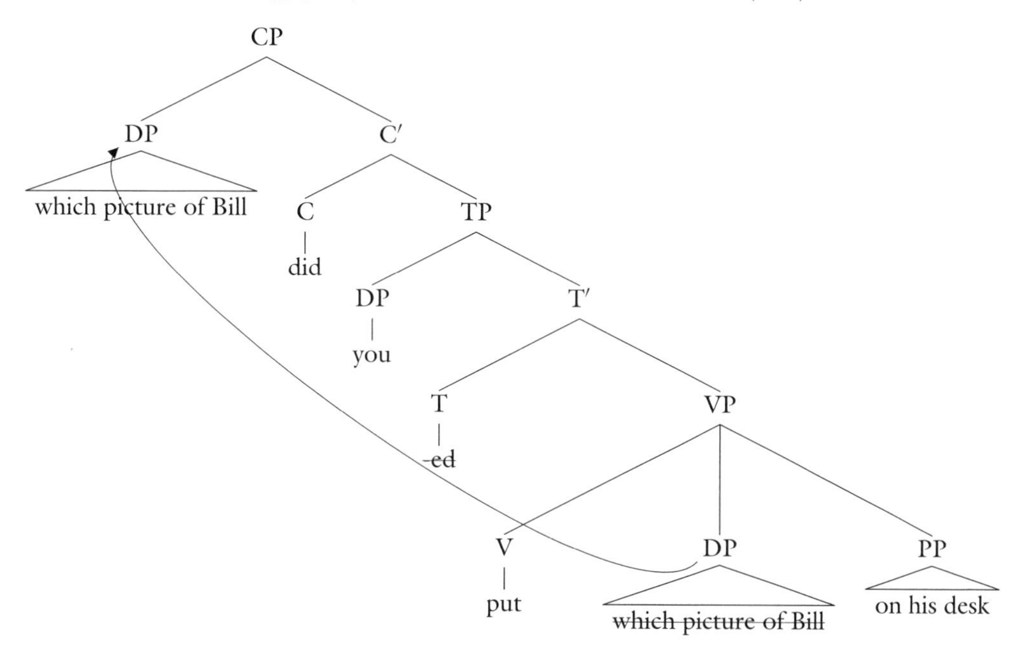

Note how we marked the preposed DP as [+q] to reflect the presence of *which*. If wh-movement in questions is restricted to wh-phrases because the subject of C must agree with C marked [+q], we see an illustration of a property that is satisfied after movement, namely agreement between a wh-phrase and a C.

Updating Table 6.1 on p. 138 with what is found in small clauses, we see that the categories that allow subjects are D, T, P, A, and V. (We did not find subjects for Num, though. Since Numerals are optional, we treated them as adjuncts rather than as subjects.) With this analysis of wh-questions, we now see that the category C also allows subjects: a wh-phrase can become the subject of a C when it is displaced by wh-movement. Again, we see that a prediction of uniformity made by X-bar theory is borne out.

8.5.2 Raising to subject

We now return to another of the sentences mentioned on p. 210 in Section 8.5, and we apply what we learned about how to determine selection and what it means for the existence of movement:

(52) Time seems to elapse slowly in the tropics

We want to determine what selects the DP *time*. There are several reasons to conclude that this DP is selected by the verb *elapse*, not by the verb *seem*. As we saw earlier, if we change *elapse* to a verb that requires a different kind of subject, like the verb *swim*, we must change this DP (and nothing else) to get an acceptable sentence:

(53) *Time seems to swim slowly in the tropics
(54) Sharks seem to swim slowly in the tropics

Secondly, it is possible to even have a "tightly selected" subject of an idiom as the subject of *seem* (cf. Section 8.4.2):

(55) The cat seems to be out of the bag
(56) The shit seems to have hit the fan

Here, the idiomatic readings associated with the expressions *the cat (be) out of the bag* or *the shit hit the fan* are available even though the subject appears in the matrix clause with the verb *seem*. We conclude that the subject of the main clause is selected by material in the embedded clause. To handle these violations of locality of selection, we – by definition – invoke Move.

The conclusion that movement is involved in these constructions with *seem* is corroborated by other cases of tight selection, such as the distribution of existential *there*. Recall that existential *there* can occur as the subject of clauses only with certain main verbs:

(57) a. There is a nurse available
b. * There run many people
c. * There stabbed an animal
d. ? There arrived many people

Now observe the following sentences:

(58) a. There seems to be a nurse available
b. * There seems to stab an animal
c. * There seems to run many people
d. ? There seemed to arrive many people

This supports our conclusion: the DP *there* is licensed by material in the infinitival clause. It may appear as subject of *seem* (in these sentences) only if it is selected by material in the infinitival clause.

In all the sentences we have just looked at, the only property of the DP subject of the main clause that mattered was whether or not it was selected by a predicate (a verb) in the infinitival clause. There was never any additional condition to impose on this DP that could have come from a specific requirement imposed by the verb *seem*. This is important to establish; otherwise we could not be sure that what we were seeing was **lexical selection** only by the infinitival verb.

The idea that *seem* is not selecting these subjects is confirmed by two pieces of evidence. First, the fact that idiom chunks can appear as the subject of *seem*, idiom chunks which are not, and cannot, be selected by *seem*. One such example is given with the idiom *keep (close) tabs on*. The relevant aspect of this idiom is that the noun *tabs* does not mean anything relevant outside of the idiom: it is only selected by *keep* (the whole phrase is non-compositionally interpreted). Nonetheless, it can appear as the subject of the *seem* clause:

(59) a. Close tabs seem to have been kept on John

The second reason is the well-formedness of the following sentences:

(60) a. It seems that John left
b. It seems that time elapses slowly in the tropics

Here we see that the subject of the main clause can also be a meaningless pronoun, a pronoun that does not refer to any particular thing. Again, such a pronoun has no content to select.[2] It is called a *pleonastic* or *expletive pronoun*.

The conclusion that we reach then is the following. In a sentence like:

(61) Time seems to elapse slowly in the tropics

the subject of the main TP is selected by the infinitival verb *elapse*, not by the main verb *seem* combining with T. To resolve the conflict between these conclusions and our ideas about locality of selection, we conclude that the DP *time* originates in the embedded clause. The simplest idea is that it originates as the subject of the TP. Then the structure of this sentence **before movement to the subject position of tensed T** looks like this:

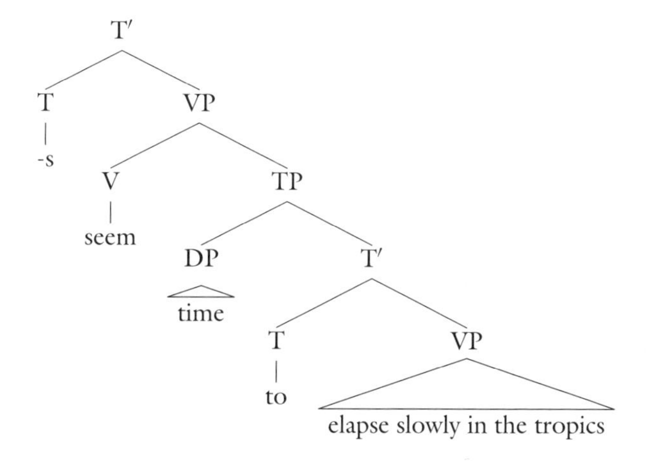

[2]It could, however, perhaps be selected as part of an idiom as in, e.g., *Beat it!*.

Notice that locality of selection is satisfied before movement applies, as *time* is the subject argument of *elapse*. *Seem* selects for an infinitival complement, which could be just a TP, as shown here (or a CP with a special silent C; see the discussion on p. 254 in Section 9.5.3).

The structure before movement is not an acceptable English sentence yet (even once T-to-V has applied). Not only do the affixes need to combine properly with the verbs, but English seems to require that a tensed clause have a nominative subject. We will return to this requirement in the next section.

For now, note that we can satisfy this requirement by moving *time* to the subject position of the tensed clause.

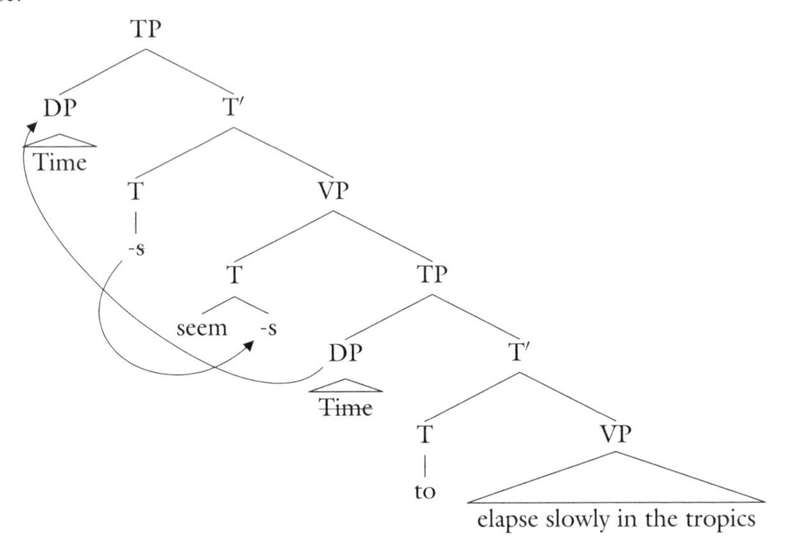

This movement of *time* to [Spec, TP] is called **raising to subject**. A verb like *seem*, whose superficial subject comes from elsewhere (i.e. from its complement) is called a **raising verb** (because it induces raising (of a DP) to subject [Spec, TP]).

Confusion alert: Do not mistake a **raising verb** like *seem* with **verb raising**. A raising verb is a verb that, like *seem*, triggers the movement of something else, e.g. the subject of an embedded verb. Raising verbs do not select a subject. Verb raising is often used to describe the movement of a verb, for example a verb climbing up the tree, i.e. undergoing V-to-T.

Remember that we said that whenever movement is involved, a pair of sentences is involved. This is the case here too. The sentence:

(62) Time seems to elapse slowly in the tropics

is well-formed if and only the following is well-formed too:

(63) Time elapses slowly in the tropics

The verb *seem* also allows small clause complements from which raising of a DP takes place:

(64) Several people seem sick
(65) Several people seem [$_{AP}$ ~~several people~~ sick]

It also allows a tensed CP complement:

(66) it seems (to Bill) [$_{CP}$ that Mary is sick]

Seem also optionally allows an experiencer to-PP:

(67) Mary seems (to Bill) [$_{CP}$ ~~Mary~~ to be sick]
(68) Mary seemed [AP ~~Mary~~ sick] (to Bill)

Given these observations, the lexical entry for *seem* will now look like this (assuming that *seem* takes a *to*-TP complement, see p. 254 in Section 9.5.3):

seem: V (PP–*exp*), TP–*to*
CP–*that*
AP

This indicates that *seem* may optionally take a *to*-PP that names the experiencer, that it takes as complement either a *that*-CP, a *to*-TP, or an AP, and that it does not select a subject.

Raising predicates are not very numerous, but they are not limited to verbs such as *seem, appear, happen*, especially when we look at infinitival clause complements. Raising is also found with adjectives such *likely* and *liable* as in *the shit is likely to hit the fan*.

8.5.3 EPP properties

In the previous section, we saw that raising to subject was required when the raising verb *seem* took an infinitival complement. We related this requirement to the observation that tensed clauses must have a subject in English. This requirement that tensed clauses have a subject is sometimes called the **Extended Projection Principle**, abbreviated to **EPP**. The name comes from the fact that this requirement does not look like a lexical requirement (of verbs) that would be satisfied just by enforcing the projection principle.

EPP: A tensed TP must have a subject.

In the case of a raising verb, after the raising to subject movement, this principle is satisfied. Of course, the raised DP will be nominative, a property that we have coded as selection for a nominative DP subject.

How should we encode this property in the grammar? We need to say that a +finite T requires a subject. We can code this as a lexical requirement of +finite Ts: they have a special feature – called an EPP feature – which has this effect. This EPP feature on T is a lexical property of T, and is satisfied when the syntax provides a subject for T. Accordingly, we can rewrite the lexical entry for past tense T in either of the following two ways:

-ed: T; [+tense], bound; epp:DP[+nominative]/CP; V; past tense
-ed: T; [+tense], bound; epp$_{nomDP/CP}$; V; past tense

Further questions: The advanced reader may have noticed that what we just said raises new questions. In particular, does expletive insertion only apply when the raising verb takes a tensed clause complement? If we allowed expletive insertion in all cases, we would derive:

* It seems to time elapse slowly in the tropics

Clearly this is excluded (and this is not a fact that is limited to English).

One way of thinking about this links this phenomenon to abstract Case (with a capital C, to distinguish it from case endings), which can be realized as case endings. The proposal (due to Jean-Roger Vergnaud) is that DPs such as the DP *time* need to bear Case. This is formulated as the **Case Filter**:

Case Filter: Overt DPs must have Case.

How does the DP get its case? Recall that tensed T has a nominative subject. If the DP *time* can only get a Case by associating with tensed T, e.g. by becoming its subject, this explains why the DP must move.

Conversely, why can't raising apply when *seem* takes a finite complement?

(70) it seems (to Bill) [$_{CP}$ that Mary is sick]
(71) *Mary seems (to Bill) [$_{CP}$ that ~~Mary~~/she is sick]

Pursuing this line, we could appeal to the fact that *Mary* already gets Case in the embedded clause. The DP *Mary* thus does not need to move further, and this could be the reason it cannot do so. This recalls the problem of why *do*-support cannot apply to support an affix if there is an alternative strategy (such as V-to-T). We described this property of insertion rules as **last resort**: it only applies if there is no alternative. Principles such as last resort are called **Economy Principles**. An alternative explanation is couched in terms of the notion of locality, to which we return in Chapter 10. See also Section 8.5.4 for a case of insertion not obeying last resort in this sense.

Past tense T is thus +tense, and it is a bound morpheme selecting a V as a sister. It also selects a VP complement, but all Ts do, so this is part of being a T and thus need not be stated in the lexical entry. Finally, we add the EPP feature: the notation epp:D[+nominative]/CP (or $\text{epp}_{nomDP/CP}$) is meant to indicate that such Ts require a subject, which can either be in the nominative case and of category D (in other words a DP) or a CP (which may well be nominative too, but this is harder to tell).[3]

We can now understand the appearance of expletive *it* in sentences such as:

(69) **It** seems (to Bill) [$_{CP}$ that Mary is sick]

Pleonastic *it* must be supplied when nothing occupies the subject position of a tensed TP, so that the EPP property of T can be satisfied. This rule is often called **expletive *it* insertion**. In a tensed clause with the verb *seem*, if raising has not taken place, this rule applies, inserting *it* in the subject position of the tensed TP. This will only happen when the verb *seem* takes a tensed CP clause as complement.

Underlying structure: Present seem that John past left the room
No raising⇒expletive insertion applies: It seems that John left the room

8.5.4 Simple clauses and locality of selection

Now that we can see that there is a rule of *raising to subject*, we can wonder where else it applies. In this section, we see that it routinely applies in simple clauses, and that this leads to the promised simplification of LoS.

Raising to subject in simple clauses
Let us compare the following sentences:

(72) a. John considers [$_{AP}$ several people sick]

[3]Since all +tense Ts have this feature, technically, we need not include it in our lexical entry: it is a subproperty of being +tense (at least in English). Still we indicate it as a reminder for the reader.

b. There are [$_{AP}$ several people sick]
c. Several people seem [$_{AP}$ ~~several people~~ sick]
d. Several people are sick

We have already seen that, in the first sentence, *several people sick* is a constituent (because it can be conjoined, as in *John considers [several people sick] and [several people healthy]*). We also concluded that this constituent is an AP headed by the adjective *sick*, which takes the DP *several people* as subject. We have the same analysis for the second sentence. In the third sentence, the string *several people sick* is also an AP. Since *seem* is a raising verb, movement takes place, displacing the subject *several people* from the subject position of the AP, and raising it to the subject position of the main TP.

Based on these three cases, we could conclude that the adjective *sick* requires a DP subject that is realized as a subject of the AP headed by *sick*.

For the fourth example, we have so far provided a different analysis. We have assumed that the subject required by the adjective *sick* could be realized syntactically as the subject of the TP containing this adjective. However, the other related structures suggest another analysis, namely one in which the subject DP required by the adjective *sick* is the subject of the AP underlyingly, and is raised to the subject of TP by Move (we leave it up to the reader to verify that the 3rd person plural present tense of the verb *be* undergoes V-to-T):

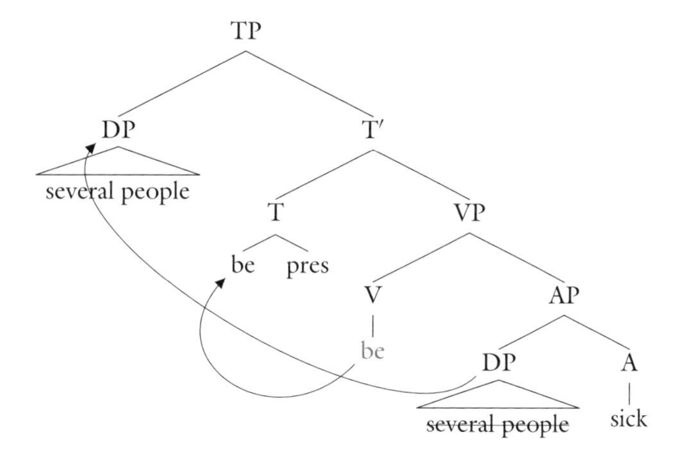

This analysis is in fact required by our assumptions: the verb *be* does not select for a subject at all. So if the DP *several people* appeared in the underlying structure as the subject of the TP, it would not be selected by anything.

This analysis can be generalized to all cases of subjects. Consider for example an idiom like this:

(73) The shit will [$_{VP}$ hit the fan]

The subject of the idiom is selected by *hit*, not by *will*, and now we have a way to make sense of this. Nothing prevents us from supposing that the subject DP appears as the subject of VP in the underlying tree, and moves to the subject of TP by raising to subject.

If this is generalized to all VPs, a number of advantages ensue. First, it will now be routinely true that APs or VPs have subjects. Second, it considerably simplifies how we can state the principle of locality of selection. We formulated that principle this way:

(74) **Locality of selection for syntax (preliminary)**:
  a. If a α selects β as complement, β is a complement of α.
  b. If a α selects β as subject, β is the subject of α or the subject of the clause containing α.
  c. If α selects β as an adjunct, β is the adjunct of α.

Now we can switch to a simpler idea:

(75) **Locality of selection (LoS), final version**: If a head α selects β, β appears as a complement, subject, or adjunct of α.

This desirable consequence was noticed and defended in Koopman and Sportiche (1991a) and has come to be known as the **VP-Internal Subject Hypothesis** or the **Predicate-Internal Subject Hypothesis**, as it applies to the selected subject of all predicates. This makes the statement of locality of selection extremely simple.

Adopting the new LoS principle, what a head lexically selects as a subject is always projected as the subject of this head in syntax. If it appears elsewhere, it has been moved.

(76) Bill is [~~Bill~~ sick]
(77) [The shit] will [~~the shit~~ hit the fan]
(78) [The girl in the red coat] will [$_{VP}$ ~~the girl in the red coat~~ [put a picture of Bill on your desk]] in two seconds

Do we sometimes see the subject of VP not raised to the subject of TP? We have seen this is the case for VP small clauses as, e.g., in *I saw [John leave], I made [John leave].*

Raising from infinitives

As a consequence of the VP-internal subject hypothesis, we need to slightly revise the structural derivation of raising to subject from inside an infinitive clause, to take into account the point of origin of the raised subject. We thus replace the derived tree on p. 214 (the second tree in Section 8.5.2) by the following, showing the subject starting VP-internally.

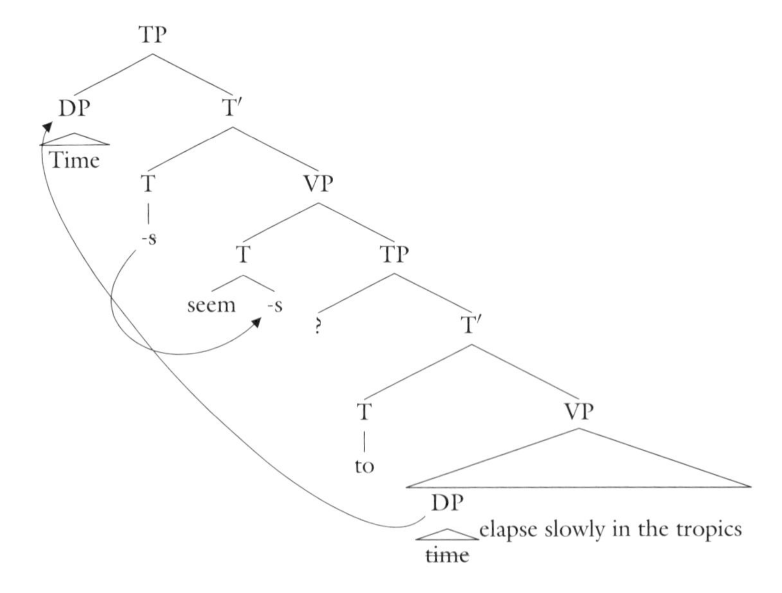

Note the question mark as the subject of the lower TP. Is there anything there? There could be, if tenseless Ts have an EPP feature like tensed Ts. In which case, the subject would have to first raise to the subject position of the infinitival T to satisfy that requirement, and next move to its surface position.

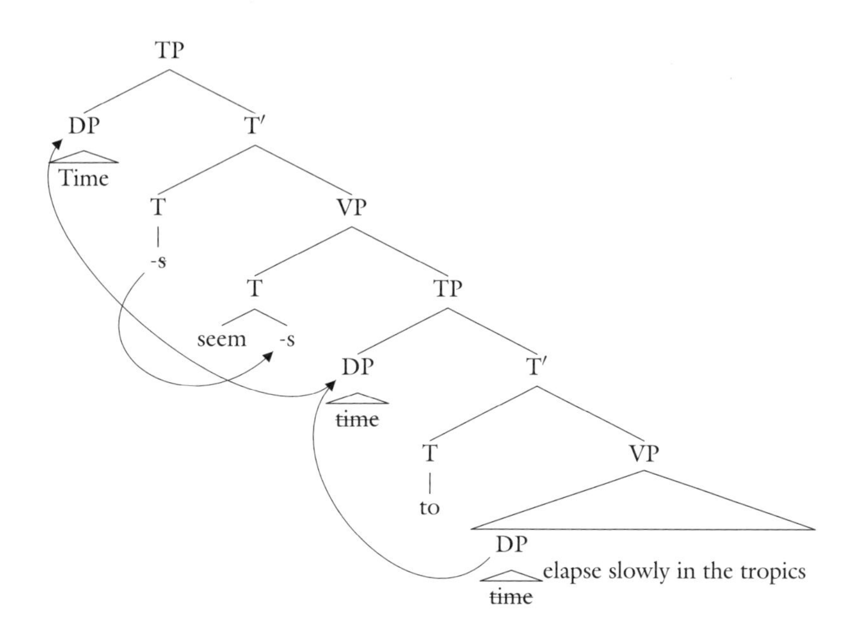

This is not a question we will decide here.

Detecting subjects in VP
In some cases, we can see a portion of the subject remaining in VP. Consider first a DP like *all the children*. *The children* is a DP, and *all the children* is also a DP. This suggests that *all* can be an adjunct to DP.

(79) [$_{DP}$ all [$_{DP}$ the children]]

If a DP like *all the children* starts as subject of a VP, it is possible to raise this entire DP to the subject of TP, but it is also possible to raise the slightly lower DP, leaving the adjunct *all* behind (as we have done with VP preposing: we could prepose a VP but leave a VP adjunct behind).

These options are illustrated below:

(80) **Underlying structure**: Will [$_{VP}$ [$_{DP}$ all [$_{DP}$ the children]] leave]
Whole DP moved:
[$_{DP}$ All [$_{DP}$ the children]] will [$_{VP}$ [$_{DP}$ ~~all [$_{DP}$ the children~~]] leave]
Only the smaller DP moved:
[$_{DP}$ The children] will [$_{VP}$ [$_{DP}$ all [$_{DP}$ ~~the children~~]] leave]

This phenomenon is called **Quantifier Floating** (because *all* is a quantifier and it appears to have "floated" away from the DP it modifies). It is discussed in Sportiche (1988) and provides evidence for the VP-internal subject hypothesis, or more generally, the predicate-internal subject hypothesis.

Back to subject–aux inversion

One might be tempted to entertain the idea that this is what happens in subject–auxiliary inversion. Take the following examples:

(81) Will John leave
(82) Will [$_{TP}$ John [$_{T'}$ will [$_{VP}$ ~~John~~ leave]]]
(83) [$_{TP}$ Will [$_{VP}$ John leave]]

Instead of saying that *will* has raised from T to C (as in (82)), one could imagine an analysis in which *John* has failed to raise from inside VP to TP as in (83). This analysis finds no support, however. First recall that whether T-to-C can apply crucially depends on what kind of material occurs in front of TP. The overt presence of a C in subordinate clauses, for example, blocks T-to-C. Under the analysis mentioned, the presence of an overt C blocking DP-movement to the subject of TP would remain mysterious. Second, certain adjuncts intervene between T and VP, and do so in the case of subject–auxiliary inversion as well. Under the T-to-C analysis this is entirely expected, but not under any analysis in which the subject fails to move to the subject of TP position in root questions:

(84) John will probably leave tomorrow
(85) Will John probably leave
(86) *Will probably John leave

Third, under VP ellipsis in yes/no questions, the subject, which would be in VP, would be expected to disappear:

(87) Speaker A: John is leaving tomorrow
(88) Speaker B: Oh yeah? Is he [$_{VP}$ ~~leaving tomorrow~~]
(89) * Is [$_{VP}$ ~~he leaving tomorrow~~]

Finally, in view of the discussion of **quantifier floating**, the following sentence provides yet another reason to reject this analysis of subject/aux inversion:

(90) Will the children often [all come]

Back to existentials

As a final remark, consider again the example:

(91) There are [$_{AP}$ several people sick]

We concluded that the verb *be* does not select a subject. We also noted that the existential *there* appearing here does not denote a location. Rather, it is an expletive. This means that the rule of expletive insertion also applies in existential *there* constructions. With a number of verbs, like *be*, that take small clause complements, the subject of the small clause may raise to the subject of TP, but does not have to. When it does not, expletive insertion can insert *there* in the subject position.

(92) Several men are sick
Underlying structure: pres be [$_{AP}$ several men sick]
Raising to subject, T-to-V hopping⇒surface structure:
Several men be+pres be [$_{AP}$ several mean sick]

(93) There are several men sick
Underlying structure: pres be [$_{AP}$ several men sick]
there **insertion, V-to-T⇒surface structure**:
There be+pres be [$_{AP}$ several men sick]

8.6 How Selection Drives Structure Building

Violations of the locality of selection have led us to postulate the existence of movement. The examples all had the same structure: a phrase or a head appears on the surface structure in a position that is not local to what it selects (in the case of moved heads) or what selects it (in the case of moved phrases). We construe such heads or phrases as having moved to their surface positions from positions where they were entertaining local selection relations.

Sometimes, selection is satisfied after movement. For example, in the case of DPs raising to the subject position of tensed TPs, the EPP property of T is only satisfied after movement has taken place. In other cases, if raising to subject does not take place, expletive insertion satisfies selection by T (its EPP property). This means that we cannot say that all selection is satisfied in underlying structures. In fact, we can construe many (perhaps all) movements as being triggered by the need to satisfy some lexical selectional requirement of a head in the landing site of movement.

Let us review cases of movement. In the case of head movement (affix hopping, V-to-T, T-to-C, Num-to-N), a head is moved or attracted to another head because one of the two heads is an affix, a bound morpheme. This need that affixes have is a selectional requirement. In the case of wh-movement in questions, movement to the subject position of a [+q] must take place. This need of a [+q] C is also a selectional requirement. In the case of raising to the subject position of a tensed clause, raising takes place to satisfy the EPP selectional property of T.

One question that arises concerns which selectional properties are satisfied when. That not all selectional requirements are satisfied in underlying structures means we must refine and further specify our model of syntactic organization. In order to do this, let us think about the steps that are involved in building a syntactic structure.

- We want to end up with a surface structure.
- To build a surface structure, we need first to build an underlying structure.
- To build an underlying structure, we need to select lexical items and organize them in constituents.

This involves two operations:

Merge: This operation actually puts lexical items and derived objects together to form more complex objects.

Move: This operation moves a previously selected and merged element to a subject position, "re-merging" it.

We may need some other operations, like ellipsis and *do*-support, to derive surface structures, but let's begin by considering how Merge and Move interact. The previous considerations yield something like the following model, inspired in part by recent work in Chomsky's (1993, 1995) Minimalist Program and Kayne's (1994) antisymmetry theory.

Here is a bottom-up (we could also do it top-down by reversing everything) step-by-step derivation of the sentence **John will see the movie** (treating *will* as having category T in order to avoid head movement):

- Using the notation for lexical entries from Section 6.8.3, assume the lexicon has the noun *movie* and the empty, singular number (writing *e* to signify that the singular number is not pronounced, as in Section 8.3.3).

movie: N
e: Num, NP

Step 1. Since this noun does not select anything, it is a complete phrase by itself. Since the number selects the noun, we use **Merge** to form the phrase, projecting the selector:

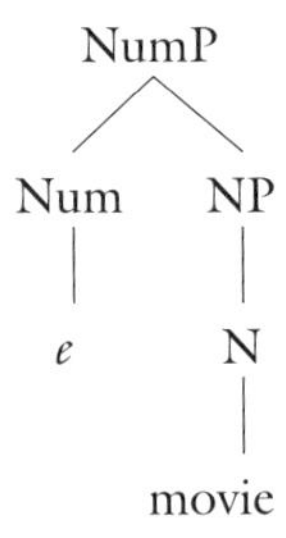

- Assume the lexicon includes a determiner that selects NumP complements:[4]

the: D, NumP

Step 2. We use Merge to combine the determiner with the previously built NumP, projecting the selector:

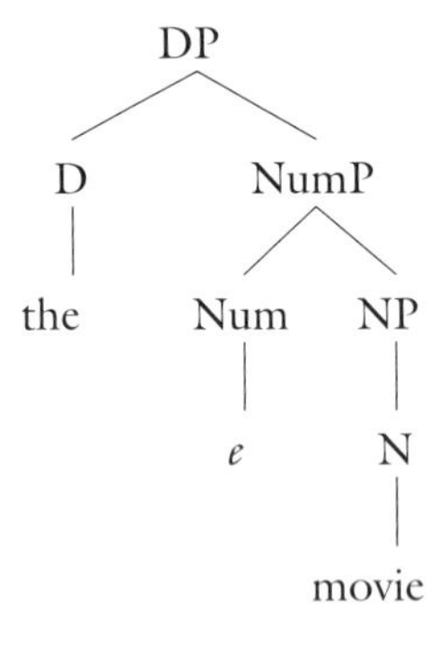

[4] It may be that all Ds select NumP, in which case we could drop this information from the lexical entry, as it would be redundant.

- Assume the lexicon includes the name *John*. (We list it as a DP, in order to set aside the question of exactly what internal structure DPs with names might have.)

John: DP

- Assume the lexicon includes the verb *see*, underlining an argument to indicate that it is the subject:

see: V, <u>DP</u>*exp*, DP*theme*

Step 3. We Merge the verb with the previously built DP, filling the complement (theme) position, projecting the selector:

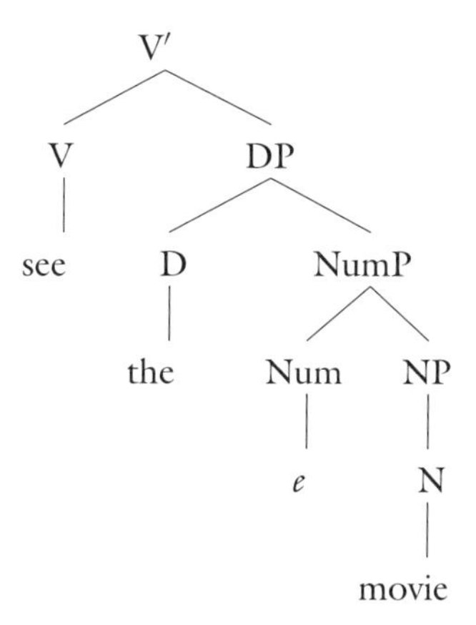

Step 4. The V′ has only one of the verb's arguments filled, so we now Merge the subject into the specifier position, projecting the selector once again:

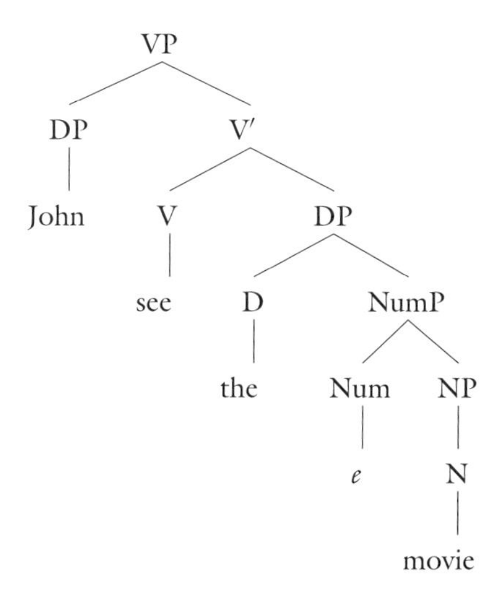

- Assume the lexicon includes *will*, selecting VP,[5]

will: T, [+tense] epp:DP_{nom}/CP

Step 5. We Merge this tense element with the previously constructed VP:

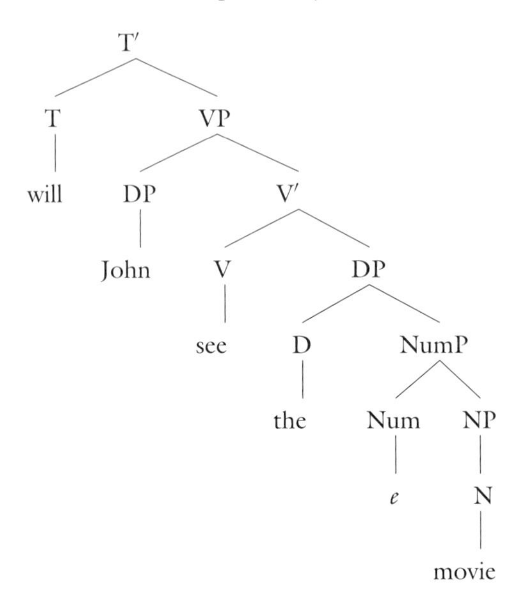

Step 6. Since the EPP feature of T is not satisfied, **Move** applies, putting the subject into the specifier of T, where the EPP feature can be satisfied locally:

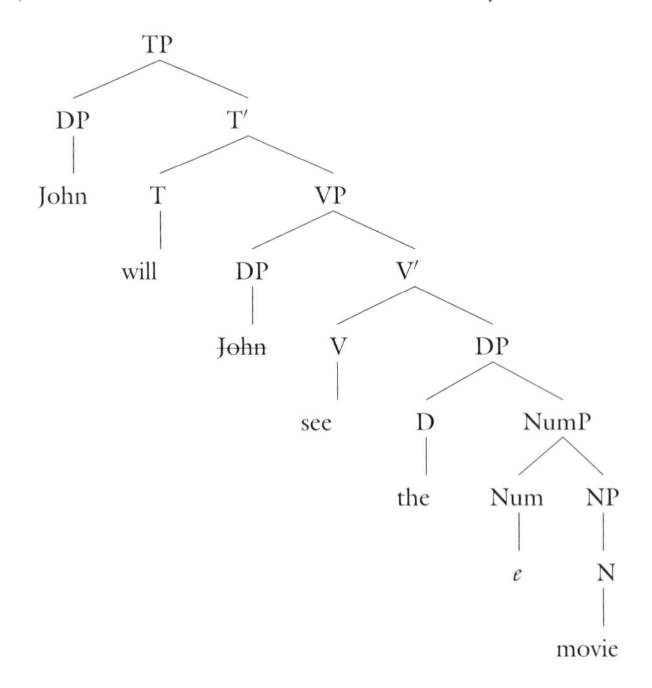

[5]We simplify this here. Remember that *will* is in fact just a defective verb that must raise to T.

- The lexicon may include a +tense silent complementizer (which automatically selects a +tense T) that appears in declarative main clauses. Let us assume so:

e: C, +tense

Step 7. We Merge the complementizer with the previously built TP, completing the clause:

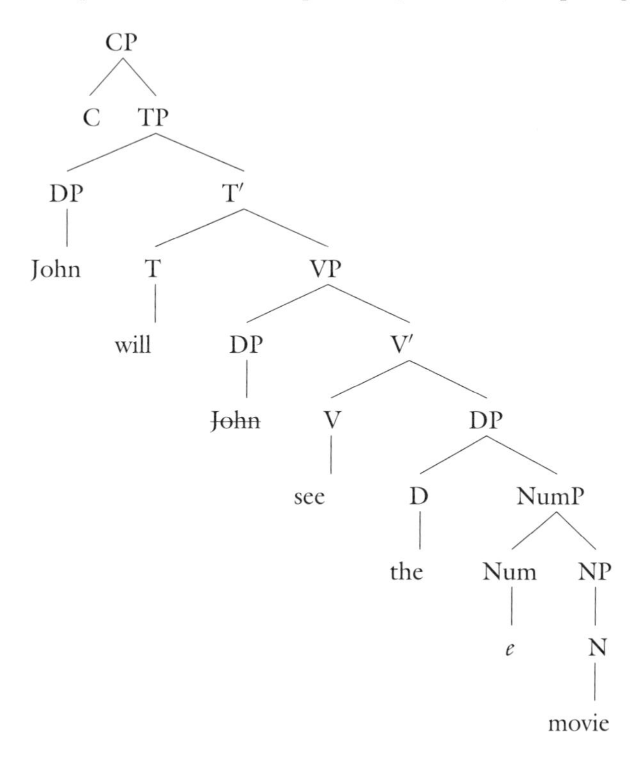

Comparing this perspective with the figure at the beginning of this chapter, we see that the definition of Merge and the way categories are projected guarantees that X-bar, projection, and selection locality principles are respected: each phrase has the category of its head, and lexical requirements are met by (underlying) adjacent constituents. Structural adjustments are accomplished by phrasal movement for EPP and wh-licensing (and by affix hopping and head movement for morphological requirements). Since EPP-driven movement and the like take place to satisfy an EPP property or feature, this kind of movement is sometimes called **Feature Checking**.

It is also interesting to notice that building the structure bottom-up highlights a similarity between Move and Merge: the only difference is that movement looks *inside* the tree for a phrase to "re-merge" instead of merging two completely independent objects. Recent work has aimed to treat Merge and Move as instances of the same basic structure-building mechanism. Move is therefore sometimes called Remerge, or Internal Merge, while Merge is called First Merge or External Merge. Binding theory and other semantic principles are defined on the structures that these mechanisms create.

8.7 Addressing some Previous Puzzles

We are now in a position to outline the general direction towards solving some problems we left unresolved in Chapter 3 (Section 3.11.3). The problems revolved around constructions like gapping or right node raising, which suggested that simple clauses could have two superficially incompatible structures. For a sentence like *they play unusual music*, "standard" tests support the rightmost structure, while right node raising suggests the leftmost structures.

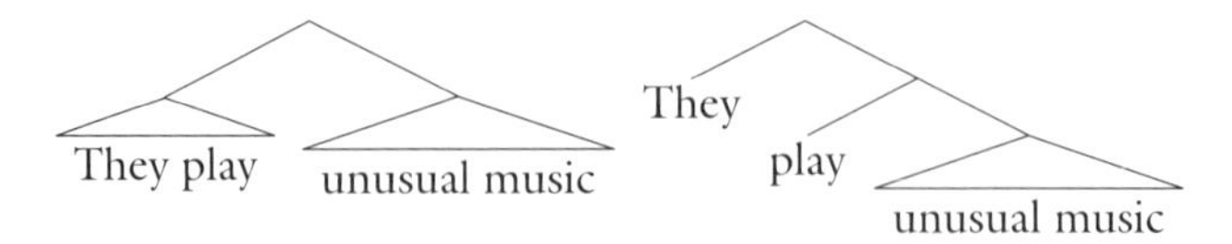

And for a sentence like *Sue will go to the theater*, standard tests support the following rightmost structure, while gapping supports the following leftmost structure:

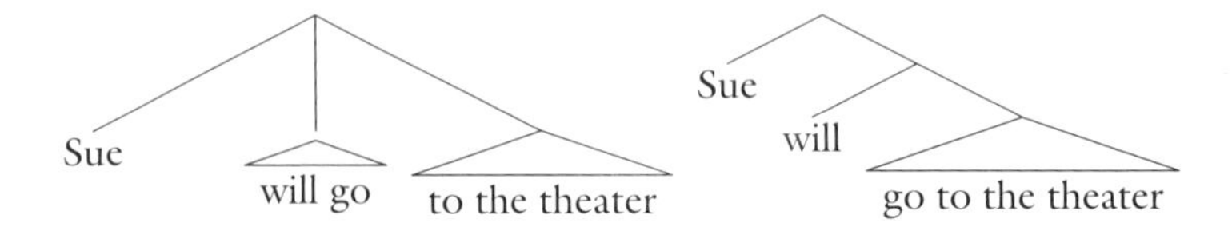

These rightmost structures are those in which selection is satisfied (more) locally. This is why we put the leftmost structures aside, until we had built some understanding of what drives constituency in the cases of local selection. Given the theory we have developed, the only analytical option that we have is to assume that the leftmost trees are derived by a reordering process, i.e. by Move. This makes a correct prediction: since the leftmost structures are derived, they should be allowed only if the rightmost structures are allowed.

Although this reasoning extends to a large variety of cases we have not talked about, it is important to note that **not every substring can be directly treated as a constituent**. As an illustration, take a seemingly exotic type of ellipsis, called **Pseudo-Gapping**, which elides a non-constituent string. (We will not discuss this in detail, but see e.g. Lasnik (1995).)

(95) John gave Bill a lot of money
(96) And Sue will Susan (Pseudo-Gapping)
(97) Sue will ~~give~~ Susan ~~a lot of money~~

The second sentence suggests that ellipsis has applied to the non-continuous string crossed out in the third. Needless to say, studying these kinds of phenomena, precisely because they appear exotic, can be extremely informative regarding the structure of syntactic theories.

8.8 Synthesis

We have now introduced enough of the fundamental mechanisms to have a good overall picture of the reasoning so far. This section takes stock of the whole approach.

We have seen that sentences or fragments of sentences are structured in particular ways, and that a wide range of linguistic phenomena are sensitive to such structures. We have called such structures trees, in line with the graphical representation we have used.

Trees contain three types of information:

i. They contain information about constituency, that is, about how sequences of elements are grouped together. We have called the basic grouping operation Merge.
ii. They also contain information about temporal ordering, coded by how elements are written down on a page, interpreting "to the left of" as meaning "precedes".
iii. They contain labels, which, via our labeling conventions, provide information about the nature of these constituents, and an indication of why they behave the way they do.

A potential structure for gapping

Here is a structure that potentially underlies gapping: rightward movement of the focused constituent, followed by "gapping" – ellipsis at least of the boxed T′ (perhaps TP, depending on whether the focused subject has undergone movement).

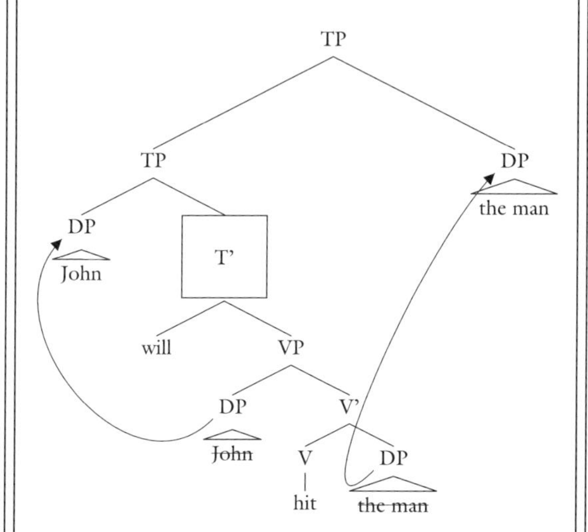

This leads to the expectation that, in gapping, T and its complement must be left unpronounced, while the focused subject and (at least) one other focus constituent remains. The following sentences are consistent with this expectation.

(94) a. I will want to eat a pear tomorrow, and
you will ~~want to eat an apple tomorrow~~ an apple

b. My mother said to Susan that she should go to art school, and
my father ~~said to Susan that she should go to law school~~ that she should go to law school

c. (Talking about some flowers) I'll probably put some on the piano, and
Susan ~~will probably put them on the table~~ on the table

d. Mary took advantage of Susan, and Bill ~~took advantage of John~~ of John

For example, we label a particular constituent XP (e.g. VP) to indicate that it shares properties with other XPs (e.g. other VPs) and to indicate that it behaves the way it does because it has an X (e.g. a V) as a head.

In addition, we have been led to the conclusion that a given sentence can be simultaneously analyzed as having different structures, e.g. what we have called surface or derived structures, and what we have called underlying structures. How did we get there?

This conclusion was based on the fact that lexical properties of lexical items are realized in tree structures (as they must be, given the projection principle), sometimes locally (this has a technical meaning), sometimes not. For example, if a given lexical item LI obligatorily c-selects a DP complement, this DP must always appear as an immediate complement of this LI in the tree (selection is satisfied locally). But sometimes this DP does not appear in a local relationship with this LI, violating locality of selection. We needed to construct rules telling us exactly how locality of selection can be superficially violated. We called these rules "movement rules," and defined a movement operation, Move. We conceived of Move as modifying an underlying tree, in which all selection is satisfied locally, and producing a derived tree, in which some selection is not satisfied locally. (Move could also modify a derived tree, creating another one.) Understanding exactly how locality of selection can be superficially violated requires understanding how Move works and is allowed to work in natural languages (something we will more systematically explore in Chapter 10).

To detect constituents, we have used constituency tests. The basic tests we have discussed are subdivided into:

Replacement (=a.k.a. substitution) tests:
pronominalization; *do so* replacement; ellipsis, such as VP-ellipsis, NP ellipsis, and gapping (which is only possible in coordinated structures).

Coordination: conjunction and disjunction.
Displacement/distortions: topicalization, wh-movement, clefts, pseudoclefts

Given a string S that we subject to one of these tests, the test probes the kind of structure a string S can have. A few reminders and remarks are important. **First**, any string manipulated as a block by some test is a constituent. This is true by definition. The kind of constituent involved, however, may be unfamiliar or difficult to identify. **Second**, different tests could give us different, apparently inconsistent, results. This type of situation would show that our string S is structurally ambiguous: it may allow different structural analyses. We have already encountered simple instances of this. If we apply different tests to the following string:

(98) I will hit the man with the binoculars

we find different results: one in which *[the man with the binoculars]* is a constituent as shown in (99), and one in which *[hit the man]* is a constituent and *[with the binoculars]* is an VP adjunct, as shown in (100).

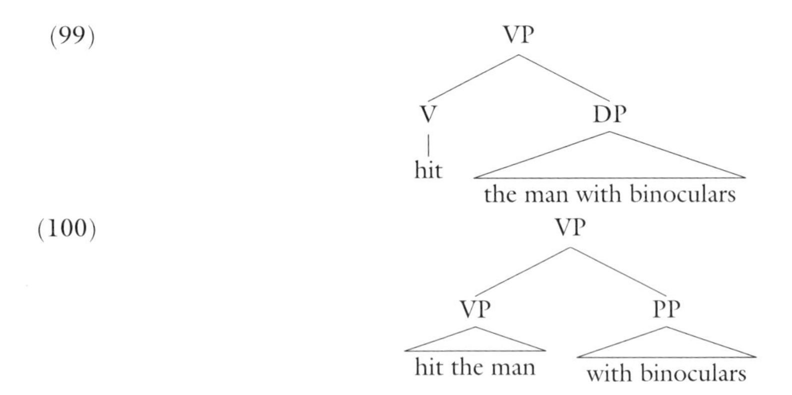

The first structure is supported by clefting:

(101) It is the man with the binoculars that I will hit

The second by VP ellipsis:

(102) John will [[hit the man] with shoes] and I will [[~~hit the man~~] with binoculars]

This distinction correlates with two different meanings (in which, respectively, the man had binoculars, and the hitting was done with binoculars). Intuitively, this meaning difference can be read off the tree representations. (This is due to the principle of compositionality. We have not provided precise rules to compute meaning but see, e.g. Heim and Kratzer (1998).)

Sometimes, however, while the conclusions are just as sound, it is less clear what the difference in structures correlates with. Consider the following sentence:

(103) John will push the man

This sentence can have a structure (104) in which *push the man* is constituent, as evidenced by, say, disjunction or VP ellipsis:

(104) a. John will [push the man] or [leave the area]
b. Mary will [push the man] and John will [~~push the man~~] too

But it can also have a structure as in (105), in which *will hit* is a constituent, as demonstrated by gapping:

(105) Mary will push the girl and John ~~will push~~ the man

These results may seem contradictory, but there is no contradiction: it just means that the sentence can be structurally ambiguous. Note that in the second instance, there is a contrast established between *Mary* and *John* on the one hand and between *the girl* and *the man* on the other. This contrast is absent in (104), so there is also a difference in meaning, but of a different kind from that found between (99) and (100).

Given the general conclusions we have reached, either structure (104) or structure (105) must involve movement(s). We concluded it must be structure (105). Why? Fundamentally, because there is an asymmetry between these sentences: if a gapped structure is well-formed, there must be a corresponding well-formed non-gapped structure, but not vice versa.[6] We model this asymmetry by deriving the gapped structures (by movement) from the other structures (and we have seen an example of how this could be done on in Section 3.11.3).

Note that the two structures are not simultaneously available.

(106) *Mary will [rob a bank] and [steal a car], and John ~~will rob~~ a store

It is not possible to have a structure with VP conjunction, which requires a particular constituency, being a context for gapping, which requires another.

Crucially, binding theory, introduced to deal with regularities among the referential dependencies that DPs hold with one another, both capitalizes on and confirms what we found regarding constituency. As we will see in Chapters 11 and 12, binding theory can be used a lot more, to great efficacy.

Third, while tests tells us something about the structure a sentence can have, they do not tell us anything about the derivational history of the sentence: tests only provide information about *derived* trees. For example, in the sentence:

(107) Which book about Galileo did you say you wanted to buy

we know that the wh-moved phrase **can** form a constituent with the verb *buy* as in the sentence:

(108) Who said you wanted to buy which book about Galileo

But no test that we have seen so far will tell us that the underlying structure of (107) contains *[buy which book about Galileo]* as a constituent.

This raises the following question: are there ways to probe for underlying structures? The answer to this question is positive. One type of positive answer arises by definition: since we define underlying structures as encoding local satisfaction of selectional relations, any reliable indication that some element E is actually selected remotely by another A will suggest that E has moved from a position in a structurally local relation with A.

[6]The advanced reader may, of course, be aware that this can be contradicted by "island repair" under ellipsis, a topic that we cannot address here, which would require a somewhat more abstract formulation of this regularity. See, in particular, Merchant (2001).

We have already discussed a variety of constructions exhibiting these properties (see Section 8.4):

- An idiom chunk separated from the rest of the idiom (*the cat seems to be out of the bag ...*).
- A case-marked element bearing the Case licensed by a remote element (cf. *whom does the queen appreciate*? vs. *who appreciates the queen?*
- Existential *there* licensed only in certain contexts but appearing remotely from these contexts (*there seems ~~there~~ to be some problem here*) (see Section 8.4.4).

Are there other ways to probe structures? We will answer positively, particularly in Chapter 11.

8.9 Terminology and Notation

We have defined **Merge** and **Move**. As mentioned previously, Merge is sometimes called **first merge** or **external merge**, while Move is also referred to as **remerge**, or **internal merge**.

Raising to subject is a species of what is sometimes called **A-movement**, and sometimes **NP movement** (though the latter is now a misleading and confusing term, as it seems we are actually moving DPs). This type of phrasal movement only moves DPs (or subject clauses).

Wh-movement and topicalization belong to the category of **A-bar movement**. This type of movement can move several types of XPs (DPs, VP, PP, APs, . . .).

Satisfying selection by movement is sometimes called **feature checking**: for example, moving to subject of TP checks the EPP feature of T. Saying that features must be checked is equivalent to saying that selection must be satisfied.

When a piece of structure is moved, we have represented the launching site as containing crossed out material. This crossed out material is called a **trace** of the moved material. Sometimes, instead of representing traces as follows:

(109) Bill is [~~Bill~~ sick]
(110) [The shit] will [~~the shit~~ hit the fan]
(111) [The girl in the red coat] will [$_{VP}$ ~~the girl in the red coat~~ [put a picture of Bill on your desk]] in two seconds

we represent them as here:

(112) Bill$_k$ is [t_k sick]
(113) [The shit]$_k$ will [t_k hit the fan]
(114) [The girl in the red coat]$_k$ will [$_{VP}$ t_k [put a picture of Bill on your desk]] in two seconds

The notation t_i is just another way of notating the unpronounced copy, the trace (widely used in the original literature before 1993). To identify what the trace is a trace of, we coindex the moved phrase and its trace. Note that a phrase c-commanding its trace **binds** it, by definition (see Chapter 7).

8.10 Conclusion

8.10.1 Summary

This chapter is very important. We have introduced many ideas and it is essential to understand the logic that led to them.

First, we have noticed that lexical selection is sometimes not satisfied locally. These structures form a well-defined set: they have the property that they are systematically related to structures in which locality is not violated. To make sense of this, we have postulated that the former are derived from the latter. We called the deriving process Movement, or Move. Move displaces a constituent away from the position where it is selected. You must be very clear about this. Movement is **the** mechanism by which such violations of locality arise.

We have discussed several ways of diagnosing selection relations, all involving some form of covariation (idiom chunks, Case distribution, existential *there*). You should know how to use these diagnostics.

Movement of a phrase is involved in topicalization and in wh-questions. Movement of a head is involved in affix hopping, V-to-T, T-to-C, and Num-to-N. Movement of a phrase is also involved in *raising categories*: these are categories that trigger raising to subject. Remember not to confuse this with "verb raising" which is another name for V-to-T movement. Raising categories include verbs like *seem*, auxiliary verbs like *be* and *have*, and generally the category T since, even in simple clauses, the subject of TP always originates elsewhere. You should know what kinds of movement there are and their basic properties.

We have also found that tensed clauses in English always require subjects – something we call the extended projection principle – and that subjects can be supplied by movement, as in raising to subject cases, or by expletive insertion of *it* or *there*.

It is important to distinguish two aspects of this proposal about the existence of movement operations. One is that there are cases in which selection is local and cases in which it is non-local. It is a **terminological** decision to call all cases of actual non-local selection movement.

The other aspect concerns how movement should be formalized. We have developed a view according to which movement is a relation between two trees. We represent this relation as a derivation of one tree from the other by an operation that transforms the first (this is why this approach is sometimes called **transformational grammar**). The claim that all of topicalization, wh-movement, T-to-C, raising to subject, etc., are cases of movement, means that the relations they express are best analyzed as transformations in the sense given above.

8.10.2 What to remember

There is a lot to remember in this very important chapter. Minimally, you should know the different types of movement or (Move operations) that are found: head movement such as T-to-C, A-movement such as raising to subject, and A-bar movement such as wh-movement. You should be clear about why we postulate the existence of movement dependencies. You should also know how to detect movement, by detecting selectional relations that are-non local by using e.g. the distribution of idiom chunks, and the driving force behind the existence of movement (satisfaction of selection).

8.10.3 Puzzles and preview

Noticing non-local selection and postulating Move to derive it has brought along many new questions, some of which we will progressively address.

What kinds of movement are there? What is allowed to move? Under what conditions? The movement types we have seen are representative. They differ in terms of what they move, but a certain uniformity holds across movement types:

- Movement between two positions always involves one position c-commanding the other.
- Move seems "triggered": movement takes place, as in head movement, wh-movement, or raising to subject, to satisfy some lexical requirement of some head (often referred to as "feature checking" in the syntactic literature).
- Movement is subject to what is called the "attract closest" principle, which prohibits movement of an element to some position if a movement to this position (of something

else) spanning a smaller structure is allowed. The already evoked head movement constraint is one instance of this principle in action, of which we will see more in Chapter 10.
- There are certain boundaries that Move cannot cross (bounding nodes or phase boundaries), which we will also see in Chapter 10, and this constitutes one of the major diagnostics for movement, and distinguishing between types of movement.

Among the questions that are raised are whether or not non-finite Ts have an EPP feature too (we will not discuss this question here, but there is some evidence in favor of a positive answer), and how common EPP features are (as we will see in Chapter 12, quite a bit more common than we have seen so far). We have also evoked the last resort principle, which we will not discuss here, but see, e.g. Chomsky (1991).

8.10.4 Further exercises

(1) Writing lexical entries

(i) Using the format given in this chapter, write the lexical entry for the C +q, *have, be,* and *will.*

(ii) Give the surface tree for the following questions:

a. Has John studied Russian?
b. Are your two brothers in London right now?
c. Will Bill have been writing chapters?
d. Did your friend like the movie?

(2) Tree drawing: *if* clauses and -*ing*

Your task is to construct a tree for the sentence in (1):

(1) If you had just thought of bringing her the groceries, she would have been delighted

(i) Break down the string into big subconstituents, and work these out before you start drawing the tree. This will require you to apply tests and figure out how we should motivate the constituent structure: see what the issues are and tell us why you made certain decisions (and which tests you used).

(ii) The following sentences will be helpful for figuring out some of the fragments. (Determine what each example shows and for each example state what conclusion(s) you can (minimally) conclude.) Once you are done, put it all together.

(2) My grandmother said that if you had thought of just bringing her the groceries, ...

(3) a. Bringing her the groceries is important
b. Quickly bringing her the groceries is important
c. To bring her the groceries is important
d. That you bring her the groceries is important
e. *The bringing her the groceries is important
f. *The quick bringing her the groceries is important

For the grand tree in (1), make sure that you obey the principle of locality of selection everywhere in your tree.

(iii) List two adjuncts, two complements, and two heads in your tree for (1).

(3) Ambiguity and structure

The sentence in (1) is ambiguous. (The ambiguity has to do with whether the *chicken* is interpreted as the agent or the theme of the verb to *eat*)

(1) The chicken should have been ready to eat

Give the tree structures corresponding to each interpretation and provide an unambiguous paraphrase for each of these structures.

(4) *If* clauses, head movement

(1a) can be expressed as (1b) with no (discernible) change in meaning:

(1) a. If you had thought of just bringing her the groceries, the chicken would have been ready to eat now
b. Had you thought of just bringing her the groceries, the chicken would have been ready to eat now

Some forms, however, are not possible:

(2) a. *Had if you thought of just bringing her the groceries
b. *If had you thought of just bringing her the groceries...
c. *Had you had thought of just bringing her the groceries
d. *You if had/had if thought of just bringing her the groceries ...
(i) Discuss how we could treat (1b) (short answer).
(ii) Can your proposal account for the impossible forms in (2)? For each, state how.
(iii) Draw a likely structure for "of just bringing her the groceries" (see the previous exercise as well).

Consider (3b):

(3) a. Had you been thinking of . . .
b. *Been you had thinking of . . .
(i) Is the ungrammaticality of (3b) expected or not? Why? Why not?
(ii) If the principles we have seen are universal, would you expect a form like (3b) to be possible in any language? Why? Why not? (This will require some thought; the answer(s) can be short, but should be clearly formulated.)
(iii) What if principles could vary for individual languages? Would you expect in that case that (3a) and (3b) could *both* occur in the same language? Why? Why not?

(5) French and English

The following sentences compare the distribution of French and English finite verb forms.

The first line is the French sentence, and the second line is the literal gloss (this is the line relevant for the analysis). Sometimes a third line is given with the English translation. Your task is to find out how exactly French and English differ and to articulate the difference. To do this: start by looking at each example carefully; do a structural analysis for English (i.e. apply your constituent structure tests and draw a tree) and see what you need to say about how to go from English to French, using the general theory developed in the book. For the purpose of this exercise, you may assume that French is (sufficiently) like English (e.g. same X-bar parameters, same distribution of adjuncts, same VPs, same TPs, etc.) but obviously there are some differences you need to figure out.

(1) a. Il devient parfois grognon
he becomes sometimes cranky
"He sometimes gets cranky"

b. Il peut parfois devenir grognon
he can sometimes become.INF cranky

c. Il est parfois devenu grognon
he is sometimes become.PART cranky
"He sometimes got cranky" (lit: He has sometimes gotten cranky)

d. Il a parfois pu devenir grognon
he has sometimes can.PART become.INF cranky
"He could sometimes get cranky"

e. Il n'est pas souvent devenu grognon
he NEG'is *pas* often become.PART cranky
"He did not often get cranky" (lit: He has not often gotten cranky)
Here and below, ignore the (optional) negative particle *ne* in your trees. Assume that *pas* is exactly like English *not*.

f. Il ne devient pas souvent grognon
he NEG becomes *pas* often cranky
"He doesn't often get cranky"

g. de ne pas souvent devenir grognon est important
to NEG *pas* often become.INF cranky is important
"It is important to not get cranky often"

(i) Give the English trees for (1a), (1b), (1c), and (1f); and show how you get to French from these trees.
(ii) State in one sentence what the difference(s) between English and French is (are). Be brief and precise.
(iii) Feel free to add any comments, questions, or remarks.

(Inspired by Emonds (1978) and Pollock (1989). This exercise does not compare the similar placement of *être* and *avoir* and modals in French infinitival complements with the similar behavior of these elements in English tensed clauses.)

(6) Benglish problem: phrase structure and head movement

(i) Krenglish is a (hypothetical) language that is identical to English in every respect except that main verbs move to T (instead of T lowering onto V) and Ns move to Num (instead of Num lowering onto N).

Translate the following English sentence into Krenglish. (You should draw the tree before spelling out the Krenglish sentence.)

(1) John often reads new books

(ii) Xenglish is a (hypothetical) language that is identical to English in every respect except for the fact that T never selects a subject. (i.e. in Xenglish the lexical entry of T is T: VP (for any value of T)).

Translate (1) into Xenglish.

(iii) Menglish is a (hypothetical) language that is just like English, expect for the fact that all Specifiers/Subjects follow X′.

Translate (1) into Menglish.

(7) Constituency (and some affix hopping)

Draw the tree for each of the numbered sentences below. Make sure your tree reflects the facts in the lettered examples below each numbered example. The facts given there do not necessarily represent all the information you need to know to draw the tree; rather, they are guidelines for the potentially tricky parts. Notate affix hopping where it occurs.

(1) The nervous guitarist wanted the singer to remove his aesthetically unconscionable hat before the show
  a. . . . to remove the aesthetically unconscionable hat before the show
  b. *. . . to remove his aesthetically one before the show
  c. . . . to remove his aesthetically unconscionable one before the show
  d. . . . to remove his one before the show
  e. He wanted the singer to do so
  f. He wanted the singer to do so before the show
  g. He did
  h. *He did before the show
  i. What he wanted was the singer to remove his aesthetically unconscionable hat before the show
  j. The nervous one wanted the singer to remove his aesthetically unconscionable hat before the show.
  k. He wanted him to remove it before the show

(2) The chancellor baked every regent a highly unusual cake for Christmas
  a. He did so
  b. He baked them a highly unusual cake for Christmas
  c. He baked them the highly unusual cake for Christmas
  d. He baked every one a highly unusual cake for Christmas
  e. *He baked every one for Christmas
  f. *He baked every regent a highly one for Christmas
  g. He baked every regent a highly unusual one for Christmas
  h. It was for Christmas that he baked every regent a highly unusual cake
  i. The chancellor did so for Christmas
  j. *He did so a highly unusual cake for Christmas

(Exercise inspired by Peter Hallman.)

(8) Review

This exercise asks you to draw trees. Now you have to draw trees as consistently as possible with the textbook. Relevant elements: basic phrase structure of CP, TP, DP, VP, etc., small clauses, argument/adjunct distinction, treatment of Number in DPs, treatment of auxiliary verbs, head movement, and *wh*- movement.

(i) Draw the derived (or surface) trees for the following sentences. Throughout, if there is movement, indicate the starting (underlying) position and the derived (surface) position.
  a. For the Lakers to win would greatly please several students.
  b. The tropical storm covered the mountains with snow on Saturday
  c. When had he heard Bill sing?
  d. The governor's report on the situation is truly frightening

(ii) Answer the following questions.
  a. Is the constituent *with snow* in (1b) a complement or an adjunct?

b. Justify your answer to (iia). (Provide an argument in support of your answer. This should take the form of a little explicit reasoning based on some piece of data you come up with illustrating the behavior of this constituent.)
c. Is the constituent *on the situation* in (1d) a complement or an adjunct?
d. Justify your answer to (iid). (Provide an argument in support of your answer. This should take the form of a little explicit reasoning based on some piece of data you come up with illustrating the behavior of this constituent.)

(9) Review 2

Drawing trees involves two things: deciding constituency and labeling nodes. At this point – when in doubt – it is more important to get the constituency right than the labels right. If you do not know how to label a node or if you are not sure, write X with your guess in parentheses (e.g. X (DP) = I am not sure what it is: I think it is a DP).

(i) Draw the tree for the following sentences or expressions. Throughout, if there is movement, indicate the starting (underlying) position and the derived (surface) position.
  a. Whose friend's new neighbor would she have told how to properly lean the ladder against the wall?
  b. My few half-hearted attempts to build complete listings of my record collection
(ii) Write the lexical entry for the verbs *tell*, *lean,* and the noun *listing* (see end of Sections 6.8.2 and 6.8.3 for the format).
(iii) Are the selectional properties of these items satisfied locally in YOUR trees for (ia) and (ib) in the sense of the principle locality of selection given on p. 244. Justify your answers. (Here it is more important to give an answer consistent with YOUR trees even if your trees are wrong.)

(10) Tree drawing and explaining ill-formedness

(i) Draw the surface tree for the following sentences. Apply the principle of locality of selection (i.e. determine the lexical entries of the individual verbs).
  If you have difficulty, remember and apply your constituency tests! And, as always, if you encounter unsolvable problems, draw the tree in the way that seems most appropriate and write down what the problems are.
  (1) The director's sister has decorated the three large tables adjacent to the leftmost door
  (2) It did not seem to the soldiers that they had a good strategy
  (3) Has Mary indeed shown you the reviews of her movie?
  (4) John didn't climb these six high mountains yet, did he?
  (Treat the tag questions as an adjunct to the main TP/CP.)
(ii) Explain why the following strings are ill-formed (using the hint given for each question). Be precise in your explanation.
  (5) * Mary had been reading but Sophie did not
  (Hint: Draw the tree for the first conjunct and think about how VP ellipsis would apply to it.)
  (6) *You did not have eaten the soup
  (Hint: draw the tree and ask why *do*-support is unnecessary in this case.)

(11) Head movement constraint and negation

Section 8.5.2 discusses negation and two possible structural analyses of *not.*

(i) Give the two trees for the following sentences, one for each structural analysis of *not:*

(1) John will not eat soup

For the rest of the problem, assume that the following principle is correct:

(2) *Head Movement Constraint:*
A head can only move to the closest head that c-commands it or that it c-commands.

You are going to have to construct arguments. In each case, you have to think in structural terms (i.e. what is the tree for this sentence and how is it derived? If the HMC is true, what does it allow or disallow in either structural analysis of negation?).

(ii) On the basis of the following sentence, construct an argument against the leftmost (in Section 8.5.2) option:

(3) John has not eaten

(iii) On the basis of the following sentence, construct an argument against the rightmost (in Section 8.5.2) option:

(4) John did not eat

(iv) (Bonus question): Assuming both arguments are correct, explain which argument is worse (which argument is more damning). That is, if you had to choose one of the two structural analyses for negation, which one would be preferable? Explain why.

(12) **Benglish problem: phrase structure, head movement, and EPP**

The data in (1) are sentences in Benglish (hypothetical language) and their English translation. Your task is to tell (i) what the X-bar structure looks like in this language; (ii) whether this language has V-to-T or T-to-V for auxiliary verbs; (iii) whether it has V-to-T or T-to-V for main verbs; and (iv) whether [Spec,TP] selects for a nominative subject or not (i.e. whether or not it has the EPP)?

Other than those things, you can assume Benglish has ALL of the rules of English (for instance, there is a T-to-C requirement for questions, and the right-hand rule applies, etc.).

(1)

	Benglish	English translation
a.	Girl tall the	The tall girl
b.	Her sister	Her sister
c.	Sue sister's	Sue's sister
d.	She cake the bakes	She bakes the cake
e.	She cake the not bakes	She doesn't bake
f.	She cake the baking be not will	She will not be baking the cake
g.	She house the in not is	She is not in the house
h.	It raining is	It is raining
i.	It raining be to seems	It seems to be raining
j.	She cake baked?	Did she bake a cake?

(13) **Categories**

The Danish linguist Jespersen (1860–1943) proposed that *few* is an adjective. Consider the following examples:

(1) a. He saw few people
a. He saw fewer people
b. He saw the fewest people

(i) Briefly state why these examples show *few* is an A. Be explicit.
(ii) Provide at least one additional argument that presents additional support for the fact that few is an A. (Hint: think modifiers.)
(iii) If *few* is an adjective, this raises the question of what to do with strings like the following:
(2) A few books

Explain what the puzzling fact about (2) is, taking into account the examples below:

(3) a. A book/*a books
b. A nice book/* a nice books
c. *A few book /a few books

(iv) Formulate a hypothesis about the syntactic structure of the string in (2), and draw the tree. (Hint: take the projection principle and the principle of locality of selection into account, i.e. what do we know about the lexical entry for *a*? What does it always combine with as a lexical property?)
(v) (Optional further explorations): You might want to explore if your hypothesis gives you some handle on the following contrasts.

(4) a. Give me a few (of your candies)
b. *Give me a nice/red (of your candies)

(Based on Kayne (2005))

8.10.5 Further readings

The literature on movement is extensive and diversified depending on the type of movement, or particular construction (or language), one is looking at. For the principle of locality of selection – which goes back to Chomsky (1965) – as formulated here and used throughout the book, see Sportiche (2005).

There is an extensive literature on the English auxiliary system and the distribution of different verbal forms, starting with Chomsky (1957). Much of what is presented here is inspired by further pioneering work by Emonds (1976) on what we call V-to-T, or den Besten (1983) on what we call T-to-C.

An important work on this topic, Pollock (1989), is due to Jean-Yves Pollock, currently (in 2012) an emeritus professor at the university of Paris-Est in France and depicted here. In this work he shows that much more articulated structures are needed to account for the distribution of verbs forms across clause type. V-to-T, T-to-C, and T-to-V are particular instances of what is is generally known as head movement. Among the extensive literature on this topic, see Koopman (1984), Travis (1984), and Baker (1988).

Further readings were introduced in the body of the chapter.

9
Infinitival Complements: Raising and Control

This chapter is devoted to a discussion of (some) infinitival clause structures. As we will see, there is a rich and somewhat intricate typology of such structures, which the tools that we have developed will allow us to characterize. We will start with the only kind of violation of LoS from the list (50) on p. 234 that we have not yet discussed: **(Subject) Control** constructions. Superficially, these resemble raising to subject constructions but, as we will see, they are structurally different:

(1) **Susan** hopes/wants/tries to sleep — Subject control
(2) **Susan** seems to sleep a lot — Raising to subject

We will show that, unlike what happens in raising to subject cases, in subject control constructions, the subject of the main clause is selected both by the main verb and by the embedded verb. This will lead us to postulate the presence of a silent subject in the infinitival clause, which we will call PRO. In this chapter, we will explore various issues about the nature and behavior of PRO. One of its properties is that it is bound by the main clause subject. As we will see, this will allow simple solutions to some intricate problems for the binding theory.

We find not only raising to subject and subject control constructions, which establish relations between a main subject and the subject of a *to*-infinitival, but also parallel cases involving a superficial object in the main clause and the subject of the infinitival:

(3) a. John believes Bill to have slept
    b. John convinced Bill to sleep

We will see that *Bill* is not selected by *believe* in (3a). Verbs like *believe* are known as **Raising to Object** or **Exceptional Case Marking** verbs. But *Bill* can be shown to be selected by *convince* in (3b). This pattern is known as Object Control.[1]

To understand this chapter, it is important to remember the basics of binding theory as discussed in Chapter 7. Furthermore, it is essential to have mastered the content of Chapter 6, and to know in particular how to determine selectional properties of individual verbs.

[1] This terminology is discussed in Section 9.5.3.

An Introduction to Syntactic Analysis and Theory, First Edition.
Dominique Sportiche, Hilda Koopman, and Edward Stabler.

9.1 Subject Control

Let us start with:

(4) **Susan** hopes to sleep

We are going to show that the subject in bold is selected as an argument by both the verb *sleep* in the infinitival complement, **and** by *hope*. As a first indication, note that we can provide a close paraphrase of (4) with a tensed clause complement instead of an infinitive:

(5) Susan$_j$ hopes that she$_j$ will sleep

As usual, coindexation indicates that the DP *she* refers to *Susan*. Clearly, these two sentences are synonymous (or almost – we will see later that there is a subtle difference between the two): they seem to be true or false in the same situations. In the latter, we clearly see (because of what we know about sentence structure) that *she* (meaning Susan) is selected by the verb *sleep* and *Susan* is selected by the verb *hope*.

Second, changing the bottom verb can lead to unacceptability:

(6) * Susan hopes to elapse

This is clearly an incompatibility between *Susan* and *elapse*, not between *hope* and *elapse*. We see in the following sentence that the verb *elapse* can perfectly well be the main verb of a clause complement of the verb *hope*:

(7) Susan hopes [that time will elapse]

Conversely, we can see that a DP subject selected by the infinitival verb must still be compatible with – i.e. selected by – the main verb:

(8) * Time hopes to elapse

Here *time* satisfies the selectional requirements of *elapse*, but not of *hope*.

More generally, in a sentence frame of the form *X hopes to VP**, where VP* is a particular VP, X must simultaneously be allowed to occur in a frame such as *X hopes for this* and in a frame such as *X VP**. For example, *X hopes to sleep all day* is allowed only if both *X hopes for this* and *X sleeps all day* are. So, in this case, the main subject must satisfy the requirements of *hope*, i.e it must denote an experiencer, an entity with a mind. In addition, it must be possible as a subject for an infinitival verb too.

How can both the verb *sleep* and the verb *hope* select the subject of the main clause? By the principle of locality of selection, this subject must be both the subject of the VP headed by *hope* and the subject of the VP headed by *sleep*. The only way to resolve this problem is to suppose that, although we hear only one DP, there are actually two DPs in the syntactic structure. Each one is selected as a subject by its own verb in accordance with the principle of locality of selection and the projection principle.

The question we address now is this: what is the nature of the silent subject? One thing we know is that the main subject and the silent subject are interpreted in the same way, more or less, as the name and the pronoun in Section 9.1, and they must corefer. How can we represent the silent subject to get this result? Here it is useful to compare these cases with cases where both DPs are pronounced. There are several possible options, listed below.

(9) The silent subject could be an exact copy of the subject of *hope*, and as such it would covary with the subject of *hope*.

(10) The silent subject could be an anaphoric expression, like a pronoun, or an anaphor.

Let us explore these options in turn. Suppose first it is an exact copy. Accordingly, this is what we would get if the main subject is *Susan* or *everyone*.

Is there a silent version of the pronounced subject in the infinitival?

(11) Susan hopes [~~Susan~~ to sleep]
(12) Everyone hopes [~~Everyone~~ to sleep]

While the meaning we get with (11) seems fine and has the potential of enforcing coreference between the silent DP and the subject of *hope* (assuming that there is only one Susan), this option predicts a wrong meaning when the subject is *everyone*. We can bring this out clearly if we paraphrase these structures by replacing the infinitival clause by a tensed clause counterpart:

(13) Everyone hopes to sleep
(14) a. Everyone hopes [that everyone will sleep]
b. Everyone hopes [that he will sleep]

Clearly the sentence in (a) does not have the meaning of (13): (13) is true even if someone hopes that someone else will not sleep, but (a) would be false in such a case. So we give up on this first option. Note that Principle C leads us to the same conclusion, namely that the two DPs cannot really be identical. Indeed the silent DP would not be free (it would be coreferential with a c-commanding DP, namely the other DP *Susan*.) This would violate Principle C of the binding theory. To see this, let us draw a tree: to distinguish the two occurrences of *Susan*, each independently selected, let's label the first one *Susan1* and the second *Susan2* and, since they must corefer, they have to be coindexed:

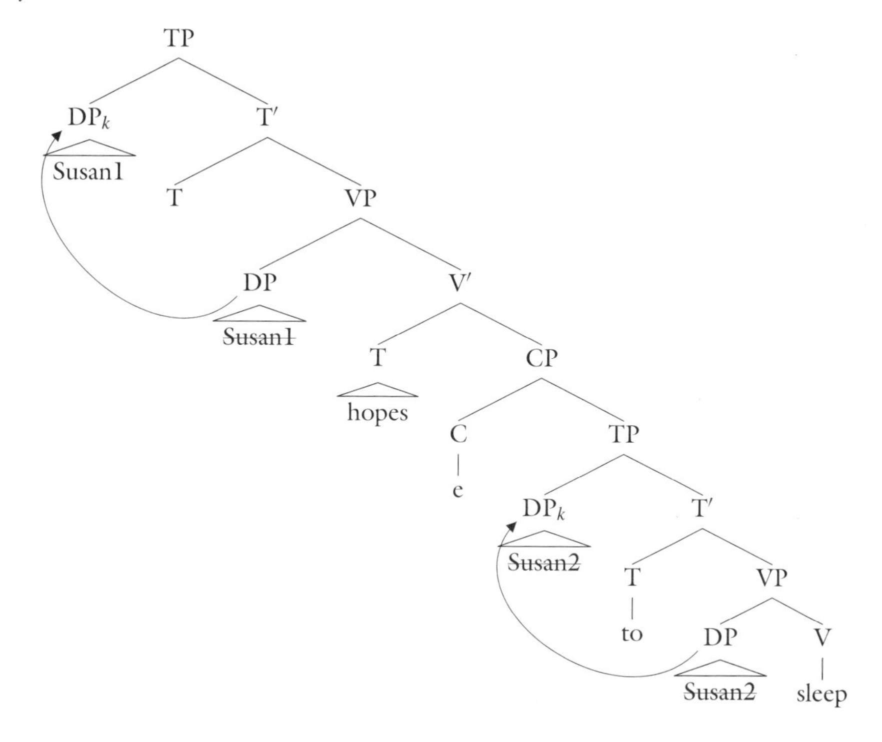

Two remarks on this tree: First, we take the infinitive clause to be a CP with a silent C. We justify this in Section 9.5.3. Second, we have represented the silent subject of the infinitive as having moved from VP-internal position. Whether this happens or not depends on whether infinitival *to* has an EPP feature. Nothing in this chapter depends on this: trees could also be drawn without this movement, with the subject remaining in VP.

We see that the DP *Susan1* has the main T' as a sister, which contains everything else in the clause. So it c-commands everything, including *Susan2*. Since *Susan1* and *Susan2* are coreferential, this is a Principle C violation. But note that *Susan1* also c-commands its trace, ~~Susan1~~. Isn't this also a Principle C violation? We of course want to define things so that it is not (we want movement of this sort to be possible): Principle C does not apply to an antecedent/trace pair. This extends to cases like *Susan seems to be ~~Susan~~ sleeping*. Susan is only the argument of *sleep*, and counts as a single instance of *Susan* for Principle C.

Back to our example, we conclude that a non-pronominal expression (a name, a referential expression, or a quantified expression) does not appear to be an option, because of interpretative differences and Principle C.

Now note that sentences (13) and (14b) seem to be true and false together, suggesting that taking the silent DP to be a pronoun has a better chance of working. We could try a pronoun, as in the tensed clause we used to describe the meaning of our original sentence. This means our sentence would behave similarly to (15) or, even closer, to (16):

(15) Susan$_j$ hopes [that she$_j$ will sleep]
(16) Susan$_j$ hopes [for her$_{i,?*j}$ to sleep]

However, there are differences between these cases and our original sentence. In the tensed sentence (15), the pronoun *she* may be, but does not have to be, coreferential with the main subject *Susan*. Thus (15) (without the coindexing) can mean that Susan hopes that some other female will sleep. This option does not exist for (4). The same is true of the closer analogue (16), or worse, since coindexing is marginal at best. Thus, the silent element cannot really be a pronoun.

Since we want to guarantee that the silent DP is interpreted with the same reference as the subject of *hope*, the best option would be some kind of silent anaphor: this would have the potential to guarantee coreference (since anaphors must be bound) but how can we tell whether this is the right idea?

To do this, consider the following examples, the discussion of which we adapt from Fodor (1980), which references a famous radio speech made during World War II by the British Prime Minister Winston Churchill. These examples illustrate a different construction, referred to as a gerund. This contains a VP marked with -ing and, what is most relevant here, it allows a silent subject interpreted as coreferential with the main subject, but also a variety of pronounced subjects, including names, pronouns and reflexives:

(17) a. Only Churchill remembered [[$_{DP}$??] giving the Blood, Toil, Tears, and Sweat speech]
b. Only Churchill remembered [himself giving the Blood, Toil, Tears, and Sweat speech]
c. Only Churchill remembered [Churchill giving the Blood, Toil, Tears, and Sweat speech]
d. Only Churchill remembered [his giving the Blood, Toil, Tears, and Sweat speech]

Assume that it is true that young Macmillan heard this speech, and vividly remembers hearing it on the radio. Then it is true that he also remembers Churchill giving the speech. Or he remembers his (=Churchill's) giving the speech. So Churchill would not be alone in remembering this. (Note incidentally that (17c) is awkward because it is a Principle C violation.) Under such circumstances, (17a) is still true, but both (17c) and (17d) are

"*De se*" or the case of mistaken identity: The difference in interpretation between the sentence with PRO and the ones without can be brought out in special scenarios, which involve a speaker not recognizing himself. Let us imagine the following scenario:

Imagine a radio singing contest in which Susan participated. The radio show is rebroadcast prior to the announcement of who won. Listening to this rebroadcast, Susan does not recognize herself when she hears herself sing,

> but she says: "this contestant is surely the best one. I hope she wins first prize." In such contexts, we can truthfully report Susan's hope with the first sentence, but not with the subject control sentence below:
>
> (19) Susan hopes that she will win the first price
> (20) Susan hopes to win the first price
>
> This is a subtle, but clear judgment. In order to be able to truthfully utter the subject control structure to report Susan's hope, she must know that she is talking about herself. She would have to have said: "I hope **I** win". So PRO should be more like a silent "I" standing for the subject of the verb *hope*. This is called a *de se* (literally, *about oneself*) interpretation. You should be able to construct examples showing that overt reflexives do not have to be interpreted *de se*. This is further discussed in Chapter 13, and it matters for the proper classification of anaphors.

false. This is unexpected if the silent DP is either a silent name (*Churchill*) or a silent pronoun coreferential with *Churchill*. We thus corroborate our earlier conclusion that names or pronouns are not the way to go. Is (17b) also true? The fact is that for some speakers the answer is positive, but not for all: many speakers can hold this sentence to be false. They would say: *No, Churchill is not the only one who remembers himself giving this speech, Macmillan also remembers him giving this speech.* This means that a silent reflexive cannot be the general solution to this problem. What seems to be needed is a special kind of silent anaphor: let us call this special silent anaphor **PRO**, following Chomsky (1981). Accordingly, we would have:

(18) Susan hopes [PRO to sleep]

PRO needs to be construed so that it is interpreted as bound by the subject of *hope*. And it should be interpreted in such a way that, in the above context, (17a) is the only sentence that is true for all speakers (read the next text box if you are curious about this fascinating topic; it is further discussed in Chapter 13).

Taking all this into account, we get the following tree:

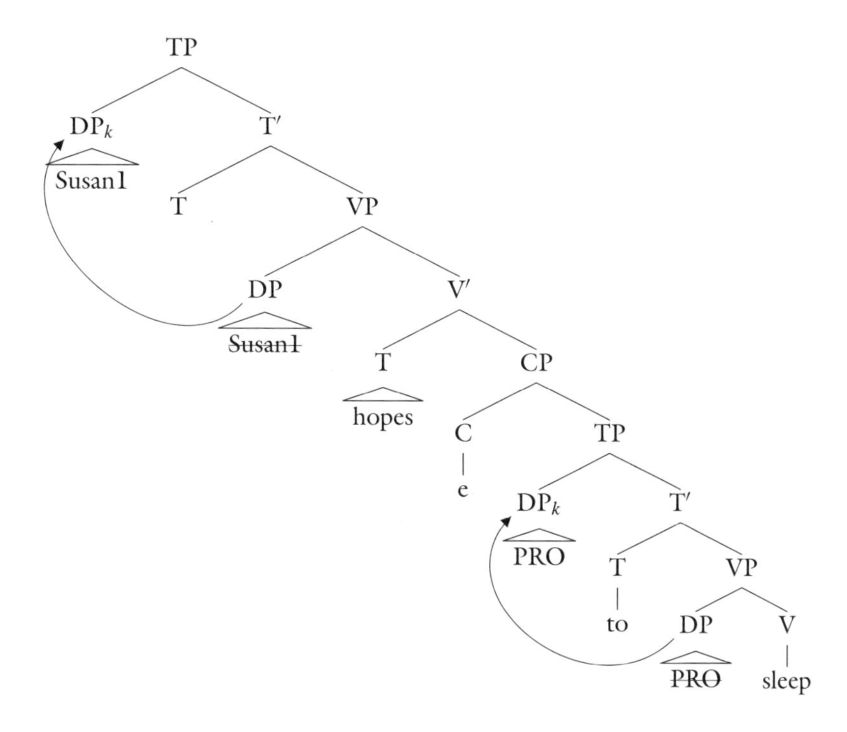

In such sentences, the interpretive value of PRO is determined by the subject of the main clause, as we have indicated by coindexing. We say that PRO is **controlled** by the subject of *hope*: this is why this is called a **subject control construction**. What determines whether we have a control construction or not, is the verb that takes the infinitive complement. This is why *hope* is called a **subject control verb**.

Besides subject control verbs, there are also object control verbs, to which we turn below. The control relation is similar to (but not quite the same as) the relation between an antecedent and a reflexive anaphor. It is no surprise that they agree in person, number, and gender. The class of subject control verbs is large: it contains verbs such as *hope, wish, try*, and *attempt*, among others.

"Big" PRO, "small" pro: PRO is always written with capital letters and read as "big PRO." It is distinguished from *pro* written in lower case, which is referred to as "little pro" or "small pro." Small *pro* is the silent counterpart of regular pronouns, found for example as the null subject of tensed sentences in languages like Italian, Spanish, or Mandarin, but not English, where an overt subject pronoun is required. (See Rizzi (1982), and the collection of articles in Jaeggli and Safir (1989).)

(21) parliamo inglese Italian
hablamos ingles Spanish
speak.1PL English
*(we) speak English

9.2 Using the Theory: Control and Binding

9.2.1 Subject infinitives

Principle A: Consider the following two sentences:

(22) a. [For [John to hurt his friends]] is stupid
b. [To hurt one's friends]] is stupid

In both cases, the infinitival clause is the subject of the main clause. We can replace the DP *his friends* by the anaphor *himself* in the first sentence and by the anaphor *oneself* in the second and the results are fine:

(23) a. [For [John to hurt himself]] is stupid
b. [To hurt oneself]] is stupid

To see how Principle A is satisfied, we must first determine the structure of the tree, which looks something like the following:

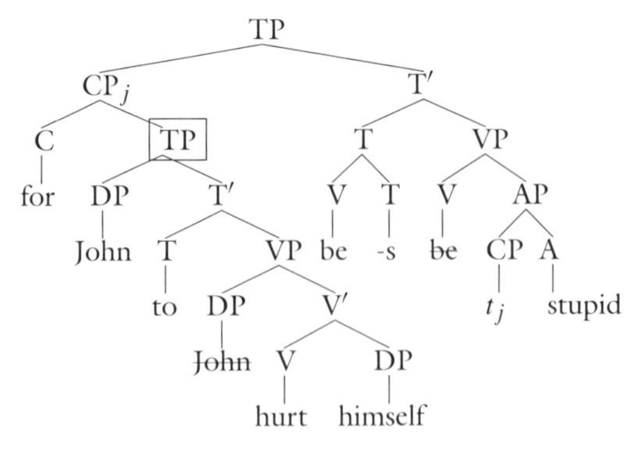

Instead of showing a whole copy of CP$_j$ as the subject of the AP, where it originated, we use the abbreviated trace notation t_j introduced on p. 230.

Control as movement: The analysis of control constructions we have presented does two things. First, it postulates the presence of a silent subject. Next, it identifies some properties of this silent DP, which we have called PRO. The reader may have realized that PRO could perhaps simply be analyzed as a trace of movement. Accordingly, the name *Susan* would be first merged as the subject of the verb *sleep* and would move to the subject position of the verb *hope* once the verb *hope* is merged into the structure:

(24) Susan sleep
(25) Susan hope to ~~Susan~~ sleep

Such an analysis would have to be construed so that the trace is interpreted with the *de se* reading mentioned in the framed box on p. 268. In effect, under such a proposal, a PRO is a trace left by a DP moving to a theta-position, a position entering into a thematic relation with a predicate. Note that this is different from saying that we have two independent instances of the DP *Susan* both referring to the same person.

This analysis was proposed, for certain cases of control, in an influential article Hornstein (1999). Norbert Hornstein is currently Professor of Linguistics at the University of Maryland, and is pictured here. Distinguishing this analysis from the treatment of PRO as a kind of silent reflexive is an advanced topic, and is discussed, for example, in Landau (2003).

In (23a), the anaphor *himself* satisfies Principle A of the binding theory: it has a c-commanding antecedent in its local domain, which is the first TP with a subject, indicated by a box. The only antecedent available is *John*.

What about the second sentence? How is Principle A satisfied? Clearly in the same fashion, but now the anaphor has PRO as a local antecedent. (Check the tree below.) We don't need to say anything more.

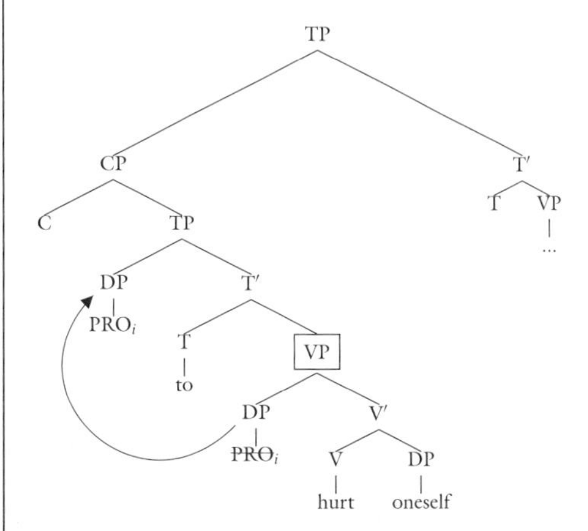

Once PRO is added, we see that this sentence does not violate Principle A of the binding theory after all. The anaphor has a local domain (the boxed VP – make sure you see why) and a licit antecedent, the subject of the boxed VP. This antecedent is just silent. Note that by the same token, PRO itself cannot be an anaphor – at least not always – as we mentioned earlier, since clearly it does not have a c-commanding antecedent in this last sentence.

Contrast this with an alternative theory where the silent subject would not be represented in the syntax at all. For this alternative, we might try the following hypothetical subjectless structure:

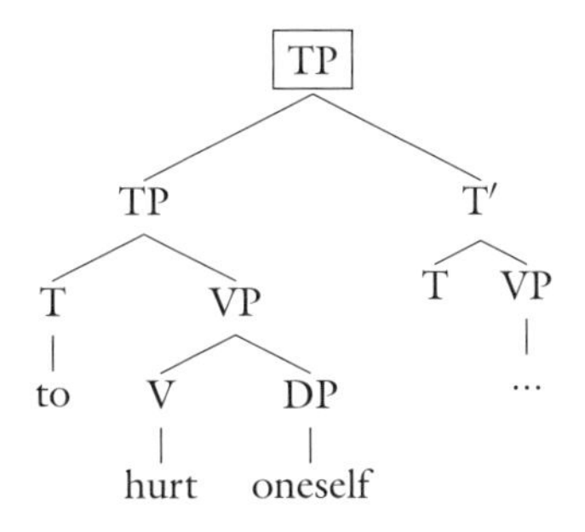

Here, Principle A seems to be violated for the anaphor *oneself* since there does not seem to be any antecedent. The domain for the anaphor is now the boxed TP, the first with a subject. Within this local domain, there isn't any possible antecedent for the reflexive, and so this sentence is wrongly predicted to be ill-formed. We would need to fix binding theory in some way to allow it. So this alternative may superficially look "simpler", in the sense that the structures contain fewer symbols, but this may be deceptive. We would have to give up the principle of locality of selection, and the projection principle, and complicate Principle A the binding theory.

So we see that the existence of PRO, postulated purely to satisfy the lexical requirement of verbs under the principle of locality of selection, also finds important confirmation in Principle A of the binding theory.

The same reasoning applies to cases involving Principle B of the binding theory. Let us next examine the following sentences:

(26) a. [For [John$_i$ to hurt him$_{*i,j}$]] is stupid
b. [[To hurt him]] is stupid

Here we see that we have a Principle B effect in the first case: *him* must be disjoint in reference from *John*. This follows straightforwardly from Principle B. Note that in the (b) sentence, we also have a Principle B effect: *him* cannot refer to whoever is doing the hurting. Again, this straightforwardly follows if the subject of *hurt* is syntactically realized as PRO, but not otherwise.

Practice

Draw the tree for (a) and check that Principle B would be violated under coreference. Then draw the trees for (b), with and without PRO, and check that Principle B would not be violated if PRO is absent, but would under coreference between *him* and PRO if PRO is present.

9.2.2 PRO in infinitival complements

We can illustrate the same positive effects of the presence of PRO in other cases. Consider the following sentence (which is only possible in certain varieties of English), which can be paraphrased as: John made a promise to Bill that he, John, would leave:

(27) John promised Bill to leave

We can paraphrase this by replacing the infinitive clause by a tensed clause. (It is always a good strategy to try to do this, to get a quick idea of the kind of infinitive you are dealing with. It will only be successful with verbs that do alternate.)

(28) John$_i$ promised Bill that he$_i$ (John) would leave

This paraphrase suggests that:

i. *Bill* is a complement of the verb *promise*;
ii. the infinitival clause is also a complement of the verb *promise*;
iii. this infinitive has a missing subject – a PRO – interpreted as coreferential with the subject *John*, so we are dealing with a subject control verb.

The structure of this sentence is now roughly given as:

(29) John_j promised Bill $[_{CP}[_{TP}$ PRO_j to control X]]

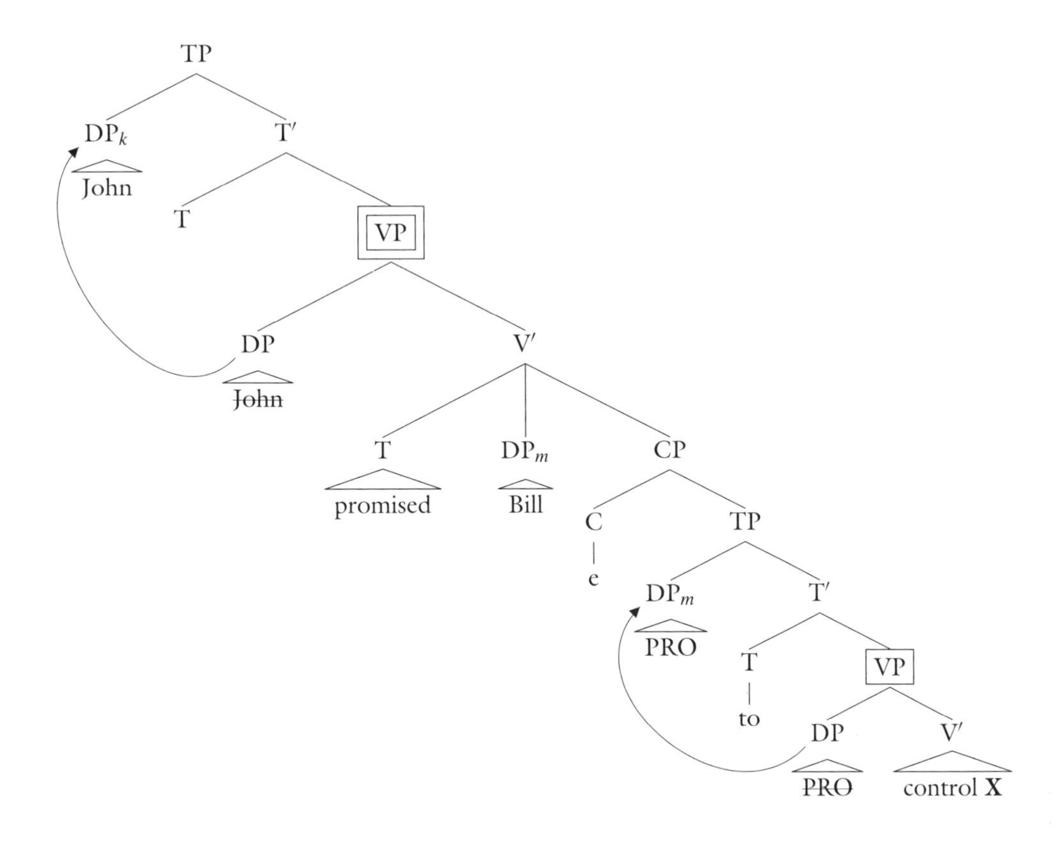

Now consider the following sentences in which X in the tree above is an anaphor:

(30) a. John promised Mary to control himself
b. * John promised Mary to control herself

Why is the first sentence ok, but the second sentence deviant? Here are the respective structures of these sentences:

(31) a. John_j promised Mary $[_{TP}$ PRO_j to control himself]
b. * John_j promised Mary $[_{TP}$ PRO_j to control herself]

In both cases, the anaphor is c-commanded by either *John* or *Mary*. In both cases, the domain of the anaphor is the smallest XP with a subject, that is the embedded VP (the singly boxed TP in the tree above). So the only antecedent allowed is PRO. Since PRO is controlled by *John*, the reflexive can only corefer with *John*. If we do not appeal to the presence of PRO, the anaphor would be c-commanded by either *John* or *Mary*. In both cases, the domain of the anaphor would be the smallest XP with a subject, that is the main clause VP (the doubly boxed TP in the tree above). Incorrectly, both sentences would be predicted to be fine.

9.3 Interim Summary: Inventory of *To*-infinitival

How to analyze an infinitival complement depends on the choice of the verb that selects it. We have seen how to identify raising to subject expressions, like *seem, appear, be likely*, etc. These verbs select an infinitival TP. The following table lists their properties:

(32) **Raising to subject verbs or adjectives**:

Raising is obligatory	*it seems Bill to sleep all day
	*John seems Bill to sleep all day
Do not take for-infinitives	*John seems for Bill to sleep all day
No not select a subject	*John seems that Bill sleeps all day
Allow weather *it*	it seems to be sunny
May allow expletive subjects	it seems
if CPs are allowed,	... that Bill sleeps all day
	*... to sleep all day
Allow existential *there*	there seems to be no problem
Allow idiom chunks as subjects	the cat seems to be out of the bag

In the case of a raising verb like *seem*, if nothing can raise to the subject position of the clause, expletive *it* is inserted, because TPs need subjects.

Subject control@ These verbs come in at least two kinds: verbs of wanting or hoping, or **W(ant)-type verbs** (*wish, want, long, yearn, desire, need, itch, pine, thirst, etc.),* which may be, but do not have to be, subject control verbs. The other kind is Try-type verbs [b (*attempt, endeavor, aim, venture, strive, dare* ...), which are subject control only old]. (Further differences in control are discussed in Section 9.3 below.) All these verbs take CP complements.

(33) **Want/hope-type subject control verbs**:[2]

Control not obligatory	John hopes that Bill will sleep
Can take for-infinitives	John hopes for Bill to sleep
Select a subject	John hopes that Bill will sleep all day
Disallow weather *it*	*it hopes to rain
Disallow expletive *it*	*it hopes that Bill will sleep
Disallow existential *there*	*there hope to be two fireman available
Disallow idiom chunks	*the cat hopes to be out of the bag

(34) **Try-type subject control verbs**:

Control obligatory	*John tried that they sleep
Disallow for-infinitives	*John tries for Bill to sleep
Selects a (sentient) subject	*time tries to elapse
Disallow weather *it*	*it tries to rain
Disallow expletive	*it tries that Bill will sleep
Disallow existential *there*	*there try to be three fireman available
Disallow idiom chunks	*the cat tries to be out of the bag

[2] It is worth noting that, for all verb classes, speaker variation is found.

Exhaustive and partial Control: Verbs like *try* are also different from verbs like *want* or *hope* in that they impose different control requirements. This can be seen with the help of some (intransitive) verbs that require a plural subject: *meet* and *gather*. These can occur under control verbs with a singular controller like *want* and *hope*, but not under control verbs like *try* (the subscript $\supset i$ here indicates the referent bearing the index i is included in the reference of the plural subject):

(35) a. *He_i tried [$\text{PRO}_{\supset i}$ to meet at 6 o'clock]
b. He_i hoped [$\text{PRO}_{\supset i}$ to meet at 6 o'clock]
c. She_i wanted [$\text{PRO}_{\supset i}$ to meet at 6 o'clock]

This suggests that for some verbs, like *want*, it is sufficient that the reference of the controller be included in PRO. This is called **Partial Control** (PC). For other verbs, such as *try*, this is not possible – they require what is called **Exhaustive Control** (EC). (See Landau (2000).) This makes control unlike anaphor binding but similar to pronominal binding, viz:

(36) a. *John_i showed Bill $\text{themselves}_{\supset i}$
b. OK [No player from any $\text{team}]_i$ revealed $\text{their}_{\supset i}$ strategy

We see that the configurations in which each of these verbs (raising verbs, w-type verbs and try-type verbs) can occur are all different: each represents a different class.

9.4 Raising to Object/ECM and Object Control

There are two more important patterns for infinitive complements exemplified by the following examples:

(37) a. John believes Bill to have slept
b. John convinced Bill to sleep

Verbs exhibiting the first pattern are called **exceptional case marking** or **raising to object**, abbreviated as ECM verbs.[3] The ECM class includes *believe, expect, prove, know, assume.* ... Verbs exhibiting the second pattern are called Object Control, abbreviated as OC. The OC class of verbs include verbs like *convince, persuade, order.* ... The difference lies in whether the surface object DP is a selected argument of the preceding verb or not.

When we compare these two classes systematically, we see the patterns of grammaticality are different from the patterns seen so far, and they differ from each other:

ECM/Raising to object	**Object control**
John believed Bill to have slept	John convinced Bill to sleep
John believes that Bill has slept	* John convinced that Bill should sleep
* John believes Bill that Mary slept	John convinced Bill that Mary should sleep
*John believed to be sick	*John convinced to sleep

An ECM verb seems to allow either a direct object or a clause complement, but not both, while object control verbs allows both. All this suggests that we are dealing with two new patterns. What are they? The crucial question we ask is the following:

(38) For each case, is the surface "object" (here *Bill*) selected by the verb that immediately precedes it?

[3]The origin of this terminology is explained in Section 9.5.4. We will use these terms interchangeably.

This is what we find when we apply the diagnostic tests for selection: with ECM verbs, the object can be expletive *it*, weather *it*, existential *there*, or an idiom chunk (with idiomatic meaning preserved), but none of these are possible with object control verbs:

(39) a. John believes it to be obvious that Bill left
b. John believes it to be raining
c. John believes there to be several firemen available
d. John believes the cat be out of the bag

(40) a. *John convinced it to be obvious that Bill left
b. *John convinced it to be raining
c. *John convinced there to be several firemen available
d. *John convinced the cat to be out of the bag

This tells us that the DP following *believe* is only the subject of the following infinitival clause, but the DP following *convince* is not.

Since we are dealing with objects, there are also some new tests. One test involves active/passive pairs as below:

(41) Bill cooked the rice/The rice was cooked by Bill
(42) Bill visited Mary/Mary was visited by Bill

In simple cases such as the above, the two sentences of the pair have the same truth value: they are true and false in the same situations. But note what happens under ECM verbs and object control verbs:

(43) a. John believes Bill to have cooked the rice
b. John believes the rice to have been cooked by Bill
(44) a. John believes Bill to have visited Mary
b. John believes Mary to have been visited by Bill

With *believe*, the sentences do not change in truth value if we apply passive in the infinitive.

(45) a. John convinced Bill to cook the rice
b. *John convinced the rice to be cooked by Bill
(46) a. John convinced Bill to visit Mary
b. # John convinced Mary to be visited by Bill (#=ok but wrong meaning)

With *convince*, the sentences do change in truth value (and sometimes acceptability) when we apply the passive in the infinitive.

We can make sense of all these differences if the "object" of an object control verb is selected by this verb, while that of an ECM verb is not, so it is not really the object of the ECM verb. This is consistent with our judgments about the meaning of *believe* and *convince*:

Believe is the name of a relation between two objects: a thinker and a proposition (a state of affairs) that the thinker takes to hold true. The thinker is realized as a DP subject, while the proposition is realized as a clausal object.[4]

[4]This explains the ECM terminology: the accusative case on the DP following the verb is clearly licensed by the verb even though the verb does not select the DP. Hence the terminology.

Convince is the name of a relation between three entities: a convincer (a DP), someone (also a DP) being convinced, and a state of affairs or an action (CP) that the convinced party ends up holding true, or acting out.

This translates into the following structures:

Important: We code the complement of object control verbs as a CP with a silent C, and the complement of ECM/raising to object verbs as a TP. We discuss this in Section 9.5.3.

(47) a. John believes [$_{TP}$ Bill to have slept]] (inf-TP complement)
b. John convinced Bill$_k$ [$_{CP}$[PRO$_k$ to sleep]] (inf-CP complement)
c. John believes [$_{CP}$ that [Bill slept]] (+tense CP complement)
d. John convinced Bill [$_{CP}$ that [Mary should sleep]] (+tense CP complement)

Given these structures, we can understand the observations we made: with an ECM verb, expletive *it* is allowed – (39) – as long as it is allowed in the clause embedded under the ECM verb. It is disallowed with OC verbs – (40) – because the postverbal DP is selected by the OC verb and needs to be sentient, i.e. able to believe or to act. This is also why passive under ECM poses no problem – (43) – and does not change truth value: the active/passive alternation happens in the embedded clause. For OC verbs however, passive changes who the second thinker is. With *rice* – (45) – passive fails because *rice* cannot act or believe. In the other case – (46) – the second actor changes: it is *Bill* in one case and *Mary* in the other, so the meaning changes.

Here are tables summarizing the behavior of each class:

(48) **ECM/Raising to object verbs**:

Followed by accusative DP	John believes him to have slept
PRO subject disallowed	*John believes to have slept
Allow *that*-CP	John believes Bill to have slept
Disallow *for*-CP	*John believes for Bill to have slept
Select experiencer subject	*Time believes Bill to be honest
Allow weather *it*	John believes it to be windy
Allow existential *there*	John believes there to be firemen available
Allow idiom chunks	John believes the cat to be out of the bag
Active/passive: meaning preserved	John believes the rice to have been prepared by Bill John believes Bill to have prepared some rice

(49) **Object control verbs** :

Followed by accusative DP	John convinced Bill/him to sleep
Allow *that*-complement	John convinced Bill that he should sleep
Disallow *for*-infinitives	*John convinced Bill for himself to sleep
Select an *exp* subject	?*Time convinced Bill to be honest
Disallow weather *it*	*John convinced it to be windy
Disallow expletive	*John convinced it to be possible that
Disallow existential *there*	*John convinced there to be fireman available
Disallow idiom chunks	John convinced the cat to be out of the bag
Active/passive: meaning not preserved	John believes Bill to have prepared some rice *John convinced some rice to have been prepared by Bill

9.5 Conclusion

9.5.1 Summary

This chapter was devoted to investigating the syntactic of (some) infinitival clauses in English. One important subcase is that of infinitive clauses with silent subjects. The presence of such silent subjects was corroborated by the binding effects they create. Trying to understand the properties of these silent subjects has led us to classify infinitives in different subclasses: subject and object control, raising to subject or to object (or ECM).

9.5.2 What to remember

In this chapter, we have discovered two important things. First, the subject of infinitive clauses can sometimes be silent and interpreted like a special reflexive anaphor. We called such subjects **PRO**. Their presence is detected because of s-selection, and also because of their interactions with the binding theory.

The other discovery has to do with the variety of verbs embedding infinitival complements: such verbs can be **raising to subject** verbs, which trigger raising of a DP. They can be **control** verbs, where the subject or object of the selecting verb determines the meaning contribution of the silent PRO subject in the infinitive clause. Finally, we have discovered the class of **raising to object** (also called **exceptional case marking**) verbs (like *believe*) which do not involve control.

As a general rule, we code infinitival complements that contain PRO as CPs with a silent C, and complements of raising verbs as TP.

The main tool used for discovery has been the assessment of selection relations: this illustrates just how essential it is to master the procedures to do this.

Here is a table listing all the different characteristics of the infinitival complement taking verb types that we have so far discovered:

	Raising		Control		
	to subject	to object	subject control		object control
			try-type	*W*-type	
Expletive subject	Yes	No	No	No	No
Expletive object	No	Yes	No	No	No
Truth changing passive	No	No	Yes	Yes	Yes
For-infinitives	No	No	No	Yes	No
Control type	NA	NA	EC	PC	PC
Example	*seem*	*believe*	*try*	*hope*	*persuade*

Here is a list of simplified lexical entries for each of these verbs:

seem	V			(PP[to]$_{exp}$) TP[to]$_{theme}$/CP[that]$_{theme}$
hope	V	$\underline{DP_{exp}}$		TP[to]/CP[that]/CP[for]$_{theme}$
try	V	$\underline{DP_{agent}}$		CP[e]$_{theme}$
believe	V	$\underline{DP_{exp}}$		TP[to]$_{theme}$/CP[that]$_{theme}$
persuade	V	$\underline{DP_{agent}}$	DP$_{goal}$	CP[e]$_{theme}$/CP[that]$_{theme}$
convince	V	$\underline{DP_{agent}}$	DP$_{goal}$	CP[e]$_{theme}$/CP[that]$_{theme}$

9.5.3 Puzzles and preview

This chapter has introduced the core properties of raising and control constructions, and focused on the motivation for PRO and its interaction with the binding theory. There are many issues that we did not touch on, but here are some remarks.

Verb classes
Within a particular verb class, some properties correlate. Some of these correlations are not accidental (e.g. disallow idiom chunks and weather *it*), but others do seem accidental: for example, raising verbs do not allow *for* infinitive complements. If this is not accidental, we should try to construct an account. To decide whether it is accidental or not, we need to have a full picture of which verb classes there are and what properties each exhibits. Although we have documented some classes, we are far from finished: indeed, there are other verb classes than the ones we have talked about. There are, in particular, several different varieties of ECM verbs. Recent, and very advanced discussion, of these can be found in e.g. Moulton (2009) for English or Sportiche (2011) for French.

Can a verb simultaneously belong to several classes? Yes and no. Yes, because a verb like English *expect* allows both subject control (*They expect [PRO to win]*) and ECM (*They expect me to win*), and a verb like French *sembler/"seem"* allows both raising to subject *Le temps semble s'écouler lentement/Time seems to elapse slowly* and object control *Il me semble m'être parjuré/it seems to me that I perjured myself*). However, this could just mean that these verbs have two distinct lexical entries. No, because no verb seems to allow this simultaneously: there is no verb that is both ECM (or object control) and raising to subject at the same time, in that it allows both a direct object and some other DP raising to subject. This requires an explanation. (One exists in terms of what Move is allowed to do, but we set this aside for now.)

Remarks on the distribution and interpretation of PRO
We have seen two kinds of English *to*-infinitival with silent subjects:

(50) a. John hopes [PRO to win]
b. [[PRO to leave on time]] is important

In the first, PRO requires a syntactic antecedent and receives an interpretation as a special reflexive (the *de se* reading). Not so in the second: PRO receives the so-called arbitrary interpretation (so the sentence means *for people/anyone to leave in time is important*), and for this reason it is called **Arbitrary PRO**.

Whether these two PROs are in fact the same object is a complex question that we cannot fully address here. Nonetheless, these two PROs share important distributional properties:

- They cannot occur in a position in which an overt DP can occur.[5]
- They cannot occur in a position in which a trace could occur (except, of course, a trace of PRO itself).

It is not clear that the second property is independent rather than derived (it could reduce to a requirement that such a PRO moves in these cases). The first property, however, is not known to follow from anything, and surely needs an explanation. Here are some examples:

(51) a. * PRO left school vs. They left school
b. *They removed PRO vs. They removed [someone/them/themselves]
c. *They talked [about PRO]
vs.
They talked [about someone/them/themselves]
d. *They believe [PRO to be sick] vs. They believed [someone/them/themselves to be sick]

[5]There are apparent counterexamples, e.g. *I remember Churchill speaking/I remember PRO speaking, I expect John to win/I expect PRO to win* but, in each case, it can be shown that the two members of the pair are structurally different.

e. * They saw/heard/made [PRO sing] vs. They saw/heard/made/ [someone/them/themselves sing]
f. They hope/wish/try [PRO to sing] vs. *They hope/wish them/themselves to sing

> **The PRO theorem**: Chomsky (1981) suggests that this could be derived by postulating that PRO is both an anaphor and a pronoun. This would lead to potentially conflicting requirements imposed by Principles A and B of the binding theory, which would yield the desired distribution. The evolution of the binding theory since 1981 has made this interesting attempt (known as the **PRO Theorem**) difficult to maintain.

TP versus CP and PRO
Why did we code infinitival complements containing PRO as CPs with a silent C, and complements of raising verbs as TP? This is a difficult problem. Here are some remarks about this distributional property. Infinitivals with PRO pattern like CPs in that they can occur in certain CP positions that tolerate neither TPs nor VP small clauses. One such position is the subject position of a finite clause.

(52) **TP vs. CP: subjects**:

CP can be a subject:	[For [someone to go to the store]] bothered Bill
	[For [it to be sunny today]] bothered Bill
	[[That someone drove to the store]]bothered Bill
	[PRO to drive to the store] bothers Bill
TP cannot be a subject	*[someone drove to the store] bothered Bill
	*[someone to drive to the store] bothered Bill
	*[someone drive to the store] bothered Bill

This suggests that the constituent containing a PRO is a CP, not just a TP.[6]

(53) PRO can only occur as subject of a TP if this TP is inside a CP headed by a silent C.

This makes it reasonable to suppose that subject control and object control constructions involve CPs.

How about raising constructions? Notice the following pairs:

(54) a. John expects [Mary to have won]/John expects [PRO to have won]
b. John believes [Mary to have won]/*John believes [PRO to have won]

The verbs *believe* and *expect* form a **minimal pair**. Both allow ECM, but only the former allows PRO. What is the difference between these verbs? The following pair, involving a passive version of the above sentences (where the object has been moved to subject position – something not discussed in any detail in this book, suggests that the two complement clauses have different internal make-ups:

(55) a. * [Mary to have won] was expected by John
b. [PRO to have won] was expected by John

[6]We are talking about Standard American English. There are different varieties of English, of course, witness the two verses, *In the desert, you can remember your name, 'caus there ain't noone* **for to** *give you no pain*; in "Horse with no Name," written by Dewey Bunnel (1971), which probably involves a PRO subject with a non silent C. For Belfast English, see in particular Henry (1995).

CP or TP? What are the issues? First, it is important to know that, ultimately, these are not the only options. Indeed, it turns out that CP is actually several projections (see Rizzi, 1997). Second, the ungrammaticality of (9.5.3a) could be due to something other than the subject clause being a TP:

(57) a. [[That someone drove to the store]] bothered Bill
b. * [[someone drove to the store]] bothered Bill

We see that silent discussed in Chapter 4 is excluded (see Stowell (1981) for a discussion of the distribution of Maybe (9.5.3a) could be excluded because the subject clause is a CP that has a silent C, e.g. ~~*for*~~, similar to ~~*that*~~: this would mean that the infinitival clause complement of an ECM verb could be a CP with a silent C, e.g. silent ~~*for*~~. This is made all the more plausible by the well-formedness of examples like *for Bill to have won is hard to believe*, involving what is called **Tough Movement** (see Chapter 14), in which, normally, whatever occurs as main subject could occur as object of *believe*. Third, there is a **three way** distinction involving ECM verbs, subject control verbs like *expect*, and (some) w-type verbs:

(58) a. John believes (*for) Bill to have won/*PRO to have won
b. John expects (*for) Bill to have won/PRO to have won
c. John wants (for) Bill to win/PRO to win

If there is a silent ~~*for*~~, it plausibly occurs with *want* when it is not visible: this makes *want* look like an ECM verb. However, it still does not behave like *believe* with respect to something like the passive: compare *John is believed to have won* and **John is wanted to win*. This is discussed in Kayne (1981), where it is related to systematic differences between English and French.

The ill-formedness of the first example could be accounted for if the bracketed constituent[7] is a TP instead of a CP. Next, notice the following minimal pairs contrasting *likely*, which is a raising adjective, and *possible* which is not:

(56) John is likely [~~John~~ to be hungry]
It is likely [that [John is hungry]
*John is possible [~~John~~ to be hungry]
It is possible [that [John is hungry]

We can make sense of this observation if we suppose that raising to subject and ECM/raising to object predicates take infinitival TP complements rather than CP complements. This is the standard convention and we will adopt it here without further explanation (but see the texbox below if you are curious). In Chapter 13, we will see a further reason why the raising verb classes behave similarly.

9.5.4 Further exercises

(1) Raising and control

For each of the following sentences, identify the type of underlined verb (subject control, object control, raising to object, raising to subject verb, or none of the above). For each of your answers, give one argument justifying it, and support your argument with an example sentence. (Your argument must show whether there is a selectional relation between the underlined predicate and the italicized DP, and, if relevant, draw a conclusion concerning the type of the predicate (raising vs. control).)

Give the lexical entries for *attempt* and for *presume*. (Make sure your entries are consistent with your answers.)

[7] That it can be a constituent can be shown by using coordination or right node raising.

ECM or raising to object: Few theoretical issues have generated so much debate as the different analyses behind these terms, and for good reason. The theoretical importance of these constructions, which play a pivotal role in assessing, for example, the relationship between syntactic structures and semantic interpretation, and thus the overall architecture of grammatical models, is hard to overestimate.

The names ECM and raising to object reflect the two ways in which these constructions have been analyzed in the literature. In ECM accounts, the DP is treated as occupying the subject position of the infinitival TP: the class of verbs that can take objects must be able to search inside the TP to license the accusative. In Chomsky (1981) and some later works this is done by the notion of **Government** (stated informally as a relation between a head and its sister or the subject of its sister). In more recent minimalist works, this is achieved by Chomsky (1995b)'s **Agree**: a head can search its c-command domain to agree with some DP (provided that no "blocking" material intervenes).

In raising to object accounts, most vigorously defended in Postal (1974), the object obligatorily raises outside the TP into the main clause. This brings up the problem of what the derived tree should look like. We return to this topic in Chapters 12 and 13 where we will look at some binding issues left open in Chapter 7. At that point we will have gained a greater understanding of the structure of VPs, which will allow us to better understand how to approach such structures.

(1) *John* attempted to run the marathon
(2) Mary convinced *Sue* to burn the wood
(3) Anna presumed *Bill* to be on his boat
(4) *Elena* tends to be late
(5) It is important for *it* to start snowing
(6) *Albert* is certain to win the race
(7) *John* tried cutting the meat

(2) **Tree drawing (raising and control)**
Draw trees for the following sentences. Notate movement with indexed traces. Use diagnostics for raising if in doubt about whether a verb is a raising or control verb. Note also that predicate adjectives can behave like raising or control predicates. (Compare the behavior of *be likely* with *be reluctant.*)

(1) Bert is likely to decide to sell the Jeep
(2) Beowulf neglected to record his expenses
(3) The princess predicted Moritz to win the lottery
(4) It is certain to rain on the weekend
(5) Moritz planned carefully for Max to fall into the trap
(6) Harriet was reluctant to appear to have believed Moritz to have written the letter
(7) The musician offered to recommend his friend to the committee
(8) The officers tried unsuccessfully to extract the kitten from the chimney
(9) This accompanist is liable to forget to turn the pages

(3) Raising and control

(i) The following two sentences are well-formed and (nearly) synonymous. Explain what this shows about the predicate *likely.*

(1) a. John is likely to be happy
b. It is likely that John is happy

(ii) Draw the **complete** derived tree for the following sentence. Put in **everything** that needs to be there; indicate traces (= point of origin of moved elements) as crossed out items (as it is done in the textbook) and draw arrows for movement. (Assume the singing takes place in the classroom.)

(2) Which classroom had they been likely to hear him sing in?

(iii) Does your tree in (ii) correctly reflect the well-formedness of the following sentence? If so, how? If not, suggest a way that captures the fact.

(3) They had been likely to hear him do so

(4) The verb "expect"

(i) In the following sentence, the pronoun *him* must be disjoint in reference from the matrix subject *Bill.* That is, *him* cannot corefer with *Bill.* Explain why.

(1) Bill_i expects to teach $\text{him}_{*i/j}$ syntax

(ii) If we add *I wonder who* to the above sentence, *him* can corefer with *Bill.* Explain why. (Hint: start with the tree. We always reason on the basis of the (underlying and derived) trees.)

(2) I wonder who Bill_i expects to teach $\text{him}_{i/j}$ syntax

(5) What can we conclude? (Raising and control)

In this exercise, your task is **not** to determine whether or not the conclusion is correct, but rather to evaluate the validity of the argument; that is, you are supposed to determine whether you can draw the conclusion on the basis of the given data.

1. You are at a conference as a linguistic expert, and a presenter offers the following piece of evidence in support of the conclusion that the verb *request* is a control predicate.
   (1) *There requested to eat up the cookies
      (i) Circle one. The conclusion is: (a) valid (b) not valid.
      (ii) Explain why you think so (short answer).
2. English has an idiom *spill the beans*, which means "divulge a secret." The idiomatic meaning of this phrase is preserved in the following sentence.
   (1) John began to spill the beans. (Meaning: John began to divulge a secret)

Therefore, we can conclude that the verb *begin* is a raising to subject verb.

   (i) Circle one. The conclusion is: (a) valid (b) not valid.
   (ii) Justify your answer.

3. The following example comes from a Google search; the question concerns the boldfaced material.
   (1) There was a massive buzz around the playoff game throughout the whole of the village, and there **promised** to be a massive crowd of supporters
      (i) In what way is the verb *promise* used in the sentence above (raising, control, neither, etc.)? Circle one: (a) raising (b) control (c) neither.
      (ii) Explain why you reached this conclusion.

(6) Binding and control

Section 9.2.2 discussed the following examples, and stated that the tree predicts that, in both cases, the anaphor is c-commanded by either *Bill* or *Mary*:

(1) a. Bill_j promised Mary [$_{TP}$ PRO_j to control himself]
    b. *Bill_j promised Mary [$_{TP}$ PRO_j to shave herself]

Can you support this independently? One way would be to modify the sentence and use Principle C to show that either the subject or the object of *promise* c-commands the object of the embedded verb. Go ahead and do this.

(7) Binding and PRO

(i) Discuss how understanding the syntactic structure, binding theory, and PRO account for the patterns below. (You can use simplified structures with triangles, or bracketed structures, to show your point.)

(1) a. John persuaded [Mary and Bill]i to see [each other]$_i$
b. *They$_i$ persuaded him to see [each other]$_i$
c. *Mary threatened John$_i$ with hurting himself$_i$
d. Mary$_i$ threatened John with hurting herself$_i$

(ii) Explain the contrasts below:

(2) a. John struck Mary as angry of himself
b. *John struck Mary as angry at herself
c. *John regarded Mary as happy with himself
d. John regarded Mary as happy with herself

(8) "Prove"

(i) Draw the full tree for the underscored constituent in the following sentence: (you will need to insert all traces if any, think about the kind of infinitive complement, etc.)

(1) Which argument proved to prove Bill to be guilty?

(ii) Justify the way in which you have analyzed the infinitival complement of the first verb *prove* (= provide one reason why you treat it like a subject control, object control, raising to subject, or raising to object verb).

(iii) Justify the way in which you have analyzed the infinitival complement of the second verb *prove* (= provide one reason why you treat it like a subject control, object control, raising to subject, or raising to object verb).

(iv) It should be clear that the syntactic contexts in which the two instances of the verb *prove* appear are different. Do the two instances of the verb have the same meaning? Try to unambiguously paraphrase each. Can you briefly speculate as to where the difference (in syntactic contexts) comes from?

9.5.5 Further reading

Control structures were known as Equi-NP deletion in the early literature, but have been referred to as Control since the introduction of PRO in ?) or Chomsky (1981). For the many further issues surrounding control, Landau (2003) is a good starting point. For analyses that take certain cases of control to be movement, see in particular Hornstein (1999). For some patterns of cross-linguistic variation in control structures, see Polinsky and Potsdam (2002).

10

Wh-questions: Wh-movement and Locality

So far, when we have talked about movement, we simply noted that movement is one property that syntactic structures display. It is a certain kind of relation between two positions in a tree. We have not worried about how exactly movement works. We have not tried to systematically investigate when it is allowed or when it is not. In this chapter, we are going to ask such questions about the movement of wh-phrases involved in interrogative structures, i.e., questions. The same questions could be asked about head movement, or DP movement involved in raising to subject, or any other kind movement we could be led to postulate. We will begin with a basic review of some of the properties of wh-phrases and wh-movement, then try to formulate an elementary theory of when wh-movement is allowed in English.

10.1 Introduction

10.1.1 Wh-words

As we saw in Chapter 8, "wh-movement" refers to the movement of "wh-phrases" to clause-initial positions as in e.g.:

(1) a. Bill ate something
 b. Bill ate what ⇝ What did Bill eat?

A wh-phrase is a phrase that contains interrogative material that, in English, typically starts with the characters "wh." Wh-phrases are used in questions and in relative clauses, which we will discuss in Chapter 14. Much, although not all, of what we discuss in this section applies to both. There are two basic types of wh-phrases:

- The bare wh-type: *who, what, where, when, why,* and *how*. These wh-words can normally occur by themselves and we will treat them like pronouns.
- The complex wh-type: *which x, what x,* and *how many x* or *how much x, how x*. We will treat all these as determiners (D) except for *how* as in *how tall* or *how often*, which we will treat as an adjunct to AP or AdvP.

An Introduction to Syntactic Analysis and Theory, First Edition.
Dominique Sportiche, Hilda Koopman, and Edward Stabler.

Bare wh-phrases are wh-equivalent to the category in question:

(2)

DP	PP	AdvP
|	|	|
who/what	when/where/why/how	why/how

Like pronouns and certain other elements, these words behave like full phrases; compare *him, it, then, there.*

We can paraphrase *where, when, why,* and *how* above by *at/in/into what place, at what time, for what reason/purpose, in what way/manner,* etc. These interrogative words are used to ask for the identity of a person/thing, a location, place, reason, or manner.

(3) Who did you visit? A: Bill, the student, my mother...

A sentence with a bare wh-phrase typically presupposes the sentence containing it stripped of the wh-element. Thus, we could paraphrase what the speaker means when uttering (3a) by (4a) (where we replace the wh-phrase with *something/someone/*etc.). For the sentence above, a speaker uttering it typically expresses the following thought (with the presupposition in italics, and the "tell me" part reflecting the fact that, as a question, this is a request for information):

(4) *(Given that I think) you visited someone,* (tell me) who it is.

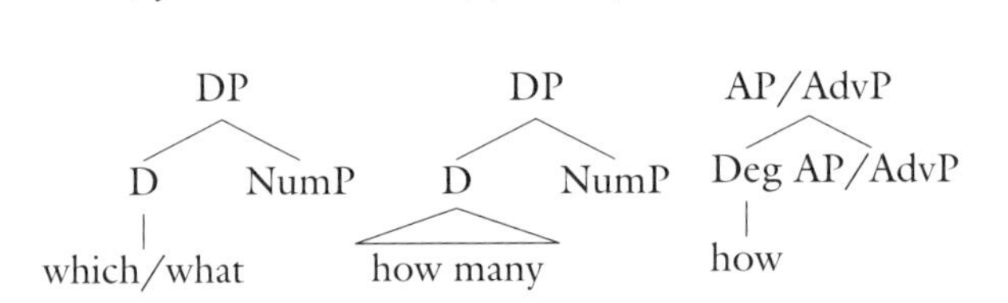

The structure we give for *how many* (or *how much*) is simplified but it will do for our purposes. The degree adjunct *how* replaces the degree/measure phrase that modifies the adjective or the adverb (as *very* in e.g. *very big*). Note how it can also be an AdvP by itself meaning "in what way."

10.1.2 Some questions about wh-movement

Since we would like to understand how wh-movement functions, we can start with the following questions:

a. What exactly does wh-movement move?
b. Where does it move to?
c. What can intervene between its launching site and its landing site?
d. Why does wh-movement exist at all?

Question (d), as why-questions often are, is difficult to answer; it depends on what exactly wh-movement is supposed to do, and this depends on the answer to the other questions. We should keep the existence of this question in mind for the future, but we will not try to answer it here. We will limit ourselves to providing preliminary answers to question (a) and (b) which we have already discussed to a certain extent. We will explore question (c) in some detail.

10.2 The Landing Site or Target Position of Wh-Movement

In Chapter 8, we already reached some conclusions about the landing site of wh-movement in questions. In main clauses, a wh-question is built "on top of" a yes/no question, that is on top of a structure in which T to C has applied, yielding subject–aux inversion.

The inverted auxiliary in the yes/no questions precedes the subject in the [Spec,TP]. The auxiliary verb in T moves to C.

Yes/No question ⇝ wh-question

(5) a. Do [$_{TP}$ you know Bill]? ⇝[$_{CP}$ Who$_i$ do [$_{TP}$ you know t_i]]?
  b. Will [$_{TP}$ you be reading it]? ⇝ [$_{CP}$ What$_i$ will [$_{TP}$ you be reading t_i]]?
  c. Has [$_{TP}$ she cried much]? ⇝ [$_{CP}$ How much$_i$ has [$_{TP}$ she cried t_i]]?
  d. Will [$_{TP}$ you leave then]? ⇝ [$_{CP}$ When$_i$ will [$_{TP}$ you leave t_i]]?

Because of this, we concluded that wh-phrases moved to [spec,CP].

Notation: First, recall that we use "subject of" or "specifier-of" synonymously. The notation **[spec,XP]** means the position subject of X or specifier of X. Note that "specifier" is *not* the name of a node. It is a way to identify a position occupied by some XP. Second: throughout this chapter, we use the t_i (called a "trace") to indicate the position from which movement is launched. This is a notational variant of equivalent to striking-out the wh-phrase, and widely used . We return to the question what's in a "trace" exactly in Chapter 11.

We also concluded that the moved wh-phrase showed +q agreement with a silent +q complementizer. This +q complementizer, being a bound, morpheme attracts T to it, that is, it triggers T-to-C a.k.a. subject–aux inversion (leading to *do*-support if T itself is a stranded bound morpheme).

(6)

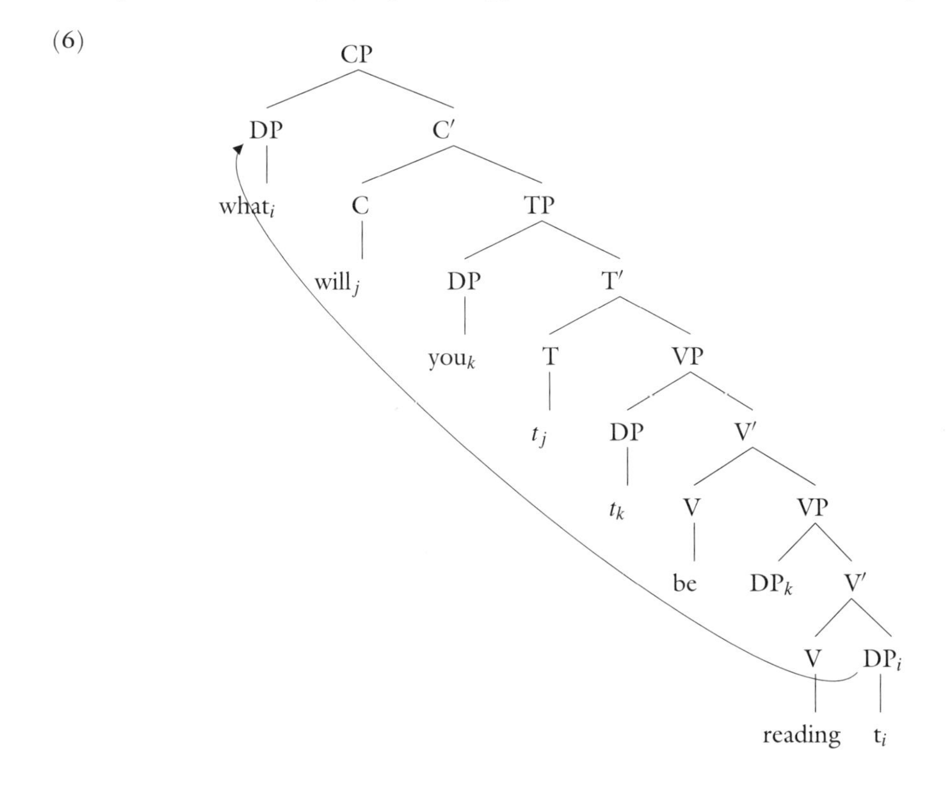

However, as we also noted earlier, T-to-C does not take place in indirect questions (except in certain varieties of English).

(7) Main clause interrogatives (questions):
  a. Who should I talk to?
  b. I don't know who I should talk to
  c. * He wondered who should he talk to

As we saw, what makes an indirect question is selection of a +q C by an embedding verb such as *wonder*. In turn, just as in the main clause case, this +q C attracts a wh-phrase, but fails to trigger T-to-C. We need to code the following properties:

- SAI occurs in main clauses.
- SAI does not occur in embedded clauses.

Ultimately, we would like to understand what is general and what is arbitrary about these properties, in part by surveying the complementizer system of many languages – in particular of many varieties of English – to see which properties cluster together and which properties seem accidental. For now, we can code this by brute force by postulating that there are two [+q] silent Cs, $e_{[+root(+T)]}$ that only occur in tensed main clauses, and a general unmarked C *e* that occurs elsewhere. In addition, we need to say, at least in the embedded case, that this C requires the presence of a wh-phrase as subject. In other words, we need to postulate an EPP feature requiring a +q phrase.[1] Here are their lexical entries:

$e_{[+root]}$: C, [+root], [+q], [+tense], EPP: XP_{+q}, bound, T
e: C, [+q], EPP:XP_{+q}

Note the following few features of these lexical entries.

First, we add the feature [+root] to the first one to indicate that it occurs only in root clauses. The second is unmarked for +/–root or +/–tense. The reason is that it occurs in both tensed and tenseless embedded questions:

(8) a. I asked what we should do
  b. I asked what to do

But it also **does** seem to occur in infinitival root clauses, witness:

(9) What to do?

Note that in all these contexts, and unlike $e_{[+root]}$, it does not trigger T-to-C. This means it is not a bound morpheme attracting a T, unlike $e_{[+root]}$. Finally, we need to state that these Cs require a wh-phrase (which is an XP, as we see in the next section). We code this requirement for a subject as EPP:XP_{+q} property.

This raises several questions: first, if such [+q] Cs are also the ones we find in yes/no questions, as they seem to be, why does there seem to be nothing in [spec,CP] in yes/no questions? This is question we cannot address in detail here, but there is actually good evidence (due to Larson (1985)) that:

- *Whether* is not a C, as we have assumed so far, but rather a wh-phrase (the wh version of *either*) moved to the subject of CP by wh-movement.[2]

[1] We saw in Chapter 8 that it is the C that has this requirement, not the moving wh-phrase.
[2] In previous chapters, we have used the distribution of *whether* in two ways: as occurring at the left edge of CP and this is still true; as being selected or as selector, and this is still indirectly true given the presence of the silent C with these same selected or selecting properties. So these incorrect assumptions are harmless.

Main clause subject questions: T-to-C movement does not occur in matrix clauses when extraction takes place from the matrix subject position:

(10) a. Who left?/*Who did leave?
b. What happened yesterday?/*What did happen yesterday?

This last question is well-formed, but it is not the question corresponding to the statement *something happened yesterday*. The *do* that appears must be stressed (unlike the "neutral" *do* inserted by *do*-support). It cannot be paraphrased by: *Something happened yesterday. What?* Instead, it can be paraphrased by: *Something did happen yesterday. What?*, where *did* must carry stress. This construction uses what is called emphatic *do* (which we can think of as an ordinary auxiliary verb like *have* or *be* or *will*). It does not just assert that something happened, but also denies a presupposition that something didn't happen. This is a property only of the matrix subjects. Wh-phrases that start out as embedded subjects still trigger SAI:

(11) a. *[$_{CP}$ Who [$_{TP}$ you think [$_{CP}$? [$_{TP}$ t left early]]]] ?
b. [$_{CP}$ Who do [$_{TP}$ you think [$_{CP}$? [$_{TP}$ left early]]]] ?

(12) a. *[$_{CP}$ What [$_{TP}$ you said [$_{CP}$? [$_{TP}$ t happened yesterday]]]] ?
b. [$_{CP}$ What did [$_{TP}$ you say [$_{CP}$? [$_{TP}$ t happened yesterday]]]] ?

There are several proposals in the literature regarding how to treat this phenomenon. In the present terms, the simplest is to suppose that $e_{[+root]}$, being more specialized than the other silent +q C, **must** be used unless it can't. (This is similar to why the plural *children* must be used instead of the regular *childs*). Assuming that $e_{[+root]}$ is ruled out with main subject wh-questions, the other silent +q C is used, which does not trigger T-to-C. This of course raises several questions: (i) what is the theory of this "competition" between the silent Cs? (ii) What prevents $e_{[+root]}$ from occurring in such contexts? We will return to (ii) later in Section 10.6.

- *Whether* has a silent counterpart marked +root which occurs as the subject of the C $e_{[+root]}$ in main clause yes/no questions.

Second, since both of these Cs **can** occur in tensed main clauses, why is T-to-C required? This is a complex and quite interesting question that we need not discuss here. It is tied to the question of why there is no *do*-support in main clause subject questions (viz. *who left?*). See the framed box here if you are curious.

10.3 What Wh-movement Moves

The conclusion that wh-movement displaces a syntactic chunk to [spec,CP] makes the prediction that wh-movement moves a phrase, an XP that can count as +q. This is correct. In English this means a +q DP, AP, or PP.

In the simplest cases, when the wh-word is a whole XP, this wh-XP moves. But this is not always true. For example, if a wh-word DP is a possessor, it cannot move by itself. Rather, the bigger DP containing the wh-DP must move.

(13) a. Whose book did you read?
b. *Who did you read *t*'s book
c. *Whose did you read *t* book

When we must move something bigger than the element that "triggers" the movement, that is the wh-word, we call this **Pied-Piping**, following Ross (1967).

In complex cases, when the wh-word is a determiner or a modifier, the wh-word alone cannot move either, a larger phrase must move. This is another case of pied-piping (we mark the launching site, the trace, with *t*):

(14) a. *How is the house [*t* big]?
b. *Which did you read [*t* book]?

c. *How did you see [*t* many] movies?
d. *How many did you see [*t* movies]?

(Recall that the # sign indicates that a string is well formed, but not with the right structure or with the intended meaning.)

(15) a. #How do you visit your parents [*t* often]?
b. #How did he fix your car [*t* successfully]?
c. #How can you leave [*t* quickly]?
d. #How do you [*t* deeply] resent my statements?

Wh-phrases inside PPs: DP-type wh-phrases (bare or complex) can appear as complements of a P. Recall that the orthography of *whose* reflects the syntactic structure below:

(16)

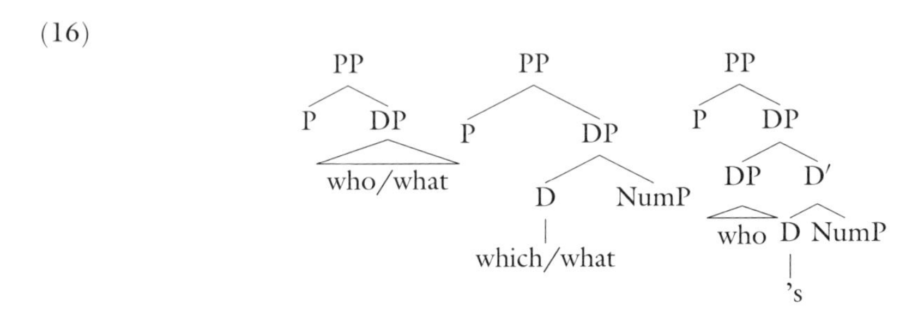

In such cases, wh-movement can proceed in two different ways:

- The entire PP can move. This would be another case of pied-piping.
- Only the DP can move and leave the P behind. This is called **P-stranding**, ubiquitous in English, found in other languages, but excluded in many.

Pied-piping: The entire PP is being moved. The *who/whom* distinction is preserved only in this context in modern colloquial English (in most instances, pied-piping itself has a formal flavor).

(17) a. [To whom]$_i$ did you speak t_i about our problem?
b. [In which box]$_i$ have you been hiding my valuables t_i?
c. [For whose grandmother]$_i$ are we baking this cake t_i?
d. [At what time]$_i$ did they arrive t_i?

However, not all prepositions are capable of pied-piping. Typically the prepositions that are relatively more idiosyncratic (less compositional), and contribute to the meaning of the verb, resist pied-piping.

(18) a. *[For which book]$_i$ are you looking t_i?
(cf. Which book are you looking for?)
b. ??[With whose personal belongings]$_i$ are you messing t_i?
(cf. Whose personal belongings are you messing with?)
c. *[To whose intuitions]$_i$ are we sticking t_i?
(cf. Whose intuitions are we sticking to?)
d. *[Off which bus]$_i$ did you get t_i?
(cf. Which bus did you get off?)

Pseudopassives: These examples are related to another fact about English prepositions: the object of a P can be passivized with some verbs, leaving P stranded. These constructions are called pseudopassives:

(19) a. This book was looked for (by Mary)
b. These examples should not be messed with
c. These data should be sticked to
d. This bed was recently slept in by the dog

P-stranding under wh-movement has a much wider distribution than P-stranding under passivization.

In some cases, it is even worse:

(20) a. You turned on the radio → **On which radio did you turn?
(cf. Which radio did you turn on?)
b. You woke up your neighbor → **Up which neighbor did you wake?
(cf. Which neighbor did you wake up?)

These Ps are called Particles or Intransitive Prepositions: particles never form a (complete) constituent with a following wh-phrase.[3]

P-stranding: The preposition is left behind and the DP that contains the wh-phrase moves up on its own. (Notice that the *who/whom* distinction blurs again in this context.)

(21) a. Who_i did you talk [to t_i]?
b. What_i have you been banging [on t_i]?
c. [Whose mother]$_i$ have you been talking [about t_i]?
d. [Which knife]$_i$ did you cut the bread [with t_i]?

P-stranding is usually the preferred version in colloquial modern English. However, P-stranding with some adjunct PPs is degraded for many speakers.

(22) a. ?What time_i are we going to take a break [at t_i]?
(cf. [At what time]$_i$ are we going to take a break t_i?)
b. ?[Which class]$_i$ did you sleep [during t_i]?
(cf. [During which class]$_i$ did you sleep t_i?)

There seems to be a sharp contrast with the next examples:

c. *[Whose foolishness]$_i$ did we end up in this situation [due to t_i]?
(cf. [Due to whose foolishness]$_i$ did we end up in this situation t_i?)
d. *[Which law]$_i$ do we have to declare bankruptcy [because of t_i]?
(cf. [Because of which law]$_i$ do we have to declare bankruptcy t_i?)

Conclusion: What exactly moves looks rather arbitrary. First, wh-movement can only move phrases. Next, which phrases move depends in part on what is **allowed** to move as we will see when we investigate a portion of this problem in the next section: some arbitrariness will disappear. A detailed investigation would reveal that the system is in fact quite regular.

[3]Here is a difference between prepositions and particles: particles can be separated from the verb by a DP (which is referred to as **Particle Shift**, see: **I have been looking War and Peace for*, **I am messing his things with*, **I always stick Sue's intuitions to*, **I got that bus off* vs. *You turned the radio on, you woke me up*.

10.4 Locality I: The Problem

In the simple examples that we have covered so far, a wh-phrase can be moved out of its original position to the specifier of the matrix CP, no matter how far down in the tree its base position is.

(23) a. What$_i$ did Bill see t_i?
b. What$_i$ did you say [$_{CP}$ that Bill saw t_i]?
c. What$_i$ does Sue think [$_{CP}$ that you said [$_{CP}$ that Bill saw t_i]]?
d. What$_i$ does Bill suspect [$_{CP}$ that Sue thinks [$_{CP}$ that you said [$_{CP}$ that T saw t_i]]]?
etc.

All these are cases where a CP appears as the complement of the higher verb, and it appears that the movement of the wh-phrase is unbounded. However, this apparent freedom of movement is misleading. It is clear that the movement of the wh-phrase is not so free and unbounded. We have already seen such cases, although we did not recognize what they meant, when we talked about pied-piping. The simplest way of thinking about wh-movement is to formulate it as:

(24) **Wh-movement**: Move a wh-word to some [Spec,CP] (that allows it).

However, we have already seen that such a simple formulation fails in all cases of obligatory pied-piping. For example, using # to indicate acceptable but with the wrong meaning:

(25) Which book did you see? vs *which did you see book
How intelligent was she? vs #how was she intelligent

We can fix this problem by requiring wh-movement to move the smallest XP containing the wh-word. (This gives us a better description but, ultimately, we also want to know why wh-movement moves phrases rather than words.)

(26) **Wh-movement**: Move the smallest XP containing a wh-word phrase to some [Spec,CP] (that allows it).

But of course, this is not going to be enough. First, there are cases when we are allowed to pied-pipe a bigger phrase (e.g. with certain PPs). Second, and more importantly for our present purposes, because we are sometimes required to move a bigger phrase (e.g. with non-strandable Ps or with movement of *whose*, which is with obligatory pied-piping). Third, and most importantly, because there are cases in which we cannot do anything at all:

(27) a. A picture of some monster scared the entire population
b. *Who did [a picture of ___] scare the entire population

(28) a. Bill accused the people fond of candies of greed
b. *What did Bill accuse the people fond of ___ of greed

10.4.1 The A-over-A principle

The first systematic attempt to capture the contexts that blocked the movement of wh-phrases was Chomsky's (1964) **A-over-A Principle**, which essentially states that it is not possible to move a category from a context that is embedded inside the same type of category (A-over-A):

(29) * [... Y ... [$_A$ ... **A ...**]

The bold-faced A is contained in another A. So according to the A-over-A principle, this lower A cannot be wh-moved out of the bigger A. The practical application of this principle was that a DP (at the time, they were called NPs) inside another DP was not allowed to move out. This principle covered a number of different constructions (given the assumptions of the day), including cases of wh-movement from inside a relative clause. (Do not worry about the structure of the relative clause at this point. The only thing to remember is that the relative clause is an adjunct to NP.)

(30) a. You talked to the man that read a magazine
b. You talked to [$_{DP}$ the [$_{NP}$ [$_{NP}$ man] [$_{CP}$ that read [$_{DP}$ a magazine]]]
c. You talked to [$_{DP}$ the [$_{NP}$ [$_{NP}$ man] [$_{CP}$ that read [$_{DP}$ what]]]
d. *What$_i$ did you to [$_{DP}$ the [$_{NP}$ [$_{NP}$ man] [$_{CP}$ that read t_i]]?

We can see that the DP *what* tries to leave the DP *the man that read what*, which is the complement of the P *to*, and the result is bad, as shown. The application of the A-over-A principle in this case is that the DP *what* is not allowed to leave the DP that contains it. Similarly, the impossibility of extracting a conjunct out of a coordination immediately follows from the A-over-A principle:

(31) a. You ate some chicken and rice
b. You ate [$_{DP}$ [$_{DP}$ some chicken] and [$_{DP}$ rice]]
c. You ate [$_{DP}$ [$_{DP}$ what] and [$_{DP}$ rice]]
d. *What$_i$ did you eat [$_{DP}$ t_i and [$_{DP}$ rice]]?

Here, we attempted to extract a DP (shown as t_i) out of a larger DP. Furthermore, it is clear that this would generalize to trying to extract an AP out of an AP coordination, a VP out of a VP coordination, etc.

A-over-A was a very simple and quite general principle with some explanatory power but it had two problems:

- It was too weak: it did not block cases that were ill-formed even though they looked very much like the excluded cases (suggesting a single principle is at play). For example, the movement of APs out of a relative clause is just as bad, if not worse, but A-over-A cannot stop them from moving because they are APs not contained inside APs. In other words, they are not the same type of category as the domain that they attempt to escape.

(32) a. You talked to a man that looks very intelligent
b. You talked to [$_{DP}$ [$_{DP}$ a man] [$_{CP}$ that looks [$_{AP}$ very intelligent]]]
c. You talked to [$_{DP}$ [$_{DP}$ a man] [$_{CP}$ that looks [$_{AP}$ how intelligent]]]
d. *[$_{AP}$ How intelligent]$_i$ did you talk to [$_{DP}$ [$_{DP}$ a man] [$_{CP}$ that looks t_i]]?

One other case of weakness was found with coordination. In fact, wh-extraction of anything out of a coordination is excluded (with one exception called Across the Board or (ATB) extraction to which we return on p. 279).

(33) a. You like rice from India and some chicken
b. You like [$_{DP}$ [$_{DP}$ rice from India] and [$_{DP}$ some chicken]]
c. You like [$_{DP}$ [$_{DP}$ rice from [$_{PP}$ which country]] and [$_{DP}$ some chicken]]
d. *Which country $_i$ did you like [$_{DP}$ [$_{DP}$ rice from t_i] and [$_{DP}$ some chicken]]?

In themselves, these are not damning problems. It may well be that we need another principle, another constraint on wh-movement to handle this case (but it looks suspicious that this case and the cases that the A-over-A principle does exclude are so similar). Much more serious is the following problem.

- It was too strong: it blocked cases that it should not block. For example, A DP inside a direct object may be wh-questioned as shown below, but A-over-A cannot differentiate these cases from those that must be blocked, such as the context above.

(34) a. You saw a picture of some students
b. You saw [[DP a picture of [[DP some students]]
c. You saw [[DP a picture of [[DP which students]]
d. [[DP Which students]$_i$ did you see [[DP a picture of t_i]?

If a hypothesis is **too weak** in the sense that it does not exclude certain ill-formed structures, this may suggest that this hypothesis is wrong, for example if we have some good reasons to think that the excluded data and the unexcluded data form a natural class. However, this does not demonstrate that this hypothesis is wrong. If a hypothesis is **too strong**, in the sense that it excludes certain well-formed structures, this demonstrates that the hypothesis is wrong. It **must** be revised.

As a result, some modification had to be introduced, and no simple and general enough way was found to be satisfactory. Consequently, the A-over-A principle was replaced by a number of independent constraints, most of which are due to Ross (1967) and (1986), as was the criticism of the A-over-A constraint we discussed above. Ross conducted a systematic investigation of when wh-movement was allowed and when it was not allowed and proposed a large catalogue of what he called "island constraints." The term "island" is meant to evoke a place that is difficult to leave. The existence and nature of islands has defined an important research agenda, which is still being actively pursued.

10.4.2 The constraints

All the constraints we are going to see have the general format:

Constraint XYZ: Movement cannot extract anything from a certain type of structure that looks like this . . .

These constraints (or conditions) that are stated below are simply observations and generalizations. Saying that a given wh-movement cannot move to a given [Spec,CP] because it would violate some constraint or the other is not an explanation. It is a descriptive statement. We will have a better description of what happens than with the A-over-A principle, but we have lost the kind of more general explanation that the A-over-A principle provided as to why these constraints hold. This is why the search went on to try to understand why the particular constraints that were found to exist.

If we wanted to discover what "constraints" there are, one good way to proceed would be to try systematically to extract from all possible embedded constituents and note when this succeeds and when this fails. For example, suppose we want to extract from inside a clause. To organize the data, we could try to extract systematically from clauses that are complements, clauses that are subjects, and clauses that are adjuncts. And we could also vary what these clauses are complements of, subjects of, or adjuncts to. If we were trying to extract from inside DPs, we could do the same thing: try to extract from DPs that are subjects, or objects, or adjuncts of verbs, then of nouns, prepositions, etc. Incidentally, note how important it becomes to know exactly what the constituent structure is if we are going to be successful in describing what happens.

We are not going to do this systematically here, but if we were investigating this problem thoroughly, we would have to.

Extraction out of clauses
Here we will be a little bit less systematic. We will begin with the following extraction from clauses (CP) in the following positions:

(35)

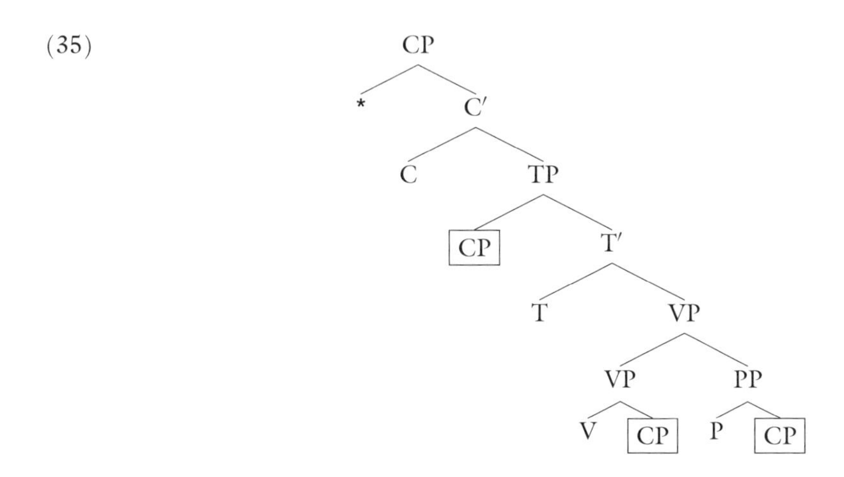

That is, we begin with clauses that are either the subject of a clause, complement of V, or (in an) adjunct to VP (which means it is typically inside a PP adjunct to VP). We are going to ask the question of whether wh-movement from within these CPs to the star position is possible.

Unboundedness: The first thing to notice is that, in principle, wh-movement in questions, direct and indirect, is unbounded in the following sense: there is no bound on the distance (measured, for example, in number of nodes intervening) between the launching site and the landing site; it can be made as large as we want. Here are some examples to illustrate this important property.

(36) a. What did you eat ___
b. What did you say that Bill thinks that I ate ___?
c. Who should I tell your mother that you are going to visit ___tomorrow?

The first example in (5), that is, the movement of *what*$_i$ from the DP$_i$ position to [Spec,CP] of its clause, is **short distance** since it involves a single clause. Wh-movement can also take place across clausal boundaries as the other examples show. In these instances, **long distance** wh-movement, a wh-phrase that originates in a lower clause moves to the [Spec,CP] of the matrix clause. We see in this case that the wh-phrase can cross over CP boundaries, not just one but apparently many. The same is true of indirect questions: embedded wh-questions can have the wh-phrase move short or long distances as well:

(37) a. I don't know who I should talk to *t*
b. Sue told Bill that I don't know who I should talk to *t*
c. I don't know who Sue told Bill that I should talk to *t*
d. Mary doesn't know who I think that Sue told Bill that I should talk to *t*

Movement unboundedness: The unboundedness of wh-movement is one important difference with the raising to subject kind of movement that usually can never cross tensed CP boundaries. Compare for example:

(39) a. [$_{CP}$ Who$_i$ did [$_{TP}$ you say [$_{CP}$ that [$_{TP}$ I pushed t_i]]]]?
b. * [$_{TP}$ You$_i$ seem [$_{CP}$ that [$_{TP}$ I pushed t_i]]]?

This is one of the systematic differences between A-movement (movement of the raising kind) and A-bar movement (movement of the wh-kind).

Note also that what happens in a higher clause is independent of the wh-movement that takes place in the lower clause.

(38) a. I wonder who Mary would like to invite *t* for dinner tonight
b. Do you wonder who Mary would like to invite *t* for dinner tonight?
c. Why$_j$ do you wonder t_j [who$_i$ Mary would like to invite t_i for dinner tonight]?

Wh-islands: We have seen that wh-extraction out of complement clauses is sometimes possible, whether they are tensed clauses or infinitives:

(40) a. What$_i$ did Bill persuade John [$_{CP}$ PRO to buy t_i]?
b. What$_i$ did you say [$_{CP}$ that Bill saw t_i]?

There is one class of cases, however, in which extraction is always difficult: embedded wh-questions, be they tensed or tenseless questions. This constraint is called the **wh-island constraint**. The data below is organized as follows: the first line represents the baseline sentence, the second replaces one DP with a second wh-phrase, and the third line shows the result of the extraction of that wh-phrase:

(41) a. You wonder [$_{CP}$ who bought the wine for the party]
b. You wonder [$_{CP}$ who bought what for the party]
c. *What$_i$ do you wonder [$_{CP}$ who bought t_i for the party]?

(42) a. Sue asked [$_{CP}$ where PRO to hide your keys]
b. Sue asked [$_{CP}$ where PRO to hide what]
c. *What$_i$ did Sue ask [$_{CP}$ where to hide t_i]?

The wh-island constraint is further illustrated below.

(43) a. You know [$_{CP}$ why Bill called the police]
b. You know [$_{CP}$ why who called the police]
c. *Who$_i$ do you know [$_{CP}$ why t_i called the police]?

(44) a. Bill wonders [$_{CP}$ who filed for divorce yesterday]
b. Bill wonders [$_{CP}$ who filed for divorce when]
c. *When$_i$ does Bill wonder [$_{CP}$ who filed for divorce t_i]?

The complementizers that are [+wh] also trigger wh-island effects:

(45) a. You wonder [$_{CP}$ whether Sue will present her talk tomorrow]
b. You wonder [$_{CP}$ whether Sue will present what tomorrow]
c. *What$_i$ do you wonder [$_{CP}$ whether Sue will present t_i tomorrow]?

(46) a. Mary asked [$_{CP}$ if John had left something on the table in the morning]
b. Mary asked [$_{CP}$ if John had left what on the table in the morning]
c. *What$_i$ did Mary ask [$_{CP}$ if John had left t_i on the table in the morning]?

(47) **The Wh-island Constraint (paraphrased):**[4] A wh-phrase cannot move out of a [+q] CP (i.e. a CP that has a wh-phrase in its [Spec,CP] or a +q C in its C position).

A wh-island blocks the movement of a wh-phrase if the [Spec,CP] that is filled with another wh-phrase is not the one from which we extract, but is higher in the tree.

(48) a. You wonder [$_{CP}$ when Bill suggested [$_{CP}$ that John should visit his mother]]
b. You wonder [$_{CP}$ when Bill suggested [$_{CP}$ that John should visit who]]
c. *Who$_i$ do you wonder [$_{CP}$ when Bill suggested [$_{CP}$ that John should visit t_i]]?

(49) a. You wonder [$_{CP}$ who believes [$_{CP}$ that aliens abducted Mary]]
b. You wonder [$_{CP}$ who believes [$_{CP}$ that aliens abducted who]]
c. *Who$_i$ do you wonder [$_{CP}$ who believes [$_{CP}$ that aliens abducted t_i]]?

Here is an example of structure involving a wh-island violation, with the island appearing as a boxed node, and the offending movement as the long arrow:

(50)

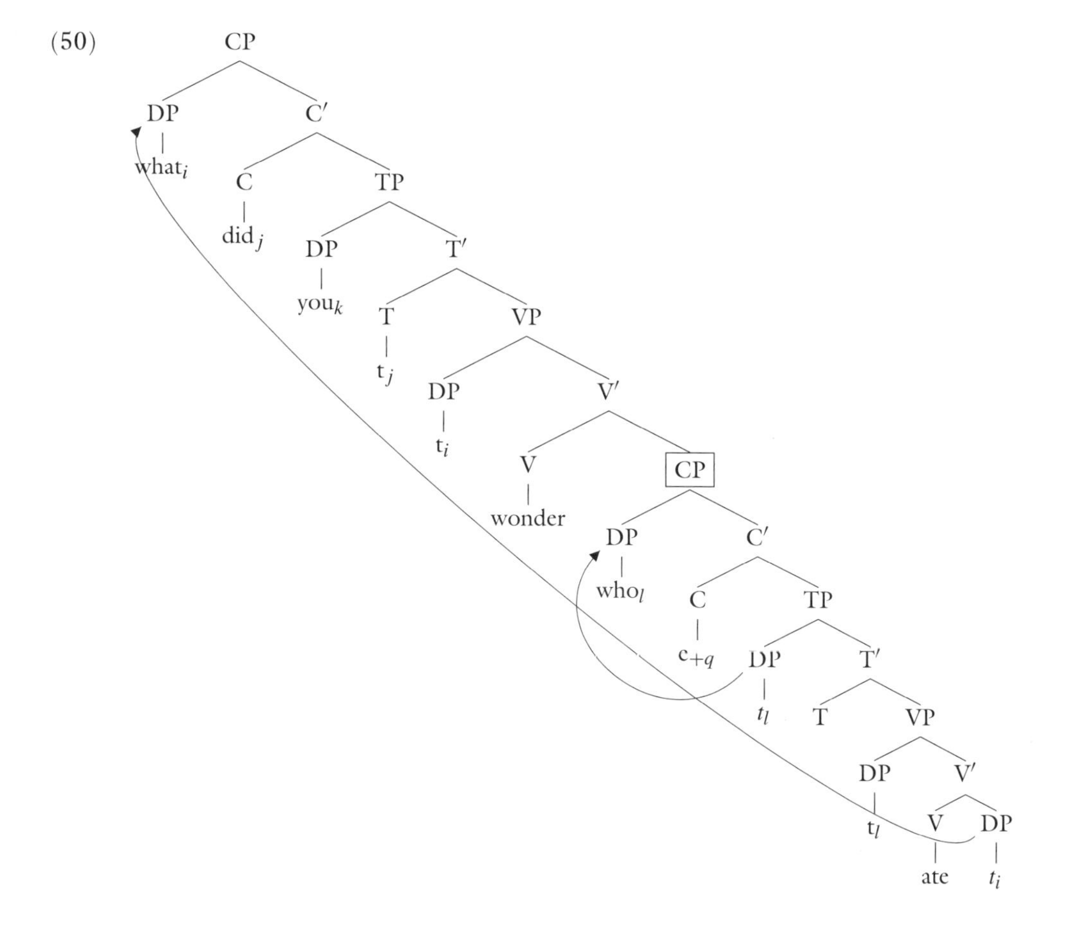

[4]Here and below we use *paraphrased* or *adjusted* to signify that we use words to describe the constraints.

The movement of wh-phrases out of a wh-island is blocked, so an adverbial that starts out in the lower clause inside the wh-island cannot raise to the matrix [Spec,CP]. As a result, sentences that have an adjunct wh-phrase in the matrix [Spec,CP] will be construed as if the wh-phrase started at some point *outside* the wh-island, not *inside*:

(51) a. You wonder [$_{CP}$ who the aliens abducted why]
b. *Why$_i$ do you wonder [$_{CP}$ who the aliens abducted t_i]?

(52) a. You wonder [$_{CP}$ who the aliens abducted] why
b. Why$_i$ do you wonder [$_{CP}$ who the aliens abducted] t_i?

(53) a. John asked [$_{CP}$ what T ate when]
b. When$_i$ did John ask [$_{CP}$ what T ate t_i]?

(54) a. John asked when [$_{CP}$ what T ate]
b. When$_i$ did John ask t_i [$_{CP}$ what T ate]?

Practice

(i) For each example sentence in this chapter, make sure you know how to draw the trees. (ii) Draw the trees for (52) and (54). Thinking about the answers to these questions, why is it reasonable to have the t_i of the reason adjunct follow rather than precede the CP in (52)? What about (54)? Why is it reasonable to have the the t_i of the temporal adjunct preceding the CP in (54), rather than following the C? Why is this also problematic, i.e. what principle is apparently violated in (54)? Think about two possible ways to pursue an analysis to this particular problem, keeping the principle fully general.

Sentential Subject Constraint: We have examined cases of extraction out of complement clauses (of V). Now we turn to extractions from clauses that are subjects. A clause that is a subject is called a sentential subject. Note that in technical jargon, a sentential subject is *not* the subject of a sentence, it is a subject that is a clause.

(55) a. [$_{CP}$ that Bill threw your things out of the room] really annoyed you
b. [$_{CP}$ that Bill threw what out of the room] really annoyed you
c. *What$_i$ did [$_{CP}$ that Bill threw t_i out of the room] really annoy you?

(56) a. [$_{CP}$ that most people didn't vote last year] was terrible
b. [$_{CP}$ that most people didn't vote when] was terrible
c. *When$_i$ was [$_{CP}$ that most people didn't vote t_i] terrible?

(57) a. [$_{CP}$ for you to charge this boat on your credit card] would be a disaster
b. [$_{CP}$ for you to charge what on your credit card] would be a disaster
c. *What$_i$ would [$_{CP}$ for you to charge t_i on your credit card] be a disaster?

The impossibility of extraction is not tied to the sentential subject being in the main clause:

(58) a. Bill thinks [$_{CP}$ that [$_{TP}$ [$_{CP}$ for you to charge this on your credit card] would be fine]]
b. Bill thinks [$_{CP}$ that [$_{TP}$ [$_{CP}$ for you to charge what on your credit card] would be fine]]
c. *What$_i$ would Bill think that [$_{CP}$ for you to charge t_i on your credit card] be fine?

Here is an example of a sentential subject constraint violation with the island shown as a boxed node (simplifying the tree):

(59)

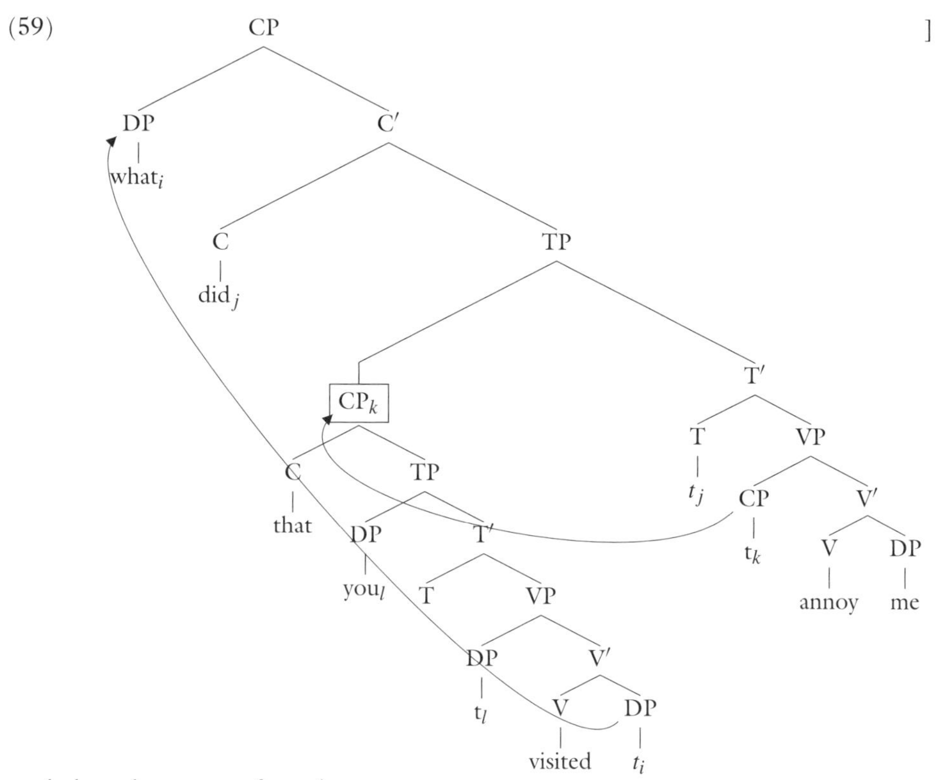

To exclude such cases, we formulate:

(60) **The Sentential Subject Constraint (paraphrased)**: No element can move out of a CP that is in the subject position.

The Adjunct Island Condition: The Adjunct Island Condition prohibits extraction from inside an adjunct. Here is an example illustrating this impossibility:

(61) a. He went home [$_{PP}$ before [$_{CP}$ Mary finished what]]
b. *What$_i$ did he go home [$_{PP}$ before [$_{CP}$ Mary finished t_i]]

(62) **The Adjunct Island Condition (adjusted)**: No element in a CP inside an adjunct may move out of this adjunct.

We illustrate this in the tree below with the adjunct island boxed:

(63)

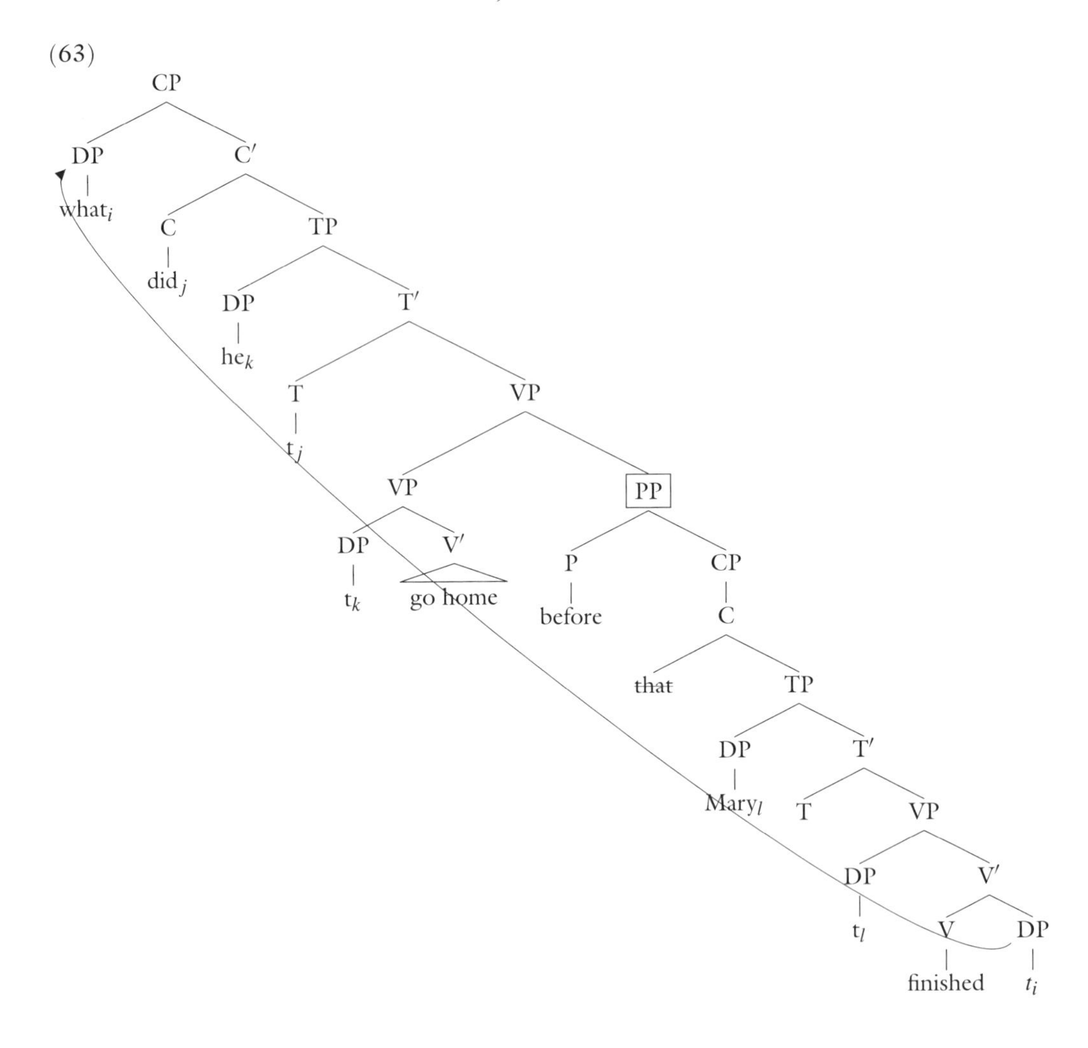

Complex NP Constraint (CNPC): We now turn to extraction out of clauses that are either complements or adjuncts in the N system as in the diagram below:

(64)

NP
NP CP
N CP

The Complex Noun Phrase Constraint is a constraint putting together two configurations: the impossibility of extracting out of a clause that is the complement of a noun and the impossibility of extracting out of a clause that is an adjunct to an NP.

Noun–Complement Type CNPC Violations: Nouns like *claim, rumor, story, suggestion*, etc. take CP complements (note the correlation with verbs: *to claim that John left, to suggest that John left.*)

(65) a. You heard [$_{DP}$ the [rumor [$_{CP}$ that Bill has broken the vase]]]
b. You heard [$_{DP}$ the [rumor [$_{CP}$ that Bill has broken what]]]
c. *What$_i$ did you hear [[$_{DP}$ the rumor [$_{CP}$ that Bill has broken t_i]]]?

(66) a. Bill is spreading [$_{DP}$ the [news [$_{CP}$ that Mary is going to buy a new car]]]
b. Bill is spreading [$_{DP}$ the [news [$_{CP}$ that Mary is going to buy what]]]
c. *What$_i$ is Bill spreading [$_{DP}$ the [news [$_{CP}$ that Mary is going to buy t_i]]]?

(67) a. You dislike [$_{DP}$ the [suggestion [$_{CP}$ that Sue should go to Death Valley]]]
b. You dislike [$_{DP}$ the [suggestion [$_{CP}$ that Sue should go where]]]
c. *Where$_i$ did you dislike [$_{DP}$ the [suggestion [$_{CP}$ that Sue should go t_i]]]?

The structure of such sentences is exemplified below (with the island appearing as a boxed node):

(68)

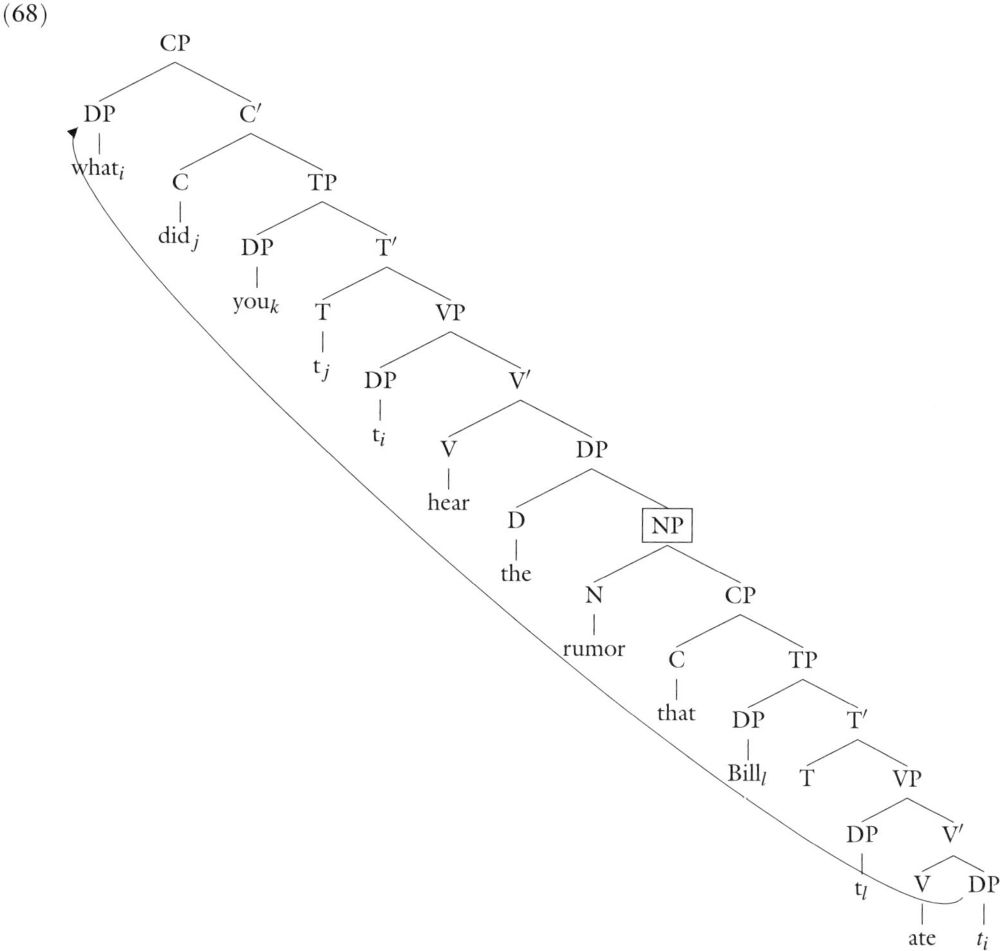

Relative Clause Type CNPC Violations:

(69) a. You sharpened [$_{DP}$ the [$_{NP}$ knife [$_{CP}$ which Tom cut the bread with]]]
b. You sharpened [$_{DP}$ the [$_{NP}$ knife] [$_{CP}$ which Tom cut what with]]
c. *What$_i$ did you sharpen [$_{DP}$ the [$_{NP}$ knife] [$_{CP}$ which Tom cut t_i with]]?

(70) a. Bill knows [$_{DP}$ the [$_{NP}$ man] [$_{CP}$ who yelled in the hallway yesterday]]
b. Bill knows [$_{DP}$ the [$_{NP}$ man] [$_{CP}$ who yelled where yesterday]]
c. *Where$_i$ does Bill know [$_{DP}$ the [$_{NP}$ man] [$_{CP}$ who yelled t_i yesterday]]?

(71) a. Sue watched [$_{DP}$ the [$_{NP}$ movie] [$_{CP}$ which Bill liked]]
b. Sue watched [$_{DP}$ the [$_{NP}$ movie] [$_{CP}$ which who liked]]
c. *Who$_i$ did Sue watch [$_{DP}$ the [$_{NP}$ movie] [$_{CP}$ which t$_i$ liked]]?

The structure of such sentences is exemplified below (with the island appearing as a boxed node):[5]

(72)

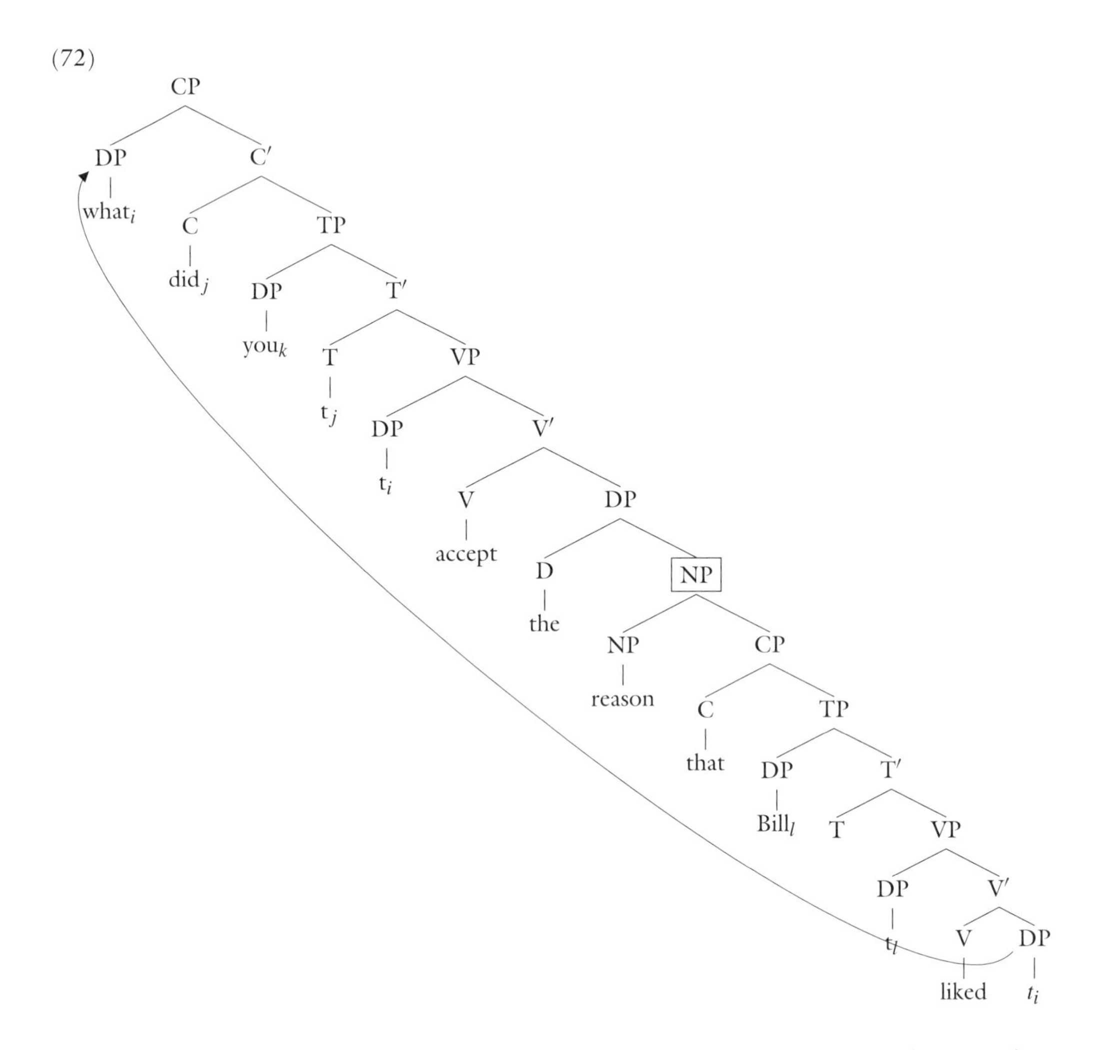

The impossibility of wh-extraction from inside these types of clause is known as the **Complex NP Constraint** or **CNPC**. The CNPC is one of Ross's (1967) constraints. A "complex NP" (in this context) refers to a DP that contains a CP. The CP can be (a) a complement of the noun, where

[5] Relative clauses themselves involve wh-movement that we do not indicate here. [Spec,CP] of the relative clause holds a (here silent) wh-phrase (clearly related to a position inside the clause, much as in wh-questions). We return to the structure of relative clauses in Chapter 14.

the noun takes a CP-internal argument, or (b) an adjunct on the NP, which is a relative clause. The CNPC is formulated as follows:

(73) **Complex Noun Phrase Constraint (adjusted)**: No element inside a CP dominated by a NP can be moved out of this NP.

CNPC cases are classic A-over-A contexts, though this particular formulation (CNPC) of the restriction blocks all cases of movement, including [+ q] APs, AdvPs, etc.

Extraction out of DPs

As we did in the case of clauses, we can try to perform a wh-extraction from within DPs. We will limit ourselves to the following two cases. (For the moment, we leave aside adjuncts, which raise all sorts of complication.)

(74)

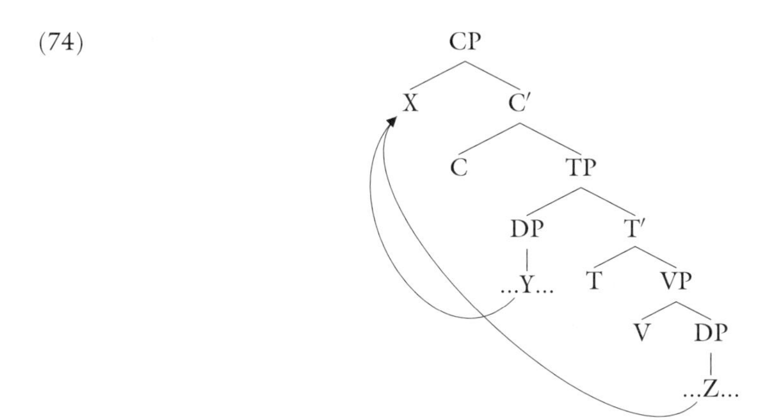

We have already seen that we can extract a DP out of a DP object of a verb (this created a problem for the A-over-A principle):

(75) a. You saw [$_{DP}$ a picture of [$_{DP}$ some students]]
b. You saw [$_{DP}$ a picture of [$_{DP}$ which students]]
c. [$_{DP}$ Which students]$_i$ did you see [$_{DP}$ a picture of t_i]?

The Subject Condition: Extracting a DP out of a DP that is the subject of a verb (and thus usually shows up as [Spec,TP]) yields deviant results:

(76) a. [$_{DP}$ a picture of [$_{DP}$ some students]] appeared in the newspapers
b. [$_{DP}$ a picture of [$_{DP}$ which students]] appeared in the newspapers
c. [$_{DP}$ Which students$_i$ did [$_{DP}$ a picture of t$_i$] appear in the newspapers?

To exclude such cases, we can formulate the following constraint:

(77) **The Subject Condition (adjusted)**: A DP cannot be extracted from a DP subject of a clause.

Left Branch Constraint (LBC): The two cases we looked at above (extraction of a DP out of a DP subject or out of a DP complement) were both cases in which the extracted DP was itself a complement. If the extracted DP is a subject, extraction is always impossible, as illustrated below:

(78) a. You are eating [$_{DP}$ [$_{DP}$ whose cake]]
b. *Whose$_i$ are you eating [$_{DP}$ t$_i$ cake]?
c. *Who$_i$ are you eating [$_{DP}$ t$_i$'s cake]?

To exclude this kind of extraction, Ross (1967) postulated the **Left Branch Constraint**:

(79) **The Left Branch Constraint (adjusted)**: The DP subject of a larger DP cannot be extracted out of this larger DP.

As a result of this constraint, one way we can form a wh-question that questions the subject of a DP is to do pied-piping: when we want to question the subject of a DP, we pied-pipe the entire DP, if this is possible:

(80) a. You are eating [$_{DP}$ [$_{DP}$ whose] cake]
b. [Whose cake]$_i$ are you eating [$_{DP}$ t_i]?

This suggest that many cases of pied-piping exist in order to circumvent the effects of a constraint on extraction.

There are several other constraints on extractions that arise in particular configurations. We will only talk about one of them here: the **Coordinate Structure Constraint** or **CSC**.

The CSC is also one of Ross's (1967) constraints, and it prohibits extraction from inside one of two or more conjuncts.

(81) **Coordinate Structure Constraint (adjusted)**: No conjunct or element contained within a conjunct of a coordination can be moved out of this coordination.

Notice that the first part of the CSC bans the movement of either conjunct.

(82) a. You ate [$_{DP}$ [$_{DP}$ some chicken] and [$_{DP}$ rice]]
b. You ate [$_{DP}$ [$_{DP}$ what] and [$_{DP}$ rice]]
c. *What$_i$ did you eat [$\boxed{\text{DP}}$ t$_i$ and [$_{DP}$ rice]]?

(83) a. You ate [$_{DP}$ [$_{DP}$ some chicken] and [$_{DP}$ rice]]
b. You ate [$_{DP}$ [$_{DP}$ some chicken] and [$_{DP}$ what]]
c. *What$_i$ did you eat [$\boxed{\text{DP}}$ [$_{DP}$ some chicken] and t$_i$]?

The second part if the CSC bans the movement of some wh-phrase from inside one of the conjuncts. (Note the change in the tense in both conjuncts.)

(84) a. You [$_{VP}$ [$_{VP}$ ate some pie] and [$_{VP}$ drank some coffee]]
b. You [$_{VP}$ [$_{VP}$ ate what] and [$_{VP}$ drank some coffee]]
c. *What$_i$ did you [$\boxed{\text{VP}}$ [$_{VP}$ eat t_i] and [$_{VP}$ drink some coffee]]?

(85) a. You [$_{VP}$ [$_{VP}$ ate some pie] and [$_{VP}$ drank some coffee]]
b. You [$_{VP}$ [$_{VP}$ ate some pie] and [$_{VP}$ drank what]]
c. *What$_i$ did you [$\boxed{\text{VP}}$ [$_{VP}$ eat some pie] and [$_{VP}$ drink t_i]]]?

(86) a. Bill thinks [$_{CP}$ that [$_{TP}$ [$_{TP}$ Tom gathered the data] and [$_{TP}$ you wrote the paper]]]
b. Bill thinks [$_{CP}$ that [$_{TP}$ [$_{TP}$ Tom gathered what] and [$_{TP}$ you wrote the paper]]]
c. *What$_i$ does Bill think [$_{CP}$that $\boxed{\text{TP}}$ [$_{TP}$Tom gathered t_i] and [$_{TP}$ you wrote the paper]]]?

(87) a. Bill thinks [$_{CP}$ that [$_{TP}$ [$_{TP}$ Tom gathered the data] and [$_{TP}$ you wrote the paper]]]
b. Bill thinks [$_{CP}$ that [$_{TP}$ [$_{TP}$ Tom gathered the data] and [$_{TP}$ you wrote what]]]
c. *What$_i$ does Bill think [$_{CP}$ that [$\boxed{_{TP}}$ [$_{TP}$ Tom gathered the data] and [$_{TP}$ you wrote t_i]]]?

There is a systematic class of exceptions to the CSC. An element can be moved out of one of the conjuncts if a "parallel" element is also moved from the others. This is called **Across-the-Board Extraction** or **ATB**.

(88) a. Bill thinks that Tom wrote the paper and you criticized it
b. Bill thinks [$_{CP}$ that [$_{TP}$ Tom wrote the paper] and [$_{TP}$ you criticized it]]
c. Bill thinks [$_{CP}$ that [$_{TP}$ Tom wrote what] and [$_{TP}$ you criticized what]]
d. What$_i$ does Bill think [$_{CP}$ that [$_{TP}$ Tom wrote t_i] and [$_{TP}$ you criticized t_i]]?

The structure for CSC varies with the constituent that is coordinated. A simplified example tree for DP conjunction is as follows.

(89) *

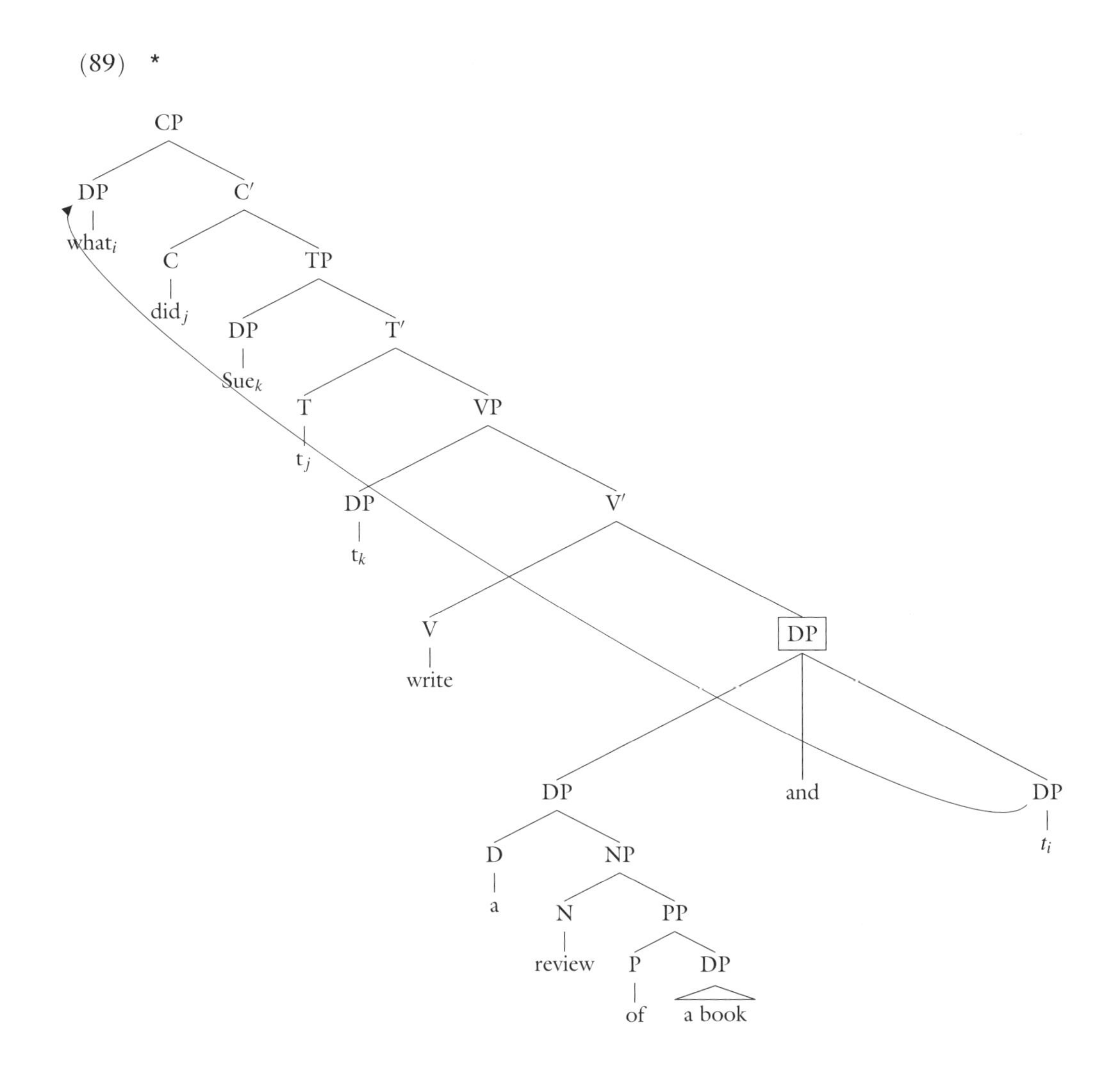

Note that the exception to the coordinate structure constraint by ATB must be formulated so as not to allow extraction of a whole conjunct. Indeed, the following variant of (89), which has undergone ATB, is ill-formed:

(90) *

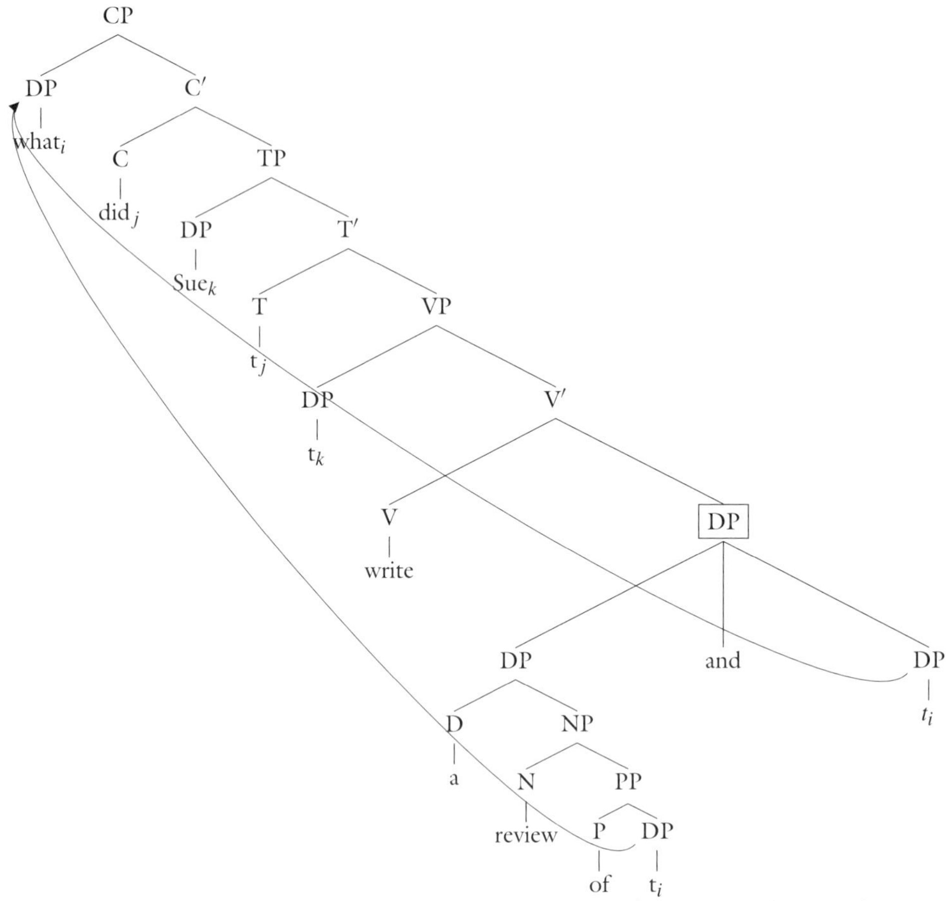

Note also that ATB extractions will create many cases of violation of the A-over-A principle – one more reason to give it up.

10.4.3 Summary

Ross (1967) was successful in providing a catalogue of constraints on the way in which wh-movement operates. It introduced a number of isolated constraints (or conditions), each of which was stating the context out of which the movement was not allowed. We list the sample we have looked at:

(47) **The wh-island constraint (paraphrased)**: A wh-phrase cannot move out of a [+q] CP (i.e. a CP that has a wh-phrase in its [Spec,CP] or a +q C in its C position).

(60) **The sentential subject constraint (paraphrased)**: No element can move out of a CP that is in the subject position.

(62) **The adjunct island condition: (adjusted)**: No element inside a CP in an adjunct may move out of this adjunct.

(73) **The complex noun phrase constraint (adjusted)**: No element inside a CP dominated by a NP can be moved out of this NP.

(77) **The subject condition (adjusted)**: A DP cannot be extracted from a DP subject of a clause.

(79) **The left branch constraint (adjusted):** The DP subject of a larger DP cannot be moved out.

(81) **Coordinate structure constraint (adjusted)**: No conjunct or element contained within a conjunct can be moved out.

This is descriptively adequate but in a way unsatisfactory, because it does not tell us why we find the constraints that we find rather than other imaginable constraints. This is why researchers have been trying to find more general conditions that have these particular constraints as consequences.

10.5 Locality II: Theory of Constraints

10.5.1 Introduction

To facilitate our review of the constraints on wh-movement we have discovered so far, let's present a little structural diagram that exemplifies the kind of movement that it excludes:

(47) **The wh-island constraint (paraphrased)**: A wh-phrase cannot move out of a [+q_{wh}] CP.
wh [$_{CP}$ wh-element [... **wh** ...]]
└────────×────────┘

(60) **The sentential subject constraint (paraphrased)**: No element can move out of a CP that is in the subject position.
wh [$_{TP}$ [$_{CP}$ ... **wh** ...] ...]
└────×────────┘

(62) **The adjunct island condition (adjusted)**: No element inside a CP in an adjunct may move out of this adjunct.
wh [$_{adjunct}$ [$_{CP}$ ... **wh** ...] ...]
└──────×──────────┘

(73) **The complex noun phrase constraint (adjusted)**: No element inside a CP dominated by a NP can be moved out of this NP.
wh [$_{NP}$ [$_{CP}$ ... **wh** ...] ...]
└────×────────┘

(77) **The subject condition (adjusted)**: A DP cannot be extracted from a DP subject of a clause.
wh [$_{TP}$ [$_{DP}$ ... **wh** ...] ...]
└────×────────┘

(79) **The left branch constraint (adjusted)**: The DP subject of a larger DP cannot be moved out.
wh [$_{DP}$ [$_{DP}$ ... **wh** ...] ...]
└────×────────┘

(81) **Coordinate structure constraint (adjusted)**: No conjunct or element contained within a conjunct can be moved out (except for ATB cases).
wh [$_{YP}$... [$_{XP}$ ... **wh** ...]] and YP]

The question we now ask is this: why do we find these constraints rather some other conceivable constraints? As far as we know, these constraints are very general within English, but also very general cross-linguistically. Is there nothing more to say about them, beyond simply listing them? If this was the case, they would constitute arbitrary properties of language. Surely, it would be more satisfying if we could show that these constraints are superficial reflections of some deeper mode of organization. We are going to try to construct such a deeper theory.

The basic idea we are going to try to pursue is the following: there is only one very general constraint. When we look at such a general constraint from different angles, we see different effects, which are the various constraints that we have seen. The situation is similar to what happens when we are presented with several pictures and we come to realize that all these images are pictures of the same object (say a house) that have been taken from different angles (the front, the back, the top, etc.).

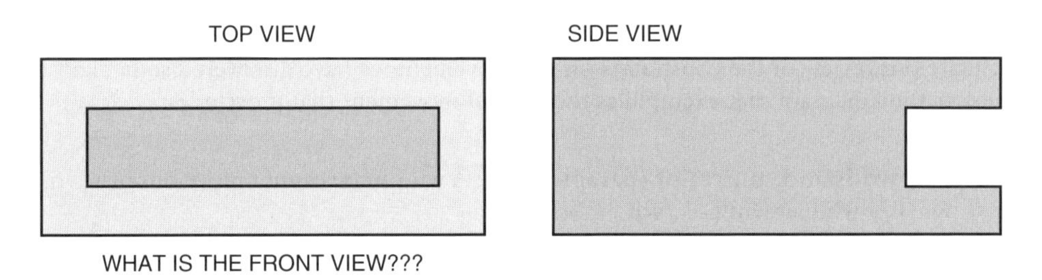

Depending on our point of view, we see different features of the house, yet, all these views are views of the same object seen from different angles. Here is an example: what is the 3D shape of an object that has the front view shown on the left and the left view shown on the right? Try to solve this problem before you look at the answer on the last page of this chapter.

The plan we are going to follow more or less summarizes (an idealized version of) the historical development of these ideas. We choose to do this because it nicely illustrates the kind of reasoning underlying not only what leads to hypotheses, but also how to revise them in the face of potential counterexamples and how this leads to new insights and to a picture that truly seems to capture the right generalizations and is rather simple. Here it is:

1. We start with wh-islands and we will explore the **Subjacency Condition** and the notion of **Bounding Node** to explain this constraint. We will see how it seems to extend to the complex NP constraint.
2. This will create a problem for allowed unbounded movement, and we will introduce a crucial innovation: **Successive Cyclic Movement** (with a short discussion of the **cycle**). This will create a problem for our treatment of the complex NP constraint.
3. Next we will examine the sentential subject condition and we will see that we have to refine how we define what a bounding node is. This will have the effect of deriving again one half of the complex NP constraint (but not the other half).
4. To cover the second half of the complex NP constraint, we will be led to further refine our notion of bounding nodes. This modification will allow covering of the adjunct island condition.
5. We will then extend the notion of a bounding node in a way that will cover the subject condition.
6. We will examine predictions made by our account: this will lead us to some understanding of pied-piping of PP and P-stranding, and of extraction out of DP.

After these steps, we will reassess what remains to be done.

10.5.2 Subjacency

The wh-island constraint suggest that wh-movement cannot span too long a distance. The reason why the c-sentence below is out is that we cannot move *what* to [Spec,CP] of the embedded clause since the position is already taken by *why*. And we cannot move the wh-phrase directly to the [Spec,CP] of the main clause because this is too far.

(91) a. Sue wonders why Bill broke what
b. [$_{TP}$ Sue wonders [$_{CP}$ why$_i$ [$_{TP}$ Bill broke what t_i]]]
c. [$_{CP}$ What$_j$ does [$_{TP}$ Sue wonder [$_{CP}$ why$_i$ [$_{TP}$ Bill broke t_j t_i]]]]

If we look at the diagram above, we see that moving the wh-phrase from the embedded clause to the main clause would *cross over two TP nodes*. A proposal was made that in certain cases, crossing over two nodes like this was forbidden. The name given to his condition was the Subjacency Condition (Chomsky, 1973). It states the following:

(92) **Subjacency Condition**: Move cannot relate two positions across two bounding nodes.
$*\ldots XP_i \ldots [_\alpha \ldots [_\beta \ldots t_i \ldots$, if α and β are bounding nodes.

We see immediately that if we take TP to be a bounding node, wh-island condition violations are derived. That is, if we look at a wh-island configuration,

(93) [$_{CP}$ wh-XP$_i$ [$_{TP}$...[$_{CP}$ wh-element [$_{TP}$ ... t_i ...]...]...]...],

we see that this movement of wh-XP to [Spec,CP] of the top clause crosses over two TP boundaries and is thus excluded by the subjacency condition, if we assume that TP is a bounding node. So it looks like the subjacency condition (including TP as a bounding node) subsumes the wh-island violation. We see more detail in a tree representation:

(94)

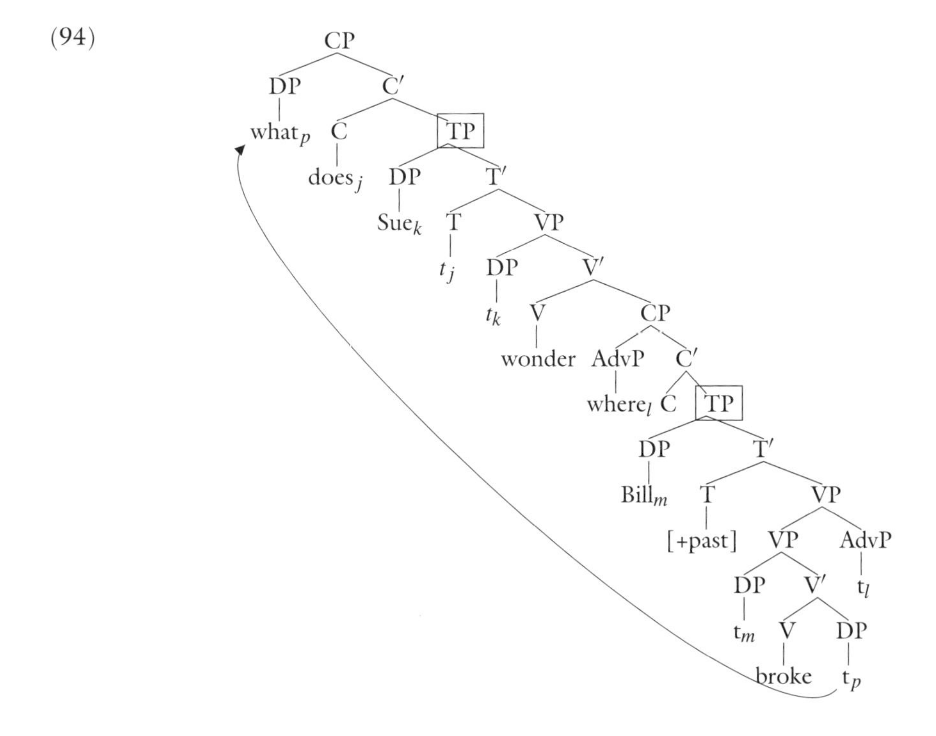

We will take this condition to apply to trees after we have performed movement (i.e. we take this to apply once we have performed all movements). That is, we make all the movements we want, and once we are done, we check whether this condition is verified.

Terminology: Two positions that are not separated by at least two bounding nodes (i.e. they are separated by none or just one) are said to be *subjacent* to each other, or one is said to be *subjacent* to the other.

What good does this do? We have replaced one condition (the wh-island condition) by another (the subjacency condition). It would seem that we have gained nothing at all. This, however, would not be correct. One immediate advantage of postulating the subjacency condition is that it has the effect of subsuming other constraints as well. To see this, observe the kind of extraction we want to exclude:

(95)

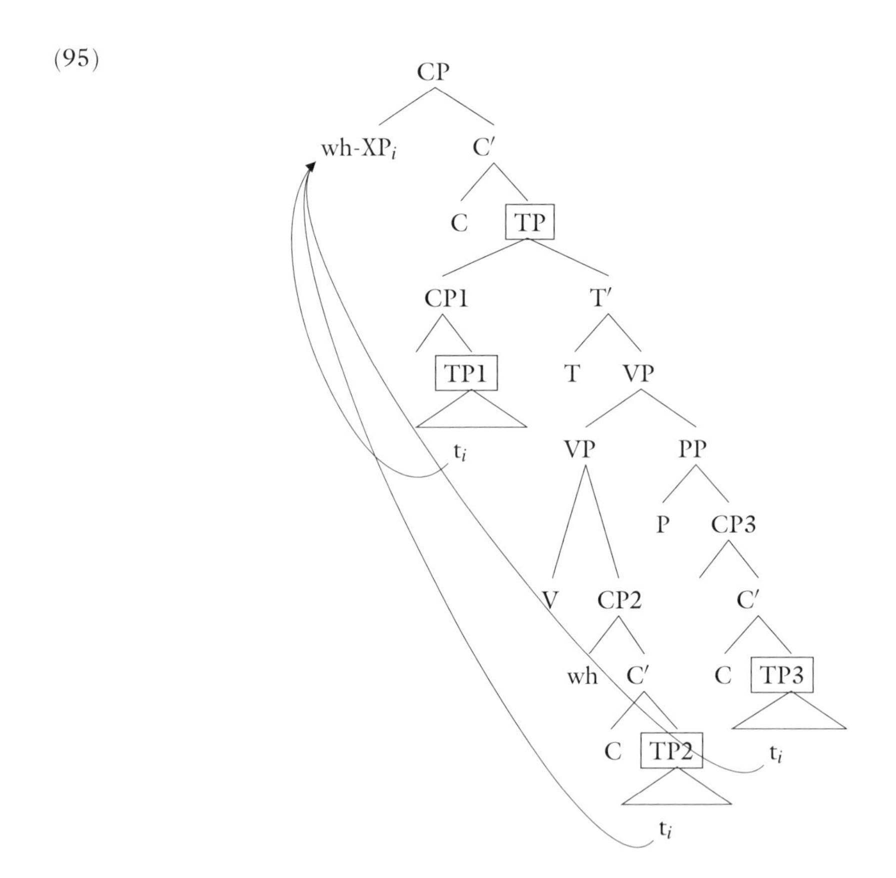

This tree illustrates three island contexts: extraction from inside CP1 is excluded by the sentential subject constraint, while CP2 is a wh-island, and CP3 an adjunct island. In every case, the movement crosses two TPs. Similarly, in complex noun phrase cases:

(96)

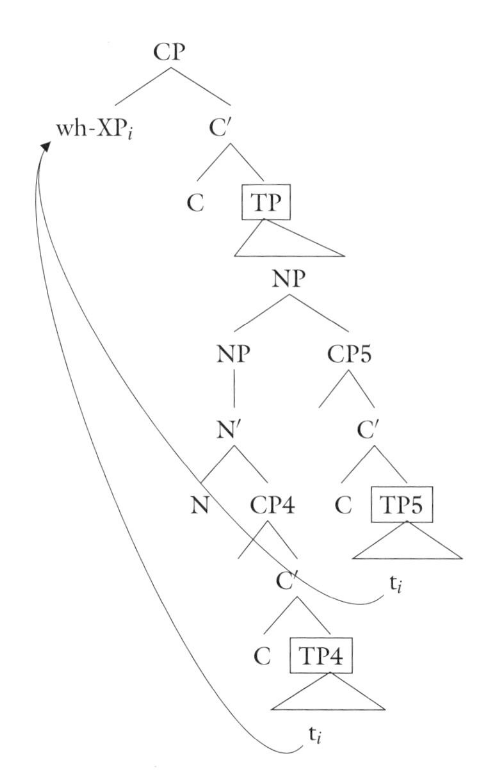

Here again, extraction would cross two TP boundaries. So we see that the subjacency condition subsumes a range of constraints.

Subjacency: a problem

Unfortunately, things are not so simple. It now looks like we have created a new problem. We have made the subjacency condition so constraining that it now excludes well-formed sentences. To see this, recall that wh-phrases are capable of moving long distances:

(97) a. Bill thinks that Sue said that I broke what
 b. [$_{\boxed{\text{TP}}}$ Bill thinks [$_{\text{CP}}$ that [$_{\boxed{\text{TP}}}$ Sue said [$_{\text{CP}}$ that [$_{\boxed{\text{TP}}}$ I broke what]]]]]
 c. [$_{\text{CP}}$ What$_i$ does [$_{\boxed{\text{TP}}}$ Bill think *[$_{\text{CP}}$ that [$_{\boxed{\text{TP}}}$ Sue said [$_{\text{CP}}$* that [$_{\boxed{\text{TP}}}$ I broke t_i]]]]]]

We see that such instances of wh-movement should be excluded since they cross two (or – if we include the italicized material – even three) bounding nodes. It is furthermore clear that we could further embed the launching site without creating deviance: a solution that would just augment the number of crossable bounding nodes is bound to fail. To solve this problem, we have two options:

i. We may rethink the way in which the subjacency condition works; or
ii. we may rethink the way in which movement works.

In some cases, potentially infinite embedding does not result in deviance. This suggests the following crucial observation: extraction seems to be sensitive not to how deeply embedded a position we extract from but to the **kind** of embedding we extract from. How can we take this into account? As we will see (it will take a little bit of time and effort), it is advantageous to try to solve the problem along the lines of (ii), i.e. to keep the Subjacency Condition as it is (for the moment) and to rethink how movement works.

Recall first that wh-movement can target an embedded [Spec,CP], i.e. can move a wh-phrase to the [Spec,CP] of an embedded clause (when it is selected as a [+q] clause by a verb or another category).

(98) a. Sue asked [$_{CP}$ where PRO to hide your keys *t*]
b. You know [$_{CP}$ when Bill called the police *t*]

Suppose that, whenever we move a wh-phrase, we must always *move it to the closest available [Spec,CP] there is.* By closest available, we mean the first [Spec,CP] we find up the tree from where we are moving that is not already occupied by something else.

A survey of when movement is possible leads to the following conjecture:

Movement and c-command: Movement is always to a c-commanding target: *a moved phrase is attracted to a c-commanding head.*

As we have seen, movement is (typically) triggered: some feature of some head is satisfied by the moved phrase. This conjecture states that this head always c-commands the trace of the moved phrase. This is very general conjecture true of all movement.

So another way of defining the notion that wh-movement moves to the [Spec,CP] *closest* up the tree is to say that it is the [Spec,CP] of a C c-commanding the launching site, which c-commands no other available C c-commanding the launching site.

We can also define "crossing a (bounding) node by movement." It means moving from a position inside this node to a head c-commanding that node.

This will not change anything when we form a question like *what did you see t*. But observe the effect it would have in the following case:

(99) a. What$_i$ does Bill think Sue said that I broke t_i
b. [$_{CP}$ What$_i$ does [$_{TP}$ Bill think [$_{CP}$ t$_i$ that [$_{TP}$ Sue said [$_{CP}$ t$_i$ that [$_{TP}$ T broke t_i]]]]]]

If we want to bring the wh-phrase to the top [Spec,CP], we would have to move it in several steps. In other words, movement would take place in *successive* steps. The immediate effect of this approach is that allowed unbounded extractions will no longer violate the subjacency condition! Let us then assume the following:

(100) **Conjecture**: wh-movement can proceed in steps, from [Spec,CP] to [Spec,CP]. This is called *successive cyclic movement.*

First, if we are going to pursue this idea, we have to modify slightly what we said about wh-movement. Recall that a verb (any other head) that selects a CP complement which is an embedded question is said to select a [+q] C to head this CP. A verb (any other head) that selects a CP complement that is a declarative clause is said to select a [-q] C to head this CP. Then the relevant parts of what we need to modify are these, where the crucial part is underlined.

(101) **Wh-movement**: Move the smallest XP containing a wh-word phrase to a [Spec,CP] (that allows it).

So far we have assumed that CPs come as [+q] or [-q], and that we move a wh-phrase to the spec of a [+q] CP. Now we allow a wh-phrase to move to any kind of [Spec,CP] (as long as we are moving to a c-commanding position). But we do not want a wh-phrase to stay in a [-q] CP. Otherwise we would allow bad sentences such as: *I said [who you saw t]*. So we will postulate that:

(102) A wh-phrase can transit through the specifier of a [-q] C but can only remain in [Spec,CP] of [+q] C.

Another way of thinking about this is that in the surface tree, a C and its [Spec, CP] must agree in wh-features (i.e. both be [+q] or both be [-q]) so that a [+q] wh-phrase cannot remain in the specifier position of a [-q] C (note further that the movement requirement can be coded by stating that [+q] Cs have an obligatory EPP feature, while [-q] Cs can optionally have one). Second, we must make sure that we do not lose anything by moving wh-phrases in successive steps. In the wh-island constructions, the intermediate [Spec,CP] is occupied by another wh-phrase.

(103) *[$_{CP}$ What$_j$ does [$_{TP}$ Sue wonder [$_{CP}$ when$_i$ I broke t_j t_i]]]
  a. the movement of *when* to the subordinate [Spec,CP]
  b. the movement of *what* to the subordinate [Spec,CP]
  c. the movement of *what* to the matrix [Spec,CP]

Once *when* moves to the lower [Spec,CP], *what* cannot move to the same [Spec,CP]. In other words: movement (103a) blocks movement (103b). When movement (103b) is blocked, movement (103c) is blocked too, by the subjacency condition.

We conclude that movement to the matrix [Spec,CP] takes place via the lower [Spec,CP]. If the wh-phrase cannot go to the lower [Spec,CP] it cannot go to the matrix [Spec,CP].

Unfortunately, allowing successive cyclicity reintroduces the possibility of extracting out of certain islands. As can be seen in diagrams (95) and (96), although in CP2 and CP5 the presence of wh-phrase in subject position of CP blocks a successive cyclic derivation, extraction again becomes possible in CP1, CP3, and CP4 by first moving to the subject of such CPs and next to the star position: each movement only crosses one bounding node. For example, we saw that in the complex NP construction CP4, we have the configuration:

(104) [$_{CP}$ wh [$_{TP}$...[$_{NP}$...[$_{CP}$ ♡ [$_{TP}$ ... **wh** ...]...]...]...]...]^F

If we allow stepwise or successive cyclic wh-movement, nothing seems to prevent XP in the diagram above to first move to the position marked by ♡, and then to move again. Each movement will only cross one TP. We have lost some of the benefits of switching from the wh-island condition to the subjacency condition. As we will shortly see, this is only a temporary setback.

As things stand, we have the following table. The hypothesis is that the subjacency condition holds. The first line lists different contexts in order: wh-islands, sentential subjects, adjunct island, CNPC the relative clause case, CNPC the complement CP case, and finally a simple CP complement. In all but the last case, wh-movement is excluded. The second line indicates what happens if we take TP to be a bounding node. A star indicates a wrong prediction, a check mark a right prediction. The third line is the result of allowing successive cyclic movement (Succ Cycl).

Constraint⇒ ⇓Hypothesis	WhI	Snt Sub	AdjIsld	CNPC R	CNPC C	Compl CP
TP Bounding	✓	✓	✓	✓	✓	*
+Succ Cyclic	✓	*	*	✓	*	✓

A hypothesis predicting that extraction is impossible in a context where it is possible, as the first line predicts, demands that the hypothesis be modified.

Sentential subject constraint and bounding nodes
Recall what kind of configurations were excluded by the sentential subject constraint, for example when we extract a wh-phrase from the clausal subject of a clause:

(105) [$_{CP}$ wh [$_{TP}$ [$_{CP}$ ♡ [$_{TP}$ ... **wh** ...]...]...]...]

Is such movement excluded by the subjacency condition as we understand it now? The answer is negative. We could move the wh-XP to ♡ first, and then out, each time crossing only one TP node. Is there a way to subsume this condition under the subjacency condition? If there is, it will have to be designed so that it does not rule out wh-extraction from an embedded clause in cases when it is allowed, as for example in:

(106) a. What$_i$ does Bill think that I broke t_i
b. [$_{CP}$ What$_i$ does [$_{TP}$ Bill think [$_{CP}$ t_i that [$_{TP}$ I T broke t_i]]]]

What difference is there between the two cases? One prominent difference is the following: notice that in the bad case, the CP is a subject, while in the good case, the CP is a complement of a verb. We can take advantage of this difference in the following way: suppose we say that not only is TP a bounding node, but CP is also a bounding node, when the CP is not a complement of V.

The consequence of this assumption is immediate. In (105), even if the wh-XP moves first through ♡, the second movement will cross a subject CP boundary and a TP boundary. This second step will violate the subjacency condition and will thus be excluded. In (106), by contrast, the embedded CP is a complement. As a result, this CP boundary does not count as a bounding node, and no movement step crosses two bounding nodes. Here is what this modification does to our table:

Constraint⇒ ⇓Hypothesis	WhI	Snt Sub	AdjIsld	CNPC R	CNPC C	Compl CP
TP Bounding	✓	✓	✓	✓	✓	*
+Succ Cyclic	✓	*	*	✓	*	✓
CP Bounding unless a Comp of V	✓	✓	✓	✓	✓	✓

Note, for example, that this modification will not affect the wh-island condition at all. But it will affect the case of the CNPC, for example. Remember the CNPC configuration, repeated from (104):

(107) [$_{CP}$ wh [$_{TP}$... [$_{NP}$... [$_{CP}$ ♡ [$_{TP}$ ... **wh** ...]...]...]...]...]

Since we allowed stepwise (or successive cyclic) wh-movement, not all such extractions were excluded because it was possible to first move to ♡ (not in the relative clause case, but in the CP complement case CP4), and then out, each time only crossing one TP node. According to our new way of thinking about bounding nodes, this lower CP now becomes a bounding node since it is not a complement of V. Even if we move in two steps through ♡, the second step will cross a bounding CP and a bounding TP. This configuration is therefore excluded by the subjacency condition. Consider these examples:

(108) a. [$_{TP}$ You heard [$_{DP}$ the rumor [$_{CP}$ that [$_{TP}$ Mary broke the vase]]]]
b. [$_{TP}$ You heard [$_{DP}$ the rumor [$_{CP}$ that [$_{TP}$ Mary broke what]]]]
c. [$_{TP}$ You heard [$_{DP}$ the rumor [$_{CP}$ what$_i$ that [$_{TP}$ Mary broke t_i]]]]
d. *[$_{CP}$ What$_i$ did [$_{TP}$ you hear [$_{DP}$ the [$_{NP}$ rumor [$_{CP}$ t_i' that [$_{TP}$ Mary broke t_i]]]]]]

The first step of the movement across the lower TP is of course fine, since it is part of the derivation for all good cases of wh-movement. The second step of the movement goes across the lower CP, and the matrix TP. The lower CP is a bounding node, since the CP is a complement of the noun *rumor*. Consequently, this bad sentence is excluded by our system of principles. It is thus a good idea to modify our subjacency condition by assuming that CPs that are not complements of Vs and TPs are bounding nodes.

(109) **Subjacency Condition**: Move cannot relate two positions across two bounding nodes.
*$\ldots XP_i \ldots [_\alpha \ldots [_\beta \ldots t_i \ldots$, if α and β are bounding nodes.
Bounding nodes: CPs that are not complements of V and TPs

10.5.3 Bounding nodes: remarks

First, there is a simple way to define bounding nodes to get TP and non-complement CPs to count as bounding nodes. Notice that TP is either a complement of C or (perhaps) a complement of V (in the case of raising to subject and ECM verbs, see Section 9.5.3). So let us adopt the following definition:

(110) **Bounding Node**: Complements of V are not bounding nodes.

Note that this definition has an immediate desirable consequence: it will now allow wh-movement out of a raising complement, if needed. We have seen that raising verbs (possibly) take TP complements. This raises the question if one can extract from these TPs, and indeed this is perfectly possible.

(111) a. John seems to like some kind of movies
b. What kind of movies does John seem to like *t*?

If TPs were always bounding nodes, we would have a serious problem with the derivation of this sentence, as wh-movement would cross two TP nodes, without an intermediate CP node that would save the derivation:

(112) [What kind of movies$_i$ does [$_{TP}$ John T [seem [$_{TP}$ ~~John~~ to like t_i]]]]

However, making the bounding nature of nodes relative to their environments, as we have done above, solves our problem: the lower TP is a complement of V, hence, according to the definition above, it will not count as a bouding node. Wh-movement therefore obeys subjacency, crossing only a single bounding node, the TP boundary, complement of C:

(113) [What kind of movies$_i$ does [$_{TP}$ John T [seem [$_{TP}$ ~~John~~ to like t_i]]]]

10.5.4 Extraction from DP: the subject condition

We have concluded that, sometimes, a CP node can count as a bounding node. It does when the CP is a subject or an adjunct, it does not when the CP is a complement of a verb. Let us now see what our account looks like if we include both the subject condition context and extraction from inside a DP complement of V:

(114)

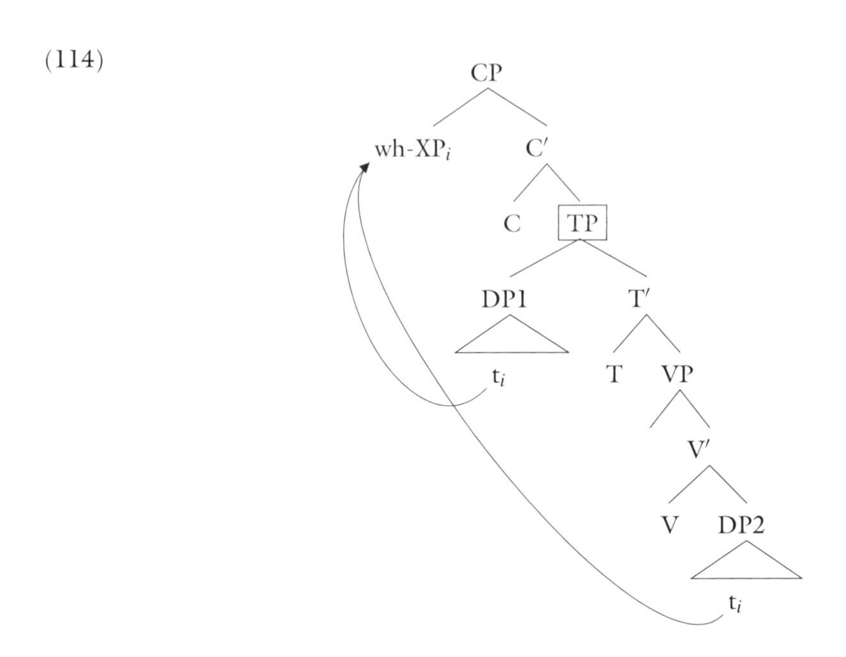

Supposing the t_is are the launching sites of extraction, we get the following results: extraction is impossible from inside DP1 (the subject condition), but sometimes possible from DP2. Recall the configurations excluded by the subject condition:

(115) [$_{CP}$ wh [$_{TP}$ [$_{DP}$ ... **wh** ...]...]...]

This condition is formulated about DP subjects, because extraction from inside DP objects is possible. This difference is illustrated by the following pair of sentences:

(116) a. You saw [$_{DP}$ a picture of [$_{DP}$ some students]]
b. You saw [$_{DP}$ a picture of [$_{DP}$ which students]]
c. [$_{DP}$ Which students]$_i$ did [$_{TP}$ you see [$_{DP}$ a picture of t_i]]?

(117) a. [$_{DP}$ a picture of [$_{DP}$ some students]] appeared in the newspapers
b. [$_{DP}$ a picture of [$_{DP}$ which students]] appeared in the newspapers
c. *[$_{DP}$ Which students]$_i$ did [$_{TP}$ [$_{DP}$ a picture of t_i] appear in the newspapers]?

If we add two columns in our table, one for the subject condition and one for extraction from within DP objects, we get the following results:

Constraint⇒ ⇓Hypothesis	WhI	Snt Sub	Adj Isld	CNPC R	CNPC C	Compl CP	Subj Cond	DP Obj
TP Bounding	✓	✓	✓	✓	✓	*	*	✓
+Succ Cyclic	✓	*	*	✓	*	✓	*	✓
CP Bounding unless a Comp of V	✓	✓	✓	✓	✓	✓	*	✓

Since these two types of extraction are from within DPs, and DP is not a bounding node, the subjacency condition has no influence on the results: the subject condition is not subsumed by the subjacency condition.

Suppose we include DP in our inventory of bounding nodes. A subject DP node is a bounding node since it is not a complement of V, as a result extraction in the unacceptable sentence (117c) will cross the two bounding nodes TP and DP. But an object DP boundary would become bounding too, blocking extraction from within DP2. There is a simple fix, however: we do for DPs what we did for CPs. If we make DP a bounding node, except if it is a complement of V, we get the right result. This does not change anything for extraction from DP1 (still bad) but in the acceptable sentence (116c), only one bounding node is crossed by the movement path, namely TP, since the DP2 node, being a complement of V, is not bounding. We get the following picture:

Constraint⇒ ⇓Hypothesis	WhI	Snt Sub	Adj Isld	CNPC R	CNPC C	Compl CP	Subj Cond	DP Obj
TP Bounding	✓	✓	✓	✓	✓	*	*	✓
+Succ Cyclic	✓	*	*	✓	*	✓	*	✓
CP Bounding unless a Comp of V	✓	✓	✓	✓	✓	✓	*	✓
CP & DP bounding unless Comp of V	✓	✓	✓	✓	✓	✓	✓	✓

10.5.5 Summary

We have reached the following conclusions. Wh-movement is constrained by the subjacency condition, which is formulated as:

(118) **Subjacency Condition**: Move cannot relate two positions across two bounding nodes.
$*\ldots XP_i \ldots [_\alpha \ldots [_\beta \ldots t_i \ldots$, if α and β are bounding nodes.
Bounding Node: A node is bounding if it is a TP, a CP, or a DP and it is not a complement of V.

In addition, we have concluded that wh-movement can proceed stepwise through intermediate [Spec,CP] positions.

It is worth stressing that this is an approximate version of what is understood today. Its main value is its illustration of how we go about developing a theory. It leaves many questions open:

- Why are TPs, DPs, and CPs singled out? How about other XPs?
- Why do Vs have a special status? How about Ns or As?

Nevertheless, even this simplified version makes predictions as to what should be acceptable or not, some of which we now turn to.

10.5.6 Independent evidence for successive cyclicity

The hypothesis that movement proceeds cyclically was put forth in an effort to find some way to subsume all the constraints under one more general condition. This effort, leading to the postulation of the subjacency condition, was successful. It would be nice if we could find independent evidence for the hypothesis that movement proceeds in successive steps. And, in fact, there is quite a bit of more direct evidence for this idea from different constructions in different languages. Here is one example of such evidence for successive cyclicity (movement of [Spec,CP] to [Spec,CP], in English dialects) from West Ulster English studied by James McCloskey (2000) of UC Santa Cruz.
Expressions like *what all* and *who all* in Irish English (W. Ulster) optionally strand their *all* in positions from which wh-movement takes place. We can thus study the behavior of the stranded *all*, as a probe into the structures and history of the derivation, rather like the distribution of the floated quantifier *all* under movement that we will discuss in the next chapter, it has helped provide information on the structure of the clause (see also Sportiche (1988)).
Irish English (W. Ulster) has *all* stranding in DP position:

(119) a. What all did you give ___ to the kids?
b. What did you give ___ all to the kids?
(120) a. Who all did you send ___ to the shops
b. Who did you send ___ all to the shops
(121) a. Tell me what all you got ___ for Xmas
b. Tell me what you got ___ all for Xmas

In West Ulster English, we have *all* stranding in the specifier of declarative CP with the silent version of the declarative complementizer *that*:

(122) a. What all did he say [he wanted ___]
b. What did he say [___ all] he wanted ___

West Ulster *all* stranding in the specifier of infinitival C (*for to*) is not allowed:

(123) a. You arrange for your mother to meet them at the party
b. Who did you arrange [___ all] for your mother to meet ___ at the party

W. Ulster *all* can be stranded in a specifier of CP with overt complementizer *that*, seen here with two levels of embedding:

(124) a. What all do you think [that he'll say that we should buy all at the store]
b. What do you think [that he'll say [all that we should buy at the store]]
c. What do you think [all that he'll say [that we should buy at the store]]

What is particularly interesting for us, of course, is that *all* can be stranded in a position immediately adjacent and to the left of the complementizer, exactly where we would expect it if wh-movement was proceeding in successive steps going through intermediate [Spec,CP] positions.

10.5.7 Consequences

The empirical coverage of the subjacency condition extends beyond the classical constraints formulated above. It can even be further extended in natural ways (although this is not without problems). One such extension would take PPs to be bounding nodes unless they are complements of V. This makes the following prediction: it should be possible to extract from a PP complement of V but not from a PP adjunct to VP. This is by and large correct. Compare:

(125) a. [Which student]$_j$ did you talk [PP to t_j]
b. *[Which meeting]$_j$ did you sleep [PP during t_j]
c. [During which meeting]$_j$ did you sleep t_j

In the first sentence the PP is a complement of the verb and the extracted DP is a complement of the P. In the second the PP is a adjunct to the verb: this is why extraction of the DP is excluded. We can now view some cases of pied-piping – here of the preposition during – as a way to circumvent a violation of the subjacency condition. Note that the extraction of the whole PP adjunct *during which meeting* only crosses VP and TP.

Since adjuncts are typically PPs, this means that the adjunct island condition (subsumed under the subjacency condition if PP is a bounding node) can be formulated more generally as precluding all extractions from adjuncts. This is exemplified below:

(126) a. John went to sleep [without [having eaten his dinner]]
b. *What did [$_{TP}$ John go to sleep [$_{PP}$ without [$_{CP}$ *e* [$_{TP}$ PRO having eaten *t*]]]]

Notice that the CP complement of the P *without* is a gerundival clause: it has a PRO subject and the suffix *-ing* is in T and corresponds to Pres or Past in a tense clause, or to in an infinitive.

(127) a. I voted for it [because Mary knew him]
b. *What did [$_{TP}$ you vote for it [$_{PP}$ because [$_{CP}$ *e* [$_{TP}$ Mary knew *t*]]]]

In both cases, extraction of *what* will cross the adjunct PP boundary and the higher TP boundary, both bounding nodes. The same results would be found with other adjuncts:

Manner adjunct PP:
Mary built it in this way ⇒ **Which way did Mary build it in?*

Temporal adjunct PP:
Sue slept before the meeting ⇒ **What did Sue sleep before?*

Clausal temporal adjuncts:
Sue slept after you called him ⇒ **Who did Sue sleep after you called* t.

10.6 Special Cases

All the constraints we have seen prohibit extraction out of a certain kind of constituent. Does this exhaust the cases of extraction prohibition? The answer is negative. There are other kinds of prohibition that do not seem to be expressible in terms of constraints reducible to the subjacency condition or its kin. We now look at a couple of examples.

10.6.1 Subject extraction: complementizer–trace effects

Wh-movement shows special effects with subject extraction. These effects are called **Comp–trace Effects** (where Comp means C, not complement), ***That*–t Effects**, or **ECP Effects**. Here are two instances of these effects.

First, in main clauses, when a wh-question is formed, we would expect T-to-C, movement as is shown for the object below:

(128) John will see what → what will John will see *t*
John saw what → what did John past see *t*

But this fails when a subject moves – see the text box on at the end of Section 10.2 – (and if T-to-C took place, it would put T too far from V and would trigger insertion of dummy *do*):

(129) John saw Mary → *Who did *t* past see Mary
→ Who *t* saw Mary

Second, with extraction of the subject of an embedded tensed clause, the complementizer *that*, which may optionally be silent, suddenly must become silent:

(130) a. [$_{TP}$ you think [$_{CP}$ Ø [$_{TP}$ John left early]]]?
b. [$_{TP}$ you think [$_{CP}$ that [$_{TP}$ John left early]]]?
c. [$_{CP}$ Who do [$_{TP}$ you think [$_{CP}$ Ø [$_{TP}$ *t* left early]]]]?
d. *[$_{CP}$ Who do [$_{TP}$ you think [$_{CP}$ that [$_{TP}$ *t* left early]]]]?

(131) a. [$_{TP}$ you say [$_{CP}$ Ø [$_{TP}$ this happened yesterday]]]?
b. [$_{TP}$ you say [$_{CP}$ that [$_{TP}$ this happened yesterday]]]?
c. [$_{CP}$ What did [$_{TP}$ you say [$_{CP}$ Ø [$_{TP}$ t happened yesterday]]]]?
d. *[$_{CP}$ What did [$_{TP}$ you say [$_{CP}$ that [$_{TP}$ *t* happened yesterday]]]]?

In certain cases, the complementizer *that* is not allowed to drop (for some speakers). In such cases, the subject of the embedded clause cannot be questioned by wh-movement:

(132) a. *[$_{TP}$ it is obvious [$_{CP}$ Ø [$_{TP}$ this happened yesterday]]]?
b. [$_{TP}$ it is obvious [$_{CP}$ that [$_{TP}$ this happened yesterday]]]?
c. *[$_{CP}$ What is [$_{TP}$ it obvious [$_{CP}$ Ø [$_{TP}$ *t* happened yesterday]]]]?
d. *[$_{CP}$ What is [$_{TP}$ it obvious [$_{CP}$ that [$_{TP}$ *t* happened yesterday]]]]?

Exactly the same is true with extraction of subjects of infinitives. The verb *want* allows a complementizer *for*, but does not require it:

(133) a. [$_{TP}$ you want [$_{CP}$ for [$_{TP}$ John to win the race]]]?
b. [$_{TP}$ you want [$_{CP}$ Ø [$_{TP}$ John to win the race]]]?
c. *[$_{CP}$ Who do [$_{TP}$ you want [$_{CP}$ for [$_{TP}$ *t* to win the race]]]]?
d. [$_{CP}$ Who do [$_{TP}$ you want [$_{CP}$ Ø [$_{TP}$ *t* to win the race]]]]?

but with a verb like *hope*, which disallows dropping *for*, we get the same paradigm as we did with *be obvious* that:

(134) a. [$_{TP}$ you hope [$_{CP}$ for [$_{TP}$ John to win the race]]]?
b. *[$_{TP}$ you hope [$_{CP}$ Ø [$_{TP}$ John to win the race]]]?
c. *[$_{CP}$ Who do [$_{TP}$ you hope [$_{CP}$ for [$_{TP}$ *t* to win the race]]]]?
d. *[$_{CP}$ Who do [$_{TP}$ you hope [$_{CP}$ Ø [$_{TP}$ *t* to win the race]]]]?

If the infinitive allows a subject and is not introduced by an overt complementizer, there is no problem extracting the subject. For example, with the ECM verb *believe*:

(135) a. [$_{\text{TP}}$ you believe [$_{\text{TP}}$ John to have won the race]]?
b. [$_{\text{CP}}$ Who do [$_{\text{TP}}$ you believe [$_{\text{TP}}$ *t* to have won the race]]]?

In conclusion, the generalization that emerges is that a subject cannot be extracted if it is immediately preceded by an overt complementizer. We will call this the comp–trace effect (often also called the ***that*–trace effect**) and we will formulate this as a filter that rules out any sentence containing such a configuration:

(136) **Comp-trace (or *that*–trace) Filter**: * [. . . C [$_{\text{TP}}$ *t* . . .],
where C is "overt" (= pronounced).

There is a lot more to say about this topic and there is an extensive literature dealing with it. You will sometimes see references to the ECP or Empty Category Principle that cover this effect. Among the questions that are investigated are the following:

- Is this a property of subject extraction? The answer is not definitely known. Does it matter if the subject does not immediately follow the complementizer? The answer seems to be positive.
- How cross-linguistically general is this prohibition? Some other languages do exhibit similar phenomena (e.g. French *que/qui* phenomena or Vata special subject pronoun) but not all. Some varieties of English are said to lack it, and so do some other languages such as Mandarin Chinese, Italian, or Spanish. An important research agenda is to understand the nature of the difference between these languages.

10.6.2 Superiority: attract closest

The case of multiple questions illustrates a different kind of locality condition than the subjacency/bounding node type of locality. Recall that multiple wh-questions are questions that contain more than one wh-phrase. They call for answers that are called "pair list" answers (that is, answers that are lists of pairs).

(137) Who studied what?
answer:
(1st pair) John studied wh-questions,
(2nd pair) Mary, relative clauses
(3rd pair) and Bill, possessive constructions.

This type of question must be distinguished from echo questions, which are simply questions for clarification of some string, which we failed to parse.

(138) Speaker A: John said [zshhgrof] yesterday? Who said [zshhgrof] yesterday?
Speaker B: John said WHAT yesterday? Who said WHAT yesterday?

What can we say about multiple wh-questions, i.e. questions when more than one wh-phrase is relevant for the answering patterns for the question? First, one wh-phrase must raise to CP, and the other one remains unmoved, i.e. it remains **in situ**, that is not moved by wh-movement (the symbol # is meant to indicate that the (b) sentence is fine, but as an echo question only):

(139) a. Who did you tell *t* to buy what?
b. # You told who to buy what

Because a wh-phrase can remain in situ, this suggests that the reason for movement is not some inherent property of the wh-phrase. Rather it must be a property of the landing site, [Spec,CP], that is related to a property of C. This confirms what we have assumed so far that, in essence, the trigger for the movement is a selectional property of the landing site (which must match a property of the moving phrase, namely +q).

Second, the issue of which wh-phrase has to move and which one does not is usually not free:

(140) a. Who prepared what
b. *?What did who prepare ~~what~~

c. Who did you persuade ~~who~~ to prepare what?
d. *?What did you persuade who to prepare ~~what~~

e. What did you put on which plates?
f. *? Which plates did you put what on?

g. What did you give ~~what~~ to who
h. *?Who did you give what to

For each pair, we observe a contrast, with the second question degraded with respect to the first. If we consider the tree representations, we see that the good questions are questions in which the wh-phrase "closest" to the C_{+q} has moved to CP. Given that wh-movement is always to a c-commanding position, the degraded examples can be excluded if a wh-phrase is not allowed to move over a c-commanding wh-phrase:

(141) * wh2. . . X. . . wh1. . . ~~wh2~~

This condition is historically referred to as the **Superiority Condition** when applied to multiple wh-questions. It can be seen as an instance of the attract closest principle, which regulates what happens when there are two potential[6] candidates for movement (as we have seen previously in various cases, e.g. the head movement constraint):

(142) **Attract Closest**: Only the closest potential candidate can move to an attracting head (which selects for it).

Changing the terminology slightly to the current jargon, we call the selecting head the **Probe**. A probe will satisfy its selection by "sending out a probe" to find a **Goal** and "attract" the first goal candidate that it c-commands to its specifier or, if it selects for a head, by attracting the head through head movement. Notice that the attract closest condition (also known as the Relativized Minimality Condition, or the Shortest Move condition, or the Shortest Step Condition) subsumes the head movement constraint or HMC discussed earlier (and to which we return in Chapter 12, Section 12.2) as a special case.

It is clear that in order to work properly, the attract closest condition must be finely tuned (see e.g. Rizzi (1990a)) in ways that we cannot discuss here. For example, note first that superiority

[6] Defining "potential" precisely, that is, what disrupts the relation between an attractor (probe) and an attractee (goal), is a complex endeavor.

effects seem to disappear with complex wh-phrases, where speakers in general find the contrast absent or much weaker (cf. (143) vs. (144)).

(143) a. Who prepared what
b. *?What did who prepare
(144) a. Which people prepared which dishes
b. Which dishes did which people prepare

Second, while the effect is present if we consider two wh-phrases, it seems to weaken or disappear if we add another wh-phrase in situ lower in the structure. We take (140) and simply add a third wh-phrase:

(145) a. Who prepared what
b. *?What did who prepare ~~what~~
c. What did who prepare for who?

Finally, not all languages show expected superiority effects. In German, for example, simple cases do not seem to show superiority effects (though of course it could be that more complex cases reveal superiority, i.e. the simple cases have some way of overcoming the effect!).

(146) a. Ich weiss nicht, wer was gesehen hat
I know not, who what seen has
"I do not know who saw what"
b. Ich weiss nicht, was wer gesehen hat
I know not, what who seen has
"I do not know who saw what"

10.6.3 Beyond subjacency: phases

As we said, the theory of constraints we have presented here (subjacency) is not the last word on the topic: far from it. One problem is to understand why such a condition exists at all and why it cares about the following:

- Why are TPs, DPs, and CPs singled out? How about other XPs?
- Why do Vs have a special status? How about Ns or As?

In the **minimalist program** (Chomsky, 1995) an effort is made to link the existence and functioning of such constraints to a very general hypothesis about the architecture of grammars and how structures and meanings are computed incrementally. Accordingly, the subjacency condition has been replaced by the **Phase Impenetrability Condition** or **PIC** (Chomsky, 2001) and bounding nodes by **Phases**.

To get the flavor of this approach, take as point of departure the fact that extraction from inside complements of V is possible, but not otherwise. This would prevent extraction from inside DP subjects (the subject condition), from inside adjuncts (the adjunct condition and the relative clause case of the CNPC), from inside complements of N (the other case of the CNPC). This would of course allow extraction from inside direct objects of verbs and clausal complements to verbs. But it would also allow wh-island violations (since an indirect question can be a complement of V). Note, however, that this case is excluded on different grounds than the other cases: the [Spec,CP] of the indirect question is already taken: this means we are extracting from inside TP, which is not a complement of V, hence a bounding node.

Let us define a phase as a CP constituent, C the phase head, [Spec,CP] the subject of the phase head. Let us further postulate that:

Phase Impenetrability Condition (PIC): The complement of a phase head cannot be seen from outside the phase.

We see immediately that this allows movement from inside a TP to the closest [Spec,CP] up the tree but no further, and thus excludes wh-island violations. The nice idea here is this: once a constituent of a certain size (a CP) is built by Move and Merge, its edge and head are still visible, but everything else has been "processed" and is thus opaque to any further computation. As formulated, phase theory is not as good as the subjacency condition in ruling out constraint violations (it excludes wh-island violations, relative clause CNPC violations, some adjunct island violations, but not sentential subject or subject condition violations), but what it does exclude, it excludes in a way that fits well with reasonable computation principles. Needless to say, this short sketch is a very rough approximation of what phase theory is and does. But it is sufficient to give an idea of what current research is trying to accomplish.

10.6.4 Attract closest and phases

Since we need attract closest, the question arises as to the division of labor between the subjacency condition or phase theory and attract closest. Do we still need the theory of locality as we have elaborated it, or could subjacency or phases be subsumed (in part or entirely) under attract closest? We will limit ourselves to a couple of remarks. First, note that attract closest does not impose an absolute extraction prohibition: a wh-phrase WH2 cannot move because a closer WH1 could. But, if in the position of WH1 there is no wh-phrase, WH2 could move as far as attract closest is concerned. Subjacency/phase theory, on the other hand, does impose an absolute prohibition: if WH2 is inside a relative clause, it can't leave, period. This makes a "Grand Unification" implausible. It looks like both subtheories are needed. This may be supported by a language like German which, as we saw in Section 10.6.2, shows different superiority effects than English. No correlated difference regarding subjacency/phase theory seem to exist, however.

10.7 Conclusion

10.7.1 Summary

This chapter has introduced a very substantial amount of material. The study of wh-movement has played and continues to play an important role in driving theoretical developments. Through the study of wh-movement, we developed a theory of locality constraining how movement is allowed to function, initially formulated in terms of **bounding nodes** and the **subjacency condition**, and ultimately in tems of **phases**. An important discovery is the surprising existence of **successive cyclic movement**. We also discovered the existence of **complementizer–trace effects** (which we have not explored in detail but on which there is a large literature) and the **superiority effects**, handled in terms of the **attract closest** requirement.

10.7.2 What to remember

One of the main objectives of this chapter was to try to understand what constrains the operation of Move as applied to wh-phrases, and to explore the possibility that some unique, general mechanisms yield the observed effects. To this end, a large number of observations was introduced as well as a number of conjectures regarding how to understand them.

You should most of all remember the démarche: how we (almost) systematically explored the empirical space; how we tried to formulate generalizations; how we tried to derive these generalizations from more general principles. You should also remember the individual constraints and what they say. They are part of the standard vocabulary of syntax. You should understand what successive cyclicity is: this is a major – and really surprising – theoretical innovation that has received support from all sorts of angles. You should know how the subjacency condition is stated and what the bounding nodes are, and how this condition applies. Current theory is formulated in terms of phases, and understanding the subjacency condition can help you see what phase theory has yet to accomplish.

You should know about comp–trace effects or *that*–trace effects, they are also part of standard syntactic vocabulary. Finally, you should know that movement is to a c-commanding position, what superiority effects are, what attract closest is and how it derives them, as well as the head movement constraint.

10.7.3 Puzzles and preview

Movement and c-command

We have seen in passing that wh-movement is to a c-commanding probe. That this is true of all movement is widely assumed, although some researchers have advocated the existence of movement to non-c-commanding positions – known as **Sideward Movement**. If movement is indeed to a c-commanding position, we may wonder why: nothing in anything we said requires this. One possible type of answer has to do with why wh-movement exists – a question on which we have gained no insight. The answer to these two questions may be rooted in the compositional nature of the meaning computation algorithm. A good place to start would be in, e.g., Heim and Kratzer (1998).

Movement and constraints

Wh-movement expresses a relation between two positions. We have seen that this relation must obey the subjacency condition. We may wonder whether any relation between two positions is subject to this condition. The answer is negative. For example, the relation between a quantified antecedent and a bound pronoun as in (147a), or a preposed element (said to be **Left Dislocated**) and a pronoun as in (147b), is not subject to, say, the CNPC, and that between a licenser and an NPI, as (147c), is not subject to, say, the subject condition:

(147) a. **Every boy** knows many [*NP* people [*CP* who like **him**]]
b. **Bill**, I know many [*NP* people [*CP* who like **him**]]
c. **None of us** said [that [*DP* **anyone** 's suggestions] were stupid]

It is in fact widely held (and this looks quite reasonable given what is known) that **sensitivity to the constraints is a property of movement relations only**.

Extensions

The study of wh-movement can be expanded in a variety of ways. One way is to look at wh-questions cross-linguistically. Another is to investigate what kind of constructions show the same properties as wh-questions. Obvious candidates are relative clauses, which also contain wh-words. We explore this in Chapter 14 and document that there are a great many constructions that display almost identical properties to wh-questions and relative clauses even though no wh-phrase seems to be involved.

And here is one possible answer to the earlier puzzle!

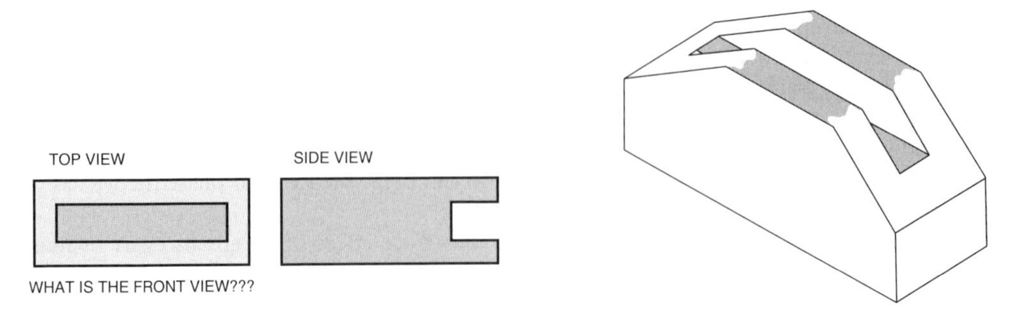

10.7.4 Further exercises

(1) Tree drawing

Give the full derived syntactic representation for each of the following sentences (indicate traces as crossed out material and movement with arrows):

(1) Which languages does your brother seem to want to learn?
(2) The man from India completely forgot to ask what to bring for Bill tomorrow
(3) What would you prefer for Bill to read to you?
(4) Whose friend's car did you tell me is sitting in the driveway?
(5) Who believed himself to be completely crazy?
(6) How many many people did you try to befriend last year?

(2) Island

For each of the following pairs of sentences, the ill-formed forms in (b) are derived from the string in (a).

(1) a. He dismissed the assertion that Bill slept on the boat
b. * Where$_i$ did he dismiss the assertion that Bill slept t_i?
(2) a. That John is against this proposition made you angry
b. *Who$_i$ did that t_i is against this proposition make you angry?
(3) a. They wondered what John should give to who
b. *Who did they wonder what John should give to?
(4) a. You thought that the students of physics were unhappy
b. *Which subject did you think that the students of were unhappy?
(5) a. I thought that the students from Germany were coming tomorrow
b. *Which country did you think that the students from were coming tomorrow?
c. Which country did you think that the students were coming from tomorrow?

(i) Draw the trees for each (a) example; check the constituency.
(ii) Examine how (b) could be derived from (a); is the (b) sentence excluded by one of the island constraints? State by which one(s).
(iii) Explain the contrast between (5b) and (5c).
(iv) (*In preparation for the subjacency account*) List, for each (b) example, all the XP nodes that lie on the "direct path" between the position where the wh-phrase merged (originates), and the position where the wh-phrase is pronounced in the string. (Be precise!) (*Example*: [who did [$_{TP}$ his mother [$_{VP}$ his mother speak [$_{PP}$ to ~~who~~]]]] Answer: (TP, VP, PP)

(v) (*After subjacency*) Give the final subjacency definition in Section 10.5.5, and discuss/show the data in (5) following from it.

(3) Subjacency

Is the following sentence ruled out by the subjacency condition as formulated in the text? If not, suggest a way to rule it out (but take care not to rule out well-formed sentences).

(1) *Which lighthouse did Susan copy John's story about?

(4) What can we conclude?

Consider the following example.

(1) Mary thinks that John's mother will join the party
As shown below, *John's mother* cannot undergo wh-movement.
(2) *Who$_i$ does Mary think that t_i will join the party?

The ungrammaticality of the above example demonstrates that *John's mother* is not a constituent in this sentence.

Circle one. The conclusion is: (a) valid (b) not valid.

Justify your answer.

(5) Follow-up on problem 4, Chapter 5

In problem 4 of Chapter 5, we noticed that replacing *the hat* with *which hat*, in (1) results in an unambiguous sentence (2).

(1) They will slap the portly cook with the hat
(2) Which hat will they slap the portly cook with?

You should now be able to fully explain this curious fact.

Draw the two structures for (1), and consider wh-movement. Explain, using subjacency, why only one structure can survive.

(6) Left branch extraction

The following examples have traditionally been explained in terms of Ross' left branch constraint.

(i) Explain if/how the patterns in (1) follow from the general assumptions about movement, the assumptions about DP structure, and the lexical properties of *'s*.
(1) a. Whose brother do you like?
b. *Whose do you like brother?
c. * Who do you like 's brother?
(ii) Will this account extend to the following? Discuss.
(2) a. *My I like brother
b. *Mine I like this brother of

(7) Wh-movement, islands, and subjacency

Consider the following sentences.

(1) How many movies did your brother buy and your sister sell?

(2) Why did everyone's friend think that Mary said that you were fired?
(3) Who do you really expect to send each other flowers?

(i) Show for each how the subjacency condition is satisfied.
(ii) Sentence (2) is ambiguous in three ways. Indicate how each interpretation arises. (Use triangles, but make sure your structure is clear enough to show the point.)
(iii) If we change *think that* to *wonder if* in (2), how many readings do you predict this sentence can have? Why? (Be explicit.)
(iv) Sentence (3) contains an anaphor. Is binding theory satisfied? How?

(8) "Decide on"

Consider the following sentence.

(1) They decided on the boat

This sentence is ambiguous. For example, it could be used as an answer to the two different questions below:

Question 1: (John and Mary were hesitating between buying a boat or a car.)
What did they finally buy?
Question 2: Where did they make the decision? Was it at home, in the car, or at sea?

(i) Draw the two trees corresponding to the two interpretations, and indicate which tree corresponds to which meaning.
(ii) Support the constituency of each tree by using VP ellipsis or VP preposing.

The following example is sometimes claimed to be unambiguous.

(2) Which boat did they decide on?

More specifically, while it is clear that the meaning in (3a) is available, the reading in (3b) has been claimed to be unavailable.

(3) a. Which boat did they choose?
b. Which boat did they make their decision on?

It is sometimes quite difficult to decide if one reading is unavailable or just more difficult to access. This in turn is important because we would like to know whether this judgment reflects the workings of the syntactic component or if it is due to the interference with different factors (say a competition between two syntactic structures, where one is easier to parse or access than the other).

(iii) Discuss if the claim about ambiguity above is expected given the theory of locality or not (use your trees!).
(iv) Evaluate, using the examples in (4), whether you find it plausible that (1) is indeed unambiguous, or not.

(4) a. They decided (on their new car) on the boat.
b. They [decided (to buy a new car)]on the boat
(5) a. Which boat did they decide (on their new car) on?
b. Which boat did they decide (to buy a new car) on?

(v) What is your overall conclusion?

(9) Relative clauses

The formation of a relative clause in many cases involves what looks like a wh- phrase. (This is not true for all types of relative clauses in English. This part of the homework only looks at those that have a wh-phrase.) Consider the following sentences.

(1) a. You were talking to the man *who I introduced to you*
b. I bought the book which I told you about
c. This is the room where Bill keeps his drum set
d. This was the time when Mary decided to quit her job
e. I spoke to the girl whose mother was not feeling well

(i) Give one argument that shows the underlined string in (1a) is a constituent.

(ii) For (1a) and (1b), by what element are *who* and *which* respectively selected? Is the principle of locality of selection respected in (1a) and (1b)? If so, how?

(iii) Postulate a source for the wh-phrase in (1c) and (1d) (i.e. where does the wh-phrase originate?), and show how (1d) is ambiguous (i.e. say what the ambiguity is, and how this follows from the structure).

(iv) Give one argument showing whether the underlined string in (1c) is an island for wh-question formation.

(v) Next, consider the relation between the source position and the pronounced position. Does this relation show the properties of wh-movement (i.e. moving a wh-phrase to [Spec,CP]), or is this a different type of dependency that we have not yet encountered (maybe more anaphor-like)? One way to answer this question is by examining the properties of the relation. If it is derived by wh-movement (i.e. movement to [Spec,CP]) we expect it to show the same properties of wh-question formation. That is,

it should be apparently unbounded;

it should obey subjacency;

it should show comp–trace phenomena/*that*–trace effects.

Test these three properties for two of the sentences in (1). (Make sure for subjacency that you test at least three different island configurations. This makes a total of five test sentences for each (so ten in total, no more and no less).) Give one sentence in which you give an example that shows if relativization (i.e. the distance the wh-phrase can travel) is unbounded or not, three sentences that test if it obeys different islands, and one that shows if there are *that*–trace phenomena or not. If you are unsure what to do, look at what we did for wh-questions.

(vi) Present a complete tree for (1e).

(vii) Benglish problem:

English has a (hypothetical) sister language *Tenglish,* which is in all respect like English, except for the fact that CP adjuncts to NP precede the NP (in fact all adjuncts precede the constituent they modify in Tenglish).

How would you translate (1e) into Tenglish? (Proceed as usual. Construct the tree structure for English first, and then identify where Tenglish is expected to vary according to the information given above, construct the Tenglish tree, insert the lexical items and "pronounce" from left to right.)

10.7.5 Further reading

There is a very substantial literature on the subject of the locality of wh-movement (and locality in general). Virtually all syntax textbooks discuss the constraints and the subjacency condition. In this chapter we have kept the names of the subjacency condition and bounding nodes constant, for reasons of clarity: if you read the literature you will see a slightly different terminology, changing over time as progress is made: e.g. Barriers, or Phase Node instead of bounding nodes. Many of Noam Chomsky's publications deal with the theory of locality including *Aspects of the Theory of Syntax* (1965), *Conditions on Transformations* (1973), *Lectures on Government and Binding* (1981), *Some Concepts and Consequences of the Theory of Government and Binding* (1982), *Barriers* (1986) (the analysis presented in this chapter is a "close cousin" of Barriers), *Principles and Parameters* (1991), to the latest reformulations in *Derivation by Phase* (2001). Also very influential works are Kayne's *Connectedness and Binary Branching* (1984) and Rizzi's *Relativized Minimality* (1991, 2004). For a study of Superiority effects see Kitahara (1997) and Norvin Richards' influential 1997 MIT Ph.D. dissertation.

11
Probing Structures

11.1 Introduction

In previous chapters, we saw that sentences or fragments of sentences are structured in particular ways and that a wide range of linguistic phenomena are sensitive to such structures. We have also seen that a given unambiguous sentence or fragment can be associated with multiple syntactic structures as its surface structure may have been derived by multiple applications of Merge, and in particular of Move, which changes the structural relations between what is moving and other structures in its tree. To detect constituents, we have constituency tests, and also the binding theory, which, through its sensitivity to c-command, can help us determine the geometry of a tree. But these tools only give us information about surface structures, once all Moving and Merging is done. To detect underlying structures, we can only use the diagnostics for selection discussed in Section 8.4. In this chapter, we will explore new ways of detecting constituency, some of which will be able to probe underlying structures. In other words, we will introduce ways to decide whether movement is involved in the structure of a string. These will prove quite useful, and sometimes surprising.

11.2 Probing Derived Structures

11.2.1 *Only*

We begin with the so-called focus particle *only*. *Only* associates with some linguistic material X, which we call its focus, and which is usually marked with distinctive prosody. It places X in contrast with implicit alternatives. If *only* associates with the material X, we can often (but not always) paraphrase the meaning effect of *only* as follows:

...only ... *X* = *X* is the only thing/person/time/manner/place/ such that ...

For example:

(1) Mary only **goes to the market** on Mondays:
= **Go to the market** is the only thing that Mary does on Mondays
(2) Mary only goes to the market **on Sundays**
= **Sundays** is the only time that Mary goes to the market

An Introduction to Syntactic Analysis and Theory, First Edition.
Dominique Sportiche, Hilda Koopman, and Edward Stabler.

(3) Mary only **goes to the market on Sundays**
= **Go to the market on Sundays** is the only thing Mary does

(4) Only **Mary** goes to the market on Sundays
= Mary is the only person who goes to the market on Sundays.

This association of a string X with *only* obeys two properties. The first one is that the material associated with *only* is a constituent, either a head or a phrase. This is illustrated in the sentence below.

(5) a. This cook will only put pepper on these tomatoes
b. This cook will only put pepper on these tomatoes
c. This cook will only put pepper on these tomatoes
d. This cook will only put pepper on these tomatoes
e. This cook will only put pepper on these tomatoes
f. This cook will only put pepper on these tomatoes

For example, the last case, which must be read with focal stress on *tomátoes*, means:

f′ = "it is only these tomatoes that this cook will put pepper on, not these pizzas or anything else"

The associate must be a constituent. Consider for example:

a. This cook will only put pepper on these tomatoes

That string does not seem be able to mean something like: "It is only pepper that the cook will put somewhere and the only place where he will put pepper is on top of these tomatoes (as opposed to under these tomatoes)."

As usual, this is a necessary but not a sufficient condition. If some material can be associated with *only*, it forms a constituent. If a string cannot be associated with *only* it does not follow that it is not a constituent. There is at least one reason for this. In addition to the constituency requirement for the associate, there is also a structural requirement of some sort. This is illustrated below with the associate in boldface:

(6) a. John had only **said that Bill saw Sue**
b. John had only **said** that Bill saw Sue
c. John had only said **that Bill saw Sue**
d. John had only said that **Bill** saw Sue
e. John had only said that Bill **saw Sue**
f. John had only said that Bill saw **Sue**
g. John had only said that Bill **saw** Sue
h. ***John/THIS person** had only said that Bill saw Sue
i. ***John had** only **said that Bill saw Sue**

In this example, pretty much anything to the right of *only* can be an associate, but not material to its left. Indeed the last example cannot be paraphrased as *John is the only person who said that Bill saw Sue*, or with focal stress on this, it cannot be paraphrased as *THIS person is the only person who had said that...* Note also that the whole sentence (which contains *only*) cannot be an associate either (the sentence cannot be paraphrased as meaning *the only that happened is that John had said that Bill saw Sue*). Perhaps this is the right way then to characterize the restriction involved. Let's call this proposal *the **Linear Precedence Hypothesis***:

(7) *Only* must be to the left of its associate.

In order to verify the predictions of this hypothesis, or consider alternatives, the very first thing to do is to unpack the string and determine the constituency of sentences with *only*. Here we appeal to the basic constituency tests: these allow us to probe the structure of any unfamiliar string. Let's examine what happens if we probe the structure with *do so* replacement and VP ellipsis:

(8) The cook will only do so
(9) This cook will only put pepper on these tomatoes, and that cook will ~~pepper on these tomatoes~~ too

We see that *only* forms a VP constituent with the VP *put pepper on these tomatoes*. Coordination points to the same conclusion:

(10) Noemie will [roast the chicken] and [only roast the chicken]

These results indicate that *only* forms a constituent with a VP. We will treat *only* as a left adjunct to VP, and label it Adv (the reader is invited to consider what an alternative structure would look like in which *only* were treated as a head taking a VP complement). If we draw the relevant (simplified) trees for the examples in (6a) above, another option seems plausible too:

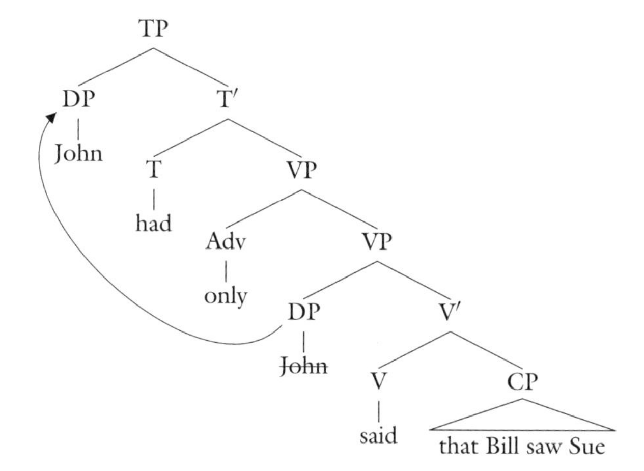

Is linear precedence (7) the right notion? We were led to this hypothesis on the basis of the structure above. But due to the fact that this tree is right-branching (rightmost nodes have daughters), being *to the right of* also means *being c-commanded by*. An alternative idea could be:

(11) *Only* must c-command its associate.

The following sentences discriminate between these two hypotheses. In the unacceptable sentences, *only* has material to its right that it cannot associate with:

(12) a. John said he only **wanted to visit Mary** to his mother
b. John said he only wanted to **visit Mary** to his mother
c. John said he only wanted to visit **Mary** to his mother
d. * John said he only wanted to visit Mary to **his mother**

(13) a. That John only **saw Bill** bothered Mary
b. That John only **saw** Bill bothered Mary
c. That John only saw **Bill** bothered Mary
d. *That John only saw Bill **bothered** Mary
e. *That John only saw Bill bothered **Mary**

Practice

Draw the trees and give the paraphrases for the intended meanings of each ungrammatical example.

Drawing the trees for such sentences reveals that in each well-formed case, *only* c-commands the material associated with it, while in each ill-formed case, it does not. This reinforces hypothesis (11) above.

Restrictions on *only*: For example, **John talked to only Mary, the picture of only several people was published* are ill-formed. This follows neither from the c-command requirement, nor from the associate not being a constituent. Rather it suggest that there are intrinsic constraints on where *only* can occur.

If this hypothesis is correct, it should be clear why failure of association with *only* does not disqualify a string from being a constituent. One reason can be failure of c-command. There may be other reasons too.

Let us now return to the base sentences in (5) and complete the paradigm with the sentences below. Here we observe that focus may not be put on *cook*, on *will*, or on *this.*

(14) g. * This <u>cook</u> will only put pepper on these tomatoes
h. * This cook <u>will</u> only put pepper on these tomatoes
i. * <u>This</u> cook will only put pepper on these tomatoes

For example, this last sentence cannot mean "this cook is the only one who will put pepper on these tomatoes." Why would this be the case? Let us inspect just the relevant portion of the tree, paying close attention to movement, i.e. the relation between the underlying tree and the derived tree:

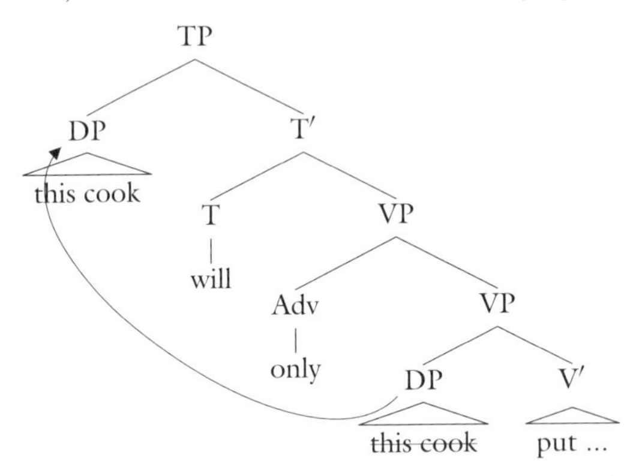

We observe that *only* does not c-command [Spec,TP], not because the subject of TP precedes *only*, but because it is not a sister of *only. Only* cannot put *the cook* in focus, because of lack of c-command. But note now that we also have an underlying tree in which *only* does c-command the subject. This tells us that association with *only* requires c-command in the surface tree.

(15) *Only* must c-command its associate in the surface tree.

Do other focus particles, like *also, even, too, just* behave similarly? We will not explore these here, except for *also* in Section 11.3.2. There we show it is similar to *only* in its sensitivity to c-command, but crucially different in the sense that c-command in the underlying tree yields fine associations.

Thus, by judiciously placing *only* in a structure we are trying to probe, we can get some valuable information about c-command relations.

Let's apply this test and consider what *only* can tell us about the question of at what level the temporal DP *tomorrow* should be attached.

(16) John will write to his parents **tomorrow**

It would not be unreasonable to take *tomorrow* to always be a TP adjunct, as it seems to entertain selectional relations with tense: *that John left tomorrow* is a strange sentence, intuitively because of the clash between past tense T and *tomorrow*. However, adding *only* suggests that it can be otherwise:

(17) John will only write to his parents tomorrow (OK for only tomorrow)

Since this is well-formed, and *only* is clearly below T, it follows *will* and precedes V. it must be that *tomorrow* is (allowed to be) attached lower, e.g. as a VP adjunct. This conclusion is further supported by VP ellipsis and VP preposing.

(18) a. Write to his parents tomorrow, John will
b. Will John write to his parents tomorrow? Yes, he certainly will!

This conclusion raises a new interesting question: if adjuncts are adjoined to a constituent they modify, as they must be given our understanding of X-bar theory and our understanding of what may merge with what, then what exactly is the property that characterizes the VP to which the temporal modifier may attach?

11.2.2 NPI licensing

A second new diagnostic is based on the behavior of certain elements that are not allowed to occur in a sentence unless some other element appears there as well. This is the case for a class of elements called **Negative Polarity Items** abbreviated as NPI. NPIs typically appear in clauses that contain negation. Such clauses are said to have negative polarity, which contrasts with clauses that have positive polarity. The presence of negation suffices (when it is well placed) to license the occurrence of a NPI. Here is an example with the NPI determiner *any*:

(19) a. *John bought anything
b. John did not buy anything

We see that *any* is only allowed in the presence of a **licenser**, here negation. There are many expressions qualifying as negative polarity items, and there are many important questions NPIs raise. We focus here on the following question:

(20) Is there any structural relation that must hold between a licenser and a NPI? And if so How should this structural relation be characterized?

We start investigating these questions with *any*, building on (19). With the licenser in boldface, and the NPI underlined, we vary first the location of the licenser and then the type of licenser.

(21) *Any*: licenser is negation or negative NP
a. *anyone **didn't** buy a book
b. * I told anyone that John didn't buy a book

c. I told **no one** that anyone bought a book
d. I told **no one** that you saw anyone
e. *That **no one** bought the book annoyed anyone

(22) *Any*: licenser C[+q].
a. **Did** John buy any book?
b. **Did** anyone buy a book?
c. I asked you **whether** John bought any book
d. *I asked anyone **whether** John bought a book
e. *The question **whether** John bought a book annoyed anyone

These examples show that the mere presence of a licenser in the same sentence as the NPI *any* is not sufficient. Nor is it the case that the licenser needs to be in the same CP as the licenser ((21c) (21d)), or can never be a subject ((21a) vs. (21c) and (22b)). These examples also show that it is not sufficient that the licenser precede the NPI: if that were the case both (21e) and (22e) should be fine. If we examine the tree structure for each example, we see that in all the good cases the licenser c-commands the NPI, and in all the bad cases, there is no c-command.

Practice

Draw the trees for the two sentences in (19), and for (21a), (21c), and (21e) and verify that the relation of c-command plays a determining role in distinguishing between the good and bad cases. Check that the other examples fall under the same generalization.

This suggests the following licensing condition:

(23) A licenser must c-command the NPI *any*.

Is this condition specific to *any* or more general?

Free choice *any* and NPI *any*: A word of caution about *any*: *Any* is said to be used either as an NPI (c-commanded by a licenser) as in *I did not see anyone* or as free choice as in *anyone can do this*. To make sure you are using NPI *any*, always use (declarative) sentences in the past tense without modal verbs. These contexts don't allow for free choice *any*.

* anyone came	* *because the NPI is not c-commanded by a licenser, and this sentence is a past declarative, without a modal, and the free choice reading is not available in this context.*
anyone can come	*OK as free choice, but * as NPI*

To distinguish the two, a good approximation is that free choice any can be modified by *almost*, but NPI any cannot.

There are many different types of NPI expressions; all are licensed by negation. Different classes are sensitive to different licensers. But what all classes have in common, regardless of the type, licenser, or domain in which an NPI must find a licenser, is that the licenser c-commands the NPI. This is illustrated below, for a few different NPIs and different licensers.

Here is a small sample of NPIs, with the NPI expression underlined and the licenser in bold. (The reader is invited to explore further NPIs like *a bit, all that, yet. ...*)

(24) give a red cent; give a damn
  a. John did **not** give a red cent to Arthur
  b. * John gave a red cent to Arthur
  c. * John gave a red cent to no one
  d. *The person **no one** likes gave a red cent to Arthur
(25) lift a finger
  a. Max did **not** lift a finger to help me
  b. * Max lifted a finger to help me
  c. * Max lifted a finger to help **no one**
  d. *The girl who likes no one lifted a finger to help Arthur
(26) in ages
  a. **No one** had seen Rip van Winkle in ages
  b. * Everyone had seen Rip van Winkle in ages
  c. * The girls with **no** fear had seen Rip van Winkle in ages
(27) bother to/bother V-ing
  a. Bill did**n't** bother to show up
  b. * He bothered to do so
  c. **Only** Bill bothered to show up
  d. * Bill bothered to **only** show up
(28) ever
  a. John must **not** ever do this
  b. * John must ever do this

These data are sufficient to show that c-command plays a determining role in distinguishing between the good and bad cases:

(29) **NPI Licensing**: The licenser must c-command the NPI.

There are other factors at play as well, and there are many complex questions that we set apart, for example. what are the NPIs in English, or any given language? What properties make an element an NPI? For a given NPI, what are its licensers? How is the licensing relation defined? More generally, for English: are all NPIs licensed by the same licensers? Is the licensing relation unique or does it depend on the pair (licenser, NPI)? The description above is only an approximation of what is known. However, it is correct in a great many cases and we can make the simplifying assumption that this description is accurate. Granting this simplification, we can illustrate how we can exploit it to probe structures.

Given an NPI, say *any*, and a licenser for *any*, say some negative item α, we can reason as follows: a sentence with *any* which is ill-formed but becomes well formed by the addition of α, suggests that the position containing α c-commands *any*. If it does not become well formed, then this **may** suggest that α does not c-command *any* (as usual, we should be very careful about failure).

As we have seen, sentences can have more than one tree associated to them, an underlying structure, and a derived structure. Does NPI licensing hold for the underlying structure or of a derived structure? In all the licit cases so far, NPI licensing holds of the derived structures.

Could NPI licensing be assumed to hold for underlying structures as well? If that were the case, it would be sufficient for an NPI to be c-commanded in the underlying structure, but it could be outside the c-command domain in the derived structure, after movement. This fails, as the following examples show: c-command in underlying structures (i.e. before movement) is not enough to license well-formed NPIs. This means we cannot use NPIs to probe for underlying trees.

(30) a. *Anyone **didn't** ~~anyone~~ buy a book
b. It seemed to no one that Bill was unhappy *at all*
c. Bill seemed to no one ~~Bill~~ to be unhappy at all
d. *Anyone seemed to no one [~~anyone~~] to be unhappy *at all*

Positive polarity items? Just as there are NPIs, there are also Positive Polarity Items (PPIs) e.g. *some*, which dislike being in negative "environments." It is a little less easy to see, but we can give the flavor of what happens with PPIs. A sentence like

(31) John did not look for someone

is a little bit strange and cannot mean the same as

(32) John did not look for anyone

This is somewhat unexpected. We should be able to interpret this last sentence just as the negation of

(33) John looked for someone

Since (33) can mean that John looked for someone or other, its negation should be able to mean "That John looked for someone or other is not the case," i.e. (33) should be able to mean "John did not look for anyone." This is not what (31) means. Rather, if it is acceptable at all, it means that there is someone who John did not look for, in which "someone" does *not* count as negated. (Another way of stating this is to say that *someone* – because it is a PPI – cannot be in the scope of negation; see Section 11.4.3 for a definition of the notion of scope.)

The whole picture about NPIs, PPIs, and their interaction is an extremely intricate domain. There is an enormous literature on this topic, pioneered in Klima (1964). See e.g. the most recent Homer (2011b).

11.3 Probing Underlying Structures

As the previous section illustrates, the properties of focus particles like *only* or the properties of NPIs can help determine constituent structure and can thus help corroborate or sharpen the results we can get by using constituency tests. However, they are not helpful in determining underlying constituent structures. Now we turn to a variety of means we can use to help corroborate or sharpen the results we get from the principle of locality of selection, that is, when we "undo" movement.

11.3.1 Quantifier floating: distribution of *all*

We have already discussed quantifier floating, also called **Q-float**, in Section 8.5.4 as a diagnostic for the underlying position of subjects. Recall that Q-float refers to the non-local relation between a DP and a quantifier like *all* to its right. The quantifier is a DP adjunct (you may want to check how constituent structure tests support this structure). This yields an underlying structure, from which two surface trees can be derived, with the discontinuous DP…, all constituent resulting from movement of the smaller DP.

(34) **Underlying structure**: will [$_{VP}$ [$_{DP}$ all [$_{DP}$ the children]] read books]
Whole DP moved:
[$_{DP}$ all [$_{DP}$ the children]] will [$_{VP}$ [$_{DP}$ ~~all [$_{DP}$ the student~~]] read books]
Only the smaller DP moved:
[$_{DP}$ the children] will [$_{VP}$ [$_{DP}$ all [$_{DP}$ ~~the students~~]] read books]

Since Q-float can diagnose a movement relationship, Q-float can be used as a diagnostic for underlying trees. In a large number of cases, the relation between a floated quantifier and the DP it modifies is one in which we have good independent reasons to postulate a movement relationship. So this increases our confidence about the interpretation of this test.

In turn, then, we can use this hypothesis to probe the nature of underlying structures in cases in which we are not sure whether movement has taken place: a stranded *all* indicates a position from which its associated DP has moved. Here is how we will use this diagnostic: when quantifier floating succeeds, we can conclude movement has taken place. When it fails, it is difficult to know why. It could be there is no movement, but it could also be that there are other reasons behind the failure, for example, we could be wrong about the exact structures of underlying trees. Some care is needed, however, due in particular to the fact that some non-trace DP, can be silent, such as PRO. So, for example:

(35) a. To all leave together would bother the girls (the girls would be bothered if all of them were leaving together)
b. The girls wanted to all meet at 5 (the girls' wish was that all of them meet at 5)

As the meaning in parentheses indicates, each *all* semantically modifies *the girls*. Does it mean *the girls* has moved away from *all*? The answer is negative: there may well have been Q-float, but of a silent PRO:

(36) a. PRO to all ~~PRO~~ leave together would bother the girls
b. The girls wanted PRO to all meet at 5

So Q-float can be seen to reveal where silent DPs are located, be they traces or PROs.

In effect, Q-float is a case of a superficial discontinuous DP constituent. There are other such cases of discontinuous DP constituents. Exploring their properties can yield important information about the trees that lead to surface trees. Here are a couple of examples from other languages:

(37) Numeral floating under "Object Scrambling" in Japanese (stranding a numeral classifier) see e.g. Miyagawa and Arikawa (2007) .
a. Gakusei-ga [hon-o san-satu] yonda.
student-nom [book-acc 3-CL] read
"The student read three books."
b. [Hon-o] gakusei-ga [~~hon-o~~ san-satu] yonda.
book-acc student-nom [3-cl] read
"The student read three books."

(38) Object topicalization in German (stranding a negative quantifier, see e.g. Van Riemsdijk (1989)):
a. Ich habe keine Kinder gesehen
I have no children seen
"I have seen no children"

b. Kinder habe ich keine ~~Kinder~~ gesehen
Children have I no seen
"I have seen no children"

Similar examples, although stylistically marked, can also be found in English as in this riddle drawn from Smullyan (1978), a fun, non-technical introduction to logic:

> A man was looking at a portrait. Someone asked him; "whose picture are you looking at?" He replied: "**Brothers and sisters have I none**, but *this man's father is my father's son*."(This man's father means, of course, the father of the man in the picture.) Whose picture was the man looking at?

Besides illustrating the structure in bold, this puzzle also illustrates that we can make a quick judgment on syntactic well-formedness of a string (for example of the italicized string above), without immediately understanding this string: the interest of this puzzle rests on this difference. And of course you may try to find out what the answer to the riddle is (or how the example in bold could be analyzed).

11.3.2 *Also* association

Another tool, similar to the one provided by floating quantifiers, is provided by the focus particle *also*. This particle is similar to *only* in that it can associate with the same material as *only* (in bold in the examples below):

(39) a. John had also **said** that Bill saw Sue ("said" in addition to "implied")
b. John had also said **that Bill saw Sue** ("Bill saw Sue" in addition to "Mary called Ann")
c. John had also said that **Bill** saw Sue ("Bill" in addition to "Henri")
d. John had also said that Bill **saw Sue** ("saw Sue" in addition to "kissed Ann")
e. John had also said that Bill saw **Sue** ("Sue" in addition to "Ann")
f. John had also said that Bill **saw** Sue ("saw" in addition to "heard")

It fails in the same contexts:

(40) a. John said he also **wanted to visit Mary** to his mother
b. John said he also wanted to **visit Mary** to his mother
c. John said he also wanted to visit **Mary** to his mother
d. * John said he also wanted to visit Mary **to his mother**

(41) a. That John also **saw Bill** bothered Mary
b. That John also **saw** Bill bothered Mary
c. That John also saw **Bill** bothered Mary
d. *That John also saw Bill **bothered** Mary
e. *That John also saw Bill bothered **Mary**

This suggests the same rule is involved:

(42) *Also* Association:
Also associates with a constituent.
Also must c-command its associate.

Interestingly however, *also* is more permissive than *only* as the following association is possible (it was not with *only*) with the associate superficially to the left of (and not c-commanded by) *also*:

(43) **John** had **also** said that Bill saw Sue (in addition to Mary saying so)

This may be taken to suggest that the rule of *also* association is wrong, but note the severe restrictions on this association of *also* with material to its left:

(44) Ann said that Bill would also come
This cannot mean: Ann also, in addition to someone else, said that Bill would come.
(45) Bill promised Mary to also invite Sam
This cannot mean: Bill, in addition to someone else, promised Mary to invite Sam. And it cannot mean: Bill promised Mary, in addition to someone else, to invite Sam.
(46) Bill persuaded Mary to also invite Sam
This cannot mean: Bill persuaded Mary in addition to someone else to invite Sam.

That is, it is not true that anything to the left of *also* qualifies as an associate of *also*. The same type of reasoning we use in the case of floating quantifiers applies here. It turns out that the cases in which a constituent that *also* does not c-command can be associated with *also* are cases in which there are independent reasons to postulate that the associate has moved from a position in which it was c-commanded by *also* in the underlying structure.

In other words, in many cases only what may reasonably be postulated (for independent reasons) to have moved from the right of *also* qualifies as an associate. Once again, we may be able to deduce something about underlying constituency from the distribution and meaning contribution of *also*.

11.4 Probing with Binding

Recall the principles of the binding theory we introduced previously in Chapter 7:

Principle A: An anaphor must be bound, and it must be bound in its domain.
Principle B: A pronoun must be free in its domain.
Principle C: An R-expression must be free.

Remember that a good approximation of the notion of domain is this: the domain of x is the smallest constituent that has a subject and that contains x. But so far we have not discussed in detail the question of whether the binding principles apply to derived trees, to underlying trees, to both, or to some complex combination of the first two options. We are not going to settle this intricate question here, but some results can be simply illustrated, which are relevant for the question of determining underlying constituent structure.

11.4.1 Principle A

Let us begin with Principle A. If we consider the following two sentences:

(47) * They knew that I liked the pictures of each other
(48) They knew which pictures of each other I liked

The first one is, correctly, ruled out by Principle A since the domain of the reciprocal anaphor is the VP of the embedded clause that does not contain the only qualified potential antecedent *they*. But the second is fine, even though without movement it would have the structure:

(49) past they know [past I like which pictures of each other]

Which looks very much like (47). If we had to enforce Principle A on underlying structures, (47) would be incorrectly ruled out. This shows that we have to allow Principle A to ignore underlying structures, imposing a requirement instead on surface structures.

To make the same point differently, if we look at the relevant portions of the derived/surface structure of (48),

(50) They knew [which pictures of each other [I liked ~~which pictures of the other~~]]

we see both the surface position and the underlying/trace position of the anaphor. Clearly, if each instance of the anaphor had to satisfy Principle A (the underlying position in the underlying structure and the surface position in the derived structure) the sentence would be wrongly predicted to be ill-formed. We conclude that the **trace of an anaphor** is not an anaphor.

Does Principle A have to be satisfied in derived trees? The answer would seem to be positive since we established Principle A by looking at the distribution of anaphors in derived trees. However, certain other data suggest that the answer is negative. This is illustrated by the following cases:

(51) I know which pictures of each other they liked
(52) I know which pictures of each other John said they liked

Clearly, in their surface positions, the anaphors do not have c-commanding antecedents. This is shown by the relevant portion of the (simplified) derived tree for the first one:

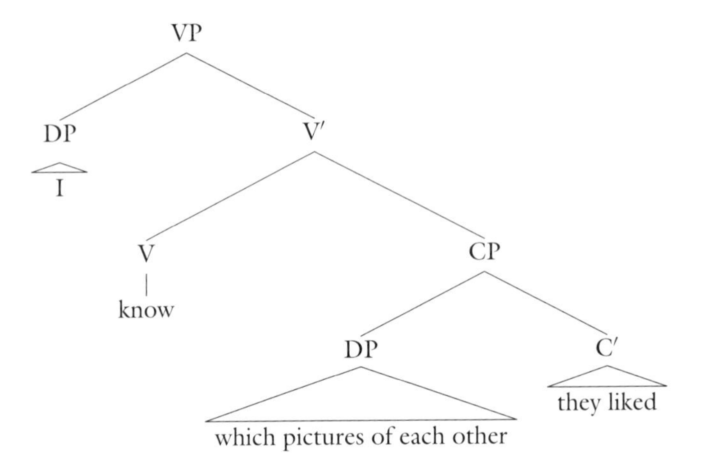

But they do in underlying structures prior to wh-movement, as we can see by looking at the structure of the subordinate clause (we indicate the antecedent in bold):

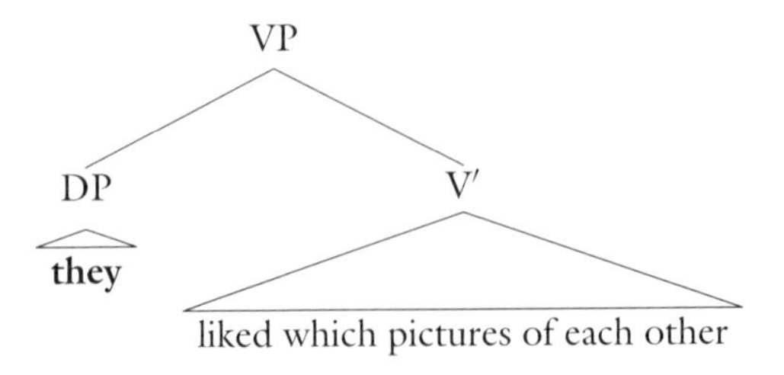

Here, the antecedent c-commands the anaphor in its local domain and hence Principle A is satisfied.

The reason moved material is struck out: The fact that Principle A can be satisfied before wh-movement provides one of the main reasons why we represent the trees the way we do, i.e. by striking through the moved material: this shows that at some point in the derivation, the material was present in that position.

(53) I knew which pictures of each other **they** liked ~~which pictures of each other~~
(54) I knew which pictures of each other John said **they** liked ~~which pictures of each other~~

Note that in order to handle these last data, it is *not* good enough to say that Principle A only applies at surface structure and that anaphor traces are not anaphors.

This shows then that Principle A does not have to be satisfied in the derived structure either. Naturally, we cannot conclude that Principle A never needs to be satisfied. Instead, what this suggests is the following:

(55) An anaphor must satisfy Principle A at some point in the derivation.

If a sentence (fragment) contains an anaphor, Principle A must be satisfied in some tree (underlying or derived) for this sentence (fragment). Of course, this conclusion holds only if we suppose that, in the sentences above, movement has taken place, that is, only if the binding theory is telling us how underlying structures are organized (which is of course extremely plausible in this case).

This conclusion can now be used to postulate certain underlying structural relations. If an anaphor appears in a sentence deemed to be acceptable, and its relation with its antecedent does not satisfy Principle A, it is reasonable to hypothesize that it satisfied Principle A in some underlying structure.

Here is a case in which this reasoning would lead one to postulate some non-obvious underlying structure (that is to postulate movement that is not obvious):

(56) This struck Bill as being crazy

By appropriately placing an anaphor and an antecedent as below:

(57) The stories about each other struck them as being false

We obtain a good sentence, yet one in which the anaphor *each other* is not c-commanded by its antecedent *them*. This suggests that the subject of the main clause has moved from a position c-commanded by the pronoun *them*. Since this subject is interpreted as an argument of *false*, this suggests that we are dealing with a raising to subject structure with the following underlying/derived structure pairs:

(58) Struck them as being [the stories about each other] false
(59) The stories about each other struck them as being ~~the stories about each other~~ false

This conclusion is corroborated by the fact that the verb *strike* does not seem to select its subject, as witnessed by the possibility of having an expletive *it* as subject in other contexts:

(60) It struck them that the stories were false

11.4.2 Pronominal binding

In Chapter 7, we saw that pronouns can have antecedents in two different ways. If the antecedent is a referential expression (that is, can be understood as picking out a concrete or abstract object or entity in the world), the pronoun and its antecedent can refer to the same object (corefer), and we can get the meaning of the pronoun by replacing it by its antecedent (recall that we use indices to code the pronoun/antecedent relation):

(65) John$_j$ believed he$_j$ could get elected
= ?? John$_j$ believed John$_j$ could get elected,

When the antecedent of the pronoun is not a referential expression, however, this replacement procedure fails:

(66) Everyone$_j$ believed he$_j$ could get elected
≠ Everyone$_j$ believed everyone$_j$ could get elected

Instead we need a more complex procedure to express the meaning of the pronoun, which has the following effect: as the antecedent cycles through the various "values" it can take, the pronoun each time takes the same value. For example, when we are talking about everyone (say in a classroom) everyone acts as shorthand for a big conjunction. If the students in the class are John, Bill, Mark, etc. *everyone* means John and Bill and Mark, etc.

(67) Everyone believed he could get elected
= John$_j$ believes he$_j$ could get elected
and Bill$_j$ believes he$_j$ could get elected
and Mark$_j$ believes he$_j$ could get elected
and ...

We have described this by saying that the relation between the pronoun and its antecedent is not a coreference relation but rather a **binding** relation: the pronoun is bound by its antecedent.

In binding theory, binding requires c-command, so we may expect this to also be necessary for pronominal binding, and indeed pronominal binding fails in clear cases where c-command does not hold, as in the following example:

(68) * That no one$_i$ succeeded displeased his$_i$ teacher.

Movement and Principle B and C: We just discussed how Principle A applies to structures in relation to Movement, concluding that it may be satisfied before or after movement. What about Principle B or C? For these, matters are somewhat more complicated. We briefly illustrate these complications here. AP topicalization, for example, suggests that violation of Principle C before movement yields ill-formed sentences.

(61) * Proud of Bill$_i$, he$_i$ thinks that Mary is
(62) He$_i$ thinks that Mary is proud of Bill$_i$,

The ill-formedness of the first sentence is surprising as *he* does not c-command *Bill*. However, the pre-movement structure, which essentially is the second sentence, violates Principle C as *he* does c-command *Bill* in it. We could conclude from this that Principle C cannot be violated anywhere, neither before nor after movement. The following sentence however, with its pre-movement structure, seems to contradict this conclusion:

(63) After movement: Which picture that Bill$_i$ liked did he$_i$ sell
(64) Before movement: He$_i$ sold which picture that Bill$_i$ liked

See Sportiche (2006), for a survey of some of the issues involved.

We considered this hypothesis:

Condition on Pronominal Binding: A pronoun can be bound by an antecedent only if the antecedent c-commands the pronoun.

Just as in the case of Principle A, the existence of this c-command requirement provides us with a way to get information about underlying structures. To see how, consider the following examples in which a pronoun can be interpreted as being bound even though it is not c-commanded by its antecedent:

(69) I know which of his poems every poet prefers, namely: the first one he wrote

In this example, the pronoun *his* is bound by the antecedent *every poet*.

(70) It is a picture of their home town that few football players keep in their locker

For each football player, there is a different hometown: the pronoun *their* is bound by the non-referential (plural) expression *few football players*.

Obviously there is no surface c-command between the (non-referential) antecedent and the pronoun, yet the pronoun can clearly be interpreted as bound by the antecedent. How should we handle such cases? One option, as usual, is to try to modify our hypothesis concerning the allowed pronominal binding configurations. The other is to trust that we have the right structural characterization of the binding configuration and to suppose that we are tapping some hidden structures not directly reflected in the surface constituency we observe.

In these two cases, there is a natural proposal to make, namely that it is some underlying structure that it is relevant to determine whether our condition on pronominal binding is satisfied. Indeed, in the first case, for example, the underlying structure of the embedded clause is revealing:

(71) -s every poet prefer which of his poems

In it, the antecedent *every poet* c-commands the pronoun *his*. Once again, then, we can infer some information about underlying structures.

Strong and weak cross-over

As introduced, c-command is a necessary condition for pronominal binding, but is it sufficient? Here are some surprising cases, named **strong and weak cross-over violations** in Postal (1971), which suggest a negative answer. A wh-phrase can act as an antecedent for a pronoun, as in the sentence below.

(72) Who_i ___ thinks he_i is clever?
   a. John thinks he (John) is clever
   b. Bill thinks that he (Bill) is clever

However, sometimes, even if the wh-phrase clearly c-commands a pronoun, this pronoun cannot be interpreted as bound. In the following example, attempting to coindex the pronoun and the wh-phrase should allow answers such as those given below. But this is clearly not possible.

(73) * Who_i does he_i think ___ is clever
   Possible answer if this was good: *John and Bill!*, with the meaning:
   a. He (John) thinks that John is clever (= John thinks that he is clever)
   b. He (Bill) thinks that Bill is clever (= Bill thinks that he is clever)

The same result holds in the following type of example:

(74) Who$_i$ ___ thinks his$_i$ brother is clever?
(75) * Who$_i$ does his$_i$ brother think ___ is clever?
Possible answer if this last example were good: *John and Bill!*, with the meaning:
  a. His (John's) brother thinks that John is clever (= John's brother thinks that he is clever)
  b. His (Bill's) brother thinks that Bill is clever (= Bill's brother thinks that he is clever)

Two related hypotheses have been proposed for these and related constructions:

Strong Cross-Over (SCO): Wh-movement cannot cross over a c-commanding pronoun that it binds.
Weak Cross-Over (WCO): Wh-movement cannot cross over a c-commanding phrase containing a pronoun that it binds.

One may wonder why this is forbidden. We can understand why strong cross-over would be bad: prior to wh-movement, the pronoun *he* c-commands *who* in the underlying structure, and this could be a violation of Principle C. But this would not take care of WCO. A general requirement that "movement cannot feed binding" would wrongly exclude cases such as:

(76) Everyone$_i$ seems to [his$_i$ mother] to be handsome

Here *everyone* has moved to the position from which it binds the pronoun *his*, yet the sentence is fine. From this point of view, raising to subject behaves differently from wh-movement. The former can feed binding, while the latter cannot. This is one of the central bases for distinguishing A-movement (the former) from A-bar movement (the latter) introduced in Section 8.9. See e.g. Koopman and Sportiche (1991b), Lasnik and Stowell (1991), and Ruys (2000).

11.4.3 Quantifier scope

Indefinite DPs, such as *someone, a young student, a surfer from Montana*, etc., can be used to introduce a referent in the discourse as in:

(77) I met a young student. She told me ...
(78) There is someone waiting for you in your office. His name is Bill.
(79) I bought a book. I found it at the Selexyz bookstore.
(80) A book was on the table. It was open.

In each case, the sentence is talking about just one person or one book. This is not surprising since these DPs are singular DPs.

But such expressions can be used differently, as illustrated in the sentence below:

(81) Every student bought a book

Here the indefinite description of a book can refer to a particular book, say *War and Peace*, but it can also function as referring to a different book depending on which student is the buyer. In other words, this sentence could be talking about many books, in fact as many as there are students.

This interpretation can be made more prominent by adding the adjective *different*, as in

(82) Every student bought a different book

Different here can either mean different from some book previously mentioned, or it can mean that the books bought are different from each other.

Understood this way, the sentence really is a summary of a list of statements. Thus if the students in question are Sophie, Samantha, and Chloe, this sentence is equivalent to:

(83) Sophie bought a book and
Samantha bought a book and
Chloe bought a book

Where the DP *a book* can be interpreted as referring to a different book in every one of these three sentences. Clearly, the ability for this DP to have this type of variable interpretation depends on the presence of the DP *everyone*. If we replace *everyone* by *I* as earlier, or by *the student*, this possibility disappears. This behavior is very similar to what we have seen with pronouns interpreted as bound (i.e. books vary with students).

This immediately brings up the following questions:

(84) What other pairs of expressions behave like the pair everyone/a book?
(85) Under what (structural) conditions can this interpretation of an indefinite description arise?

It turns out that this type of phenomena is pervasive in natural languages. Portions of this important problem are understood, much beyond what can be covered here, but some parts of this problem are still mysterious. Here we will limit ourselves to giving a preliminary answer to the second question.

First let us introduce some terminology. We will call (non-referential) expressions like *everyone* **quantifiers**. If the interpretation of an expression depends on another, the way the indefinite description's depends on the universal quantifier *everyone*, we say that the former is (or can be) in the **scope** of the latter. In this sense, a bound pronoun is in the scope of its antecedent. The question (85) above then translates as the following challenge: how can we characterize this notion of scope?

One aspect of this question is rather clear. If an expression like *everyone* c-commands the indefinite description, the indefinite description is in the scope of *everyone*. This is the case in the examples above and in the following:

(86) Everyone said that a man left

Clearly, this can mean that each person was talking about a different man. The converse is very often true, but not always. Here are a couple of cases in which it is: the universal quantifier does not c-command the indefinite, and does not have the indefinite in its scope.

(87) A man said that everyone left

If the group of people we are talking about is constituted of Anne, Joaquim, and Lea, this sentence cannot mean:

(88) A man said that Anne left. Another man said Joaquim left. Still another man said that Lea left.

Here are two more examples showing the same point:

(89) The book read by everyone described a far away place
(90) The book read by a boy described every far away place

In the first, there is only one far away place being talked about and in the second only one boy. Neither would be true if the universal quantifier *everyone* or *every place* could have the indefinite in its scope.

Here are two cases in which the converse is false: there is no c-command of the indefinite by the universal quantifier, yet the former can be in the latter's scope.

(91) A doctor has examined every patient
(92) A soldier is standing on every roof

Clearly, the first sentence can describe a situation in which there are as many doctors as there are patients (showing that the doctor talked about can depend on the patient talked about). In the second, the most natural reading is one in which there is a different soldier on each roof.

We can summarize these preliminary observations as follows:

(93) a. If A c-commands B, B can be in the scope of A.
b. If B cannot in the scope of A, A does not c-command B.
c. If B can be in the scope of A, A does not necessarily c-command B.

Notice that (93c) denies the converse of (93a). Despite the apparent failure of the converse to be true, we can still use quantifier scope properties to probe structures in the following way:

(94) If an indefinite cannot be interpreted in the scope of a quantifier, it cannot be c-commanded by it.

Later, we will see cases where such inference is useful.

One may also wonder if the failure of the converse (93c) is not due to the fact that we are looking at the wrong tree structure. As previously, it is conceivable that allowing access to underlying structures might allow us to get rid of exceptions to the converse. This very intriguing and promising possibility is being actively investigated in current research, but it is too early to tell whether it is generally correct.

Here is a case suggesting that it is correct some of the time. Consider the following sentences

(95) a. Elena drank a glass of beer
b. Elena always drank a glass of beer

In the first sentence, there is only one glass of beer talked about. In the second, there could be many glasses of beer. One way of understanding what the sentence means is to imagine that it is talking about occasions on which Elena was in a bar, and it is stating that whenever this happened, Elena drank a glass of beer, obviously not the same glass of beer every time. We see that this singular DP, *a glass of beer*, can refer to many glasses of beer, but just in case the adverb *always* is present. This reminds us of the situation with *everyone* and *a book* discussed above and we can take this to mean that *a glass of beer* is in the scope of the adverb *always*. And this is not surprising as the tree clearly shows that the adverb *always* c-commands the direct object *a glass of beer*.

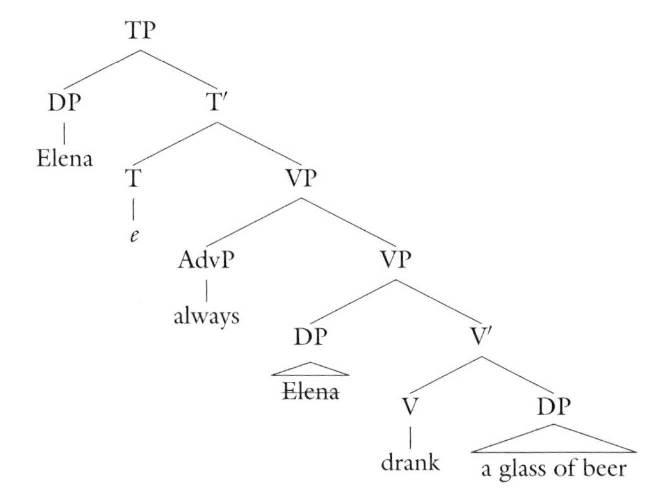

But now, consider the following case, and let us worry about the meaning of the underlined clause:

(96) If a man always wins the election, women will get discouraged

Clearly, this may be talking about different men. The sentence does not necessarily say that women will get discouraged in case the same man always wins. It can also mean that they will get discouraged if the election is always won by a man, even if it is a different man every time. In other words, *a man* can be interpreted in the scope of *always*.

The (simplified) tree structure shows that there is no c-command between *always* and *a man*.

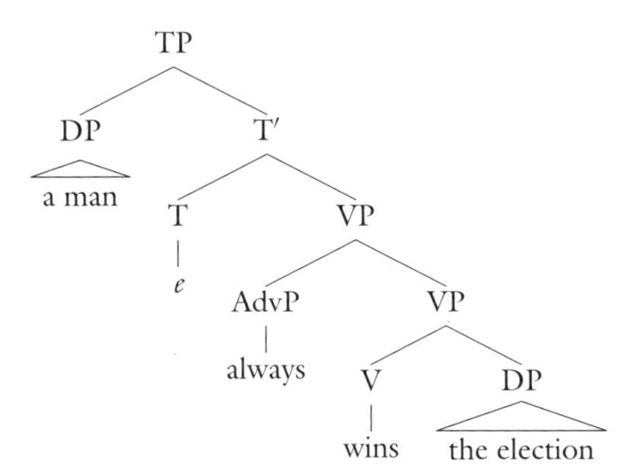

This looks like a case where the converse fails: there is no c-command of *a man* by *always*, but still *a man* can be in the scope of *always*.

But recall what we concluded the underlying structure of such clauses was. Because of the fact that the subject has to be locally selected by the verb, or the distribution of floated quantifiers, we concluded that the subject of TP had moved from the position subject of VP:

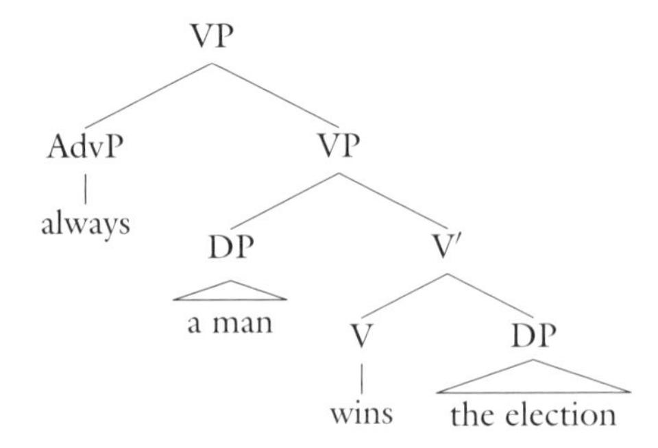

In this structure, *always* **does** c-command *a man*. If we are allowed to compute scope on the basis of this underlying structure, this case would not constitute an exception to the converse.

11.5 Conclusion

11.5.1 Summary

In this chapter, we learned about ways to probe structures, both derived and underlying. Thus, we looked at ways to corroborate the kind of derived constituent structure analyses we are led to by binding considerations (through c-command) or by using constituency tests. We also learned a bit about focus particles, polarity items, and scope, for example (all of them complex and fascinating topics). We also introduced ways to corroborate or discover what underlying structures look like, that is to corroborate what should be the normal, local, expression of selectional relations. This also used focus particles, binding, or scope considerations, but also the analysis of some discontinuities, such as floating quantifiers.

11.5.2 What to remember

You should understand how probing works, know what probing tools we have seen, and know how to apply them and interpret the results. Some methods, like constituent tests, or what can be the focus of particles like *only*, or NPI licensing, are useful to detect surface constituent structures. Others can be used to detect *underlying* constituent structures. These all have the same logic: some dependency requires c-command but c-command is not satisfied on surface trees. In many cases, c-command can plausibly be hypothesized to hold underlying, pre-movement structures. We saw this was the case with:

1. A floating quantifier such as *all* and its antecedent.
2. A focus particle such as *also* and its focus.
3. The antecedent of an anaphor and the anaphor.
4. The binder of a pronoun and the bound pronoun.
5. A quantified expression and an indefinite DP in its scope.

In all cases, postulating movement can corroborate conclusions reached on the basis of the principle of locality of selection. And superficial violations of c-command were resolved once movement was "undone." Sometimes, selectional relations are particularly hard to detect (e.g. cases of non-semantic selection such as that imposed by EPP properties).

11.5.3 Puzzles and preview

Such methods to probe structures will become very useful, as we will see in the coming chapters, where we will discuss theoretically important topics such as:

- The boundary between syntax and morphology.
- The internal structure of verb phrases, and VP shells in particular.
- The proper analysis of (accusative) subject of infinitives (ECM/raising to object).

It is thus important to understand how these probing methods work.

11.5.4 Further exercises

(1) C-command test

For each of the following sentences, we wonder whether DP1 c-commands DP2. Provide motivated answers by using the c-command tests introduced in Chapter 11.

(1) a. I introduced [the new guest]$_1$ to [the audience]$_2$
b. I$_1$ introduced the next guest to John after the dinner$_2$
c. I introduced [the next guest]$_1$ to John after [the dinner]$_2$
d. Susan told me$_1$ that [the winner of the contest]$_2$ would be announced tonight
e. I gave John$_1$ a present$_2$
f. I gave a present$_1$ to John$_2$

(2) *Only, also,* and *even*

The following sentence is structurally ambiguous (*keep* can mean "retain ownership" or "store somewhere"):

(1) Bill's mother has kept the letter in the drawer

(i) Give the two trees, paraphrase their meanings clearly, and show which meaning corresponds to which tree.

(ii) Next we add *only* to the structure, and put focal stress on *drawer.*

(2) Bill's mother has kept **only** the letter in the drawer.

(2) cannot mean *it is only the letter that she stored in the drawer,* nor can it mean *it is only in the dráwer that she stored the letter.* It can have the retain-ownership-of reading. Explain for each case why.

(iii) We put focal stress on *Bill,* and find that *only* cannot associate with it:

(3) *Bill's mother **only** keeps her letters in the drawer

Write what the expected reading would be if this were possible (use the paraphrase "it is only ... but not ..."). Explain whether this can be accounted for given what we know about *only* and if not, how it could be explained (ambiguity is not relevant for this question).

(iv) We change (3) to (4), and find a licit association between *also* and *Bill:*

(4) Bill's mother **also** keeps her letters in the drawer

Paraphrase the expected meaning, and discuss how this is possible.

(v) Next, replacing *the drawer* in (1) with *which drawer* as below yields an unambiguous sentence:

(5) Which drawer did she keep her letters in?

Explain why the ambiguity of (1) is lost. (Show from which tree structure in (1) you can or cannot form a wh-question. Here you should consider what prerequisites for movement there are, and whether locality (i.e. subjacency is satisfied).)

(vi) Finally, consider the following example.

(6) Bill will **even** drive to San Diego

The question is whether the focus particle *even* behaves like *only* or like *also* (or perhaps it is different from either). Illustrate, with annotated commented examples, whether *even* behaves like *only* or like *also*, or like neither. Propose a preliminary analysis for *even*. You will need to determine, and illustrate with examples:

a. if *even* needs to c-command its associate;
b. if the relevant condition can be satisfied before movement or after movement.

(3) Everything is in order

Consider the following sentence.

(1) They will cook the bread in order to prepare the meal

(For the purpose of this exercise, treat *in order* as being of category C.)

(i) Justify, by providing one argument, that the sequence S "in order to prepare the meal" is a constituent.

(ii) Justify by providing one argument using *only* that S can be a VP adjunct.

(iii) Provide one additional argument (not using focus particles) showing that S can be a VP adjunct.

(iv) S contains a silent subject. Decide and provide one reason to justify whether this silent subject is a trace of movement or a PRO. (= Does this sentence involve raising to subject or object (and if yes from where to where) and/or control (and if yes, of what by what)?)

(v) Draw the surface tree for this sentence. Make sure that your tree is consistent with your arguments in (i)–(iv).

(vi) Next consider (2):

(2) They did not cook the bread in order to prepare the meal.

Draw a (surface) tree for (2) so you can reason on it. In this problem, treat *not* as heading a VP adjunct.

(vii) The sentence in (2) is ambiguous (i.e. it has two different meanings). Provide a paraphrase for each of the two readings. (Warning: make sure your paraphrases are not ambiguous.)

Draw the two trees and pair them up with their paraphrases. (You do not need to draw everything in detail. Just draw enough details to clearly illustrate the difference between the two).

(viii) Explain precisely and concisely why the following sentence is ill-formed.

c. * He_k will not cook bread in order to help Bill_k's mother

(ix) Explain why, given the ill-formedness of the above sentence, we expect the following sentence to be well-formed.

d. No one_k cooks bread in order to help his_k boss

(x) The following sentence is not ambiguous. Explain why.

e. They did not cook the bread in order to please anyone

(xi) (Advanced): The following sentence is reported as well-formed by some. Explain why the co-indexing is surprising. Any ideas on how to solve this problem?

f. They will undercook [no bread]$_k$ in order to sell it_k faster

(4) Focus particle *only*

The VP of the following sentence is structurally and semantically ambiguous.

(1) He mailed the fat letter to Bill
   (i) Draw the two structures this VP can have in a rough way (no labeling, no traces: just indicate constituency) and unambiguously paraphrase the meaning of each structure (indicate which meaning goes with which tree).
   (ii) Explain why if we make *fat letter* the focus of *only* as in (2),
(2) He mailed only the fat letter to Bill
   the VP is predicted to lose its ambiguity, and state which of the two meanings is predicted to remain.

(5) Icelandic: floating quantifiers, PRO, and trace. This exercise can also be done in Chapter 9

In this chapter, we discussed "floating quantifiers" like *all* in the following example:

(1) The boys have all eaten

This problem set uses floating quantifiers from Icelandic to help provide some insights into a theoretical debate about two alternative theories of control.

Background: The theory of control outlined in Chapter 9 posits PRO (a silent argument with a specific interpretation and distribution), when its antecedent is selected by the control verb.
This theory assumes that:

(i) A single argument cannot bear two thematic roles: each argument ends up receiving one and no more than one thematic role, and each theta role ends up being associated with one and only one argument (cf. theta-criterion in Chomsky, 1981).

(ii) In addition, it is assumed that each selected argument that ends up in the syntactic subject position [Spec,TP] gets at most one case in the derivation. (This means that, if there are multiple steps of movement, only one of the positions is a case position. Or in linguistic lingo, an *argument chain* (either one-membered, or a sequence of movements) receives one case and one thematic role.)

An alternative theory of control treats control like raising to a thematic position (i.e. as movement). This theory allows an argument to accumulate thematic roles through movement. This theory of control also needs to assume that a selected argument carries no more than one case. This is to rule out forms like:

(2) *He saw

This string cannot be interpreted as:

(3) a. *He$_i$ saw himself$_i$
   b. * He$_i$ saw him$_j$.

Yet the reading in (3a) would arise if the DP could accumulate two thematic roles. The DP "he" would start out as the object of "see" and move to the subject [Spec,] position of "see" to pick up the subject experiencer role. Then it would move to the [Spec,TP], where it would have to surface as a nominative:

(4) *He$_i$ saw ~~he~~ $_i$.

To exclude such cases, it is assumed that each selected argument gets case in no more than one position. This will exclude (4), as it would get both accusative and nominative case.

Icelandic:

The Icelandic data below have bearing on the question of which theory we should adopt. These data should allow you to construct an argument for one or the other theory.

<u>*About case in Icelandic:*</u>
Icelandic floating quantifiers agree in case, number, and gender with the DPs that they modify. Also, Icelandic verbs may assign any of a number of different cases to their subjects; some verbs simply idiosyncratically require dative subjects, for instance. These two facts combine to yield paradigms like the one in (5):

(5) a. Strákarnir komust **allir** í skóla
boys-NOM got all-NOM.PL.M to school
"The boys all got to school"

b. Strákana vantaði **alla** í skólann
boys-ACC lacked all-ACC.PL.M in school-the
"The boys were all absent from school"

c. Strákunum vantaði **öllum** í skóla
boys-DAT bored all-DAT.PL.M in school
"The boys were all bored in school"

d. Strákanna var **allra** getið í radunni
boys-GEN was all-GEN.PL.M mentioned in speech-the
"The boys were all mentioned in the speech"

Now consider the sentences in (6):

(6) a. Strákarnir vonast til að komast **allir** í skóla
boys-NOM hope to get all-NOM.PL.M to school
"The boys hope to all get to school"

b. Strakarnir vonast til aðvanta ekki **alla** **í** skólann
boys-NOM hope to lack not all-ACC.PL.M in school-the
"The boys hope to not all be absent from school"

c. Strakarnir vonast til að leiðast ekki **öllum** í skóla
boys-NOM hope to bore not all-DAT.PL.M in school
"The boys hope to not all be bored in school"

d. Strakarnir vonast til að verða **allra** getið í ræðunni
boys-NOM hope to be all-GEN.PL.M mentioned in speech
"The boys hope to all be mentioned in the speech"

Evaluate how these facts bear on the two theories of control against the background given above.

(7) The position of wh-subjects

We are investigating the structural analysis of the following sentence in English:

(1) Who did the children know?

There are two analytical options:

<u>*Hypothesis 1*</u>: the sentence has a structure in which *who* is subject of TP, *did* is in T, and *the children* is the subject of vP.

<u>*Hypothesis 2*</u>: the sentence has a structure in which *who* is the subject of CP, *did* is in C, and *the children* is the subject of TP.

(i) Draw the two trees on the basis of the two hypotheses.

(ii) Using the following sentence, construct an argument that shows that the structure described in Hypothesis 2 is available.

(2) Who did the children all see?

To answer this question, consider the fact that the following sentence is ill-formed.

(3) *I saw the children all.

(iii) On the basis of the fact that the following sentence is ill-formed, construct an argument showing that the structure described in Hypothesis 1 is not available.

(4) *Who has the children seen?

(8) Sluicing

Consider the following examples of a particular type of fragment in English:

(1) He spoke to someone but I don't know **who**
(2) He bought a couple of books but I don't know **how many**
(3) He left from Los Angeles, but I don't know **when**

The problem here is deciding what the syntactic structure for the boldfaced string is. You are given two hypotheses: your task will be to argue for one of them (and against the other) based on further data below.

Hypothesis A: proposes to treat these in the syntax as a XP selected by the V *know*)
If Hypothesis A turns out to be correct, we will have to (i) complicate lexical entries to allow such strings; (ii) account for what these sentences can or cannot mean in some other component (most likely the semantics or pragmatic component), i.e. the meaning for (1) is "I don't know who he spoke with," and we cannot interpret (1) as meaning, for instance, "I don't know who you are married to".

Hypothesis B: assigns a more complex syntactic structure to the string, and assumes some kind of ellipsis has taken place which leaves the boldfaced element as a remnant. (Under this hypothesis, the interpretation can be directly read off from the string.)

(i) Give the surface tree for the string "I don't know when" under Hypothesis B, filling in the specific details (nodes, etc.).

Data set 1:

Consider the following sentences from English, which contain *each other*:

(4) a. They looked at some pictures of each other but I don't know where.
b. They looked at some pictures of each other, but I don't know exactly which pictures of each other

(ii) State in precise terms why *each other* is allowed in (4a). (You need to refer to the right principle and say exactly how that principle is satisfied in this structure.)

(iii) Sentence (4b) also contains *each other*. Evaluate this example with respect to the two hypotheses above. (Your answer must mention whether or not these data follow from each hypothesis and how. Reason on the basis of tree structures.)

(iv) Based on your answer to (iii), give the full tree structure for *I don't know exactly which pictures of each other* in (4b), and state exactly how *each other* is allowed here.

Data set 2:

The second part of this exercise has data from German, which (like many languages) has a construction that behaves pretty much in the same fashion. (You do not have to provide trees for the German examples.)

German differs from English in that common nouns and their dependents in the DPs carry case morphology. This allows us to see other properties of the construction that are harder to see in English. The following piece of information is relevant: for some verbs, the case of the object depends on the verb. For example, *schmeicheln* "flatter" takes a dative object (DAT), but *loben* "praise" an accusative (and *wissen* "know" takes an accusative (ACC)):

(5) Er will dir schmeicheln
he wants you.DAT flatter
"He want to flatter you"

(6) Er will dich loben
he want you.ACC praise
"He wants to praise you"

(7) Sie wissen die Antword nicht
they know the answer.ACC not
"They don't know the answer."

Consider now the following examples:

(8) er will jedenden schmeicheln, aber sie wissen nicht wem/ *wen/*wer
he wants someone.DAT flatter, but they know not who.DAT/*who.ACC/ *who.NOM
"He wants to flatter someone but they don't know who"

(9) Er will jedenden loben, aber sie wissen nicht *wem/ wen/ *wer
he wants someone.ACC praise but they not know who.DAT/ who.ACC/who.NOM
"He want to praise someone, but they don't know who"

(v) Under Hypothesis A, what case on *who* is expected in (8); and what is the expected case under Hypothesis B? What hypothesis do these facts support? (This does not require a lengthy answer: be succinct and to the point.)

(vi) Do you reach the same conclusions for English and German or not? Sketch all the ingredients of your analysis. (Consider: what complement *know* takes in this environment, and what processes, if any, apply to the syntactic tree.)

11.5.5 Further reading

In this more advanced chapter, we have inserted most further readings in the text at the point where the relevant discussion takes place. We list some particularly important works here again. To read about NPIs and negation, Klima (1964) is an important early work. On focus particles like *only* and c-command, see also McCawley (1998). For very recent wok on the syntactic distribution of polarity items, see Homer (2011b). To learn more about the semantics of association with focus, the reader should start with Rooth (1992). For an exploration of the syntactic distribution of focus particles with important theoretical implications, Kayne (2000), chapter 13. This should only be undertaken by advanced students. On reconstruction, binding, and scope, see Sportiche (2006).

12

Inward Bound: Syntax and Morphology Atoms

In this chapter,[1] we address a number of the empirical and theoretical problems that have come up so far. We now have sufficient theoretical understanding, and sufficiently developed tools, to explore these questions further.

This chapter unfolds as follows. We start with questions about the relation between morphology and syntax, which will lead us to the question of how to treat de-adjectival verbs (verbs derived from adjectives such as $[_A \text{wet}] \rightsquigarrow [_V \text{wet}]$, $[_A \text{dry}] \rightsquigarrow [_V \text{dry}] \ldots$). A closer look at inchoative/causative and anticausative verbs (we will define these terms below), and the distribution of silent morphemes, will lead us to a refinement of VP-internal structure, and to the introduction of so-called "VP shell" structures: some elements that look like simple Vs in fact turn out to be complex syntactic structures, composed of different syntactic heads. The introduction of these VP shell structures will allow us to look at questions and puzzles we have already seen in new ways.

- The fact that certain heads (C, T, D, Num, A ...) take single sister complements, while others (Vs, Ns) can have more than one.
- Conflicting results of constituency tests with these types of verbs or nouns.

The general conclusion is that syntactic atoms can be generally quite small, morpheme-like, and this raises the question of where the boundary lies between morphology and syntax. The discussion of the models of syntax and morphology in Section 6.11.3 compared these models and highlighted how similar they were. Both models have the same basic organization, they employ the same kind of operation of Merge and recursive application of Merge, with atoms defined in terms of categories. Atoms can be bound or free. In morphology, we saw *both* bound morphemes and words as input to Merge. In syntax we have seen something similar: some atoms are bound morphemes, (T(past/present), plural(Num), C+q), others are words. This leaves us without a clear boundary between the two components.

We also saw in Chapter 8 how structure building in both components is driven by the projection principle and locality of selection. Our initial formulation of locality of selection was much more complicated in syntax than in morphology. Recognizing that syntactic strings can have more than

[1]The title of this chapter is inspired by that of a book by Abraham Pais (Pais, 1986) describing the research leading, among other things, towards ever smaller fundamental physical particles.

An Introduction to Syntactic Analysis and Theory, First Edition.
Dominique Sportiche, Hilda Koopman, and Edward Stabler.

one tree structure associated with them allowed us to simplify the definition of locality of selection in syntax: elements entering selectional relations with a head H, H′, or HP must be sisters to H, to H′, or to HP (see Chapter 8, in particular Section 8.5.4).

We will conclude that there is a single model, a single computational engine, driving both syntactic and morphological composition.

Note that this is an intricate topic at the edge of a lot of current research, and with a long history in the field. The intention of what is covered here is to give a general idea of the type of reasoning used to address these problems. It should be construed as a simplified, though well supported, picture of what is understood today.

12.1 The Size of Atoms

As a starting point, note that we no longer have a good definition of what counts as an atom for syntactic computation. We started informally by taking words – that is, free morphemes – to be the smallest pieces that syntactic rules can manipulate. One problem under such a view is that being free or bound seems to be an arbitrary **phonological** property that a morpheme can have. This left us without an explanation of why *these* pieces are the atoms of syntax. Well, perhaps this is the way things are and there is no rhyme or reason to it. However, even if this is arbitrary, the situation is worse as we quickly discovered that syntax can also manipulate smaller pieces than free morphemes, e.g. bound T, or bound C morphemes, as we saw in various head movement processes such as V – T, T – V, T – C or even VP ellipsis. This means that both words and morphemes can be morphological atoms and syntactic atoms. This leaves us without clear boundaries between syntax and morphology from this point of view and raises the question of whether there is a well defined boundary, and if not why not?

One fundamental idea we explore in this chapter is that the atoms of syntax (the engine for the formation of phrases) are the same as the atoms of morphology (the engine for "word" formation), that is no bigger than the smallest pieces with meaning (as e.g. the prefix *pre-* which can mean "before") or function (as the Japanese suffix *-ga* which signals nominative case). The other fundamental idea we discuss is that the reason why the atoms of syntax and morphology are the same is precisely because syntax and morphology use exactly the same engine.

12.2 Head Movement and the Head Movement Constraint

12.2.1 Lexical entry for T: formal features

Consider sentences such as the following:

(1) The towel is wet

What kind of syntactic analysis should we provide for such sentences? In (1), we see that the verb *be* exhibits some complex morphological structure that has led us to postulate V-to-T (recall that *be* raises to T – see Section 8.3.1). Since the subject of the sentence is selected by the adjective, we have also analyzed the sentence as involving raising to subject position of TP from the subject position of the AP small clause headed by *wet*:

(2) The towel [be+ past [~~be~~ [~~the towel~~ wet]]]

Two movements are required: let us try to think about this a bit more precisely. Movement of the subject is required because the adjective *wet* has the following lexical entry coding its category and the fact that it c-selects a theme DP subject (recall we underline the DP to signify this):

wet: A, $\underline{\text{DP}}_{theme}$, meaning ...

Raising of V-to-T is triggered by the fact that the past tense head normally pronounced *-ed* is a bound morpheme which selects a V as its left sister. We first coded these properties as follows (see p. 146 at the end of Section 6.8.3):

ed: T, [+tense], bound, V, $\underline{DP_{nom}/CP}$, meaning: past

Let us examine the lexical entry for *-ed* a bit further. First, recall that it does not list the fact that T c-selects VP. Since Ts always select for VP (in English), this is predictable, and it does not need to be stated as a property of the specific lexical item.

This kind of requirement, c-selecting for VP, is related to what it is to be a T. Roughly speaking, tense resembles a preposition like *before* or *after*: in simple clauses, T orders the time at which some event takes place or some state holds true with respect to the moment of speech. Our sentence states that *the towel being wet* was true before now (the moment of utterance), in the past. The VP that T takes as complement describes what is ordered with respect to now, namely the towel being wet. So the fact that T selects a VP relates to the meaning of T.

Some of the requirements in the lexical entry are **formal** requirements (i.e. requirements related to form), and are sometimes called **formal features**. Formal features code requirements about allowable forms. For example, the requirement that tensed TPs must have a subject is such a formal requirement: it does not seem to relate to the meaning of T. We revised the lexical entry of past tense *-ed* at the beginning of Section 8.5.3 as follows:

-ed: T; [+tense], bound; $epp_{nomDP/CP}$; V; past tense

Another formal requirement is that past tense *-ed* be bound. This is just because this T happens to be an affix, and not all Ts are, so clearly this is a lexical property. What category this T needs to attach to is expressed by c-selection for V. This is also a formal requirement, as there is no meaning reason why T should attach to anything.

One way of satisfying this requirement is by *do*-support under certain circumstances (VP-ellipsis, presence of negation . . .). Such insertion of *do* is strongly reminiscent of what happens with the EPP feature of T which requires a subject: when there is no DP around that could be raised to become a subject, a meaningless expletive pronoun is inserted. Similarly, when there is no "real" verb to attach T to, a meaningless V such as *do* is inserted, which makes *do*-support into a kind of expletive verb insertion.

In order to capture these formal requirements in a uniform way, we need to express the property "bound" in terms of an EPP feature: instead of stating that *-ed* is bound, and c-selects V, we will say T has an EPP feature requiring a V, and notate it as an epp_V feature.

EPP properties: From this point on, we indicate all formal properties in lexical entries as EPP properties. With respect to the property of requiring a nominative subject, instead of underlining it, as was done in Section 6.8.3, we code it as $epp_{DPnom/CP}$, and the bound property selecting for X, as epp_X. This codes both the fact that they are bound morphemes and the fact that they are required to attach to a V.

Here are the old entries for T and *-al*, compared with the new entries:

"old":	-ed	T	[+tense]	bound	V	DP_{nom}	meaning: past
"new":	-ed	T	[+tense]	epp_V		$epp_{DPnom/CP}$	meaning: past
"old":	-al	A	bound	N . . .			
"new":	-al	A	epp_N	. . .			

Practice writing the entries for the atoms of nationalizations using the new format given above. Keep adjusting the lexical entries when necessary.

Note that the lexical entry for *-ed* above states that this T requires a nominative subject. But this property is not a specific property of past T, it is a general property of any +tense T (and the property of requiring a subject is perhaps characteristic of -tense T too). This means that this is part of being a +tense T, thus predictable: it should therefore be removed from the specific lexical entry. But we leave it in as a reminder (there is no harm in this).

12.2.2 Lexical entries and the head movement constraint

Looking at this modified lexical entry for T, we may wonder whether it is accidental that T takes a **VP** complement and the EPP-property requires a **V** (rather than, say, *P*). It is not. There are good reasons why the two require the same category, having to do with the functioning of head movement. Essentially, only the head of the complement of the T is allowed to combine with T by head movement.

Recall that the HMC is subsumed under the **attract closest** condition: two heads can be related by head movement if they are as close as two heads can be in the following technical sense:

(3) Two heads X and Z are as close as can be if X c-commands Z and there is no other head Y "in the middle," that is where (i) Y c-commands Z, and (ii) Y is c-commanded by X, but not vice versa.

In other words, in accordance with the attract closest condition, there is no intervening head between two heads related by head movement. This condition will be met if, for example, one is the head of the complement of the other. Thus, in a structure like this where X, Y, and Z are heads, head movement from Z to X is prohibited due to the presence of the intervening Y:

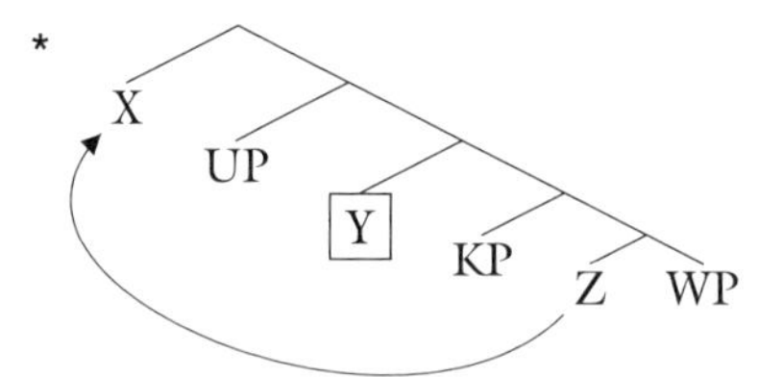

If we take this into account, it is (probably)[2] sufficient to rewrite epp_V as epp_{X^0} (where X^0 is a head). The fact that X^0 must be V in this case would follow from the head movement constraint since nothing but the head of the complement of T can move to T. In the rest of the text, we may continue to identify the category of a selected head, to make lexical entries easier to read, but it is important to remember that this is not necessary.

The effects of the **head movement constraint** were discussed as early as Emonds (1976), Koopman (1984), and Travis (1984), who coined the name of the constraint, and Baker (1988).[3]

[2] *A priori* the EPP feature of a head T could be satisfied by moving the T to a C. Movement, however, is always triggered by the attractor, never by an attractee (the attractor is called the **probe**, and the attractee the **goal**).

[3] Further questions arise: can the head of a phrase in subject position undergo head movement to the closest c-commanding head, and what about the head of an adjunct phrase? (The trees below represent two island configurations (cf. Chapter 10). Can you name these?)

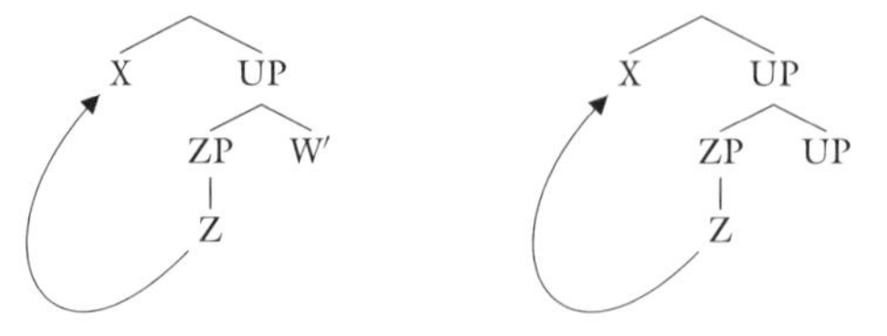

These questions have been explored in Baker (1988) who argues that such cases are not allowed: only the head of a complement can undergo head movement to an immediately c-commanding head.

12.2.3 Possible lexical entries and the head movement constraint

The HMC is in fact relevant to explain a generalization concerning the functioning of T-to-C movement, for example in the yes/no questions discussed in Chapter 6 and Section 8.3.2. This generalization is the following: only verbs that move to T (such as *have* and *be*) can move to C. Thus, non-auxiliary verbs, which do not raise to T, do not raise to C either. We can code this property by stating that this (kind of) C c-select for T. But why couldn't a C c-select for a V? If this were possible, we would expect the following to be possible:

(4) John could be there
(5) Could John ~~could~~ be there?
(6) * Be John could ~~be~~ there?

Instead of forming the yes/no question for the first example as in the second, we would do it as in the third. The fact that such cases do not seem to occur shows that this is not a matter of c-selection. Rather, this type of movement is prohibited in general by the **HMC**. This is the same point as above: a head cannot simultaneously require a complement of a certain category K, and demand as sister a head of category L different from K. In other words, certain imaginable lexical entries cannot surface in well-formed strings, and thus, presumably, cannot exist.

12.3 Causative Affixes: Syntax or Morphology?

12.3.1 Causative verbs: built in the syntax?

Let us consider the following sentences, which all contain the A *wet* and the argument selected by *wet*:

(7) The towel was wet
(8) They will wet the towel
(9) This will wet the towels

In (8) and (9), we see the de-adjectival causative verb *wet*. The selectional properties of the adjective are still present (*the towel* is interpreted as the subject of *wet*); so there must be a silent V in the structure: this V contributes a causative meaning (roughly: *they/this caused the towel to be(come) wet*), and selects an agent/causer *they* or a cause *this* as a subject. This shows that there are two syntactic atoms, an A and a V, each responsible for introducing an argument, and that these two atoms form a complex word that looks like (10). (The silent causative head is given in small caps. The particular spelling CAUS is used to suggest that it contributes a causative meaning, but is not an exact counterpart of the causative verb "cause" (which itself might be a denominal verb).)

(10)

If such words are formed in the syntax in the same way as the past tense of *be*, the properties of this composed element should follow from the lexical entries of its parts and the syntactic principles we have motivated. Just like *be* is formed by head movement to T to form *was*, the verb *wet* is formed by head movement of the adjective *wet* to the silent causative V CAUS.[4] The respective lexical entries of the adjective *wet* and the causative morpheme CAUS would look like this:

wet	A		$\underline{DP}_{theme}$,	meaning: ...
CAUS	V	epp_A	$\underline{DP/CP}_{agent/cause}$, AP	meaning: "cause to be/come"

These items merge in a tree in the normal fashion yielding:

(11)

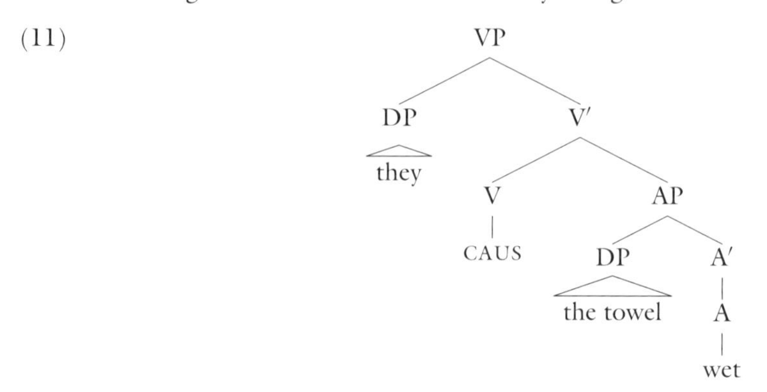

In addition, the epp_A property of CAUS will have to be satisfied. There are two ways in which this could in principle be achieved: by moving A to CAUS (similar to T-to-C, or V-to-T movement, i.e. movement of a head to the closest c-commanding head), or by moving CAUS to A (similar to affix hopping). A-to-CAUS movement immediately allows us to account for the fact that the argument of the A follows the A + combination:

(12)

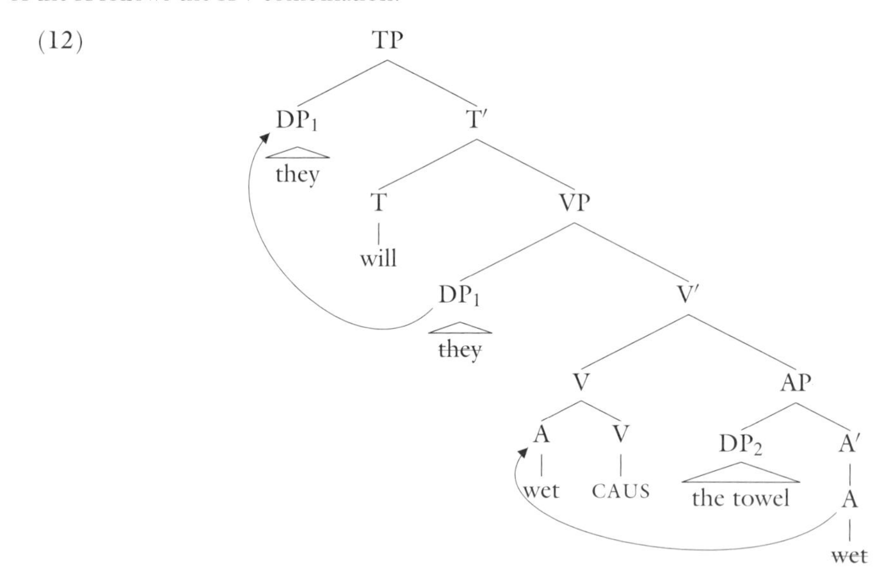

Attract closest (see Section 10.6.2) will lead to the fact that the agent/causer DP_1 moves to [Spec,TP] and not DP_2. This is of course because the agent is closest to T in terms of c-command. If the verb further needs to combine with T (to form the past tense *wetted*), we would get the following substructure after affix hopping (T-to-V):

[4] An even closer analogy is found with verbs like *hit* that do not change their pronunciation when they are suffixed with the past tense head. Thus, the pair of verbs *wet/shorten* is analogous to the pair of past tense forms *hit/danced*.

(13)

12.3.2 Causative verbs: built in the morphology?

Another analysis is possible that is a combination of syntax and morphology: the verb *wet* is projected *as is* in the syntax; word formation (or word regularities) are handled presyntactically in a separate morphological component. Because of this account, forms like *wet* are generally referred to as **lexical causatives**.

Under this option, the verb *wet* is a syntactic atom, and it is the task of the morphological module to form it from the adjective A and the silent causative V CAUS. This would yield the following syntactic structure:

(14)

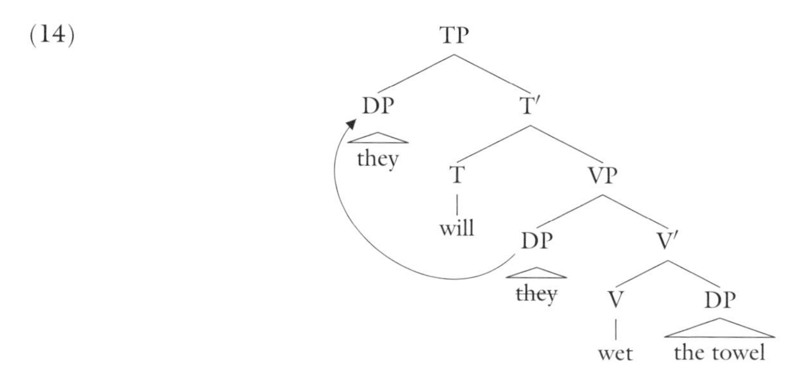

The morphological entries of the two morphemes composing the verb would look approximately as follows:

(15) CAUS: V, bound[5], $\underline{DP}_{agent}$, AP, meaning: "cause to be(come)"
(16) wet: A, $\underline{DP}_{theme}$ meaning: ...

From the point of view of syntactic merging, the verb behaves much like any other verb and it must have a lexical entry of the following form:

(17) wet: V, $\underline{DP}_{agent,cause}$, DP_{theme}, meaning: "make wet"

But this is not all. These three lexical entries are not accidentally related. There must also be some rule that tells us what the relation is between the adjective *wet* and the CAUS morpheme, and the lexical entry for the verb *wet*.

Such a rule could, for example, say that the head CAUS preserves its properties (as we would expect since it is the head of complex verb). But it should also say that the selectional properties of the non-head (the A *wet*) become properties of the complex verb in some modified form: the subject selected by the adjective *wet* as a theme subject becomes the object of the verb *wet*, and not its subject or its indirect object.

[5] This is a morphological entry so there is no EPP feature, but it would be equivalent to code the bound property of morphological atoms in EPP terms, here: epp_A.

If this is the way to go, this would raise theoretical questions. If there are rules relating lexical entries in this way, what form are they allowed to take? Can two lexical entries combine in any way we like, combining properties arbitrarily? Surely not. What then are the limitations? And why?

12.3.3 How to decide between these analyses?

How to determine which analysis to pursue? There are clear advantages to the syntactic treatment. One is that it is simpler since there is no need for a lexical entry for the verb *wet*. The verb *wet* is actually a piece of syntactic structure created by A-to-V. The other is that there is no need for any rule telling us how the **three** lexical entries for the verb *wet*, the adjective *wet*, and the silent verb CAUS are related. It all falls out of the way (head) movement and syntactic merging works. But third, the only way to prevent the generation of the de-adjectival verb by syntactic means is to explicitly prohibit CAUS from being a syntactic atom. Convincing reasons must be provided to do this. Later in this chapter (Section 12.6) we will see one further empirical argument in favor of the syntactic account, based on facts that cannot be easily captured under the morphological option: syntactic projections can have phrasal adjuncts. Indeed if there are several syntactic projections, each one should be able to be independently modified, and we might expect meaning differences depending on which projection is modified.

At a more general level, the syntactic account is a step in the direction toward making sense of the surprising similarity between the two systems. While all this is not a guarantee that it is the correct account, it looks like the null hypothesis, the hypothesis we can make in the absence of any evidence to the contrary. Existing principles account for these data, and there is no need to adopt any new mechanisms or rules. This is why we will adopt it.

12.3.4 Consequences

If this conclusion – namely that morpheme or word merging is done by syntactic merging – can be shown to be fully general, it would have far-reaching consequences. It would mean that morphemes, whether they are bound or not, are syntactic atoms, entering into tree structure, satisfying X-bar theory, etc. Their lexical properties are locally satisfied within the XP they project, in accordance with the principle of locality of selection, and the resulting morphologically complex items are put together by the general available syntactic means such as Merging (putting elements together to form a constituent) and Moving (head movement or other kinds of movement). Thus when we observe a piece of complex morphological structure, what we are seeing is the output of the syntactic structure-building algorithm. We return to what this implies for our model of morphology and syntax in Section 12.9.

This idea that syntax and morphology belong together has been present for a long time, in various forms and guises. In recent years, the framework of Distributed Morphology, developed by Morris Halle (left) and Alec Marantz (right) and many others, argues for the conception just described: aside from questions of phonological realization and postsyntactic morphological rules, morphological composition is just syntactic composition.

12.4 VP Shells

Silent CAUS brings up further questions, which we turn to next.

- CAUS is a verb, and verbs select many different types of complements. Are there categories besides As that can combine with CAUS? Can CAUS select Vs? What do we expect such a case to look like? We turn to this question in the next section.
- CAUS has been seen to combine with some intransitive A. Can it combine with any type of A? If not, what can we conclude from this failure (see Section 12.4.3)?
- English has a silent CAUS, but also pronounced causatives *make, let, have, get*. Is silent CAUS exactly like these pronounced causatives? If not, what are the differences?
- How general are VP shells? We turn to the verb *give* and *put* and the problem of ternary branching in Section 12.5. This is also related to the question of what CAUS can combine with.

12.4.1 Anticausative verbs

Let us next look at the question of whether CAUS can combine with other categories besides As. If it does, what we can expect to find?

Since CAUS is bound and silent, we should see another lexical category X superficially looking like a verb, yielding a causative meaning, i.e. with the subject interpreted as the agent/causer, and the object as an argument of X undergoing a change of state (as in *this wet the towels*). This lexical category X should also be able to occur independently when we substract CAUS, as X projects its own syntactic phrase, *the towels were wet*. In the latter case, the surface subject of X is a selected argument of X.

More concretely, here is what we expect if X is V:

(18) DP_1 V-ed DP_2 *meaning this* CAUSE*-ed DP to (become) V*
DP_2 V-ed *meaning: DP was/became V*

There is a large class of verbs in English that exhibits this pattern of alternations. Verbs like *burn, open, close, sink, melt,* etc. can occur in two environments, without any change in the verbal form.

(19) a. The wood burned (inchoative/anticausative)
b. Sam burned the wood (causative verb)
c. The ice melted
d. The sun melted the ice
e. John melted the ice
f. He melted the ice
g. The glass broke
h. Someone broke a glass
i. The water boiled
j. I boiled the water

These verbs describe a change of state undergone by some object, for example the glass that becomes broken; in their intransitive usages, that is when they occur without a direct object, these verbs are often called **inchoative** verbs. In their transitive use, when they occur with a direct object, they are called causative verbs, here we see the effects of CAUS in the interpretation and in the selection of the subject. The alternation is referred to as the causative/inchoative alternation.

The intransitive forms are also often referred to as **anticausative** verbs, a descriptive term we adopt here for expository reasons.[6]

The interpretation of the DPs *the wood/the ice/the glass* remains constant in these alternations. They are interpreted as referring to an object undergoing a change of state by burning or melting or breaking, i.e. as themes. There is a clear regularity here. How should this alternation be analyzed?

> The full picture of this problem is more complicated than we will sketch out here: some of our basic conclusions would not be affected if we took it into account. See Levin and Rappaport Hovav (1995) and references cited therein for extensive discussion.

The analysis for causative *wet* can be directly extended, if we assume that CAUS can have either an epp_A feature *or* an epp_V feature.

wet	A	$\underline{DP}_{theme}$,	meaning: "be(come) wet"
burn	V	$\underline{DP}_{theme}$	meaning: "become burned"[7]
CAUS	v	epp_V, $\underline{DP}_{agent/cause}$ VP	meaning: "cause to be/come V"

This will yield the following syntactic trees.

(20)

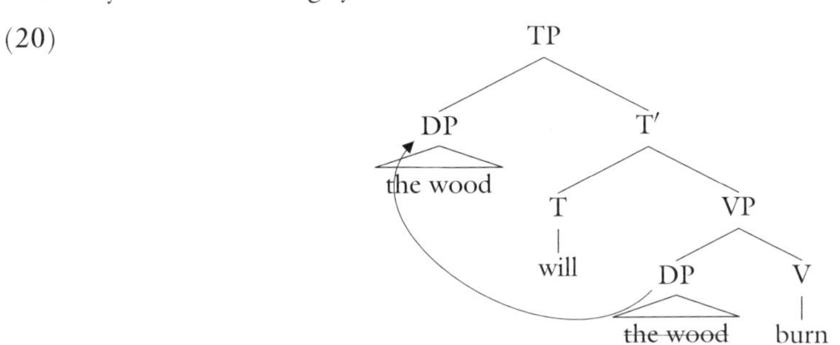

In this tree, *the wood* moves to [Spec,TP], because it is the closest DP to T.

(21) (VP shell)

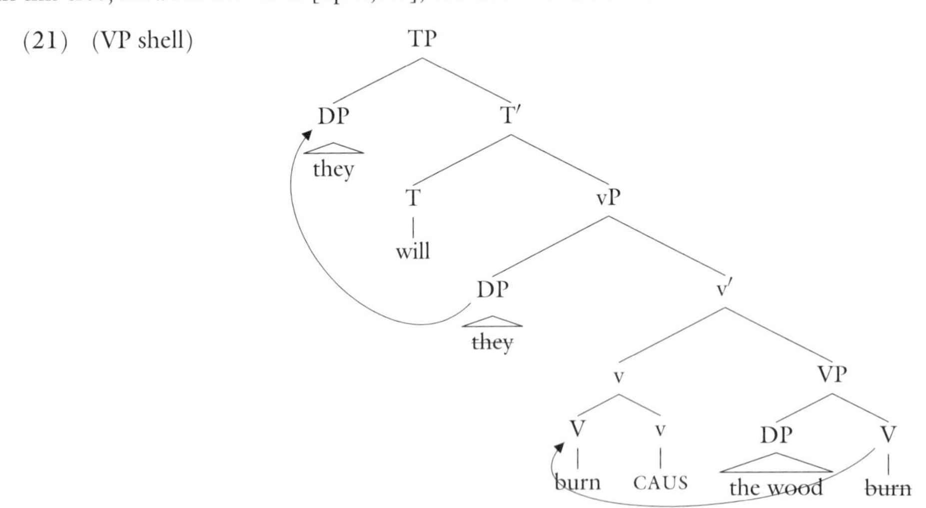

[6]At issue here is whether the intransitive forms are derived from transitive bases by adding an "anticausative," or whether the transitives are formed from intransitive bases by adding a causative. See also the framed box on at the end of Section 12.4.3, "anticausative or inchoative/causative."

[7]The second line says somewhat arbitrarily that the theme is selected by "big" V as a subject. Since it is the only element that is selected, there is in fact no difference between complements and specifiers.

In this tree, *they* will move to [Spec,TP], because it is the closest to T. Now note that the causative version has an extra layer of structure on top of the VP structure. This extra layer of structure is the VP headed by the CAUS V, referred to as "little v" for convenience.

Because what looks like a single verb (causative *burn*) seems to be associated simultaneously with two VPs, this type of structure is said to have a **VP shell** structure, with a causative *v* shell combining with an (inchoative) VP.

12.4.2 The optional agent selection account

In order to account for the data in (19), we could also pursue an alternative account in which anticausative verbs would optionally select for an agent. There would be a single VP, and hence no shell structure. We would indicate this optional selection by putting parentheses around the first part:

(22) burn: V, ($\underline{DP}_{agent}$) DP_{theme}

This lexical entry implies that these verbs can appear in the two types of VPs, given X-bar theory and the principle of locality of selection, with the theme argument always projected as the complement of V:

(23) (to be revised)

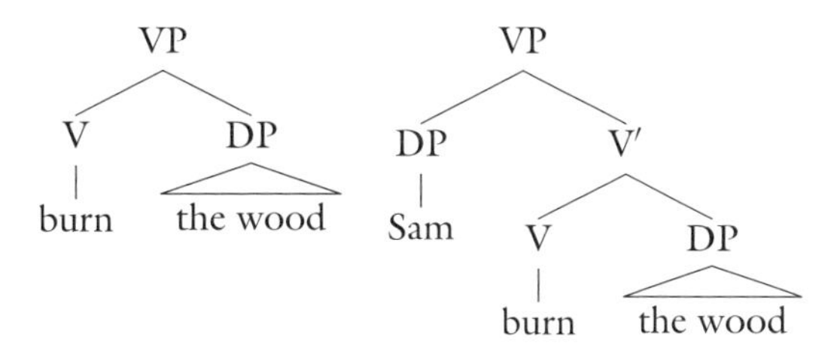

But this account of the causative/anticausative alternation in terms of the presence of an optional agent raises a problem: what should we put down as meaning for the lexical entry of *burn*? The difficulty is that in the presence of an agent "the causative version" the verb means "cause the burning of," while in the absence of an agent – the anticausative version – the verb means "reach a state of burnedness" without implying the presence of an agent. This difference means that we are really dealing with two different verbs. We have encountered optional elements in lexical entries. For example, the verb *eat* allows but does not require a direct object theme DP. We represent this by putting this DP in parentheses in its lexical entry. This, however, does not mean that the thematic role *theme* disappears. It just means that there is no DP in the syntax expressing this thematic role, this "theta role" – and in fact *John ate* entails that John ate something: in other words the theta role is not optional. The case of *burn* just discussed is different in this respect, and rather exceptional if the theta role Agent were optional. For example, we could code this by postulating two lexical entries:

(24) a. $burn_1$: V, DP_{theme}, means "reach a state of 'burnedness' "
b. $burn_2$: V, DP_{agent}, DP theme, means "cause the burning of theme"

But we are back to the same kind of problems we had with the pair $[_A$ *wet*$]/[_V$ *wet*$]$: what possible relations are there between lexical entries? What are the syntactic atoms? . . . It is clear that the VP shell analysis does not meet with these problems.

12.4.3 Silent CAUS and pronounced causatives

So far, we have seen that the silent causative CAUS can either have an A or a V EPP feature.

(25) I clean-CAUS [$_{AP}$ the table ~~clean~~]
(26) I wet-CAUS [$_{AP}$ the towel ~~wet~~]

In this respect, it looks very much like the overt causative verb *make*, which also takes AP or VP complements, [8]

(27) I made [$_{AP}$ the table clean]
(28) I made [$_{AP}$ the towel wet]

(29) a. They made [$_{VP}$ the wood burn]
b. They made [$_{VP}$ John laugh]
c. Mary made [$_{VP}$ John burn the wood]

And we just saw that CAUS can also combine with a verb. We showed that this alternation can receive a very simple syntactic treatment if we suppose that, in addition to allowing AP complements, the little v CAUS also allows VP complements.

But note now that the overt causative *make* and silent little v CAUS do not behave exactly in the same way. CAUS is much more "picky" regarding the kind of APs or VPs that it allows as complements:

(30) a. I made [$_{AP}$ John happy]
b. * I [[happy] CAUS]ed] [$_{AP}$ John ~~happy~~]
(31) a. I made [$_{AP}$ the towel wet]
b. I [[wet CAUS] ed] [$_{AP}$ the towel ~~wet~~]
(32) a. They made [$_{VP}$ the wood burn]
b. They [[burn CAUS] ed] [$_{VP}$ the wood ~~burn~~]
(33) a. They made [$_{VP}$ John laugh]
b. * They [[laugh CAUS]ed] [$_{VP}$ John ~~laugh~~]
(34) a. Mary made [$_{VP}$ John burn the wood]
b. * Mary [[burn CAUS] ed] John ~~burn~~ the wood[9]

Acquisition: Interestingly, children acquiring English seem to go through a phase where they produce forms like "giggle me!" (make me giggle), "laugh me!" (make me laugh), which are impossible in the adult grammar, and hence do not occur in the input (incidentally showing that children cannot be argued to simply parrot the input). This raises intriguing questions about the form of the child's grammar (clearly the child at this stage could be argued to have a silent causative head) and how the child gets to the adult grammar where the distribution of this silent causative head is much more restricted, since such forms are no longer possible. The difference may either lie in how the child analyzes the silent causative, or in how verbs like *giggle* are analyzed. This is still an open research question.

As (30) shows, identifying v CAUS as an exact but silent equivalent of *make* overgeneralizes: it predicts that too many forms are possible. What can we conclude from this? What we see is that

[8] Other overt causative verbs – *let, have, cause, get* – each have slightly different properties with regard to the range of selected complements.
[9] For some people this sentence is fine, but with the meaning "they burned some wood **for** John".

there are differences between causatives, and we want to understand what these differences are, and whether they are predictable or not. What we cannot conclude, though, is that this proves that the syntactic account to causative/inchoative alternations is wrong. It looks like silent CAUS is much pickier about its complement than *make*. One way of encoding this is by modifying the lexical entry for CAUS accordingly, first to indicate that it can either combine with an A or a V, second to indicate that it selects a VP or an AP complement of a certain (semantic) kind only (e.g. it must indicate change of state of a particular kind) – see for example Levin and Rappaport Hovav (1995) and Ramchand (2008).

(35) CAUS: V, $epp_{A/V}$, $\underline{DP}_{agent/causer,}$ $\underline{cause}$, AP/VP with certain semantic properties . . .

> **Which verbs alternate?** Just as certain verbs lack a causative counterpart, certain transitive verbs lack an "anticausative" counterpart. The causative/anticausative alternation seems to be typical of change of state verbs, but not, for example, of other types of transitive verbs. For example:
>
> (36) a. They ate the rice
> b. * The rice ate
> *(with the rice interpreted as theme, meaning something like the rice got into an eaten state)*
> c. I found 10 dollars
> d. * 10 dollars found *(with 10 dollars being interpreted as the theme)*
>
> We would of course like to understand why this is so. One possibility might be that such verbs do not contain a silent verb CAUS, but are built up with a different little v, namely silent verb DO.

12.4.4 Derivation direction

Anticausative or causative/inchoative? The terminology here reflects the basic direction of the derivation: is the anticausative verb *burn/melt* (*the wood burned, the ice melted*) derived from the causative form (*the fire burned the wood*), or is the causative form derived from the inchoative one, or are both options attested but for different verbs? It is not easy to answer this question on general grounds and on the basis of English alone as the morphology is silent. However, languages with non-silent anticausative and causative morphology can yield some insight into these question. Typological and comparative studies can be particularly useful (see e.g. Nichols and Bickel (2005), Haspelmath (1993), and Haspelmath et al. (2005)) in such cases. Here are some data that bear on this issue from Wolof, a West-Atlantic, spoken in Senegal. With change of state predicates, Wolof does not have a silent causative, but a pronounced one *-al*; it also does not have a silent anticausative morpheme, but again a pronounced one *-(k)u* (often called "middle" voice). Many many verbs are visibly derived from the inchoative V by adding causative v *-al*:

bax	"boil(inchoat)"	bax-al	"boil(caus)"
wow	"dry(inchoat)"	wow-al	"dry(caus)"
seey	"melt(inchoat)"	seey-al	"melt(caus)"
fees	"fill(inchoat)"	fees-al	"fill(caus)".

With these predicates, the V is basic, and a causative VP shell is added to form the causative form. A few verbs, however, are visibly derived from the transitive base, by adding a middle voice *-u* (note that the forms for "open" are derived from "close" by adding a "reversive" morpheme: lit. "unclose"):

yaq(tr.)/yaq-u "break"
ub/ub-u "close"
ubbi/ubbi-ku "open".

This last pattern is frequent in many languages (Romance, Slavic, etc.) Here are some examples from French (F) and Spanish (S):

(37) le vent a cassé la branche (F)
the wind has broken the branch

(38) la branche s'est cassée (F)
the branch SE.is broken
"the branch broke"

(39) la porte s'est ouverte
the door SE.is opened
"the door opened"

(40) El vidrio se quebró (S)
the glass SE shattered
"The glass shattered"

(41) Se está hundiendo el barco (S)
SE be sinking the boat
"The boat is sinking"

12.4.5 The English suffixes *-ify*, *-en*

We briefly turn to derived change of state verbs – that is, verbs that morphologically show that they are composed of subparts. For example, there are change of state verbs that are themselves derived from adjectives – or perhaps nouns – (as *solidify*, *liquefy*). These verbs behave like anticausatives and like causatives.

(42) a. The oil is solid
b. The oil solidified (the oil became solid)
c. The cold solidified the oil (the cold made the oil (become) solid)

First we need to explain how the adjective *solid* and the verb *solidify* meaning "to become solid" are related. One way (although not the only way) this could be done is as follows: we can understand -*ify* as basically forming a change of state verb from an AP, which introduces the argument undergoing change:

(43) *ify*: V, epp$_{A/N}$, AP/NP, means "become"

A historical note: The analysis for morphologically complex words we have presented has a long and controversial history. Few issues have lead to more divisions in the field. Some scholars, like the philosopher Jerry Fodor for example, have argued, on various grounds, that some such analyses are erroneous (Fodor and Lepore, 1999). The arguments often compare the morphological forms to fully sentential forms, and argue that they are not exactly parallel in meaning and distribution. In the current type of analyses, the structure of a CP contains (many) more atoms than VP shells do: differences in meaning and distribution should follow from these independent syntactic differences. Note also that such arguments made a lot of sense given the theoretical understanding at the time, when syntactic structures were quite shallow. It took much further theoretical development, and the development of much more sophisticated probing tools to come to the current analysis that what looks like a simple verb in fact hides a more complex syntactic structure. This issue has also played a decisive role in the history of the field: so called "generative semanticists" in the 1960s essentially proposed analyses of the type given above. The theory at that point lacked our current understanding of the properties of phrase structure, the properties of movement, binding, and the different c-command tests. Such analyses were abandoned by many in favor of "lexicalist" theories that hold that the internal structure of words is a question of morphology or the lexicon, not of syntax. Since the mid 1980s, some basic insights from generative semantics have been incorporated in syntactic theories and certain conclusions are now mainstream (little v, and more generally the syntactical decomposition of apparently simple lexical items into several syntactic atoms). Thus the general notion that "words" are the atoms of syntactic structures, and the status of "morphology" in the overall architecture of the grammar still remains a highly controversial issue, often one which is not really subject to open debate or scrutiny. Finally, note that current generative frameworks, such as some versions of Chomsky's minimalist framework (Fodor and Lepore, 1999), have a mix of lexicalist and decompositional accounts. Some minimalist theories hold that words are listed in the mental lexicon with a complex set of syntactic features. It is these features that drive the syntactic derivation so that transitive *melt* will project a vP and a VP. Other strands of minimalism, such as the "cartographic" approaches of Cinque (1999) and Rizzi (1997), (2002), and Kayne's "antisymmetry" approach (1994), assume partly or fully decompositional approaches to syntax and morphology and claim that these are in fact necessary when one wants to understand language variation. For those interested in the morpho-syntactic side, see amongst others Baker (1988), Julien (2002), Hale and Keyser (2002), Pylkkänen (2002), Pylkkänen (2008), Di Sciullo and Williams (1987), Marantz (1997), Embick (2010), and Koopman and Szabolcsi (2000).

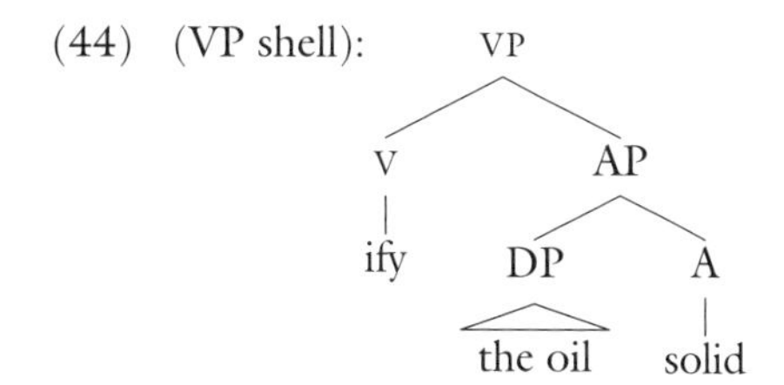

Embedding this form under T yields (42b). Thus *-ify* is basically the bound equivalent of a raising to subject predicate, like *seem* or *become* (*the oil seems solid; the oil became solid*). The verb *-ify* creates a change of state V ("become solid") and behaves like the anticausative *burn*. In particular, this VP can now be selected for by the silent V CAUS which selects for VP yielding a structured VP shell with three layers (two VPs and one AP):

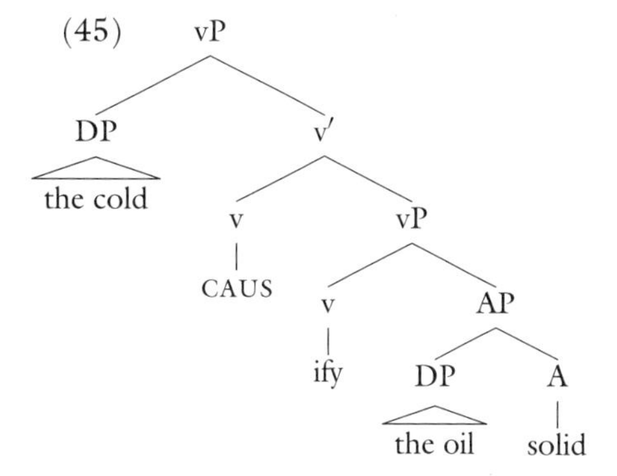

As this account uses general principles and mechanisms that are independently needed, these analyses look extremely appealing and revealing of the systematic nature of these at first glance quite surprising patterns.

This kind of structure is also found with verbs showing no morphology at all. Thus, parallel to *liquid*, *liquify*, *liquify*$_{caus}$, or *white*, *whiten*$_{V}$, *whiten*$_{caus}$, we have triplets such as *open*$_{A}$, *open*$_{V}$, *open*$_{cause}$, or *dry*$_{A}$, *dry*$_{V}$, *dry*$_{cause}$:

(46) a. This thing is liquid/white/open/dry
b. This thing liquified/whitened/opened/dried
c. She liquified/whitened/opened/dried this thing

Thus for the causative verb *dry*, we would have to postulate the following structure:

(47)

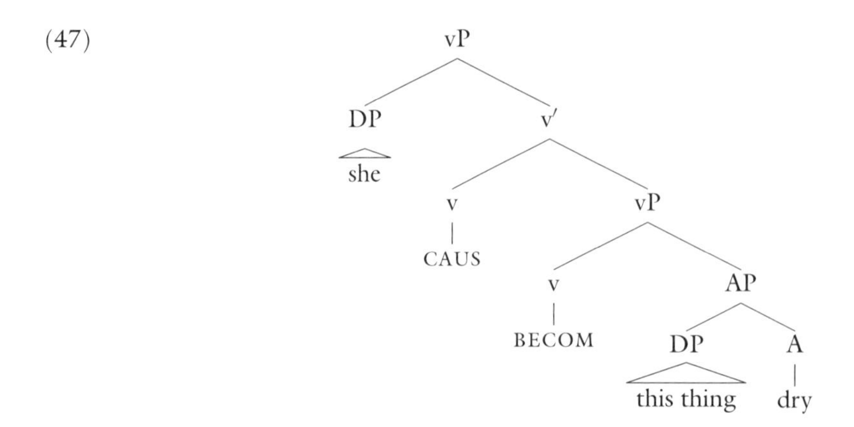

In which there are two silent "little" v's: CAUS and BECOM (the silent counterpart of *-ify*). Since both CAUS and BECOM are bound morphemes, the A *dry* will have to raise to BECOM and the resulting complex raise to CAUS yielding:

(48)

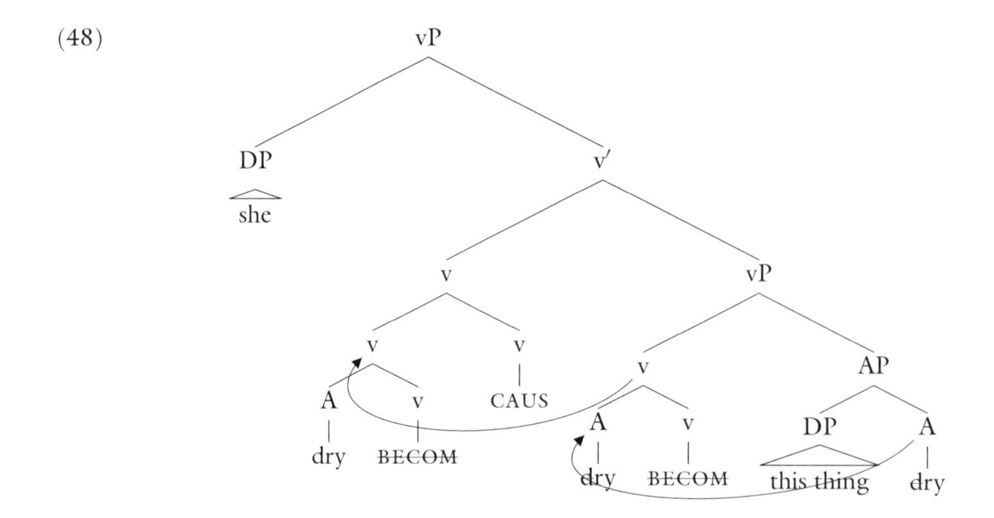

Of course, the next thing we want to do is find some independent evidence for this particular constituent structure. Can we probe these structures with the diagnostic tools that we have at our disposal? We will see that a positive answer can be given to such a question.

Finally, taking *-ify, en* to be overt versions of BECOM, does not mean that they should have all the same properties. There may be differences (in fact there are some) but core properties are similar.[10]

[10]One of them is that the silent version does not seem to affix to open scale adjectives such as *rich, wet*, that is, adjectives for which there is no maximum (it is always possible to be richer than someone else) as opposed to adjectives such as *empty, dry* (when something is completely empty or dry, it can't be emptier or drier).

12.4.6 Generalized VP shells

The conclusions we have reached can be straightforwardly extended to cases that are superficially more opaque. Recall, for example, how we treat an irregular past tense like *was* for the verb *be*, or *went* for the verb *go*. These forms have the usual internal structure derived by head movement:

(50)

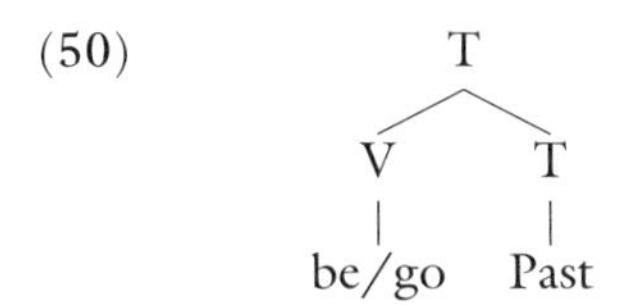

A special pronunciation rule "spells out"/"phonologizes" the abstract verbal form *go+past* as *went* and *be+past* as *was*.[11] In effect just like (semantic) idioms (e.g. *kick the bucket*) have a meaning not computable from their parts by regular rules, these are phonological idioms whose pronunciation cannot be computed from their parts by regular rules.

> **VP-internal movement?** Let us examine the following substructure of (47):
>
> (49)
>
> 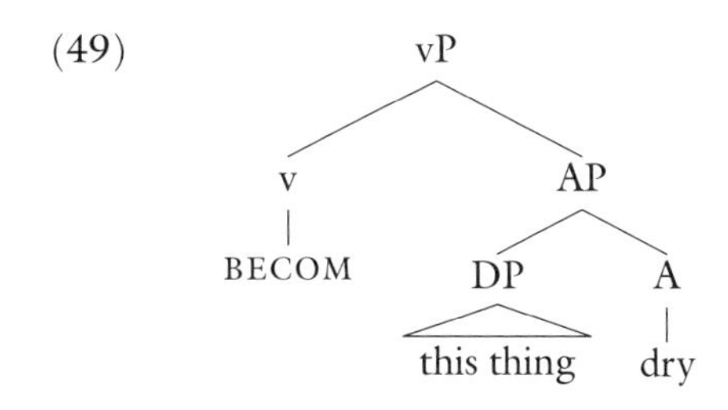
>
>
> This looks very much like the substructure of a raising to subject structure such as *this thing became t dry* since the verb *become* is a raising verb. Is there raising to subject in (47)? It is conceivable and this would mean that there is a bit more structure between the VP headed by CAUS and the VP headed by BECOM. One reason why raising may be happening is Case: the DP *this thing* must have its accusative case licensed, and the licenser is CAUS (it is the portion of the structure that makes the whole verbal complex a transitive verb – see Burzio's generalization at the end of this section). What is at stake here is whether Case can be licensed at a distance or not. If not, raising of the DP must take place. We leave this question open here.

Consider now the case of a verb like *kill*. *Kill* is a transitive verb, which from the point of view of meaning can be thought of as the causative version of the verb *die* (itself de-adjectival on the adjective *dead*) that is as "cause to become dead." Given the previous discussion, there is a straightforward way to think of the syntax of a VP headed by *kill*, such as *someone kill the fly*, as composed of abstract forms as follows:

(51)

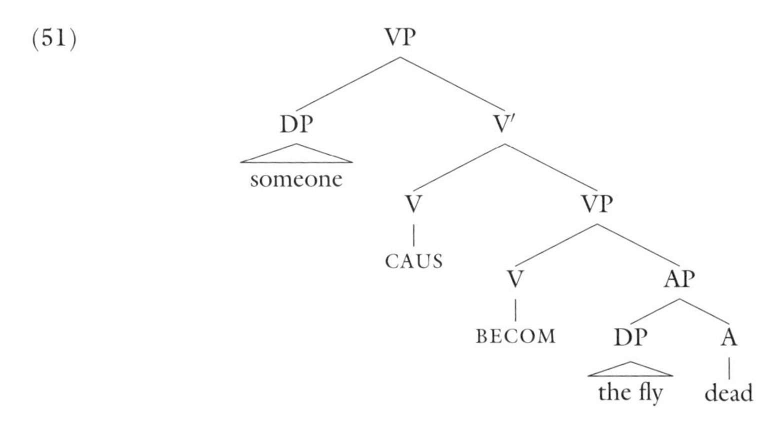

Each of these parts are syntactic atoms, which select a complement, an argument, and project a XP. Head movement forms the complex anticausative V *dead +becom*, which is a phonological idiom,

[11] For example, the structure [[GO] past] is looked up in the phonological dictionary, where it is associated with *went*.

pronounced *die* in English (head movement also forms the complex *[[dead* +BECOM*]*+ CAUS*]* which is idiomatically pronounced *kill* in English).

(52)

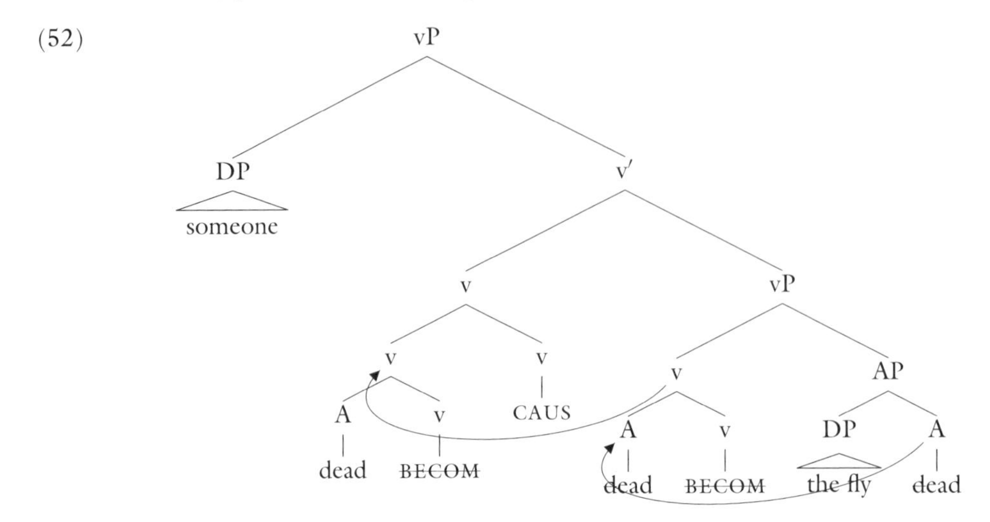

Note that if this is what *kill* means we would expect that in some languages these atoms show up, and this is the case: in the Polynesian language Tongan, for example *tā-mate-ʾi*, *tā* is a causative, and *mate* means *die* (*ʾi* is related to the accusative case). Should all transitive verbs be syntactically decomposed into different units, each representing a particular meaning component, even when these verbs do not have a morphologically complex structure or show alternations? While this is a likely analysis, in particular for verbs like *kill*, it is difficult to determine exactly what the pieces of the decomposition should be. For example, activity verbs like *eat* or *work* seem to involve a V like *do*. Also it has to be done in such a way that we can explain why *eat* does not have an optional agent, as we saw earlier.

Here we will gloss over these difficulties and use VP shells for all transitive structures that have an agent, cause, or experiencer as subject, there are two Vs, i.e. two VP projections. This in fact is the standard current analysis for the syntactic structure of active transitive verbs, not only because of the semantic properties of verbs, but also because it allows an understanding of how to characterize the property that certain verbs have of assigning accusative case, which, current research suggests, crucially depends on the presence of a v (DO, CAUSE, TAKE, etc.). The latter generalization is known as Burzio's Generalization, see Burzio (1986). These are also the verbs that by and large can occur in the passive construction in English.

John ate an apple	An apple was eaten (by John)
Many people like this movie	This movie is liked (by many people)
I burned the papers	The papers were burned (by me)
Mary considered John smart	John was considered smart by Mary

This said, to simplify trees, we will not always represent the full VP shell structures. When the presence of a VP shell is not relevant, we sometimes will use "old-style" abbreviated trees.

12.5 Ternary Branching

We have concluded that it is likely that there may not be an independent morphological component. If this is the case, all composition, all constituent formation, all structure building – which we call Merging – is syntactic. The fact that we found many similarities between the functioning of the two components, such as the following, is not surprising:

Similarities: Same atom types (morphemes)
Merge operation
Obey the projection principle
Obey locality of selection (in the same way)[12]

However, if this approach is correct, we need to explain away the apparent differences between syntax and morphology. This is a large project and we are not in a position to undertake it fully. However, we can show that some differences can be accounted for, or can be derived from other properties.

One apparent difference is the fact that morphological trees seem to be strictly binary while syntactic trees are not. More specifically, non-binary branching trees appear to be found in the complement structure of verbs (and nouns), but not in the complement structure of C, or T, or Num for example. Certain classes of verbs, like *put* or *give* have been assumed to have the following structure:

(53)

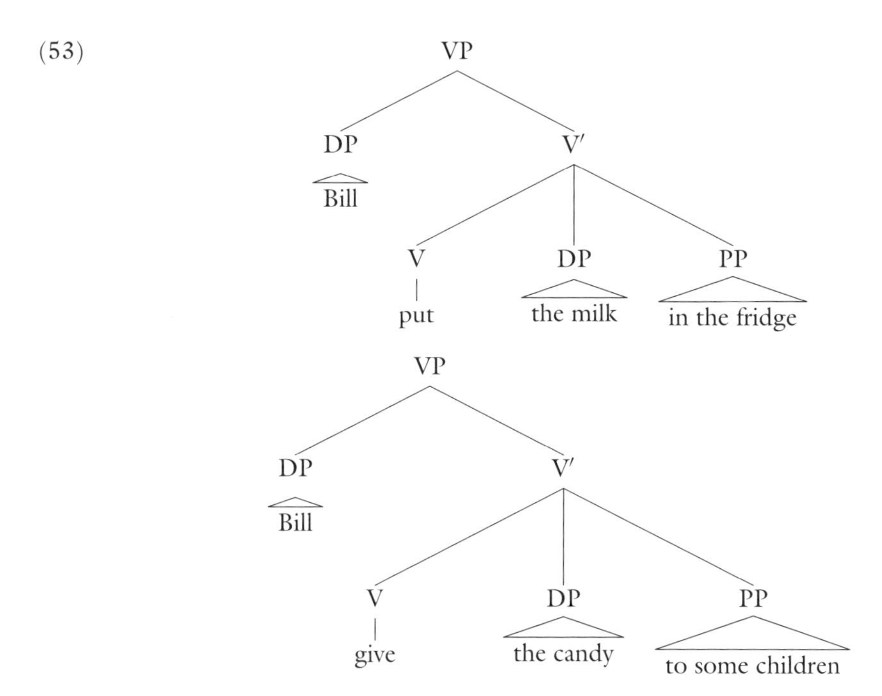

For *put*, for example, locality of selection forces *Bill* to be a sister to V′, and the DP *the milk* and the locative PP to be sisters to V, as they are both selected as complements by *put*.

This constituent structure gets further support from some of our constituency tests, but not by all. Let's contrast the two following strings which have different constituent structures:

(54) a. You put [Bill's drawing] [on the fridge]
b. I like [Bill'[s [drawing [on the fridge]]]]

As expected, these behave differently with respect to wh-question formation: the string *Bill's drawing on the fridge* fails to undergo wh-movement in (54a), but not in the context in (54b):

[12]This similarity can be hidden by the notation we used. In syntax we use X, X′, and XP, while in morphology we say that X is the head of a compound like [Y X] without calling this XP. We could use exactly the same notation for both morphology and syntax.

(55) a. Whose drawing did you put ~~whose drawing~~ on the fridge
b. *Whose drawing on the fridge did you put ~~whose drawing on the fridge~~?
c. Whose drawing on the fridge do you like ~~whose drawing on the fridge~~?

But if we look at coordination, we encounter an apparent problem. If the surface constituency is indeed as in (53), we expect that the string *the milk in the fridge/Bill's drawing on the fridge* will not behave as a constituent. The coordination test therefore is expected to fail yet it does not: as the following examples show such examples are acceptable.

(56) Sarah put *the potatoes in the pantry* and *the milk in the fridge*
Sophie gave *potatoes to the children* and *potato skins to the pigs*
They put [*Bill's drawing on the fridge* and *Mary's painting on the shelf*]

Some explanation must be found for (56). Those examples suggest the following (surface) constituent structure for the VP:

(57)

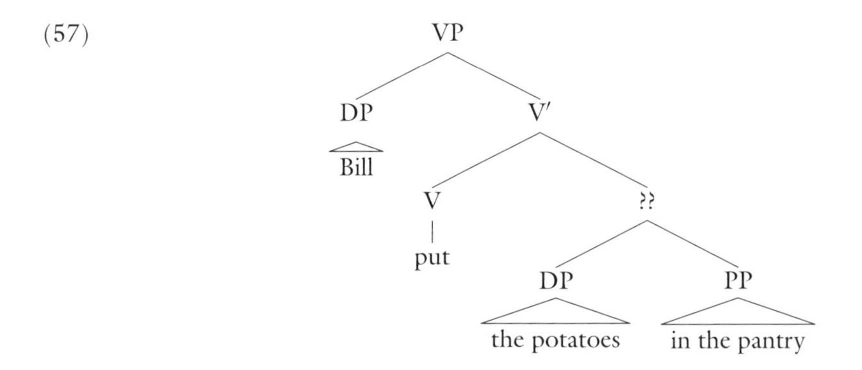

Before we proceed, let us consider a reasonable alternative: if the verb *put* had moved out of the VP, the ?? constituent could simply be a V′ with a V trace in it. Of course, this would require modifying our assumptions about what can occur between T and VP (to provide an intermediate position to which V could move), something independently plausible. Yet, there are good reasons why this would be insufficient. First, the same coordination facts hold in small clauses which seem not to contain the kind of intermediate structure to allow for this verb raising):

(58) John saw Sarah put *the potatoes in the pantry* and *the milk in the fridge*
(59) I heard Sophie give *potatoes to the children* and *potato skins to the pigs*
(60) Let them put [*Bill's drawing on the fridge* and *Mary's painting on the shelf*]

Second, if there was such a verb movement, we should expect the verb to appear separated from its direct object by a left VP adjunct. This is not possible (with light direct objects to control for the effects of **heavy constituent shift**):

(61) * Sarah had put slowly milk in the fridge

Third, much additional evidence for the tree geometry in (57) and against that shown in (53) will be provided below.

Such a structure raises many questions regarding many of our assumptions.

- What is the our mysterious ?? constituent? What is its head?
- If the verb *put* does select two complements, how would locality of selection be satisfied in this particular structure?

This problem is not confined to a single verb, it is in fact fully general. It is found with any verb that selects more than one complement. Of particular interest here are so-called double object constructions because they involve verbs that seem to take two DP complements. These will allow us to further probe structures in particularly enlightening ways. We can derive general consequences from the behavior of such constructions that can be applied to the *put* case and other cases.

(62) John gave Mary a book
(63) Sue sent Bill the new package

A reasonable VP structure for such a construction would look like this:

(64)

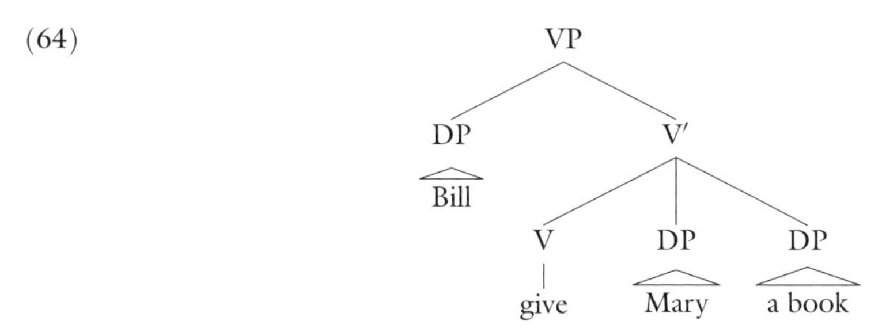

But such a proposal faces the same problem we encountered with *put*, since the following coordination is acceptable:

(65) John gave Mary a book and Sue a CD

Suggesting instead a tree like this:

(66)

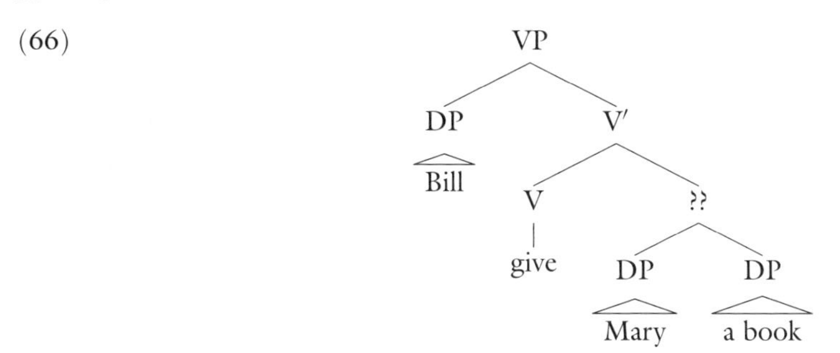

It turns out that there is a lot of support for the existence of such a constituent. Most of the data in support comes from Barss and Lasnik (1986), but the analysis we will motivate for this construction is inspired in part by Kayne (1981) and Larson (1988).

The first piece of evidence comes from Principle A and Principle C of the binding theory (see Chapter 7). Regarding the former, recall that an antecedent must c-command its anaphor in some local domain. Regarding the latter, recall that a name cannot be c-commanded by a coindexed pronoun. In this light, what do the following data suggest?

(67) I showed Mary_k herself_k
(68) *I showed herself_k Mary_k

The first sentence shows that the first object c-commands the second and that the two objects are in the same domain. Furthermore, it shows that the second object (which is a (reflexive) pronoun) does not c-command the first: if it did, this would trigger a Principle C violation. This is consistent with the second example: if the second object does not c-command the first, Principle A is not satisfied, and if the first object c-commands the second, Principle C is violated. These conclusions are corroborated by the next examples (draw their trees before you read on):

(69) I showed $Mary_k$ pictures of $herself_k$
(70) I showed [the $girls]_k$ [[each $other]_k$'s cousins]
(71) *I showed [[each $other]_k$'s cousins] [the $girls]_k$

To simplify matters, we use the content of the DPs to refer to the DPs themselves: *Mary* can bind *herself* in the first example. *The girls* can bind *each other* in the second. This suggests *Mary* c-commands *herself*, that is, *herself* is inside the sister of *Mary*. The third example shows again that the second object, *the girls*, does not c-command the first one (otherwise it would also c-command *each other*).

The simplest structure that allows this result is one that looks this:

(72)

Since DP_1 c-commands DP_2, DP_2 must be a sister of DP_1, or inside a sister of DP_1. Since DP_2 does not c-command DP_1, it cannot be a sister of DP_1, so it must be inside a sister of DP_1. Such a structure makes many correct predictions.

First, it predicts, correctly, that there should a Condition C effect in (73) but not in (74). Recall that Condition C states that R-expressions such as names cannot be coindexed with a c-commanding pronoun:

(73) *I showed $[her_k]$ $[Mary_k$'s mother]
(74) I showed [the mother of [the girl who $won]_k$] [the girl who $won]_k$

Here are the respective (portions of) trees for these two sentences:

(75)

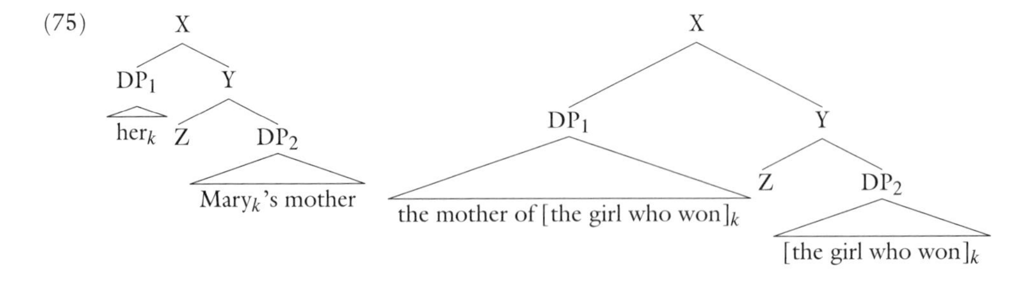

Second, it correctly predicts whether a pronoun can be bound by a non-referential antecedent or not. (Recall that in such cases, the pronoun must be c-commanded by its antecedent, see Chapter 7, Section 7.6.2.) We get the following data:

(76) I gave [every worker]$_k$ his$_k$ paycheck
(77) *I gave [its$_k$ owner] [every paycheck]$_k$
(78) I gave [every journalist]$_k$ [a copy of the article [he$_k$ wrote]]
(79) *I gave [the journalist [who wrote it$_k$]] [every article]$_k$

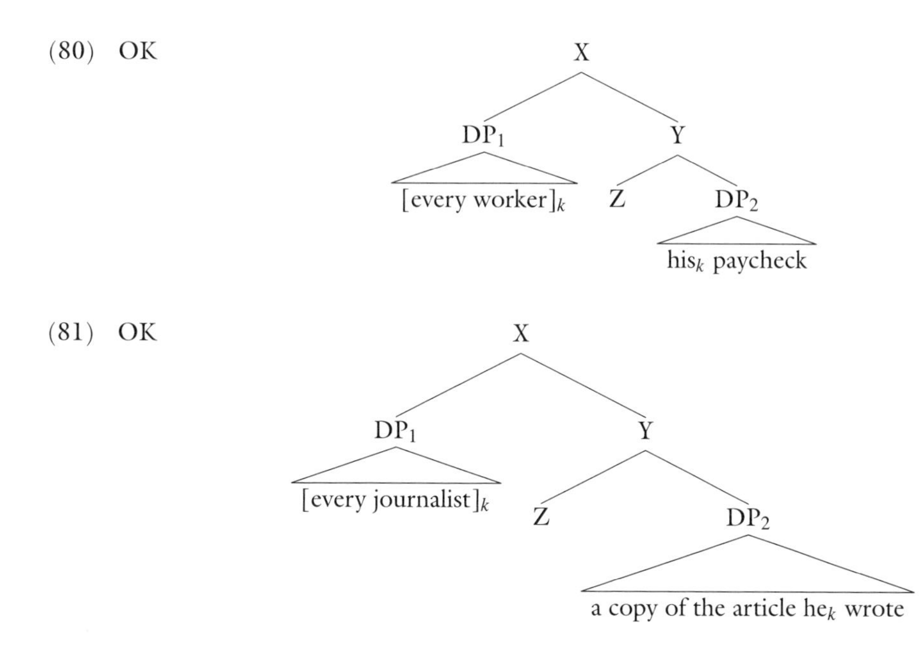

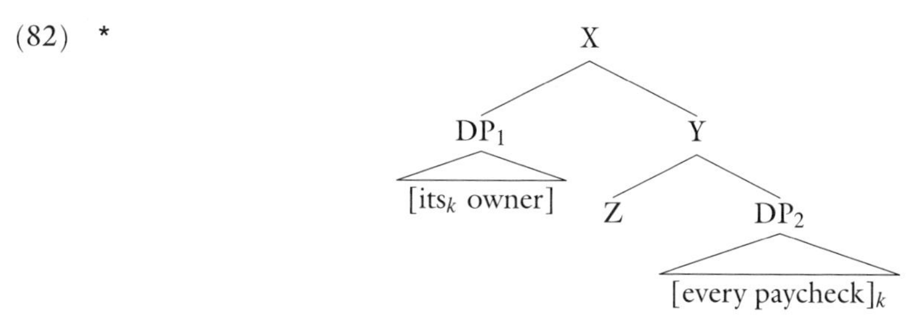

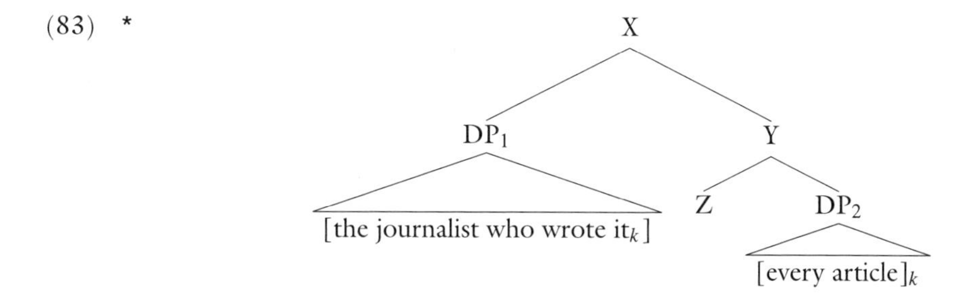

Third, it correctly predicts the following asymmetry in NPI licensing (recall that NPIs must be c-commanded by an NPI licenser, see Chapter 11, Section 11.2.2).

(84) I showed nobody anything
(85) *I showed anyone nothing

(86)

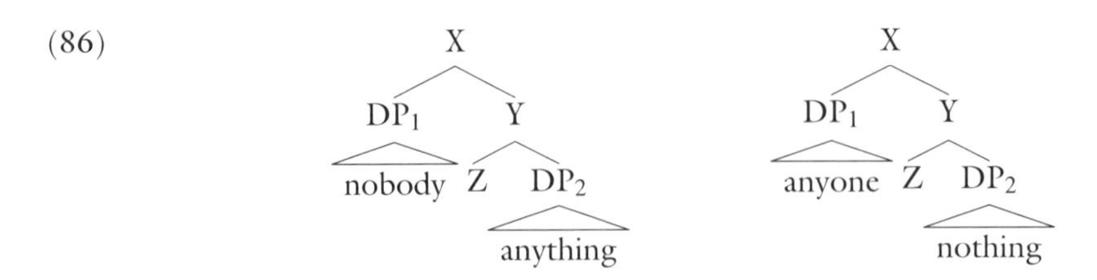

Finally, recall that an indefinite description can always be interpreted in the scope of a universal quantifier if the latter c-commands the former (see Chapter 11, Section 11.4.3). The structure above correctly predicts the following facts:

(87) I showed every boy a nice book

DP_2 is predicted to be in the scope of DP_1. This sentence should therefore be able to mean that I showed each boy a different book, and it does. The prediction is borne out. However, in:

(88) I showed a boy every book

DP_1 not is predicted to be in the scope of DP_2. It may be or it may not be. As it turns out, it can't be: this sentence cannot mean that each book was seen by a different boy. There is only one boy in total. This is not unexpected if DP_2 does not c-command DP_1.

> **A puzzle:** This last fact is somewhat surprising in other respects. We know that sometimes, a subject can be in the scope of its direct object as in the sentence below (which can mean: for each US embassy, there is a different well-trained agent protecting it).
>
> (89) A well-trained agent is protecting every US embassy
>
> It something of a surprise that this is not possible in (88) – a phenomenon called "scope freezing." This is a topic on which there is quite a bit of current research.

There is a lot more evidence favoring the structural analysis we postulated. For example, the interpretation of the following construction available in the first sentence requires *the others* to be c-commanded by *each boy* (it is a subcase of pronominal binding):

(90) Each boy visited the others (= each boy visited the other boys)
(91) The others visited each boy (≠ the other boys visited each boy)

Predictably, we have the following facts where the sign # means that the relevant meaning is not available:

(92) I gave each man the others' books
(93) # I gave the others each man's books

We can conclude that the constituency suggested by the coordination facts is actually very well supported.

Further, we see that at least in double object constructions, the first object asymmetrically c-commands the second object. For *John gave Mary a book*, this yields an overall VP structure like this:

(94)

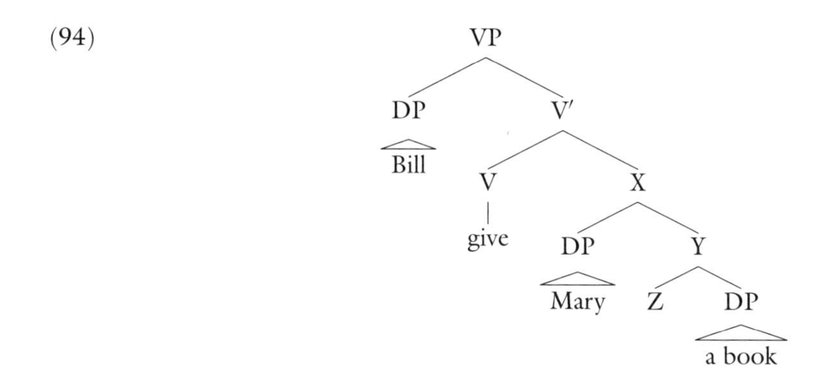

We are left with many new questions: what is the nature of the constituents X, Y, and Z? How does this help us to solve the problem we saw with *put*? Are there constituency tests that X fails? (We know that such failures would not be immediately informative, but we would of course like to understand why they occur.)

We will now outline a general type of answer to such questions inspired by the ground-breaking work of Kayne (1981) and Larson (1988). We concentrate on the general logic of the answers, leaving details aside.

Recall that in the case of causative and anticausative verbs, the leading idea was that the syntactic structures for these verbs were built by taking the verb apart into some (relevant) pieces of meaning, assuming that these pieces were syntactic atoms, and projecting them according to X-bar theory and other principles of tree structure, satisfying locality of selection. One way to think about a verb phrase like *give someone something* is as containing a causative verb that combines with a piece of structure that is related to possession, i.e as a structure with roughly the meaning "cause [someone to have or to get something]." This immediately suggests the following analysis for the node X, Y, and Z, modeled on what we have seen in other cases of VP shells:

(95)

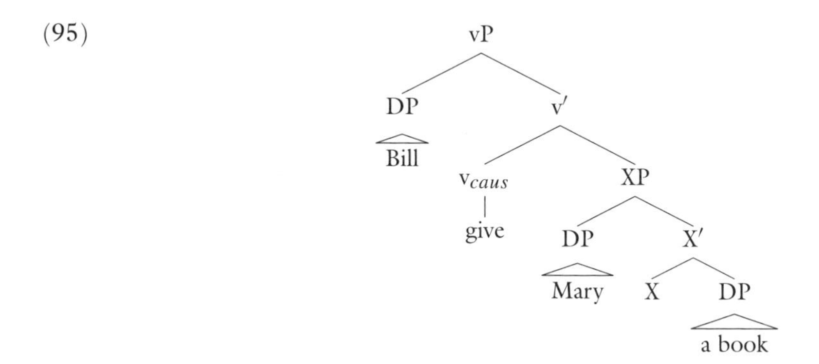

XP is a complement of CAUS; where X could be a verb HAV similar to *have* which is attracted to CAUS (by its EPP property) to form a complex verb and [HAV+CAUS] is spelled out as *give*. Here we will simply assume that X= $[\text{HAV}]_V$ and thus XP=VP (though there are various other ideas about X's identity being entertained).

Note that this structure fits well with our previous conclusion about the VP shell structure. So far, we have seen that CAUS can combine with a change of state AP or VP complement with V selecting a theme. But that leads to the expectation that there should be cases where the VP complement of CAUS takes *two* arguments, both a subject and a complement, which as a VP should be able to occur independently (*John has a book, Mary got a cold*).

This type of solution can immediately extend to others verbs such as *put*, which show the same constituency properties. A VP headed by *put* can be assumed to roughly have the following structure, which leaves the possibility that the constituent XP can be coordinated:

(96)

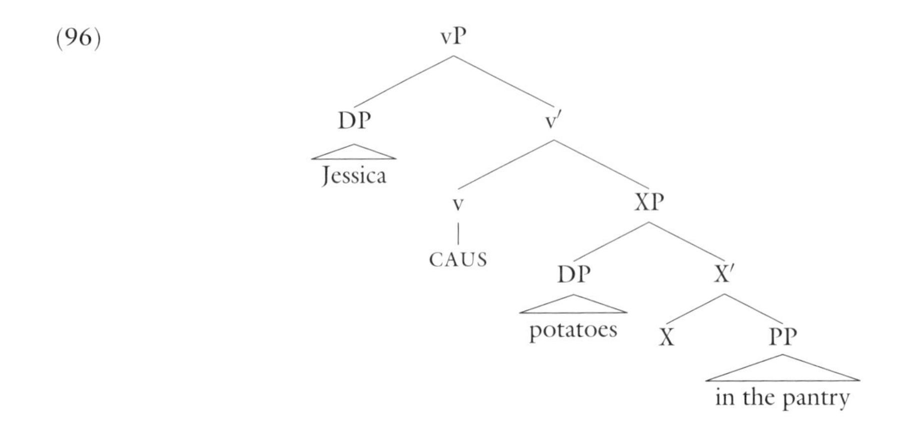

Heidi Harley

Gillian Ramchand

What is the category of X? The exact nature of the category X is still being debated in current research and various ideas about X's identity are being entertained, e.g. X being a kind of locative P by Heidi Harley, professor at the University of Arizona in Tucson, or Gillian Ramchand, professor at the university of Tromsø in Norway. It could also be that XP is more complex and is itself a shell of some sort, but the general form of the solution is clear: both constituency and c-command properties can be accounted for.

As usual X (which may be be a silent locative BE_{loc}) moves to CAUS to form [X+CAUS]. This combination is spelled out as the phonological idiom *put*.

The same remark as above applies. While it is clear that the solution lies along these lines, the precise nature of X needs to be determined by careful investigation, since only indirect effects of its presence are visible. One simple option is that X is (a version of) the verb *be* (taking a locative PP as complement) so that *put* is roughly "cause to BE." This is what we will suppose here. If X=V, then XP=VP. We can now understand the following results we encountered earlier:

(97) a. Whose drawing did you put ~~whose drawing~~ on the fridge
b. *Whose drawing on the fridge did you put ~~whose drawing on the fridge~~?

The previous explanation was that *whose drawing* is a DP by itself, but *whose drawing on the fridge* is not a constituent. Clearly, this explanation is no longer tenable. If X is the verb *be*, we get an explanation if we examine the VP shell structure. Wh-movement always moves a wh-constituent (DP, AP, PP), but never a VP constituent. The ill-formed string would have resulted from fronting the VP containing the wh-phrase, a pattern that is generally excluded in English (hopefully on principled grounds).

(98)

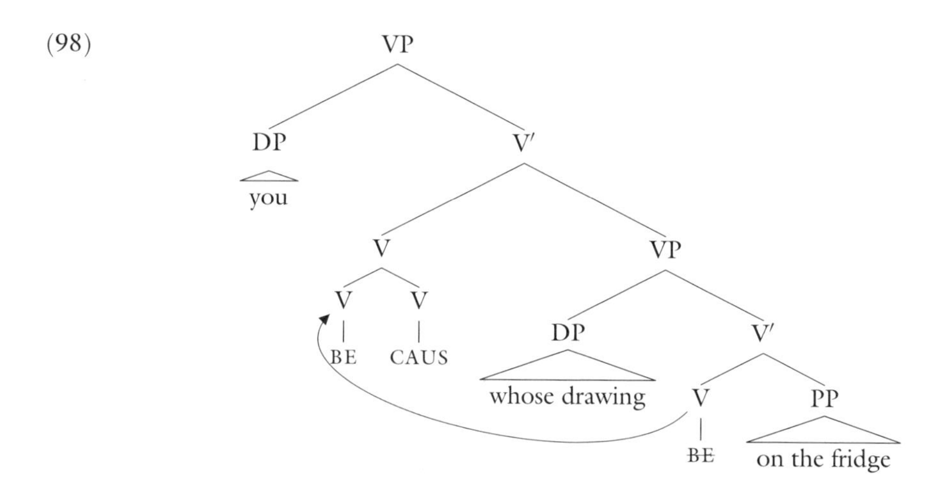

12.6 Using VP Shells: VP Shells and Adjuncts

That VPs are in fact more complex syntactic structures is an important discovery. As we said, this discovery goes back to work done in the 1960s. This work remained dormant for some years (it had in fact been a topic of heated theoretical debate) until it was revived in somewhat different forms in Kayne (1981) and Larson (1988).

One important consequence for our current discussion is that it opens the door to the idea that all syntactic trees are binary branching, an important idea pioneered by Richard Kayne (pictured here), in Kayne (1981) and republished in Kayne (1984).

Richard Kayne, photographed by Cynthia Munro Pyle, 2007

It also explains away one apparent difference between morphological Merging and syntactic Merging, making it even more plausible that morphological composition is simply syntactic composition.

Since VPs can have an intricate internal constituent structure, with simple verbs being build out of some (relevant) pieces of meaning that are syntactic atoms, the usual questions about constituency apply to this internal structure. Adopting, for ease of reference, the convention that only the most deeply embedded VP is called V, and all others are little v, what kinds of little *v*s are there? What heads can select for VP? What heads can select for v? Can VP be modified? Can vP? Can VPs (as opposed to vPs) be coordinated? Elided? Moved? Replaced? . . . If VPs can be structured as shells, how about PPs? NPs? APs? . . . (It turns out most of them can have shell structures, although we will not discuss this here.)

Here is an expectation of the VP shell analysis: if there are two VPs, we expect that each should in principle be able to support an adjunct. We will now discuss facts that support this expectation. This discussion draws on original work done by McCawley (1968) and developed by von Stechow (1996). It has been extended to new cases in Beck and Johnson (2004).

The basic facts we want to describe have to do with the meaning contribution of an adverb like *again*. In a sentence like:

(99) John slept
(100) John slept again

The first sentence describes the occurrence of a "situation" namely one of John sleeping in the past. The meaning contribution of *again* is to assert that this situation of John's sleeping is a second occurrence: it had occurred in the past and then occurred once more. *Again* is a straightforward (right) VP adjunct, as shown by, say, VP preposing or VP coordination:

(101) Sleep again, John will [$_{VP}$ ~~sleep again~~]
(102) John will [$_{VP}$ eat a sandwich again] and [$_{VP}$ leave]

It is worth noting that the following sentence is infelicitous if Bill had not slept before:

(103) John slept and Bill slept again

We have seen above, the adverb *again* is a VP adjunct. What is repeated, however, is not just that sleeping occurs. Otherwise the sentence above should be fine (there was sleeping before, namely by John, and then sleeping again, this time by Bill). Rather what is repeated is that there was sleeping by Bill. We can handle this, given that Bill is within the VP in the underlying tree.

(104) Bill [~~Bill~~ slept] again]

Now *again* modifies the VP [Bill sleep] and thus requires the repetition of sleeping by Bill.

The problem is how to capture the ambiguity of sentences like the following, the two meanings of which are described:

(105) Sally closed the door again
(106) a. Sally closed the door, and she had done it before (**repetitive**)
b. Sally closed the door, and the door had closed before (say, by itself)(**restitutive**)

On both interpretations, what makes the sentence in (105) appropriate is the existence of some previous situation. On the repetitive reading – the repetition of an action by the same agent – that situation has to be a previous closing of the door by Sally. For example in the following situation.

*"I am going to get mad at Sally. When she closed the door to the basement yesterday, I told her I did not want *her* to do this. But today,* **she closed it again**.*"*

On the restitutive reading, by contrast, that situation is the door closing: it had closed before, but Sally had nothing to do with it. For example, this reading would appropriate in the following situation:

"When the contractors built my house, and installed the door leading to the basement, the door frame was badly defective and the door could not stay open and it was closing by itself. Sara is handy with tools and managed to get it to stay open, I had hoped permanently. Unfortunately, when Sally visited us, I am not sure what she did, but **she closed it again**.*"*

Clearly, Sally had never before closed the door. Yet, the sentence in bold is appropriate.

How to obtain the repetitive reading is straightforward. The adverb *again* is an adjunct to the VP *[Sally close the door]*, with the result that the situation of Sally closing the door is said to be repeated.

More challenging is the restitutive reading, since what is occurring again does not correspond to what the VP [Sally close the door] denotes. Normally, *again* modifies some constituent. What we would like to say is that the situation being repeated is one which could be expressed by the following VP:

(107) [the door close]

The problem is how to derive this result from the syntactic structure of (105). It is clear how VP shell analysis can help, and this is what von Stechow does (von Stechow, 1995, 1996), elaborating on earlier suggestions in McCawley (1968) among others. The basic idea is that a constituent with the meaning in (105) is in fact part of the structure of (107). Since there is no obvious constituent with the meaning "the door is open" in our example, this analysis relies on a more abstract structure for VPs with the verb *open* (and other verbs that show a similar ambiguity). As we discussed earlier in Section 12.4.1, we can analyze the causative *close* as composed of the anticausative *close* plus a CAUS part contributing a causal component. This decomposition is reflected in the syntactic structure. *Again* adjoins to, and hence modifies, the lower VP constituent on the restitutive reading of the sentence, but adjoins to the higher VP on the repetitive reading. The ambiguity of this and similar examples is thus analyzed as purely structural in nature. To illustrate, we would get the following two tree structures (the trees are simplified: the causative verb *open* is actually composed of CAUS, BECOM, and the Adjective *open*: there is an AP we do not represent):

(108) Structure for the repetitive reading

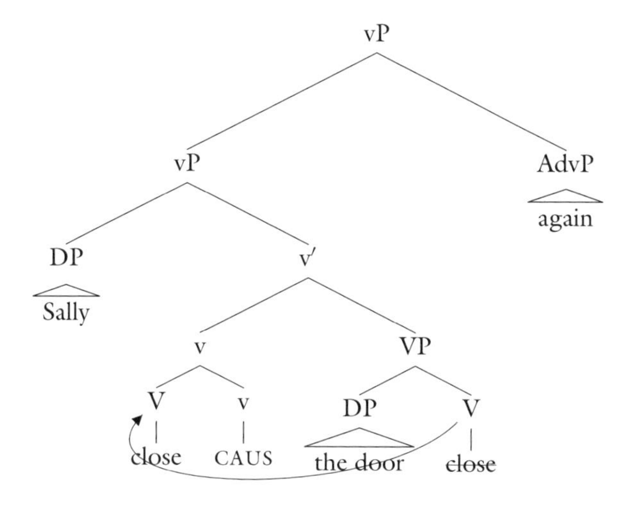

(109) Structure for the restitutive reading

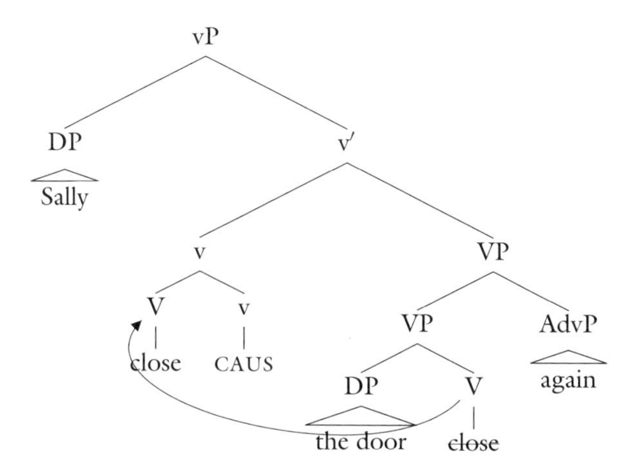

The beautiful aspect of all this is that there is nothing special to say to derive these facts once we have VP shells. The adverb *again* is a VP adjunct and, as such, it is free to adjoin to whatever VP it is compatible with. Since there are two such VPs, there are two adjunction sites, each corresponding to a different meaning.

Once more, we can use the analogy between CAUS and the pronounced causative verb *make* to illustrate what we are doing. The following sentence is also ambiguous:

(110) Sally made the door close again

It also has the two readings:

(111) a. it happened again [that Sally made the door close] (repetitive)
b. The door closed again; this time, it is due to Sally (restitutive)

And these two readings correspond to two different trees:

(112) Structure for the repetitive reading

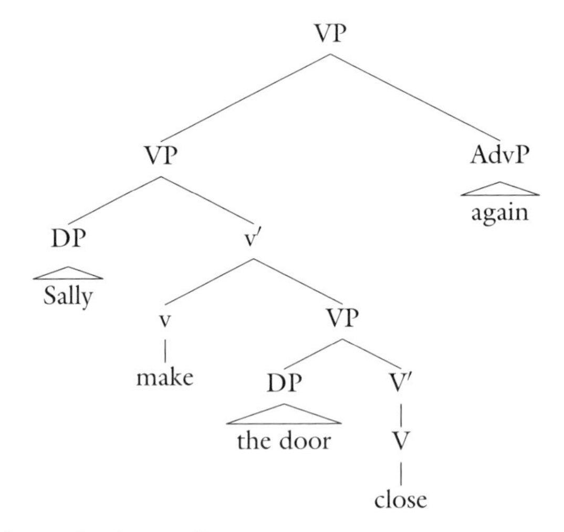

(113) Structure for the restitutive reading

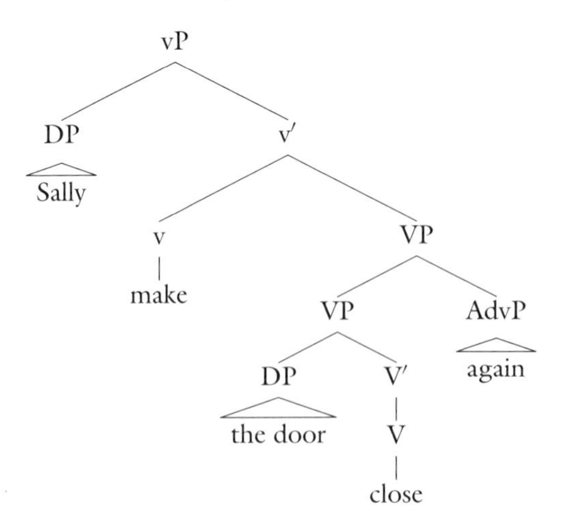

The trees in (112) and in (113) are essentially the same. The only difference is that in the former, the causative verb is a bound morpheme, it has an epp_V feature which attracts the second verb. In sum, VP shells and the idea that word formation can take place in the syntax help us derive rather complex and subtle facts about the meaning of sentences.

Finally, note the prediction made by this account if all branching is binary in the way we have indicated. We have concluded that verbs such as *give*, or *put*, etc. all have a kind of VP shell:

(114) Give = [HAV+CAUS]

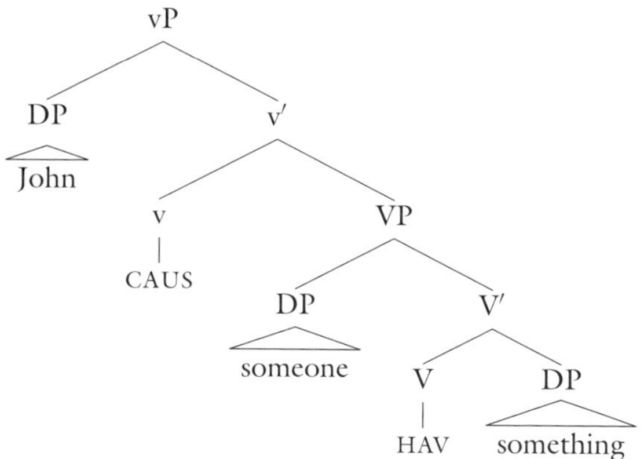

(115) Put = [BE+CAUS]

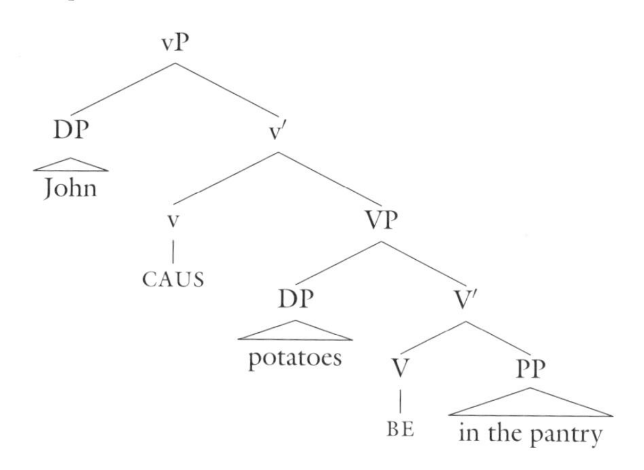

We expect that an VP adjunct like *again* should be able to attach to either VP giving rise to repetitive/restitutive ambiguity in each case (as discussed in detail in the case of double object constructions in Beck and Johnson (2004)). This seems to be true:

(116) a. Repetitive: Last year, Mary gave John a book. This year she gave him a book again.
b. Restitutive: Last year, Mary gave John a book. This year Sally gave him a book again.

(117) a. Repetitive: Yesterday, I had to put the broom in the closet, and today I put the broom in the closet again.
b. Restitutive: The broom belongs in the closet and I put it there yesterday, why is it here? Please put it in the closet again.

As final note, let us reflect on what we have shown. There are a number of convincing reasons why what we may initially think of as a simple Vs can in fact stand for a rather complex syntactic structure, a shell of some sort. This could mean that verbs always are complex objects built from several pieces. While at present it is not always clear what the pieces are – only painstaking, deep, and wide investigations will tell what the building blocks, the atoms of syntactic chemistry, are – it seems clear that there are pieces. We will thus be led to postulate shells where we know what the sum is like but we remain, for now, agnostic about what the pieces are. It is also important to understand what kind of claims this makes and does not make. For example, it seems that in some cases at least, the meaning of the sum is entirely predictable from the meaning of the parts (triplets like causative *open*, anticausative *open*, and adjective *open* could be an example of this). At other times, it clearly is not: for example, we treat *give* and *send* very much in the same way regarding their basic component. They share aspects of meaning (say: cause something to be somewhere, cause someone to have something) which allows us to make sense of certain meaning entailment relations, but they clearly differ on other counts.

How do we deal with this? One way is that there may still be other components of meaning we have not identified (e.g. adjuncts) whose meaning contribution is wrapped into the meaning of these verbs. There is also another option: we should not expect more from VP shell structures than we do for other syntactic structures. Complex syntactic structures can give rise to all sorts of idiomatic meanings. At one extreme, for example, while *shoot the breeze*, or *kick the bucket* demonstrably are VPs with a verb (that can be tensed independently) and a NP that can be modified (*kick the proverbial bucket*) by an adjective (as expected), its overall meaning is "die" (although a version of "die" that can be shown to behave like a transitive verb). A milder case could be an idiom like *throw in the sponge*, where the literal meaning is fine but metaphorical, meaning "giving up." From a syntactic point of view, we do see that *throw in the sponge* is a transitive verb with a particle, whatever it ends up being interpreted as.

It is thus conceivable that despite having a motivated internal syntactic structure made up of identifiable parts each with its own well identified meaning contribution, many VP shells may have some idiosyncratic meaning property .

12.7 Terminological Changes

Taking into account the introduction of VP shells, we need to clarify some terminology, e.g. verb, subject, or complement of V. What is traditionally called a "verb" V* may now well stand for a whole shell composed of a sequence of heads H1, H2 (e.g. little v followed by big V, etc.). An argument of this V* is now in fact an argument of some head part of this sequence (e.g. v or V). The subject of V* (as can been seen in a VP small clause) is the highest argument of this shell, that is, the subject argument of the highest head of this sequence (which we call little v in the case of causative verbs). What was previously called a DP complement of V* now corresponds to an argument of some lower head. Such a complement may well be the subject of this head. In other words, what is encoded by the first tree can now be encoded by the second.

```
   VP                vP
  /  \              /  \
DP    V'          DP    v'
     /  \              /  \
    V    DP           v    VP
                          /  \
                        DP    V
```

We still use terms like subject, verb, and object as abbreviations. It is important to remember (when relevant) what these terms may refer to in case a verb is actually part of a VP shell.

12.8 Raising to Object

Here we briefly follow up on some previous puzzles with the analysis of ECM/raising to object verbs, like *believe*, in light of the finer VP shell structure.

We start out with a quick reminder of the two dominant analyses in the literature, which are responsible for the hybrid name we have been using. In ECM (exceptional case marking) analyses, the accusative object DP is treated as occupying the subject position within the TP complement. ECM refers to the "exceptional" case marking of V across the TP boundary. Why the "exceptional" terminology? It is due to what was then considered "normal" case marking of objects: as sister to V. With the introduction of VP shells, what was exceptional has in fact become the "norm" now (in a shell, Case is licensed by v, but the object appears to be in the lower part of the shell). According to raising to object analyses, the accusative DP has risen out from the TP complement to somewhere inside the main clause: the major problem was understanding how this structure could possibly arise given the theoretical principles, and diagnosing the surface tree.

Let us revisit raising to object given the VP shell structure and current understanding, and see what kind of structure *believe* could have, when it selects a *to*-infinitival. Consider the verb *allege* for example. It introduces an agent/actor (the exact theta role is unclear) and licenses an accusative (it allows passivization). This shows the structure contains a v introducing the agent/actor. This v is also responsible for the accusative case (though exactly how is still not fully understood). *Allege* then consists of two VPs, with the lower V taking an infinitival TP, and V raising to little v. This affords a possible treatment for raising to object, where the object raises to some position between v and big V, perhaps the "free" specifier of the big VP *allege*, in which case ?? is VP, or some other projection, yielding something like the following structure in which the X+v combination is spelled out as *allege*:

(118)

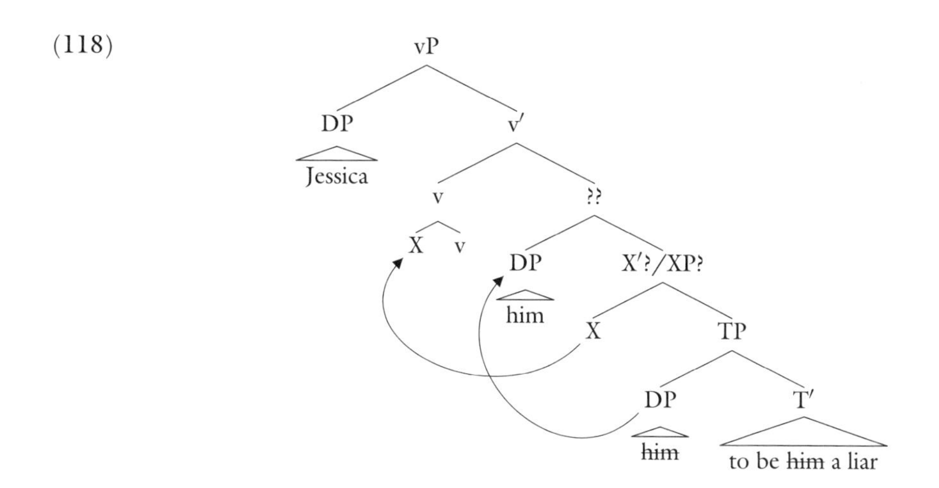

Although the details of the derived structures are not completely clear – the dust has not yet settled – it is clear that the accusative DP at least **can** be outside TP, somewhere in the VP shell structure of *allege*, as initially argued in the late 1960s and most thoroughly in Postal (1974).

In some circumstances, this can be made more visible. For many speakers, the idiomatic verb-particle combination *make out* can be close in meaning to *allege*, meaning "imply/suggest" or "falsely state." Many such speakers allow the following string:

(119) Jessica made him out to be a liar

Such a string receives an immediate analysis along the lines of (118):

(120)

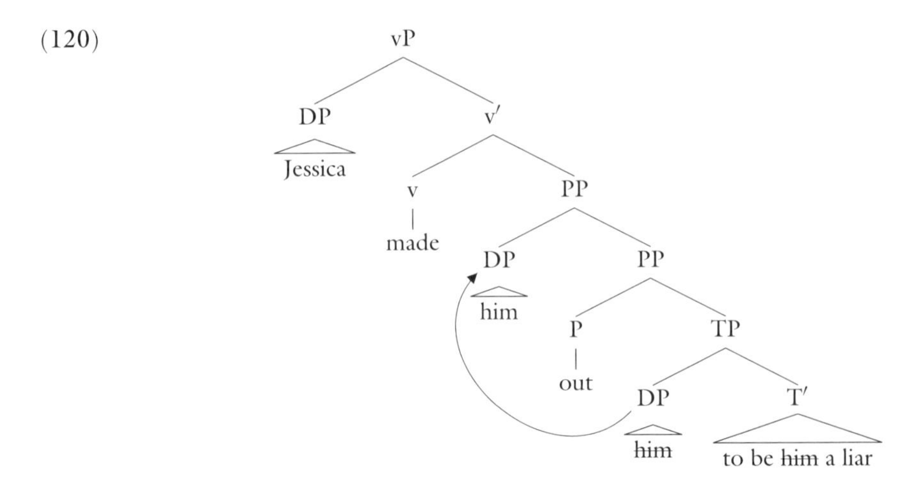

This conclusion is consistent with fact that the object supports quantifier float: which taken as a diagnostic can only occur when a DP has undergone movement:

(121) Jessica made them out all ~~them~~ to be liars

Such raising into the main clause also makes immediate sense of another puzzle that was discussed in Chapter 7: pronouns and anaphors behave as if they are in the *believe* clause. We return to this issue in Chapter 13.

(122) a. He$_i$ believes him$_j$ to be happy
b. He$_i$ believes himself*i* to be happy

12.9 The Model of Morphosyntax

Putting all our conclusions together means replacing the previous models of morphology and syntax presented in Sections 6.1 and 6.11.1. We reproduce diagrams of each of those models here:

Now, to obtain a unified model, we remove any specific reference to syntax and morphology, update the syntax model with our findings (namely concerning locality of selection, and binary Merge),

More about objects: Needless to say, this is not the end of the matter. First, many speakers also allow:

(123) Jessica made out him to be a liar

in which the accusative DP can follow the particle: this may suggest that the accusative DP can actually stay inside the embedded clause (or that both *out* and *him* are in the matrix). Furthermore, evidence due to Lasnik and Saito (1991) suggests that the accusative DP can raise out of the TP to an even higher position inside the main clause. Thus, in the readings where the adjunct modifies the matrix clause, we have:

(124) a. The DA proved the defendants to be guilty during each other's trials
b. *The DA proved [that the defendants were guilty] during each other's trials
c. The DA proved none of the defendants to be guilty during any of the trials
d. *The DA proved [that none of the defendants were guilty] during any trial

The sentences (124a) and (124c) show the defendants *can* c-command an adjunct of the matrix verb in raising to object configurations, but that this fails when it is clearly inside the complement TP as in (124b) and (124d). This suggests a raised object c-commands the matrix adjunct after movement. In order to do this, the raised accusative DP must be higher than the position of this adjunct. What is at stake here is the position of such adjuncts, and how accusative case is licensed by v. We will not discuss here these issues at the forefront of current research.

and remove from the new models elements that seem different (X-bar theory and the RHHR; head–complement order).

This unified model can make sense of a variety of observations that pervade the literature. Some were left as problems in Chapter 2. For example, non-atomic words made up of an adjective or a noun and a "particle" *en*, (such as *enlarge, endanger*) at least seem to have a head initial substructure (headed by *en*). This is no longer surprising since this is allowed by syntactic rules of composition. Similarly, Benveniste (1968) notes that French nominal compounds such as *pot de chambre "chamber pot"* have the structure of syntactic phrases (head initial) but morphological properties (no determiners) (the contrast between English and French is striking), leading Benveniste to call this "micro-syntax." In fact, this contrast between English and French illustrates a general type of cross-linguistic variation: independent/free items in one language correspond to bound morphemes in another. Such differences appear shallow from the point of view of a unified model.

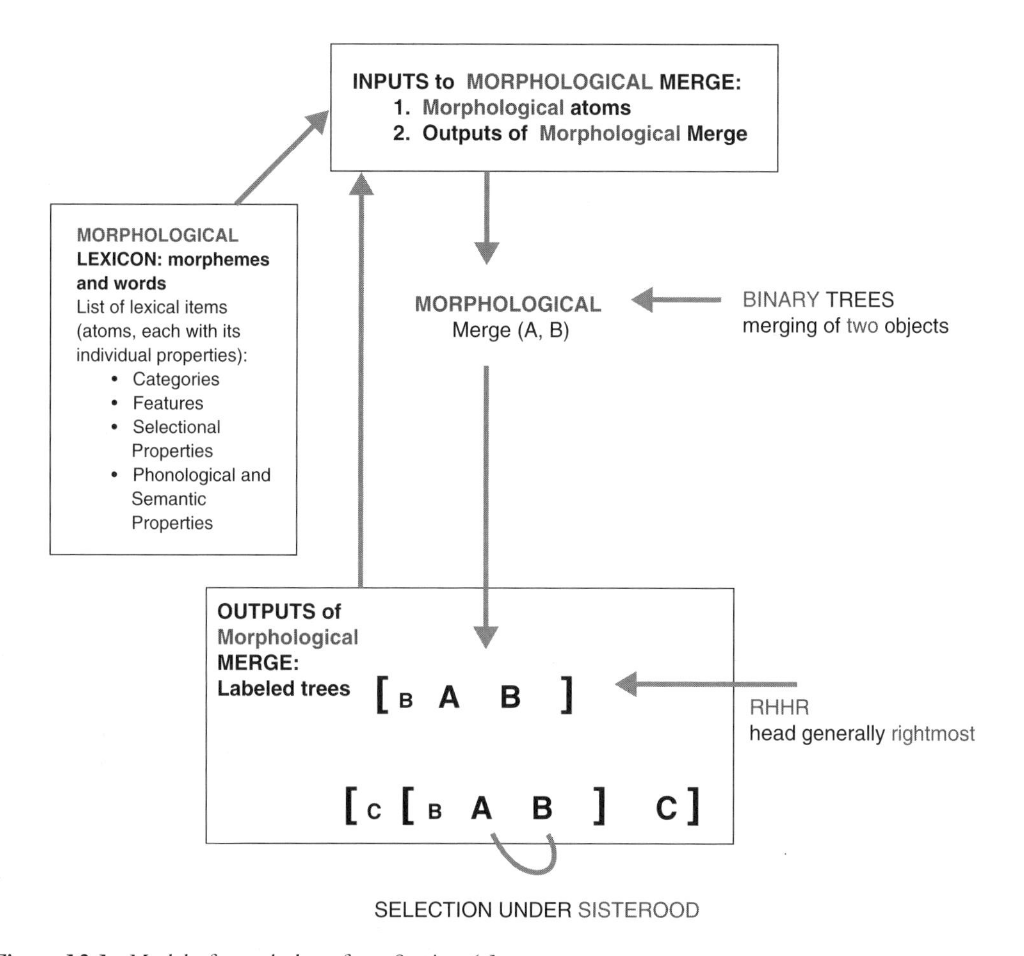

Figure 12.1 Model of morphology from Section 6.1

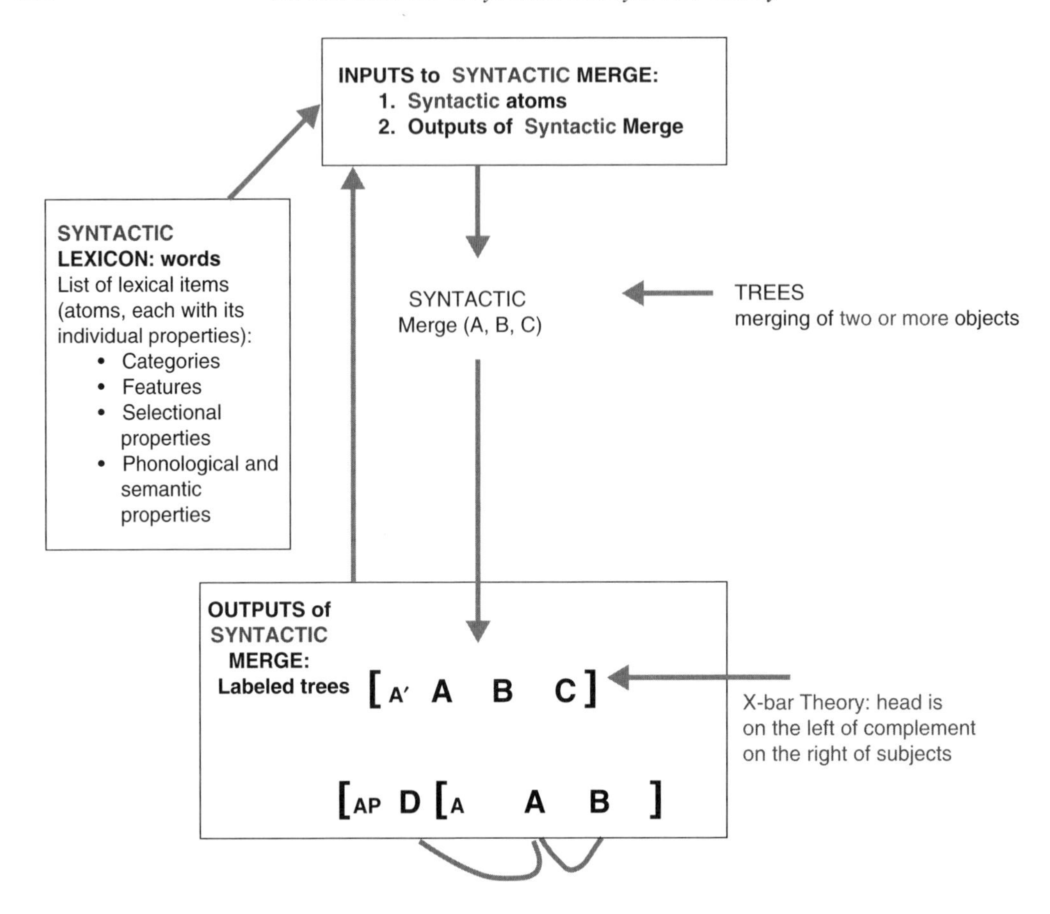

Figure 12.2 Model of syntax from Section 6.11.1

At the same time, the portions of the old models that do not seem to be common to both immediately evoke some of the questions that need to be answered to fully realize the unification of morphology (or more precisely of morphosyntax – that is, excluding phonological considerations) and syntax.

- Is there a unified theory of possible tree structure akin to X-bar theory?
- Where do e.g. head–complement word order differences come from?

We also see further differences. "Syntactic" composition seem to be unconstrained: whatever respects the composition rules is possible. This is not true of "morphological" composition. Thus, *dry* can be an adjective, an inchoative verb, or a causative verb, but *wet* can only be an adjective or a causative verb. This may be predictable, but if it weren't, it would mean that a mechanism is needed to check whether possible forms (perhaps only for word-level categories) are actual forms. This property is sometimes called "listedness" (it also applies to some (idiomatic) syntactic phrases).[13]

[13]Fundamentally, this means divorcing the units on which syntactic computation takes place that are abstract elements devoid of phonological properties (technically equivalence classes of what we call here lexical entries under the relation "has the same syntactic behavior as") from phonological realizations that need to look up whether particular combinations involving bound morphemes exist, and which can be done postsyntactically. Go to the Distributed Morphology website (http://www.ling.upenn.edu/ rnoyer/dm/) for a particular instantiation of these ideas.

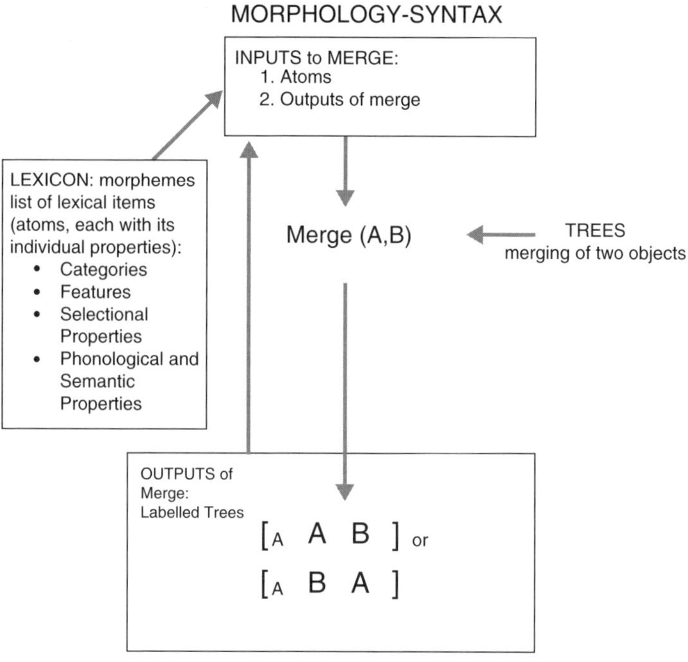

Figure 12.3 Model of the Morphology-Syntax component

Similarly, syntactic strings can use Move (or Remerge). Is there movement in morphology? If not, this must be explained away. Recent cross-linguistic research suggests that the traditional answer that there is no movement in morphology is far from obvious (see e.g. Koopman, 2005).

For all these questions, there are reasonable proposals in the research literature (for example, noting the crucial role played in "syntax" by atoms that seem *not* to occur in "pure" morphological composition, i.e. so called functional categories such as Num, T, C, D . . .). Yet it may be that a unified model of the kind we have discussed here is not quite the right answer. However, at the very least, the very substantial similarity between syntactic and morphological composition suggests that stipulating that there are two independent components is not the right answer: these must be derived.

12.10 Conclusion

12.10.1 Summary

In this chapter, we looked at the division of labor between the morphological component and the syntactic component. In order to do this, we probed syntactic structures much more deeply than before. This has led us to conclusions suggesting the following general proposition:

1. All morphological atoms are also syntactic atoms.

Along the way, we reached conclusions in particular cases suggesting the following general conclusions (the first two anticipated in Kayne (1984)):

2. Syntactic Merge is a binary operation: no head takes more than one complement, and thus syntactic trees are at most binary branching.

3. Some lexical heads (V, P, N ...) are silent.
4. Some apparently simple verbs are not mono-morphemic and are in fact parts of VP shells.

Needless to say, this is far from exhausting the questions we can ask about the relationship between syntactic structures and morphological structures, but these results suggest that strings of morphemes and of strings of words are built by the same algorithms using the same principles. This is a very far-reaching conclusion, suggesting that all morphological atoms are syntactic atoms too and that there is a unique computational engine responsible for structure building.

12.10.2 What to remember

From the point of view of results, the most important concept to remember is the idea that there may be a single computational engine to form complex units, and the research agenda that such a conjecture defines. From a practical standpoint, it means trying to determine the smallest units of composition, be they words, morphemes – silent or not, or even morphemes hidden by idiomatic composition.

In pursuing this agenda, we have used two important tools. First, once again, is the principle of compositionality, which expresses the idea that there is a close match between syntactic structure and meaning computation. In postulating VP shells, for example, it is useful to think about how the meaning of a particular verb could be built on the basis of more elementary elements of meaning, how they could be syntactically arranged to give rise to the meaning of the verb compositionally, and to try to corroborate such syntactic structures with the various probing tools at our disposal.

A second important tool is the systematic exploration of the division of labor between the lexicon and Merge. If we observe a particular grammatical property, is this a property of some lexical entry, or is it a property of the merging algorithm and the general properties that constrain it? Of course, we cannot answer this question *a priori*, but there are guidelines. What appears in the lexical entry of some atom is an idiosyncratic property of this atom. What reflects the effects of Merge is a general property of a derived object arising in a systematic fashion from the component parts of this object: in effect, this is a consequence of the compositionality property that we discussed regarding how the meaning of non-atoms is calculated, but which is much more general: all properties of the whole are computed by general rules from the properties of its parts.

This gives us boundary conditions on what property comes from where, hence on what property should be listed in the lexicon. By definition, properties listed in the lexicon are idiosyncratic, unpredictable, and specific to particular items.

12.10.3 Puzzles and preview

One major puzzle arising from what the chapter has covered has to do with the richness of syntactic structures: VPs can be internally far more structured than we initially thought. This opens up the possibility that we are substantially underestimating the amount of structure present in all constituents, including VPs themselves (and if you have read the boxes in Section 12.8, this point should be clearer). A substantial amount of research suggests exactly this, for example Rizzi (1997) for what we call C, or Koopman (2000, 2010) for what we call P. Perhaps the most striking example is the result of a detailed typological survey done on, and taking into account, the idea that morphemes project their own phrases in the syntax, called **the Cinque Hierarchy** discussed in Cinque (1999). Based on the distribution of adverbs and typological generalizations about the ordering of particles and bound morphemes (i.e. heads) that express the semantic notions encoded by adverbs, the Italian linguist Guglielmo Cinque, depicted here and currently (2013) professor at University Ca Foscari in Venice, Italy,

has proposed a universal "cartography" of the structure of the clause. Here is the 1999 version of this hierarchy for a portion of a single clause. This hierarchy uses traditional descriptive terminology to talk about different notions. Though his terminology will be largely unfamiliar to the reader, the possible candidates from English for each category should make most meanings clear. The page numbers from Cinque (1999) are indicated in parentheses (where the particular portion of the tree is discussed):

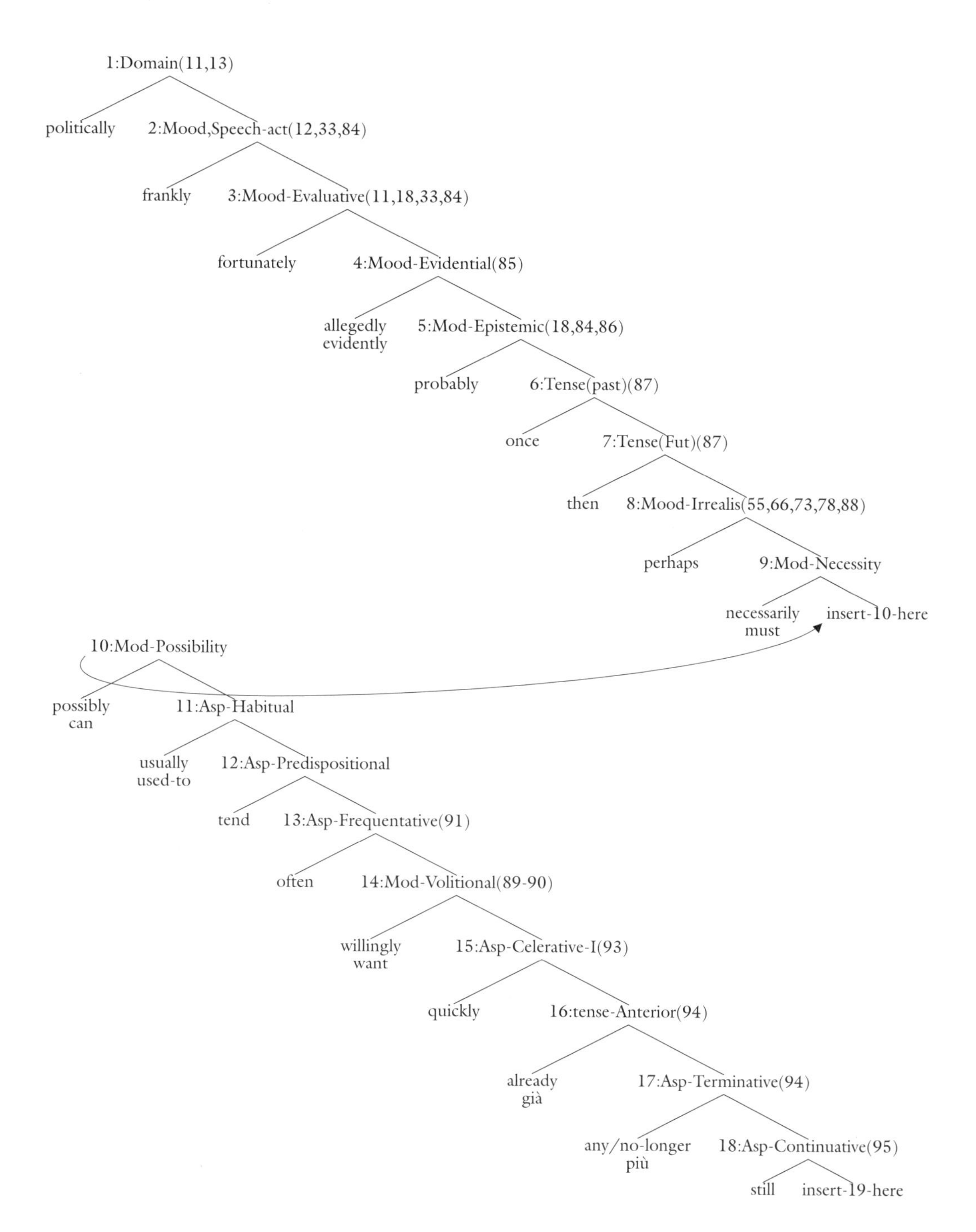

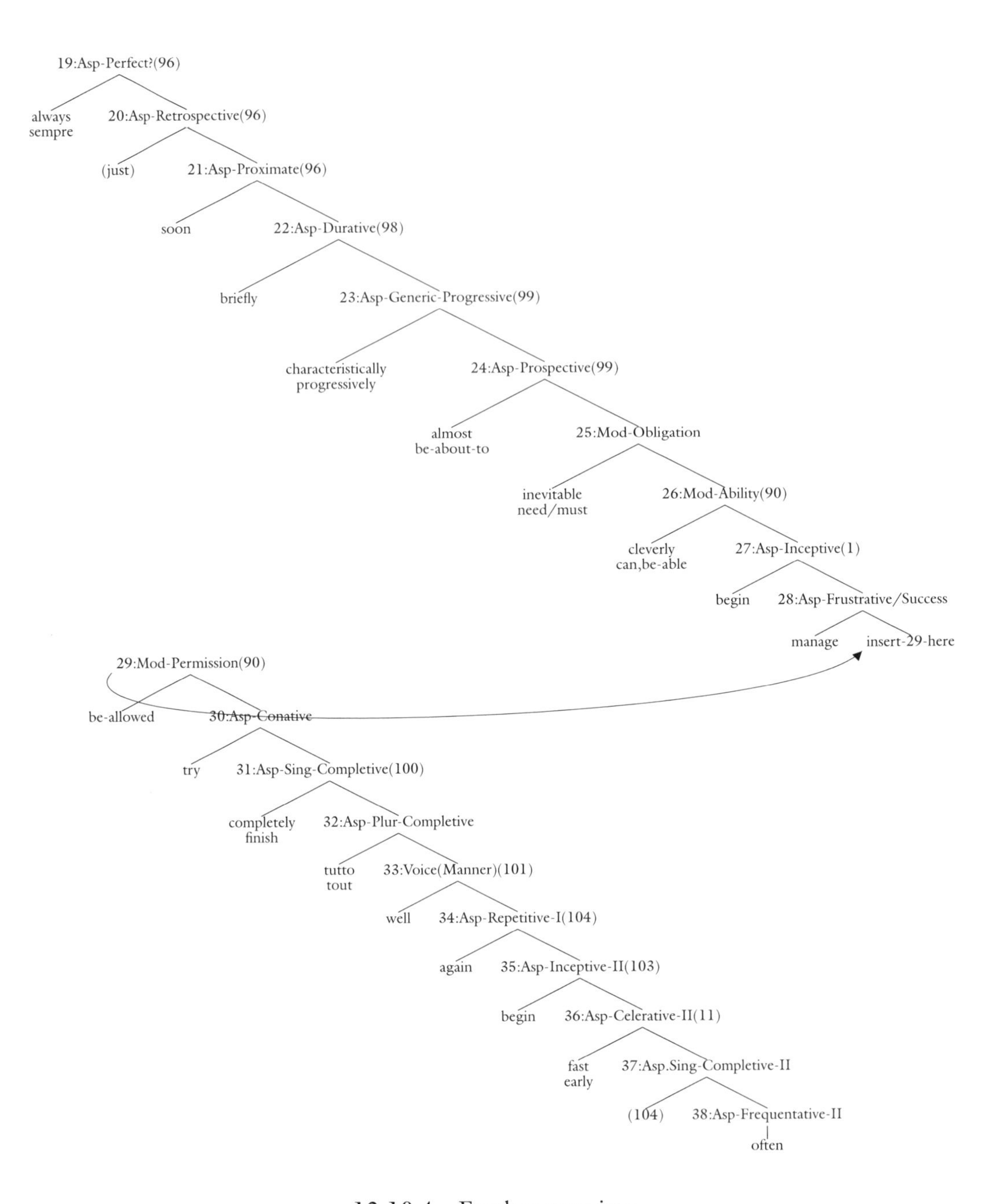

12.10.4 Further exercises

(1) *Only, any*, VP shell, and sentential subject

PART 1: only

Consider the following sentences.

(1) a. The fact that **only** Bill went to the movies saddened the girls.
b. The fact that Bill could **only** go to the movies saddened the girls.

(i) Give the VP shell structure for *sadden*. (Feel free to discuss any questions or problems you may have about (1a) and (1b).)

(ii) This sentence contains *only*.

a. Explain why *only* can only be associated with *Bill* in (1a).

b. Explain why *only* can be associated with *to the movies* or *go to the movies* in (1b). Give the paraphrases.

c. Explain why *only* cannot be associated with *the girls* in (1b). (Give the paraphrase of what this could mean.).

PART 2: any

Consider the sentences in (2):

(2) a. Nothing saddened anyone
b. *Anything saddened no one
c. Did anything sadden anyone?

(iii) Explain how the judgments in (2a) and (2b) follow from your structure.

Next consider the examples in (3)

(3) a. *These pictures about nothing saddened any girl
b. These pictures about nothing saddened Mary

(iv) Given (3), the following contrast between (4a) and (4b), on the one hand, and (4c) and (4d), on the other, should be surprising. Explain why it is surprising.

(4) a. They$_j$ like [each other]$_j$'s brothers
b. *[Each other]$_j$'s brothers like them$_j$/the boys$_j$
c. These stories about [each other]$_j$ saddened the boys$_j$
d. These pictures of themselves$_j$ saddened the girls$_j$

(2) The verb "donate"

Consider the following example from English:

(1) These politicians will all donate money to charities

Consider also the following related sentences. (Assume the grammaticality judgments as given.)

(2) a. These three politicians will all have donated clothes and shoes to charities
b. The politicians will all have donated them to charities
c. The politicians will all donate money to charities or to institutions
d. How much money should they all donate to charities?
e. *How much money to charities should they all donate?
f. These politicians will all donate clothes to charities and books to public institutions
g. These politicians will all donate something to charities, but those ones won't

The sentences in (2) show something about the constituent structure in (1). State what (if anything) each of these sentences shows about constituency. (Example: *John saw Mary and Bill saw Susan:* coordination shows that "Bill saw Susan" is a constituent of the same type as "John saw Mary," i.e. a tensed TP.)

(i) Give the lexical entry for *donate*, using the format in the chapter. (Make sure you include category, free or bound, c-selection, and s-selection/thematic roles, and underline the element selected as a specifier.)

(ii) Give a tree representation for (1). (Label the nodes in your tree: indicate movement with strikeouts and arrows.)

(iii) Briefly explain what each of the sentences in (2) shows about constituent structure and whether your tree representation accounts for the judgments. Where relevant, discuss problems or conflicts that may arise.

(iv) Consider the c-command relations in your tree representation for (1): for each DP that you have identified in your tree, list all the XPs they c-command.

(To think about: consider phenomena that require c-commands. What predictions do you make on the basis of your tree structure? Can you set up sentences that would test your predictions?)

(3) VP shell: causatives

English has a (hypothetical) sister language, *Wenglish,* which is in all respects like English, except for the fact that it has two bound heads, ***-et*** and ***-ake***, both of which yield a causative meaning (as indicated in the translations). You may assume that these heads are productive.

The general distribution of these causative heads can be illustrated in the following Wenglish examples, with the English translations below them. (You are supposed to reason on the basis of the Wenglish forms, and think about *v*P/VP shells. The English translations help you understand what the Wenglish strings mean ....)

(1) a. The bowl burn-ed
"The bowl burned"
b. They burn-**et**-ed the bowl
"They burned the bowl"
c. They walk-**et**-ed Lucy to America
"They made Lucy walk to America"
d. They laugh-**ake**-ed the child
"They made the child laugh"
e. They give-**ake**-ed the child a present to Bill
"They made the child give a present to Bill"

(i) Based on these examples, formulate the lexical entry of (hypothetical) *-et* and *-ake*. This means you need to state what category these elements belong to; whether they are bound or not, what subject and complement they select; what EPP properties they have.

(ii) Can you determine from the examples in (1) if *v*/V raises to *-ake/-et*, or if *- ake/-et* lowers to *v*/V? Explain. (You may want to come back to this after you do the next question.)

(iii) Give the Wenglish structures for (1a), (1b), and (1e).

Consider next the following examples:

(2) a. They give-**ake**-ed each other a present to the boys
b. I give-**ake**-ed the boys a present to each other
c. They give-**ake**-ed me a present to each other

You are told Wenglish *each other* obeys Principle A of the binding theory. Based on this information and the tree structure you drew for (1e),

(iv) Do you expect (2a), (2b), and (2c) to be well-formed? Discuss each case individually.

(v) For each sentence, discuss what you expect these sentences to mean in English (reason on the basis of the trees).

(4) VP shells

(i) Draw the trees for the following two sentences.
 (1) John unexpectedly left (= it was unexpected that John left)
 (2) John left slowly (= John's leaving was slow)
(ii) Justify that the adverb (or AdvP) *slowly* is a VP adjunct (by running a relevant constituency test or c-command test if you can find a way to do it).
(iii) Consider now the following sentence:
 (3) John unexpectedly cooked the bread slowly

Observation #1: This sentence means: it was unexpected that John's cooking of the bread was slow.

Observation #2: This sentence cannot mean: John's unexpectedly cooking the bread was slow.

a. Assume first that there is no VP shell (meaning that you are supposed to use a single VP structure). Given that these AdvPs are VP adjuncts, draw the two trees that should, in principle, be available.
b. For each tree structure, write the meaning that the tree should have under it.
c. Your answer to the previous question should lead to a problem. Explain the nature of the problem.

(5) The verb *threaten*

We would like to understand what happens in sentences such as the following (all the (a) sentences are from Google). Suppose in each case, someone said the (a) sentence, but I did not hear it and I ask you: what is it about? Sometimes the (b) answer is well-formed, sometimes not:

(1) a. Putin threatens to aim missiles at Ukraine
 b. Putin's threat to aim missiles at Ukraine
(2) a. Global warming threatens to redraw the world's wine map
 b. *Global warming's threat to redraw the world's wine map

The fact that sentence (2b) is not possible underscores the existence of a difference among the (a) sentences. Your main task will be to analyze the form *threaten* in a way that can lead to an explanation of the difference between the (a) sentences by providing different syntactic structures for them.

(i) One could think the difference has to do with the difference between the DPs *Putin* and *global warming*. Formulate a simple hypothesis about what this difference could be and explain why the following well-formed example shows this hypothesis is incorrect.
 (3) Yesterday's threat was more ominous than today's
(ii) Taking into account the following sentence (from Google), provide a **complete** surface tree for sentence (2a), and provide two justifications for how you treat the verb *threaten* in (2a).
 (4) There threatened to be a late twist in the game
(iii) Using the fact that the following sentence fragment is out and the fact that (1b) is good, provide a complete surface tree for sentence (1a), and provide two justifications for how you treat the verb *threaten* in (1a).
 (5) *There's threat to be a late twist in the game
(iv) Given the ill-formedness of sentence (5), formulate a hypothesis that explains why (2b) is ill-formed. (Note: you are not required to give a syntactic analysis for the sentence with the noun *threat.)*

(v) Suppose we add the word *again* after the verb *threaten* in (1a) and (2a). For each modified sentence, explain whether we expect it to be ambiguous (due to the presence of *again*) and justify your answer. (Note: do not worry about the fact that *again* separates the infinitive from the verb – there is a process which is called extraposition that has taken place.)

(6) Syntax and morphology

A much debated question in the literature is whether English morphology is strictly right-headed, or overwhelmingly right-headed (DiSciullo and Williams, 1981). The discussion turns around the issue how examples of the following kind should be analyzed. What is their head? What exactly is their morphological structure?

(1) *emprison, embody, empower, embolden, embitter, enchain, endanger, enlist, entrain, enslave, ensnare, entangle, enlarge*

(i) Discuss this issue from the perspectives pursued in this chapter (i.e. there is no difference between syntax and morphology).

(ii) Propose and motivate a syntactic analysis for the examples above, using VP shells.

(7) A case study of *near* (categories and silence)

The way we determine the label of a word is by distributional criteria. When we start looking at a language in detail, we sometimes encounter surprises. A case in point is the word *near* in English.

(1) He lives near/in/under the forest

(i) Based on this distribution, how should we label *near*? Why?

(ii) The answer to the previous question is reasonable, but when we probe a bit further, we also see that *near* is different from *in/above/under*. (This discussion goes back to the Danish linguist, Otto Jespersen (1860–1943).)

(2) Of all these people, it was Robin Hood who lived nearest/*innest/*underest the forest
(3) John lives nearer/*inner/*underer the forest than Bill
(4) near/nearer/nearest/nearness/*inness/*underness
(5) This was a near miss/a close miss /*an in miss, *an under miss

(iii) Based on these sentences, what can you conclude about the category label of *near*? (Say this for each sentence, e.g., in (2), *near* behaves like a ... because ... etc.))

Putting an analysis together

The final part asks you to think about how to put an analysis together that would capture these properties. (You are not required to give a full account, but simply try and see how far you can get.) Start by evaluating the analytical options below, and tell us why A is unavailable, why B does not help, and why something like C must be part of the analysis.

Hypothesis A: near is an A and a P simultaneously. (This would imply it has two heads.)
Hypothesis B: *near* is lexically ambiguous: sometimes an A, sometimes a P.
(This means there would be two lexical entries for *near*.)
Hypothesis C: near is always an A, even when used in the context of (1) above. *Near the forest* is a PP because it behaves like one. This must mean there is a P in the structure as well.

(iv) Try to come up with an analysis (and provide a tree structure) which seems a reasonable account for the properties above, taking the following examples into account. Then list which examples you can account for, and which examples you cannot.

(6) He was very poor/sad/intelligent/afraid *(of) the forest
(7) He was very near the forest
(8) *He was very in the forest
(9) He was right in the forest/right under the tree/right near the tree
(10) He was near to the forest

(Based on Maling (1983) and Kayne (2005)).

(8) Twice

Here is a sentence that differs in meaning, depending on what *twice* modifies:

(1) Mary will knock on the door twice

Describe the two meanings, and line them up with two different structures.

(9) VP shells and resultatives

1. Consider the data below for so-called resultative constructions. Use these data to motivate an analysis for (2a) that accounts for the data in (1)–(3).

(1) a. I painted the table red
b. I painted the table red and the chair blue
(2) a. I painted the table red drunk.
b. *I painted the table drunk red
(3) (I painted the table red drunk)
a. ... and he did so sober
b. *... and he did so green drunk
c. ... and he did so too

2. Next consider the examples in (4).

(4) a. She sang the children to sleep
b. *She sang the children
What is surprising about this pair of sentences? Is "the children" selected by "sing"or not? If it is not, what is it selected by? What other construction does (4a) (partially) look like?

3. Given the data in (1)–(4) what can you minimally conclude about the syntactic structures of (5) and (6)?

(5) The children were sung to sleep
(6) The table was painted red drunk

(10) Verb particles.

Consider the following two sentences, which contain the P *up*.

(1) a. John picked up the money
b. John ran up the stairs

Your task is to determine (some) properties of the constituent structure, in particular whether the P *up* forms a constituent with the following DP or not in (1a) and (1b).

(2) a. *John picked out a coin and up the money
b. John ran down the corridor and up the stairs
(3) a. John picked the money up
b. *John ran the stairs up
(4) a. *Up the money he took
b. Up the stairs he ran
(5) a. *John picked only up the money
b. John picked up only the money
(6) a. *John picked and Mary hoisted, up some heavy weights
(cf. John picked up and Mary hoisted up some heavy weights)
b. John ran, but Bill walked, up the stairs

(i) Make a (reasonable) proposal for the constituent structures of (2a) and (2b), and discuss whether your proposal accounts for all the properties listed above.
(ii) If it does not, state (remaining within the example sentences shown above) what property/ies is/are not captured; briefly discuss whether existing principles/mechanisms could be made to capture these properties easily, and be bold enough to make a (tentative) proposal.

12.10.5 Further reading

In this more advanced chapter, we have inserted most further readings in the text at the point where the relevant discussion takes place. Some works are particularly important and we list them (again) here.

Chomsky (1970) has played a seminal role in the discussion of how and where properties of morphological complex words should be treated. This is a difficult but important background paper to read to understand the current landscape of formal theories. Harris (1995) is a good overview of the developments of theoretical ideas in the 1960s and 1970s relevant for what is discussed in this chapter. Of the many references cited in this chapter, the following are particularly important: Hale and Keyser (2002), Marantz (1997), and Levin and Hovav (2005).

13
Advanced Binding and Some Binding Typology

13.1 Basics: Reminders

Here are some relevant examples of relations we talked about previously.

(1) Mary$_j$ left after she$_{j,k}$ had lunch
(2) If his$_{j,k}$ mother agrees, John$_j$ will sing
(3) Every boy$_j$ said he$_{j,k}$ was sick
(4) Juno$_j$ looked at herself$_j$

As we saw, we need to distinguish between several types of expressions:

- Anaphors: reflexive/reciprocals: *-self, each other, one another.*
- Pronouns: *she, they, me, his,* (perhaps PRO?), etc.
- Everything else, which we called R-expressions.

Among R-expressions, we distinguished between referential expressions, which point to some real or imaginary, concrete or abstract, object, and non-referential expressions which do not. Coindexing between referential expressions means coreference. This is, for example, what happens in (1) or (2). Coindexing involving a non-referential expression, as in (3), denotes a relation of referential dependence that we will not discuss in detail but is intuitively clear enough for our purposes.

The reason why we distinguished among these expressions is that they behave differently from each other. We can see this by looking at coindexing possibilities in simple cases. In English, we found two types of situation. First, there are contexts in which anaphors require coindexing, while pronouns and R-expressions prohibit it:

(5) a. She$_j$/[Every girl]$_j$ saw herself$_j$/*her$_j$/*Susan$_j$
b. They$_j$/Many$_j$ saw [each other]$_j$/*them$_j$/*Susan$_j$

Second, there are contexts in which R-expressions prohibit coindexing, while anaphors and pronouns allow it:

An Introduction to Syntactic Analysis and Theory, First Edition.
Dominique Sportiche, Hilda Koopman, and Edward Stabler.

(6) They$_k$ saw their$_k$ brother/*[John and Mary]$_k$'s brother/[each other]$_k$'s brothers

The first case shows that anaphors have some property A and the other two do not (they have property −A). The second case shows that R-expressions have property R, while the other two do not (they have property −R). No binary distinction will suffice to describe this, as the following table illustrates:

Property	+A	−A
+R		R-expressions
−R	Anaphors	Pronouns

To account for the behavior of these expressions, we began with a formulation of the binding conditions (see Section 7.2.2 for the final version), roughly as follows. Some preliminary definitions set the stage:

(7) a. A DP1 is *bound* by another DP2 just in case DP2 c-commands DP1 and they are coindexed. A DP which is not bound is *free.*
b. Node A *c-commands* node B iff a (non-reflexive) sister of A (reflexively) contains B. (We say "non-reflexive sister" to emphasize that no node is its own sister in this sense. But on the other hand every node "reflexively contains" itself.)
c. The *domain of a DP pronoun* is the smallest XP that has a subject and that contains the DP.
d. The *domain of a DP anaphor* is the smallest XP that has a subject and that has a DP c-commanding the anaphor.

Then we can formulate the binding conditions as follows:

Principle A: An anaphor must be bound, and it must be bound in its domain.
Principle B: A pronoun must be free (= not bound) in its domain.
Principle C: An R-expression cannot be bound.

From a theoretical point of view, there are a couple of challenges that we should meet. First, we should be able to explain how the binding conditions are acquired by speakers. (We briefly touched upon this fascinating and complex question in Chapter 7.) Second, we should be able to explain what the relation is between the form of an expression and its behavior with respect to binding theory. For example, it seems unlikely that there would be a variety of English in which the

Practice

First part: go through each of the sentences and make sure you know how the statements of the binding conditions predict the predicted status column. (If you speak another language, construct a similar table.) Second part: The judgments reported in the actual status column are the standard judgments given in the literature. As grammars vary from individual to individual, these judgments may be different for you. Write down what they are and, if they differ from the standard ones, see if you can formulate some descriptive generalization about your own variety of English. *Caveat*: when testing sentences with reciprocals, of the form *the Xs . . . each other*, make sure you are interpreting the sentence as *each of the Xs . . . the other Xs* (just to make sure you are looking at the reciprocal interpretation). For example, make sure you interpret *the boys talked to each other* as meaning *each of the boys talked to the other boys.*

expression *himself* behaves as a pronoun only, and the expression *him* behaves as an anaphor only. If correct, this correlation between form and behavior should be explained. We are not going to try to do this here.

Here are a number of sentences with pronouns and anaphors. The binding principles should be able to predict their status.

We can survey the predictions of this first proposal in the table below. In italics, we indicate the anaphor (or the pronoun) and its antecedent. Then we list the "Actual Status" – standard judgments given in the literature, and the "Predicted Status" – what the binding principles say about these structures.

(8) Table 1

Sentence/Condition A	Actual Status	Predicted Status w/o Shells	Predicted Status w Shells
John likes *himself*	✓	✓	?
John talked with/to *himself*	✓	✓	✓
They put the rug [around *themselves/each other*]	✓	✓	*
They saw a snake near *themselves/each other*	✓	✓	?
Himself/Each other left (the boys)	*	*	*
Pictures of *each other* are on sale	*	*	*
They read *each other*'s books	✓	✓	?
I read *each other*'s books	*	*	*
The boys saw pictures of *themselves/each other*	✓	✓	?
The boys saw Bill's pictures of *themselves/each other*	*	*	*
The boys expected that Mary would see *themselves/each other*	*	*	*
The boys bet that pictures of *themselves/each other* would be selected	✓	✓	*
The boys bet that *themselves/each other* would be selected	*	✓	✓
The boys heard that I would select pictures of *themselves/each other*	*	*	*
They expect [Mary to see *themselves/each other*]	*	*	*
They expect [Mary to read some stories about *themselves/each other*]	*	*	*
I consider *them* (to be) *each other*'s friends	✓	✓	*
They consider me (to be) *each other*'s friends	*	*	*
The boys hoped for *each other* to win	✓	✓	*
The boys hoped for Bill to invite *each other*	*	*	*

(9) Table 2

Sentence/Condition B	Actual Status	Predicted Status w/o Shells	Predicted Status w Shells
He likes *John*	*	✓	*
They read [*their* books]	✓	✓	✓
The boys saw pictures of *them*	*	*	?
The boys saw Bill's pictures of *them*	✓	✓	✓
The boys expected [*they* would win the race]	✓	✓	✓
The boys expected [that Mary would see *them*]	✓	✓	✓
They expected [that [pictures of *them*] would be on sale]	✓	✓	✓
John talked with/to *him*	*	*	*
They consider me proud of *them*	✓	✓	✓
They consider *them* proud of me	*	✓	?

We see that some sentences, however, do not behave as predicted. Some of these were already discussed in Chapter 7, but others have stopped behaving as predicted because we modified the syntactic structures with the introduction of VP shells. We will consider some of these now.

First we will discuss problems we encounter with Principle A without taking into account VP shells. Then we turn to the question of how to incorporate shells in our treatment of both Principle A and Principle B. We can face two kinds of problems: good sentences that are excluded, and bad sentences that are allowed. The latter requires us to think about how to adjust our predictions but are less threatening than the former: they warrant investigation of course, their deviance could be due to some unknown principle. The former requires our immediate attention: if we exclude good sentences, it means that some of our principles are too strong: they exclude too many sentences and we must reformulate something somewhere.

13.2 Reminder About Principle A

A case of the former type was discussed in Section 7.2.2. There, we introduced the idea that the domain of an anaphor needed to contain at least some DP distinct from the anaphor c-commanding the anaphor precisely because a good example was being excluded. This adjustment was needed to capture examples of the following kind:

(10) *They* read *each other*'s books

This is what had led to the following two modifications:

(11) **A node does not c-command itself**.
(12) The *domain of a DP anaphor* is the smallest XP that has a subject **and that has a DP c-commanding the anaphor**.

This change has a welcome consequence for such a well-formed example as the following (part of the table above):

(13) The boys bet that pictures of each other/themselves would be selected

As you should be able to check, both of the above modifications are required to prevent it from being excluded.

13.3 Subjects of Tensed Clauses

A case of the latter type of sentence that does not behave as expected is the following:

Sentence/Condition B	Actual Status	Predicted Status
They said (that) *themselves* were leaving	*	✓
They said (that) *each other* were leaving	*	✓
The boys expected [*themselves/each other* would win the race]	*	✓

These sentences are predicted to be fine: the smallest XP with a subject containing the anaphor and containing a DP c-commanding the anaphor would be the main clause VPs which contain (the trace of) *they*. Some modification must be introduced to exclude such cases. There is a long history of trying to find the right generalization. One way we could go about this – and this has been explored in various ways – is to modify the notion "domain of an anaphor" to prevent an anaphor subject of a tensed clause seeking an antecedent outside of its clause. This is not easy: sometimes anaphors are allowed to seek an antecedent outside of the tensed clause containing them, as is the case for example in (13) above. This sentence is fine despite the fact that the anaphors are inside the tensed clause complement of the verb *bet*, and their antecedent is outside of it.

We can also gain some insight about what is going on by looking at what happens in other languages. This is what Luigi Rizzi, an Italian linguist, currently (2013) professor at the university of Siena in Italy (and seen on the left here) did in 1990. He discovered an interesting effect that we will call the **Anaphor Agreement Effect**. The effect is this: when we look at English, it seems that anaphors that appear as the subject of tensed clauses are excluded. But an examination of some cross-linguistic data suggests that this is not the right generalization. Rather, what seems to matter is whether or not an anaphor triggers (normal visible) agreement on T (as it does in English). When it does, as in English, Icelandic, or Italian, it is not allowed. But when it does not, as in Khmer, Vietnamese, Chinese, Korean, and Thai, it is fine (and allowed to seek an antecedent outside its clause).

(14) **The Anaphor Agreement Effect** (Rizzi, 1990b): Anaphors are prohibited from positions triggering agreement (on T).

The reasoning can be illustrated by the following Italian data from Rizzi (1990b, 15a),

(15) A loro importa solo di se stessi
to them.DAT matters.3S only of themselves.GEN
"All that matters to them is themselves"

Here we have a dative subject (*a loro*) binding a genitive anaphor (*di se stessi*) complement of the verb, and the tensed verb carrying 3rd singular agreement. Italian allows the object of the verb to be nominative as well, in which case agreement on T must be obligatorily plural, as indicated below. In this situation, the object cannot be an anaphor as shown in the second sentence.

(16) a. A me interessano/*interessa solo loro
to me.DAT interest.3PL/interest.3S only they.NOM
"I am interested only in them"
b. *A loro interessano solo se stessi
to them.DAT interest.3PL only themselves.NOM
"They are interested only in themselves"

We show the same effect with a DP with different person and number features and a different verb:

(17) a. A voi importa solo di voi stessi
to you.DAT.PL matters.3SG only of yourselves.GEN
"All that matters to you is yourselves"
b. A me importatete solo voi
to me.DAT matter.2PL only you.NOM.PL
"All that matters to me is you"
c. *A voi importatete solo voi stessi
to you.DAT.PL interest.2PL only yourselves.NOM
"All that matters to you is yourselves"

There are many superficial counterexamples to the anaphor agreement effect: for example, it has been reported that Tamil, Modern Greek, Georgian, Albanian, Jacaltec, Selayarese, and French, exhibit configurations that violate it. However, in a remarkable study, Ellen Woolford discovered that all such counterexamples were only apparent and, once the particulars of each language were taken into account, the counterexamples disappeared.

To conclude this section, we can attribute the ill-formedness of sentences listed in the table at the beginning of this section to the anaphor agreement effect. Naturally, we would like to know why such an effect holds. This is a more advanced topic that we will not pursue here. Both Rizzi (1990b) and Woolford (1999) make theoretical proposals in this regard.

> In Woolford (1999), Ellen Woolford showed that either agreement was a special form only found with anaphors (thus not normal agreement), or that the anaphor was not itself triggering the agreement (because it was not the subject, or because the agreement appearing on T was a default agreement). Just as remarkably, Woolford showed that the same phenomenon could be duplicated with objects. In languages in which objects trigger the presence of an agreement marker, e.g. Nez Perce, Inuktitut, Swahili, etc., anaphors are excluded, or have a special behavior (e.g. a special agreement form). It should be pointed out that the facts discussed are mostly about reflexive anaphors. The case of reciprocals is perhaps more complex. Thus, while speakers of English usually disallow the first sentence below, some allow the second:
>
> (18) *They said that each other were leaving
>
> (19) Before deciding, they asked what each other was doing.
>
> We will leave this question open here.

13.4 VP shells and the Binding Theory

We now turn to the consequences of adopting the theory of VP shells for functioning of the binding theory. Recall that we motivated the existence of VP shells by looking at morphological properties, by looking at cases of verbs superficially taking two complements or by looking at the interpretation of adverbs. We saw that even apparently simple transitive verbs like *close*, *open*, or *dry* had to be analyzed as involving a VP shell too. As a result, we adopted the idea that simple transitive verbs such as *buy* in *John bought a book*, or *invite* in *Athena invited Juno*, involve two VPs one on top of the other.

> How can we be sure that a verb like *invite* involves a VP shell, rather being a simple verb taking a subject and an object? One way is to look at how *again* works with it. If it is possible to say (truly): *John invited Mary and then Bill invited her again*, in a case in which Bill never invited Mary before, it suggests that a restitutive reading is available, that is that we have at least two VPs. This is in fact the case with *invite.*

Accordingly, *Athena invited Juno* is analyzed as having a VP as below; that is, *invite* is analyzed as the complex [V+v] (the identity of the v and V pieces does not matter here as long as the two together yield the pronounced verbal form "invite").

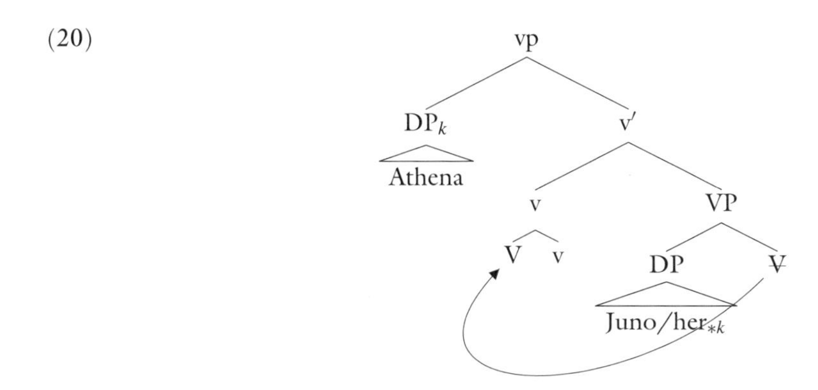

13.4.1 Revising binding domain for pronouns

Suppose now that the direct object is a pronoun, like *her*: coreference between *Athena* and *her* is not possible. But is it predicted to be good or not by our binding theory? It is predicted to be good! The problem is that the domain of the pronoun is VP and not vP. And within VP, the pronoun is free as required by Principle B. Something needs to be modified to fix this. There are several nearly equivalent ways to do this with slightly different predictions. One option that will not work is to do what we did with Principle A. If we require the presence of a c-commanding DP, this will correctly rule out (20), but it will also rule out *they like their books*, as should be easy to see. So we will adopt a way that will generalize straightforwardly to some more complex cases we will see later (but it is important to keep in mind that there are a few slightly different alternatives). The result we want to obtain is that the domain of the pronoun *her* is vP and not VP: this would exclude coindexing of *her* and *Athena*, since *her* would be bound in its domain. To get this, let's modify the notion of domain, as follows: if the domain of an anaphor of a pronoun contains the trace of a head, it must also contain the antecedent of this trace.

Here are the new definitions for domain with the new requirement added in (21b–22b):

(21) The domain of a DP pronoun is the smallest XP with a subject
  a. which contains the DP, and
  b. which contains the antecedent of every head trace it contains.

(22) The domain of a DP anaphor is the smallest XP with a subject and
  a. which has a DP c-commanding the anaphor, and
  b. which contains the antecedent of every head trace it contains.

Note that we modified the definition of domain for pronouns and for anaphors. But we have only discussed the case of pronouns. We return to anaphors below.

It is clear how this revised notion of domain for pronouns would exclude the illicit coreference above. Now the domain of the pronoun cannot be VP. Since VP contains the trace of V (written V above), it must contain V too. As a result, the smallest XP with a subject (i) which contains the DP and (ii) which contains, the antecedent of every head trace it contains is vP, as desired.

Practice

Now you should be able to verify that the following table is accurate, namely what the predicted outcomes were under the old notion of domain with or without VP shells, and under the new notion of domain with VP shells.

Sentence/Condition B	Actual Status	Predicted Status		
		Old domain, no VP shell	Old domain with VP shell	New domain with VP shell
They showed her *them*	*	*	✓	*
She showed *the boys them*	*	*	✓	*
They showed *them* a book	*	*	✓	*
They showed her to *them*	*	*	✓	*
She showed *the boys* to *them*	*	*	✓	*

Let's return now to the following case, discussed in Section 12.8:

(23) They expect them to see Mary

Expect is a raising to object (RtoO) verb, which means that it does not select its superficial direct object (know how to show this!). Rather, this direct object is selected by some predicate in the infinitival complement clause. What exactly is the structural analysis, the tree, for such structures? In particular, how does the superficial direct object fit in the surface structure tree? Is it the subject of a TP immediately preceding the non-finite T *to* (this is the so-called ECM analysis mentioned in Chapters 9 and 12). Is this TP included in a CP? Is the superficial direct object in the main clause? We discussed empirical evidence that the direct object was indeed in the VP shell structure of the RtoO verb (cf. Section 12.8). The binding facts further corroborate these earlier findings. To see this, let us evaluate the predictions that would be made by assuming that *them* is the subject of TP (within a CP complement or not) in the kind of structure sometimes assumed for ECM complements.

We would have the following (partial structure, shown without a CP here):

(24)

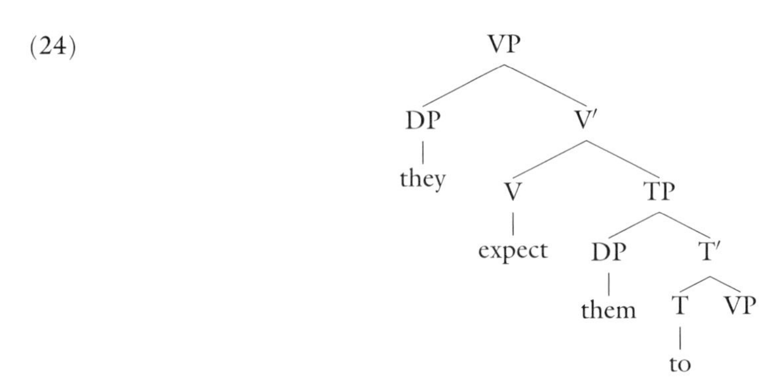

Clearly, such a structure makes the wrong prediction regarding possible coindexing between *they* and *them*. It should be clear that the domain of the DP *them* is TP. This predicts incorrectly that coindexing between *them* and *they* should be allowed: if it were, this sentence should be able to mean "they expect themselves to . . . ".

What we need is for the domain of the pronoun *them* to be a constituent that contains the subject *they* (or its trace); this means the structure has to be different from the one above. Let us think about the kind of structure we would assign to a sentence like:

(25) They expect them

Given the discussion we had above about the verb *invite*, and the necessary disjoint reference between the subject and the object pronoun, we can postulate the following structural analysis:

(26)

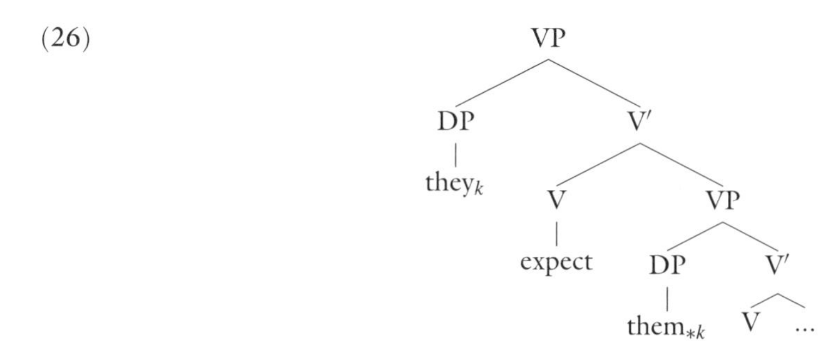

If this structure was somehow also part of the structure for (23), we would have the right prediction with respect to Principle B. But there is an important difference between (23) and (25): in the latter, *them* is selected by *expect* (in fact by V). In the former it is not (it is selected by *see*). This means that a structure like (26) cannot be an *underlying* structure for (25). This is a by now familiar situation: we would like a certain derived structure, but this derived structure cannot be an underlying structure. We have encountered this before, for example in raising to subject structures (where the subject of a main clause has raised from an embedded clause position). By the same reasoning, this suggests that *them* in (26) has raised into its surface position. Hence the following derivation (where again we represent the complement clause as a TP, leaving open the possibility that a silent CP layer is present):

(27)

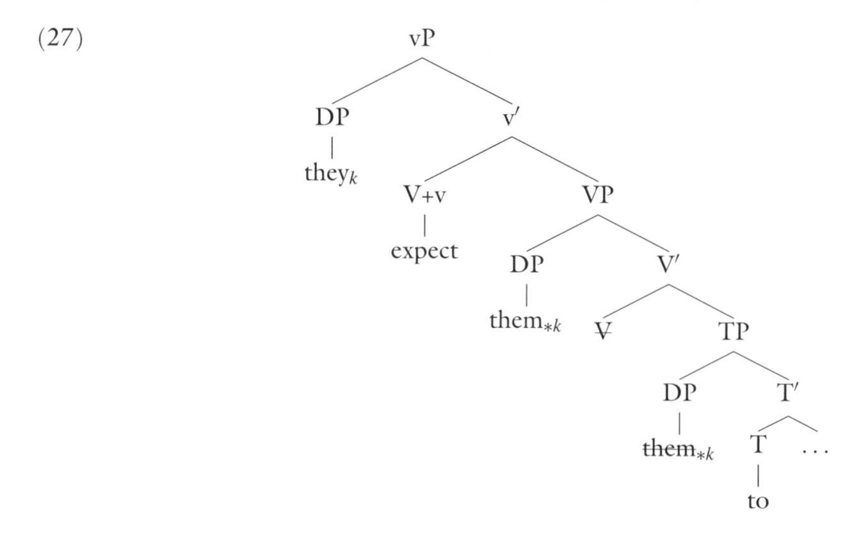

In other words, raising to object applies, and so-called ECM structures – exceptional case marking structures – are not so exceptional from the point of view of case marking. They are called this because it seems that the subject of an embedded clause receives accusative case from a main verb, but in fact, this case marking is expected once the subject of the embedded clause raises to a position where direct objects are normally getting Case. This is why verbs such as expect (*believe, assume*, etc.) are also called RtoO verbs, a name that fits their syntactic derivation well. There is something exceptional about ECM verbs, but it not that their case-marking behavior is exceptional, rather that they trigger raising to object unlike other verbs taking infinitival complements.

The structures given above for RtoO/ECM verbs are good enough for our purposes here. It is important to keep in mind that they are just approximations of what we think is the truth today. From a theoretical standpoint, the following question arises: is the distinction between raising to object/ECM verbs and other verbs taking infinitival complements but disallowing raising to object arbitrary, or is there a deeper explanation for this difference? The same questions can of course be asked about raising to subject verbs. In the latter case we know that a precondition is that raising to subject verbs should not select for a subject, but not much more than this. These are open questions requiring further research.

13.4.2 Revising binding domain for anaphors

We have already indicated the change for the notion of domain for anaphors that we repeat here:

(28) The domain of a DP anaphor is the smallest XP with a subject
  a. which has a DP c-commanding the anaphor, and
  b. which contains the antecedent of every head trace it contains.

Let us now see why the modification in (28b) is required. Here is a table summarizing the problem created by introducing shells:

Sentence/Condition B	Actual Status	Predicted Status		
		Old domain, no VP shell	Old domain VP shell	New domain VP shell
He introduced *himself* to them	✓	✓	*	✓
She showed John a picture of *herself*	✓	✓	*	✓
They showed him *each other/themselves*	✓	✓	*	✓
They showed it to *each other/themselves*	✓	✓	*	✓

We can illustrate this with the help of a tree for a sentence like *He*$_k$ *introduced himself*$_k$ *to them*. As before, we treat *show* as V+v (e.g. [see+CAUS], but again, we do not worry about the parts as long as V+v = *show*).

(29)

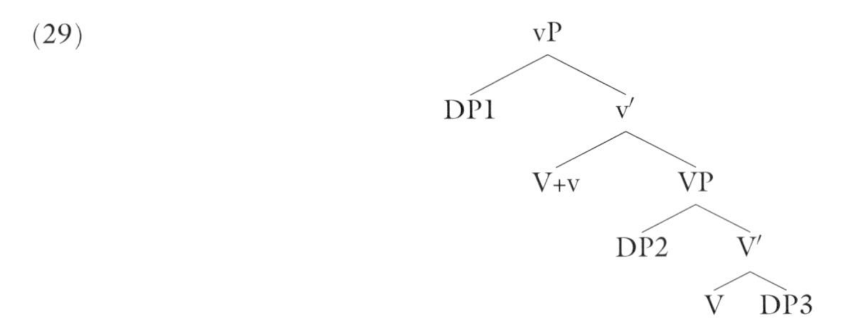

In *He*$_k$ *introduced himself*$_k$ *to them*, DP2 is the anaphor that must be bound by DP1. This result follows even without the modification, because the domain of an anaphor must contain a DP c-commanding the anaphor. In *She*$_k$ *showed John a picture of herself*$_k$, DP2 is *she* and DP3 is *a picture of herself*. Without the modification, the domain of DP3 is VP: this wrongly predicts that the sentence is ill-formed. With the modification, the domain is extended to vP and correctly allows DP1 to be an antecedent for *himself*. The same reasoning applies to the other sentences in the table.

Practice

Provide a syntactic analysis for the following well-formed sentence (paying attention to the surface position of the knights):

(30) Lancelot considered the knights all loyal to the king

Then provide a syntactic analysis of the very last example of the table in (9) that explains why Principle B, as we have formulated it, correctly explains its deviance.

13.5 Binding Variation and Typology

To what extent is what we have seen in English representative of the binding systems found across languages? Put more concretely, are there other kinds of anaphors we have not talked about? And are the notions of binding, domains, or the formulation of the binding principles uniform across languages or do we find variation? As of today, it is fair to say that we can only give very sketchy answers to these questions, which are the focus of intense research activities. Still we can illustrate a few things linguists have learned about anaphoric systems.

The binding conditions we have formulated obey the following general format:

(31) **Binding Condition Format**: DP of type x must (not) be bound within domain (x).

One way of reformulating the questions is to ask, for each language, whether we find other types than anaphors, pronouns, or R-expressions, whether there are other notions of binding, and whether there are other notions of domain. It turns out that we find positive answers to all three questions.

As usual, the existence of this kind of variation raises two related questions that we will not try to address here. One is whether there is a general theory that can tell us what is a possible binding system and what cannot be. Second, since different languages seem to have different systems, language learners must be able to zero in on their language system on the basis of simple exposure to it. Determining how this can be accomplished is an important research question that will teach us a lot about human cognition and how it develops in the mind.

We find that there are other types than these, in particular one type that has been called a **logophor**. We will see that the relevant notion of binding and of domain for logophors is different from what we have seen so far, but we will also see that even for anaphors, differences are found in the notion of domain, and differences are found with respect to what can count as an antecedent.

Regarding the notion of domain for anaphors, it seems we find at least the following options represented in languages of the world:

An element must be bound/free within Domain D where D is defined as:

Subject Domain: Smallest XP with a subject.
Extended Subject Domain: Smallest XP with a subject and a c-commander.
Tense Domain: Smallest tensed clause.
Root Domain: Sentence.

Regarding what can count as an antecedent (a property also called "orientation"), it seems we find at least the following options represented in languages of the world:

C-command Orientation: A c-commanding antecedent.
Subject Orientation: A subject antecedent.
Anti-subject Orientation: A non-subject antecedent.
Discourse Orientation: Not syntactically determined.

All these notions are straightforward except the last one (discourse orientation). When an anaphor is discourse oriented, it is often called a **logophor**. A logophor selects its antecedent according to the role this antecedent plays in the discourse. Different logophors (in different languages) seem to function differently. The linguist Peter Sells (Sells, 1987) has documented the existence of the following options. The antecedent of a logophor can be:

A Source: Someone (or a DP referring to someone) who is the intentional agent in a communication. For example, normally the subject of the verb *say*, or the object of *hear from* ... is a Source in this sense: in the sentence *John said that it was raining*, *John* is a

Source. Similarly, the utterer of a sentence is a Source (e.g. if I say: *it is raining*, I am a Source).

B Self: Someone (or a DP referring to someone) whose mental state or mental attitude the content of the proposition describes. This, for example, would be the case of the (referent of) the subject of the verb *want*, or *hope*, or *think*; in the sentence *John feels that he should leave*, the subject *John* is a Self. *John* is also a Self in a case like: *John's opinion is that you are right*.

A Pivot: Someone (or a DP referring to someone) with respect to whom (space-time) location or deixis is evaluated. For example, suppose I report what John said by uttering: *John said: "the book is here,"* the meaning of *here* is evaluated with respect to *John*. We understand that the book is near John, and not necessarily near me. *John* is considered a Pivot.

We will briefly illustrate these possibilities with data drawn from languages other than English.

13.5.1 Mainland Scandinavian (Danish, Norwegian, Swedish)

Data for these languages are drawn from Vikner (1985), Hellan (2008), and Riad (1988) via Safir (1992). In these languages, we can distinguish three components:

- regular pronouns *ham/hende/dem* (him, her, them);
- "reflexive pronouns" *sig* (which can be possessive);
- the noun *selv* (self).

The noun *selv* can freely combine with either pronouns or reflexives yielding four possible forms:

hamselv	ham
sigselv	sig

Here are some representative examples from Danish (to avoid certain complications found in these languages, we use embedded clauses) illustrating the behavior of these elements (this, to a certain extent, is valid for Dutch *hem/hemzelf, zich/zichzelf*):

(32) ...at Sue fortalte Ann om X
that Sue told Anne about X
If X = Sue: *hende, *hende selv, *sig , sig selv
If X =Ann: *hende, hende selv, *sig , *sig selv

(33) ...at Sue bad Anne$_k$ [om PRO$_k$ at ringe til X]
that Sue asked Anne$_k$ [for PRO$_k$ to ring to X]
If X = Sue: hende, *hende selv, sig , *sig selv
If X = Ann: *hende, *hende selv, *sig , sig selv

This gives us the following rough overall description (many details left open). *Selv* is a "localizer": it makes the element it affixes require a c-commanding binder within the domain of tense. Elements without *selv* behave like pronouns in that they obey Principle B. *Sig* on the other hand is subject oriented while *ham* is anti-subject oriented. Since *selv* can combine with *sig* or *ham*, it gives us four cases:

	Selv: Bound within smallest XP	Free in smallest XP
Sig: Subject-oriented and bound in its tense domain	*Sigselv*: locally bound by a subject within smallest XP	Must be locally free but bound by a subject in its tense domain
Ham: Anti-subject-oriented	*Hamselv*: bound by a non-subject within smallest XP	Must be free from a subject within its tense domain

Although we have not described English the way we have Mainland Scandinavian, the English system can be described in a similar way. Accordingly, English has pronouns (*he, she, them*, etc.) and a "localizer" *self* (which can independently occur as a noun or as a bound noun/prefix). Just as in Mainland Scandinavian, pronouns are subject to a disjoint reference requirement (Principle B). However, when affixed with *self*, they turn into anaphors that must be bound locally (Principle A).

What seems to be special about these Scandinavian languages is the existence of a specialized subject-oriented element *sig*. Its presence seems to force regular pronouns to become anti-subject oriented. Some other languages are said to have a similar subject-oriented anaphor requiring c-command by its antecedent, e.g. Kannada, or Hindi/Urdu.

An interesting theoretical question to address is this: how should the binding system of these languages be constructed so that we guarantee that subject orientation (for *sig*) or anti-subject orientation (for *ham*) is enforced. Simple notions of c-command or domain will in general not be good enough.

13.5.2 Icelandic

Data for Icelandic are drawn from Thráinsson (1976), Maling (1984, 1986), Anderson (1986), and Sigurðsson (1990). Icelandic, which is also a Scandinavian language, is very similar but not identical to Mainland Scandinavian. Just as in mainland Scandinavian, we find pronouns (*han*) and a subject oriented reflexive pronoun *sig*. This reflexive inflects for case: *sig* (various cases), *ser* (dative), *sin* (genitive), *sin* (possessive). In addition, the possessive forms inflects for number, gender, and case. Finally there is a self form, *sjalfum*, which is suffixed to pronouns or reflexives and is a "localizer": it makes them mandatorily require an antecedent within a certain domain.

We thus get the following four possibilities (ignoring case differences):

han sjalfum	han
sig sjalfum	sig

Again simplifying somewhat, the behavior of these four expressions is reported to be close to what happens in Mainland Scandinavian. A pronoun is anti-subject-oriented and must be free within its subject domain, while a reflexive is subject-oriented and must be bound by a c-commander within its tense domain. For example, Thráinsson (1976) provides the following sentences:

(34) a. Jón$_i$ skipaði mér$_j$ [að PRO$_j$ lemja sig$_i$]
John ordered me to hit-infinitive SIG

b. *Eg$_j$ hótaði Jóni$_i$ [að PRO$_j$ lemja sig$_i$]
I threatened John to hit-infinitive SIG

c. *[$_{DP}$ Skoðun Jóns$_i$]$_j$ virðist [t_j vera hættuleg fyrir sig$_i$]
opinion John's seems t be-infinitive dangerous for SIG

"John's opinion seems to be dangerous for SIG"

In the first one, we see *sig* taking an antecedent outside of its own (infinitive) clause. The second illustrates the fact that *sig* is subject-oriented, and the third shows that a non-commander will not qualify as an antecedent, even if it is part of a subject.

One difference between Mainland Scandinavian and Icelandic concerns *sig*: in Icelandic, it doesn't need to be locally free. In the Icelandic equivalent of (32), it would be OK to use *sig* if X=Sue. Similarly, in (34a), sig_j would be fine too (with a different meaning).

There is another difference, however: sometimes *sig* is allowed to look beyond what appears to be its tense domain, for example if it is found in a subjunctive clause. Thráinsson (1976) provides the following sentences to illustrate this. In all three, *sig* is a direct object.

(35) a. Jón$_j$ skipaði Pétri$_i$ [að PRO$_i$ raka sig$_{i/j/*k}$
John$_j$ ordered-indicative Peter$_i$ to shave himself$_{i/j/*k}$
á hverjum degi]
every day

b. Jón$_j$ veit [að Pétur$_i$ rakar sig$_{i/*j/*k}$
John knows that Peter shaves-indicative himself$_i$/*him$_j$/*him$_k$
á hverjum degi]
every day

c. Jón$_j$ segir [að Pétur$_i$ raki sig$_{i/j,*k}$
John$_j$ says that Peter$_i$ shaves-subjunctive himself$_i$/him$_j$/*him$_k$
á hverjum degi]
every day

In the first two, *sig* must be bound by a c-commanding subject within its tense domain (which is the indicative clause). But, as the third shows, *sig* may take a "long-distance" antecedent when the clause that contains it is subjunctive. In this case, the antecedent of *sig* does not have to be a c-commander. Instead it must be a source or a self antecedent, which may be a c-commander, but does not have to be, and can even be implicit:

(36) a. [$_{DP}$ Skoðun Jóns$_i$] er [að sig$_i$ vanti hæfileika]
opinion John's is that SIG-accus lacks-subjunct talents
"John's$_i$ opinion is that he$_i$ lacks talents" (cf. Maling 1984, 222)

b. [$_{DP}$ Álit Jóns$_i$]$_j$ virðist [t$_j$ vera [að ég hati sig$_i$]]
belief John's seems be that I hate-subjunct SIG
"John's$_i$ belief seems to be that I hate him$_i$"

c. Björn sagði Pétri frá [$_{DP}$ ósk Jóns$_i$] um [að Ari
Björn told Peter about wish John's about that Ari
sýndi sér$_i$ virdingu]
showed-subjunct SIG respect
"Björn told Peter about John's$_i$ wish that Ari showed him$_i$ respect"

The following pair shows that source or self is crucial. In the second sentence, the fact that we are talking about the child's appearance does not suffice to make it an antecedent for *sig*.

(37) a. Barnið$_i$ lét ekki á ljós [að það hefði verið hugsað vel
the-child put not in light that there had-subj been thought well
um sig$_i$]
about SIG
"The child didn't reveal that SIG had been taken good care of"

b. *Barnið$_i$ bar þess ekki merki [að það hefði-subj verið hugsað
the-child bore it not signs that there had been thought
vel um sig$_i$]
well about SIG
"The child didn't look as if SIG had been taken good care of"

We describe this by saying that *sig* can be either an anaphor (when it is bound by a c-commander in its tense domain) or a logophor (when it takes a source or self antecedent).

It is worth noting that Rizzi's anaphor agreement effect holds in Icelandic. *Sig* cannot appear in a situation where it triggers agreement on T. Rizzi (1990b) provides examples from Maling (1984) contrasting a grammatical case, where *sig* does not agree with T (being inside a PP), with an ungrammatical case in which *sig* does agree (Subjunc = subjunctive in the examples below):

(38) a. Sigga$_i$ telur að mér lõ'ki vel vid sig$_i$
Sigga thinks that me(DAT) likes(Subjunc) well with self
"Sigga thinks that I like himself"
b. *Sigga$_i$ telur að mér lõ'ki sig$_i$
Sigga thinks that me(DAT) likes(Subjunc) self(NOM)
"Sigga thinks that I like himself"

Icelandic also allows dative subject constructions. In such a case, T does not agree with the Dative subject, but with the nominative DP. Dative *sig* (= *ser*) is possible in such cases. Thus we have the following contrast, from Maling (1984, (8b)) and Rizzi (1990b, (15b)), respectively:

(39) a. Hún sagði að sér þae+tti v+nt um mig
She$_i$ said that selfi(DAT) was(Subjunc) fond of me
b. *Jón segir að sig elski Maria
Joni says that selfi(NOM) loves(Subjunc) Maria

In the first sentence, the subject anaphor is dative, does not trigger agreement, and is allowed; in the second, it is nominative, triggers agreement, and is disallowed.

13.5.3 Chinese

As our last example, we take a look at Chinese. Chinese has of course many different dialects, which seem to differ in subtle ways with respect to binding theory. Our discussion is drawn from the work of Huang and Liu (2001), and from personal communications with Professor C.-T. James Huang, presently (in 2013) professor at Harvard University, whose pioneering work on Chinese syntax has been very influential. He is pictured here on the left.

This data are drawn from a particular variety of Mandarin Chinese that is similar to English, Scandinavian, and other languages. It has pronouns (e.g. *ta/him*) and a morpheme *ziji* meaning *self*. When combined, the result (e.g. *ta-ziji*) behaves very much like English *himself*. It is an anaphor that is subject to Principle A. One significant difference is that since subjects of TP do not trigger agreement on T, subject anaphors are fine, as expected under Rizzi's generalization concerning the anaphor agreement effect. Here are some examples to illustrate this:

(40) Zhangsan$_i$ piping-le ta-ziji$_i$
Zhangsan criticize-Perf himself
"Zhangsan criticized himself"

(41) Zhangsan ji-le yi-ben shu gei ta-ziji
Zhangsan send-Perf one-Cl book to (him)self
"Zhangsan sent a book to himself"

The following example illustrates the lack of anaphor agreement effect:

(42) Zhangsan shuo ta-ziji kanjian-le Lisi
Zhangsan say (him)-self see-Perf Lisi
"Zhangsan said that he saw Lisi"

This example illustrates that Principle A is operative:

(43) *Zhangsan$_i$ shuo [Lisi piping-le (ta)-ziji$_i$]
Zhangsan say Lisi criticize-Perf himself
"Zhangsan$_i$ said Lisi criticized him$_i$"

The behavior of monomorphemic *ziji* (that is, *ziji* by itself) is very reminiscent of what we saw with Icelandic *sig*, an intriguing similarity since the two languages are obviously not closely related.

Fundamentally, *ziji* can behave like a subject-oriented anaphor, subject to Principle A. In this case, just like Scandinavian *sig*, Chinese *ziji* is subject oriented: its antecedent must a subject and must be in the domain of *ziji* as defined by Principle A. In other words, *ziji* behaves like *ta-ziji* above and shows subject orientation:

(44) Zhangsan$_i$ song (gei) Lisi$_j$ yi-zhang (ta)-ziji$_{i/*j}$-de xiangpian
Zhangsan give to Lisi one-CL self?s picture
"Zhangsan$_i$ gives Lisi$_j$ a picture of himself$_{i/*j}$"

In the above example, the subject of the clause, *Zhangsan*, can be an antecedent for *ziji*, but *Lisi* cannot.

Ziji can also behave like a logophor. In this case, there is no locality requirement but its antecedent must meet the properties that antecedents of logophors must possess (in Chinese): (roughly) it must be a source, a self, or a pivot. In the following example, *ziji* allows a long-distance antecedent, *Zhangsan*, which is a source (and *Lisi* could also be antecedent for *ziji*):

(45) Zhangsan$_i$ shuo Lisi kanjian-le ziji$_i$
Zhangsan say Lisi see-Perf self
"Zhangsan$_i$ said that Lisi saw him$_i$"

A source can also be implicit. In the following example, it remains implicit (in which case the antecedent of the logophor is understood to be the speaker of the utterance). Hence, in the following examples, *ziji* would be replaceable by a 1st person pronoun *I*, *me*, or reflexive *myself*.

(46) Zhe-ge xiangfa, chule ziji, zhiyou san-ge ren zancheng
This-CL idea, besides self only three-CL people agree
"As for this idea, besides myself, only three other people agree"

(47) Zhe-pian wenzhang shi Ann he ziji he-xie de, (qing duoduo zhijiao)
This-CL article be Ann and self co-author DE, (please many advise)
"This article was co-authored by Ann and myself; please give me your advice"

The literature on Chinese *ziji* documents two additional interesting properties which we have not seen yet. First, when it is used as a logophor, *ziji* must be interpreted *de se* (see the discussion of the *de se* interpretation of PRO). What this means is that the sentence in (45) must be interpreted as meaning:

Zhangsan said: "Lisi saw me"

This, for example, would not be the case if Zhangsan had said: "Lisi saw him," not realizing that the "him" in question was Lisi himself. In other words, the source or self or pivot must be aware that *ziji* refers to *him*. We have seen that PRO – which is silent – has to be interpreted *de se* as subject of certain infinitives in English (as in French and Spanish, etc.). What Chinese *ziji* illustrates is that some overt expressions must also be interpreted thus. Second, when *ziji* is used as a logophor, there are blocking effects. We are not going to discuss them in detail, but we can exemplify them. Roughly they occur when the wrong kind of DP occurs between the logophor *ziji* and its antecedent. In such cases coreference becomes impossible:

(48) * Antecedent_k... Blocking DP... ziji_k

This for example is the case if a first or second person intervenes between *ziji* and a 3rd person antecedent.

(49) Zhangsan_i renwei [ni_j hen $\text{ziji}_{*i/j}$]
Zhangsan think you hate self
"Zhangsan thinks that you hate yourself"
"*Zhangsan_i thinks that you hate him_i"
(but this is ok if *ni* is replaced by *Lisi*)

These two properties are very important as they distinguish *ziji* the anaphor from *ziji* the logophor. *Ziji* the anaphor does not

- care about interveners blocking coreference (like 1st or 2nd person pronouns as above); and
- need not be interpreted *de se*.

On the other hand, *ziji* the logophor

- is sensitive to the status of the antecedent as source, self, or pivot; and
- is subject to intervention effects.

We can illustrate this dual behavior of *ziji* with the following examples. Before we do so, here is the reasoning behind what we are going to do. Imagine that the following example is a Chinese example with English words (where we mean *self* to stand for *ziji*):

(50) Paul said that the weather had damaged a picture of self

What do we expect if *self* is an anaphor? The domain of *self* for Principle A does not contain *Paul*. The sentence should be out with *self* taking *Paul* as antecedent. If *self* is a logophor however, *Paul* should qualify as antecedent since it is a source. But there should be an additional requirement: *self* should also be interpreted *de se*. According to Huang and Liu, the latter is the case. The *de se* reading is required (if *self* is interpreted as meaning Paul, Paul cannot be mistaken about who is in the picture: he must know it is him).

Now, what about a sentence like this:

(51) Paul said that a picture of self had burned

What do we expect if *self* is an anaphor? The domain of *self* for Principle A contains *Paul.* The sentence should be acceptable with *self* taking *Paul* as antecedent. No other condition is required. If *self* is a logophor, however, there should be an additional requirement: *self* would have to be interpreted *de se.* This provides us with a test: if the *de se* interpretation is required, *self* in this sentence is a logophor. Otherwise, it is an anaphor. The following Chinese examples are modeled on this last case and they show that *ziji* is sometimes an anaphor and not a logophor.

(52) a. Zhangsan yiwei ziji de erzi zui congming
Zhangsan think self DE son most clever
"Zhangsan thought that his son was the cleverest"
b. Zhangsan yiwei Lisi zui xihuan ziji de erzi
Zhangsan think Lisi most like self DE son
"Zhangsan thought that Lisi liked his son most"
(53) a. Zhangsan shuo ziji kanjian-le Lisi
Zhangsan say self see-Perf Lisi
"Zhangsan said that he saw Lisi"
b. Zhangsan shuo Lisi kanjian-le ziji
Zhangsan say Lisi see-Perf self
"Zhangsan said that Lisi saw him"

In all these examples, *ziji* may be bound by the matrix subject *Zhangsan*, which – as subject of the verb *say* – qualifies as a source. If the interpretation is not meant to be *de se* (when the coreference is reported purely as the speaker's knowledge from the speaker's own perspective), *ziji* may be bound by the matrix subject *Zhangsan* in the (a) examples but not in the (b) examples. In the (b) sentences, under the non-*de se* scenario, the reflexive is only naturally bound by the embedded subject Lisi. This is consistent with the view that, when logophoric conditions do not hold, Principle A of the binding theory must be met (as in the (a) examples). If it is not (as in the (b) examples), the sentence is excluded.

The same scenario holds for blocking effects. Suppose we have our Chinese/English sentence again:

(54) Paul said to me that a picture of self had burned

What do we expect if *self* is an anaphor? The domain of *self* for Principle A contains *Paul.* The sentence should be acceptable with *self* taking *Paul* as antecedent. No other condition is required. If *self* is a logophor, however, the sentence should be ill-formed because of the presence of *me*, which acts as a blocker. This provides us with a second test: if such a sentence is good, *self* in this sentence can be an anaphor and does not have to be a logophor; if it is bad, *self* in this sentence must be a logophor.

As shown below in the (b) and (c) examples, a 1st person pronoun blocks the long distance binding of *ziji* in the embedded object. This is expected: since Principle A is not satisfied, *ziji* must be a logophor subject to blocking effects. However, as shown in the (a) examples, a 1st person pronoun does not induce blocking when *ziji* occurs in or within an embedded subject position. It suggests that, in such case, it is an anaphor.

(55) a. Zhangsan$_i$ dui wo shuo ziji$_i$ piping-le Lisi
Zhangsan to me say self criticize-Perf Lisi
"Zhangsan$_i$ said to me that he$_i$ criticized Lisi"
b. ??Zhangsan$_i$ dui wo shuo Lisi piping-le ziji$_i$
Zhangsan to me say Lisi criticize-Perf self
"Zhangsan$_i$ said to me that Lisi criticized him$_i$"
c. *Zhangsan$_i$ shuo wo piping-le ziji$_i$
Zhangsan say I criticize-Perf self
"Zhangsani said that I criticized him$_i$"

Again, it is only *ziji* the logophor that shows sensitivity to these blocking effects. *Ziji* the anaphor does not.

In sum then, Chinese has a double system in a way that is very similar to the Icelandic system. It has an anaphoric system appealing to some locality principle such as Principle A. And it has a logophoric system working along different lines and displaying special interpretive properties and effects.

13.5.4 How exotic is all this?

One might think that such properties as are displayed by Icelandic or Chinese are special and unusual. Nothing could be further from the truth. The blocking effects, for example, were first documented for Chinese by Huang, but they can be found elsewhere, for example in French from Dominique Sportiche.

French has an expression *soi* meaning "self". It does not require an antecedent in the same sentence:

(56) Voilà ce qu'on se disait à ce moment là: Si la radio parle de soi, c'est que tout va bien
"This is what we were telling ourselves then: If the radio is talking about us, all is fine"

and allows covert antecedents in the same sentence (the object of *persuade*):

(57) Ces circonstances persuadent de l'utilité que les armes personnelles ne protègent pas que soi
"These circumstances persuade (one) of the usefulness that personal weapons protect not only oneself"

but when it has an overt antecedent, it must be indefinite:

(58) Dans ces cas là, on ne se rend pas compte que la télé parle de soi
"In such cases, one does not realize that the tv is talking about oneself"

We are not going to discuss this in detail here (e.g. is it a logophor?), except to show that it exhibits strong intervention effects.

(59) Aujourd'hui, on (personne ne) pense que la nation/le président/*tu a(s) besoin de soi
"Today, one (nobody) thinks that the nation/the president/*you need(s) one"

Similarly, overt expressions that need to be read *de se* are also found in familiar languages. *Soi* in Sportiche's French is one such expression. Here is another example from Italian:

(60) P. crede che i suoi pantaloni siano in fiamme. Ma non si è accorto che i pantaloni sono i propri.
Pavarotti believes that the his pants are in flame but not realize that the pants are the own
"Pavarotti believes that self's pants are on fire, but he hasn't realized that the pants are his own"

(61) P. crede che i propri pantaloni siano in fiamme. Ma non si è accorto che i pantaloni sono i propri.
Pavarotti believes that the self pants are in flame but not realize that the pants are the own
"Pavarotti believes that self's pants are on fire, but he hasn't realized that the pants are his own"

The first discourse is fine. But the second is strange. This is because the expression *propri* (his own) is coreferential with the subject *Pavarotti*, but, unlike *suoi* (his), must be read *de se*. In the second discourse, the second sentence contradicts the *de se* meaning by stating that Pavarotti was unaware that his own pants were on fire. The example, inspired by the work UCLA philosopher David Kaplan, comes from Gennaro Chierchia, portrayed on the right, an Italian linguist, presently professor at Harvard University, who realized that discussions of the *de se* readings in the philosophical literature were directly relevant for linguistic theory.

In very recent work, Charnavel (2012) showed that the expression *son propre*, which is the French equivalent of the English *his own* (and similar to the Italian *proprio*), behaves very much like the Chinese expression *ziji*. It can have a long distance antecedent, but in such a case, it behaves like a logophor (its antecedent must be a source or a self) and it must be read *de se*. Otherwise, it must be bound within its local domain just like a short distance anaphor, need not be read *de se*, and allows all sorts of antecedents, including inanimates and non-subjects.

Comparative syntax and universal grammar: Most of what we have motivated has been on the basis of English. One reason for this is that the target audience for this book is primarily the English-speaking community. That almost everything was motivated on the basis of English allows the reader to better evaluate the validity and the limits of what is proposed. But this presentation may mislead one into thinking that almost everything presented here has been historically motivated on the basis of English. This is not the case. Many important insights have come from the study of other languages from all over the world. We can see why in this chapter. The study of the basic anaphoric system of Italian, Scandinavian, or Chinese leads one to notions (anaphor agreement effect, logophor, subject orientation), that are not apparent in English. More often than not, such notions are in fact relevant for English (and other languages) too, but they are much more hidden in English. Once these notions have been discovered, it becomes much easier to see that they are relevant in English and this is why we have been able, most of the time, to motivate what we have said with English examples. We can draw two important lessons from this.

First, studying the grammar of many languages is crucially important for linguistic theory, not only in order to discover the basic relevant ingredients shaping human languages, but also because comparison between human languages can tell us about what can vary from one language to another and what cannot vary, that is, what are the fixed principles and what are the parameters of linguistic theory. Second, such research underscores the deep unity of human languages. Despite what looks like enormous diversity, research has strongly suggested time and time again that the fundamental – albeit sometimes hidden – governing principles of linguistic organization are common to all. The idea that Universal Grammar, the invariants of human grammars, should be viewed as a system of fixed principles interacting with parameters whose value is fixed by exposure to linguistic data, is called the **Principles and Parameters** framework, expounded in part in Chomsky and Lasnik (1993).

13.6 Conclusion

13.6.1 Summary

In this chapter, we discussed recent developments in binding theory, incorporating the finer understanding of syntactic structure we have currently achieved, as well as a sample of an impressive body of knowledge that has accumulated over the years concerning binding patterns in many languages. Despite a surprising variety of systems, some notions seem to recur consistently, both for plain anaphors (e.g. c-command) and for other kinds, such as exempt anaphors (e.g. logophoricity). Clearly much remain to be done in this domain.

13.6.2 What to remember

In this chapter we updated Principle A and B of the binding theory, introduced in Chapter 7, in light of the discoveries in Chapters 11 and 12. You should understand how we proceeded and reasoned. You should know how to work with binding conditions, and how the behavior of pronouns provides arguments in favor of subjects having been raised to an object position in raising to object constructions. You should know how this evidence converges with independent empirical evidence. You should be able to follow the descriptions of the relevant data patterns in different languages and understand how these bear on the formulation of the binding theory.

13.6.3 Puzzles and preview: exempt anaphora

The study of Chinese anaphors shows that a single expression such as *ziji* can behave either as an anaphor subject to Condition A of the binding theory, or as a logophor not subject to Condition A. When such a situation arises, sorting out the various behaviors of such expressions requires careful, thorough analyses, see e.g. Charnavel (2009) in which it is done for some French anaphors). To avoid prejudging the results of such investigations, we can call an expression a *plain* anaphor in contexts in which it can be shown to be subject to Condition A of the binding theory, and an *exempt* anaphor in contexts in which it is not subject to Condition A. In turn, we need to decide whether an exempt anaphor is a logophor or not, and if not how exactly it behaves.

Such a situation is in fact found in English. As we have seen, the distribution of reflexives such as *herself* is regulated by Condition A, but this is not always the case. For example, the following sentence is reportedly fine even though the anaphor is not bound in its Condition A domain:

(62) Sue was sad because Henri had invited everyone but herself

This means that a more complete description of the grammar of English should include a general characterization of the cases in which reflexives behave like plain anaphors and of the cases in which they behave like exempt anaphors. Furthermore, it would be necessary, just as was done in Chinese, to provide an account of the behavior of exempt anaphors (are they logophors in requiring a source, self, or pivot as antecedent? Or do they instantiate yet another type of anaphoric dependency?). The literature contains various attempts to sort out plain anaphors from exempt anaphors in English, for example the influential Pollard and Sag (1992) or Reinhart and Reuland (1993), or more recently Charnavel (2012).

An anaphor like *herself/himself* can be exempt, and in particular need not always have a c-commanding antecedent. As a result, it is important to check that, whenever we use Principle A of the binding theory to establish that some c-command relation must hold or have held prior to movement between an anaphor and its antecedent, we are not dealing with a case of exempt anaphora. It is in fact possible to do this, and all the cases in which we have (e.g. in Chapter 11) or will (e.g. in Chapter 14) reason in this way in this book can be so controlled. This question is discussed, for example, in Chapter 3 of Charnavel (2012).

13.6.4 Further exercises

(1) Super equi

Start by considering the following sentences, which show an alternation between the two forms:

(1) a. It is possible that Mary will take a train to Boston
  b. It is possible to take a train to Boston
(2) a. To take a train to Boston is possible
  b. That Mary will take a train to Boston is possible

Assuming these sentences are related by Move, (meaning is preserved) there are two possible ways in which one could account for the alternations between the sentences in (1) and (2). Draw the two trees that show each hypothesis clearly, and label these as hypothesis 1 and hypothesis 2. Determine if you can decide between these based on these (few) data. (You are not supposed to draw conclusions on the basis of data that you have not been presented with!)

Another alternation: disturb

The verb *disturb* also participates in the same kind of alternations, as shown in the following examples. (You can assume for the purposes here that the alternations are derived in the same way as the ones above.)

(3) a. It disturbed John to have to take a train to Boston
  b. To have to take a train to Boston disturbed John
  c. Having to take a train to Boston disturbed John

These set the stage for the following example. (Pay attention to the indexation!)

(4) It disturbed [every boy]$_j$ that Mary had forgotten about him$_j$

(i) What is the name of the relation between the quantificational phrase *every boy* and the pronoun (indicated with the indices)? Additionally, write down the condition that it is subject to.
(ii) What information do we get from (4)? Draw the tree for (4) which is consistent with it.
(iii) What does it show about the validity of the two hypotheses? (Short answer.)

Next set of data

Consider next:

(5) a. It disturbed John to perjure himself/*herself
b. Perjuring himself/*herself disturbed John
c. It disturbed John that Mary perjured himself

(iv) Explain the data in (5a) and (5b). Make sure you say for each how exactly binding theory is satisfied. Be careful to check if there are any PROs in the structure. Draw a rough tree for both (5a) and (5b). (The tree should show the relevant properties that enter into the account.)

(v) What conclusion can you draw from the contrast between (5a) and (5b) regarding Hypotheses 1 and 2? (One or two sentences should suffice.)

Further embedding

We embed (5a) under *know*, and we find the following contrast:

(6) a. Mary knew that it disturbed John to perjure himself/*herself
b. Mary knew that perjuring himself/herself disturbed John

(vi) Explain exactly how binding theory is satisfied in (6b).
(vii) What, if anything, is surprising about this fact?
(viii) Tell us briefly what you can conclude about the contrast between (6a) and (6b).
(ix) What is your overall verdict on the two hypotheses?

(Super equi. Based on Landau (2000).)

(2) VP shells and the binding theory

With the introduction of VP shells, where all transitive structures (i.e. structures with an agent/experiencer and an accusative object have two shells), we must make sure we don't get into trouble with binding theory. In this problem, you are asked to evaluate different formulations of the binding principles, and evaluate their predictions.

Binding Principles A and B state:

Principle A: an anaphor must be bound in its domain.
Principle B: a pronoun must be free in its domain.

Here are four versions of the notion *binding domain:*

The domain of some element E is (i) a constituent containing E, and (ii) is the smallest phrasal constituent (XP) possible ...

Version 1: which is a TP
Version 2: which has a subject
Version 3: which has a subject distinct from E
Version 4: which contains a subject and the head X

- Version 3 = roughly equivalent to (66) in Section 7.2.2 (p. 171).

The domain of a DP pronoun is the smallest XP with a subject that contains the DP.

The domain of a DP anaphor is the smallest XP which has a subject and which has a DP c-commanding the anaphor.

- Version 4 has as an effect that when the head moves to a c-commanding position (like V to *v*), it is the position of V (i.e. vP) that counts.

For the purposes of this exercise, objects of transitive verbs are merged as subjects of big VP; agents as subjects of v. For each of the following sentences, answer the following questions. (Use the table presented below.)

a. What is the relevant principle?
b. Does it correctly predict the status of the sentence?
c. Give the relevant domain, its head underlined and the first and last word of the domain according to each version:

Sentences:
1. OK John$_k$'s sister likes him$_k$
2. * Sue$_k$ thought that herself$_k$ had left
3. OK Mary$_k$ saw her$_j$
4. OK I gave Mary$_k$ her$_k$ book back
5. * Sue showed himself$_k$ Bill$_k$ in the mirror
6. * Andrew$_k$ resented Henrietta's comments about himself$_k$
7. OK Henri$_k$ believed himself$_k$ to be crazy
8. * Himself$_k$ is sick
9. OK Mary told me$_k$ when to prepare myself$_k$
10. OK John$_k$ likes his$_k$ book
11. OK They$_k$ like each other$_k$'s books

(3) Engelnese

A recent article published in the journal *Schmience* claims to have uncovered the existence of Engelnese, a close relative English. It is identical to English in every way except:

(i) for its anaphoric system: in Engelnese, the only reflexive form there is an invariable DP: SELPF (Thus Engelnese has no *himself, herself, myself* etc.).
(ii) for what is exemplified in the following sentences from Engelnese.

(1) a. I saw SELPF in the mirror
"I saw myself in the mirror"
b. The weather was unkind to SELPF
"The weather was unkind to me"

(2) John want Mary to help SELPF
(i) "John wants Mary to help herself" or
(ii) "John$_k$ wants Mary to help him$_k$" or
(iii) "John wants Mary to help me"

(3) John believe that SELPF will win
"John$_i$ believes that he$_i$ will win"

(4) a. John love SELPF
"John loves himself"
b. John want me to understand SELPF
"John wants me to understand myself"
"*John$_k$ wants me to understand him$_k$"

(5) Johni said to Sue_j that $Maria_k$ love SELPF $_{i,*j,k}$
"John told Sue that Mary loves herself/*her_j/him_i"

Some scientists suspect a hoax. You are called as an expert witness and must testify in front of a panel whether this is a possible human language.

(i) Decide for yourself and then write down what you would tell the panel. Part of this will be to explain for each sentence what meaning it can have or not.

After your testimony, you decide to read an Engelnese manuscript allegedly recovered from an archeological site. You come across the following passage:

"Thyrsten had too much &**y$#0 to drink, to the point he could not recognize me or even selpf. I think he did not really know who he was. Pointing to all the graves in the cemetery, he turned towards me and said he was sad and lonely because the war had killed many friends of selpf's."

(ii) Does this passage bear on your opinion about Engelnese? Explain why or why not

(4) Where does binding theory apply?
For each of the following examples, show if binding theory must apply before movement or after movement (or whether it is irrelevant). Assume the given judgments, and explain in precise terms.

(1) a. How proud of $himself_i$ do you consider $Bill_i$ to be?
b. *He_i sent Mary a present after $John_i$ went to the states
c. After $John_i$ went to the States he_i sent Mary a present
d. He_i wondered [which picture of $himself_i$ [they posted on the board]]
e. Which picture of himself did she say that he thought I liked

13.6.5 Further readings

After this chapter you should be able to critically read and understand the extensive literature on binding theory. In addition to the basic literature already cited in Chapter 7, and the literature throughout this chapter, we recommend in particular the foundational papers on binding: Chomsky (1981), Chomsky (1986), and the chapter "Pronouns and Their Antecedents" in Kayne (2005). For still broader issues, such as what the study of binding theory tells us about boundary conditions on the study of language, see Sportiche (2012).

14
Wh-constructions

So far we have studied only one kind of wh-movement construction: direct questions and indirect questions. The question that we are now looking at is the following: are there other instances of wh-movement and how do we recognize them? The obvious strategy is to establish some diagnostic properties of wh-movement and look for constructions that display them. One property that would seem to be a reliable indicator that we are dealing with a wh-movement construction is the presence of a clause initial wh-word. As we will see, however, this is not a reliable indicator: there are constructions that have all the properties of wh-constructions, but sometimes do not, or even in some cases never, have an audible wh-word.

14.1 Diagnostic Properties of Wh-movement

Before proceeding, let us summarize the kind of properties that wh-movement exhibits in wh-questions.

1. Wh-movement leaves a gap. This is simply the observation that the copy of a moved wh-element, its trace, is left unpronounced both in direct question and indirect questions:

(1) a. What$_i$ did Bill see ~~what$_i$~~?
b. What$_i$ did you say [$_{CP}$ that Bill saw ~~what$_i$~~]?

(2) a. Sue asked [$_{CP}$ where PRO to hide your keys ~~where~~]
b. You know [$_{CP}$ why Bill called the police ~~why~~]

2. The distance between a wh-phrase and the gap can be arbitrarily large. Wh-movement is unbounded in the sense that it can cross-over CP boundaries. (Even if we know that, in reality, movement proceeds in short steps.) This is the fact that the trace can be left in a complement clause of a complement clause of a complement clause, etc.

(3) a. What$_i$ does Sue think [$_{CP}$ that you said [$_{CP}$ that Bill saw t_i]]?
b. What$_i$ does Bill suspect [$_{CP}$ that Sue thinks [$_{CP}$ that you said [$_{CP}$ that T saw t_i]]]?

3. Wh-movement obeys the subjacency condition. That is, it obeys all the constraints subsumed under the subjacency condition).

An Introduction to Syntactic Analysis and Theory, First Edition.
Dominique Sportiche, Hilda Koopman, and Edward Stabler.

4. Wh-movement exhibits funny effects with subject extraction. We have called these effects complementizer–trace (or comp–trace). They were discussed in Section 10.6.1.
5. Wh-movement shows what is called the strong cross-over effect (see also Section 11.4.2). When we discussed the condition on pronominal binding we saw that a pronoun can be interpreted as a bound pronoun when it has a quantified antecedent which c-commands it.

(4) Everyone$_i$ thinks you like him$_i$
for all x, x thinks you like x
(5) I told no one$_i$ that you liked him$_i$

Wh-phrases behave like other quantified antecedents in this respect (we only look at the bound pronoun readings below):

(6) Who$_i$ thinks that you like him$_i$
for which x, x thinks you like x.
(7) Who$_i$ did you tell that you liked him$_i$
for which x you tell x that you like x.

There are contexts, though, in which a pronoun cannot be bound by a wh-phrase: these contexts are contexts where a wh-phrases "crosses" over a pronoun, as in the following example:

(8) Who$_i$ does he think Mary saw t$_i$

In this type of context the pronoun cannot be bound by the wh-phrase, i.e. (8) cannot receive the following interpretation (not that this interpretation is expressed by (6)):

(9) *Who$_i$ does he$_i$ think Mary saw t$_i$
for which x, x thinks Mary saw x

In (8) the pronoun c-commands the trace of the wh-phrase who and in this context pronominal binding fails. This context is called Strong Cross-over.

(10) **Strong Cross-over**: A bound pronoun cannot c-command a wh-trace.

We would like to find out why (10) holds. A simple hypothesis is that a wh-trace counts as an R-expression, and is thus subject to Principle C of the binding theory. The strong cross-over effect would thus follow in the same way as the fact that *he* and *John* cannot be coindexed:

(11) *He$_i$ thinks that Mary saw John$_i$

The status of (11) follows from Principle C of the binding theory:

(12) *Who$_i$ does he$_i$ think Mary saw t$_i$
*He$_i$ thinks Mary saw someone$_i$
*He$_i$ thinks Mary saw the bastard$_i$
* He$_i$ thinks Mary saw John$_i$

So no new principle is needed. But now, we can use the strong cross-over prohibition to see if we have a wh-trace somewhere. The presence of such a trace should trigger a Principle C violation if we choose the right kind of example.[1]

[1] Recall that in addition to the strong cross-over configuration, there is also the weak cross-over configuration which we will not get into (here "weak" refers to the fact that the judgments of deviance are somewhat less strong). This context refers to cases in which the bound pronoun does not c-command the trace of wh-movement (**Who*$_i$ *does his*$_i$ *mother love ti*). See Section 11.4.2 and for recent discussion, see Kayne (1994).

We now turn to various constructions that we will show exhibit the properties of wh-movement constructions. We will conclude that all of these constructions involve movement of a wh-phrase to some [Spec,CP] position proceeding cyclically.

14.2 Relative Clauses

14.2.1 Relative clauses involve wh-movement

The formation of a relative clause clearly involves a wh-phrase in many cases (but not in all cases as we see below). To distinguish these wh-phrases from the wh-phrases occurring in interrogatives, the latter are often called interrogatives, while the former are called relative wh-phrases (or pronouns, in the case of wh-words). This is exemplified below:

(13) a. You were talking to [$_{DP}$ the [$_{NP}$ man]$_i$ [$_{CP}$ who$_i$ [$_{TP}$ I introduced __ to you]]]
b. I bought [$_{DP}$ the [$_{NP}$ book]$_i$ [$_{CP}$ which$_i$ [$_{TP}$ I told you about __]]]
c. This is [$_{DP}$ the [$_{NP}$ room]$_i$ [$_{CP}$ where$_i$ [$_{TP}$ Bill keeps his drum set __]]]
d. That was [$_{DP}$ the [$_{NP}$ time]$_i$ [$_{CP}$ when$_i$ [$_{TP}$ Mary decided to quit her job __]]]

It is also clear that corresponding to this wh-phrase, there is a gap in the relative clause indicated by __. It is thus natural to postulate that the wh-phrase is in [Spec,CP] of the relative clause and moved there by wh-movement. We should therefore find all the properties of wh-movement before we proceed.

Note that we have the wh-phrase coindexed with the "head NP," to indicate how the relative clause is interpreted (roughly *the man who I saw* means the man such that I saw this very man). The wh-phrase which we will term, following traditional usage, a relative pronoun or a wh-relative pronoun is plausibly generated at the gap position and moved to the [Spec,CP]. The gap itself is the trace. We will conclude that this process – call it relative clause formation – is indeed a case of wh-movement.

(14) a. You were talking to [$_{DP}$ the [$_{NP}$ man]$_i$ [$_{CP}$ who$_i$ [$_{TP}$ I introduced t_i to you]]]
b. I bought [$_{DP}$ the [$_{NP}$ book]$_i$ [$_{CP}$ which$_i$ [$_{TP}$ I told you about t_i]]]
c. This is [$_{DP}$ the [$_{NP}$ room]$_i$ [$_{CP}$ where$_i$ [$_{TP}$ Bill keeps his drum set t_i]]]
d. That was [$_{DP}$ the [$_{NP}$ time]$_i$ [$_{CP}$ when$_i$ [$_{TP}$ Mary decided to quit her job t_i]]]

It is clear that movement of the wh-relative pronoun is unbounded.

> **Practice**
>
> Construct examples showing the unboundedness of the movement of the wh-relative pronoun, following that which we did for wh-questions.

We now verify that the relation between the relative clause "operator" wh-phrase and its trace obeys the island constraints:

Wh-island:

(15) a. *The [man]$_i$ [$_{CP}$ who$_i$ [$_{TP}$ I wondered [$_{CP}$ who$_j$ [$_{TP}$ I introduced t_i to t_j]]]]
b. *The [book]$_i$ [$_{CP}$ which$_i$ [$_{TP}$ I know [$_{CP}$ who$_j$ [$_{TP}$ t_j told you about t_i]]]]

c. *The [room]$_i$ $[_{CP}$ where$_i$ $[_{TP}$ Bill asked $[_{CP}$ what$_j$ $[_{TP}$ I keep t_j t_i]]]]
d. *The [time]$_i$ $[_{CP}$ when$_i$ $[_{TP}$ Mary wonders$[_{CP}$ why$_k$ $[_{TP}$ she decided to quit her job t_j t_i]]]]

Complex NP constraint (noun–complement):

(16) a. *The [man]$_i$ $[_{CP}$ who$_i$ $[_{TP}$ I heard $[_{DP}$ the claim $[_{CP}$ t_i that $[_{TP}$ I introduced t_i to you]]]]]
b. *The [book]$_i$ $[_{CP}$ which$_i$ $[_{TP}$ you forgot $[_{DP}$ the fact $[_{CP}$ t_i that $[_{TP}$ I told you about t_i]]]]]
c. *The [room]$_i$ $[_{CP}$ where$_i$ $[_{TP}$ I head $[_{DP}$ the rumor $[_{CP}$ t_i that $[_{TP}$ Bill keeps his drums t_i]]]]]
d. *The [time]$_i$ $[_{CP}$ when$_i$ $[_{TP}$ you believed $[_{DP}$ the story $[_{CP}$ that $[_{TP}$ I quit my job t_i]]]]]

Complex NP Constraint (relative clauses): Here we provide a step-by-step construction of the relevant example, which is (d).

(17) I introduced the man to the woman
a. The [woman]$_j$ $[_{CP}$ $[_{TP}$ I introduced the man to who]]
b. The [woman]$_j$ $[_{CP}$ who$_j$ $[_{TP}$ I introduced the man to t_j]]
c. The [man] $[_{CP}$ $[_{TP}$ I like the [woman]$_j$ $[_{CP}$ who$_j$ $[_{TP}$ I introduced who to t_j]]]]
d. *The [man]$_i$ $[_{CP}$ who$_i$ $[_{TP}$ I like the [woman]$_j$ $[_{CP}$ who$_j$ $[_{TP}$ I introduced t_i to t_j]]]]

(18) I told the publisher about the book
a. The [publisher]$_j$ $[_{CP}$ $[_{TP}$ I told who about the book]]
b. The [publisher]$_j$ $[_{CP}$ who$_j$ $[_{TP}$ I told t_j about the book]]
c. The [book]$_i$ $[_{CP}$ $[_{TP}$ I criticized the [publisher]$_j$ $[_{CP}$ who$_j$ $[_{TP}$ I told t_j about which]]]]
d. *The [book]$_i$ $[_{CP}$ which$_i$ $[_{TP}$ I criticized the [publisher]$_j$ $[_{CP}$ who$_j$ $[_{TP}$ I told t_j about t_i]]]]

(19) Bill keeps his drums in this room
a. The [drums]$_j$ $[_{CP}$ $[_{TP}$ Bill keeps which in his room]]
b. The [drums]$_j$ $[_{CP}$ which$_j$ $[_{TP}$ Bill keeps t_j in his room]]
c. The [room]$_i$ $[_{CP}$ $[_{TP}$ I adore the [drums]$_j$ $[_{CP}$ which$_j$ $[_{TP}$ Bill keeps t_j where]]]]
d. *The [room]$_i$ $[_{CP}$ where$_i$ $[_{TP}$ I adore the [drums]$_j$ $[_{CP}$ which$_j$ $[_{TP}$ Bill keeps t_j t_i]]]]

(20) Mary quit her job that time
a. The [job]$_j$ $[_{CP}$ $[_{TP}$ Mary quit which that time]]
b. The [job]$_j$ $[_{CP}$ which$_j$ $[_{TP}$ Mary quit t_j that time]]
c. The [time]$_i$ $[_{CP}$ $[_{TP}$ I am doing the [job]$_j$ $[_{CP}$ which$_j$ $[_{TP}$ Mary quit t_j that time]]]]
d. *The [time]$_i$ $[_{CP}$ when$_i$ $[_{TP}$ I am doing the [job]$_j$ $[_{CP}$ which$_j$ $[_{TP}$ Mary quit t_j t_i]]]]

Sentential subject constraint:

(21) a. *The [man]$_i$ $[_{CP}$ who$_i$ $[_{TP}$ $[_{CP}$ that $[_{TP}$ I introduced t_i to you]] annoyed Bill]]
b. *The [book]$_i$ $[_{CP}$ which$_i$ $[_{TP}$ $[_{CP}$ that $[_{TP}$ I told you about t_i]] surprised Sue]]

c. *The [room]$_i$ [$_{CP}$ where$_i$ [$_{TP}$ [$_{CP}$ that [$_{TP}$ Bill keeps his drum set t_i]] is a good idea]]
d. *The [time]$_i$ [$_{CP}$ when$_i$ [$_{TP}$ [$_{CP}$ that [$_{TP}$ Mary quit her job t_i]] angered her mother]]

Left branch constraint:

(22) a. *the [man]$_i$ [$_{CP}$ whose$_i$ [$_{TP}$ I introduced [t$_i$ mother] to you]]
b. *the [book]$_i$ [$_{CP}$ whose$_i$ [$_{TP}$ I told you about [t$_i$ cover]]]

Compare with cases where the whole constituent is pied-piped:

(23) a. The [man]$_i$ [$_{CP}$ [whose mother]$_i$ [$_{TP}$ I introduced t_i to you]]
b. The [book]$_i$ [$_{CP}$ [whose cover]$_i$ [$_{TP}$ I told you about t_i]]

> **Practice**
>
> Construct similar examples showing that relative clause formation, i.e. the movement of a wh-relative pronoun, also obeys the subject condition and the adjunct island condition.

Comp–trace effects: We can easily illustrate that relative clause formation triggers them:

(24) a. The man [$_{CP}$ who [$_{TP}$ you think [$_{CP}$ [$_{TP}$ t left early]]]]?
b. *The man [$_{CP}$ who [$_{TP}$ you think [$_{CP}$ that [$_{TP}$ t left early]]]]?
c. The man [$_{CP}$ who [$_{TP}$ you want [$_{CP}$ [$_{TP}$ t to win the race]]]]?
d. *The man [$_{CP}$ who [$_{TP}$ you want [$_{CP}$ for [$_{TP}$ t to win the race]]]]?

Strong cross-over effects: Similarly, we can show the presence of strong cross-over effects:

(25) a. The man$_j$ who$_j$ t_j thinks Mary saw him$_j$
b. *The man$_j$ who$_j$ he$_j$ thinks Mary saw t_j

The second sentence cannot have *he* coindexed with *who* and its trace *t*. It is of course fine if *he* has a different index than *who*.

14.2.2 Relative clauses with silent wh-phrases

Now we have verified that relative clause formation has all the properties of wh-movement, and is therefore a case of wh-movement. However, in some cases or relative clauses, there is no relative pronoun at all. Are such cases also cases of wh-movement?

Here are examples of relative clauses in English without a wh-phrase relative pronoun.

(26) a. You were talking to the [man]$_i$ [$_{CP}$ (that) [$_{TP}$ I introduced __ to you]]
b. I bought the [book]$_i$ [$_{CP}$ (that) [$_{TP}$ I told you about __]]
c. This is the [room]$_i$ [$_{CP}$ (that) [$_{TP}$ Bill puts his drums [in __]]]
d. That was the [time]$_i$ [$_{CP}$ (that) [$_{TP}$ Mary decided to quit her job __]]

- In these structures *that* still seems to be the complementizer, but not the wh-phrase itself. Note that *that* is optional (as the complementizer often is):

(27) a. You were talking to [$_{DP}$ [$_{DP}$ the man] [$_{CP}$ who [$_{TP}$ __introduced me to you]]]
b. You were talking to [$_{DP}$ [$_{DP}$ the man] [$_{CP}$ that [$_{TP}$ __introduced me to you]]]
c. *You were talking to [$_{DP}$ [$_{DP}$ the man] [$_{CP}$ [$_{TP}$ __introduced me to you]]]

Note the (c) sentence with a subject wh-phrase: in this case the complementizer must be present – in Standard American English. This is another funny subject extraction effect that we will not deal with here.

- There cannot be pied-piped material when the wh-relative pronoun is not present. For example, prepositions cannot be pied-piped. They must be stranded (if possible).

(28) a. You were talking to the [man] [$_{CP}$ to whom [$_{TP}$ I introduced you ___]]
b. You were talking to the [man] [$_{CP}$ who [$_{TP}$ I introduced you [to ___]]]
c. *You were talking to the [man] [$_{CP}$ to that [$_{TP}$ I introduced you ___]]
d. You were talking to the [man] [$_{CP}$ that [$_{TP}$ I introduced you [to ___]]]

Nor can a bigger DP be pied-piped if the gap is its subject:

(29) a. *You were talking to the [man]$_i$ [$_{CP}$ (that) [$_{TP}$ I introduced [___mother] to you]]
b. *I bought the [book]$_i$ [$_{CP}$ (that) [$_{TP}$ I told you about [___cover]]]
c. *You were talking to the [man]$_i$ [$_{CP}$ [___mother]$_i$ [$_{TP}$ I introduced t_i to you]]
d. *I bought the [book]$_i$ [$_{CP}$ [___cover]$_i$ [$_{TP}$ I told you about t_i]]

Is relative clause formation without a relative pronoun an instance of wh-movement? If we run through all the examples showing that relative clause formation with a relative pronoun is wh-movement – examples (15) to (25) – and systematically erase the relative pronoun, we will find that the presence of the relative pronoun changes nothing at all (except for pied piping noted above and the funny subject effect noted in (27c)).

Practice

Run through all these examples and verify that, indeed, the judgments remain all the same.

How then do we account for these findings? On the one hand, we want to treat these cases as involving wh-movement. On the other hand there is no wh-phrase involved at all. Very simply, we will say that wh-relative pronouns can be **silent**, that is a wh-phrase that has no phonetic content. Just as pronouns can be silent in infinitives (e.g. PRO – read "big pro"), or certain Cs (silent *that*) or Ts (when it is present in English), or D be silent (the plural version of English, *a* – i.e. the plural indefinite determiner).

These silent relative pronouns are the exact equivalent of the DPs *who* or *what*. These are often notated OP for (relative) operator (another way of terming wh-phrases) or [$_{DP[+wh]}$ who]. So OP = [$_{DP[+wh]}$WHO/WHAT] with silence indicated with capital letters.

Here are some examples where what moves up to the [Spec,CP] is a silent operator, OP:

(30) a. You were talking to the [man]$_i$ [$_{CP}$ OP$_i$ (that) [$_{TP}$ I introduced t_i to you]]
b. I bought the [book]$_i$ [$_{CP}$ OP$_i$ (that) [$_{TP}$ I told you about t_i]]
c. This is the [room]$_i$ [$_{CP}$ OP$_i$ (that) [$_{TP}$ Bill keeps his drum set [in t_i]]]
d. That was the [time]$_i$ [$_{CP}$ OP$_i$ (that) [$_{TP}$ Mary decided to quit her job t_i]]

Although we can't see the empty operator, we can tell that it has moved to the highest [Spec,CP] position, which is where the overt wh-phrases go. What is significant in this context is that relative clauses with silent operators also obey all the diagnostic properties of wh-movement, e.g. the island constraints, etc.

14.2.3 Doubly filled Comp filter

So far, all English (restrictive – see below for non-restrictive) relatives can be treated in a uniform fashion. The form of the relative follows from whether the wh-phrase is pronounced or not, and whether the C (*that*) is pronounced or not. Note, however, that this analysis predicts four types of relatives for English, and only three are attested:

(31)						
	a.	the man	who		you saw	(pronounced wh-phrase, silent C)
	b.	the man		that	you saw	(silent OP, pronounced C)
	c.	the men			you saw	(silent OP, silent C)
	d.	*the men	who	that	you saw	(pronounced OP, pronounced C)

We see here that the form that is excluded has both a pronounced wh-phrase and a pronounced C. This configuration should be excluded. We can state what is excluded in the following filter, which is called the Doubly Filled Comp Filter (Comp here refers to C, not to complement!):

(32) **Doubly Filled C(omp) Filter**: * [wh-phrase *that*], where both the wh and *that* are pronounced.

Note that this filter will also account for the following impossible indirect question in English:

(33) *I wonder who if John saw

We can thus let wh-movement operate freely, let elements be silent or pronounced in CP: the effects of illicit combinations can be ruled out by filters that apply to the output structures as was suggested (in a different context) in Perlmutter (1970).

14.2.4 Infinitival relatives

Direct questions are questions in matrix clauses that are almost always tensed. This is why (almost) all direct questions are tensed. However, we saw that indirect questions in English can either be tensed or infinitive clauses:

(34) a. I don't know whether/if you left early
b. I wonder whether/if you left early
c. I asked you whether/if you left early

(35) a. I don't know whether/*if PRO to leave early
b. I wonder whether/*if PRO to leave early
c. I asked you whether/*if PRO to leave early

Since relative clauses are adjunct clauses, we expect that they also could in principle be either tensed or infinitival clauses. Are there then infinitival relative clauses? The answer is positive:

(36) a. I finally met a $[\text{man}]_j$ $[_{CP}$ $[\text{with whom}]_j$ $[_{TP}$ PRO to dance t_j]]
b. This is the only $[\text{room}]_i$ $[_{CP}$ $[\text{in which}]_i$ $[_{TP}$ PRO to keep your drums t_i]]
c. That was the $[\text{time}]_i$ $[_{CP}$ $[\text{at which}]_i$ $[_{TP}$ PRO to start packing t_i]]

Note the meaning that such constructions take. For example, we can paraphrase the (c) sentence as meaning: this was the time at which one should start packing. In other words PRO is interpreted as meaning one or anyone (the so-called arbitrary interpretation of PRO). Secondly, there is an idea of "should" as well and it is an interesting question where this bit of meaning comes from since there is no word or morpheme that seems to introduce it.

We could show that infinitival relatives meet all the relevant properties qualifying them as wh-movement constructions even though, for some properties, it is difficult because they are subject to all sorts of additional poorly understood restrictions. These relatives, just like tensed relatives, may occur without an overt wh-relative pronoun:

(37) a. Here is [a great [book]$_j$ [$_{CP}$ OP$_j$ for [$_{TP}$ Bill to read t_j]]]
b. I am looking for [a [candidate]$_j$ [$_{CP}$ OP$_j$ for [$_{TP}$ Bill to vote for t_j]]]
c. [A [man]$_j$ [$_{CP}$ OP$_j$ [$_{TP}$ t_j to fix the sink]]] is hard to find

Unlike the case of tensed relatives, however, there cannot be an overt wh-relative pronoun if the phrase in [Spec,CP] is a simple wh-DP:

(38) a. *Here is [a great [book]$_j$ [$_{CP}$ which$_j$ for [$_{TP}$ Bill to read t_j]]]
b. *I am looking for [a [candidate]$_j$ [$_{CP}$ who$_j$ for [$_{TP}$ Bill to vote for t_j]]]
c. *[A [man]$_j$ [$_{CP}$ who$_j$ [$_{TP}$ t_j to fix the sink]]] is hard to find
d. *I met [a [girl]$_k$ [$_{CP}$ [whose$_k$ grandmother]$_j$ [$_{TP}$ PRO to respect t_j]]]

Why this is so is only understood to a certain extent. Here we will not pursue this question. Infinitival relatives also display the effects of the doubly filled comp filter.

(39) a. *Here is [a great [room]$_j$ [$_{CP}$ in which$_j$ for [$_{TP}$ Bill to rest t_j]]]
b. Here is [a great [room]$_j$ [$_{CP}$ in which$_j$ [$_{TP}$ to rest t_j]]]
c. Here is [a great [room]$_j$ [$_{CP}$ OP$_j$ for [$_{TP}$ Bill to rest in t_j]]]
d. Here is [a great [room]$_j$ [$_{CP}$ OP$_j$ [$_{TP}$ to rest in t_j]]]

Either there is a C (*for*) or an overt wh-phrase (*in which*) but not both.

14.2.5 The promotion analysis of relative clauses

In the sentences below, what is called the head NP of the relative clause is in bold (notice that this notion of head is **not** the same as the X-bar theoretic notion of head).

(40) a. I bought [$_{DP}$ the [$_{NP}$ **book about food**]$_i$ [$_{CP}$ which$_i$ [$_{TP}$ I told you about t$_i$]]
b. I bought the [**book**]$_i$ [$_{CP}$ OP$_i$ (that) [$_{TP}$ I told you about t$_i$]]
c. You were talking to the [**man**]$_i$ [$_{CP}$ OP$_i$ (that) [$_{TP}$ I introduced t$_i$ to you]]

What is the relation between the head of a relative clause and the relative clause?

Recall that we have also seen that the surface constituency of a (restrictive) relative is D [$_{NP}$ NP CP].

(41) Tom has *two violins that once belonged to my father*, and Willem has *one* too

In (41), *one* replaces *violin that once belonged to my father.*

(42) Tom has *two Italian violins* that belonged to my father, and Willem has *one* that belonged to my mother

In (42), *one* replaces *Italian violin* or just *violin.*

The meaning of a sentence with a relative clause like the first example is roughly:

(43) I bought a book. I told you about this book

Since the relative clause is saying something about the head, we have the wh-phrase coindexed with the "head-NP," to indicate how the relative clause is interpreted.

The question we now address is the following: how does this coindexing come about? There are in principle two ways. The first is to have the head NP coindexed with the NP inside the relativized DP because this latter NP is like a pronoun taking the head NP as antecedent. The other way is to have the coindexation follow from movement: the head NP moved out of the relativized DP, leaving a trace NP (note that the structure below does not show VP shells):

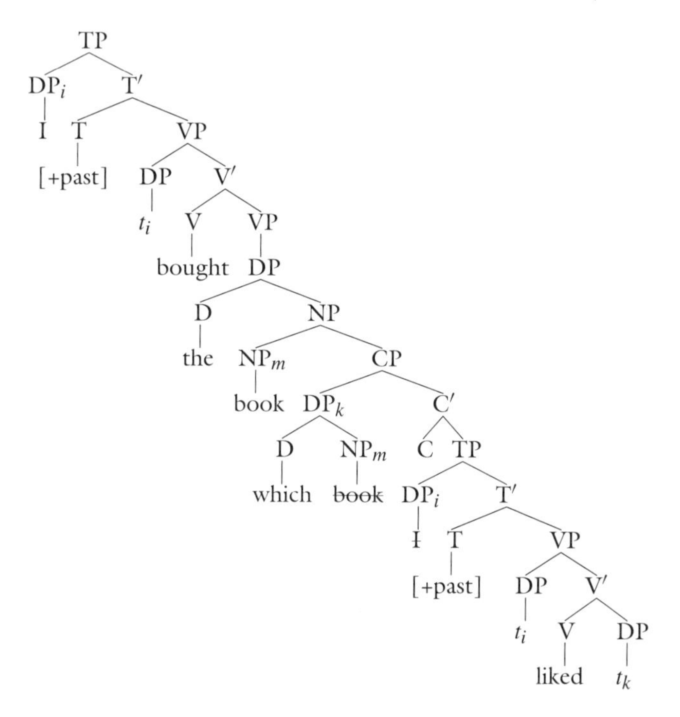

How do we decide? If it is movement, the head NP was inside the relative clause earlier in the derivation. Otherwise, this head NP was never there. In Vergnaud (1974), Jean Roger Vergnaud, pictured here, develops arguments to the effect that the head was inside the relative clause earlier in the derivation, at least in some cases of relative clauses. Below is one the most famous arguments based on the properties of idioms.

Idiom chunks:

(44) Bill is aware of the significant headway that John made *t*

This sentence is fine. But *headway* is a idiom chunk of the idiom *make headway*: *headway* is selected as complement of *make*. If *headway* is what is generated inside the relative clause and moved out, then this is not surprising. Otherwise, it is unexpected.

Another argument can be given using the binding theory.

Anaphor binding:

(45) Bill liked the **pictures of each other** which they acquired *t* yesterday

This sentence is fine. *Each other* needs to satisfy Principle A. If the head of the relative (underlined) was inside the relative (in the *t* position), then we can explain why this sentence is good: Principle A is satisfied before movement. If the head (in bold) was never inside the relative clause, we cannot explain this.

Conclusion: The head NP can be moved out of the relative clause. This is called the Promotion or Raising Analysis of relative clauses.

Does this mean that the head is always moved out of the relative clause? The answer seems to be negative. For example, there is another kind of relative clause, which is usually written with a comma between the head and the relative clause. They are read with a special intonation, and the meaning of the relative clause is a comment about the head (you can add "by the way") rather than a way to specify it further:

(46) a. I bought a [$_{NP}$ book]$_i$, which$_i$ (by the way) I had told you about t$_i$
b. You were talking to the [man]$_i$ [$_{CP}$ OP$_i$ *(that) [$_{TP}$ I introduced t$_i$ to you]]
c. I bought the [book]$_i$ [$_{CP}$ OP$_i$ *(that) [$_{TP}$ I told you about t$_i$]]

These relative clauses are called non-restrictive relative clauses or appositive relative clauses (the others are called restrictive relative clauses). They disallow silent wh-words as relative pronouns, and they disallow the kind of examples we just looked at:

(47) a. You were talking to a [man]$_i$, *(that) by the way I introduced t $_i$ to you] last year
b. I bought several [books]$_i$, *(that) by the way I had told you about t $_i$

(48) a. *Peter liked some pictures of each other, which (by the way) they acquired *t* yesterday
b. *Peter is aware of some significant headway, which (by the way) John had made *t* recently

This suggests that non-restrictive relatives do not involve promotion. They also seem to have a slightly different structure, in which the relative clause is a DP adjunct rather than an NP adjunct.

(49)

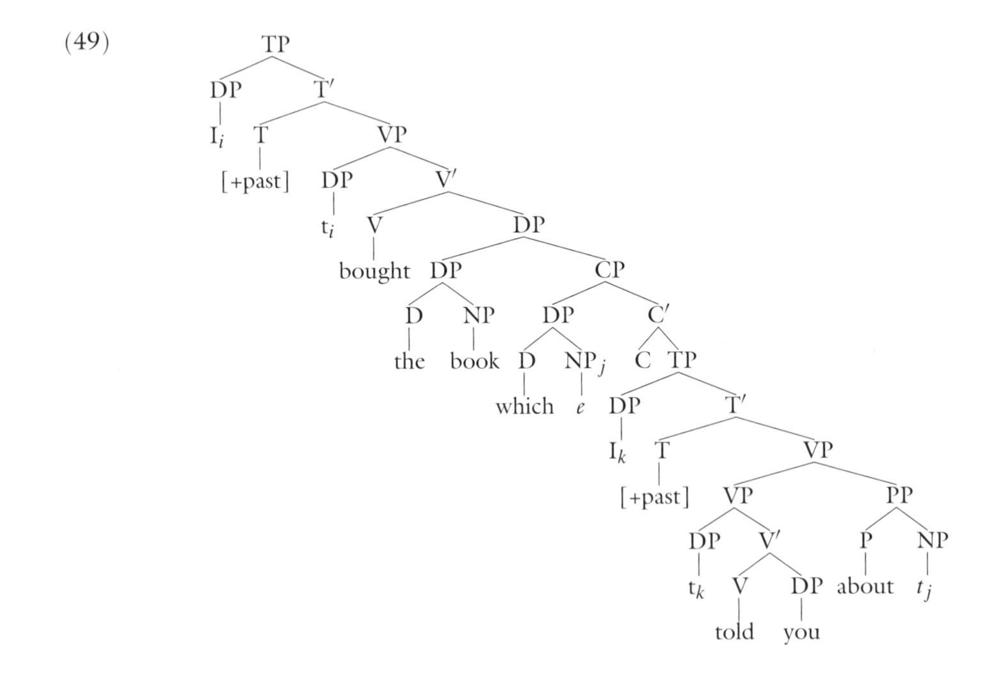

14.3 Another Case of Null Operator Movement: *Tough*-Construction

In the *tough*-construction, it appears that the object of an infinitival (lower) clause has moved over the subject of its own clause to the subject position of the matrix clause.

(50) a. Bill is tough [to work with ___]
b. This idea is easy [to sell ___]

The subject of *tough* is not necessarily a selected position (i.e. a theta-position): it tolerates expletives.

(51) a. It_i is tough [to work with $Bill]_i$
b. It_i is easy [to sell this $idea]_i$

The subject of the infinitival can be an arbitrary PRO, but it can also be an overt element.

(52) a. Bill is tough [$_{CP}$ [$_{TP}$ PRO to work with ___]]
b. This idea is easy [$_{CP}$ [$_{TP}$ PRO to sell ___]]
(53) a. Bill is tough [$_{CP}$ for [$_{TP}$ me to work with ___]]
b. This idea is easy [$_{CP}$ for [$_{TP}$ me to sell ___]]

We would thus like to say that there is movement of the object of the infinitive verb to the subject of *tough*, but this is problematic, since raising to subject does not do this:

(54) a. I am likely [___to work with Bill next year]
b. It is likely [for me to work with Bill next year]
c. *Bill is likely [for me to work with ___next year]

The movement can be long-distance in English (as long as the intermediate clauses are infinitival):

(55) a. $Bill_i$ is tough [$_{CP}$for [$_{TP}$ me to want [$_{CP}$ [$_{TP}$ PRO to work with t_i]]]]
b. [This $idea]_i$ is easy [$_{CP}$ for [$_{TP}$ me to try [$_{CP}$ [$_{TP}$ PRO to sell t_i]]]]

A one-step movement would violate the subjacency condition. Notice that we witness a strong cross-over effect:

(56) $Bill_i$ is tough [$_{CP}$ for [$_{TP}$ me to want [$_{CP}$ [$_{TP}$ him to work with t_i]]]]

If we coindex *him* with *Bill*, the result is deviant, suggesting that the trace t_i is like a wh-trace.

One general solution for this kind of construction is the following: there is movement, but of a silent operator (wh-word). A silent operator is merged as the object of the verb in the infinitival and moves up to the subordinate [Spec, CP]: it is coindexed with the subject of *tough*.

(57) a. $Bill_i$ is tough [$_{CP}$ OP_i [$_{TP}$ PRO to work with t_i]]
b. [This $idea]_i$ is easy [$_{CP}$ OP_i [$_{TP}$ PRO to sell t_i]]
(58) a. $Bill_i$ is tough [$_{CP}$ OP_i for [$_{TP}$ me to want [$_{CP}$ [$_{TP}$ PRO to work with t_i]]]]
b. [This $idea]_i$ is easy [$_{CP}$ for [$_{TP}$ me to try [$_{CP}$ [$_{TP}$ PRO to sell t_i]]]]

(59)

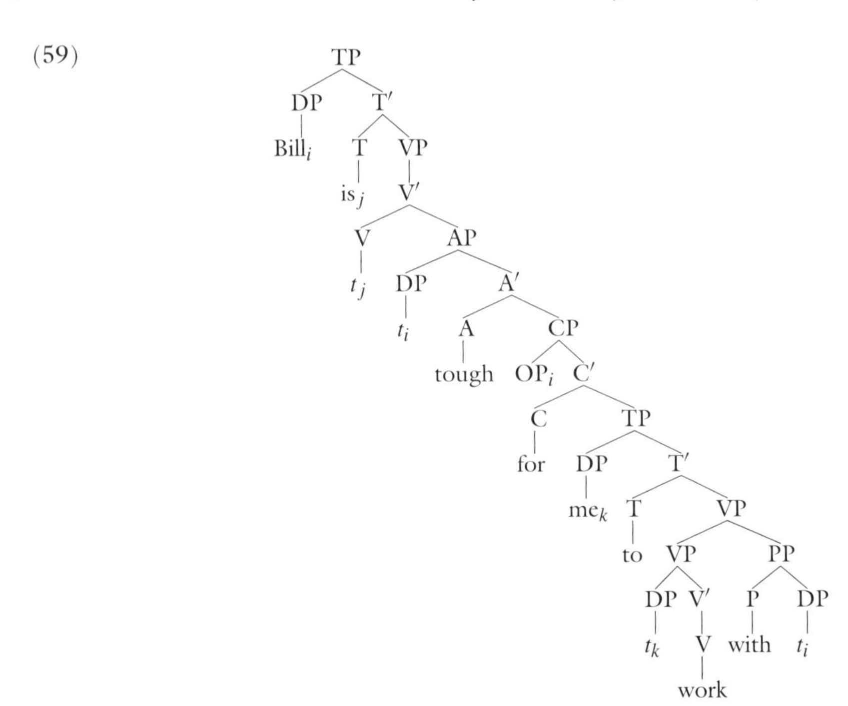

The proposal that there is a movement from the subordinate object to the subordinate [Spec,CP] is strengthened by the fact that the *tough* construction obeys the island constraints.

(60) Wh-islands:
 a. *Bill$_i$ is tough [$_{CP}$ OP$_i$ for [$_{TP}$ me to wonder [$_{CP}$ how$_j$ [$_{TP}$ to work with t_i t_j]]]]
 b. *[This idea]$_i$ is easy [$_{CP}$ OP$_i$ for [$_{TP}$ me to ask [$_{CP}$ who$_j$ [$_{TP}$ to sell t_i (to) t_j]]]]

(61) Complex NP constraint (noun-complement):
 a. *Bill$_i$ is tough [$_{CP}$ OP$_i$ for [$_{TP}$ me to spread [$_{DP}$ the excitement [$_{CP}$ [$_{TP}$ to work with t_i]]]]]
 b. *[This idea]$_i$ is easy [$_{CP}$ OP$_i$ for [$_{TP}$ me to plan [$_{DP}$ a strategy [$_{CP}$ [$_{TP}$ to sell t_i]]]]]

(62) Complex NP constraint (relative clause):
 a. *Bill$_i$ is tough [$_{CP}$ OP$_i$ for [$_{TP}$ me to make [$_{DP}$ [$_{DP}$ the time] [$_{CP}$ OP$_j$ [$_{TP}$ PRO to work with t_i t_j]]]]]
 b. *[This idea]$_i$ is easy [$_{CP}$ OP$_i$ for [$_{TP}$ me to visit [$_{DP}$ [$_{DP}$ the convention] [$_{CP}$ OP$_j$ [$_{TP}$ PRO to sell t_i [in t_j]]]]]]

(63) Coordinate structure constraint:
 a. *Bill$_i$ is tough [$_{CP}$ OP$_i$ for [$_{TP}$ me to [$_{VP}$ work with t_i] and [$_{VP}$ enjoy my job]]]
 b. *[This idea]$_i$ is easy [$_{CP}$ OP$_i$ for [$_{TP}$ me to [$_{VP}$ have some confidence] and [$_{VP}$ sell t_i]]]

(64) Sentential subject constraint:
 a. *Bill$_i$ is tough [$_{CP}$ OP$_i$ [$_{TP}$ [$_{CP}$ for [$_{TP}$ me to work with t_i]] to be pleasant]]
 b. *[This idea]$_i$ is easy [$_{CP}$ OP$_i$ [$_{TP}$ [$_{CP}$ for [$_{TP}$ me to sell t_i]] to annoy everyone]]

14.4 Topicalization and Left Dislocation

Topicalization and "left dislocation" are very similar constructions in which a constituent from inside a clause appears clause-initially. In topicalization, this constituent has a corresponding gap in its expected position; in left dislocation, there is a pronoun that corresponds to the left dislocated element. The term *left dislocation* in fact covers two different constructions with different properties, one of which is referred to as Hanging Topic Dislocation Construction and the other is called Clitic Left (or Right) Dislocation (a term coming from the Romance languages, but widely found even in languages that have no clitics). These two constructions are distinct in their intonational patterns and in their formal behavior. Here is an example of both constructions in French:

(65) Hanging topic: with a (big) intonational break existing between *Ophelia* and the TP boundary:
 a. Silvester, Ophélie lui plait
 Silvester Ophelia to-him appeals
 "Silvester, Ophelia appeals to him"
 b. Silvester, Ophélie danse avec lui
 Silvester Ophelia dances with him
 "Silvester, Ophelia dances with him"

(66) Clitic left dislocation (read continuously without a break):
 a. Ophélie il (ne) l' oublie pas
 Ophelia he (NEG) her forget-FUT not
 Ophelia he does not forget her
 b. Silvester elle lui raconte tout
 Silvester she to-him tells everything
 To Silvester she tells everything

When a pronoun is present, English only has the hanging topic construction. And this is what is illustrated below:

(67) Topicalization:
 a. Anchovies, I like ___
 b. Star Wars, I watched ___often

(68) Hanging topic left dislocation:
 a. Anchovies, I like them
 b. Star Wars, I watch it often

The gap in topicalization constructions corresponds to a trace. Subjacency effects in general serve as reliable diagnostics to determine movement, but some other of Ross's constraints do not, e.g. the coordinate structure constraint. Here we see that topicalization obeys the island constraints (and shows other properties of wh-movement), but the hanging topic construction does not obey the island constraints:

Wh-island:

(69) Topicalization:
 a. *Anchovies$_i$ [$_{TP}$ I don't know [$_{CP}$ who$_j$ [$_{TP}$ t_j likes t_i]]]
 b. *[Star Wars]$_i$ [$_{TP}$ Bill wonders [$_{CP}$ [how often] [$_{TP}$ I watch t_i t_j]]]

(70) Left dislocation:

a. Anchovies$_i$ [$_{TP}$ I don't know [$_{CP}$ who$_j$ [$_{TP}$ t_j likes them$_i$]]]

b. [Star Wars]$_i$ [$_{TP}$ Bill wonders [$_{CP}$ [how often] [$_{TP}$ I watch it$_i$ t_j]]]

Complex NP constraint (noun–complement):

(71) Topicalization:

a. *Anchovies$_i$ [$_{TP}$ I believe [$_{DP}$ the claim [$_{CP}$ that [$_{TP}$ he likes t_i]]]]

b. *[Star Wars]$_i$ [$_{TP}$ Bill heard [$_{DP}$ the rumor [$_{CP}$ that [$_{TP}$ I watch t_i often]]]]

(72) Left dislocation:

a. Anchovies$_i$ [$_{TP}$ I believe [$_{DP}$ the claim [$_{CP}$ that [$_{TP}$ he likes them$_i$]]]]

b. [Star Wars]$_i$ [$_{TP}$ Bill heard [$_{DP}$ the rumor [$_{CP}$ that [$_{TP}$ I watch it$_i$ often]]]]

Complex NP constraint (relative clause):

(73) Topicalization:

a. *Anchovies$_i$ [$_{TP}$ I know [$_{DP}$ [$_{DP}$ a man] [$_{CP}$ who$_j$ [$_{TP}$ likes t_i]]]]

b. *[Star Wars]$_i$ [$_{TP}$ I talked to [$_{DP}$ [$_{DP}$ a student] [$_{CP}$who$_j$ [$_{TP}$ t_j watches t_i often]]]

(74) Left dislocation:

a. Anchovies$_i$ [$_{TP}$ I know [$_{DP}$ [$_{DP}$ a man] [$_{CP}$ who$_j$ [$_{TP}$ likes them$_i$]]]]

b. [Star Wars]$_i$ [$_{TP}$ I talked to [$_{DP}$ [$_{DP}$ a student] [$_{CP}$who$_j$ [$_{TP}$ t_j watches it$_i$ often]]]

Coordinate structure constraint:

(75) Topicalization:

a. *Anchovies$_i$ [$_{TP}$ I think [$_{CP}$ [$_{TP}$ Bill [$_{VP}$ likes t_i] and [$_{VP}$ drinks wine]]]]

b. *[Star Wars]$_i$ [$_{TP}$ I [$_{VP}$ watch t_i often] and [$_{VP}$ admire George Lucas]]

(76) Left dislocation:

a. Anchovies$_i$ [$_{TP}$ I think [$_{CP}$ [$_{TP}$ Bill [$_{VP}$ likes them$_i$] and [$_{VP}$ drinks wine]]]]

b. [Star Wars]$_i$ [$_{TP}$ I [$_{VP}$ watch it$_i$ often] and [$_{VP}$ admire George Lucas]]

Sentential subject constraint:

(77) Topicalization:

a. *Anchovies$_i$ [$_{TP}$ [$_{CP}$ that [$_{TP}$ I like t_i]] surprises everyone]

b. *[Star Wars]$_i$ [$_{TP}$ [$_{CP}$ that [$_{TP}$ I watch t_i often]] is a well-known fact]

(78) Left dislocation:

a. Anchovies$_i$ [$_{TP}$ [$_{CP}$ that [$_{TP}$ I like them$_i$]] surprises everyone]

b. [Star Wars]$_i$ [$_{TP}$ [$_{CP}$ that [$_{TP}$ I watch it$_i$ often]] is a well-known fact]

Left branch constraint:

(79) Topicalization:

a. *John('s)$_i$ [$_{TP}$ I like [$_{DP}$ t_i mother]]

b. *Sue(s)$_i$ [$_{TP}$ I hate [$_{DP}$ t_i attitude]]

(80) Left dislocation:

a. John$_i$ [$_{TP}$ I like [$_{DP}$ his$_i$ mother]]

b. Sue$_i$ [$_{TP}$ I hate [$_{DP}$ her$_i$ attitude]]

So far, we have assumed that topicalization moves the topic to a position adjunct to TP. Current thinking (at the time of writing – 2013) on the matter suggests instead that such moved topics are in [Spec,CP] of a special kind of C to host a topic (i.e. selects for a topic as its specifier). Here we notate it C [+topic], but it is often notated as Top heading a TopP. Relevant discussion can be found in Rizzi (1997).

(81)

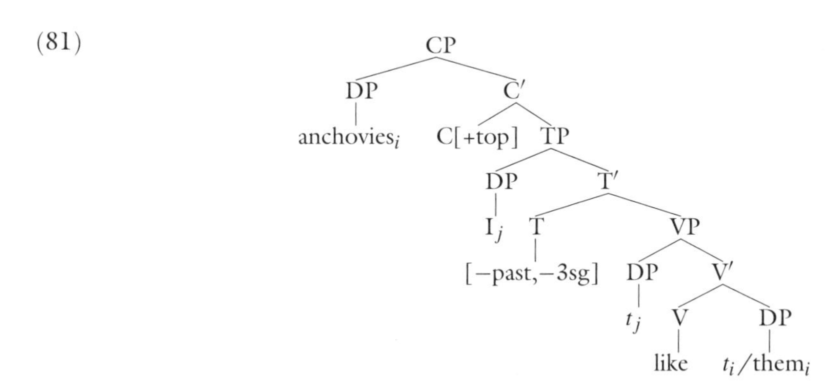

The hanging topic is not moved. It is directly merged in a clause-initial position, in fact before wh-phrases:

(82) a. ?John when did you see him?
b. *When John did you see him?

This suggests an analysis where the hanging topic is outside the CP. To make things concrete, we can treat it as an adjunct to the CP.

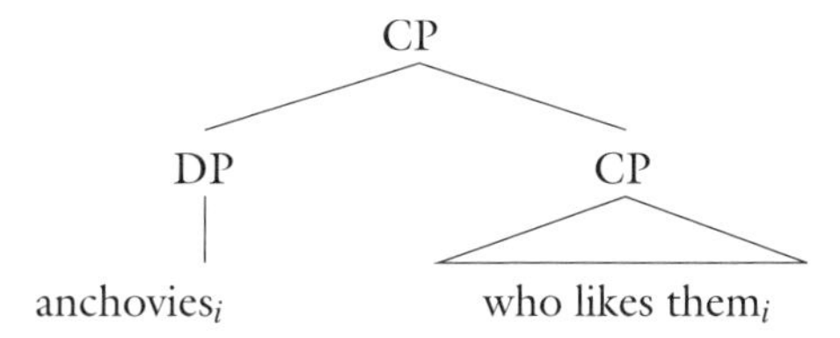

We may wonder now about left dislocation and clitic left dislocation illustrated in French respectively in (65) and (65). It turns out that left dislocation does not seem to involve movement (as it does not obey island conditions) while clitic left dislocation does involve movement much like English topicalization! This is discussed, for example, in Cinque (1977).

14.5 Other Wh-movement Constructions

We have seen that wh-movement is involved in main and embedded tensed or tenseless interrogatives, and we have established a number of diagnostic properties displayed by this kind of movement. We also saw that relative clauses, whether tensed or tenseless, involve wh-movement. A particularly interesting fact is there may not be any wh-phrase present in a relative clause, which means that wh-movement may be involved even if there is no overt wh-phrase.

Wh-questions: (direct and indirect).
Relative clauses:
a. Headed restrictive and non-restrictive relatives.
b. Infinitival relatives.
c. Free relatives or headless relatives.

Of these, we have not discussed free or headless relatives. Here are some examples.

(83) I will buy whatever you buy *t*
(84) I like who you met *t* yesterday
(85) Whenever John visits *t*, he is hungry.

Other cases of constructions involving a wh-movement-like process are English topicalization, or *tough*-movement constructions as we just saw. There are a number of other constructions that display properties similar to wh-movement that we will not discuss here in detail. What they all have in common is that they display all the diagnostic properties of wh-movement that can be tested: presence of a gap, unboundedness, sensitivity to islands, sensitivity to strong cross-over effects, funny effects with subjects. Here is a partial list with an illustration of each, where we notate as OP the moved element when it is silent:

i. Exclamatives: [What a beautiful car]$_i$ they bought t$_i$!!
ii. Cleft constructions: It is Bill$_i$ that I think we should call t$_i$
iii. Pseudocleft constructions: [what$_i$ John wants t$_i$] is a book
iv. Purposives: Mary bought it [OP$_i$ [to read t$_i$ on the train]]
v. Comparatives: Bill met more people than [OP$_i$ [John ever knew t$_i$]]
vi. Subcomparatives: Bill bought more apples than [OP$_i$ [Sue sold t$_i$ pears]]
vii. Complex adjectival constructions: John is too stubborn [OP$_i$ [to talk to t$_i$]]
viii. *As* constructions: Mary left early as [OP$_i$ [John said t$_i$]]
ix. *Which* constructions: Bill resigned yesterday, [which$_i$ Anna denied t$_i$]
x. *Though* constructions: handsome$_i$ though [you may think that Bill is t$_i$]

A last and interesting case of wh-construction is the following:

(86) Temporal clauses: John jumped before [[Mary said [he jumped]]]

This sentence is ambiguous the same way *when*-questions are ambiguous. Recall that when the wh-phrase is an adjunct/adverbial, the trace ensures that the interpretation will be construed with the right clause.

(87) When did Mary say that he jumped?
a. [$_{CP}$ When$_i$ did [$_{TP}$ Mary say t_i [$_{CP}$ that [$_{TP}$ he jumped]]]]?
b. [$_{CP}$ When$_i$ did [$_{TP}$ Mary say [$_{CP}$ that [$_{TP}$ he jumped t_i]]]]?
(a): When did Mary say that?
(b): When did he jump (according to Mary)?

We find the same ambiguity depending on where the trace is:

(88) John jumped before [OP$_i$ [Mary said [he jumped $\boldsymbol{t_i}$]]]
(89) John jumped before [OP$_i$ [Mary said $\boldsymbol{t_i}$ [he jumped]]]

This sentence could be truthfully uttered if John jumped on Tuesday at 5 p.m., earlier than the time, say 7 p.m., at which he jumped according to Mary. This corresponds to the first structure. This sentence could also be truthfully uttered if John jumped on Tuesday at 5 p.m., earlier than the time, say 7 p.m., at which Mary said something, even if what she said is: John jumped at 3 p.m. (that is, earlier than when he actually jumped). This corresponds to the first structure: because John jumped earlier than when Mary spoke. This shows that the silent OP really is a silent *when*. Since this silent *when* is a [Spec,CP], this also shows that before and after take CP complements (with a silent *that* and a silent OP), as we discussed back in Section 6.5.3.

14.6 Conclusion

14.6.1 Summary

In this chapter, we have shown that, despite their superficial differences, the properties of a great many different constructions (questions, relatives, comparatives, clefts) could be unified at an abstract level under the heading of wh-movement. We did this by showing that all of these constructions share a number of core properties. This perspective was famously developed in Chomsky (1977). This view is part of the important discovery that what traditional grammars call constructions (e.g. interrogatives, relative clauses, passives, etc.) are not, from the point of view of grammatical analysis, atomic objects. This idea, similar to atomism in chemistry, constitutes a radical break with some long held grammatical ideas, and has led to a very substantial deepening of our understanding of grammatical structures.

14.6.2 What to remember

This last point is perhaps the most important point to remember: constructions are not atomic objects. Rather, they are like very complex molecules or chemical compounds, whose properties are derived from the interaction of the much more basic constituents making them up. To see this, one has to be willing to move away from superficial differences and take seriously the idea that superficially different sentence types share a great many central, albeit often hidden, properties.

It is thus also important to remember that in order to reach such conclusions, we have to establish with great care and systematicity, the grammatical properties of the sentences we are looking at. Only very detailed analyses are likely to uncover the deep unity that may lie under the apparent superficial diversity.

14.6.3 Puzzles and preview

Many puzzles remain, the resolution of which, when solutions exist, are beyond the scope of this introductory book. With the unification of so many different constructions comes the problem of how to account for their differences. Why must a wh-word sometimes have be silent? Why is *tough*-movement constrained in the way it is in only allowing movement from sequences of infinitives, unlike say, question formation? Does the type of unification defended in English extend to other languages? And in what way?

The cases of movement that we have looked at, which we analyze as various instances of wh-movement – although sometimes of a silent wh-phrase – belong to the so-called category of A-bar, movement. This terminology is based on a typology of landing positions: A-bar also called non-A (meant to evoke non-argument) positions and A-positions. A-bar, movement thus contrasts with A-movement, which is movement to an A-position. This is the type of movement one gets typically when an argument moves to the specifier of a Case licensing head as e.g. [Spec,TP]: such movements are exemplified by raising to subject or raising to object.

This also raises new, general, questions: are there properties shared by all instances of A-bar movement? Or by all instances of A-movement? The answers seem positive (A-bar movement, for example, seems not to be related to the case properties of landing positions, unlike A-movement): this raises the question of why these clustering of properties arise in this way, and how this relates to the distinction between A-bar and A positions.

14.6.4 Further readings

This chapter follows in the footsteps of the very influential Chomsky (1977) "On wh-movement." One important reference on the syntax of relative clauses is Kayne (1994). Otherwise, this where the *Blackwell Companion to Syntax* (Everaert and Riemsdijk, 2006) is particularly useful: look for articles dealing with questions, comparatives, tough-movement, clefts, etc.

15
Syntactic Processes

We conclude by summarizing some of the main ideas of our previous chapters, but with particular attention to the question of how syntactic structure could be recognized in ordinary fluent conversation. Intuitively, it seems clear that we usually attempt to make sense of what we hear on a word-by-word basis. We do not wait for the end of each sentence, but interpret what we hear at every point. Many different kinds of psychological studies confirm this intuitive idea. Compare the apparently much simpler task of pushing the brake or the accelerator in a car in response to seeing a red light or green light. Many studies show that, even for the most attentive subjects, this kind of response follows the stimulus by at least 200 milliseconds or so – one fifth of a second (Donders, 1969; Luce, 1986). In this time the light is perceived, a response is chosen, and the motor plan is executed. So it was a surprise, in the 1970s, when Marslen-Wilson noticed that the apparently much more complex task of perceiving and reproducing speech takes approximately the same time (Marslen-Wilson, 1973). This task, called "speech shadowing," involves repeating what you hear as quickly as possible, rather like simultaneous translation but without the translation. Marslen-Wilson found that some people can shadow accurately with as little as 250 milliseconds lag time, when listening to speech in which the average length of a syllable is about 200 milliseconds. Not only that, but fast shadowers do not just repeat the sounds they hear. They analyze and understand what they are hearing, as shown by the fact that when these shadowers mistakenly substitute an incorrect word, it is usually syntactically and semantically appropriate. Since the 1970s, many better experimental methods have been found for studying the perception of linguistic stimuli, including eye tracking (Ferreira and Henderson, 2004) and various methods of "functional neuroimaging" (Hickok, 2009; Poeppel and Monahan, 2008). These methods further confirm the very rapid recognition of syntactic and semantic properties of language. How can linguistic structures, the structures we have been exploring in previous chapters, be calculated so rapidly and automatically? In some sense, the calculation must be "simple," simple enough that we can do it without apparent effort. We can recognize a sentence, plan, and execute a verbal response, in not much more time than we need to respond to a green light. The recognition, planning, and motor response can remain only about one syllable behind the linguistic stimulus.

An Introduction to Syntactic Analysis and Theory, First Edition.
Dominique Sportiche, Hilda Koopman, and Edward Stabler.

15.1 The Language Model: Defining Structure

Keeping the processing perspective in mind, let's review once more the model of language developed in the preceding chapters. Many different types of constructions have been considered, but we have seen that in very many cases, things that look at first very different turn out to be fundamentally similar. We started by observing in Chapters 2 and 12 that morphological structures seem to depend on syntactic category and have locality requirements very similar to syntactic selection. Noun phrases, verb phrases, and in fact all phrases seem to have a similar structure that we noted at first with X-bar structure in Chapter 6, and then simplified in later discussion. Wh-movement applies in similar ways to phrases of many kinds, Chapters 10–14. And all movements are subject to locality conditions, which look complex and diverse at first but fall into very general patterns when considered more carefully in Chapter 10. The emergence of these general patterns may help us understand how computing linguistic structure could be much simpler than it seems at first! Let's review the basic structure of our syntax once more and consider how we might begin to fill in the details. The basic ideas about Merge and Movement can be defined simply and precisely. And because they are so simple, it has been possible to establish mathematical results about the complexity of recognizing the structures our grammars define.

X-bar notation has some unnecessary redundancy. Let's consider again this example from Section 8.6:

```
      CP
     /  \
    C    TP
        /   \
      DP     T'
      |     /  \
    John   T    VP
           |   /   \
         will DP    V'
              |    /  \
       (John,struck) V  DP
                   |   /  \
                  see D    NumP
                      |    /  \
                     the Num   NP
                          |    |
                          e    N
                               |
                             movie
```

Notice that the category of the single complementizer head appears twice (as part of the labels C and CP); the category T of the single tense head appears three times; the category V of the verb appears three times; and so on. It is enough to represent the category of each head just once. A more succinct representation may make the tree slightly harder to read, but it will make the representation smaller and easier to calculate with. Rather than labeling the phrases with categories, let's use "<" and ">" to point to the head of a phrase. Furthermore, instead of representing a moved constituent in both its original and its moved position, let's assume that both positions are visible to the semantics but that only the moved position is visible to the syntax.[1] Then we can represent the previous structure with this more compact one:

[1] An alternative way to obtain the same succinctness is to let the single moved element appear in both the moved and the original positions, so that the structure is no longer a tree.

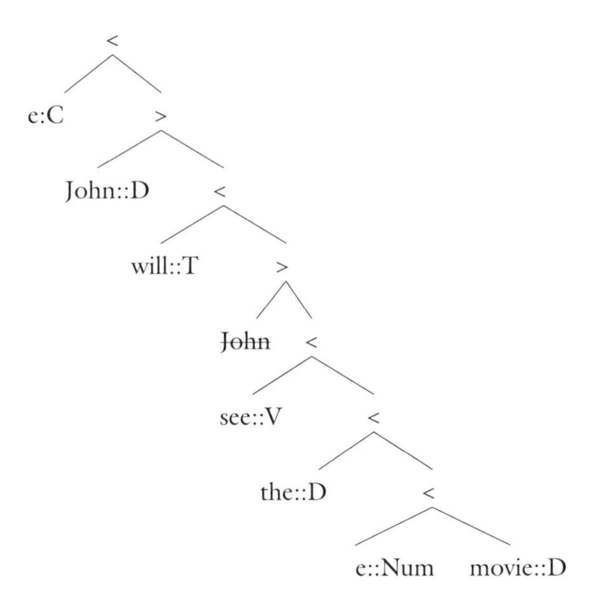

Following the "arrows" from the root, we can see that the head of this phrase has category C, so it is a complementizer phrase. And we can see that the maximal projection of *the* is $[_{\text{DP}}$*the* $[_{\text{NumP}}$ e $[_{\text{NP}}$*movie*]]] by the fact that this is the largest subtree that has *the* as its head.

15.2 Selection, Movement, Locality

In Section 8.6, the structure for *John will see the movie* was derived in seven steps. Let's go through the steps of that same derivation again, but this time using our more concise representation. To make the calculation completely definite, we will put full lexical items into our tree, but we will mark at each step which syntactic features can play a role in later derivational steps. The key feature of these grammars that allows derivations to be efficient is that the number of syntactic features relevant at any point is bounded. That is, for each grammar the number of visible features in each derived structure never exceeds some particular bound k. To illustrate how this works, we step through a simple derivation in the next section, putting boxes around the syntactic features at each point that is essential for later derivational steps.

- Using the notation for lexical entries from Section 6.8.3, assume the lexicon has the noun *movie* and the empty, singular number (writing *e* to signify that the singular number is not pronounced, as we did in Section 8.3.3).

  movie: N
  e: Num, selects N

  To be precise and succinct, let's use the symbol =N to mean "selects NP," and let's put the features in the order in which the derivation needs to consider them:

  movie: N
  e: =N Num

Step 1. Since this noun does not select anything, it is a complete phrase by itself, selected by the empty Num. Using < and > instead of labels like NP or NumP, we derive the following structure:

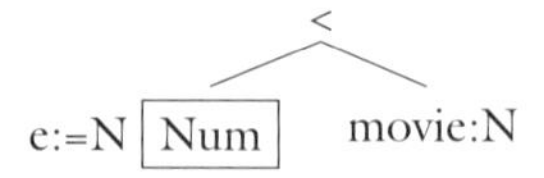

Notice that there are three syntactic features in the two lexical items, but only one of them remains visible to the syntactic calculation – the one we have put in the box. The derivation will never again need to know that *movie* was an N selected by the empty Num. Those features may matter to the semantics, but they will have no effect on the later steps in the derivation of the syntactic structure.

- Assume the lexicon includes a determiner that selects NumP complements, which we now represent this way:

the: =Num D

Step 2. We use Merge to combine the determiner with the previously built NumP, projecting the selector.

<
the:=Num D <
e:=N Num movie:N

Notice that the derivation now includes lexical items with five syntactic features, but only one of them remains visible to the derivation. The derivation will not need to know again that the determiner selected the NumP.

- The lexicon includes the verb *see*. Instead of underlining an argument to indicate that it is the subject, we simply put the selection requirements in the order they are used. And we will leave aside the semantic information about which is the agent and which is the patient, since the syntax does not need it:

see: =D =D V

Step 3. Now we can merge the verb with the previously built DP, filling the complement (patient) position, projecting the selector:

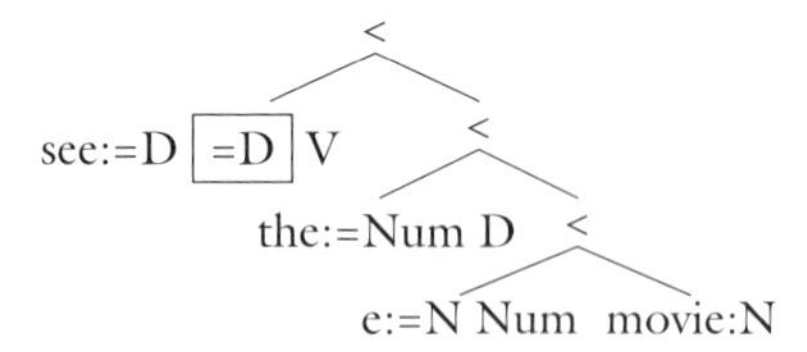

At this point, two of the eight lexical features remain visible.

- We can assume the lexicon includes the name *John* as a determiner (setting aside the question of exactly what internal structure DPs with names might have). But in English, DPs can satisfy the EPP requirements. There are various ways to capture this in our calculation – the simplest is to use a special feature –epp to mark elements that can fulfill EPP requirements:[2]

John: D –epp

The –epp feature simply indicates that this element can move to satisfy an EPP requirement.

Step 4. Following the arrows from the root down to the head of the phrase we built in Step 3, we can see that it still has a selection requirement as its first feature, so we now merge the subject (agent) into specifier position, projecting the selector once again:

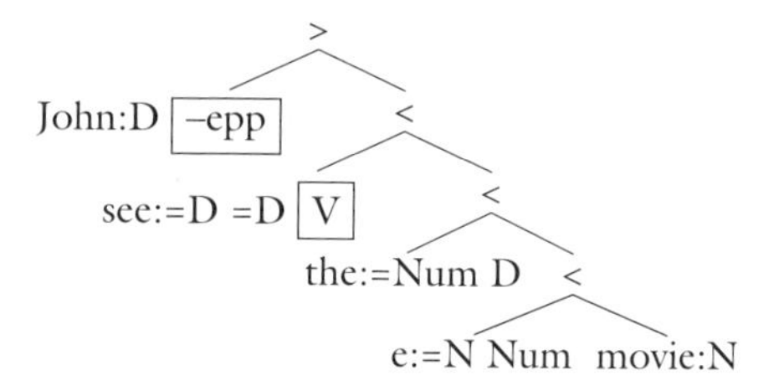

Notice that the arrow > at the root of this true shows that *John* is in specifier position, and that the head of this phrase is the V, so this is a VP. We can also see that two of the ten syntactic features in this result remain visible.

- Assume the lexicon includes *will* with category T, which selects VP and licenses an EPP element. Let's write +epp to indicate this licensing requirement.

will =V +epp T

Step 5. We merge this tense element with the previously constructed VP:

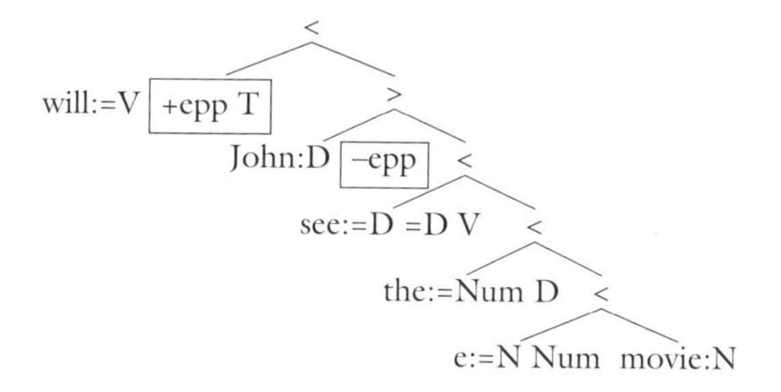

After this step, three of the thirteen syntactic features remain visible.

Notice that there is only one –epp element available to move in this structure. If we allow more than one licensee feature to be present when a licensor triggers a movement, then we need to specify what happens in that case. For the moment, let's make the simple assumption that every licensee `-f` must move to the first available `+f` position; in other words, there cannot be two `-f` features competing for the same `+f`, since both elements would have to move to that position. This simple constraint is slightly stronger than "attract closest" discussed in Sections 10.6.2 and 10.6.4, since it requires

[2] For calculating structures, this notation is slightly simpler than the suggestion in Chapters 10–12 of using EPP features indexed with the categories required, but that idea could be treated without major changes – see Theorem 2 below.

that there can only be one available element to move; this makes mathematical analysis of the grammar easier. "Attract closest" and related constraints make the picture slightly more complicated, but they can be analyzed too.

Step 6. Since the EPP feature of T is not satisfied in the result of Step 5, *Move* now applies, taking the maximal projection of the –epp head and moving it to the specifier position. In the tree on the left below, we have struck out the lower occurrence, as done earlier in the text. An alternative representation simply merges the lower occurrence again at the higher position, where it is pronounced, as shown on the right below:

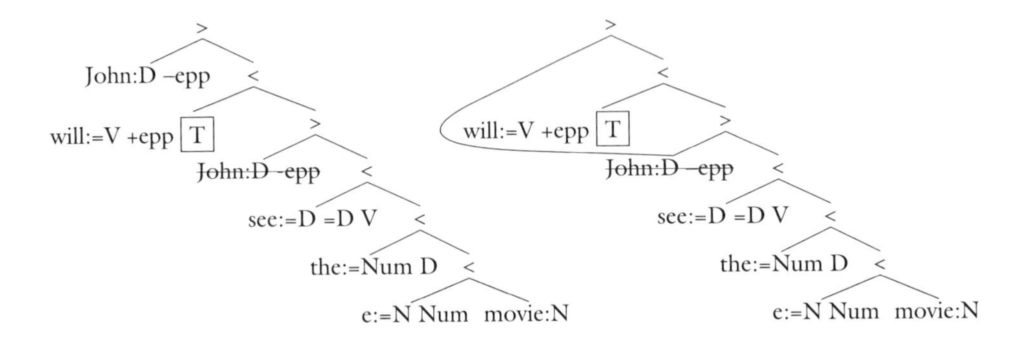

At this point, just one of the thirteen syntactic features is visible for the next step of the derivation.

- Now we assume that the lexicon includes the empty complementizer which selects T:

e: =T C

Step 7. Finally, we merge the complementizer with the previously built TP, completing the clause:

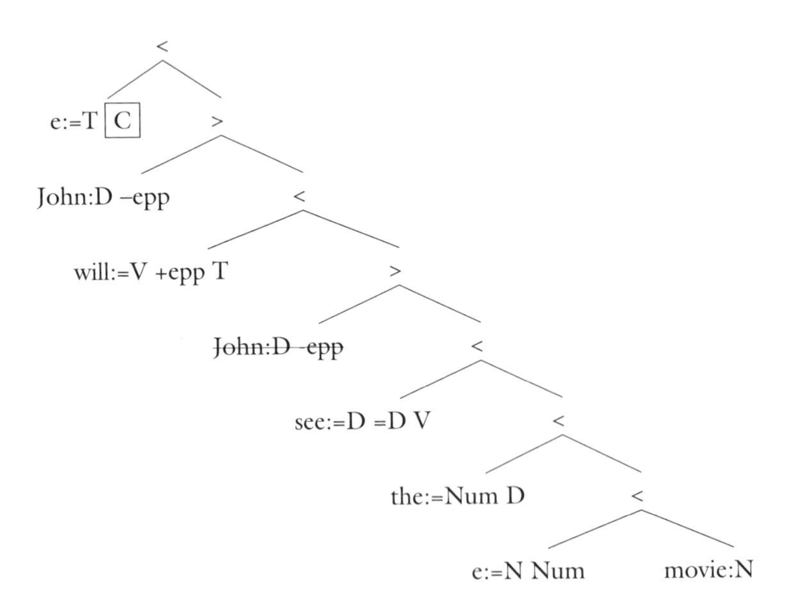

Now the only syntactic feature that remains visible is the category C at the head of the tree, which signals that we have derived a complete grammatical sentence.

Reviewing this derivation, making a list of the operations we used, it turns out that they are rather few and simple. Since every operation involves a pair of features on the heads of the trees involved, let's write $t[=\mathrm{f}]$ to represent a tree whose head (which we can find by following the arrows down from the root) has the selection feature =f as its first visible feature. And then t can be the result in which that first visible feature is no longer visible. Similarly, a tree with category c as its first visible feature is $t[\mathrm{c}]$ and t is the result in which that feature is no longer visible in the derivation. If we assume that complements are merged on the right, while additional elements in the phrase (if any) are merged on the left into specifier position, we can define Merge with two cases. Let's write $|t| = 1$ to mean that tree t has just one node (i.e. it is a lexical item, and so its complement position has not been filled).

$$\mathbf{merge}(t_1[=\mathrm{x}], t_2[\mathrm{x}]) = \begin{cases} [_{<}\ t_1\ \ t_2] & \text{if } |t_1| = 1 \\ [_{>}\ t_2\ \ t_1] & \text{otherwise} \end{cases}$$

What this rule says is that to merge a tree $t_1[=\mathrm{x}]$ and a tree $t_2[\mathrm{x}]$, we put the selected phrase on the right, in complement position; and otherwise, if the first tree has more than one node (and hence we know that its complement position is filled), we put the selected item on the left, in specifier position. In both cases, the selector feature =x and category feature x become irrelevant, invisible for later derivational steps.

We can similarly define phrasal movement as an operation on these reduced trees. Given any tree t with subtree t_1, let t_1^M be the maximal projection of the head of t_1, and let $t\{\cancel{t_1}\}$ be the result of "striking out" subtree t_1, "remerging" it to the higher specifier position:

$$\mathbf{move}(t[+\mathrm{x}]) = [_{>}\ t_1^M\ \ t\{\cancel{t_1[-\mathrm{x}]^M}\}]$$

A simple locality condition requires that this rule can only apply when exactly one -x feature is visible in the tree, but various other locality conditions have been explored and this is an area of ongoing research, as discussed at length in Chapter 10. These definitions of Merge and Move are simplified notational variants of the rules we have used throughout the text.

15.3 Computational Properties of the Model

The precise definitions of Merge and Move have been carefully studied mathematically, in order to see exactly what kinds of languages they can define, and how the derivations of sentences in those languages can be calculated. This study reveals two surprises – an "external convergence" theorem and an "internal convergence" theorem.

Taking the external convergence first, consider what can be defined with any finite lexicon, by applying the Merge and Move rules given above. Let the language of any such grammar be the set of pronounced sentences – the morpheme sequences – that have derivations resulting in the clausal category C like the one above (or any other single category). It turns out that the class of languages that can be defined by Merge and Move in this way is a class that was already known from earlier work on formal grammars. From the definition of these grammars, the following can be proven

Theorem 1: The languages definable by Merge and Move (as given above) are exactly the languages definable by "multiple context free grammars" (Seki et al., 1991), by "set

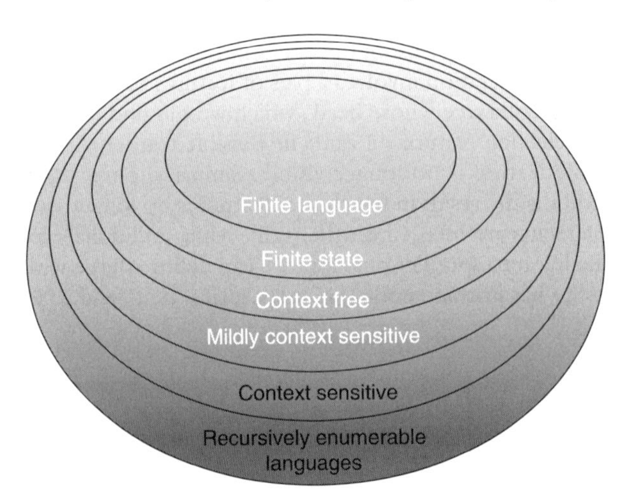

Figure 15.1 The Chomsky hierarchy of language complexity. Deciding whether a sentence is in a "recursively enumerable" language can be impossible. Some recursively enumerable languages – like the set of truths of arithmetic – are *undecidable* in this sense. Deciding whether a sentence is in a context sensitive language is always decidable but can be *intractable* – the number of steps needed to find a derivation may increase exponentially as the length of the sentence increases. But deciding whether a sentence is generated by a mildly context sensitive grammar is tractable.

local tree adjoining grammars" Weir (1988), and by a certain class of "abstract categorial grammars" (Kanazawa and Salvati, 2007; Salvati, 2007).[3]

Aravind Joshi calls languages with the fundamental properties of this class **mildly context-sensitive**, and proposes that the class of possible human languages is properly included among them (Joshi, 1985).[4] The fact that languages definable with Merge and Move are in this class provides further support for this broad hypothesis, though some important challenges remain.[5] In the 1950s, Noam Chomsky observed that languages can be classified into a hierarchy according to the kinds of rules that determine which elements can appear where (Chomsky 1956, 1957, 1963). The previous result places the languages definable by Merge and Move into this hierarchy, as shown in Figure 15.1.

In effect, the basic results mentioned above establish that our grammars for human languages are capable of defining languages that are more complex than artificial languages like arithmetic or propositional logic – these are "context-free languages." But the mildly complex languages are easier to define and recognize than the theorems of first order logic, or of standard arithmetics – these languages are not mildly context sensitive, but are "recursively enumerable."

A second surprising result about the languages definable by Merge and Move relates this simple kind of language model to a wide range of closely related theoretical proposals. For this reason, these results represent a convergence of formal proposals that are internal to this particular tradition of linguistic theory:

[3]This theorem was proven independently by Jens Michaelis and by Henk Harkema. See Michaelis (1998, 2001a,b) and Harkema (2001a,b).
[4]For further results on this mildly context sensitive class, with further references, see for example (Seki et al., 1991; Mönnich, 2010).
[5]There are challenges on a variety of fronts, including the case marking system of Old Georgian Michaelis and Kracht (1997), German scrambling Rambow (1994), Chinese number names (Radzinski, 1991), and the VP copying in certain cleft constructions in Yoruba (Kobele, 2006).

Theorem 2: To our basic mechanisms Merge and Move (as defined just above), it is possible to add head movement, affix hopping, adjunction, asymmetric feature checking, and various kinds of locality conditions on movement, without changing the class of definable languages.[6]

This result means that a large range of theories about human language will have the same "expressive power." That is, these different grammars cannot be distinguished just by what they can define, though they may differ in how succinct and illuminating they are, and how appropriate for the semantic and phonetic interfaces.

15.3.1 Parsing: calculating structure

This section is quite technical and can be skimmed or skipped on first reading. The goal is to show how the calculation of a parse can be done, and the basic idea will be clear even without understanding every detail.

We have said that the derivation of structures defined by a grammar with Merge and Move can be calculated, and that this calculation is always tractable, but we have not presented any calculation method. We will present one here, but you will see that it is a method designed for automatic calculation (e.g. by computers or brains), rather than a method that you would want to use for hand calculation.

The decision about whether a sequence of perceived morphemes is generated by a grammar is commonly called "recognition." When a recognizer outputs a representation of the derivation(s), if any, we call it a "parser." There are many different ways to calculate derivations for our grammars with Merge and Move. One of the simplest methods uses the rules Merge and Move quite directly and so is easy to explain. It is sometimes called the "CKY-like" method, after Cocke, Kasami, and Younger who developed similar methods for recognizing context-free languages in the 1960s. In effect, this parsing algorithm simply applies the grammar rules in all possible ways to derive every possible analysis of every subsequence of the input.

Step 1. Given a morphologically analyzed input sequence like *John will see the movie*, to keep track of the temporal sequence, number the positions between the morphemes:

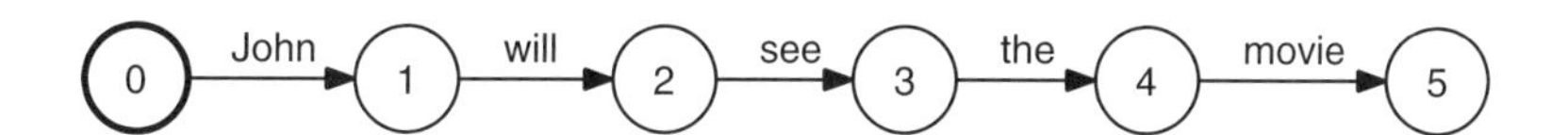

Now every subsequence can be represented by a pair of indices. For example (0,3) represents the temporal interval containing the subsequence *John will see*, and (0,0) represents the empty position before any words were heard.

Step 2. We will construct a table (sometimes called a "chart" or "matrix") to hold all the analyses found at each point, beginning with all compatible lexical elements. In the sequence *John will see the movie*, the interval (0,1) contains *John*, so we put the features of all lexical items that are pronounced this way in position (0,1), and similarly for each of the other pronounced words. And since empty elements can occur in the empty intervals (0,0), (1,1) ...(5,5), we put each possible set of features of empty elements in these positions. In the following chart, assuming the grammar has just the lexical items from our previous example derivation, we see the features of empty lexical items on the diagonal, and the features of pronounced lexical items are just above the diagonal:

[6] Stabler (2010) provides a review of these results with many further references to this ongoing mathematical work.

	0	1	2	3	4	5
0	::=T C ::=N Num	::D –epp				
1		::=T C ::=N Num	::=V +epp T			
2			::=T C ::=N Num	::=D =D v		
3				::=T C ::=N Num	::=Num D	
4					::=T C ::=N Num	::N
5						::=T C ::=N Num

We use :: to mark these items as lexical, and : to mark derived items.

Step 3. Now, we apply the simple operations of the grammar to fill in parts of the upper half of the matrix that correspond to constituents, in all possible ways. Merge was defined above with two cases, but we now must break it into three cases, where the third case allows Merge to apply to non-adjacent elements if the selected element moves – something that is signalled by a feature -f. And rather than putting trees into the table, we will keep a record of just the active features of each head together with the temporal interval spanned by its maximal projection (minus any moving elements). Proceeding in this way, the seven steps of the derivation presented above are these:

i. First we merge the adjacent Num and N lexical items, a step we can write like this,

$$\frac{(4,4)::=\text{N Num} \qquad (4,5)::\text{N}}{(4,5):\text{Num}}$$

We add the derived NumP to the chart by putting :Num into cell (4,5). This is the first case of Merge: merging with an adjacent complement.

ii. Now we merge the adjacent D and Num lexical items, a step we can write like this,

$$\frac{(3,4)::=\text{Num D} \qquad (4,5):\text{Num}}{(3,5):\text{D}}$$

This is again the first case of Merge: merging with an adjacent complement.

iii. Now we merge the verb with the adjacent DP:

$$\frac{(2,3)::=\text{D =D V} \qquad (3,5):\text{D}}{(2,5):=\text{D V}}$$

This is again the first case of Merge: merging with an adjacent complement.

iv. Now we Merge the verb with a non-adjacent specifier. Since the specifier is non-adjacent, we keep the coordinates of this moving element separate:

$$\frac{(2,5)::=\text{D V} \qquad (0,1):\text{D –epp}}{(2,5):\text{V}, (0,1):\text{–epp}}$$

Intuitively, the result of this step is a VP in the temporal interval (2,5) which includes a discontinuous element in the interval (0,1). This is what we called the third case of Merge: merging with something that is moving.

v. Now we merge the tense with the verb phrase, to form a tense phrase that still has the same moving element that the verb phrase had:

$$\frac{(1,2){:}{=}\text{V +epp T} \qquad (2,5){:}\text{V}, (0,1){:}{-}\text{epp}}{(1,5){:}\text{+epp T}, (0,1){:}{-}\text{epp}}$$

vi. Step v created a phrase whose first visible feature is the trigger for movement +epp, and we can see in the same consituent that there is a left-adjacent –epp moving phrase, so move the DP to [Spec,TP] as follows:

$$\frac{(1,5){:}\text{+epp T}, (0,1){:}{-}\text{epp}}{(0,5){:}\text{T}}$$

vii. Now we merge the TP result of the previous step with C:

$$\frac{(0,0){::}{=}\text{T C} \qquad (0,5){:}\text{T}}{(0,5){:}\text{C}}$$

Spurious step. The previous steps recapitulate the derivation we did above, by hand. When we look for all possible analyses, though, we find this step too:

$$\frac{(2,3){::}{=}\text{D =D V} \qquad (0,1){:}\text{D }{-}\text{epp}}{(2,3){:}{=}\text{D V}, (0,1){:}{-}\text{epp}}$$

This result is spurious, but harmless: nothing further follows from it.

Step 4. At this point, we have made all possible additions to the chart, using the simple lexicon of our example. The complete chart is shown below. We can see in this chart that we have found a successful derivation because we have found a clause C that spans the whole interval (0,5), and the sequence of steps leading to this successful result can be retrieved.

We can see that each of these four basic steps requires only finitely many substeps: step 1 is bounded by the finite length of the input; 2 by the finite size of the lexicon; 3 by the fact that there are finitely many rules, and no rule application increases the number of visible features; and 4 is a simple check for success. Calculating the maximum number of steps needed for an input of length n, Harkema (2000) proves that the number of steps needed is always tractable, always less than a polynomial function of n.

	0	1	2	3	4	5
0	::=T C ::=N Num	::D –epp				:T :C
1		::=T C ::=N Num	::=V +epp T			:+epp T,(0,1):–epp
2			::=T C ::=N Num	::=D =D V :=D V,(0,1):–epp		:=D V :V,(0,1):–epp
3				::=T C ::=N Num	::=Num D	:D
4					::=T C ::=N Num	::N :Num
5						::=T C ::=N Num

The completed chart for *John will see the movie*.

Calculating this kind of chart is similar to standard "matrix multiplication," as has been noted in a number of complexity analyses (Valiant, 1975; Satta, 1994). See Stabler (2001a,b) and Harkema (2000) for a more detailed presentation, and Kallmeyer (2010) for a broader introduction. It is possible that neural systems can do something like matrix multiplication – see for example Ballard (1997, p. 74). And there are some preliminary connectionist implementations of the CKY method described here (Gerth and beim Graben, 2009).

15.3.2 Garden paths and linguistic illusions

In the 1960s and 1970s there was great excitement about the possibility that developments in linguistic theory might lead us quite directly to good models of how people understand their languages. At first psychologists considered the possibility that the time needed to recognize a sentence might be a simple function of how many steps were needed in its derivation, but models of language processing, even ones that use grammar very directly, do not predict this. In particular, for most parsing methods, the number of steps depends on how many analyses are available for all possible subconstituents. That is, it depends on the whole grammar. The step from a grammar to a good parsing model is not direct and immediate even for much simpler artificial languages, like familiar programming languages.

A different kind of challenge to the transparency of the relation between grammatical structures and psychological processing comes from garden paths and linguistic illusions. These were noticed in the 1970s (Fodor, Bever, and Garrett, 1976), and still pose puzzling questions. A garden path sentence is a grammatical sentence that is not recognized as acceptable, at least not without some careful reflection. The most famous one,

(1) The horse raced past the barn fell

is not readily recognized as a grammatical sentence that means something very similar to *the horse which was raced past the barn fell.* Constructions like this have been studied extensively. One important observation made by MacDonald, Pearlmutter, and Seidenberg (1994) is that this garden path is especially difficult to recover from because the verb *raced* is rarely used as a past participle transitive verb; in one corpus, only 1% of the occurrences of *raced* had that category. The verb *carried*, on the other hand, occurs 49% of the time as a transitive past participle in the same corpus, and so the similar sentence is much easier to recognize as grammatical:

(2) The basket carried past the barn fell

This kind of result suggests that the search for grammatical analyses is rationally biased to prefer likely derivations, and much effort has gone into defining how this search for analyses is actually done in normal human language use.

Illusions offer the opposite challenge. An illusion is an ungrammatical sentence that is recognized as acceptable. Some errors are not noticed, or at least, they are not rejected as being completely ungrammatical. One example of this is provided by studies showing that while sentences in which negative polarity items (NPIs) are c-commanded by a negative phrase are accepted (3a), and NPIs without any negative phrase like (3c) are rejected, subjects rate sentences like (3b) as better than (3c) even though the negative phrase is not c-commanding (Drenhaus, Frisch, and Saddy, 2005; Vasishth et al., 2008):

(3) a. No professor who a student likes will ever say that
b. The professor who no student likes will ever say that
c. A professor who a student likes will ever say that

Judgment tasks are hard to interpret though: what standard of "grammaticality" or "acceptability" are subjects using? To sidestep this issue, a more recent study monitored neural responses – event related potentials (ERPs) – while listening to examples of these sentences, and found that examples like (3b) actually do produce a rapid response (a P600 response) to the ungrammatical NPI (Xiang, Dillon, and Phillips, 2009), a response typical for recognizing syntactic anomalies. These kinds of results suggest that even in the case of grammatical illusions, cases where we seem to accept sequences that are not fully grammatical, or misunderstand grammatical sequences, human recognition of syntactic structures (and anomalies in those structures) is remarkably fast and accurate. Ongoing research aims to reveal more detail about what is happening.

When we are actually using our linguistic abilities, the mechanisms that define grammatical structure are obviously subject to restrictions of memory, attention, and many other factors, most of them poorly understood. Theories that aim to account for these interactions are sometimes called "performance models," as opposed to the simpler "competence model" of the grammar. We find a similar distinction between algorithm and hardware implementations in computer science. The question of exactly what role the grammar plays in performance models is one that can only be answered by attempts to develop psychological and neurophysiological theories that can explain our abilities.

15.4 Conclusion

15.4.1 Summary

This last chapter does not introduce any new ideas about language structure, but instead takes some first steps towards understanding how the structures of previous chapters could be calculated quickly and automatically in ordinary language use. We can rigorously and mathematically define the operations of merging heads with phrases they select, and then move elements around in restricted ways. These movements can make the pronounced parts of a phrase "discontinuous," but the phrase is still recognized as a whole unit, and this is usually as automatic as the visual recognition of a whole object even when the view is partly obstructed, as when we see a bird in a cage. The calculation defined here is one way to automatically assemble the disconnected pieces of pronounced, surface forms to yield one coherent structure. That structure is always the projection of one single head, one projection that is the whole of the sentence.

15.4.2 What to remember

We have seen repeatedly throughout the text that the apparent diversity of linguistic forms often hides common structure, and this chapter shows how the common structure is the result of a common structural calculation, a calculation that is essentially uniform across all structures of all languages. This calculation is powerful and expressive enough to allow the very significant diversity we see among human languages, but it is not the case that it can define just anything. In Chomsky's hierarchy of language complexity (Figure 15.1), it appears that human languages, as defined by our grammars – abstracting away from limitations of memory, attention, etc. – may all be "mildly context sensitive," or very nearly so. We expect this perspective to be much enriched with the ongoing study of locality conditions and syntactic structures of the world's languages.

15.4.3 Puzzles and preview

Our first steps toward understanding the structures of sentences and how they are calculated leave very many puzzles open. In linguistic structure, many questions of detail were left unresolved, many apparent conflicts between constituency tests, patterns of movement, and binding. But here at the end of this long text, it is natural to reflect on some broader questions. For example, which properties, exactly, trigger the construction of phrase structures? Our perspective on this takes a surprising turn in Chapter 12, where the atoms of syntax are characterized as the "engines" of phrase structure and we proposed that these are also the atoms of morphology. Lexical requirements determine the whole calculation of structure. Selection requirements trigger Merge steps, and the EPP properties of a head can trigger movements. If this is roughly right, then the question is: why do heads have properties like this? This is analogous to asking why the basic elements in the periodic table have their particular properties, properties that allow them to combine into molecular compounds of various sorts. But in language, there is another, different, kind of question that should help us understand what is happening: how are the properties of sentences, in all their varieties across languages, discovered by children learning their first languages? Children apparently discover the atoms of their languages and properties of those atoms with just a few years of exposure. Since children do this so reliably and similarly in spite of quite different linguistic experiences, we must conclude that language acquisition is easy, at least in the sense that the inference of atoms and their properties is robust across rather significant variations in the data. The simple underlying structural principles that this text has aimed to identify must make that possible.

15.4.4 Further readings

The Chomsky hierarchy is commonly introduced in computer science texts (Martin, 1997: §8.4) and mathematical works (Mateescu and Salomaa, 1997: §3.1) as a kind of summary of basic complexity results. Human languages are context sensitive, as discussed, for example, in Savitch et al. (1987) but the artificial languages most often used in computer science (programming languages and the language of arithmetic) are context free, and even human languages can be approximated with context free grammars, so context sensitive languages get relatively little attention from computer scientists and computational linguists with engineering goals. Texts which properly introduce context sensitive grammars, closer to what we need for human languages and more like the grammars developed in previous chapters, have begun to appear relatively recently (Kallmeyer, 2010; Francez and Wintner, 2012). These texts introduce the math that sets the stage for the work described in this chapter.

References

Abbott, Barbara. 1976. Right Node Raising as a Test for Constituenthood. *Linguistic Inquiry*, 7:639–642.

Abney, Steven P. 1987. The English Noun Phrase in its Sentential Aspect. Ph.D. thesis, Massachusetts Institute of Technology.

Adger, David. 2003. *Core Syntax: A Minimalist Approach*. Oxford: Oxford University Press.

Anderson, Stephen R. 1986. The Typology of Anaphoric Dependencies: Icelandic (and Other) Reflexives. In L. Hellan and K. Koch-Kristensen, editors, *Papers in Scandinavian Syntax*. Dordrecht: Reidel, pages 65–88.

Anderson, Stephen R. 1992. *A-Morphous Morphology*. New York: Cambridge University Press.

Anderson, Stephen R. and D. Lightfoot. 2002. *The Language Organ: Linguistics as Cognitive Physiology*. Cambridge: Cambridge University Press.

Baayen, Harald, t. Dijkstra, and R. Schreuder. 1979. Singulars and Plurals in Dutch. *Journal of Memory and Language*, 36:94–117.

Baker, Mark C. 1997. Thematic Roles and Syntactic Structure. In Liliane Haegeman, editor, *Elements of Grammar*. Dordrecht: Kluwer, pages 73–137.

Baker, Mark C. 1988. *Incorporation: A Theory of Grammatical Function Changing*. Cambridge, MA: MIT Press.

Baker, Mark C. 2001. *The Atoms of Language*. New York: Basic Books.

Baker, Mark C. 2003. *Lexical Categories: Verbs, Nouns, and Adjectives*. New York: Cambridge University Press.

Ballard, Dana H. 1997. *An Introduction to Natural Computation*. Cambridge, MA: MIT Press.

Barss, Andrew and H. Lasnik. 1986. A Note on Anaphora and Double Objects. *Linguistic Inquiry*, 17: 347–354.

Beard, Robert. 1998. Derivation. In Andrew Spencer and Arnold M. Zwicky, editors, *The Handbook of Morphology*. New York: Elsevier.

Beck, Sigrid and K. Johnson. 2004. Double Objects Again. *Linguistic Inquiry*, 35(1):97–123.

Beneviste, Emile. 1967. Fondements syntaxiques de la composition nominale. *Bulletin de la Societe de Linguistique de Paris*, 62(1): 15–31

Berko, Jean. 1958. The Child's Acquisition of English Morphology. *Word*, 14:150–177.

Bertram, Raymond, H. Baayen, and R. Schreuder. 2000. Affixal Homonymy Triggers Full Form Storage, Even With Inflected Words, Even in a Morphologically Rich Language. *Cognition*, 74:B13–B25.

Booij, Geert E. 2005. *The Grammar of Words*. Oxford: Oxford University Press.

Bresnan, Joan. 1979. *Theory of Complementation in English Syntax*. New York: Garland.

Büring, Daniel. 2005. *Binding Theory. Cambridge*: Cambridge University Press.

Burzio, Luigi. 1986. *Italian Syntax: A Government-Binding Approach*. Boston MA: Reidel.

Carnie, Andrew. 2002. *Syntax: A Generative Introduction*, volume 4. Oxford: Wiley-Blackwell.

An Introduction to Syntactic Analysis and Theory, First Edition.
Dominique Sportiche, Hilda Koopman, and Edward Stabler.

Charnavel, Isabelle. 2009. Linking Binding and Focus: On Intensifying *son propre* in French. Master's thesis, UCLA.

Charnavel, Isabelle. 2012. On Her Own. Parsimonious Compositionality: Probing Syntax and Semantics with French *propre*. Ph.D. thesis, UCLA.

Chierchia, Gennaro. 1998. Plurality of Mass Nouns and the Notion of Semantic Parameter. In S. Rothstein, editor, *Events and Grammar*. Dordrecht: Kluwer, pages 53–103.

Chomsky, Noam. 1956. Three Models for the Description of Language. *IRE Transactions on Information Theory*, IT-2:113–124.

Chomsky, Noam. 1957. *Syntactic Structures*. The Hague: Mouton.

Chomsky, Noam. 1963. Formal Properties of Grammars. In R. Duncan Luce, Robert R. Bush, and Eugene Galanter, editors, *Handbook of Mathematical Psychology*, Volume II. New York: Wiley, pages 323–418.

Chomsky, Noam. 1964. *Current Issues in Linguistic Theory*. The Hague: Mouton.

Chomsky, Noam. 1965. *Aspects of the Theory of Syntax*. Cambridge, MA: MIT Press.

Chomsky, Noam. 1970. Remarks on Nominalization. In R. A. Jacobs and P. S. Rosenbaum, editors, *Readings in English Transformational Grammar*. Waltham, MA: Ginn. Reprinted in Chomsky, Noam. 1972. *Studies on Semantics in Generative Grammar*. The Hague: Mouton.

Chomsky, Noam. 1973. Conditions on Transformations. In Stephen R. Anderson and Paul Kiparsky, editors, *A Festschrift for Morris Halle*. New York: Holt, Rinehart & Winston. Reprinted in Chomsky, Noam. 1977. *Essays on Form and Interpretation*. Amsterdam: North-Holland.

Chomsky, Noam. 1975. *Reflections on Language*. New York: Pantheon.

Chomsky, Noam. 1977. On Wh-Movement. In P. Culicover, T. Wasow, and A. Akmajian, editors, *Formal Syntax*. New York: Academic Press.

Chomsky, Noam. 1981. *Lectures on Government and Binding*. Dordrecht: Foris.

Chomsky, Noam. 1982. *Some Concepts and Consequences of the Theory of Government and Binding*. Cambridge, MA: MIT Press.

Chomsky, Noam. 1986. *Knowledge of Language*. New York: Praeger.

Chomsky, Noam. 1991. Some Notes on Economy of Derivation and Representation. In Robert Freidin, editor, Principles and Parameters in Comparative Grammar. Cambridge, MA: MIT Press, pages 417–454.

Chomsky, Noam. 1993. A Minimalist Program for Linguistic Theory. In Kenneth Hale and Samuel Jay Keyser, editors, *The View from Building 20*. Cambridge, MA: MIT Press.

Chomsky, Noam. 1995a. Bare Phrase Structure. In Gert Webelhuth, editor, *Government and Binding Theory and the Minimalist Program*. Cambridge, MA: MIT Press, pages 383–439.

Chomsky, Noam. 1995b. *The Minimalist Program*. Cambridge, MA: MIT Press.

Chomsky, Noam. 2001. Derivation by Phase. In Michael Kenstowicz, editor, *Ken Hale: A Life in Language*. Cambridge, MA: MIT Press, pages 1–52.

Chomsky, Noam and H. Lasnik. 1977. Filters and Control. *Linguistic Inquiry*, 8.

Chomsky, Noam and H. Lasnik. 1993. Principles and Parameters Theory. In J. Jacobs, A. von Stechow, W. Sternfeld, and T. Vennemann, editors, *Syntax: An International Handbook of Contemporary Research*. Berlin: de Gruyter. Reprinted in Chomsky, Noam. 1995. The Minimalist Program. Cambridge, MA: MIT Press.

Christensen, Ken R. and M. Wallentin. 2011. The Locative Alternation: Distinguishing Linguistic Processing Cost from Error Signals in Broca's Region. *NeuroImage*, 56:1622–1631.

Cinque, Guglielmo. 1977. The Movement Nature of Left Dislocation. *Linguistic Inquiry*, pages 397–412.

Cinque, Guglielmo. 1999. *Adverbs and Functional Heads: A Cross-Linguistic Perspective*. Oxford: Oxford University Press, Oxford.

Crain, Stephen and R. Thornton. 1998. *Investigations in Universal Grammar: A Guide to Experiments on the Acquisition of Syntax and Semantics*.

Culicover, Peter W. 1997. *Principles and Parameters: An Introduction to Syntactic Theory*. Oxford: Oxford University Press.

Demonte Barreto, V. and I. Bosque. 1999. *Gramática descriptiva de la lengua española*. Madrid: Espasa Calpe.

den Besten, Hans. 1983. On the Interaction of Root Transformations and Lexical Deletive Rules. In W. Abraham, editor, *On the Formal Syntax of the Westgermania*. Amsterdam: John Benjamins Publishing Company.

Di Sciullo, Anna Maria and E. Williams. 1987. *On the Definition of Word*. Cambridge, MA: MIT Press.

Donders, Francisus C. 1969. On the Speed of Mental Processes. *Acta Psychologica, Attention and Performance*, 30:412–431.

Drenhaus, Heiner, S. Frisch, and D. Saddy. 2005. Processing Negative Polarity Items: When Negation Comes Through the Backdoor. In S. Kepser and M. Reis, editors, *Linguistic Evidence: Empirical, Theoretical, and Computational Perspectives.* New York: Walter de Gruyter.

Dryer, Matthew S. 1992. The Greenbergian Word Order Correlations. *Language*, 68(1):81–138.

Embick, David. 2010. *Localism Versus Globalism in Morphology and Phonology*, volume 60. Cambridge, MA: MIT Press.

Embick, David, A. Marantz, M. Miyashita, et al. 2001. A Syntactic Specialization for Broca's Area. *Proceedings of the National Academy of Sciences*, 97:6150–6154.

Emonds, Joseph E. 1976. *A Transformational Approach to English Syntax.* New York: Academic Press.

Emonds. Joseph. 1978. The Verbal Complex V′-V in French. *Linguistic Inquiry*, 9: 151–175.

Emonds, Joseph E. 1987. The Invisible Category Principle. *Linguistic Inquiry*, 18(4):613–632.

Emonds, Joseph E. 2000. *Lexicon and Grammar: The English Syntacticon*, volume 50. The Hague: Mouton de Gruyter.

Everaert, Martin and H. C. Riemsdijk. 2006. *The Blackwell Companion to Syntax.* Malden, MA, USA: Blackwell.

Fabb, Nigel. 1988. English Suffixation is Constrained only by Selection Restrictions. *Linguistics and Philosophy*, 6:527–539.

Featherston, Samuel, T. Münte, M. Gross, and H. Clahsen. 2000. Brain Potentials in the Processing of Complex Sentences: An ERP Study of Control and Raising Constructions. *Journal of Psycholinguistic Research*, 29:141–154.

Ferreira, Fernanda and J. M. Henderson, editors. 2004. *The Interface of Language, Vision and Action.* New York: Psychology Press.

Fiengo, Robert and R. May. 1995. *Indices and Identity.* Cambridge, MA: MIT Press.

Fodor, Jerry A. 1980. *The Language of Thought.* Cambridge, MA: MIT Press.

Fodor, Jerry A. and T. G. Bever. 1965. The Psychological Reality of Linguistic Segments. *Journal of Verbal Learning and Verbal Behavior*, 4:414–420.

Fodor, Jerry A. and Ernest Lepore. 1999. Impossible Words? *Linguistic Inquiry*, 30(3):445–453.

Fodor, Jerry A., T. G. Bever, and M. F. Garrett. 1976. *The Psychology of Language: An Introduction to Psycholinguistics and Generative Grammar.* New York: McGraw-Hill.

Fox, Danny. 2002. Antecedent-Contained Deletion and the Copy Theory of Movement. *Linguistic Inquiry*, 33(1):63–96.

Francez, Nissim and S. Wintner. 2012. *Unification Grammars.* New York: Cambridge University Press.

Gerth, Sabrina and P. beim Graben. 2009. Unifying Syntactic Theory and Sentence Processing Difficulty through a Connectionist Minimalist Parser. *Cognitive Neurodynamics*, 3(4):297–316.

Greenberg, Joseph. 1978. Some Universals of Grammar with Particular Reference to the Order of Meaningful Elements. In Joseph Greenberg, editor, *Universals of Human Language.* Stanford, CA: Stanford University Press.

Haegeman, Liliane. 1994. *Introduction to Government and Binding Theory.* Oxford: Blackwell, 2nd edition.

Haeseryn, Walter et al. 1997. *Algemene Nederlandse Spraakkunst.* Groningen: Nijhoff.

Hale, Kenneth and S. J. Keyser. 2002. *Prolegomenon to a Theory of Argument Structure.* Cambridge, MA: MIT Press.

Halle, M. and A. Marantz. 1994. Some Key Features of Distributed Morphology. *MIT Working Papers in Linguistics*, 21(275):88.

Harkema, Henk. 2000. A Recognizer for Minimalist Grammars. In: Sixth International Workshop on Parsing Technologies, IWPT'00.

Harkema, Henk. 2001a. A Characterization of Minimalist Languages. In Philippe de Groote, Glyn Morrill, and Christian Retoré, editors, *Logical Aspects of Computational Linguistics*, Lecture Notes in Artificial Intelligence, No. 2099. New York: Springer, pages 193–211.

Harkema, Henk. 2001b. Parsing Minimalist Languages. Ph.D. thesis, University of California, Los Angeles.

Harris, Randy A. 1995. *The Linguistics Wars.* New York: Oxford University Press.

Haspelmath, Martin. 1993. More on the Typology of Inchoative/Causative Verb Alternations. In B. Comrie and M. Polinsky, editors, *Causatives and Transitivity.* Amsterdam: John Benjamins Publishing Company, pages 87–120.

Haspelmath, Martin, M. S. Dryer, D. Gil, and B. Comrie, editors. 2005. *The World Atlas of Language Structures*. Oxford: Oxford University Press.

Hauser, Mark D., N. Chomsky, and W. Fitch. 2002. The Faculty of Language: What Is It, Who Has It, And How Did It Evolve? *Science*, 298(5598):1569.

Healey, Phyllis M. 1960. *An Agta Grammar*. Summer Institute of Linguistics, Philippine Branch, Manila.

Heim, Irene and A. Kratzer. 1998. *Semantics in Generative Grammar*. Oxford: Blackwell.

Hellan, Lars. 2008. *Anaphora in Norwegian and the Theory of Grammar*. Dordrecht: Foris.

Henry, Alison 1995. *Belfast English and Standard English: Dialect Variation and Parameter Setting*. New York: Oxford University Press.

Hickok, Gregory. 2009. The Functional Neuroanatomy of Language. *Physics of Life Reviews*, 6(3):121–143.

Homer, Vincent. 2011. Polarity and Modality. Ph.D. thesis, UCLA.

Hornstein, Norbert. 1999. Movement and Control. *Linguistic Inquiry*, 30:69–96.

Hornstein, Norbert, J. Nunes, and K. K. Grohmann. 2005. *Understanding Minimalism*. Cambridge: Cambridge University Press.

Hualde, Jose I. and J. O. De Urbina. 2003. *A Grammar of Basque*, volume 26. Berlin: Walter de Gruyter.

Huang, C.-T. James and C.-S. Luther Liu. 2001. Logophoricity, Attitudes, and *Ziji* at the Interface. In Peter Cole, Gabriella Hermon, and C. T. James Huang, editors, *Long-Distance Reflexives, Syntax and Semantics 33*. New York: Academic Press, pages 141–192.

Huddleston, Rodney and G. K. Pullum. 2002. *The Cambridge Grammar of English*. Cambridge: Cambridge University Press.

Indefrey, Peter, C. M. Brown, P. Hagoort, H. Herzog, and R. Seitz. 2001. Left Prefrontal Cortex Processes Syntax Independent of Lexical Meaning. *NeuroImage*, 14:546–555.

Jackendoff, Ray S. 1972. *Semantic Interpretation in Generative Grammar*. Cambridge, MA: MIT Press.

Jackendoff, Ray S. 1977. *X-Bar Syntax: A Theory of Phrase Structure*. Cambridge, MA: MIT Press.

Jackendoff, Ray S. 1990. *Semantic Structures*. Cambridge, MA: MIT Press.

Jackendoff, Ray S. 1995. *Patterns in the Mind: Language and Human Nature*. New York: Basic Books.

Jaeggli, Osvaldo and K. Safir. 1989. The Null Subject Parameter and Parametric Theory. *The Null Subject Parameter*, 15:1–44.

Johnson, N. F. 1965. The Psychological Reality of Phrase Structure Rules. *Journal of Verbal Learning and Verbal Behavior*, 4:469–475.

Joshi, Aravind. 1985. How Much Context-Sensitivity is Necessary for Characterizing Structural Descriptions. In D. Dowty, L. Karttunen, and A. Zwicky, editors, *Natural Language Processing: Theoretical, Computational and Psychological Perspectives*. New York: Cambridge University Press, pages 206–250.

Julien, Marit. 2002. *Syntactic Heads and Word Formation*. New York: Oxford University Press.

Kallmeyer, Laura. 2010. *Parsing Beyond Context-Free Grammars*. New York: Springer.

Kanazawa, Makoto and S. Salvati. 2007. Generating Control Languages with Abstract Categorial Grammars. In L. Kallmeyer, P. Monachesi, G. Penn, and G. Satta, editors, *Proceedings of the 12th Conference on Formal Grammar (FG'07)*, Stanford, CA: CLSI Publications.

Kang, A. Min, R. Todd Constable, John C. Gore, and Sergey Avrutin. 1999. An Event-Related Fmri Study of Implicit Phrase-Level Syntactic and Semantic Processing. *NeuroImage*, 10:555–561.

Kayne, Richard S. 1981a. *Unambiguous Paths. Levels of Syntactic Representation*. Dordrecht: Foris, pages 143–183.

Kayne, Richard S. 1981b. On Certain Differences Between French and English. *Linguistic Inquiry*, 12(3): 349–371.

Kayne, Richard S. 1984. *Connectedness and Binary Branching*. Dordrecht: Foris.

Kayne, Richard S. 1994. *The Antisymmetry of Syntax*. Cambridge, MA: MIT Press.

Kayne, Richard S. 2000a. *Parameters and Universals*. New York: Oxford University Press.

Kayne, Richard S. 2000b. A Note on Prepositions, Complementizers, and Word Order Universals. In *Parameters and Universals*. New York: Oxford University Press.

Kayne, Richard S. 2005. *Movement and Silence*. New York: Oxford University Press.

Kayne, Richard S. 2010. *Comparisons and Contrasts*. New York: Oxford University Press.

Kitahara, Hisatsugu. 1997. *Elementary Operations and Optimal Derivations*. Cambridge, MA: MIT Press.

Klima, Edward S. 1964. Negation in English. In J. A. Fodor and J. J. Katz, editors, *The Structure of Language: Readings in the Philosophy of Language*. Englewood Cliffs, NJ: Prentice Hall, pages 246–323.

Kobele, Gregory M. 2006. Generating Copies: An Investigation into Structural Identity in Language and Grammar. Ph.D. thesis, UCLA.

Koopman, Hilda. 1984. *The Syntax of Verbs: From Verb Movement Rules in the Kru Languages to Universal Grammar*. Dordrecht: Foris.

Koopman, Hilda. 2000. *The Syntax of Specifiers and Heads*. London, New York: Routledge.

Koopman, Hilda. 2005. Korean (and Japanese) Morphology from a Syntactic Perspective. *Linguistic Inquiry*, 36(4):601–633.

Koopman, Hilda. 2010. Prepositions, Postpositions, Circumpositions, and Particles. *Mapping Spatial PPs*, 1(8):26–74.

Koopman, Hilda and D. Sportiche. 1991a. The Position of Subjects. *Lingua*, 85:211–258. Reprinted in Dominique Sportiche. 1998. *Partitions and Atoms of Clause Structure: Subjects, Agreement, Case and Clitics*. NY: Routledge.

Koopman, Hilda and D. Sportiche. 1991b. Variables and The Bijection Principle. *The Linguistic Review*, 2:139–160. Reprinted in Hilda Koopman, 2000. *The Syntax of Specifiers and Heads: Collected Essays of Hilda J Koopman*. New York: Routledge.

Koopman, Hilda and A. Szabolcsi. 2000. *Verbal Complexes*. Cambridge, MA: MIT Press.

Ladefoged, Peter and D. E. Broadbent. 1960. Perception of Sequence in Auditory Events. *Quarterly Journal of Experimental Psychology*, 13:162–170.

Landau, Idan. 2000. *Elements of Control: Structure and Meaning in Infinitival Constructions*. Boston, MA: Kluwer.

Landau, Idan. 2003. Movement out of Control. *Linguistic Inquiry*, 34(3):471–498.

Larson, Richard K. 1985. On the Syntax of Disjunction Scope. *Natural Language & Linguistic Theory*, 3(2):217–264.

Larson, Richard K. 1988. On the Double Object Construction. *Linguistic Inquiry*, 19:335–391.

Lasnik, Howard. 1976. Remarks on Coreference. *Linguistic Analysis*, 2(1):1–22.

Lasnik, Howard. 1995. A Note on Pseudo-Gapping. In Rob Pensalfini and Hiroyuki Ura, editors, *Papers on Minimalist Syntax*. MIT Working Papers In Linguistics 27, Cambridge, Massachusetts, pages 143–163. Reprinted in H. Lasnik. Editor. 1999. *Minimalist Analysis*. New York: Blackwell.

Lasnik, Howard and M. Saito. 1991. On the Subject of Infinitives. *CLS*, 27:324–343.

Lasnik, Howard and T. Stowell. 1991. Weakest Crossover. *Linguistic Inquiry*, 22(4): 687–720.

Lasnik, Howard and J. Uriagereka. 1988. *A Course on Syntax*. Cambridge, MA: MIT Press.

Levin, Beth. 1993. *English Verb Classes and Alternations*. Chicago: Chicago University Press.

Levin, Beth and M. R. Hovav. 2005. *Argument Realization*. Cambridge: Cambridge University Press.

Levin, Beth and M. R. Hovav. 1995. *Unaccusativity: At the Syntax-Lexical Semantics Interface*. Cambridge, MA: MIT Press.

Lightfoot, David. 1982. *The Language Lottery: Toward a Biology of Grammars*. Cambridge, MA: MIT Press.

Luce, R. Duncan. 1986. *Response Times: Their Role in Inferring Elementary Mental Organization*. Oxford: Oxford University Press.

MacDonald, Maryellen, N. J. Pearlmutter, and M. S. Seidenberg. 1994. Syntactic Ambiguity as Lexical Ambiguity Resolution. In C. Clifton, L. Frazier, and K. Rayner, editors, *Perspectives on Sentence Processing*. Hillsdale, NJ: Lawrence Erlbaum, pages 155–180.

Maling, Joan. 1984. Non-Clause-Bounded Reflexives in Modern Icelandic. *Linguistics and Philosophy*, 7: 211–241.

Maling, Joan. 1986. Clause Bounded Reflexives in Modern Icelandic. In L. Hellan and K. Koch Christensen, editors, *Topics in Scandinavian Syntax*. Dordrecht: Kluwer, pages 53–63.

Marantz, Alec. 1988. Clitics, Morphological Merger, and the Mapping to Phonological Structure. In Michael Hammond and Michael Noonan, editors, *Theoretical Morphology: Approaches in Modern Linguistics*. San Diego, CA: Academic Press, pages 253–270.

Marantz, Alec. 1997. No Escape From Syntax: Don't Try Morphological Analysis in the Privacy of Your Own Lexicon. In *Proceedings of the 21st Annual Penn Linguistics Colloquium*. University of Pennsylvania, pages 201–225.

Marcus, Mitchell, B. Santorini, and M. A. Marcinkiewicz. 1993. Building a Large Annotated Corpus of English: The Penn Treebank. Principles and Parameters. *Comparative Grammar*, 19:313–330.

Marks, L. E. and G. A. Miller. 1964. The Role of Semantic and Syntactic Constraints in the Memorization of English Sentences. *Journal of Verbal Learning and Verbal Behavior*, 3:1–5. Reprinted in D. H. Kausler, editor. 1966 *Verbal Learning: Contemporary Theory and Research*. New York: Wiley. Also reprinted in L. Postman and G. Keppel, editors. 1969. *Verbal Learning and Memory*. New York: Penguin.

Marslen-Wilson, William. 1973. Linguistic Structure and Speech Shadowing at Very Short Latencies. *Nature*, 244:522–523.

Martin, John C. 1997. *Introduction to Languages and the Theory of Computation*. New York: McGraw-Hill.

Mateescu, Alexandru and A. Salomaa. 1997. Aspects of Classical Language Theory. In G. Rozenberg and A. Salomaa, editors, *Handbook of Formal Languages, Volume 1: Word, Language, Grammar*. New York: Springer, pages 175–251.

McCawley, James D. 1968. The Role of Semantics in a Grammar. In Emmon Bach and Richard Harms, editors, *Universals in Linguistic Theory*. New York: Holt, Rinehart and Winston, pages 124–169.

McCawley, James D. 1982. Parentheticals and Discontinuous Constituent Structure. *Linguistic Inquiry*, 13:91–106.

McCawley, James D. 1998. *The Syntactic Phenomena of English*. Chicago: University of Chicago Press.

McCloskey, James. 1991. Clause Structure, Ellipsis and Proper Government in Irish. *Lingua*, 85:259–302.

McCloskey, James. 2000. Quantifier Float and Wh-Movement in an Irish English. *Linguistic Inquiry*, 31(1):57–84.

McKee, Cecile. 1992. A Comparison of Pronouns and Anaphors in Italian And English. *Language Acquisition*, 1:21–55.

McQueen, James M. and Anne Cutler. 1998. Morphology in Word Recognition. In Andrew Spencer and Arnold M. Zwicky, editors, *The Handbook of Morphology*. New York: Elsevier.

Medina, Tamara Nicol and J. Snedeker and J. C. Trueswell and L. R. Gleitman. 2011. How Words Can and Cannot be Learned by Observation. *Proceedings of the National Academy of Sciences*, 108(2): 9014–9019.

Merchant, Jason. 2001. *The Syntax of Silence: Sluicing, Islands, and the Theory of Ellipsis*. Oxford: Oxford University Press.

Michaelis, Jens. 1998. Derivational Minimalism is Mildly Context-Sensitive. In *Proceedings, Logical Aspects of Computational Linguistics, LACL'98*, New York: Springer.

Michaelis, Jens. 2001a. On Formal Properties of Minimalist Grammars. Ph.D. thesis, Universität Potsdam. Linguistics in Potsdam 13, Universitätsbibliothek, Potsdam, Germany.

Michaelis, Jens. 2001b. Transforming Linear Context Free Rewriting Systems into Minimalist Grammars. In Philippe de Groote, Glyn Morrill, and Christian Retoré, editors, *Logical Aspects of Computational Linguistics, Lecture Notes in Artificial Intelligence, No. 2099*. New York: Springer, pages 228–244.

Michaelis, Jens and M. Kracht. 1997. Semilinearity as a Syntactic Invariant. In Christian Retoré, editor, *Logical Aspects of Computational Linguistics*. Lecture Notes in Computer Science 1328. New York. Springer-Verlag, pages 37–40.

Miyagawa, Shigeru. and K. Arikawa. 2007. Locality in Syntax and Floating Numeral Quantifiers. *Linguistic Inquiry*, 38(4):645–670.

Mönnich, Uwe. 2010. Well-Nested Tree Languages and Attributed Tree Transducers. In The 10th International Conference on Tree Adjoining Grammars and Related Formalisms TAG+10.

Moulton, Kellen. 2009. Natural Selection and the Syntax of Clausal Complementation. Open Access Dissertations, page 99.

Ngonyani, Deogratias S. 1996. The Morphosyntax of Applicatives. Ph.D. thesis, UCLA.

Nichols, Johanna and B. Bickel. 2005. Locus of Marking in the Clause. In Martin Haspelmath, Matthew S. Dryer, David Gil, and Bernard Comrie, editors, *The World Atlas of Language Structures*. Oxford: Oxford University Press.

Ouhalla, Jamal. 1994. *Introducing Transformational Grammar: From Rules to Principles and Parameters*. London: Arnold, and New York: Oxford University Press.

Padilla, José A. 1990. *On the Definition Of Binding Domains In Spanish: Evidence From Child Language*. Boston, MA: Kluwer.

Pais, Abraham. 1986. *Inward Bound*. Oxford: Oxford University Press.

Pallier, Christophe, A. D. Devauchelle, and S. Dehaene. 2011. Cortical Representation of the Constituent Structure of Sentences. *Proceedings of the National Academy of Sciences*, 108(6):2522–2527.

Perlmutter, David M. 1970. Surface Structure Constraints in Syntax. *Linguistic Inquiry*, 1(2):187–255.

Pesetsky, David. 1995. *Zero Syntax: Experiencers and Cascades*. Cambridge, MA: MIT Press.

Pinker, Steven. 1994. *The Language Instinct*. New York: William Morrow.

Pinker, Steven. 1999. *Words and Rules*. New York: Basic Books.

Poeppel, David and P. J. Monahan. 2008. Speech perception: Cognitive Foundations and Cortical Implementation. *Current Directions in Psychological Science*, 17(2):80–85.

Polinsky, Maria and E. Potsdam. 2002. Backward Control. *Linguistic Inquiry*, 33:245–282.

Pollard, Carl and I. A. Sag. 1992. Anaphors in English and the Scope Of Binding Theory. *Linguistic Inquiry*, 23(2):261–304.

Pollock, Jean-Yves. 1989. Verb Movement, Universal Grammar, and the Structure of IP. *Linguistic Inquiry*, 20:365–424.

Postal, Paul. 1969. Anaphoric Islands. In *Chicago Linguistic Society*, volume 5, pages 205–239.

Postal, Paul. 1971. *The Crossover Principle*. New York: Holt, Rinehart and Winston.

Postal, Paul. 1974. *On Raising*. Cambridge, MA: MIT Press.

Postal, Paul, editor. 1998. *Three Investigations of Extraction*. Cambridge, MA: MIT Press.

Prince, Alan and P. Smolensky. 1993. *Optimality Theory: Constraint Interaction in Generative Grammar*. Malden, MA: Blackwell.

Pylkkänen, Liina. 2002. Introducing Arguments. Ph.D. thesis, Massachusetts Institute of Technology.

Pylkkänen, Liina. 2008. *Introducing Arguments*. Cambridge, MA: MIT Press.

Radford, Andrew. 2004. *Minimalist Syntax: Exploring the Structure of English*. Cambridge: Cambridge University Press.

Radzinski, Daniel. 1991. Chinese Number Names, Tree Adjoining Languages and Mild Context Sensitivity. *Computational Linguistics*, 17:277–300.

Rambow, Owen. 1994. Formal and computational aspects of natural language syntax. Ph.D. thesis, University of Pennsylvania. Computer and Information Science Technical report MS-CIS-94-52 (LINC LAB 278).

Ramchand, Gillian. 2008. *Verb Meaning and the Lexicon: A First-Phase Syntax*, Volume 116. Cambridge: Cambridge University Press.

Ratcliffe, Robert R. 1998. *The 'Broken' Plural Problem in Arabic and Comparative Semitic*. Philadelphia, PA: John Benjamins Publishing Company.

Reinhart, Tanya. 1983. *Anaphora and Semantic Interpretation*. Chicago: University of Chicago Press.

Reinhart, Tanya and E. Reuland. 1993. Reflexivity. *Linguistic Inquiry*, 24:657–720.

Renzi, Lorenzo (G. Salvi (and A Cardinaletti)). 1988–1995. *Grande Grammatica Italiana di Consultazione*. Bologna: Il Mulino.

Resnik, Philip. 1993. Selection and Information: A Class-Based Approach to Lexical Relationships. Ph.D. thesis, University of Pennsylvania.

Riad, Tomas. 1988. Reflexivity and Predication. In *Working Papers in Scandinavian Syntax*. Lund, Sweden: Department of Scandinavian Languages.

Richards, Norvin. 1997. What Moves Where When in Which Language? Ph.D. thesis, Massachusetts Institute of Technology, Cambridge, MA.

Rizzi, Luigi. 1982. *Issues in Italian Syntax*. Dordrecht: Foris.

Rizzi, Luigi. 1986. Null Subjects in Italian and the Theory of Pro. *Linguistic Inquiry*, 17:501–557.

Rizzi, Luigi. 1990a. *Relativized Minimality*. Cambridge, MA: MIT Press.

Rizzi, Luigi. 1990b. Speculations on Verb Second. In J. Mascaró and M. Nespor, editors, *Grammar in Progress: GLOW Essays for Henk van Reimsdijk*. Dordrecht : Foris, pages 375–386.

Rizzi, Luigi. 1997. The Fine Structure of the Left Periphery. In L. Haegeman, editor, *Elements of Grammar*. Boston, MA: Kluwer, pages 281–337.

Rizzi, Luigi. 2002. Relativized Minimality Effects. In M. Baltin and C. Collins, editors, *The Handbook of Contemporary Syntactic Theory*. Blackwell, Oxford, pages 89–110.

Rizzi, Luigi. 2004. Locality and Left Periphery. In Adriana Belletti, editor, *Structures and Beyond: Cartography of Syntactic Structures*, Volume 3. New York: Oxford University Press, pages 104–131.

Rizzi, Luigi. 2013. *Syntax and Cognition: Core Ideas and Results in Syntax*, Special Issue, *Lingua*, 130:1–208.

Roberts, Ian G. 1997. *Comparative Syntax*. London: Arnold.

Rooth, Mats. 1992. A Theory of Focus Interpretation. *Natural Language Semantics*, 1:75–116.

Ross, John R. 1967. Constraints on Variables in Syntax. Ph.D. thesis, Massachusetts Institute of Technology.

Ross, John R. 1986. *Infinite Syntax*. Norwood, NJ: Ablex.

Runner, Jeffrey. 1998. *Noun Phrase Licensing*. New York: Garland.

Ruys, Eddy G. 2000. Weak Crossover as a Scope Phenomenon. *Linguistic Inquiry*, 31(3):513–539.

Safir, Ken. 1992. Implied Non-Coreference and the Pattern of Anaphora. *Linguistics and Philosophy*, 15:1–52.

Safir, Ken. 1996. Derivation, Representation, and the Resumption: The Domain of Weak Crossover. *Linguistic Inquiry*, 27(2):313–339.

Salomaa, Arto and M. Soittola. 1978. Automata-Theoretic Aspects of Formal Power Series. New York: Academic Press.

Salvati, Sylvain. 2007. Encoding Second Order String ACG with Deterministic Tree Walking Transducers. In S. Wintner, editor, *Proceedings of the 11th conference on Formal Grammars, FG2006, FG Online Proceedings.* CSLI Publications, pages 143–156.

Satta, Giorgio. 1994. Tree Adjoining Grammar Parsing and Boolean Matrix Multiplication. *Computational Linguistics*, 20:173–232.

Savitch, Walter J., E. Bach, W. Marsh, and G. Safran-Naveh, editors. 1987. *The Formal Complexity of Natural Language.* Boston, MA: Reidel.

Schachter, Paul and Fe T. Otanes. 1972. *Tagalog Reference Grammar.* Los Angeles, CA: University of California Press.

Seki, Hiroyuki, T. Matsumura, M. Fujii, and T. Kasami. 1991. On Multiple Context-Free Grammars. *Theoretical Computer Science*, 88:191–229.

Selkirk, Elisabeth. 1983. *The Syntax of Words.* Cambridge, MA: MIT Press.

Sells, Peter. 1987. Aspects of Logophoricity. *Linguistic Inquiry*, 18:445–479.

Sigurðsson, Halld'or 'Armann. 1990. Long Distance Reflexives and Moods in Icelandic. In G. Rozenberg and A. Salomaa, editors, *Modern Icelandic Syntax.* New York: Academic Press, pages 309–346.

Smullyan, Raymond M. 1978. *What is the Name of This Book.* Englewood Cliffs, NJ: Prentice Hall.

Spencer, Andrew. 1991. *Morphology.* Oxford: Blackwell.

Spencer, Andrew and A. M. Zwicky, editors. 1998. *The Handbook of Morphology.* New York: Elsevier.

Sportiche, Dominique. 1988. A Theory of Floating Quantifiers and its Corollaries for Constituent Structure. *Linguistic Inquiry*, 19:425–449.

Sportiche, Dominique. 2005. Division of Labor between Merge and Move: Strict Locality of Selection and Apparent Reconstruction Paradoxes. UCLA. Available at <http://ling.auf.net/lingBuzz/000163> [accessed May 2013].

Sportiche, Dominique. 2006. Reconstruction, Binding and Scope. In M. Everaert and H. van Riemsdijk, editors, *The Blackwell Companion to Syntax.* Oxford: Blackwell.

Sportiche, Dominique. 2011. French Relative *Qui*. *Linguistic Inquiry*, 42(1):83–124.

Sportiche, Dominique. 2012. Binding Theory—Structure Sensitivity of Referential Dependencies. *Lingua*, 13:187–208.

Sprouse, Jon and D. Almeida. 2011. The 469 Data Points that Form The Empirical Foundation of Generative Syntactic Theory are at Least 98% Replicable Using Formal Experiments. Ms., University of California, Irvine.

Stabler, Edward P. 2001a. Minimalist Grammars and Recognition. In Christian Rohrer, Antje Rossdeutscher, and Hans Kamp, editors, *Linguistic Form and its Computation.* Stanford, CA: CSLI Publications. (Presented at the SFB340 workshop at Bad Teinach, 1999.)

Stabler, Edward P. 2001b. Recognizing Head Movement. In Philippe de Groote, Glyn Morrill, and Christian Retoré, editors, *Logical Aspects of Computational Linguistics, Lecture Notes in Artificial Intelligence, No. 2099.* New York: Springer, pages 254–260.

Stabler, Edward P. 2010. Computational Perspectives on Minimalism. In Cedric Boeckx, editor, *Oxford Handbook of Minimalism.* Oxford: Oxford University Press, pages 616–641.

Stowell, Tim. 1978. What was There Before There was There. In *Papers from the 14th Regional Meeting of the Chicago Linguistic Society.* Chicago: University of Chicago, pages 457–471.

Stowell, Tim. 1981. Origins of Phrase Structure. Ph.D. thesis, Massachusetts Institute of Technology.

Stowell, Tim. 1983. Subjects Across Categories. *The Linguistic Review*, pages 285–312.

Thráinsson, Höskuldur. 1976. Reflexives and Subjunctives in Icelandic. In *Proceedings of the North Eastern Linguistic Society, NELS 6.* Amherst: University of Massachusetts, pages 225–239.

Townsend, David J. and T. G. Bever. 2001. *Sentence Comprehension: The Integration of Habits and Rules.* Cambridge, MA: MIT Press.

Travis, Lisa. 1984. Parameters and Effects of Word Order Variation. Ph.D. thesis, Massachussets Institute of Technology, Cambridge, Massachusetts.

Trueswell, John G., T. N. Medina, A. Hafri, and L. R. Gleitman 2013. Propose but Verify: Fast Mapping Meets Cross-situational Word Learning. *Cognitive Psychology*, 66:126–156.

Valiant, Leslie G. 1975. General Context Free Recognition in Less Than Cubic Time. *Journal of Computer and System Sciences*, 10:308–315.

Van Riemsdijk, Haider. 1989. Movement and Regeneration 1. *Dialect Variation and the Theory of Grammar*, page 105.

Van Riemsdijk, Haider and E. Williams. 1986. *Introduction to the Theory of Grammar*. Cambridge, MA: MIT Press.

Vasishth, Shravan, S. Bruessow, R. L. Lewis, and H. Drenhaus. 2008. Processing Polarity: How the Ungrammatical Intrudes on the Grammatical. *Cognitive Science*, 32(4):685–712.

Vergnaud, Jean-Roger. 1974. French Relative Clauses. Ph.D. thesis, Massachusetts Institute of Technology, Cambridge, Massachusetts.

Vikner, Sten. 1985. Parameters of Binder and Binding Category in Danish. In *Working Papers in Scandinavian Syntax 23*, Trondheim: University of Trondheim.

von Stechow, Arnim. 1995. Lexical Decomposition in Syntax. In U. Egli, P. E. Pause, C. Schwarze, A. von Stechow, and G. Wienold, editors, *The Lexicon in the Organization of Language*. Amsterdam: John Benjamins Publishing Company, pages 81–118.

von Stechow, Arnim. 1996. The Different Readings of *Wieder* "Again": A Structural Account. *Journal of Semantics*, 13:87–138.

Weir, David. 1988. Characterizing Mildly Context-Sensitive Grammar Formalisms. Ph.D. thesis, University of Pennsylvania, Philadelphia.

Williams, Edwin. 1981. On the Notions 'Lexically Related' and 'Head of a Word'. *Linguistic Inquiry*, 12: 245–274.

Woolford, Ellen. 1999. More on the Anaphor-Agreement Effect. *Linguistic Inquiry*, 30:257–287.

Xiang, Ming, B. Dillon, and C. Phillips. 2009. Illusory Licensing Effects across Dependency Types: ERP Evidence. *Brain and Language*, 108:40–55.

Index

An Introduction to Syntactic Analysis and Theory, First Edition.
Dominique Sportiche, Hilda Koopman, and Edward Stabler.